GOTHIC
ART FOR ENGLAND 1400–1547

EDITED BY RICHARD MARKS AND PAUL WILLIAMSON

ASSISTED BY ELEANOR TOWNSEND

V&A PUBLICATIONS

First published by V&A Publications, 2003

V&A Publications
160 Brompton Road
London SW3 1HW

Designed by Harry Green
V&A photography by the V&A Photo Studio under the direction
of Christine Smith: Pip Barnard, Mike Kitcatt, Paul Robins, Ken Jackson

ISBN 1 85177 401 7

FRONT JACKET ILLUSTRATION: Margaret of York's crown (cat. no. 11)

BACK JACKET ILLUSTRATION: Henry VII's Chapel, Westminster Abbey
(cat. no. 28)

HALF-TITLE PAGE: St George and the Dragon (cat. no. 58)

FRONTISPIECE: Tapestry with the arms and badges of Lord Dynham
(cat. no. 154)

Printed in Singapore

V&A Publications
160 Brompton Road
London SW3 1HW
www.vam.ac.uk

GOTHIC

CONTENTS

PATRONS AND EXHIBITION ADVISORY COMMITTEE

PATRONS

His Royal Highness the Prince of Wales

The Most Revd and Rt Hon.
The Lord Archbishop of Canterbury Dr Rowan
Williams

The Most Revd and Rt Hon.
The Lord Archbishop of York Dr David Hope

His Eminence The Archbishop of Westminster
Cormac Murphy O'Connor

The Rt Revd and Rt Hon.
The Lord Bishop of London Dr Richard Chartres

His Grace the Duke of Northumberland

EXHIBITION CURATOR
Professor Richard Marks (University of York)

ASSISTANT CURATOR
AND EXHIBITION COORDINATOR
Eleanor Townsend (V&A)

V&A LEAD CURATOR
Dr Paul Williamson

EXHIBITION ADVISORY COMMITTEE

Marian Campbell (V&A)

John Cherry (The British Museum)

Professor Eamon Duffy
(Magdalene College, University of Cambridge)

Dr Susan Foister (The National Gallery)

Dr Phillip Lindley (The University of Leicester)

Ann Payne (The British Library)

Dr Rowan Watson (V&A)

Dr Christopher Wilson (University College London)

Linda Lloyd-Jones (Head of Exhibitions, V&A)

Ann Hayhoe (Exhibition Assistant)

Diane Bilbey (Secretary, Exhibition Advisory Committee)

CONTRIBUTORS TO THE CATALOGUE

The following have contributed catalogue entries,
and are identified by their initials:

John Allan	JA	John Mitchell	JM
Janet Backhouse	JMB	Dr Linda Monckton	LAM
Peter Barber	PB	Dr Lisa Monnas	LM
Jon Bayliss	JCB	Peta Motture	PM
Claude Blair	CB	Dr Julian Munby	JTM
Dr Alixe Bovey	AB	Dr Tessa Murdoch	TM
Sarah Brown	SB	Beverley Nenk	BN
Marian Campbell	MLC	Anthony North	AN
John Cherry	JC	David Park	DP
Rachel Church	RC	Ann Payne	AP
Dr Elizabeth Cleland	EC	Dr Catherine Reynolds	CR
Barrie Cook	BC	Dr Samantha Riches	SR
Geoff Egan	GE	Graeme Rimer	GR
Andrew Elkerton	AE	James Robinson	JR
Dr Susan Foister	SF	Nicholas Rogers	NR
Prof. Miriam Foot	MF	Timothy Schroder	TS
Dr Jane Geddes	JGe	Dr David Skinner	DS
Dr John A. A. Goodall	JG	Brian Spencer	BS
Dr Christa Grössinger	CG	Andrew Spira	AS
Nicholas Hall	NH	Eleanor Townsend	EMT
John Hardacre	JH	Dr Charles Tracy	CT
Dr Lotte Hellinga	LH	Dr Pamela Tudor-Craig	PT-C
Robin Hildyard	RH	Dr Hugo van der Velden	HvV
David King	DK	Dr Rowan Watson	RW
Richard Knowles	RK	Karen Watts	KW
Philip J. Lankester	PJL	Annette Wickham	AW
Reino Liefkes	RL	Dr Paul Williamson	PW
Dr Phillip Lindley	PGL	Dr Christopher Wilson	CW
Catharine MacLeod	CM	Linda Woolley	LW
Prof. Richard Marks	RM		

PICTURE CREDITS

Illustrations have been provided by the following individuals and institutions.

Catalogue numbers are shown in bold and plate numbers are in italic, preceded by the letters *pl.* or *pls*. Page numbers are given for unnumbered contextual illustrations.

BELGIUM

Université Catholique de Louvain **215**

Musées royaux des Beaux-Arts de Belgique, Bruxelles *pl.42*

FRANCE

Bibliothèque nationale de France **72, 74,** *pl.103*

Musée du Louvre © Photo RMN–Arnaudet **10**

Musée national du Moyen Age. © Photo RMN–Gérard Blot **282, 344**

GERMANY

© Domkapitel Aachen. Photo: Pit Siebigs **11**

THE NETHERLANDS

Museum Catharijneconvent, Utrecht **92**

© Rijksmuseum, Amsterdam **323**

UNITED KINGDOM

All-Hallows-by-the-Tower church **136**

Oxford, Warden and Fellows of All Souls College **36, 99, 100, 101, 179**

Ashmolean Museum, Oxford **12, 102,** *plate p.285,* **325**

The Barber Institute of Fine Arts, The University of Birmingham **244**

Photographs by Keith Barley **67, 291, 292, 293**

Bodleian Library, University of Oxford **253, 256,** *plate p.445, pl.46*

© Bristol City Council **124,** *pl.110*

© Bristol Museums & Art Gallery **135, 159, 191, 198, 315**

Courtesy of the British Library Board **14, 15, 27, 33b, 41, 42, 43, 46, 47, 49, 52, 73, 77, 80, 85, 90, 93, 96, 116, 143, 173, 175, 214, 223, 224, 225, 254, 318, 340, 353, 354, 355, 359,** *pls 79, 87, 88*

© The British Museum **32, 34, 40, 64, 68, 70, 132, 165, 166, 189, 195, 204, 205, 206, 211, 221, 242, 252, 278, 304, 336, 342, 353**

© The British Museum. Courtesy of the Benefice of Rougham, Beyton with Hessett and Rushbrooke **301**

© The British Museum. Courtesy of the Vicar of Lacock, Wiltshire **184**

© The British Museum. Courtesy of the Warden and Fellows of All Souls College, Oxford **207**

Duke of Buccleuch and Queensberry **95**

Photograph by Ronald A. Chapman FBIPP FRPS **357**

By permission of the Duke of Devonshire and the Chatsworth Settlement Trustees **45**

Photographs by Derrick A. Chivers **53, 139, 247, 332, 333**

The Master, Fellows and Scholars of Christ's College, Cambridge **110, 111, 112, 113,** *pl.107*

The Churches Conservation Trust. Photograph by Paul Barker **273**

Colchester Museums **125, 126**

© The College of Arms **1, 76,** *pl.115*

Conservation of Wall Painting Department, Courtauld Institute of Art **298**

The Conway Library, Courtauld Institute of Art **86, 330,** *pl. 67*

The Conway Library, Courtauld Institute of Art. Reproduced by permission of the Provost and Fellows of Eton College *pl.95*

The Master and Fellows of Corpus Christi College, Cambridge **171, 358**

Corpus Christi College, Oxford **104, 105, 106, 107, 108**

Corpus Christi College, Oxford, UK/Bridgeman Art Library *pl.106*

The Country Life Picture Library **23, 145, 148,** *plate p.289*

Photographs by John Crook **109, 233, 234, 235, 356**

Photograph by C. R. A. Davies **257**

© English Heritage **339**

Reproduced by permission of English Heritage.NMR **29,** *plate p.178,* **83, 117, 261, 264, 296, 320, 343,** *pls 84, 86, 91*

Reproduced by permission of the Provost and Fellows of Eton College **24, 190**

Exeter City Council **129**

Exeter City Museums & Art Gallery **121, 265, 313, 321,** *plate p.259*

Fitzwilliam Museum, Cambridge **17, 94**

Photograph by Jane Geddes **26**

Glasgow Museums: The Burrell Collection **38, 152, 160, 178, 217, 219, 281, 288**

Courtesy of The Worshipful Company of Goldsmiths **192**

Courtesy of The Worshipful Company of Goldsmiths. Photograph by A. A. Barnes **186**

Photographs by John Goodall **51, 119**

Photograph by Peter Goodrum **294**

Guildhall Library **130, 133, 142, 308**

Martin Harrison *pl.90*

Courtesy the Henry Moore Institute, Leeds. Photograph by Jerry Hardman-Jones *plate p.400*

Herbert Art Gallery & Museum, Coventry/Bridgeman Art Library *pl.92*

The Dean and Chapter of Hereford Cathedral and the Hereford Mappa Mundi Trust **251**

Crown copyright: Historic Royal Palaces **4, 5**

The Masters of the Bench of the Inner Temple *pl.14*

Ipswich Borough Council Museum & Galleries **210, 334**

© Jarrold Publishing and Norwich Cathedral, reproduced by kind permission of the publisher **236**

© The John Rylands University Library of Manchester **172, 174, 241, 309, 341,** *pl.41*

Reproduced by courtesy of Kendal Museum, Kendal, Cumbria **268**

Anthony Kersting **237, 245,** *pl.111*

The Provost and Scholars of King's College, Cambridge **20, 21**

Lambeth Palace Library **44, 103, 227, 311, 326,** *pl.12*

Worshipful Company of Leathersellers **131**

Luton Museum Service **347, 348**

The President and Fellows of Magdalen College, Oxford **250, 255**

The Master and Fellows, Magdalene College, Cambridge **169**

Photographs by Richard Marks **50, 89, 149, 260,** *pl.121, plate p.446*

The Mary Rose Trust **16, 63**

Reproduced by courtesy of The Mercers' Company **137,** *pl.57*

Courtesy of Shrewsbury Museums Service and the Strategic Rail Authority **194**

© Museum of London **62, 71, 122, 176, 177, 200, 202, 203, 212, 221, 222, 324, 325**

© National Gallery, London **161, 162, 213,** *pl.3*

© The National Gallery of Scotland **295**

© The Trustees of the National Museums of Scotland **61**

The Board of Trustees of the National Museums & Galleries on Merseyside (Walker Art Gallery) **97, 351**

By courtesy of the National Portrait Gallery, London **2**

Reproduced by kind permission of the National Trust *pl.85*

National Trust Photographic Library **81, 158, 216, 289**

Courtesy of the Warden and Scholars of New College, Oxford **180, 181, 188, 249, 305**

Nimbus Conservation **337**

Reproduced by kind permission of The Duke of Norfolk, Arundel Castle *pl.82*

Norfolk Record Office **168**

Collection of the Duke of Northumberland **115**

Norwich Castle Museum and Art Gallery **155, 208, 276**

Nottingham University Library **312**

© Oxfordshire County Council Photographic Archive **246**

Private Collection. Copyright reserved **196, 352**

Private Collection. Photograph: Photographic Survey, Courtauld Institute of Art *pl.48*

Public Record Office **30, 33a**

Public Record Office. Reproduced by permission of the Chancellor and Council of the Duchy of Lancaster *pl.22*

© The Board of Trustees of the Royal Armouries **55, 56, 65, 66, 338**

© The Board of Trustees of the Royal Armouries and University Museum of Archaeology and Anthropology, Cambridge **57**

The Royal Collection © 2002, Her Majesty Queen Elizabeth II **209,** *pl.48*

By kind permission of the Rector, Churchwardens and Parochial Church Council of St Nicolas, Stanford-on-Avon **39**

Society of Antiquaries of London **285**

© Tate, London 2003 **286, 287**

Towneley Hall Art Gallery **300**

Master and Fellows, Trinity College, Cambridge *pl.81*

Ufford, Suffolk, St Mary's church of the Assumption **270**

© Warburg Institute *pl.89*

© Dean and Chapter of Westminster **9, 54, 114, 239,** *pl.125*

Photographs by Christopher Wilson **3, 19, 25, 28, 123, 144, 146, 147, 150, 228, 231, 258, 259, 316, 327, 329** *pls 25, 61, 62, 63, 64, 65, 68, 69, 71, 73, 74, 75, 76, 93, 105, 118, 119, 120, 128*

By permission of the Dean and Canons of Windsor *pl.96*

Photo © Woodmansterne **13**

Bishop of Worcester and Worcestershire County Record Office **118**

Produced by kind permission of the Dean and Chapter of York **48, 141, 232, 317,** *pl.5*

The York Glaziers Trust **37**

The York Glaziers Trust. Courtesy of the Rector of Stockerston church **290**

York, The Mansion House, City of York Council **82**

York Museums Trust (Yorkshire Museum) **69, 98,** *plate p.428*

U.S.A.

Bowdoin College Museum of Art, Brunswick, Maine, Bequest of the Honorable James Bowdoin III **22**

The Metropolitan Museum of Art, Harris Brisbane Dick Fund, 1936. (36.69) Photograph © 1979 The Metropolitan Museum of Art **8**

The Metropolitan Museum of Art, The Cloisters Collection, 1967. (60.127.1) Photograph © 2002 The Metropolitan Museum of Art **154**

The Metropolitan Museum of Art, Rogers Fund, 1904. (04.3.274) Photograph © 2002 The Metropolitan Museum of Art **79**

The Metropolitan Museum of Art, Rogers Fund, 1950. (50.69.1 and 50.69.2) Photograph © 1995 The Metropolitan Museum of Art **163**

National Gallery of Art, Washington. Samuel H. Kress Collection. Photo by Philip A. Charles **84**

© The Pierpont Morgan Library, New York 2002 **78, 91**

Rare Book Department, The Free Library of Philadelphia **140**

ACKNOWLEDGEMENTS

We would like to thank all those, both within and outside the Museum, who have helped with object selection and obtaining loans. At an early stage in the planning of the exhibition a series of seminars was held to discuss in detail the main themes of the exhibition, and we are most grateful to those who took part. A substantial Senior Research Grant for collaborative projects from the Getty Grant Program enabled us to fund the seminars and create an advisory panel drawing on expertise from across the museum and university sectors. Thanks to the generosity of the University of York, the grant also allowed Professor Richard Marks, the Exhibition Curator, to devote time away from his university commitments to devise the exhibition with the assistance of Eleanor Townsend, and covered travel expenses. The production of the catalogue has been made possible by a generous subvention from Daniel Katz, a notable supporter of the Museum, for which we are most grateful.

The Cathedrals Fabric Commission of England, the Council for the Care of Churches and the Diocesan Advisory Committee have been constant sources of support and advice. We are of course particularly indebted to all the lenders to the exhibition, not only for agreeing to show their precious objects, but also for their hospitality, guidance and in many cases for providing images of the works of art in their care.

The following have contributed in many ways to the organization of the exhibition and the preparation of the catalogue: Prof. Malcolm Baker, Nicolas Barker, Keith Barley, The Revd J. F. A. Bertram, Peter Brown, Reginald Bush, Dr James Campbell, Dr Tom Campbell, Derrick Chivers, Morag Clements, Patricia Collins, Dr Elizabeth Danbury, Mark Downing, Anna Eavis, Dr A. K. B. Evans, Dr Christine Ferdinand, Mr and Mrs Robert Geddes, Dr John A. A. Goodall, Stephen Gritt, Hugh Harrison, Helen Hughes, Mrs Jane Jones, John Larson, Santina Levey, Dr Julian Litten, Timothy McCann, Dr Scot McKendrick, Dr Joanna Mattingley, Jonathan Miles, Ann Oldfield, Dr Sophie Oosterwijk, Pauline Plummer, Harold W. Pond, Chloe Reddaway, Dr Sarah R. Rees Jones, Mrs Sara Rodger, Rachel Russell, Lucy Rutherford, Dr Nigel Saul, George Shaw, Andrew Singleton, Professor Jeremy J. Smith, R. J. L. Smith, Nino Strachey, Martin Stuchfield, Gavin Todhunter, Wendy Toulson, Dr Paula J. Turner, Dr Ian Tyers, Dr Malcolm Vale.

For the catalogue, we would like to thank the V&A Publications team: Mary Butler, Ariane Bankes, Monica Woods, Nina Jacobson, Clare Davis, Geoff Barlow; the editor Mandy Greenfield and the designer Harry Green.

TIMELINE

REIGNS OF ENGLISH KINGS	REIGNS OF FRENCH KINGS	REIGNS OF BURGUNDIAN DUKES	HISTORICAL EVENTS	RELIGIOUS EVENTS
1399				
1399: Henry IV accedes to throne after deposition of Richard II	1399: Charles VI on the throne	1399: Philip the Bold is duke		
1400				
1400: Richard II dies			1400: Chaucer dies	1401: Act *de haeretico comburendo* licenses the burning of heretics
		1404: Philip the Bold dies, John the Fearless succeeds		
1410				
1413: Henry IV dies; Henry V accedes to throne			1414: Lollard (Oldcastle) Rising	1414: Council of Constance begins
			1415: Battle of Agincourt (England defeats France)	
				1417: Great Schism ends
				1418: Council of Constance ends
		1419: John the Fearless is murdered, Philip the Good succeeds	1419: Revolution of Hussites in Bohemia	
1420				
1420: Henry V marries Katharine de Valois			1420: Treaty of Troyes – Henry V to inherit French throne	
1422: Henry V dies; Henry VI accedes to throne	1422: Charles VI dies; France divided between supporters of his son, later crowned as Charles VII, and the kings of England			
	1429: Coronation of Charles VII		1429: Failure of Siege of Rouen by the English – resistance led by Joan of Arc	
1430				
			1431: Lollard Rising	1431: Council of Basle begins
1440				
1445: Henry VI marries Margaret of Anjou				
1450				1449: Council of Basle ends
			1450: Battle of Formigny (French defeat English); Jack Cade's revolt	
			1451: Johann Gutenberg invents the movable-type printing press	
			1453: Battle of Castillon (last battle of Hundred Years War – remaining English lands in France lost, except Calais)	
			1455: First battle of St Albans (so-called start of the Wars of the Roses) – Duke of York takes control of the king	
1460				
1461: Edward IV deposes Henry VI	1461: Charles VII dies; Louis XI accedes to throne		1461: Battle of Towton (Yorkists defeat Lancastrians)	
1464: Edward IV marries Elizabeth Woodeville				
		1467: Philip the Good dies, Charles the Bold succeeds		
		1468: Charles the Bold marries Margaret of York		
			1469: Rebellion of Warwick and Clarence against Edward IV	

	REIGNS OF ENGLISH KINGS	REIGNS OF FRENCH KINGS	REIGNS OF BURGUNDIAN DUKES	HISTORICAL EVENTS	RELIGIOUS EVENTS
1470	1470: Edward IV deposed; Henry VI back in power 1471: Edward IV regains power; Henry VI killed in the Tower			1471: Battle of Barnet (Yorkists defeat Lancastrians); battle of Tewkesbury (Yorkists defeat Lancastrians) 1473 or early 1474: *The Recuyell of the Historyes of Troy* published in Bruges (first book to be printed in English) 1475: Treaty of Picquigny between England and France 1476: William Caxton moves to England and sets up printing press at Westminster	
			1477: Charles the Bold killed at the battle of Nancy; Burgundy seized by France; Mary of Burgundy (heiress) marries Maximilian of Austria		
1480	1483: Edward IV dies; his heir Edward V is deposed by Richard III 1485: Henry VII succeeds Richard III 1486: Henry VII marries Elizabeth of York	1483: Louis XI dies; Charles VIII accedes to throne	1482: Mary of Burgundy dies 1482: Maximilian signs Treaty of Arras by which Franche-Comté and Artois pass to France	1485: Battle of Bosworth (Henry Tudor defeats Richard III and the Yorkists; Richard III killed) 1487: Rising of Lambert Simnel	
1490				1492: Columbus discovers the Americas 1495: Perkin Warbeck's rebellion 1497: John Cabot reaches Newfoundland and claims lands for England 1498: Vasco da Gama sails round Africa to reach India	
		1498: Charles VIII dies; Louis XII accedes to throne			
1500					
	1509: Henry VIII succeeds Henry VII				
1510				1513: Battle of the Spurs (English defeat French); battle of Flodden Field (English defeat Scots)	1517: Martin Luther produces his 95 theses criticizing the sale of indulgences by the Catholic Church
		1515: Louis XII dies; Francis I accedes to throne			
1520				1520: Henry VIII and Francis I meet at the Field of Cloth of Gold 1529: Wolsey deprived of all honours except archbishopric of York	
1530	1533: Henry VIII divorces Catherine of Aragon, and marries Anne Boleyn 1536: Anne Boleyn executed; Henry VIII marries Jane Seymour 1537: Jane Seymour dies			1530: Wolsey dies	1533: Act of Restraint of Appeals – the break with Rome 1534: Henry VIII is declared Supreme Head of the Church of England 1536: Act of Parliament authorizing the suppression of the smaller religious houses; first pilgrimage sites suppressed 1539: The Great Bible, the first official English translation of the Bible, is published
1540	1540: Henry VIII marries Anne of Cleves; marriage annulled; Henry VIII marries Catherine Howard 1542: Catherine Howard executed 1543: Henry VIII marries Catherine Parr 1547: Henry VIII dies, succeeded by Edward VI	1547: Francis I dies, succeeded by Henry II			1540: The remaining monastic houses and friaries are dissolved; most pilgrimage sites destroyed; Thomas Cromwell executed

I

AN AGE OF CONSUMPTION: ART FOR ENGLAND c.1400–1547

RICHARD MARKS

1 Henry VII's Chapel, Westminster Abbey, interior (cat. no. 28)

The last phase of the Middle Ages is all around us. Some of England's most familiar and cherished man-made landmarks date from this time, several still performing the functions for which they were designed. St George's Chapel, Windsor, remains closely associated with the monarchy and is the headquarters of the Knights of the Garter (plate 70, cat. no. 25). King's College Chapel is the jewel of Cambridge and the college itself is a seat of learning, as its founder Henry VI intended (cat. no. 19). Henry VII's great chapel projects from the east end of Westminster Abbey into what is still the heart of government (plates 1, 72, cat. no. 28). All of these, and royal palaces like Hampton Court, are among England's leading tourist attractions – not just because of their historic associations, but also (and probably more importantly) through their beauty and magnificence. Outside London and its environs, visitors flock to Lavenham in Suffolk, a town retaining its late medieval layout and much of its housing stock (cat. no. 123). Its church and that of nearby Long Melford (plate 121) are among the glories of East Anglian ecclesiastical architecture. It is impossible to travel far without encountering visible traces of the England of Henry V, of the Wars of the Roses, of Henry VIII. Numerous towns and cities preserve their medieval street-pattern and many of their medieval buildings, even if concealed behind later façades and accretions. Castles and manor houses pepper the landscape. Parish churches are the most characteristic features of both the English urban and rural topography. Although they are often aggregates of different periods, it is hard to find any without some element, be it a window, bench or tomb, dating from the period 1400–1547. Especially in East Anglia, the Cotswolds, Devon and Somerset, it is common to find entire churches that were built or rebuilt in these years. Even outside these areas, most counties contain several churches whose fabric entirely dates from this time. Quantities of artefacts of secular and domestic origin survive in national and local museums, the Oxford and Cambridge colleges and the City of London livery companies. Many have been brought together for the first time in this exhibition.

In addition to the numerous buildings, books, stained-glass windows, carvings and other works of art, there is a mass of documentation. There is more for this period, and it is of a more

heterogeneous character, than for previous centuries and it increases in volume from the second half of the fifteenth century: alongside records of expenditure and inventories are contracts, churchwardens' accounts, wills, commonplace books and correspondence.[1] There are also the observations of scholars and overseas visitors and even a few constructed 'biographies'.[2] By 1400, English had become the everyday speech of the highest in the land and many of the written records, including the collections of letters, are in the vernacular. Through these, however distorted and diluted, the voices of those who commissioned and used what today we classify as art-objects are heard. And these voices represent a wider social spectrum than just the Crown, the nobility, the gentry and the upper clergy: for the first time we have numerous details of the collective and individual possessions of townspeople and villagers, of artisans, traders and tillers of the soil. Cumulatively the multivocality of the period offers insights into the art and architecture that English men and women owned, shared and enjoyed.

Late medieval art in England might be plentiful and ubiquitous, but it is neither readily comprehended nor easily defined.[3] Its principal characteristic is its variety. Qualitatively it encompasses the good, the bad and the downright ugly. It was simultaneously international and insular, progressive and provincial, diverse and diffuse, conservative yet receptive to new modes and technologies, inventive in form, vibrant in colour and rich in iconography. Above all, it was in demand. The absence from this exhibition (with a few exceptions) of artefacts made in or for Wales, and that area of Ireland which formed 'the Pale', is not to subordinate these other constituent parts of the British Isles, which at the time came under the rule of one sovereign, to an ethnically English cultural hegemony; on the contrary, it is to acknowledge that these other nations, like the Scots, trod their own paths in matters artistic.[4]

The elusiveness and complexity of the art produced in and for England between 1400 and 1547 stems partly from the inescapable fact that so many of its products had functions and meanings utterly removed from those of the twenty-first century. The pattern of survival has also been uneven and therefore distorting. A lethal combination of war, changing religious ideologies, financial imperatives, cupidity and fragility, fashion and taste has dealt severely with the products of the Middle Ages – pre- as much as post-1400. Of royal possessions, almost nothing remains for our period apart from ecclesiastical buildings funded by various monarchs. Even the last resting places of Henry VI, Edward IV and Henry VIII are no longer marked by their original or intended monuments; Richard III's grave at Leicester has disappeared without trace. As a result, exam-

ples of the best and most innovative commissions are absent. The Reformation was responsible for the almost wholesale destruction of artefacts made for the Church or private devotion. The jewel-bedecked shrines and gold and silver altarpieces have vanished entirely. The total surviving church plate from the years 1400–1547 would not suffice to have serviced even a large parish church like Long Melford, let alone a cathedral or monastic establishment. Long Melford is fortunate in preserving considerable quantities of stained glass and traces of its mural and ceiling decoration, but it has lost its rood and rood-screen, its huge high-altar reredos and other altarpieces, all of its vestments and banners, almost all of its brasses and, with one exception, its large stock of devotional images. That the dominant sculptural medium was wood is barely apparent from the handful of survivors – and even these (and statuary in stone) have been stripped of their rich polychromy.[5] Once-common categories of objects, such as painted cloths, have almost completely disappeared (cat. nos 155, 301). The number of extant illuminated books is not matched by the survival rate of wall- and glass-painting. Personal attire, that potent messenger of status and wealth, has perished, apart from jewellery. Those artefacts which have come down to us are often displaced and rarely fulfil their original function.

A second confusing factor is historiographical. The fate of the visual arts is frequently perceived to have been determined largely by political events, themselves seen in the light of the strife-torn and blood-drenched England evoked in Shakespeare's history plays. Following this reading, as English military triumphs turned to defeat in France and the country descended into internecine dynastic strife, England declined artistically into a backwater. This interpretation has been compounded by the fact that the period straddles the traditional historical divide between the medieval and early modern eras: the triumph of Henry Tudor at the battle of Bosworth in 1485 has often been seen as a cultural turning-point, when a new dawn was ushered in by a polyglot group of foreign artists charging to the rescue, introducing Renaissance modes of representation and ornamentation and restoring England to the mainstream of European visual culture. The later Middle Ages have thus been viewed as an age of transition, sandwiched between the glories of English High Gothic art and architecture of the thirteenth and fourteenth centuries and the emergence of new artistic models based on the reception of Renaissance ideals under a 'new' Tudor monarchy.

The persistence of nineteenth-century notions of what is canonical Gothic and a qualitative view of art history, which measures the artistic production of the period by the

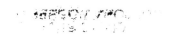

yardstick of Renaissance Italy, have contributed to this caricature. To an extent, this perception has found echoes in attitudes to northern European art as a whole in the fifteenth and early sixteenth centuries. The great Dutch historian Johan Huizinga saw in the Franco-Burgundian culture of the time both the end of the Middle Ages and the first flowering of the northern Renaissance, hence the title of his classic book, *Herfsttij der Middeleeuwen*.[6]

Attempts to define the visual arts in England are also complicated by the receptivity of leading English patrons to continental products and craftsmen. This was as true in 1400 as it was in 1547, although the influence of non-indigenous production was more pervasive in Henry VIII's reign than it had been in Henry IV's. The well-to-do, both

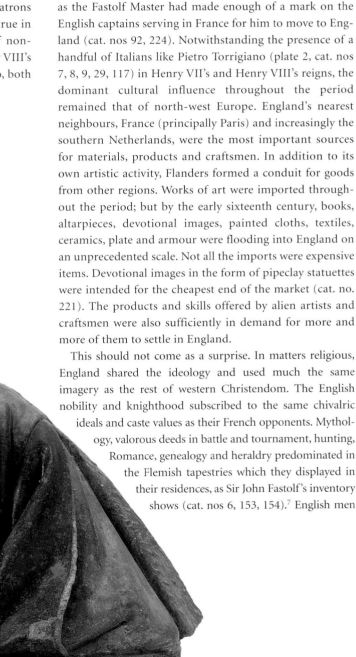

2 Bust of Henry VII,
Pietro Torrigiano (cat. no. 7)

lay and clerical, had no qualms about acquiring or commissioning works of art from abroad or from foreign artists. Major patrons, led by the Crown, went to the best available, irrespective of nationality. Archbishop Chichele's pair of silver wine flagons was made by Parisian goldsmiths (cat. no. 101). Among John, Duke of Bedford's possessions could be found luxurious illuminated manuscripts of both French and English craftsmanship (plate 87, cat. nos 72, 73). The French illuminator known as the Fastolf Master had made enough of a mark on the English captains serving in France for him to move to England (cat. nos 92, 224). Notwithstanding the presence of a handful of Italians like Pietro Torrigiano (plate 2, cat. nos 7, 8, 9, 29, 117) in Henry VII's and Henry VIII's reigns, the dominant cultural influence throughout the period remained that of north-west Europe. England's nearest neighbours, France (principally Paris) and increasingly the southern Netherlands, were the most important sources for materials, products and craftsmen. In addition to its own artistic activity, Flanders formed a conduit for goods from other regions. Works of art were imported throughout the period; but by the early sixteenth century, books, altarpieces, devotional images, painted cloths, textiles, ceramics, plate and armour were flooding into England on an unprecedented scale. Not all the imports were expensive items. Devotional images in the form of pipeclay statuettes were intended for the cheapest end of the market (cat. no. 221). The products and skills offered by alien artists and craftsmen were also sufficiently in demand for more and more of them to settle in England.

This should not come as a surprise. In matters religious, England shared the ideology and used much the same imagery as the rest of western Christendom. The English nobility and knighthood subscribed to the same chivalric ideals and caste values as their French opponents. Mythology, valorous deeds in battle and tournament, hunting, Romance, genealogy and heraldry predominated in the Flemish tapestries which they displayed in their residences, as Sir John Fastolf's inventory shows (cat. nos 6, 153, 154).[7] English men and women encountered continental products through war, diplomacy, trade and commerce, and pilgrimage.

To limit the history of art in England to what is deemed to be the work of indigenous craftsmen would thus present a very confused and distorted picture, especially at the highest levels. It is often difficult – even pointless – to characterize a work as 'English' or 'foreign'. The Donne Triptych (cat. no. 213) is self-evidently the work of Hans Memling and was executed in Bruges, but what label should be applied to the Bedford Psalter and Hours (cat. no. 73), a manuscript with illumination by several artists, including the foreign-born but domiciled Herman Scheerre? How is a cope, whose material was manufactured in Italy but with English needlework, to be classified (cat. nos 31, 248)? It is unhelpful to distinguish between the Donne Triptych and the Fairford glass (cat. no. 294) on the basis that one was painted in Flanders and the other was made by immigrant craftsmen from the same region. As at Fairford, the reception of foreign artists and craftsmen, designs and products usually involved some degree of translation into English idioms. The Fairford glazing programme had to be adapted to fit Perpendicular windows. Scheerre painted his initials and miniatures in manuscripts with traditional English decorative elements. The hybrid nature of the late Winchester and Westminster stone sculpture makes it difficult to determine the country or countries of origin of the carvers (cat. nos 234, 235, 356, 239).

Broadly speaking, the formal vocabulary of English art remained what we would define as Gothic throughout the period. Henry Bolingbroke's seizure of the throne in 1399 did not mark the emergence of a new style. By that date, the brilliance and luxurious refinement of International Gothic had already been assimilated at the highest level; indeed, Richard II's exquisite Wilton Diptych (plate 3) is one of the finest creations of its time anywhere in Europe. The salient technical and design innovations of Perpendicular architecture had been framed before 1400; thereafter it was a matter of variations on a theme. This is not to suggest that nothing changed between 1400 and 1547. Much did, but more in some fields than others. Painting (especially portraiture) was of greater significance in the early sixteenth century than it had been a century earlier. Figuratively, the illusionism propagated in Flanders supplanted the more ethereal illusionism of International Gothic that was in vogue in the early fifteenth century. The architecture of war too became transformed in respect of the defences of the realm. All'antica ornamentation was an increasingly common element in the repertoire of early sixteenth-century masons, sculptors, goldsmiths, painters and glaziers. In the dissemination of such motifs, printing

(introduced into England in the later fifteenth century) came to play an important role, as well as opening up a new and socially more diverse field for artistic endeavour.

It is possible to identify a large number of artists in the period and quite a number of their products survive. Helpful though this can be, names may mislead, by privileging centres where records are preserved; and they obscure what was for the most part the collaborative nature of artistic activity in the Middle Ages. The St William window in York Minster was principally the work of glass painters, but also involved at one remove or another were glassmakers, masons and blacksmiths (cat. nos 232, 317). A woodcarver, a painter and a leatherworker as well as an armourer (the last possibly the donor, William Vynard) participated in the making of the St George belonging to the Armourers and Brasiers' Company (cat. no. 58).

Craftsmen went wherever their patrons demanded. The sculptor John Massingham was associated with Westminster Abbey, All Souls College, Oxford, and the Beauchamp Chapel in Warwick. John Prudde, who held the office of king's glazier under Henry VI, worked at Winchester, Oxford and Warwick (cat. no. 89), as well as in the royal residences and in foundations like Eton. Even a provincial workshop such as the Malvern-based glass-painting firm of Richard Twygge and Thomas Wodshawe, through patronage networks, was able to attract important commissions at Westminster Abbey and Tattershall College (plate 19, cat. nos 37, 292). The likes of Massingham and Prudde were located in London (or Westminster) and inevitably the capital was, as always, the most important centre for much artistic production and the purchase of artefacts, notably monumental brasses, goldsmiths' work and the crafts associated with bookmaking, firstly illumination and later also printing. Across the Thames, Southwark was the principal residence of the alien craftsmen from the late fifteenth century.

Demand stimulated output. The building trades had long been established close to stone quarries and timber, but it is in this period that regional production in other fields of activity can be assessed, on documentation as well as extant work. The pattern was diverse. The alabaster carvers seem to have remained centralized in the vicinity of the alabaster quarries in the Midlands, but with retail outlets in centres like Bristol and London and a chain of agents perambulating the country, taking orders for tombs, images and altarpieces. Their stock products were offered already painted and must have presented serious competition to the work of locally based stone- and woodcarvers and painters and gilders. In prosperous eastern England there was sufficient

3 The Wilton Diptych
(National Gallery, London)

demand to support craftsmen in several urban centres, hence the range of styles exhibited by screen-paintings and glazing in Norfolk and Suffolk. Bury St Edmunds housed manuscript and monumental painters, bell-founders, brass-engravers, masons and carvers who serviced the town and its hinterland. The sparser population in the north meant that York craftsmen cast their nets more widely. William Brownfleet carved choir-stalls for Bridlington Priory and also worked in Ripon Minster, where he was probably responsible for the magnificent misericords (cat. no. 240). In York, like London, there was a sufficient concentration of masons, glass-painters and other craftsmen to support craft guilds, but in smaller towns and even centres like Bury there is no evidence that the individual guild writ ever ran.

Much regional production was distinctive and was shaped in varying degrees by tradition, the availability of materials and craftsmen, changing patterns in worship and devotion,

and wealth. The parish churches of Devon, the Cotswolds, Norfolk and Suffolk all display their own regional architectural traits. The wagon roofs favoured by the carvers, carpenters and joiners in the West Country contrast with the elaborate hammerbeam constructions of East Anglia. Rood-screens in Devon are notable for their carving, whereas better-quality figurative painting on the dado is a feature of East Anglian screenwork (cat. nos 264, 265, 266, 277). In some cases it is a matter of individual workshops, rather than a regional mode. Brownfleet was probably associated with a group of Yorkshire woodcarvers who during the early sixteenth century executed a number of roofs, stalls, screens and tombs. Stained-glass workshops in various parts of the country are identifiable by their own distinctive traits. 'Provincial' was not invariably synonymous with inferior. In the West Country, the Dominican friar John Siferwas (presumably a trained painter before he became a mendicant) in *c*.1400 produced masterpieces of manuscript illumination like the Sherborne Missal and Lovel Lectionary (plate 4, cat. no. 254), which were the match of anything by his London-based contemporaries. There are good grounds for believing that the innovators in glass-painting during the early fifteenth century were Thomas Glazier of Oxford and John Thornton of Coventry (and later York).

Thus English art was far from being entirely dominated by alien products and artists. This was particularly true of architecture, where masons continued to design and build in the Perpendicular idiom, whether a cathedral or a parish church, a college or a castle. There is nothing second-rate about the spatial articulation, the technical mastery and visual complexities of the fan vaults and architectural design of the great royal chapels at St George's, Windsor, King's College and Henry VII's mausoleum at Westminster. Without parallel on the Continent are the walls of glass in the east end of York Minster, combining kaleidoscopic translucency and iconographic ingenuity (plate 5). At their best, the alabaster men were capable of carving tailor-made tombs (plate 8, cat. nos 330, 337), images and altarpieces (cat. nos 84, 244, 282, 344) of a quality that attracted the patronage of the highest in the land.[8] Their products also found ready markets from Scandinavia to Spain. Nor should English music be overlooked. The polyphony sung in the great ecclesiastical establishments and choral foundations is one of the cultural achievements of the age, and the 'English manner' was both admired and emulated on the Continent.

The scale of expenditure by the likes of Edward IV and the first two Tudor monarchs is astounding. They called on the best available craftsmen in their particular fields. With diplomatic hyperbole, John Leland dubbed Henry VII's Chapel the wonder of the entire world. When it was conceived, the king and his advisers employed Netherlandish glass painters for the windows, the Florentine sculptor Torrigiano for the altar and royal tombs, and unidentified carvers for the stalls and for the multitude of saints that adorn the triforium and eastern chapels. The incomparable architectural frame, however, was designed by Robert Janyns, an English master mason, who also worked on St George's Chapel, Windsor.[9] Both Henry VII and his successor built a chain of royal residences that were filled with the prodigious quantities of tapestries (cat. no. 6) and plate listed in the royal inventories. Truly they were players on the international scene when it came to artistic patronage.

Outlay on this scale was not so much an exercise of individual taste as what was expected of rulers. In reminding monarchs that expenditure on buildings, furnishings and all

forms of display was an essential aspect of effective kingship, the fifteenth-century writer Sir John Fortescue was merely expressing what had been normative princely behaviour for centuries.[10] His dictum was applied in varying degrees, according to means and status, personal whim and circumstance. Henry VII was acutely conscious of the potency of regal display: the phrase 'As to a Kings werk apperteigneth' recurs in his will.[11] For him and for Henry VIII, costly buildings and furnishings projected a (much-needed) impression of permanence and stability, festooned as they were with their badges and devices.

4   The Lovel Lectionary, John Siferwas (cat. no. 254)

5   York Minster, east window, John Thornton, 1405–8

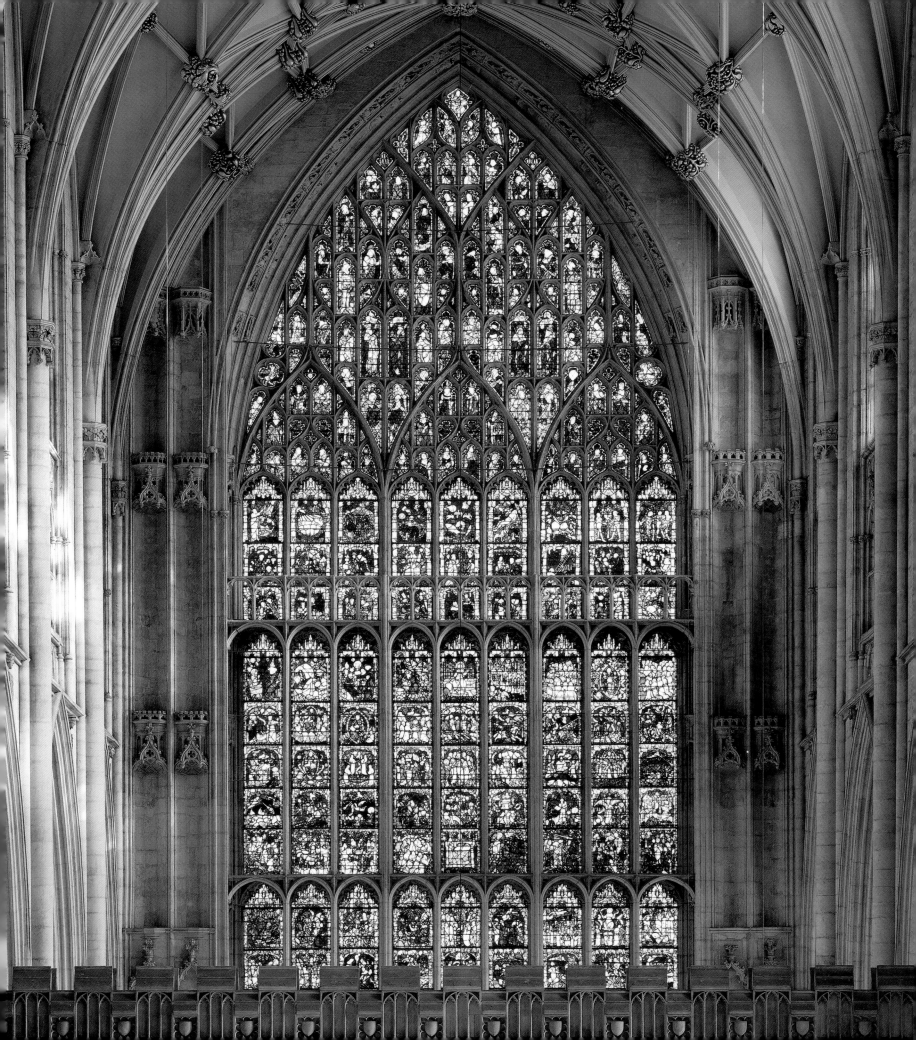

6   Hengrave Hall (cat. no. 149)

Such precepts did not just apply to the monarchy, but were adopted by the ruling caste, both secular and ecclesiastical. Late medieval English society was one in which individuals were bound to each other by ties of lineage, marriage, allegiance and clientage. It was a small world, as the Paston correspondence shows. Through its pages occur the names of monarchs, prelates, nobles and gentry, lawyers and merchants, even parochial clergy and ordinary renters of property. Within the Church, it was possible for talented individuals like Henry Chichele and Richard Fox to rise from humble origins to hold respectively the highest ecclesiastical office in the realm and one of the richest sees in Christendom. In general, however, English men and women knew their place in the order of things and behaved accordingly. Bishop Waynflete, one of Sir John Fastolf's executors, was expressing a universally-held value when he stipulated that the old warhorse should be buried 'accordyng to hys degree'.[12] By acquiring possessions according to their 'degree', status and rank were acquired or confirmed. Lords and knights accumulated and built in the same way that they fought (when necessary), managed their estates and businesses, and pursued their leisure pastimes. Fastolf and Ralph, Lord Cromwell constructed status-conscious castles and manor houses, and planned elaborate collegiate foundations for the well-being of their souls (cat. nos 50, 145, 67, 291, 292). The Pastons discharged their familial and social obligations in erecting tombs and chantries and in embellishing their local parish church or monastery.

In the fifteenth and sixteenth centuries, those engaged in trade and commerce were major consumers of luxury goods and artefacts. Merchants, especially those who made their living from the wool and cloth trades, aimed to beautify and enrich the cities and towns where they were domiciled. The brasses covering the floors of Cotswold churches like Northleach testify to the contribution made by the wool trade to the grandeur of late medieval ecclesiastical architecture in this region. The same applies to East Anglia. The profits of the cloth industry enabled John Baret to amass the staggering quantity of goods and possessions which, meticulously disposed of in his will, imprinted his personal stamp on St Mary's church in Bury St Edmunds (plate 58, cat. nos 261, 331).[13] Hengrave Hall, one of the most impressive country houses of its day, was built for a London merchant (plate 6, cat. no. 149). Their overseas peregrinations and contacts meant that merchants were no less receptive to new fashions and ideas than their social superiors. Robert Tate, a London alderman and member of the Staple of Calais, commissioned a Netherlandish altarpiece for a pilgrimage chapel adjacent to All-Hallows-by-the-Tower (plate 56, cat. no. 136). Thomas Powder of Ipswich and his wife Emme even forsook the long-established monumental brass industry in favour of the products of Flemish founders (cat. no. 334).

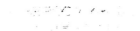

The aforementioned windows of Fairford were a by-product of the Tame family's success as wool-merchants (cat. no. 294). Merchants were not just consumers and commissioners; they also imported foreign goods. The Calais-based Celys frequented the great fairs at Antwerp and Bruges and shipped home their purchases. They also acted as agents for wealthy clients like Sir John Weston, Prior of the Knights of St John in England.[14]

As we move down the social scale, the wealthier peasants and artisans had surplus cash and goods in kind to spend on themselves and their parish churches. Urban archaeological sites have revealed pottery, base-metal and wooden plate and utensils; also items of personal adornment such as rings and rosary beads. These were pale reflections – and even, in some cases, imitations – of the silver and gold plate and jewellery owned by the wealthier echelons of society, but they show that artefact possession in this period was not the exclusive preserve of the latter. Inventories and wills reveal that the rural dwellings of the more prosperous yeomen and husbandmen and their wives sometimes contained surprising quantities of 'household stuff'. Among the possessions of Alice Cooke (d. 1521), a comfortably-off widow of Eaton Bray in Bedfordshire, were brass pots, pans, cauldrons, five platters, a basin, a chafing-dish (cat. no. 198), four saucers, candlesticks, two coffers and much bedding. And through belonging to a parish community, Alice also had a stake in more major artefacts, such as the images in her parish church; she made small bequests to the lights of several, including the Rood (cat. no. 268), the Sepulchre (cat. no. 273), the Trinity and St Nicholas.[15] As a member of the Dunstable Fraternity of St John the Baptist, Alice would have been entitled to have her body covered by the guild's magnificent pall during her funerary rites (plate 31, cat. no. 349).

For owners and users, every artefact had a function and a meaning. Possessions and commissions were used by *arrivistes* like the Pastons and Ralph Cromwell to assert their worldly success. Selfhood, status, affinity and patronage were expressed through the burgeoning popularity of personal and familial insignia. The Tudor palaces and religious foundations were quite literally dressed in the king's livery. The Beauchamp Chapel is permeated by the heraldry, badges and mottoes of the founder – on tomb, vault, stall and window (cat. nos 86, 87, 89). By donating a votive crown replete with initials and personal devices to the image of Our Lady at Aachen, Margaret of York was privileging her relationship with this famous cult image (cat. no. 11). John Baret's motto, *Grace me gouerne*, adorned many of his possessions and can still be seen on the painted roof over his tomb and on the tomb itself (cat. no. 331). *Vanitas* and self-

promotion were sometimes concealed by a thin veil of self-denial, epitomized by John Clopton's inscription on the exterior of the exquisite Lady Chapel at Long Melford (plate 121): 'Let Christ be my witness that I have not exhibited these things in order that I may win praise, but in order that the Spirit may be remembered.' Display, even in spiritual matters, might be motivated as much by competition and material betterment as by the desire for personal salvation. The 'monthly mind' of Richard Cely (1482) was used by the family to attract suitable spouses for his unmarried sons by an exhibition of their plate.[16]

To our eyes, such flaunting of wealth and status might seem vulgar and ostentatious. Yet to contemporaries it was entirely proper. Possessions not only defined personal status, their manufacture and sale also provided employment, and in the religious sphere they served God. People were also aware of the ephemeral nature of worldly goods and success. John Baret is represented on his tomb as a naked decaying corpse, with texts admonishing viewers to heed their own fate and to pray for his soul (plate 58).

Outward display was accompanied by a desire for privacy or exclusivity among the upper echelons of society. In the parish churches, as more and more individuals, as well as groups like fraternities, claimed space both for the living and for the dead, so the gentry and urban elites created separate chapels as family pews and burial sites, usually in the most prestigious parts of the building. This was not new to the period, but the process accelerated during the fifteenth and early sixteenth centuries. These chapels – and their equivalents in private residences – were lavishly equipped and the family identity stamped on them by heraldry and the other common signifiers of rank and status. The Ashwellthorpe Triptych was of a size to fit the altar of an oratory either in the Knyvett house or the chapel that still stands on the north side of the chancel of Ashwellthorpe church (plate 56, cat. no. 276). In the secular sphere, the same wish for privacy (and comfort) manifested itself in the supplanting of the great hall by the parlour or great chamber as the main focus of family life. This trend too had been in train since the middle of the fourteenth century.[17]

An increased emphasis on affective piety fuelled demand for portable devotional artefacts like Books of Hours (a demand vastly enhanced by the advent of printed books) and rosaries. A Venetian visitor in about 1500 remarked on the prevalence of personal devotional practices in England, 'the women carrying long rosaries in their hands and any who can read taking the office of Our Lady with them and with some companion reciting it in the church, verse by verse, in a low voice … '[18] Agnes Browne or her husband can be imagined walking through the streets of Stamford to All Saints church bearing her Flemish-made Book of Hours with its embossed cover and minute images on the clasps (cat. no. 140). Agnes's book may have functioned as a devotional aid, but even when closed it acted as a discreet indicator of status. It is little wonder that rosaries made from precious materials feature so much in wills and inventories (cat. no. 222). Personal items of adornment, like the Clare Cross and the Middleham Jewel, were simultaneously status symbols, financial assets, fashion accessories, apotropaic reliquaries and devotional aids (plate 7, cat. nos 209, 98). Even an iconographical ring might have romantic as well as religious connotations. The newly wedded Margery Paston gave her husband a ring engraved with her name-saint as a love token. Margery Cely dispatched to her spouse in Calais a gold fetterlock and a heart of gold as keepsakes that must have resembled those in the Fishpool hoard (cat. no. 206).[19]

In this period, many crafts offered a wide range of products to suit the needs and purses of a socially-diverse clientele. Much of the output of the monumental brass engravers was affordable by the more prosperous artisans and peasantry. The alabaster carvers too produced work for the cheaper end of the market. Even items of personal devotion, like alabaster St John's heads, which might cost as little as one shilling, were not beyond the means of the likes of Alice Cooke of Eaton Bray (cat. no. 219).[20] For some crafts, a sliding scale of charges existed. John Prudde charged from 7d. to 2s. a square foot, dependent on the amount of coloured glass used and the complexity of the imagery. His price of 1s. 2d. for 'vitri historiales' (that is, narrative subjects) at Eton College in 1450 was still the rate at Tattershall more than 30 years later (cat. nos 89, 291, 292).

There was a vast difference between the cost of artefacts commissioned at the highest level and those made more or less off the shelf for the lower end of the market. The tomb of Ralph Greene at Lowick (plate 8, cat. no. 330) was one of the more expensive products of the alabaster carvers, yet its cost of £40 pales into insignificance when compared with the £720 or so expended on the monument of Richard Beauchamp, Earl of Warwick (cat. no. 87). The latter's materials included Purbeck marble, enamel and copper-gilt, and its manufacture demanded the combined skills of a draughtsman or painter (for the design), a marbler, a carver, a goldsmith, a barber-surgeon and founders.

Textiles were extremely expensive. Throughout the period, Netherlandish tapestries were highly prized status symbols for anyone who was anybody. Edward IV paid Pasquier Grenier, the leading tapestry merchant, the enormous sum of nearly £2,500 for a series of hangings depicting the *History*

of *Nebuchadnezzar*, the *History of Alexander*, a *Judgment*, the *Passion*, several *verdure* hangings and three valances for a bed. This was more than eight times the amount contracted with the mason for building the nave of Fotheringhay church in 1434 (cat. no. 327).[21] Crimson velvet cloth-of-gold imported from Italy cost anywhere between £2 and £11 per yard (cat. no. 201). The set of vestments left by Agnes Cely to her parish church of St Olave's, Hart Street in London at her death in 1483 cost her executors £39 8s. 11½d., of which 17¾ yards of 'blue cloth of gold' were priced at 26s. 8d. per yard; the vestment maker's charge for making up the set

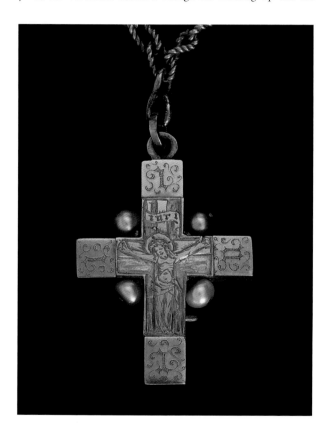

7 The Clare Cross (cat. no. 209)

came to a mere 10s. This sum far exceeded the £8 3s. 4d. disbursed to Roger Egge, a freemason and marbler, for the tomb of Agnes's late husband.[22]

Price was one of several considerations when it came to acquiring an artefact. Patrons also concerned themselves with subject-matter. Sir Thomas Stathum was very precise about what he wanted on his brass in Morley church (Derbyshire), even if the finished article did not conform exactly to his instructions (cat. no. 332). The annotations to the imagery depicted in the vidimus for a window of one of Cardinal Wolsey's projects were presumably made at the patron's behest (cat. no. 295). 'Workmanlike' is a common

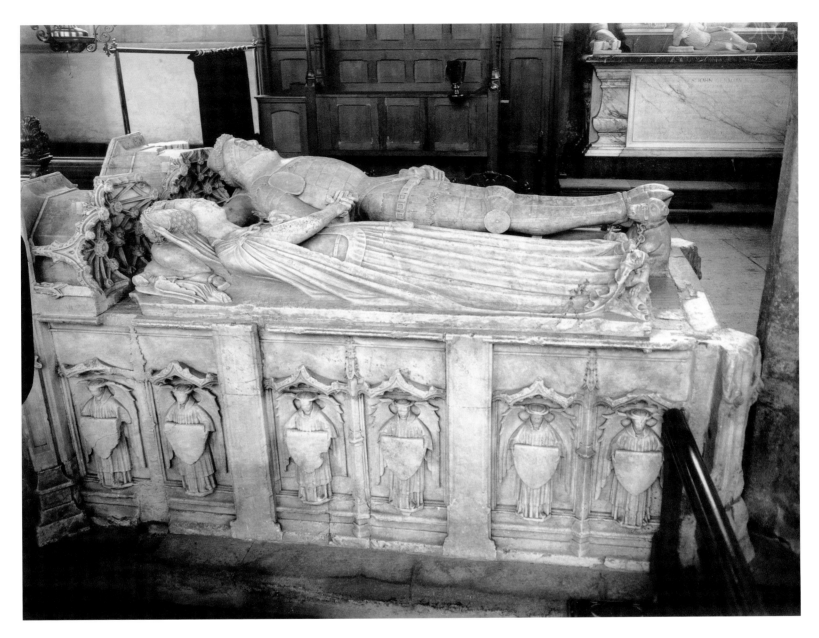

8   Tomb of Ralph Greene and his wife Katherine, St Peter's church, Lowick, Thomas Prentys and Robert Sutton (cat. no. 330)

adjective in contracts, because patrons wanted value for their outlay. A constant refrain in the Beauchamp Chapel accounts is that not only must the materials be of the highest quality, but they should be worked 'in the most finest wise', or words to that effect.[23] The more discerning (or more hard-nosed) patrons recognized inferior work when they saw it. John Paston I expressed his dissatisfaction with a tombmaker in St Bride's parish, London: he was 'no klenly portrayer' and John proposed finding someone else to design and 'grave' his brother Edmond's brass.[24]

Artistic skill was evidently valued and it would be useful to know by what criteria John Paston was judging the unfortunate tombmaker. Johan Huizinga sought to compre-hend what late medieval people admired in the artistic products of their day and how they valued their aesthetic qualities. Unfortunately a meaningful vocabulary for critical evaluation is lacking throughout the period. What qualities did Oxnead church (Norfolk) possess, to be labelled as 'resonable plesaunt'? What criteria were John Leland apply-ing to St Mary's church in Nottingham for it to be lauded as 'excellent' (plate 60)? What led Margery Kempe to charac-terize an image of a Pietà as 'fair' (the most widely used epithet)? Was it because, within her experience, this Pietà was aesthetically superior to others she had seen? Or was it because it was larger or more elaborately painted and gilded?[25]

Indicators of the aesthetic sensibilities of late medieval patrons and owners are elusive, even in the most sophisticated circles. It is impossible to say whether the magnificent manuscripts, jewels and plate listed in John, Duke of Bedford's inventories reflected his personal connoisseurship or what was expected of him by his princely status.

Ultimately, there is a clear distinction between patronal desires and perspectives and the act of creation. Richard Beauchamp 'devised' his mortuary chapel, but by this he meant ordered: he or his heirs and executors specified the chapel's iconography, but they did not design the building and its contents, any more than Archbishop Chichele was responsible for the appearance of All Souls College, Oxford. It is about those who commissioned that we know most – often their fame (or reputation) has been determined by their possessions. Those who articulated the wishes of patrons, and translated them into the works of art we still admire, have left far fewer traces in the written records. Their memorials are the wonderfully diverse buildings and artefacts they conceived and fashioned. And behind the known artists and craftsmen are hosts of anonymous masons, carvers, painters, goldsmiths, weavers and needleworkers. It is these – as much as Scheerre, Thornton, Prudde, Holbein and Torrigiano – whom we have cause to celebrate.

FURTHER READING

The essays and entries in this catalogue; Aston 1979; Davis 1971, 1976; Gairdner 1986; Hanham 1975; Harvey 1969; Stratford 1993.

NOTES

1 The most important published inventories are those of John, Duke of Bedford and Henry VIII; also those of Sir John Fastolf. Extensive correspondence survives from gentry (the Pastons, the Stonors and the Plumptons) and wool-merchants (the Cely family); from the end of the period are the letters of one of the highest in the land, Arthur Plantagenet, Lord Lisle, the bastard son of Edward IV. All of these are available in published editions.

2 The observations made by John Leland during his extensive travels are the best known. The papers of William Worcestre, secretary to Sir John Fastolf, are particularly valuable for architectural historians. The *Beauchamp Pageants* is a highly selective pictorial narrative of the life of Richard Beauchamp, Earl of Warwick (cat. nos 85, 90). Very different and more complex is the *Book of Margery Kempe*, an account of an extremely, even excessively, devout member of the mercantile elite of King's Lynn, Norfolk.

3 Unsurprisingly, few scholars have attempted an overview. See Evans 1949 (as the title shows, this covers only the first part of the period); Richmond 1995 offers a historian's perspective; Gaimster and Stamper 1997 provides an interdisciplinary approach.

4 See, for example, Edinburgh 1982.

5 For polychromed sculpture, see Boldrick, Park and Williamson 2002.

6 Huizinga 1996, esp. pp.xix–xx. The book was first published in 1919. The first English edition (1924) was entitled *The Waning of the Middle Ages*. See Aston 1979; Peters and Simons 1999; Haskell 1993, chapter 15.

7 Gairdner 1986, no. 389.

8 Most notably, the tomb of Henry IV and Queen Joan in Canterbury Cathedral.

9 Wilson 1995.

10 Plummer 1885, p.125.

11 Astle 1775, *passim*.

12 Gairdner 1986, no. 393.

13 For Baret's will, see Tymms 1850, pp.15–44. This document also names several Bury craftsmen.

14 Hanham 1975.

15 Bell 1997, no. 95, pp.59–60.

16 Hanham 1985, pp.260–63. The 'monthly mind' was a celebration in memory of a deceased individual, when prayers and alms were offered for the good of their soul.

17 Girouard 1978, chapter 3; Cooper 1999, chapter 8.

18 Sneyd 1847, p.23.

19 Gairdner 1986, no. 923; Hanham 1975, no. 222.

20 Cheetham 1984, p.31.

21 McKendrick 1987, pp.521–2; Salzman 1967, pp.505–9. The Fotheringhay price excluded materials.

22 Hanham 1985, pp.255, 269–70.

23 Dugdale 1730, pp.445–7.

24 Davis 1971, no. 37, p.54.

25 Gairdner 1986, no. 934; Toulmin Smith 1964, I, p.94; Meech and Allen 1940, p.148.

9 Map showing England and northern Europe 1400–1547

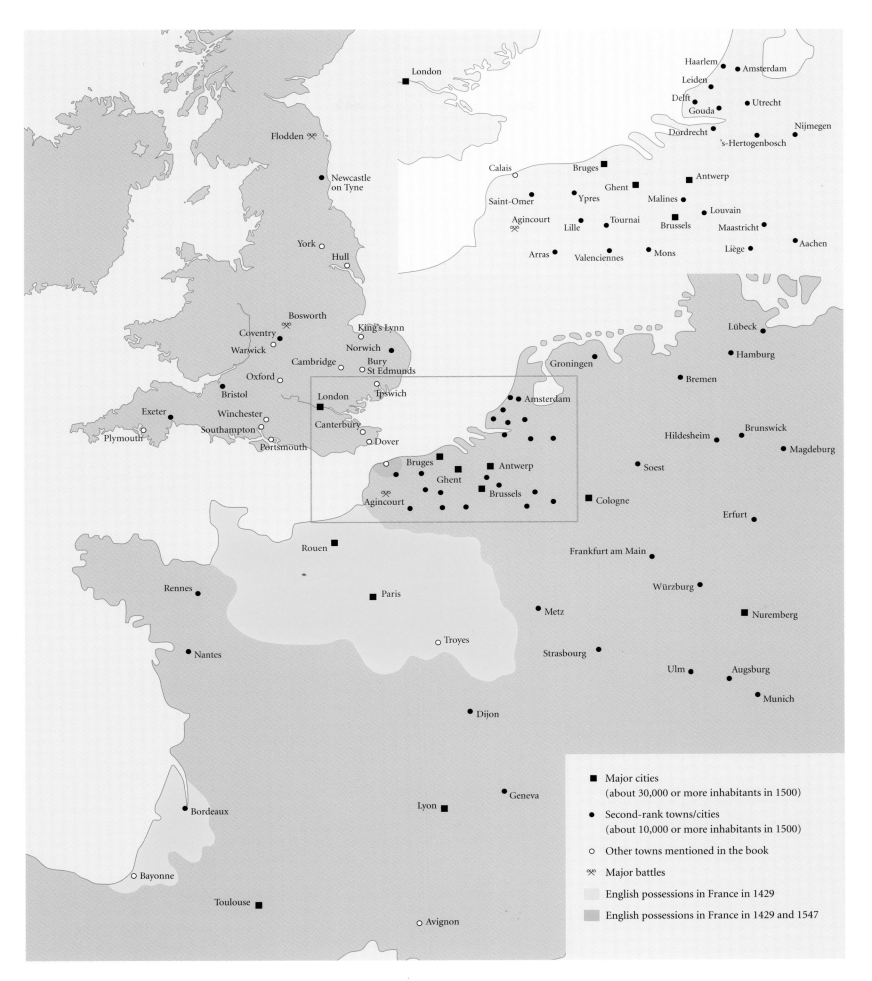

Haarlem
Amsterdam
Leiden
Delft
Utrecht
Gouda
Nijmegen
Dordrecht
's-Hertogenbosch

London

Flodden ⚔

Newcastle
on Tyne

Calais
Bruges
Antwerp
Ghent
Saint-Omer
Ypres
Malines
Louvain
Agincourt ⚔
Tournai
Brussels
Maastricht
Lille
York
Arras
Valenciennes
Mons
Liège
Aachen
Hull

Bosworth ⚔
King's Lynn
Lübeck
Coventry
Norwich
Hamburg
Warwick
Cambridge
Bury
St Edmunds
Groningen
Bremen
Oxford
Ipswich
Bristol
London
Amsterdam
Exeter
Winchester
Hildesheim
Brunswick
Southampton
Canterbury
Magdeburg
Plymouth
Portsmouth
Dover
Bruges
Soest
Ghent
Antwerp
Agincourt ⚔
Brussels
Cologne
Erfurt

Rouen
Frankfurt am Main
Rennes
Würzburg
Paris
Metz
Nuremberg
Troyes
Nantes
Strasbourg
Ulm
Augsburg
Munich
Dijon

Geneva
Bordeaux
Lyon

Bayonne

Toulouse
Avignon

■ Major cities
  (about 30,000 or more inhabitants in 1500)

● Second-rank towns/cities
  (about 10,000 or more inhabitants in 1500)

○ Other towns mentioned in the book

⚔ Major battles

English possessions in France in 1429

English possessions in France in 1429 and 1547

II

POLITICS, WAR AND PUBLIC LIFE

JOHN WATTS

The historian Susan Reynolds recently remarked on the tendency for all irrational and oppressive behaviour to be characterized with reference to the Middle Ages. 'Bosses and landlords who bully their employees or tenants are [seen as] being feudal,' she wrote. 'If they bully them fiercely, they are worse: they are positively medieval.'[1] One of the ironies of this common and casual slur on those formative ages of our civilization is that when people think of 'getting medieval', as the movie *Pulp Fiction* memorably put it, it is images from the end of the period that frequently come to mind. Ask anyone what he or she knows of the Middle Ages, and every second person will refer either to the Spanish Inquisition or to the sad fate of the Princes in the Tower. Not only are these fifteenth-century references, but they derive from virtually the same decade: Ferdinand and Isabella sent out their request for an inquisition from Seville in 1478; Richard III grabbed his infant nephew's throne in 1483. These barbarities, if that is what they were, are the work of the very end of the Middle Ages, a point fixed almost ineradicably in the English consciousness by the advent of the Tudor dynasty at Bosworth Field in 1485. To see them as 'medieval' must therefore be perverse, but there are reasons why we have often done so. Those reasons go to the heart of the period covered by this exhibition; to real conflicts and changes which took place within that period, but also to the distortions which arose from the arrival of new styles of thought and speech in a political society that was already a highly complex, vocal and self-conscious one.

Until quite recently, a period stretching from Henry IV to Henry VIII would not have made much sense to a historian of political culture. This was two periods, not one. The first saw the twilight years of the Middle Ages: the war with France was the centre of political life, and, when it subsided in the defeats of the 1450s, civil war among the overmighty aristocracy rapidly followed; the crown, weak and indebted, was passed around between the houses of Lancaster and York; bands of liveried retainers skirmished in the shires; and the English Church, groaning with corruption, languished in the loose embrace of Rome. The second period, on the other hand, was one of renaissance and reform. Tudor kings restored the power of the crown and reduced the aristocracy to order; at their magnificent courts, great

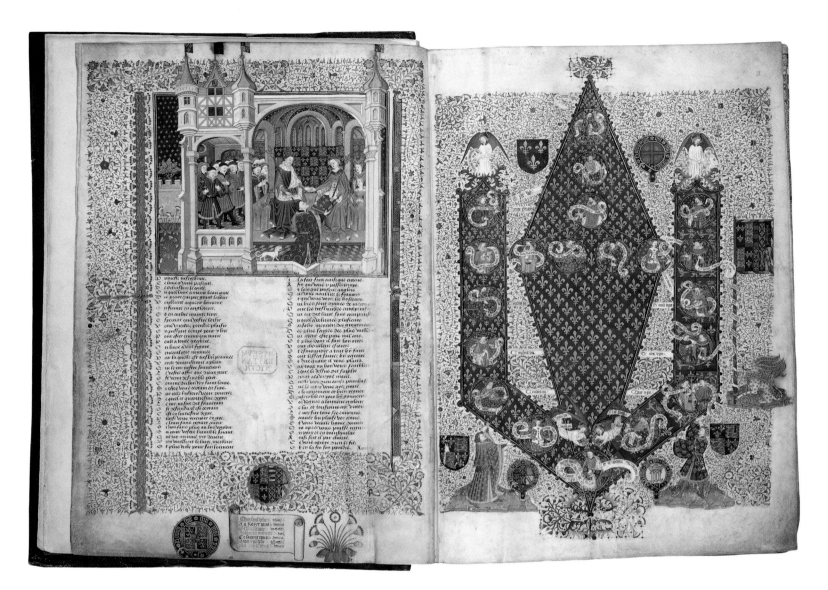

10 John Talbot, Earl of Shrewsbury, presents his book to Margaret of Anjou (left page), and genealogical table showing Henry VI's French and English royal descent, the Shrewsbury Book (cat. no. 42)

magnates gave way to educated ministers; the Church was placed firmly under royal headship; and a reforming state spread order and regulation throughout the British Isles, while print and Protestantism forged a new and insular national identity.

These *1066 and All That* myths, which have done so much to medievalize the fifteenth century, have a long pedigree behind them. In a way, the story begins with the usurping Yorkists, who made Richard II appear the last real and rightful medieval king by tracing their right to the throne back to 1399. In their propaganda, the 62 years of Lancastrian rule which followed Henry IV's usurpation became a time of almost unrelieved disorder in which the dire consequences of men's subversion of the divinely appointed law of succession became bloodily clear. The tide of polemic that accompanied the subsequent usurpations of Richard III and Henry VII did little to restore the image of the first half of the cen-

tury and merely piled up evidence of worsening depravity and the need for reform. If Edward IV had restored order in the 1470s, this was effaced by his brother's coup: Richard complained of long years in which kings had ruled without the good counsel of the lords and against justice; he condemned the late king's lustfulness and self-will; and, of course, he made his own contribution to the disorders of the century: infanticide, rebellion and tyranny. The new Tudor king, Chancellor Alcock told parliament in 1485, was like a second Joshua, leading the people out of their worst misery and restoring Ovid's Golden Age.[2] And that was just the politicians. Writers and pundits were even more extravagant in their representations of past and present: adopting the classical Latin and reformed vernaculars typical of continental humanism, they scornfully recast the learning of the last few centuries as monkish obscurantism and made articulate demands for the reform of both state and church.

To the historians of the future, therefore, the commentators of the later fifteenth and early sixteenth centuries bequeathed a view of their period in which the fault-line of 1485 was already apparent. And succeeding grand narratives of the past have tended to confirm it. For whiggish Victorians, the fifteenth century saw the collapse of medieval constitutionalism and the first signs of Tudor and Stuart tyranny in the so-called New Monarchy of Edward IV and Henry VII. For the more bureaucratically minded historians who followed them, the period saw a sharp improvement in central government, presaging the birth of the modern state in the mid-sixteenth century. It is only over the last 50 years that awareness of the continuities between the fifteenth and sixteenth centuries has really strengthened, and more recently still that the more positive, and also less romantic, features of the 85 years before Bosworth have been properly appreciated.[3] If we think that the Wars of the Roses were

pretty appalling, that is partly because the men and women who lived through them thought so too. If we imagine that they arose because of the end of the Hundred Years War, that is partly because our historians have picked up the idea from a polemic circulated to MPs in the early 1470s.[4] If we see 'overmighty subjects' in the fifteenth century, it is because Sir John Fortescue identified them in a contemporary treatise written to reform the king's government.[5] This evidence tells us that troubles existed, and they did, but it also tells us that this was a time of public debate and public concern, of persuasive writing and extensive consultation, of do-gooding and showing off. The age of Richard III and the Spanish Inquisition was also, in its way, an age of mass politics and media management. Indeed, it was as bloody and inquisitive as it was partly for that very reason: the wars that produced Richard's usurpation began in popular tumult and a messily public attempt to resolve a host of far-reaching

11 Henry VII Cope, showing royal badges and devices (cat. no. 31)

political problems. The Tudor cult of obedience and royal magnificence; the court-centred realm that grew up towards 1500: these were not just outcomes of the fifteenth century, or even solutions to its problems, they were simply later and better responses to the same problems facing government in the first age of mass public consciousness.

It is certainly true that the fifteenth century was born against a background of war and political strife. Richard II's disastrous reign had culminated in the usurpation of his throne by his most powerful subject, Henry of Bolingbroke, Duke of Lancaster, in 1399. Like all usurpers, Henry IV was vulnerable: he lacked the legitimacy of a natural successor and soon found that his promises of lower taxation and better government could not be fulfilled, as his enemies – and some of his friends – exploited his vulnerabilities and obliged him to raise money and troops in large quantities. So it was that the first few years of the fifteenth century were marked by a series of aristocratic rebellions, as well as a huge rising in Wales, led by the messianic nationalist Owain Glyndwr. Victories over the rebels, at Shrewsbury in 1403 and in Yorkshire in 1405, together with a series of brilliant campaigns in Wales led by Prince Henry, brought a measure of calm to the realm. Little by little, a new aristocratic establishment grew up and the rule of Lancaster came to be accepted. Although the sick and prematurely aged usurper was barely able to enjoy this achievement himself, his son reaped the benefits, coming to the throne with the backing of a more-or-less united political nation in 1413, and moving to strengthen royal authority and martial glory with a more active prosecution of rights to territory abroad.[6]

From the thirteenth and fourteenth centuries, the crown had inherited claims to the thrones of both Scotland and France, together with a series of titles to lands and lordships in western France and southern Scotland and a handful of allies and networks of influence. The territory in English hands at the beginning of the fifteenth century was very limited, however: none of Scotland (and only a small area of Ireland, 'the Pale', around Dublin); the towns of Calais, Bayonne and Bordeaux, and a handful of strongpoints and settlements gathered around them. Despite this unpromising situation, the desire of the kings to vindicate their claims remained as strong as circumstances permitted, and as the fortunes of the monarchy recovered from the usurpation of 1399, policy towards France, if not Scotland, became more and more aggressive. Henry V bore down upon Normandy in 1415, conquering the duchy in four years and overrunning much of northern France with his ally, the Duke of Burgundy. His splendid victory at Agincourt in 1415 (plate 12) secured the unity and admiration of the political classes,

reorienting the aristocracy towards a war of conquest in France for a generation, and effacing all memory of the usurpation of 1399. The treaty sealed at Troyes with the French king in 1420 brought Henry's recognition as heir, and meant that his son, Henry VI, went on to be crowned in an English-occupied Paris a decade or so later. This was, in fact, to be the zenith of English achievement in the Hundred Years War.

The dauphin of France rejected the treaty as soon as it was signed, and the two decades following Henry V's death, from dysentery at Vincennes in 1422, saw a prolonged and bitter struggle to preserve what has come to be known as Lancastrian France. Had Henry V lived on, this struggle might have had a different outcome, but it is one of the ironies of fate that he was succeeded by a nine-month-old baby who grew up a weakling. As the energies of the political community were turned towards making Henry VI's authority mean something, and as fighting men found themselves starved of cash and political support, the English position gradually crumbled. French confidence revived, and in two great campaigns, in which bribery was as prominent as military action, Charles VII regained Normandy in 1449–50 and Bordeaux and Bayonne in 1450–3. The English retained only Calais (plate 9), but they never lost sight of their claims in France. Not until 1801 did the kings of England cease to regard themselves as kings of France, and Edward IV, Henry VII and Henry VIII all led major expeditions, the first of them with robes suitable for a coronation stored opportunely in his baggage.[7] If their efforts were not more prolonged, or more successful, this was surely in part because of the difficulties of maintaining control in England itself until the end of the century. But where they could not prevail, they settled for lucrative pensions or the acquisition of strongholds from which future assaults might be launched. If it was Scotland, not France, that proved to be the main casualty of England's imperial ambitions under Henry VIII, it was not because the idea of continental dominion had gone cold.

The defeats of the 1450s helped to bring about the prolonged period of intermittent civil disturbance known as the Wars of the Roses. This was not, as contemporaries sometimes suggested, because a nobility deprived of war abroad decided to vent their martial energies at home. Rather, it was because of what the defeat reflected and represented: the utter failure of Henry VI's government to fulfil its responsibilities; to defend its own territory and that of its subjects, by war abroad; or to protect their property at home, by justice and the avoidance of excessive taxation. The parliaments of 1449–51 saw an explosion of anger against the king and the supposedly wicked councillors who had misled him and pillaged his resources, destroying his

capacity to fight and increasing the burdens on his true sub- jects. The men of Kent rose up in Jack Cade's rebellion of 1450, and Duke Richard of York, the greatest of English noblemen and heir to a line that Henry IV's usurpation had excluded, set himself up as the voice of a critical public opinion. In their origins, then, the Wars of the Roses were about royal misrule and its divisive consequences – the divi- sions between ministers and people when the king governed badly, and the divisions that developed among landowners when the king did not provide authority and justice. York's calls for justice upon those who had forfeited public confi- dence, for the restoration of noble counsel, sound finance and action against disorder, were countered by the men

around the king whom he sought to destroy. Their case was that York himself, his disorderly behaviour and the ambi- tions inspired by his as-yet-unvoiced title to Henry's throne were the greatest obstacles to the restoration of effective government and social peace. As the conflict escalated, with bloodshed at the battles of St Albans (1455), Blore Heath (1459) and Northampton (1460), these opposing positions were more clearly articulated and more strongly held: divi- sions among the nobility took on the character of a vendetta. York's attempt to seize the throne, when it finally came, may have been an attempt to restore the situation, by uniting royal authority with the personal capacity to rule, but divisions were now too deep and this move of 1460

12 Battle of Agincourt, *Chronicle of St Albans*, late 15th century (Lambeth Palace Library, MS 6, f.243)

simply added another, dynastic, dimension to a conflict that was raging out of control.[8]

For the next 30 years or so, English politics have a repetitive quality. A series of insecure usurpers struggled to gain control, as Henry IV had before them. They could win the throne, as Edward of York did at Towton in 1461 (or Richard III, in London, in 1483; or Henry Tudor, at Bosworth, in 1485), and they could reward their friends and try to build a new establishment, as Edward did in the 1460s, Richard in 1483–5 and Henry in the 1480s and '90s. But they found it hard to gain public confidence, because they could not rule effectively: their enemies feared and opposed them, and those enemies could often find support from a public exasperated by disorder, cronyism and a level of taxation that seemed only to benefit the king and his friends. Worse still, the Hundred Years War came back across the Channel, as the reviving kings of France and the powerful rulers of Burgundy kept the English off their shores by backing alternative claimants to the throne.[9] Edward IV, it is true, succeeded in wiping out the Lancastrian royal family, and beat off the French with a campaign in 1475. He broke the vicious cycle of usurpation

13   Sir Thomas Lovell, Pietro Torrigiano (attrib.), c.1516–20 (cat. no. 9)

and ruled effectively for more than a decade after 1471, but he had the misfortune to die young, leaving the throne to a child of 12, and the resulting instability was too much for Richard of Gloucester to resist. His usurpation revived the Wars of the Roses pattern of ineffective kingship, disgruntled public and divided nobility. Despite Henry VII's best efforts, it was a pattern that never completely went away. When the Tudor usurper was ill, in the early 1500s, a group of his advisers speculated on who might succeed him: 'some of them spoke of my lord of Buckingham, saying that he was a noble man and would be a royal ruler', others spoke of Suffolk, but none of them spoke of the young Prince Henry.[10] Even when that Henry became king, fears of a return to the Wars of the Roses hung about the Tudor court: these help to explain the king's anxiety to father a male heir, which was to play such an important role in the Reformation, and it is worth remembering that Cardinal Pole, exiled head of Catholic resistance, was also among the last surviving Yorkist claimants.

But, of course, the Tudors did bring the Wars of the Roses to an end and restore the orderly politics that England had enjoyed before the 1450s. How did they do it? The traditional answer – by the centralization of authority – is partly right, but partly no answer at all. England was already a highly centralized country, with a unified legal system, a structure of parliamentary representation, and webs of influence – both conceptual and material – stretching outwards from a powerful king (plate 14). But there was also a powerful aristocracy, whose enormous landed wealth was protected by law, and whose resulting influence over the rest of the political community was tolerated, even affirmed, by royal policy. Later medieval kings adopted a somewhat presidential mode of rule, in which the power they deployed was almost always someone else's; persuasion, leadership and the fulfilment of public obligations, such as defence and justice and sound finance, were the well-springs of their authority. In the second half of the fifteenth century, however, kings began to rule in a more direct way, relying more on men who were closely tied to them, extending and maintaining the landed estate of the crown, creating and undoing client aristocracies, and insisting on a more exacting level of order and obedience from their more powerful subjects (for example Sir Thomas Lovell, plate 13). To a large extent, this was the result of the civil wars. The magnates who usurped the crown in this period brought large estates with them; they needed, as we have seen, to build up and rely on their friends; if they could brazen out resistance, they would find themselves in a powerful position, with an unusual freedom to remake the map of power. Meanwhile, the new nobilities created by Edward IV, Richard III and Henry VII were insecurely rooted: they lacked

14   Court of the King's bench,
c.1460 (Inner Temple Library,
Inner Temple Misc. MS 188)

the inherited social power of their predecessors, and – with continuing convulsions – lacked the time to build it up.

The nobility was thus permanently enfeebled by the Wars of the Roses, and the crown stepped in to fill the vacuum, building more direct links with the lesser landowners – the knights and esquires whom historians call 'the gentry' – and taking more of a role in the ordering of local society itself. In these developments, ideology too played a part. Years of mayhem had produced a stronger desire for central direction; the importance of obedience to the king for the maintenance of order had become clear; and political discussion and burgeoning historical knowledge had awakened an interest in the institutions of royal government and a strong sense that they – and not the lords – should be the major agencies of rule. So it was that more of the business and power of government was pulled into the centre, not only to the king himself under Edward IV and Henry VII, who were busy in a way that their predecessors had not been, but also to an ever-growing bank of ministers and administrators. By Henry VIII's time this group had taken on much of the expanded task of rule, leaving the king to return to a life of aristocratic ease, with its attendant consequences of chivalry, hunting and obesity.[11]

This more centralized government soon flexed its muscles. A stream of new legislation came from the parliaments and proclamations of Henry VII and Henry VIII, regulating more and more of their subjects' lives and being enforced with greater vigour and punctiliousness. A network of councils was created, some of them charged with keeping the peace in the more distant parts of the realm; others with providing more flexible justice than the aged common law could offer; still others involved in financial management. The expanded crown lands were aggressively exploited, especially under Henry VII, and the tax system reformed so as to elicit funds for war that comprised half as much again, by the 1540s, as those enjoyed by Henry V.[12] On the back of this more intrusive government, new political configurations and a different political culture emerged. The crown's growing monopoly of power in the secular sphere helped to create a sort of nationalizing temperament, which soon had consequences for the organization of religion. That arch-pluralist and second king, Cardinal Wolsey, was already running the Church of England in a far more interventionist way in the 1520s; and when the Pope refused the king's demand for a divorce from Queen Catherine of Aragon, the assertion of a royal headship over the Church and the ensuing absorption of huge swathes of ecclesiastical lands in the Dissolution of the monasteries were not difficult steps for the government to conceive.[13] 'This realm of England is an Empire,' declared the Act in Restraint of Appeals in 1533,

and this meant that England's royal government had a complete plenitude of power, free to do anything and everything for the good of its subjects.[14] This power was felt throughout the land: by disorderly landowners in the shires, by magnates who awakened the king's suspicions, and by those few brave souls – Thomas More, John Fisher, and others – who opposed the religious changes of the 1530s. As these examples demonstrate, the new power did not go unresisted. Hostility to centralization had already been a factor in the risings of the Wars of the Roses period, most notably in 1469, when the excluded Earl of Warwick rose up against the apparatchiks of Edward IV's regime; and it is perceptible in the numerous popular and local rebellions of the early Tudor period, when the new taxes, in particular, were a source of grievance. But what Bishop Stubbs rather wonderfully called 'the recovered strength of the monarchic principle' was unquestionably the trend of the times, and most political-interest groups adjusted to the new realities, seeking places at the burgeoning court, exploiting the new opportunities for justice and joining in the metropolitan culture of humanistic letters and polemical concern for the interests of the commonwealth.[15]

So was this one period, or two? However different the world of Henry VIII was from that of Henry IV, the path between them is clear and continuous, and many features of the older time are visible later: Henry VIII's investment in the wars in France may have been more circumspect than Henry V's, but the dream of Agincourt remained a compelling one.[16] Looking at it another way, Henry VIII's more insular and imperial realm is also apparent earlier on. At the height of Henry V's success, the commons in the parliament of 1420 were at pains to restrict their liability for taxation to the defence of the wonder-king's English domains alone, and they went on to refuse taxation throughout the 1420s when Lancastrian France hung in the balance.[17] Henry V and his son sported closed imperial crowns, betokening complete authority over their realms: they dissolved ecclesiastical property, in the shape of priories linked to religious houses in France, and their subjects talked readily of a 'church of England'. Henry Chichele, who became Archbishop of Canterbury in 1414, even wrote to his king as 'your true priest, whom it hath liked you to set in so high estate'.[18] The overwhelming importance of the king to his subjects is as clear throughout the fifteenth century as it is in the age of the Holbein portrait. A great deal of high politics already focused on advising, or counselling, the king, at times roughly, but more generally in a respectful, if persistent and didactic, fashion. Thomas Hoccleve's *Regimen of Princes*, presented

to Henry V as Prince of Wales in *c.*1411, drew on the major authorities of the time to provide the prince with a model of the kinds of virtues he should cultivate and the policies he should follow. This was a hectoring and humourless work, accompanied by a thinly disguised plea for a pension for its 'poor' author (plate 15), but it was also part of a long tradition. The flattering verses that Thomas More wrote for Henry VIII's accession, and the panegyric poems of Nagonius presented to Henry VII (plate 16), breathed the new air of humanistic rhetoric, but they had essentially the same function: they flattered to inspire, to draw the king towards the kinds of behaviour that his role demanded. Poets praised and preached while politicians sought to persuade, and at times to challenge, but all of

them were caught up in a realm where everything depended on the effectiveness of the king at its centre.

This is, in fact, one of the underlying explanations both of the convulsions of the fifteenth century and of their resolution in a larger and stronger royal government. Defence, justice, the security of property and the soundness of royal finances all depended on the quality of the king. This meant a determination – perceptible throughout the century – to try to make royal government work: even the child-fool Henry VI was able to reign for more than 25 years with the united support of magnates and MPs; even in the decade of civil war that followed, a majority of lords supported him, such was their desire to uphold authority. But dependence on the king for all social goods – the common good, or

15 Thomas Hoccleve's *The Regimen of Princes* (cat. no. 41)

'common weal', in the fifteenth-century catchphrase – meant that there was also pressure to amend incompetent rule, pressure that could not but be rebellious and disruptive if the king could not see what was good for him. This pressure was felt during the reigns of incompetents, like Henry VI, and, in a different way, under bullies like Henry VII and Henry VIII,

16 Henry VII in a triumphal car; Nagonius's Latin Poems (cat. no. 48)

who reawakened in their subjects a fear that it was royal power and not disorder that posed the greatest threat to property. But it was also felt in the reigns of able but ineffective kings, like Henry IV, whose incapacity stemmed from usurpation. Since these usurpations were themselves the consequences of attempts to deal with bad kingship, it should be clear why the fifteenth century was so disrupted: not because its people, or its kings, were inherently disorderly, but because so much depended on the quality of kingship. Whether the early Tudors really solved this problem is an open question: perhaps they were lucky, in that, until 1547, one fully grown man followed another. But the bureaucratic strengthening of kingship and the reduction of the magnates did a lot to make the Tudor realm work more smoothly.

The other important theme in the politics of this time, which is also an important continuity, and an important context for the items in this exhibition, is the existence of a self-conscious and assertive political community, in dialogue with the king and his government. United by a common law and provided with many means of representation – through parliament, through networks of lordship and clientage, through petitioning and display, through their increasing literacy and the spreading use of the vernacular – the English people of the fifteenth and sixteenth centuries saw themselves as a community, to whom the government bore obligations and on behalf of whom they could speak, and even act, when necessary. This relationship between government and community was widely idealized. Fortescue's famous treatise on the 'Governance of England', for example, presented an image of the English past in which the brotherhood of Trojan warriors who founded the nation chose Brutus as their leader so that they could enjoy the benefits of kingship.[19] The vernacular poets of the turn of the fourteenth and fifteenth centuries sought a 'comun vois' with which to address both king and people for their common benefit. It was a new English, not precisely the language spoken or written before, but a stylized amalgam of the vernacular with the rhythms and vocabulary of Latin and French: it was a public language, expressive of the people in their collectivity and in their moral and political aspect.[20] John Gower switched the dedication of his *Confessio Amantis*, that great compendium of moral and political knowledge: no longer a book for 'king Richardes sake', it became a book 'for Engelondes sake', a work to teach the English how to live better with one another. Gower and Chaucer anatomized English society, and their great works reverberated through the fifteenth century, widely copied in the emerging capital and rapidly printed by Caxton in the 1480s (cat. nos 173, 226). Others did the same with less aplomb: an avalanche of didactic writings depicted and prescribed the ways of living, from table manners to French grammar; chancellors told parliaments about the social structure, with mountainous magnates charged with peace-keeping, hilly gentlemen and merchants given the tasks of justice and administration, and the flat plains or waters of the commons charged with obedience.[21] Even that word 'commons', so innocuous to us, was full of political significance. When the peasants of 1381 declared they were the true, or loyal, commons of England, they meant that they were part of the political community of governors and advisers.[22] In the minds of its inhabitants, England was a diverse but integrated political space, in which 'every estate is ordained to support the others', and even the humblest had counsel to offer the king and benefits to draw from his protection: 'the least liege man with body and rent, he is a parcel of the crown'.[23] Small wonder that the humanists of the later fifteenth century had little difficulty finding a plausible *res publica* in this most mixed of monarchies.

For this community was not only imagined, but real. The peasants of 1381 made their feelings about taxation known to the king in much the same way as the knights and burgesses of the 1376 parliament had done. A sense of participation in parliamentary politics stretched far beyond those county and urban notables who were actually elected to the assembly; indeed, it became necessary to restrict the franchise in 1430, because too many of the lower sort were turning up at elections; the rebellion of the highly politicized yeomen of Kent in 1450 was clearly intended to do for the community what MPs and magnates had failed to do in the parliament that preceded it.[24] Rising literacy, a taste for preaching, the circulation of bills, poems and ballads, even a manuscript-copying industry addressing both cheap and fancy ends of the market, meant that even before the advent of the printing press in the 1470s, a mass public with an interest in its own political, moral and spiritual health existed in England. Its agitations were frequent and dramatic enough for its existence to be ever in the minds of political leaders in both state and church. Kings took ever greater care to disseminate news of their victories and justifications of their policies; clerics made increasing efforts to control access to religious knowledge; magnates found themselves appealing directly to the people or responding to their concerns. 'Please it your Highness tenderly to consider the great grutchyng and rumour that is universally in this your realm, of that justice is not duly administered to such as trespass and offend against your laws,' wrote Richard of York in 1450.[25] Much as the people lacked formal means of representation – indeed partly *because* they lacked formal means of representation – they exerted a significant pressure on the politics of the great. This often critical mass-public was the defining feature of fifteenth- and sixteenth-century England. While its presence helped to cause, and to worsen, political conflict in the early part of the period, it also trained the elite of magnates and ministers in the arts of public relations and the science of politics. And later it became an important rhetorical and real support for royalism and reform. Just as the barbarisms

and the triumphs of the twentieth century owe much of their nature to mass-politics and mass-media, so did those of the age of Lancaster, York and Tudor.

FURTHER READING

Carpenter 1997; Gunn 1995; Harriss 1985; Keen 1990; Watts 1996.

NOTES

1 Reynolds (S) 1994, p.1.

2 *Rot. Parl.*, VI, p.267.

3 For the historiography, see Watts 1998b and Goodman 1988, pp.1–8.

4 Sheppard 1889, pp.274–85.

5 Plummer 1885, p.127.

6 For Henry IV's reign, see McFarlane 1972; for Henry V's, Harriss 1985.

7 Scofield 1923, II, p.116; Currin 1996; Davies 1998.

8 For Henry VI's reign, see Watts 1996; for the later stages of the war, Allmand 1989, pp.32–6, and Keen 1989.

9 Davies 1995.

10 Gairdner 1861–3, I, p.233.

11 For the Wars of the Roses and the subsequent recovery of royal power, see Carpenter 1997 and Gunn 1995; for Henry VIII's reign, Scarisbrick 1997.

12 Gunn 1995, pp.48–53, 62–70, 81–9, 102–8, 132, 183–90 and chapter 3, *passim*; Loach 1991, p.139.

13 Gunn and Lindley 1991b.

14 Elton 1982, p.353.

15 Stubbs 1903, p.3.

16 Davies 1998.

17 Harriss 1985, p.149.

18 Hay 1988, pp.246–7; McFarlane 1981, p.82; Steane 1993, p.35; Thompson 1994. For a wide-ranging discussion of fourteenth- and fifteenth-century precursors of features typically thought of as sixteenth-century, see Harriss 1963.

19 Plummer 1885, p.112.

20 Middleton 1978; Catto 2001.

21 For expanding literacy, see Keen 1990, pp.217–39; for parliamentary sermons, see, for example, *Rot. Parl.*, IV, p.419.

22 Dobson 1983, pp.127, 130.

23 Watts 1996, pp.22 note, 23.

24 Myers 1981, p.166.

25 Gairdner 1904, II, p.177.

17 Simplified genealogy showing the kings and queens of England 1377–1547

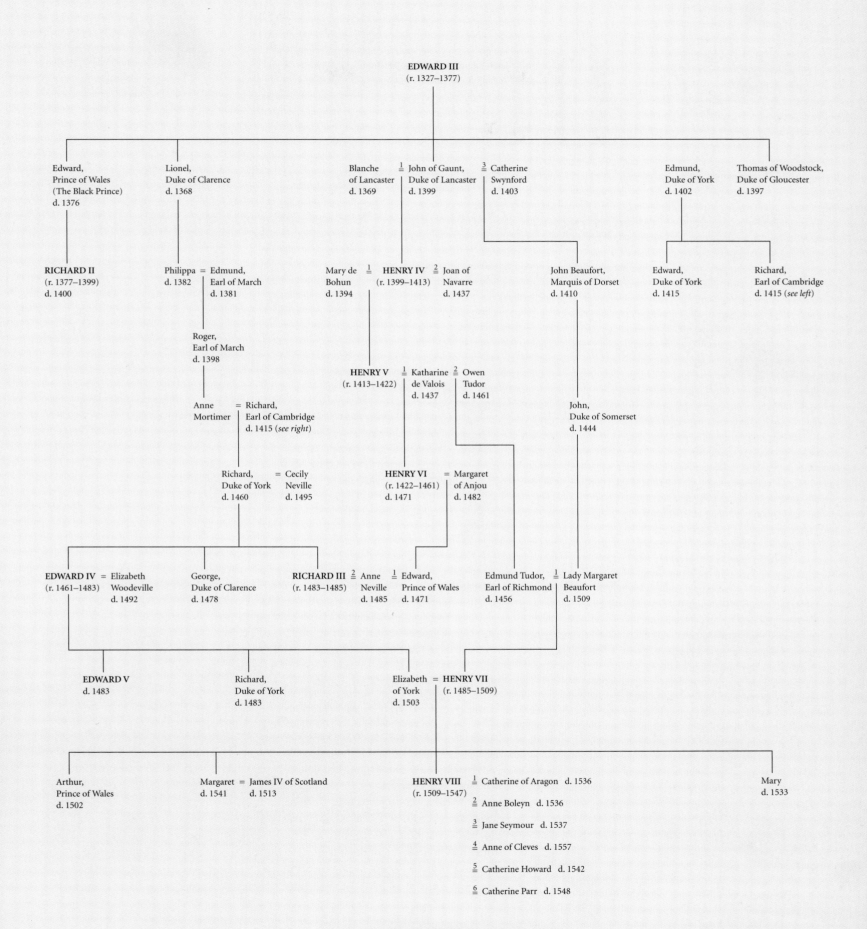

EDWARD III
(r. 1327–1377)

Edward,
Prince of Wales
(The Black Prince)
d. 1376

Lionel,
Duke of Clarence
d. 1368

Blanche
of Lancaster
d. 1369

$\underline{1}$ John of Gaunt,
Duke of Lancaster
d. 1399

$\underline{3}$ Catherine
Swynford
d. 1403

Edmund,
Duke of York
d. 1402

Thomas of Woodstock,
Duke of Gloucester
d. 1397

RICHARD II
(r. 1377–1399)
d. 1400

Philippa
d. 1382

= Edmund,
Earl of March
d. 1381

Mary de
Bohun
d. 1394

$\underline{1}$ HENRY IV
(r. 1399–1413)

$\underline{2}$ Joan of
Navarre
d. 1437

John Beaufort,
Marquis of Dorset
d. 1410

Edward,
Duke of York
d. 1415

Richard,
Earl of Cambridge
d. 1415 (*see left*)

Roger,
Earl of March
d. 1398

HENRY V
(r. 1413–1422)

$\underline{1}$ Katharine
de Valois
d. 1437

$\underline{2}$ Owen
Tudor
d. 1461

Anne
Mortimer

= Richard,
Earl of Cambridge
d. 1415 (*see right*)

John,
Duke of Somerset
d. 1444

Richard,
Duke of York
d. 1460

= Cecily
Neville
d. 1495

HENRY VI
(r. 1422–1461)
d. 1471

= Margaret
of Anjou
d. 1482

EDWARD IV
(r. 1461–1483)

= Elizabeth
Woodeville
d. 1492

George,
Duke of Clarence
d. 1478

RICHARD III
(r. 1483–1485)

$\underline{2}$ Anne
Neville
d. 1485

$\underline{1}$ Edward,
Prince of Wales
d. 1471

Edmund Tudor,
Earl of Richmond
d. 1456

$\underline{1}$ Lady Margaret
Beaufort
d. 1509

EDWARD V
d. 1483

Richard,
Duke of York
d. 1483

Elizabeth
of York
d. 1503

= HENRY VII
(r. 1485–1509)

Arthur,
Prince of Wales
d. 1502

Margaret
d. 1541

= James IV of Scotland
d. 1513

HENRY VIII
(r. 1509–1547)

$\underline{1}$ Catherine of Aragon d. 1536

$\underline{2}$ Anne Boleyn d. 1536

$\underline{3}$ Jane Seymour d. 1537

$\underline{4}$ Anne of Cleves d. 1557

$\underline{5}$ Catherine Howard d. 1542

$\underline{6}$ Catherine Parr d. 1548

Mary
d. 1533

III

KINGSHIP AND QUEENSHIP

ROSEMARY HORROX

18 Henry VII and Elizabeth of York, Church of St Nicholas, Stanford on Avon (cat. no. 39)

In the Middle Ages royal power was a reality – kings ruled, and upon that rule the whole political system was predicated. Sir John Fortescue famously defined the king's role as to maintain the peace both outward and inward.[1] Maintaining the peace inward referred to the king's role as lawgiver and judge; maintaining the peace outward was a matter of diplomacy and leadership in war. These two dimensions are embodied in the king's great seal, which showed the king enthroned in majesty on one side and mounted and armed on the other (plate 40, cat. no. 33). But there was a third dimension to the role, which Fortescue does not explicitly mention, but which is enshrined in the coronation *ordo* of medieval kings: the king's role as protector of the Church. By the late fourteenth century, with the attack by John Wyclif on some of the central teachings of the Church, this had come to include not just the defence of the Church's temporal possessions, but the protection of orthodoxy against heresy. The Pope's designation of Henry VIII as *Fidei Defensor* – Defender of the Faith – in tribute to his polemic against Luther merely acknowledged a recognized function (cat. nos 353, 354).

These three functions sound simple – and they do remind us that medieval government laid claim to a more limited supervision of its subjects' lives than would be the case today. But they are shorthand for a complex set of expectations and obligations. As lawgiver, for instance, the king stood above the law – it was his, after all, and at his coronation he promised to strengthen and maintain the law rather than to 'keep' or 'obey' it. But there was a sense that he should abide by his own rules – hinted at in the first coronation oath to ratify and confirm the law, customs and liberties granted by his predecessors.[2] It was central to medieval thinking that a king should not be coerced, but should voluntarily submit to contemporary expectations, and in the legal sphere one can see particularly clearly where that comes from. A slavish adherence to the letter of the law by the king was inappropriate for good practical reasons. It was recognized that justice might require someone who could override the law at times. So too did order. Law and order is now so generally seen as a *single* entity that it is easy to overlook that in the Middle Ages (human) law was the means, order the end. Given the enormous importance attached to order in human affairs, it followed that law could – indeed, should – be modified at times in pursuit of that goal. For a king to flout

Henricus VII R.

Elizabetha R.

the law wilfully was unacceptable; to set it aside for good reason was not. What constituted wilfulness and reason might, in individual cases, be open to argument, but the general principle was accepted. Kings had to be able to bend the rules, and this was true in all spheres of royal activity.

They did so, inevitably, with varying degrees of success. Put simply, a king who was trusted could get away with more than one who was not, and this is a reminder of the personal nature of monarchy. Although the king's role, and the resources at his disposal, changed only slowly, individual qualities were superimposed upon that underlying pattern, giving a very different 'feel' to separate reigns, and sometimes to periods within a single reign. These shifts of emphasis can make it difficult to be sure whether a more fundamental change is going on. The century and a half following the deposition of Richard II is a period which past historians thought *did* bring a change in the nature of monarchy – how could it have been otherwise when they believed that this period saw the transformation of the medieval world into a more recognizably 'modern' one? Recent historians, however, have been much less sure. Dynasties indeed changed with bewildering frequency. Richard II's deposition in 1399 brought the house of Lancaster to the throne. In 1461 Edward of York took the throne, and his family held it (with a brief gap in 1470–1) until the defeat of Richard III at Bosworth in 1485 handed the crown to the Tudors, descendants in the female line of the illegitimate branch of the Lancastrians, the Beauforts (plate 18, cat. no. 39).

Such a whirligig would seem at first sight to be evidence of diminishing respect for royal authority, and hence of an erosion of the king's power. And it is undoubtedly true that usurpers – Henry IV in 1399, Edward IV in 1461, Richard III in 1483 and Henry VII in 1485 – did take time to grow into the job. Indeed, Richard III never managed it, and some historians would argue that Henry IV and Edward IV were weakened throughout their reigns, not just in the early years, by a widespread belief that their rule was illegitimate. But the underlying perception of what the king should be remained constant – and so did the sense that he was crucial to the functioning of the medieval polity. One could even argue that the struggles of the mid-fifteenth century made effective royal government seem *more* important, not less, as offering the one safe route out of civil strife. And if that is indeed the case, then perhaps it was the actions of the kings themselves, rather than the reactions of their subjects, which were most distorted by an awareness that they had usurped power.

Subjects were, after all, under intense pressure to obey their king, whatever their reservations about his political legitimacy. There were practical reasons for this. Disobedi-

ence could mean at best loss of favour, at worst accusations of treason. But it was also ideologically unacceptable. The king was the head of the earthly hierarchy within his own realm, and as such an attack on him was an attack on order itself. And that order, for all its manifest imperfections, was the nearest fallen humanity could come to the divine order that moved the universe. Even criticism of the king could be problematic, as is shown by the contemporary convention that it was 'evil counsellors' who were to blame when things went wrong, and not the king himself.

Moralists, it is true, argued that criticism was not only acceptable but a positive duty. But they were in no doubt that in practice it happened less than it should and that kings were not, in fact, told what they did not want to hear. In any case, what they had in mind was a very specific sort of criticism: the readiness of royal advisers to tell the king frankly if they thought he was making a mistake. The availability of honest advice (what contemporaries would have called sad and substantial counsel) was essential to good governance. It was the king's job to stand above conflicting interests, and thus he had to be a free agent. But if he was to arrive at a reasoned decision, he had to listen. If coercion

19 Stained-glass panels showing Prince Edward and his sisters, Priory church of St Mary and St Michael, Little Malvern (cat. no. 37)

20   Marriage of Henry V
and Katharine de Valois,
The Beauchamp Pageants
(cat. no. 90)

were drawn up against deposed kings. But they were not, in the strict legal sense, charged. Both royal depositions in the fourteenth century (those of Edward II and Richard II) were presented as abdications. In effect, both kings were said to have been shamed into resigning their crowns: the ultimate assertion of the contemporary need for the king to be a free agent. Probably no one believed it, but it neatly side-stepped the necessity of justifying deposition.

The fifteenth-century usurpers took a different line. Although they all, at some stage, criticized the previous regime, the transfer of power was justified by dynastic considerations. In 1460 Richard, Duke of York claimed the throne not because Henry VI had been a disaster (although he had), but because York could present himself as the rightful heir of Richard II. In 1483 Richard III announced that he was his brother's heir because his brother's children were illegitimate (plate 19, cat. no. 37). Henry VII's justification was, to put it mildly, a fudge, but there were dynastic elements in there. Publicly he simply denied the legitimacy of the Yorkist intrusion and tacitly presented himself as the heir of his uncle Henry VI.

As this implies, the deposition of Richard II had injected a new element of uncertainty into the situation. Richard was childless, and his supplanter, Henry Bolingbroke, was his male heir. But if it was accepted that the crown of England could pass through the female line (as it had in the twelfth century, when Henry I's daughter Matilda, never queen herself, had transmitted the crown to her son Henry II), then Richard's heirs were the Mortimers – and it was from his mother Anne Mortimer, the last of the line, that Richard of York derived his claim. For all his public emphasis on dynasty, York did not in fact claim the throne *because* of that descent. He claimed it as the only way of breaking out of the vicious circle of confrontation and political exclusion in which he found himself in the late 1450s. But his descent gave him the means to do that. To be able to claim that the king was not in fact the king cut through the ideological difficulties of opposition at one stroke.

This was why 'high' politics were so unstable in the second half of the fifteenth century. In a hereditary monarchy the king was generally non-negotiable. Now, for a time, that was no longer quite true. Even towards the end of Henry VII's reign the muddying of the waters can be seen in the way in which men were said to be considering the succession of someone other than Henry's own son.[4] But, in spite of that much-cited example, it is clear that there was a powerful pull back towards dynastic certainty. No one ever claimed that the realm had the right to choose its ruler. Two dynasties might be contending, to devastating effect, but there was no suggestion that the crown was up for grabs.

rendered his role impossible, so did his own partiality or plain ignorance – which is why it was so important that the king should be willing to hear all points of view, however unpalatable he might find them. Once he had reached a decision, however, continuing criticism began to look dangerously like opposition, unless it could be presented as offering *more* information, hitherto unavailable to the crown. 'The king knoweth not all' was a useful face-saving device for both king and critics.[3]

Ideologically, therefore, kings were almost unassailable. They were under an obligation to rule justly and for the good of their realm, but they were answerable to God, not to their subjects, for their failure. It was accepted that tyrannical or simply inept rule was a disaster – and charge sheets

Even within that closed circle of claimants, when one side or the other achieved the throne by the fortune of war, it was taken as evidence of God's verdict, not man's. As John Paston II put it, consoling himself for the Lancastrian defeat at Barnet: 'God hath shown himself marvellously, like him that made all and can undo again when he lists, and I can think that by all likelihood shall show himself as marvellous again'.[5] When the hereditary transmission of land was fundamental to social and political standing, it could hardly be otherwise, and the power of the hereditary principle to reassert itself can be seen not only in the accession of Henry VIII, but in the ultimate accession of his two daughters.

If kings were non-negotiable, queens were not. Most kings during this period found wives for themselves when already on the throne – Richard III and Henry VIII were the only kings who had a wife at the time of their accession, and Henry, famously, went on to contract a further five marriages as king. Henry VII was the only one of these kings who found a bride for his heir in his own lifetime. This left the choice of queen open to criticism, and foreign marriages, in particular, tended to attract adverse comment. The value of the marriage to England might be challenged, or the wages of the queen's foreign servants grudged.

But once the queen was installed, it was rare for her own performance to be attacked. Henry VIII's ruthless way with wives who failed to produce the required son notwithstanding, the queen's fertility did not generally become an issue. The political elite were very well aware that the odds against producing surviving male children were uncomfortably high and it was extremely rare for there to be public criticism of a queen on those grounds, whatever tensions might be building up within the royal family itself. Motherhood apart, the queen's public role was as intercessor, whose appeal for mercy could legitimate the moderation of the full rigour of justice. It was analogous to the role of the Virgin in the political economy of heaven, since Mary was the saint who could extract divine mercy even for those sinners who most deserved punishment. And, like the mother of God, queens were praised when their efforts were successful, but remained beyond reproach if ever they were not.

But the queen's influence was not only a public matter. It was acknowledged that she could assert a more intimate influence over her husband. On the whole this seems to have been uncontentious. Like any other form of counsel, it was validated by the king's willingness to accept it, and contemporaries were unperturbed, as moderns might not be, by the private nature of the queen's promptings. It was accepted that advice could come in many forms, from private gossip to debates within the royal council. Where it could become problematic was when the king was incapable

of making up his own mind, so that the queen was in effect claiming the right to exercise unmediated royal authority. This was the situation of Margaret of Anjou in the late 1450s, when, with a mentally enfeebled husband, she sought to act (without authority) as regent for her infant son. Margaret was branded a virago – a male woman, which in the thinking of the time was a profoundly unnatural hybrid. When critics of Edward IV's marriage to Elizabeth Woodeville accused her mother of bringing about the match by bewitching the king, they may have sought to play on similar anxieties. The accusation of witchcraft was a familiar political smear, but here it carried the implication that the king could be prevented from thinking for himself.

One might expect similar anxieties to gather around the queen mother of an under-age king, although this was a relatively rare situation. In 1483 Richard, Duke of Gloucester apparently believed that the young Edward V was likely to be too much under the influence of his mother's family, the Woodvilles, but his immediate concern seems to have been with the male members of the family. The position of the mother of the infant Henry VI, Katharine de Valois (plate 20, cat. no. 90), did give grounds for anxiety, but these focused on the prospect of her remarriage. To be stepfather of the king was a distinctly anomalous position, but queen dowagers must have found it equally anomalous to marry commoners. In this respect the inclinations of queen and realm are likely to have coincided, and few queen dowagers did remarry. Margaret Beaufort, Henry VII's mother, who was already married to Thomas Lord Stanley when her son became king, quickly claimed the status of *femme sole*.

Such sensitivities are testimony to the fact that power was personal. There was, of course, a whole quasi-religious edifice sustaining the belief that royal power was, on the contrary, impersonal. The king's coronation marked him out as a man touched by divinity, and for the rest of his life his supra-normal status was manifested in the power of healing by touch. Such power could be invoked as evidence of *true* royalty. In the 1470s some sufferers preferred to seek a cure at the tomb of Henry VI rather than from the hands of his supplanter Edward IV – or so, at least, the compiler of Henry's miracles sought to imply (plate 21, cat. no. 323).[6] Court ceremonial emphasized the king's separateness in the

21 Henry VI (cat. no. 323)

22 Henry IV, in an initial of the Great Cowcher of the Duchy of Lancaster (Public Record Office, PRO DL 42/1, f.51)

can see it in the way the king presented himself. *Magnificence* was one key word here, but *intimacy* was the other. Magnificence – the splendour with which the king surrounded himself – was all about the creation of distance. But the king also had to deal with his servants (a word that subsumes a wide range of function and status) on a one-to-one basis. Edward IV was able to drive a man away from court (to wait at a neighbouring manor until he received the summons to return) just by withdrawing his gaze, but he was also famous for his affability towards the humble and overawed.[8]

Contemporaries seem to have had no problems with either element in this rather schizophrenic royal persona. Majesty was a prerequisite of the job, and approachability (whether literal or figurative) was desirable too. Kings (like God, who was their exemplar) should have the love as well as the dread of their subjects. But it must always have been a difficult balancing act for the kings themselves, and those who succeeded best were probably the larger-than-life characters, whose anger and affability were equally overwhelming. Henry VIII was in this, as in many other things, very like his maternal grandfather Edward IV.

The double nature of monarchy parallels a more general dualism that runs through medieval political life: the tension between power as a public or private phenomenon. The *ends* of power were agreed to be the public good: the common weal. But the means by which those ends were achieved put a more positive emphasis on the private (or the personal) than is generally the case in the West today. In a world in which the king had no standing army and a professional bureaucracy that would now barely be thought sufficient to run a town hall, getting things done depended on establishing obligations. There was, as we have seen, a general obligation to obey the king because he was the king, but swift and effective royal action relied upon a body of recognized and reliable servants (plate 23, cat. no. 161, where Grimston is shown holding a Lancastrian collar of SS, see cat. no. 71). Although the king was everybody's lord, he inevitably stood in a closer and more defined relationship with his acknowledged servants, and it was a relationship that put the king himself (as well as the servants) under an obligation: they to carry out his wishes; he to reward them appropriately for their obedience.

It is possible to see this as an erosion of royal authority, since by enmeshing the king in a network of obligations, it reduced him to the level of any other lord, rather than leaving him enthroned comfortably above the hurly-burly of political rivalry. Henry IV's relationship with his duchy of Lancaster retinue (plate 22), in particular, has recently been seen in these negative terms.[9] The short answer to this

formal crown-wearings, usually held at the great feasts of the liturgical year. The king's divine purpose was articulated for a wider audience during civic entries and the like, in which the image of the king as promised hero and redeemer also to be found in the more shadowy world of political prophecy was given dramatic visual expression.[7]

Late-medieval writing on kingship did not reach the dizzy heights of divinity claimed for rulers at some other periods. But that sense of the king's difference pervades it – and its very unselfconsciousness (as compared, for instance, with the highly self-conscious cult of the virgin-queen that was to develop around Elizabeth) shows how much it was taken for granted. It did not mean, however, that the exercise of royal power could just be a matter of fiat. Kings could indeed command, and frequently did, but their use of the imperative rested on a willingness to obey which had to be cultivated. Medieval kingship was an exercise in man-management as well as an expression of quasi-divine authority, and although the balance between the two might tilt under individual rulers, both elements remained essential.

This dualism lies at the heart of medieval monarchy. One

23 *Edward Grimston*,
Petrus Christus (cat. no. 161)

criticism could be that kings had no choice in the matter: they had to have servants, and servants expected their reward. But the situation was rather more complex than this answer, or the criticism itself, would allow. Service to the crown was not a straightforward commercial transaction. Even for men close to the king – servants rather than subjects – the duty of obedience must have been part of their motivation and, it may not be too optimistic to suggest, a consciousness of contributing in some measure to good governance. Of course they looked to benefit themselves as well. Royal service was its own reward: enhancing the individual's status and hence his authority. What the king added on top of that was up to him. He owed his servants favour just as he owed his subjects justice: an expectation that it would be unwise to disappoint in general, but one that he was not necessarily obliged to meet in any particular case, or in any particular way.

Fortescue, who grappled with the issue of royal favour, accepted that the king's servants should be rewarded. But he wished to see them receiving a single office apiece, to reduce favour to a level playing field.[10] Modern historians have generally been inclined to think this a good idea. Medieval kings did not. That was no doubt partly for the pragmatic reason that the hope, however remote, of significant gain was a powerful incentive to service. But, more important, Fortescue's model rejected the chivalric (and hence princely) virtue of largesse – gift-giving that was not just generous but was uncalculating. 'Calculating' in that negative sense is a nineteenth-century formulation, but the concept is powerfully present in the Middle Ages. One reason for that is that grace (and hence its more mundane cousin favour), although it could be earned, should be in the last resort unconstrained: a free gift from a superior to an inferior. But another is surely because service was seen as a personal relationship, which rendered calculation inappropriate.

The men to whom the king looked for obedience in the matters that touched him particularly closely, and who were in line for the most generous outpouring of favour, were men whom he knew and trusted – men whom, in many cases, he would probably have considered friends. Of course not all the king's servants were personally close to him. Their sheer numbers made that impossible. The royal household (office within which offered the most common way of formalizing the relationship of king and acknowledged servant) was growing steadily throughout this period. That growth was made possible by the increase in the crown lands, which allowed servants to be rewarded with a grant of office within the royal demesne rather than paid from the royal coffers. Henry IV had started the process by bringing the duchy of Lancaster and the earldom of Hereford to the crown. Edward IV added the duchy of York and the earldom of March; Richard III the earldoms of Warwick and Salisbury, although half the land was technically held for his young nephew. By the reign of Henry VII the household had become so large that the existence of an inner circle of intimates, which had, informally, been a reality much earlier, was formalized by the creation of the privy chamber.

To a modern western audience that identification of the personal and the public can seem potentially, if not inherently, corrupt. But that was not the medieval perception. 'Obedience done for love is more steadfast than that which is done for lordship or for dread.'[11] Of course personal affection could become problematic if it became favouritism. Kings owed a duty beyond their own inclinations, and the sentence quoted above praises love of subject for king – not necessarily *vice versa*. But in the real world everyone knew that the strongest political relationships were grounded in affection and liking, and contemporaries were not shy of discussing them in those terms. It is perhaps too easy now to overlook the fact that a personal monarchy had its strengths as well as, more famously, its weaknesses.

FURTHER READING

Gunn 1995; Harriss 1994; Horrox 1989; Strohm 1998; Watts 1996.

NOTES

1 Plummer 1885, p.116.

2 Sutton and Hammond 1983, pp.219–20.

3 Wright 1859–61, I , p.273, II, p.230.

4 Chrimes 1972, p.308; see the essay by John Watts in this volume, esp. p.31.

5 Davis 1971–6, I, p.438.

6 Wolffe 1981, p.354.

7 Coote 2000; Kipling 1998.

8 Horrox 1995, p.9.

9 Powell 1989; Carpenter 1997; Castor 2000.

10 Plummer 1885, p.15.

11 Buhler 1941, p.6.

IV

NATIONAL AND REGIONAL IDENTITIES

DEREK KEENE

Late medieval England had a more centralized political structure, and a more uniform culture, than most other states in Europe. As a kingdom, it stood in sharp contrast to France, its nearest and most comparable rival. The city and regional states of Germany and Italy represented quite different ways of articulating authority and control within territories where there was much linguistic, cultural and economic common interest. English identity, as a nation and as a state, was expressed in language, in culture and in a system of government that operated with a significant degree of consent at both local and national levels. That coherence was acknowledged by the English and perceived by observers overseas. Group exemptions from taxation were rare. Even within the small number of formal immunities from royal authority, central rule was normally effective. A more general delegation of control to the localities tended to strengthen the sinews of the state and consolidate a political elite. Internal warfare reflected dynastic or client-based interests and the feebleness of individual monarchs, rather than opposition between territorially entrenched powers.

This distinctive unity and strength was apparent well before the Norman Conquest in the unification of the English kingdoms in response to invasion and in the creation and persistence of strong institutions of rule. After 1066 the redistribution of landed interests among the French-speaking conquerors created a situation in which it was difficult to build up unchallenged regional bases of power. From then until the sixteenth century, England was part of a multiple state whose rulers also had important interests overseas, most notably in parts of France. Nevertheless, the rhetoric and the reality of English unity – even of an English empire with London at its head – was strong in the twelfth century and continued to evolve. During political conflict in England, war against France could be seen as a way of promoting harmony at home.

All this arose in part from England's situation on an island on the periphery of Europe and at one end of transcontinental networks of exchange that linked Britain to more dynamic and sophisticated cultures and economies elsewhere. The kingdom was not directly threatened by powerful, territorially-adjacent states. It had only one city of European standing,

Debts owed to Londoners, 1424

Debts owed to York people, 1424

Debts owed to Exeter people, 1424

24 The hinterlands of London and two regional capitals, as revealed by a sample of debts. The sample included no cases of Exeter people in debt to other residents of the city.

London, which so overshadowed other English towns that urban rivalries could not undermine the integrity of the kingdom. Conditions that promoted fragmentation in Germany and Italy, and provincialization in France, were not present in England. Moreover, since the twelfth century and earlier, notions of English identity and nationhood had been shaped by their perceptions of barbarous, Celtic people and territories to the north and west. This became a problem for subjects of the King of Scotland, whose use of English in government and trade caused them by 1500 to redefine their 'Inglis' as Scots.[1] Those regions of England most susceptible to invasion, disorder and territorial sepa-

ratism lay towards the northern and western frontiers. Legally, the subjects of foreign powers were defined as aliens, but so too were the Welsh and the Irish, who were subject to the English crown.

Overall, England was less densely settled, less commercial and less urbanized than neighbouring parts of the Continent and northern Italy (plate 9). Its aggregate wealth and power was less even than that of some smaller states then emerging elsewhere in Europe. In the later fifteenth century, for example, the English national revenue was less than a quarter that of France, less than half that of Venice, and only about three times as much as the contribution of

the county of Flanders (equivalent in area to Kent and Surrey combined) to the Burgundian state.[2] The south-eastern parts of England, however, had for long had close links with one of the poles of European economic life, just a short voyage across the sea in Flanders and near the mouth of the Rhine. During the fourteenth and fifteenth centuries the markets of Bruges and then Antwerp became ever more dynamic and more closely integrated with those of Italy, southern Germany and Iberia. London, in particular, prospered from these developments, and between 1300 and 1500 there was a marked shift in the geographical distribution of wealth from the Midland counties to those of the south-east. At the same time there was an overall improvement in the conditions of business, and a redistribution of wealth that arose from the shortage of labour consequent upon the sharp fall in population occasioned by famine and plague in the fourteenth century. From the 1370s or earlier until about 1500, when population levels began to rise again, peasants and shopkeepers enjoyed a

more varied diet, better housing and a greater range of manufactured goods than they had done in 1300.[3]

Change was not even during this period. The years between about 1375 and 1420 were notable for new growth. Town and country witnessed rapid physical change as people adjusted to new conditions. National revenue reached a peak. London, and commercial ways of doing things, became more dominant than ever before. This was as apparent in the production of illustrated manuscript books,[4] as in more mundane fields (plate 24). At the same time there was a surge in the use of English (rather than Latin or French) for business, literary and religious texts. In the fifteenth century a plateau of economic activity was followed by a mid-century slump, with a recovery during the final three decades.[5] Throughout the period, even in London, living standards were lower than those in the southern Low Countries, and the country grew ever more dependent on that region for its export markets and its imports of luxuries and manufactured goods. A notable

25 Westminster Hall, interior

change, arising from a complex interaction of production costs, tariffs and market advantage, was the increase in the English manufacture of woollen cloth for export, although a growing share of the value of the final product came to be added by workshops overseas. This industry was a prime source of the nation's wealth, and enhanced London's role as a national centre for exports and internal distributive trade. Dominant nodes overseas came to have a stronger influence. Paris continued to be a powerful model, as it had been since the thirteenth century. A newer and more pervasive influence was that of Burgundian culture, both courtly and bourgeois, mediated through the cities of Flanders and Brabant. In numerous ways they reshaped and transmitted to England, principally via London, commodities and ideas from more distant territories.

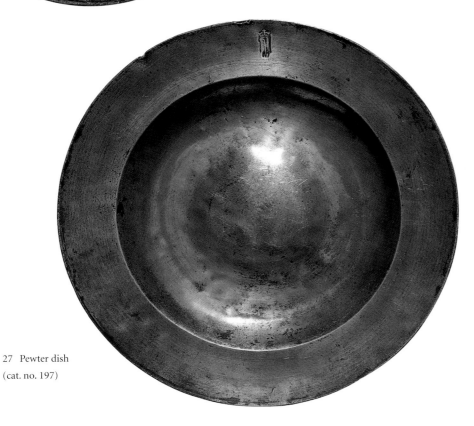

26 Seal-matrix of the Shearmen and Fullers of the Guild of the Nativity of our Lord of Coventry (cat. no. 132)

Regional identities and cultures evolved in response to these fundamental shifts. Many settlements shrank in size. Even London, which greatly increased its predominance over other towns, seems still in 1500 to have been smaller than it had been in 1300. London's role as a capital – established by the late thirteenth century as the prime seat of the monarch, political assemblies and more-or-less fixed institutions of central government – consolidated its position as the centre for elite consumption and for the circulation of news and ideas.[6] York was for much of the period the second city, but had less than one-third of London's population and a smaller proportion of its wealth. From time to time kings used York as an alternative capital. It was strategically well situated for action against the Scots and distant from the uncooperative and potentially dangerous Londoners, but could not challenge London as a place from which to rule. Significantly, it was Richard II, the monarch who most favoured York as a rival to the established capital and who perhaps had the strongest, most cosmographic sense of the identity of England and its succession of monarchs, who rebuilt Westminster Hall (plate 25) and embellished it with statues of the kings from Edward the Confessor onwards.[7] His model was presumably the *Grand'Salle* of the kings of France, at the heart of their capital, Paris. At the same time the royal practice of residing in or very close to London was becoming ever more entrenched.

The developing textile industry was associated with newly prosperous or smaller urban centres (e.g. Coventry, Colchester and Reading) and their hinterlands (plate 26, cat. no. 132), while several once-important provincial cities (including York) declined. Politically and strategically, York remained the second city, but by the early sixteenth century it had fallen to about sixth or lower rank in terms of population and wealth. On major routes small towns prospered in response to the relative increase in circulation. London entrepreneurs and capital came to have a new significance in regional economies, sometimes bypassing regional centres such as York (plate 24). In this way London was an increasingly direct stimulus to regional production, as in the cases of the West Riding woollen industry, cloth finishing at Coventry and Salisbury, and knife-making at Thaxted in Essex.[8] In many cases it made sense to locate such crafts at the cheaper, non-metropolitan sites of production. Yet London remained by far the largest and most diverse concentration of craft skills in the land and enjoyed strategic advantages as a site of production. The best and most innovative English-made goods were the products of London workshops. London dominated the goldsmiths' trade. Thaxted cutlers seem largely to have worked to orders from cutlers in London, who supplied them with exotic imported materials for handles and probably also with imported blades. In the pewter industry (plate 27, cat. nos 197, 196), which was expanding rapidly to meet the new demand from middle-ranking households for metal utensils, London offered both the established skills of its workforce and a location that enabled it readily to unite tin from the

27 Pewter dish (cat. no. 197)

south-west and lead from Derbyshire in a product that it could easily distribute at home and overseas. Around 1500, however, the London pewter industry, like many other English urban crafts, lost ground to the superior skills and market opportunities of workshops overseas.[9]

For centuries London's concentrated demand for basic foodstuffs and fuel had shaped specialized rural production and distribution over a wide hinterland. With increasing commercialization and new patterns of wealth and consumption, the city's demands – though in aggregate smaller than before – had an impact that was in some respects more marked. The influence of London markets became more apparent on cattle rearing and dairy production in distant parts of the north and west. Closer to the capital there appeared a zone devoted to growing and processing brewing grains, in response to Londoners' increased appetite for ale and the growth in London of brewing for export.[10] Rural specialization, industrial specialization and London markets thus went hand-in-hand in shaping the regions, as their inhabitants made the best use of local resources in response to wider demand.

While the influence of London was a major force for cultural change, some regions appear to have strengthened their economic independence of the capital, and so presumably reinforced their sense of identity in new ways. In the south-west it is possible to trace the way in which, during the fifteenth century, Exeter strengthened its influence as a regional economic centre and reduced its dependence on London (plate 24). Exeter profited from the increasing demand for tin, derived a more autonomous prosperity from the growth of the south-western fishing industry, and was able to engage directly in the newly dynamic commerce of the Low Countries and the Atlantic seaboard.[11] East Anglia and Norwich may similarly have benefited from their capacity for direct interaction with the Low Countries.

Despite its unity and the dominance of the metropolis, late medieval England was a country of regional identities with deep roots in the landscape, patterns of settlement, lordship, customs and beliefs, economic activity, and connections to the wider world. Many regional characteristics are readily recognizable, but the regions themselves had fuzzy boundaries and were frequently cross-cut or overlapping. Mapping the regions of medieval England, except on crude geographical or administrative criteria, is an extraordinarily complex task.

The most distinctive contrast was between the upland districts of the north and west – characterized by sparse settlement and by extensive and pastoral farming systems – and the more densely settled, intensively farmed, lowland districts of the south and east.[12] The most densely settled districts of all were in parts of East Anglia, Kent and Sussex, where conditions most resembled those across the sea in Flanders and Picardy. Indeed, the pattern of late medieval urbanization indicates that the potential for interaction and exchange was very heavily concentrated in the south-east – around London and probably along the axis of the Thames estuary – while the north and west were correspondingly remote. Contemporaries had some clear ideas of regional characteristics, associating them with linguistic and dialect differences and with the laws of the Old English kingdoms. The contrast between north and south was seen as especially strong. Southerners associated the northerners' grating speech with York and their Danish origins, while the warfare and disorder of the fifteenth century enhanced perceptions of the northerners' savagery. Certainly the contrast in wealth between north and south increased, along with northern envy of southern riches.[13] At the same time, however, contacts between the two regions became closer with the increasing prevalence of migration to London and the practice of doing business there.[14] One outcome of these centralizing tendencies was that regional variation in speech diminished.[15] East Anglia is one of those territories where several indicators suggest a common regional culture and identity.[16] This may have been promoted by its geographical shape and situation and by the dominance of Norwich as an urban centre, but close analysis does not always sustain the conclusion of East Anglian isolation and distinctiveness.

Communications were important. The principal land routes radiated from London to the furthest corners of the realm, facilitating the movement of news, administrative officials, armies, cattle and high-value goods. For long-distance trade in bulky goods, however, access to water transport was essential. Transport costs shaped the hinterlands of many regional centres, but in this respect London enjoyed advantages over all the rest. The routinely navigable stretch of the River Thames brought a large area of the south-east Midlands into its immediate hinterland, while estuarine and coastal traffic enabled it to trade easily with much of the east and south coasts.[17] Much of the east Midlands was connected to London and the North Sea trading area through the ports of the Wash. Londoners extended their reach by using southern ports such as Southampton. The use of water transport emphasizes the centrality of London for much of England, as well as its proximity to commercial centres overseas. Many regions were shaped by their outward aspect as well as by their internal resources and communications. Thus parts of the east coast looked as much to their Scandinavian, Baltic and Low Countries trading connections as to London, while Southampton looked to Normandy, Gascony and the Italian galley trade. Chester looked to Ireland and Wales, and

28 St Sitha
(cat. no. 281)

Bristol to Ireland, Gascony, Iberia and, by the late fifteenth century, to the new Atlantic trade.

Such connections promoted the exploitation of localized resources. Thus Newcastle and its hinterland prospered as a source of coal for London and other fuel-hungry cities in the Low Countries and the Baltic region. Derbyshire lead and south-western tin were widely distributed, as were alabaster from the region of Nottingham, and 'marble' from the Isle of Purbeck. All were raw materials that could accept a high degree of added value and so were especially suitable for widespread trade, as was the stone from Caen in Normandy, which was especially prized for building. By contrast, most other building stones tended to be used locally, except when prestigious projects employed quality stone from distant but accessible quarries. One of the most distinctive and visible regional characteristics, therefore, was the use of stone and other materials such as clay and timber for ordinary building.[18] Many parts of eastern England, including the London region, lacked stone. Bricks were imported from Flanders, but from the fourteenth century onwards were increasingly made in England. Following Burgundian example, they came to be characteristic of high-status building in eastern regions.

Structures of local government also encouraged the formation of regional identities and communities. Justice was to an increasing degree administered at county level by local men. The county court was an important assembly where royal proclamations were made and local views expressed. The county was the unit for administering taxes and other royal interests. County towns contained landmark buildings, such as the royal castle and the county gaol, along with major churches used by some local aristocrats and gentry as sites for prestigious burial. Aristocratic client networks were also an important force for defining territories, both within counties and across their boundaries.[19]

Cathedral cities served as places of administration, worship, commemoration and assembly for extensive diocesan regions, especially at the great feasts of the liturgical year. Along with other great churches containing relics and shrines, cathedrals drew pilgrims from far afield and so contributed to a general sense of the identity of the place and the region surrounding it. Lesser cults and commemorations also expressed regional identity. They had great historical depth and were responsive to new influences and ideas. The south-west, for example, was as remarkable for its commemoration of British saints as for its linguistic separatism.[20] The early history of Northumbria and Wessex continued to be visibly expressed in the church dedications, feasts and representations of royal and episcopal saints. The rich surviving iconography of late medieval East Anglia displays both its own group of saints – ranging from St Edmund, its martyred king (d. 870), to the mythical St Walstan of Bawburgh and his mother – and seems to have been particularly responsive to new cults from overseas largely received via Flanders.[21] Other innovations spread remarkably quickly. The cult of St Zita (usually anglicized as Sitha), introduced to London by the families of Lucca merchants dwelling there in the early fourteenth century, seems to have met a special English need for a female household saint (plate 28), and less than a century later was observed in the far north and to the west, as well as along the east coast.[22]

The nearest we have to a contemporary view of regional characteristics is in William Worcestre's account of his journeys through southern England between 1477 and 1480, which he supplemented with information from local observers and records. Worcestre got nowhere near Shrewsbury, for example, but Sir Roger Kynaston of that city provided him with an account (evidently reflecting personal experience and interests) of landscape and historical features in a region extending from mid-Wales into Derbyshire and Cheshire, while during a journey between London and Walsingham a Dublin merchant provided Worcestre with information on the Isle of Man.[23] Worcestre's jottings are far from systematic, but do reflect some consistent concerns. He noted geographically distinctive features such as islands, rivers and hills, but the matters that caught his attention were local rather than regional in character. He seems to have had little sense of county identity, except in the case of remote and isolated Cornwall. The physical connectedness of the territory he traversed is apparent from his precise records of distance and from his identification of numerous bridges. England had long been a well-bridged country.[24] Like later tourists and antiquaries, Worcestre remarked on and described noteworthy churches, castles and manor houses, in both town and country. He was impressed by new building, and in eastern regions remarked on new structures in brick. He noted local saints and cults, and related his knowledge of the history and mythology of early Britain and England to particular sites. The world of magnate patronage and regional influence, of which he had much direct personal experience, emerges clearly from his pages in his list of the building works of Richard Beauchamp, Earl of Warwick, in five Midland counties and Berkshire, and in his note of the inexplicable outbreak of violence in Norfolk between the tenants of the Duke of Norfolk and those of the Duke of Suffolk.

It is not surprising that William Worcestre's account of his journeys displays relatively little awareness of regional differentiation, for material culture seems often to defy modern attempts at analysis of regional patterns and movements.

Too often, rigid preconceptions of regional unity or identity, rather than the evidence itself, inform such attempts. Some simple and inexpensive products, such as those of many pottery kilns, did not travel very far and presumably expressed the distinctively local character of many households (plate 29, cat. no. 200). But pots shared forms with those of other regions, and some of the wealthier households that used them also purchased more expensive and less

29 Surrey ware jug
(cat. no. 200)

regionally differentiated goods in the capital. We know that many carpenters worked in highly localized environments, especially in and around towns. Yet in the timber-framed structures that were used for most small-scale domestic accommodation, it is rarely easy to identify coherent regional patterns and the dissemination of innovations, although observation by individual craftsmen and the imitation of influential examples seem to have played a part. Thus the builder of Baguley Hall near Manchester appears to have drawn directly on structural ideas circulating only in the south-east, but which – once expressed at Baguley – became a model imitated in the north-west.[25] Likewise, prestige projects of building and decoration, such as the Beauchamp chapel at Warwick (c.1442–62), where top-ranking craftsmen from London were employed, could influence the adoption of new styles in the vicinity (cat. no. 86).[26] In East Anglia the builders of church towers consciously imitated and exceeded recent examples in nearby parishes, thus reinforcing local character.[27] In the 1430s, however, the Grocers' Company of London chose as a model for the roof of their new hall in the city the Kent country house of a prominent citizen of London, erected some eight decades earlier.[28]

Such patterns of connection and influence were facilitated by the cohesiveness – commercial as well as political – of the kingdom as a whole. London, as a centre of information and skills, and the elite patronage that operated through the city made an important contribution to the circulation and exchange of ideas. Recent case studies illustrate some of the complex interactions between metropolitan and regional factors. From the late thirteenth century onwards, London was the principal site of manufacture of high-status engraved memorial brasses inlaid in marble slabs shipped in from Purbeck, while the brass plates themselves were probably imported from the Meuse valley via Cologne. In London the workshops were concentrated near St Paul's Cathedral, not only because this district of the city had a long tradition of fine metal-working and masonry skills, but also because St Paul's was the principal place of resort for wealthy visitors to the city, including the leading ecclesiastics who were among the early commissioners of the monuments. Where quality and status mattered, the bulky nature of the raw material and the final product was no obstacle to their movement over considerable distances, and London-made memorials were supplied to a wide region around the city, including much of the south and east Midlands.[29] In the fifteenth century London bell-founders supplied churches within an even wider region, shaped by the availability of water transport.[30] The highest-status commissions could travel yet further: the shrine and reredos presented to Durham Cathedral by Lord Neville of Raby in 1372 and 1380 were carved in London using Nottingham alabaster and Caen stone, and then shipped to Newcastle for carting to Durham.[31]

During the early fourteenth century, workshops in several provincial cities, including Lincoln and York, supplied their immediate regions with monumental brasses, but for almost a century from about 1360 the London workshops had a virtual monopoly on home-produced brasses. This represents a striking parallel to the changes in the fortunes of provincial towns in relation to London and to the development of the capital's distributive trade. In this period the London workshops achieved remarkably high and uniform standards of production. Subsequently their quantity of output was maintained, but quality declined and provincial centres of brass engraving, with products no better than London's, re-emerged to serve their hinterlands (plate 59, cat. no. 333). In East Anglia at this time, as in York, there appear to have been links between the designs for brasses, locally produced manuscripts, painted glass, screens and perhaps even panel paintings.[32] Such lack of specialization suggests connections between workshops supplying a new, growing and less discriminating demand for all these products, which could be supplied on a local basis. It may be that the production of carved alabaster panels followed a similar trend, with the large-scale production of relatively simple pieces at Nottingham workshops following on from a period when the industry was dominated by high-quality products worked in London.[33] These changes seem not to have been the outcome of new, widespread provincial prosperity, or of any associated strengthening of regional identities, but due to a broadening of the demand for products and styles no longer desired by elite consumers. The new demand may also have been stimulated by religious experimentation and renewal.

In London itself, and among the elite groups that it supplied from the mid-fifteenth century onwards, the higher standards seem increasingly to have been set by Low Countries' styles in manuscript production, metal-working and painted glass. Native workers may have adopted old-fashioned versions of those styles, but increasingly immigrant craftsmen from the Low Countries established themselves in London and its suburbs to meet the new demands.[34] At the highest levels, English patrons could presumably provide rewards comparable to (or approaching) those to be obtained from Burgundian patrons, but many of those immigrants presumably saw London as a less competitive market than the one at home.

The register of the guild of the Holy Trinity, founded at Luton in 1474–5, shows how relatively humble provincials could associate themselves and come into contact with the tastes of ambitious patrons and leading Londoners.

30 The Register of the Guild
of the Holy Trinity, Luton,
Bedfordshire (cat. no. 347)

The guild primarily served the inhabitants of Luton and its neighbourhood, but its original patron was Thomas Rotherham, at that time Bishop of Lincoln – in whose diocese Luton lay – and Chancellor of England. Rotherham donated the register, which contained a magnificent frontispiece painted by a Flemish artist who almost certainly worked in London (plate 30, cat. no. 347). Other founder members or people commemorated in the original register included a London draper known to have owned a book decorated by a Low Countries artist, and a deceased mayor of London who had married a local heiress. Subsequently the register appears to have been sent to London annually for new names to be added and periodic embellishment. The quality of this later work, in a mundane English style, fell far short of the original. Later members of the guild, including Londoners but also people from the port of Boston (Lincolnshire) and Kendal (in Westmorland, a source of widely traded cloth), indicate the widespread connections that even a small town like Luton could have.[35]

A recent study of Ewelme in Oxfordshire casts light on related issues.[36] Work at the parish church in the early fifteenth century, patronized by Sir Thomas Chaucer, son of the poet, drew on designs used by a mason who worked in the region around Oxford. Chaucer's daughter Alice, however, married the Earl of Suffolk, who, when he remodelled the church from 1437 onwards, did so with reference to East Anglian forms, and especially to the earl's family church at Wingfield in Suffolk. This explicit advertisement of the titles of the founders of God's house at Ewelme cut across regional cultures and identities. Alice survived her husband and was commemorated at Ewelme by an alabaster tomb, probably carved in London in about 1470–75, having herself commissioned a memorial from famous London makers for her husband at his burial place in Hull.

Late medieval England, with its long history of unity and centralized power, was a country where ideas of language and nationhood conferred a stronger sense of a single identity than ever before. Commerce, focusing increasingly on London and influenced by new forces overseas, did much to sustain these developments. Trade, the movement of people and magnate patronage all tended to promote contact between the regions, increase dependence on London and reduce cultural variation, but at the same time enabled certain districts to enhance their distinctive character. Many long-established perceptions of regional difference remained. Warfare and regional shifts in prosperity increased the sense of a contrast between south and north. Economic change, language, literature, religion, and material and other cultural expressions interacted in complex ways to shape distinctive features of both national and regional society.

FURTHER READING

Dyer1989; Galloway 2000; Miller 1991; Palliser 2000; Pollard 2000; Prevenier and Blockmans 1986 (Blockmans and Prevenier 1999 is a revised edition of the text, but lacks the illustrations).

NOTES

1 Robinson 1985.

2 Calculations based on data in Bonney 1995 and 1999, and on Spufford 1986.

3 Dyer 1989; Hatcher 1994.

4 Scott 1996, pp.27–8.

5 Hatcher 1996.

6 Keene 1989.

7 Colvin 1963, pp.528–32; Lindley 1997b; Wilson 1997.

8 Keene 1995, 1997, 2000a.

9 Keene 1997.

10 Campbell et al. 1993; Galloway, Keene and Murphy 1996; Galloway 1998; Keene 2000b.

11 Kowaleski 1995, 2000; Keene 2000a.

12 Campbell 2000.

13 Turville-Petre 1996; Pollard 1990, 2001.

14 Keene 2000b.

15 Milroy 1992; Görlach 1999; Wright 1996, 2000.

16 Beadle 1991.

17 Campbell et al. 1993.

18 Clifton-Taylor 1965; Salzman 1967.

19 Carpenter 1992, especially chapters 9 and 10.

20 Orme 2000.

21 James 1987.

22 Sutcliffe 1993; Cullum and Goldberg 2000, pp.220–30.

23 Harvey 1969, pp.66–71, 168–9.

24 Harrison 1992.

25 Stenning and Andrews 1998, p.139.

26 Marks 1993, p.190.

27 Salzman 1967, pp.547–9.

28 Nightingale 1995, pp.412–13.

29 Blair (J) 1987.

30 Barron 1994.

31 Wilson 1980b.

32 Badham 1990, Marks 1993, pp.195–6; Scott 1996, p.28.

33 Ramsay 1987.

34 Marks 1993, pp.205–9; Geddes 1999, pp.261–72; see also the essays by Catherine Reynolds and Kim Woods in this volume.

35 Marks 1998b; Scott 2000a.

36 Goodall 2001.

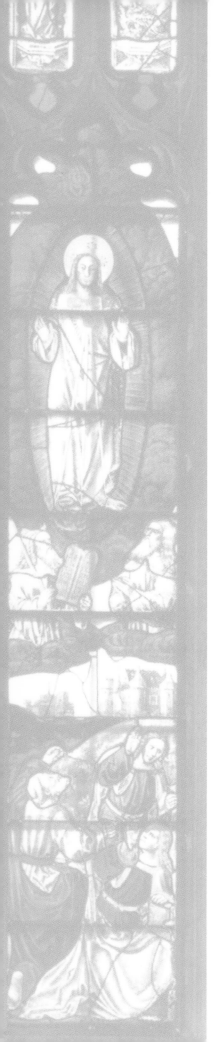

V

LATE MEDIEVAL RELIGION

EAMON DUFFY

Between the death of her husband Henry in 1470 and her own in December 1485, the wealthy Bristol widow Alice Chester showered a series of major benefactions on her parish church of All Saints, in the heart of the city. She continued and extended the chantry established by her husband 'for the loving of almighty God and the augmenting of divine service'. This chantry provided the parish with the services of an auxiliary priest, who conducted masses and prayers of intercession for Alice Chester's family every Friday in the year and on the anniversary of Henry's death. She paid for the installation of a riverside crane for loading and unloading merchandise by the Marsh Gate, a crucial amenity in this city devoted to maritime trade. Above all, she funded an extensive programme of renewal of the church's liturgical furnishings and devotional imagery. She commissioned a statue of the Trinity 'over the image of Jesus', standing in a gilded tabernacle covered with a curtain, which could be closed or drawn back 'when it shall please the vicar and the parishioners'. She gilded the Lady Altar, paid for a painted frontal, and commissioned a carved tabernacle with three of the most popular late medieval representations of Mary – the Pietà (cat. no. 344), the Annunciation and the Assumption. She had the Rood Altar gilded and carved with images of the saints – St Anne, St Mary Magdalene, St Giles, St Erasmus, St Anthony – and she provided another painted veil to cover these images 'at certain times'. She presented a long linen towel or 'houselling-cloth' to be held under the chins of her fellow-parishioners as they knelt in rows to receive their annual communion on Easter day. She gave a great brass basin for the ritual washing of the church's relics on Relic Sunday, and a new cross of enamel and silver-gilt to be carried in the weekly processions before the main Sunday Mass. And 'taking to her counsel the worshipful of this parish with others having best insights in carving, to the honour and worship of almighty God and his saints, and of her special devotion unto this church', she commissioned a new rood-loft, the great partition separating the chancel and high altar from the body of the church, filled with 22 carved and gilded images, arranged in pairs on pillars and tabernacles round the principal image of the Trinity, which was flanked by statues of St Christopher and St Michael the Archangel. Finally, considering that 'there was no hearse cloth in the church of any reputation in value … for the love and honour she had unto almighty God and all Christian souls, and for the ease and succour of all this parish unto whom she owed her good will and love in her day', she presented the church with a black pall, decorated with her own and her husband's initials and an inscription in Latin asking for prayers for their souls, for use at the funerals of other parishioners. This would probably have resembled the funerary pall on which the Fayrey family is depicted, used by the Dunstable guild of St John the Baptist (plate 31).[1]

Mistress Chester's bounty epitomizes many of the preoccupations at the heart of late medieval lay piety. It was a Christianity rooted in the concrete, nourished by the sight of images and the touch of relics and of 'sacramentals' (sacred objects and ceremonies) like holy water, focused on the Passion of Christ and the intercession of the saints – above all the Virgin Mary (cat. no. 278), but also practical helper saints like Christopher, protector of travellers (cat. nos 283, 290, 296); Michael, protector of the death-bed (cat. no. 279); and Erasmus, protector against disorders of the stomach and bowels (cat. no. 285). It was a piety much concerned with death, with the power of prayers and pious works to ease the souls of the departed through the cleansing pains of Purgatory, and with the mutual obligations of prayer and charity, which bound the living to the dead. It was a ritual piety, intensely reverential towards the sacraments, above all the Eucharist. It was keyed to the annual cycle of the liturgy, processions and Masses, the feasts of the saints and their relics, and the church's seasons – Lent, when the many images in the church were concealed behind veils painted with tokens of the Passion, and Easter, when the community celebrated and consolidated its often fragile unity by reconciling quarrels and kneeling shoulder-to-shoulder to receive communion together. It was a Christianity that coloured, and was coloured by, the structures and values of society, emphasizing the virtues of neighbourhood, and hence attributing religious merit

to practical benefactions such as the riverside crane; it was acutely conscious of rank and precedence, endearingly and competitively sensitive to appearances and respectability.

Planning her munificence, Mistress Chester consulted the vicar and the leading parishioners, the 'worshipful' of the parish. The element of pride of wealth and conspicuous consumption in her giving was crystallized in the gift of the hearse cloth or pall prominently embroidered with her own and her husband's initials. Those embroidered names must have had the effect of annexing every funeral at which the cloth was used, thereby exacting repayment in the form of the perpetual reciprocity of the parish's prayers. Through Mistress Chester's benefactions we catch a vivid glimpse of the social dynamics of an urban community, in which skilled and articulate craftsmen expected even lavish benefactors to observe the courtesies of consultation and group decision-making. These were communities used to transacting business, dealing with the demands of ecclesiastical and secular authorities, electing their own churchwardens and guild officers, managing their own funds, mounting their own ambitious schemes of decoration and rebuilding. We glimpse, too, the physical layout of a prosperous late medieval church, crammed with altars and images and lights, the theatre for a liturgy which sanctified matter by blessing and venerating it, which sanctified space by processing around it or by dividing it into holy corrals with decorated screens and partitions, and which sanctified time in the cycle of fast and feast, penitence and celebration, that made up the ritual year.[2]

31 Fayrey funerary pall
(cat. no. 349)

Stendit ypus sup celos ↄ ↄparauit sue castissime matri
immortalitatis locum et hoc est ista preclara festiuitas omⁱ
sanctoↄ festiuitatibↄ incomparabilis in qua gloriosa ↄ felix
mirantibↄ celestis curie ordinibↄ ad ethereum peruenit thalamum cuⁱ
pia sui memorum immemor nequaquam existat
sancta dei genitrix super coros angeloↄ ad celestia regna

Exaltata es

Deus qui virginalem aulam in qua habitares
eligere dignatus es da quesumus ut sua nos
defensione munitos iocundos faciat sue interesse
festiuitati qui viuis et regnas cum deo patre in
vnitate spiritus sancti deus per omnia secula seculoↄ amen

32 The Assumption of the
Virgin, Book of the Fraternity
of Our Lady's Assumption
(cat. no. 133)

33 Archbishop Richard Scrope
and suppliant, Bolton Hours
(cat. no. 141)

Alice Chester and All Saints church can serve as emblems of late medieval English religion because, if the high Middle Ages was the age of the Great Church, of cathedral and monastery, then the century and a half after the Black Death was emphatically the age of the parish church, and of the lay people who worshipped there. The drive to instruct and motivate laymen and women initiated by the Fourth Lateran Council, and formulated for England in Archbishop Pecham's constitution *Ignorantia Sacerdotum* of 1281, bore pastoral fruit in a host of vernacular guides and devotional treatises aimed at instructing the laity – catechisms, saints' lives, meditations on the Passion or on the art of dying well (cat. no. 341). It also inspired a series of handbooks, beginning with William of Pagula's *Oculus Sacerdotis*, designed to equip parish priests to implement this programme. The emergence in the course of the fourteenth century of the vernacular theologies associated with so-called 'mystics' like Richard Rolle of Hampole, Walter Hilton and, later, Julian of Norwich was another manifestation of the ferment produced by this democratization and vernacularization of religion, which found many expressions. At the end of the fourteenth century the writings of William Langland, of the Pearl poet and of the writer of the verse legend of St Erkenwald all belong within this wider movement, as does, at a further point on the spectrum, the popular heretical movement known as Lollardy.[3]

Ironically, reaction against the anti-sacramental and anti-clerical polemics of the Lollards may have curtailed the scope and vigour of this vernacular movement as a whole. Censorship designed to eradicate heresy not merely made the direct citation of scripture in English suspect, but also resulted in the disappearance from English religious writing of the originality evident in the writings of Langland and Julian of Norwich: intellectual adventurousness gave way to a duller and defensive devotionalism.[4] But lay people of the middling ranks remained intensely and increasingly interested in religion. Religious texts to serve their needs abounded, above all the Book of Hours. This Latin prayer book, composed of psalms, hymns and prayers, was divided into the seven monastic 'hours' of prayer and arranged around two themes – devotion to the Virgin Mary (and hence to the Incarnation and death of her son Jesus Christ) and prayer for the dead: the twin landmarks in the religious world of Alice Chester, also. Books of Hours, sumptuously illuminated and bound, had at first been the prerogative of royalty and aristocracy (cat. nos 44, 45, 73, 93, 94, 115, 215, 223, 224). By the early fifteenth century, however, they were being mass-produced by commercial stationers all over Europe, not only for the gentry, but even for prosperous guildsmen of the towns and their wives (plates 33, 113, cat. no. 140), and they had moved

decisively downmarket. Supplemented by regional calendars and a range of Latin and vernacular devotions added to order or written in by the owners themselves after purchase (cat. no. 326), they became the most important religious books of the later Middle Ages, handed on from parents to children and setting the tone of much lay piety. With the

advent of printing, their mass-production reached new heights (cat. no. 225), and almost 120 editions of the Sarum Book of Hours were printed for the English market before 1530. The early fifteenth-century Lynn merchant's wife and aspiring visionary, Margery Kempe, is often thought of as illiterate, and she certainly could not write, but she owned and used a Book of Hours, taking it to church to 'say her Matins … her book in her hand'.[5]

Margery's search for sanctity, modelled on the lives of continental women visionaries, was extraordinary by any standards, but she shared the main features of her devotional landscape with her more conventional neighbours. Even after she began her restless journeyings to the great shrines of Christendom, her parish church of St Margaret in

Lynn was one of the focal points of her spiritual life – she went there to pray and to hear notable visiting preachers, reported on the emotional impact of its Holy Week liturgy, knelt as the sacrament was carried from it through the streets to the sick during pestilence, took (and sometimes gave) spiritual advice from (or to) the local clergy and from notable members of the four orders of friars active in the town. Like her neighbours she travelled to regional holy places, as well as to national shrines like Canterbury, Walsingham and the Holy Blood of Hailes. She and her husband made a special journey to see the Corpus Christi plays at York and to pray before the relics in the Minster. She collected indulgences, attended her neighbours' death-beds, and listened to or read conventional saints' lives and popular devotional treatments of the Passion. Between the religion of this aspiring saint and that of her bourgeois neighbours there was a difference of degree and intensity, rather than of kind.[6]

The popularity of the Book of Hours among the gentry and the urban bourgeoisie has been associated by some historians with other manifestations of privatization in religion, such as the emergence of the gentry pew. Built inside the parish church, yet not altogether part of it, such pews or family chapels constituted, it has been suggested, a private enclave in which the gentry could get on with the practice of an elite religion that was increasingly remote from the public religion of the parish: 'they were, so to speak, getting their heads down, turning their eyes from the distractions posed by their fellow worshippers, [and] at the same time taking them off the priest and his movements and gestures'.[7] It has even been suggested that the spread of the Book of Hours posed a 'challenge' to 'institutional, parish-orientated religion'.[8]

But this is perhaps to confuse personalization with privatization. Devotional use of these books certainly represented a search for greater interiority, a more engaged lay piety, but the contents of the Book of Hours were highly conventional and most closely related to the liturgy and the widely shared repertoire of symbols that the liturgy made familiar. The very idea of a Book of Hours was to provide lay people with a simplified version of a clerical or monastic breviary, and so enable them to share the official prayer of the church. A fundamental component of all such books was the *Dirige* or Office of the Dead, celebrated before most funerals and hence one of the parts of the medieval church's worship that was most familiar to the laity. Most religious guilds celebrated *Diriges* for deceased members, and encouraged or enforced attendance by guild members (those who were unable to read said the rosary). The additional prayers bound into or written in the margins of so many of these books were just as familiar – prayers to be recited at the elevation of the Host at Mass, or while gazing at such universal devotional emblems as the Cross, the Vernicle (Wounded Face of Christ), the Pietà and the 'Image of Pity' (the half-figure of the dead Christ, displaying his wounds and surrounded by the instruments of the Passion). All these emblems were endlessly repeated in the decoration of churches as well as in devotional books and prints.

Individual focus on the public symbols that nourished *everyone's* interiority cannot sensibly be considered a symptom of privatization. The Image of Pity is a case in point: reproduced in myriads of fifteenth-century devotional books, in blockprints, engraved on funeral brasses, carved on bench-ends and altars, and displayed on panel and wall-paintings, it was a powerful evocation of the suffering of Christ in the Passion (cat. no. 345). It was also closely associated with the Mass, the wounded body of the Man of Sorrows being equated with the bread of the Eucharist. Hence it was a favourite choice all over Europe for the decoration of Eucharistic vessels such as pyxes, and for the doors of the sacrament-houses and tabernacles used for storing the consecrated bread. In the late fifteenth century the Chudleigh family, landlords of the parish of Ashton in Devon, decorated their burial chapel at the east end of the church's north aisle (plate 34, cat. no. 260). The panels of the screens that separated their chapel from the body of the church and from the high altar were decorated with figures and scrolls illustrating the liturgy of the new Feast of the Visitation, in a style derived from contemporary woodcuts, and markedly superior to the doll-like figures of the saints with which the parish had painted its rood-screen.[9] The Chudleigh chapel had its own altar and carved or painted images, and probably its own priest. The dominant religious image, however, was a huge representation of the Image of Pity, painted high on the north wall and looming above the separating screen-work, where it could be seen, and prayed before, by the whole parish. Gentry and plebeian piety – private and public – here converged and overlapped.

The Chudleigh chapel at Ashton alerts us to a fundamental fact about the late medieval parish church, which is also a fact about late medieval religion. Most churches were examples of 'complex space', based not on a single focal point – the high altar or the pulpit – but subdivided into a series of distinct but overlapping enclaves, some more important or more private than others, and representing different sub-groups and interests within the broader community.[10] This complexity reflected the nature of the late medieval parish itself, which was rarely a single hierarchical unit, but rather a constellation of groups, families and individuals who often cooperated and sometimes conflicted.

34   Church of St John the
Baptist, Ashton (cat. no. 260)

Most urban and many rural parishes, for example, contained one or more religious guilds (plate 32, cat. nos 347, 348). These were voluntary religious bodies dedicated to a saint or religious mystery (such as Corpus Christi or the Trinity): guild members met for Mass and vespers on their patronal day, when they elected officers for the year, held a feast at which all the brethren and sisters were expected to be present (women were often members, but rarely officers) and alms were distributed to the poor. They attended funerals and held obits for their dead members. Guilds offered their members other benefits too: in both town and country they were often substantial property-owners, able to lend money or to rent out buildings, land or livestock at attractive rates. In many communities guild office was one of the recognized ways of establishing or consolidating one's weight, and could function as an apprenticeship for more demanding parochial office. Most guilds maintained one or more lights before a patronal image in their local church. Many employed clergy as chaplains, and churchwardens' accounts

from all over the country show that guilds often contributed significantly to parish devotional, charitable and building projects – many Corpus Christi guilds, for example, paid for the candles burned around the Easter Sepulchre in Holy Week, or maintained lights before the reserved sacrament, or paid for torches to burn at the Elevation of the Host at the parish Mass on Sundays. Guilds offered ordinary people a form of sanctified sociability, and an opportunity to express devotion to favourite saints, or to the Body of Christ. In scattered rural communities or large towns, guilds might also maintain meeting halls or chapels that could serve as a local focus of identity, and their stipendiary clergy might function as assistant parish priests, providing crucial religious services, especially in winter, when travel to a distant parish church was difficult. The precise relationship between guild and parish varied from place to place, but it should not be conceived in terms of rivalry: the official, 'compulsory' religion of the parish and the voluntary religion of the guild were complementary, not opposed.

Guilds were not the only contributors to the complexity of the late medieval parish. Every parish church in England had one or more altars in addition to the high altar. Some of these were tucked away in screened-off gentry chapels, and staffed by chaplains paid to pray primarily for their employers, as the Chudleigh family chantrist would have been. Other altars were placed prominently in front of the rood-screen or against pillars in the body of the church, their attendant clergy paid for by wealthy parishioners on short-term contracts, from one to 20 years (the arrangement for Alice Chester's priest). But even private chantrists were expected to assist in the religious activities of the parish at large, and many of them played key roles, training the choir, playing the organ or writing out the parish liturgical books and the wills of parishioners.[11]

Chantries were private institutions, attached to families or individuals. In many parishes, age- or gender-specific groups – the Wives, the Young Men or 'Grooms', the Maidens – organized themselves for festal and religious activity, and maintained their own religious symbols in their parish church. These were rarely altars, but more often candles in front of favoured images, although they include one of the most famous (albeit heavily restored) collections of stained glass surviving from the early Tudor period, the windows paid for by the Young Men, the Maidens and the Wives at the western end of the Cornish parish church of St Neot.[12] These groups were often organized geographically. Within the sheep-grazing Norfolk parish of Salle in the fifteenth century there were regional plough-lights and maiden-lights – at Marshgate, Kirkgate, Lunton and Steynwade, all of which maintained lamps in the church. Such groups of people were regularly remembered in local wills, like that of Alice Martyn, who left 6d. to the plough-light and 'to the daunsyng lights of the maydens to eche of them 3d.';[13] or that of William Kechyn, parishioner of Sloley, in Norfolk, who left 20d. in 1506 to 'the plough light of the street ther I dwell ynne', and 12d. 'to every of the odir vii plough lights in the same town'.[14]

Salle, with a population of about 500, had seven guilds: of the Blessed Virgin Mary (the Assumption guild), St Thomas, St Paul (the parish dedication), St John the Baptist,

35   Stained-glass panel showing a donor couple,
Church of St Nicholas, Stanford on Avon (cat. no. 293)

36   Stained-glass window showing the Appearance of the Risen Christ to the Virgin Mary, the Transfiguration and the Three Marys at the Sepulchre, Church of St Mary the Virgin, Fairford (cat. no. 294)

37   Church of St Peter and
St Paul, Salle (cat. no. 257)

St Margaret, the Trinity (which had its altar and priest in Thomas Roos's chapel) and St James, which had its altar in the chapel of the south transept, built for it by Thomas Brigg (d. 1444).[15] Brigg's initials are on bosses in the roof and on the outside cornice of the chapel, which is filled with Brigg burials, while Thomas and his wives kneel before St Thomas Becket, his name-saint, in the upper registers of the stained glass. It was therefore very much a family chapel, partitioned from the rest of the church as Brigg's land, no doubt, was fenced off from that of his neighbours. But his chapel was also the St James's guild chapel and, along with the Brigg family name, the scallop shell of St James can be seen carved on its parapet. Similar sharing arrangements between guilds and local gentry operated in the north transept. We need to beware of deducing too much from these arrangements. It remains true that late medieval gentry were less closely involved with parish and guild than their humbler neighbours: often guild members, they were rarely guild officers, and almost never served the parish as churchwardens. But in many parishes the gentry remained a significant and influential presence, initiating or supporting parish projects, and were part of the social complexity reflected in the physical complexity of the parish church building itself.

And so the interior of Salle church (plate 37), now a vast, cathedral-sized auditorium without partitions, was not originally a single open space, but an interconnecting network of sacred zones based around a multitude of altars and images, some privately owned, others the property of guilds in which many parishioners were sharers. Many of these zones were adorned with lights paid for by young people's gender-groups, all of them in some sense part of a common symbol-system and set of resources, and manned by a transient population of salaried chaplains, many of them the sons of local families; they were financed by guilds, by local landowners and by short-term benefactions, like that of the yeoman Robert Pull, who left eight marks in 1510 as wages for 'a pryst that shalbe able to synge in the church of Saul a yere'.[16] We get some sense of how these sacred spaces were viewed, at least by the chaplains, from the bequest by one of the former chaplains in 1399 of three sets of vestments 'to serve the *common* altars'; and the bequest by another chaplain in 1456 of his missal, to be used at two of the guild altars (*not* ones that he himself had served while alive) in the church.[17]

All Saints, Bristol, and Salle church, Norfolk, were filled in the late Middle Ages with devotional furniture, stained glass, altars, images, lights and the vessels, vestments and books needed for the celebration of the liturgy. Some were bought by the parish, acting through its elected wardens,

as required by ecclesiastical law. But much – perhaps most – was provided by individual or group benefactions (see plate 35, cat. nos 290, 293). Late medieval Christians believed that after death all but a handful of people would go, not straight to heaven, but to a place of painful cleansing and renewal called Purgatory. The pains of Purgatory could be eased by the loving prayers of friends and relatives, and by good works done by oneself while still alive, or by others on one's behalf after death. Prominent among those good works were contributions towards 'the increase of divine service'. Late medieval church buildings were therefore 'antechambers of purgatory', paved with funeral slabs and brasses appealing for prayers, and stuffed full of ritual furniture donated to improve the religious amenities of the parish. Such gifts pleased God and obliged one's neighbours, and they were often prominently labelled (as Alice Chester's hearse-cloth was), reminding the grateful parish of its obligation to pray for its benefactor.

It was these convictions that funded the massive rebuilding and refurbishment of so many late medieval English parish churches. Late medieval piety responded vividly and immediately to the visual. Devotional pictures of the wounded Christ promised special blessings to those who 'piteously behold' the image (cat. no. 345). Devotees were encouraged to weep in empathy with the sufferings of Christ or the afflicted Virgin by the Cross, portrayed in wall and window and altar, or painted, or printed on the page: the devotional gaze was accorded special power and privilege.[18] Accordingly, late medieval donors were intensely alert to the visual quality of their devotional gifts, looked around them for patterns to imitate or exceed, and wanted the very best. In 1522 Sir John Spencer paid for a statue of the Virgin for his parish church of Brington in Northamptonshire 'to be made after the patron [pattern] oon maister X [name illegible] caused to be made at Banbury, and to be made by the same man that made his, orells by some other'; in 1545 the little Devon parish of Morebath commissioned a new rood from the carver William Popyll, 'after the pattern of [the neighbouring parish of] Brushford, or better', while an early sixteenth-century Norfolk donor required that his gift should be 'aftyr the best faschone of anny her abowth'.[19] Late medieval donors, therefore, knew what they wanted, but were also willing to give the craftsmen they commissioned some room for manoeuvre. The Ludlow Palmers' guild, whose patron was St John the Evangelist, commissioned elaborately carved imagery for their chapel in the parish church in 1524: they told their craftsman that he must make 'on the north side ... one substantial story according to his paper, that is to be known St John

Evangelist, standing beneath in a godly story and the Palmers receiving a ring of him, and over him St Edward in a godly story ... and the Four Latin Doctors of the Church, with other divers saints such as he thinketh best with two or three miracles of St John Evangelist'.[20]

The most spectacular surviving examples of late medieval parochial patronage are the painted and carved rood-screens that remain in large numbers in East Anglia and in central and southern Devon (plate 38, cat. nos 265, 266, 277, 357). These screens supported the principal image in the church, the great crucifix or rood from which they took their name (cat. no. 268). They divided the chancel and high altar from the nave or body of the church, and so formed a ritual threshold between the profane and the holy, this world and the next. They were themselves often the back-drop for nave altars at which the daily Masses funded by guilds or private benefactors were celebrated. For all these

reasons, the screens were densely covered focuses of reli-gious art and much-favoured targets for pious benefaction. Along the loft, below the rood, there were usually carved or painted 'pageants', single figures or narrative scenes from sacred history, while along the lower border or dado were generally painted rows of saints. Where altars stood against the screen, the panels above the altars were often painted to form a reredos. The decoration of such screens was often applied after the woodwork itself was in place, and its fund-ing reflected the complex interplay between individual and community, which was so striking a feature of the late medieval parish. Decorative schemes might be funded by the parish as a whole under its wardens, by coordinated benefactions from groups or individuals, or added to piece-meal, as individual donors or testators provided the money. Coordinated schemes might have rows of conventional saints (commonly the 12 apostles and Old Testament

38   Rood-screen, St Mary's church, Attleborough (cat. no. 264)

prophets) or matching sets of the Four Evangelists and the Four Latin Doctors. Even such sequences might be interrupted in obedience to donors, as the set of the Four Evangelists at Barton Turf is, having St Loy or Eligius, patron saint of metal-workers, instead of St Luke; presumably the local farrier or blacksmith had paid for the pictures. They might also vary hugely in quality from figure to figure, as they do at Aylsham in Norfolk, where the apostles and prophets paid for by Thomas Wymer in 1507 were painted on paper and glued to the screen. Evidently by a highly skilled painter who was probably trained in the Netherlands, they are of a different order altogether from the crude figures further along the screen, paid for by poorer neighbours and executed by a local artist.[21] Screens in small country churches might have extraordinarily miscellaneous rows of ill-matched saints and scenes, reflecting the devotional preferences of the donors of individual 'panes' or panels, as they do at Wellingham in Norfolk, and at Westhall in Suffolk.

We will close this survey of late medieval religion with a glance at the iconography of the last-documented rood-screen of the Middle Ages, that at North Burlingham in Norfolk. Begun in the mid-1520s and funded by a series of small benefactions from parishioners, its rows of painted saints were not completed until 1536, two years after Henry VIII's momentous break with Rome. The screen was decorated with the patron saints of the donors: St Benedict and St Thomas Becket on panels paid for by Thomas Benet; St Cecilia and St John on panels paid for by John and Cecily Blake; St Catherine on a panel paid for by Robert and Katherine Frennys. Here, the Company of Heaven is conformed to the community of the parish. But other images reflect the devotional world beyond the parish, depicting the patron saints of some of the region's most popular shrines: St Etheldreda of Ely, and her sister St Withburga of East Dereham (portrayed carrying her pilgrimage church); St Edmund of Bury; and the uncanonized local pilgrimage saint, Walstan of Bawburgh, patron of the farmers' workers and farm animals, who provided the prosperity of North Burlingham.[22] Within two years of the completion of this screen Henry VIII would ban pilgrimage altogether and order the destruction of all images of Becket: the saint's image on the screen at North Burlingham would be scraped out to the knees. So even as the tide of Reformation lapped at their doors, Burlingham's parishioners were filling their church with images that reflected the unique combination of the local and the universal, the material and the ideal, which gave the religion of the people of late medieval England its distinctive cast.

FURTHER READING

Duffy 1992; French 2001; French, Gibbs and Kümin 1997.

NOTES

1 Details of these gifts are contained in Burgess 1995, pp.15–17.

2 See also the essay on the parish church by Paul Williamson in this volume, for the case of Long Melford.

3 Pantin 1980, Part III; Watson 1999.

4 Watson 1995.

5 Meech and Allen 1940, pp.212, 216.

6 The literature on Margery Kempe is immense, but a good introduction is to be found in Atkinson 1983.

7 Richmond 1984, p.199.

8 Hughes 1997, p.123.

9 Glasscoe 1987 and cat. no. 260.

10 See the comments of Graves 1990.

11 Burgess 1985.

12 See Rushforth 1937, Marks 1993, p.6, and Mattingley 2000. It is not strictly accurate to describe these groups as 'guilds'.

13 Norwich Record Office (NRO), Archdeaconry of Norwich Wills (ANW), 222 Gloys, Will of Alice Martyn, 1510; cf. NRO, ANW, 173 Cooke, will of Margaret Greeve, 1508 (bequest of 3d. to the plough-light of Kirkgate); parish organizations for women only are discussed, using evidence mainly from the south-west of England, in French 1998.

14 NRO, NCC, 444 Ryxe.

15 His will is in NRO, PCC 44/45 Wylbey.

16 NRO, NCC Spyltimber 291; Pull also left 6d. to each plough-light.

17 Salle, 83 (John Lutting, chaplain d. 1399), 98–100 (Robert Luce, chaplain d. 1456).

18 Scribner 1989.

19 Cox 1913, p.286; Duffy 2001, p.78; Duffy 1997, p.147.

20 Duffy 1997, p.155.

21 Mitchell 2000b, pp.374–5.

22 Duffy 1997, p.159.

VI

THE USE OF IMAGES

MARGARET ASTON

39 Figure of Christ Crucified
(cat. no. 268)

Our age is accustomed to the ubiquity and multiplication of imagery, and to worries about possible dangers in their usage. The later Middle Ages, as Johan Huizinga long ago made us aware, was likewise a period saturated with images, and as the Lancastrians and early Tudors added their contribution to the rich artistic inheritance of the Plantagenets, this process might have seemed as unstoppable as some organic growth. Yet, already in 1400, anxiety was being expressed about the spiritual dangers inherent in the church's use of images. A controversy had been initiated that was a harbinger of what was to come.

The accession of Edward VI in 1547 and the arrival of the most fundamental variety of continental reform imposed what proved to be a disastrous caesura in ecclesiastical art in England. Iconoclasts, in the same cause of eliminating idolatry that had earlier moved followers of John Wyclif (c.1327–84), began their sweeping clearance of churches, virtually eliminating some of the most familiar imagery. The singular radicalism of this assault is reflected in the demolition of the image that was central both to church interiors and to church art: the crucifix. In 1400 roods were to be found in all churches, on the shared assumption that (as the homilist John Mirk put it) faith should be strengthened by often seeing and having 'mynd of' Christ's passion. 'Ther ben mony thousaund of pepul,' he said, 'that couth not ymagen in her hert how Crist was don on the rood, but as thai lerne hit be syght of ymages and payntours'.[1] Others had different convictions. For them the law of God and worship of the cross were incompatible. On the night of 16–17 November 1547 the great rood was pulled down in St Paul's Cathedral in London, killing and injuring several workmen in the half-lit church. A new world was inaugurated under cover of darkness. And now we have only a handful of the figures of carved roods from the thousands known to Mirk's contemporaries (plate 39), while countless wooden carvings of saints that generations of parishioners had used, painted and repainted were reduced to ash in Tudor bonfires.

The concept of worship is central to the understanding of late medieval images, both ecclesiastical and secular. 'What is honour?' This was a question that was being disputed in the schools before 1400, thanks to Wycliffite opposition to church images. But it related to society as a whole, to depictions of all kinds, not only those of Christ and the saints. Worship was a large word, not confined to religious respect, and though it took a later generation to demonstrate fully the dangerous relationship between images of spiritual and temporal powers, idolatry was already an issue in the fourteenth century and still a risky matter in the mid-fifteenth, when Bishop Reginald Pecock wrote some unusually perceptive observations. He recognized (and was not alone in this) that while religious imagery, properly used, had moral value, it was counter-productive to have too much of it. Holy images of cult saints should 'not be multiplied so wijde that at ech chirche, at ech chapel, at ech stretis [street's] eende, or at ech heggis [hedge's] eende in a cuntre be sett such an ymage, for certis thanne tho ymagis schulden be as foule or of litil reputacioun and schulde be undeinteose [unpleasing] for the grete plente of hem'. They would no longer hold respect through delight, thereby serving their essential purpose of being 'rememoratijf or [re]mynding signes'. Excess reduced value. Pecock went so far as to propose a kind of image rationing, so that in any one area only a certain number of places should house such reminders of Christian sainthood (churches and chapels being permitted images of God, the Virgin and saints).[2]

Contemporary theory on the use of images was of ancient origin, but it related only to those of the church, and it was elaborated by churchmen whose thought processes centred on letters.[3] They assumed an equivalence between written word and seen depiction. The image was a transmitter, recalling into the viewer's mind known persons and events and the virtues and qualities of the absent. This process might bring into recollection the holy figures of the past, or the rulers of the present. In either case, representation and presentation were more nearly allied than they are now, to the extent that it was accepted that the signifying image was worthy of the honour of the signified. Since the image partook of the nature of its prototype, much more than reading was involved in its use.

If honour could be defined as the testimony of virtue and excellence in another,[4] what then were the proper expressions of it where imagery was concerned? Was it right to kiss, kneel or light candles before depictions of Christ, God the Father and saints, or did this amount to idolatry? The matter was complicated by the fact that there were different kinds of image and different kinds of worship. The church maintained that the highest worship of all should be given to imagery of Christ: the Wycliffites regarded worshipping roods as idolatry and the image of the Holy Trinity as an abomination. Some of their followers acted on such beliefs by deliberate denials of worship, like the Lollard incumbent who prevented his parishioners creeping to the cross, or the knights who turned their backs and went on talking when the procession with the consecrated Host passed along the street. As the arguments in defence of images showed, this question of honour could not be treated as a purely religious matter.[5] For precisely the same kind of veneration, expressed by gestures of kissing, removing hood or cap from head, bowing the head or kneeling, was given in other circumstances. In particular honour was due in such ways to the image of the king, his seal and banner. As Archbishop Arundel put it to the well-informed Wycliffite, William Thorpe, in 1407:

> For, lo, ertheli kyngis and other lordis, which usen to senden her lettris enselid with hir armes or with her privy sygnetis to men that ben with hem, ben worschipid of these men; [for whanne these men] resceyven her lordis lettris, in which thei seen and knowen her willis and the heestis of her lordis, in worschip of her lordis thei don of her cappis or her hoodis to her lettris.[6]

Even though the Lollard challenge cannot be said to have significantly affected the making or use of church imagery throughout the course of the fifteenth century (unless perhaps by promoting some purposeful sponsorship in response),[7] it raised contemporary awareness of some fundamental issues involved in the interlocked responses to spiritual and secular signs. It also gives some pointers to us. It may help a little towards answering an all-important question: how well could contemporaries read images? How wide a gap do we have to posit between those of courtly and gentry status (who, increasingly as time went on, might own or commission images) and the humble unschooled, whose access to sculpture and painting must largely have been limited to what they saw in church or the occasional play or pageant, and whose possession of images was unlikely to reach beyond pilgrim badges, indulgence woodcuts or pipe-clay statuettes (plates 41, 42, cat. nos 221, 324, 325, 326)?[8]

Arundel's reported remark only tells us that retainers were familiar with their overlord's seals and cognizances. At the end of our period, Bishop Stephen Gardiner, involved in a similar argument in 1547, made explicit claims for the illiterate's capacity to read visual imagery. This, he claimed, was effectively a pillar of the state, since it enabled everyone to read and reverence the king's standards, banners and the coats of arms worn by his pursuivants, as well as the cognizances of the nobility. Gardiner made much of the Great Seal (plate 40, cat. no. 33), to which any honest man 'wil put of his cap', recognizing, if the inscription was beyond him, 'Sainct Georg on horsback on the one side, and the Kinge sitting in his majestie on the other side'.

Protector Somerset, the recipient of this letter, must have hooted with delight when he read it. As an architect of the iconoclastic designs of Edward VI's regime, he naturally made the most of the bishop's extraordinary mistake. If he, well educated as he was, believed St George to appear thus on the Great Seal, what could one expect of the visual literacy of ordinary men and women?[9]

Ultimately we cannot answer that question (though we may wonder whether Gardiner's mistake is any reflection of the widespread popularity of St George – with or without the dragon) (cat. nos 58, 84, 256, 284, 297). It is not made any easier by the fact that the literate – especially, of course, image critics like Somerset – took a superior, supercilious view of popular capacity. Scenes of country bumpkins discussing the iconography of stained-glass windows high above their heads perhaps became something of a literary topos. But it has to be admitted that construing the content of some stained glass (including the typological windows in Canterbury Cathedral choir) was and is difficult, and demands knowledge of their arrangement and esoteric content.[10] Different images addressed different users, and painted windows intended for monks were not like the ones seen by pilgrims, such as those making their way to St Thomas Becket's shrine, who could look at the depictions of his miracles in the glass. Still other kinds of church glass, such as the series of Creed windows still surviving in some village churches, could well have helped parochial teaching of this necessary learning, including as they did the text, clause-by-clause, beside the apostle to whom it was attributed. There were many kinds of image that were conjoined, one way or another, with words.[11] And there is evidence (some of it hostile and thus prejudiced) of learning through imagery in the writings of the time.

John Bale, preaching new doctrine – including the learning of the Creed in English – in his parish of Thorndon in Suffolk in the late 1530s, warned his listeners against old depictions of Christ's descent into hell and warring with devils 'as they see it set forth in painted cloths, or in glass windows, or like as myself had before time set it forth in the country there in a certain play'.[12] A retrospective account by William Turner told the story of a Cambridgeshire painter, John Warde, who in about 1535 set up in his church pew a picture of St Christopher 'very lyvely in a table', together with 'a devout interpretacion' of the saint's life, in order 'to learne to be a ryght Christophor'. But (hence the telling of this tale) what was intended as instruction turned into worship, when other parishioners started to set candles

40   Reverse of Henry IV's Great Seal (cat. no. 33b)

before the image.[13] A popular saint like St Christopher (plates 41, 42), so often viewed – even momentarily, in wall-paintings glimpsed through an open church door – scarcely needed commentary, thanks to his credited protective powers, but could still provide a useful homiletic example (cat. nos 283, 290, 296). John Mirk explained that the image of St Margaret, who was commonly called on by women in childbirth, was painted and carved with a dragon under her feet and a cross in her hand to show how she triumphed over the fiend by virtue of the cross (plate 43, cat. no. 280).[14] Also early in the fifteenth century a vernacular commentary on the Ten Commandments, which was printed twice in the 1490s and again in 1536, gave an unusually full explanation of the iconography of the saints. The dialogue form of *Dives and Pauper* made possible the kind of freedom that existed in academic debate against Wycliffites. Discussion of the first precept began with the danger of image-worship becoming idolatry. The devil was allowed his advocacy of burning images, and in return Pauper told Dives how properly to 'rede in the book of peynture and of ymagerye', explaining what the various emblems of the saints stood for; the lily or rose in the hand of the Virgin, the keys of St Peter, St Catherine's wheel, the evangelists' symbols, the bare feet of the apostles.[15]

How images were 'read' in practice remains elusive. The well-known example of Margery Kempe, which shows how the sight of the crucifix or Pietà (cat. no. 344) could trigger

41 St Christopher indulgence
woodcut, German, dated 1432
(John Rylands University
Library of Manchester, 17249)

42 *The Annunciation* (detail),
The Master of Flémalle or
workshop, *c.*1425–30, showing
a woodcut of St Christopher in
a domestic context (Musées
royaux des Beaux-Arts de
Belgique, Brussels, inv. 3937)

43 St Margaret (cat. no. 280)

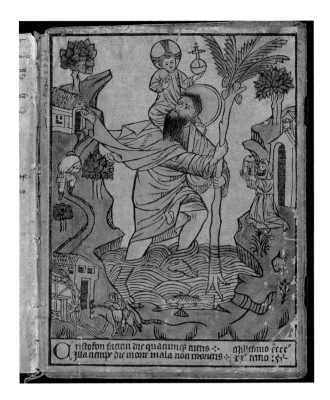

could be translated into the timeless post-mortem stare of a
funeral effigy, directed towards a favoured saint (cat. no.
87). Thomas More made fun of this kind of image use when
he described the London wives who looked so long at a
carving of the Virgin that they believed it smiled at them. It
is easy to be dismissive, but perhaps we all have an innate
yearning to find life in works of art, and gazing does not go
out of fashion. As recently as 1985 the miracle of a concrete-
and-plaster statue of the Virgin, which two women had seen
move, caused hundreds of people to travel to Ballinspittle in
County Cork, to gaze in baited expectation.[17] It was Martin
Bucer who remarked in 1549 that people 'are always disposed to believe in magical changes in things';[18] we await
the consolation of the inexplicable. Although William
Thorpe rebuked the people who left his sermon at Shrewsbury to watch the elevation of the Host, it was the reformers
of the sixteenth century who made gazing a suspect activity,

spasms of affective devotion, reminds us that there were and
always are different ways of looking and seeing.[16] Using
images did not necessarily mean learning from and through
them, though that was accepted theory and the author of
Dives and Pauper believed that proper teaching could cure
the errors of false worship. Devotion included a form of
seeing that was far from intellectual; rather, it was a matter
of contemplation through inert gazing – something that

linking it with false worship of the Eucharist. The idolatrous eye was most dangerous when its viewing held a sacramental dimension. What began in the fifteenth century as the alarm of a minority later became an obsession that changed the church – and moved it away from the visual.

Were there not problems with secular honour too? Secular imagery served king and government in the same ways as church imagery served God and the saints. It elevated through splendour, and its representations served to instil respect and evoke attitudes and gestures of worship. Throughout most of this period, recognition of the monarch, for all but the tiny inner circle of the court, did not depend on his personal features. Royalty was identified by magnificence of appearance in dress, furnishing, followers and lavish trains. The example of the posthumous impersonation of Richard II reflects the nature of contemporary visual consciousness, as does Henry VI's loss of respect by continually going about 'in a long blew goune of velvet as thowth he hadd noo moo to chaunge with'.[19] The king was present in his essence and dignity wherever his arms were, and his authority was known in the heraldic bearings of his representatives. Armorial shields, badges and devices, and the genealogical pedigrees that might consist of a series of stylized images of kings whose lineaments were totally unknown, together formed a familiar visual vocabulary. Past power validated present power, just as the virtues of dead saints validated present virtues, and in either case it was conveyed by formulaic imagery. The royal arms signified the earthly king, just as the crucifix signified the heavenly king. One significant difference, proved by Henry VIII's treatment of the Earl of Surrey in 1547, was that arrogation of the arms and ensigns ('armes feldes beastes fowles or other suche lyke thinges') of the Tudor king could result in the death penalty.[20]

Heraldry and genealogy were central to the representation of king and nobility. Churches and secular buildings alike proclaim their worldly donors and sometime owners with fierce proprietorial ostentation (plate 44). King's College Chapel in Cambridge is dressed inside and out with the Tudor dragon and Beaufort greyhound, crowned roses and portcullises, which Henry VIII added to Henry VI's foundation (cat. no. 19). The glazing of Henry VII's Chapel at Westminster, as much as that of the Great Hall at Fawsley in Northamptonshire, was liberally blazoned with shields of arms, fulfilling the royal desire that the king's 'armes, bagies and cognoissaunts' should shine alongside the scenes from Old and New Testaments (cat. no. 152).[21] There seemed to be no conflict to such patrons, just as there had seemed no incongruity in the Benedictines of Gloucester celebrating the prowess of Edward III's fighting nobility by an armorial roll call in the huge new east window of their church (now the

cathedral).[22] Boundaries of place did not separate religious and secular images.

Worldly achievements could be commemorated in glass windows by both text (including the names of donors) and image:

Wyde wyndowes y-wrought y-written full thikke,
Schynen with schapen scheldes to schewen aboute,
With merkes of marchauntes y-medled bytwene[23]

– which might be a means of invoking prayer for the donor, as well as telling present and future church-goers about his fame (plate 35, cat. nos 290, 293). But glorification of this kind had long been reprimanded. Did not God forbid the inscribing of such deeds and donors, 'leste prude be peyntid there and pompe of the worlde'?[24] The wrong sort of imagery could be found even in church, and could detract from true devotion:

His sight schal so be set on sundrye werkes,
The penounes and the pomels and poyntes of scheldes
With-drawen his devocion and dusken his herte.[25]

There was also the possible contingency of punishment in this world, if local enmities were wreaked on a rival's family stained glass – as seems to have happened at Buxlow in Suffolk in 1450, when two men smashed a window in the chancel containing the arms of the Bokele family, ancestors of the church patron.[26]

The imagery of funeral monuments seemed to run the same risks. Did they not lavish gilding and painting and artistic talent on portrayals of personal greatness? Those who could afford it lay in state in the style that befitted their position in life. That, with the genealogical record which established their place in society, was what mattered, not a faithful likeness. The alabaster image of Ralph Greene (d. 1417) and his wife at Lowick (Northamptonshire) was ordered to be 'a counterfeit of an esquire armed at all points … with a helm under his head and a bear at his feet; and the other … of a lady lying in her open surcoat, with two angels holding a pillow under her head, with two little dogs at her feet' (plate 8, cat. no. 330).[27] Yet such images of the dead belonged to two worlds and spoke visually to both. They could simultaneously claim admiration and call for prayer – *ora (orate) pro anima (animabus)* … – and the coupled word and image invoked from future passers-by the words of spoken prayer which, at best, would aid the deceased's salvation by bringing his or her name into the mind of God. So-called *transi* tombs, with their double images of finery and finality, advertised the individual's temporal glories and mortal decay with a self-reflexiveness that addressed both the memory of posterity and the inevitability of death and decay (plate 105).[28] The

44 Stained-glass panel showing Yorkist and other badges, Holy Trinity church, Tattershall (cat. no. 67)

image of the dead appropriately recorded rank and office, with identifying emblems that might still count at the ultimate weighing of souls. A priest shown on his brass vested for Mass holding chalice and Host would take his chalice into the grave with him, ready to rise again with the instrument of his sacramental bond with Christ. The memorial image could be read as his passport to eternity, the picture that he would present to the judge at the great Day of Judgement.[29]

Another way of looking at the interweaving of temporal and spiritual interests attached to images is to examine their role in miracles. Expectation of the miraculous, as something that might suddenly appear round some corner of the daily experience of an image, certainly hung audibly in the fifteenth-century air. It was helped by sermons whose exemplars included tales of talking and moving images. The Virgin went to release the imprisoned son of a widow who boldly stole the sculpted Christ child from his mother's arms; a prostitute repented after witnessing a conversation between a carved Virgin and the Child on her lap.[30] Or there were the demonstrative movements of crucifixes, one of which stopped its ears when prayers were offered for a man who had signally failed to hear divine service, while another leaned down from the cross to embrace a knight who had forgiven his father's murderer.[31] Such exempla, like the stories in the popular *Golden Legend* (from which some of them derived) (cat. no. 226), though they leave us in the dark about the attitudes of those who heard or read them, are suggestive of what might have been in the minds of pilgrims who visited Our Lady of Walsingham or the Rood of Grace at Boxley – whose Christ was equipped to express miraculous responses with

mechanical devices like those used in contemporary drama. From 1400 up to the Reformation people pilgrimaged to holy shrines in high holiday hopes of special sights and cures, and images were central to their experience. The pilgrims' own images connected them with the shrines they visited, both in the shape of the *ex-voto* objects (plate 45, cat. no. 321) they left behind as thank-offerings (including miniature silver heads, limbs, hearts and eyes), and in the medals, badges and ampullae of holy water they went away with, which could be worn on hats or collars, or nailed up somewhere at home (cat. nos 324, 325). These souvenirs of miraculous cures might additionally themselves acquire prophylactic powers and be used in time of need.

Miracles still happened, even if their status was becoming more questionable and sometimes uncomfortably tinged with politics. They were inextricably associated with imagery. In 1471, when Edward IV was marching south towards London to reclaim his throne from Henry VI, he reached Daventry by Palm Sunday, 7 April. If this seemed auspicious to some, what happened as Edward joined the procession (with its initial anthem 'Behold, O Sion, thy king cometh') and moved to honour the unveiled rood (to 'Ave Rex Noster') had to be taken as a remarkably fortunate sign. While the king knelt and honoured the rood, the painted wooden tabernacle (shut fast for Lent), which enclosed a small alabaster statue of St Anne on the pillar in front of him, creaked open. 'Sodaynly … the bords compassynge the ymage about gave a great crak, and a little openyd', as was observed by Edward and others nearby. And then 'the bords drewe and closed togethars agayne, withowt any mans hand, or touchinge, and, as thowghe it had bene a thinge done with a violence, with a gretar might it openyd all abrod, and so the ymage stode, open and discovert, in syght of all the people there beynge'.[32] It was hard not to read this adventitious opening as being related to a royal advent of more than one kind.

The events of 1471, which set Henry VI on the road to sainthood, produced the last large English burst of miracles and associated celebratory imagery. The final Lancastrian king was never canonized, but the pilgrims who went to his sanctuary at Windsor ensured that his miraculous abilities were publicized through badge, medallion and woodcut (plate 46, cat. no. 324i). The new cult could transform a parish's income, as it did at Yarmouth in the 1480s, thanks to a new image of Henry VI.[33] One of the king's recorded miracles concerned a pilgrim badge from Canterbury, perhaps bought in the year of St Thomas's jubilee in 1470. In 1486 this memento was swallowed by an infant, whose life was saved by a desperate appeal to the saintly power of 'the glorious King Henry'.[34] The relieved father, who went to Windsor to render thanks, left the offending badge as a thank-offering at the royal shrine. It was an event that mirrored the changing fashions in saints and shrines, though the worship of Henry VI – as much as that of Thomas Becket – owed more to the manner of his death than to the devout humility of his life.

The time was coming – and was already visible in the 1530s – when miracles were to be measured by the rule of scripture; authenticity pushed back into the early years of Christian history. The only miracle for which Thomas More claimed first-hand knowledge, and which for him proved that God still worked miracles at shrines, concerned the image of the Virgin at Ipswich. Anne Wentworth, the 12-year-old daughter of Sir Roger Wentworth, who was a friend of More's, suffered from seizures in which she blasphemed ('vexed and tourmented by our gostly enemye the devyll'). After a vision in which she saw the Virgin in the form of Our Lady of Grace, she was taken to Gracechurch, Ipswich, and 'layde before the ymage of our blessyd lady … grevously tourmented and in face, eyen, loke, and countenance so grysely chaunged … that it was a terrible syght to beholde'. There, in the presence of the whole company, she was restored, 'perfytely cured and sodeynly'.[35]

By the end of our period the situation was very different from what it had been in 1400. Secular authority was in command of the church. The time when religious imagery could speak for and assist the souls who were suffering in Purgatory was coming to an end for ever. Images of saints in parish churches, though still officially acceptable unless they were provably abused with idolatry, were already under threat, and dangerously contested in some parts of England. Image making was changing, and new kinds of art (particularly portraits of courtiers) were inaugurating new forms of image use and perhaps new kinds of worship. The gentry of sixteenth-century England could see and hold in hand depictions of both known and unknown individuals, portrayed to the life with sufficient realism to feel their living presence – even to choose a marriage partner through reading the features of the image (plate 50, cat. nos 163, 164). Lucas Horenbout's portrait miniature of Henry VIII, of about 1525–7, was followed by the more famous miniatures and paintings of Holbein, whose supremely telling portrayals of Christina of Denmark and Anne of Cleves contributed to the king's matrimonial adventuring (cat. nos 17, 18).[36] The king himself acquired a more formidable presence-in-absence in the corridors of power. As the attributes of honour that commanded respect began to be whittled down, images of temporal lordship seemed to gain at the expense of the spiritual.

It is supremely ironical that Henry VIII, having earned from Pope Leo X in 1521 the title of Defender of the Faith for his book against the heresies of Martin Luther (cat. no. 354), gained parliamentary sanction for this style after he had

effectively hereticated himself in the eyes of many of his subjects. The ending of pilgrimage shrines seemed to make the king into a Lollard and Lutheran, as he publicly destroyed the revered cult Virgins of Walsingham and Ipswich and the rood of Boxley, and confiscated the Holy Cross of Bromholm, which had been the butt of Lollard attacks. The future hung on a knife edge – but not for long. Already Archbishop Cranmer was worrying about images of the Holy Trinity and St Michael weighing souls, as well as about the dangers inherent in worship of the cross. Even before Henry died, the royal arms had begun to take the place of the rood in some churches. After the accession of Edward VI the images of England's churches began to pay a heavy price to the Old Testament law of the Decalogue. We are still counting that cost.

45   Wax votive offerings
(cat. no. 321)

46 Woodcut showing
Henry VI as a saint, *c*.1500?
(Bodleian Library, University of
Oxford, MS Digby 227, f.376v)

FURTHER READING

Aston 1988; Aston 1993; Dimmick, Simpson and Zeeman 2002;
Kamerick 2002 (which appeared after this essay was written);
Marks forthcoming (a).

I am grateful for the help I have received from Richard Marks,
James Simpson and John Watts.

NOTES

1 Erbe 1905, p.171.

2 Camille 1989, pp.268–71, 291–7; Camille 2002, pp.151–71; Babington
1860, 1, pp.136–7, 160–61, 183–4. The practicality of this idea is not
enhanced by the suggestion that the places and images were to be
'appointed and chosen by God or by man'.

3 Duggan 1989.

4 British Library, MS Harl. 31, f.190r; Hudson 1988, p.93, n.205; Aston
1988, pp.104–24.

5 Anglo 1992, pp.5–39. I have benefited much from this discussion.

6 Hudson 1993, p.57; British Library, MS Harl. 31, f.188v.

7 Catto 1985, pp.107–11; Nichols 1994, pp.99–120.

8 Marks forthcoming (a).

9 Muller 1933, pp.274–5.

10 Caviness 1992, pp.109–11; Henry 1987, pp.17–18; Kemp 1997.

11 Camille 1987, pp.33–40; Camille 1985, pp.26–49.

12 Fairfield 1976, pp.46–7; from Public Record Office (PRO) SPI/111,
f.183v; Aston 1988, p.351. Painted cloths (whose existence in churches is
evidenced in Edwardian inventories) disappeared through their own
perishable nature as well as by reforming destruction.

13 Turner 1555, ff.20v–21r (STC 24361); cf. Duffy 1992, p.166.

14 Erbe 1905, p.201.

15 Barnum, I, pp.82–99; on burning images, Aston 1988, pp.133–9;
Aston 1993, chapters 8 and 10.

16 For the Pietà, see Marks 2002b.

17 Paul Johnson, 'A wholly moving experience', *Guardian*, 2 September
1985, p.21. Weeks later the statue was attacked with axe and hammer by
a gang who told off worshippers for adoring 'a lump of stone' (*Irish
Times*, 1 November 1985, p.1).

18 Whitaker 1974, p.88.

19 Thomas and Thornley 1938, pp.212, 215.

20 Watts 2002; Anglo 1992, pp.38–9.

21 Marks 1993, pp.97–8, 213–15; Marks 1995, pp.158, 160, 168–9.

22 McHardy 2001, pp.186–7; Marks 1993, pp.87, 165.

23 *Pierce the Ploughman's Crede*, 11.175–7, in Barr 1993, p.68; cited in
Scattergood 1997, p.85.

24 Skeat 1886, 1, p.67, C Text, Passus iv, 1.70; cited in Marks 1993, p.229.

25 *Pierce the Ploughman's Crede*, 11.561–4, in Barr 1993, pp.84–5;
Scattergood 1997, p.85.

26 Richmond 1981, pp.199–200, n.171.

27 Crossley 1921, p.30; Stone 1972, p.179.

28 Binski 1996, pp.139–52.

29 Biddle 1990, 1, pp.789–99; Butler 1987, pp.248–9.

30 Erbe 1905, p.247; Ross 1940, pp.160–62.

31 Brandeis 1900, pp.110, 252–3.

32 Bruce 1838, pp.13–14; Scase 2002, pp.172–84; Duffy 1992, pp.23–7
on Palm Sunday ceremony.

33 Swanson 1991, p.169.

34 Spencer 1978, p.237; Spencer 1998, pp.189–92.

35 Lawler 1981, 1, pp.92–3; Marius 1985, pp.344, 446–7; MacCulloch
1986, pp.143–6.

36 Hearn 1995, pp.118–19.

VII

ENGLAND AND THE CONTINENT: ARTISTIC RELATIONS

CATHERINE REYNOLDS

I n Rouen in 1420 the Welshman William Bradwardine hired a Norman scribe and illuminator to work for him for three years, with all materials and accommodation provided. Bradwardine's service as surgeon to Henry V's troops had been rewarded with Norman lands and he also engaged in Anglo-Norman trade. By financing a scribe for a specific time, instead of for individual volumes for his own use, he was probably helping to provide a steady supply of books for the English market.[1] Eighty-seven years later, in Rouen, a Norman printer was producing English liturgical books for the Netherlandish stationer Gerard Freez, who had settled in York. Freez's purchases in France were partly financed by the York goldsmith Ralph Pulleyn and by the London-based Netherlander Maynard Vewick (Meynnart Wewyck), painter to Henry VII and Henry VIII and later one of Freez's executors.[2] In both 1420 and 1507, therefore, complex international connections ensured that the deficits of English book production were partly met with Norman imports. Against the great changes of the intervening years, notably the French reconquest of Normandy and the development of printing, this continuity is striking. Neither political nor technological change had altered the failure of English book producers to satisfy demand and the consequent rewards for astute traders who bridged the gap were plentiful.

What was true for books applied in varying degrees to many art forms: paintings, sculpture, prints, tapestries, embroideries, metalwork, glass and ceramics. The English, already notoriously xenophobic, imposed a succession of revenue-raising controls on resident aliens, mostly Netherlandish, German or French, and on imports – controls from which the book trades were exempted between 1484 and 1534 – yet alien goldsmiths, metalworkers and woodworkers were numerous throughout the period, with more painters, illuminators and glaziers apparent from the later fifteenth century.[3] What is apparent, however, may mislead. Origins are obscured by anglicized names and imprecise terms, since Dutch, Almain and German could all refer to Netherlanders or Germans. Does the difference between the workforce for the Beauchamp Chapel of the mid-fifteenth century, with two recognizable aliens (cat. no. 87), and for Henry VII's Chapel, with Vewick among several foreigners (cat. nos 29, 117), accurately reflect reality? Surviving records and artefacts – an arbitrary and perhaps

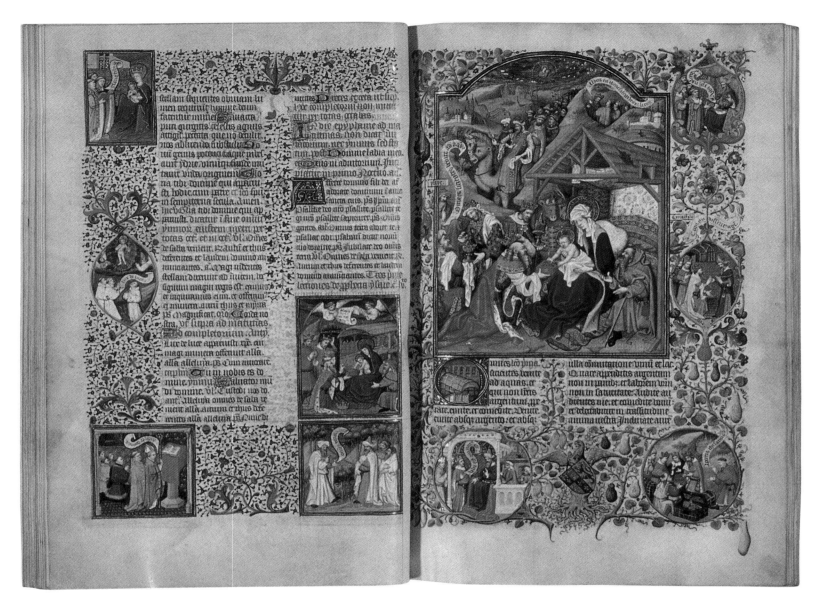

47 Salisbury Breviary
(cat. no. 72)

unrepresentative selection – permit only tentative deductions on England's artistic dependence on foreigners and its causes, where unsatisfactory home production (in quantity, quality or price) interacted with England's changing relations with the Continent.

English power was only just retreating from France and many of all ranks, from Richard II and Edward IV downwards, had been born abroad. This legacy of foreign experience was evident materially, as in the embroidered bed hangings carefully protected in cotton covers for Henry VIII, which over a century earlier had been highly valued when the Duke of Bedford received them as part of the Duke of Alençon's ransom.[4] The wars enabled such acquisitions and also encouraged them. In 1445 Henry VI could present himself to French ambassadors as Charles VI's

rightful successor before a word was spoken. As the ambassadors noted, he appeared surrounded by French armorial tapestries from Charles VI's collection.[5] Politics rather than commerce governed the gains of war and made French markets readily accessible to expatriate Englishmen before the loss of Paris in 1436, Normandy in 1450 and Gascony in 1453.

By the fourteenth century Paris had become the greatest artistic centre in Europe, although not especially geared to the export market. As part of the vital local clientele, the English from 1420 were therefore significant, despite their limited resources. Illuminated books, the only extensive surviving results of English patronage, show that the Duke of Bedford's commissions fostered the leading Parisian workshop, which now bears his name (plate 47), while a Rouen

style was established by the artists dubbed the Fastolf and Talbot Masters (plate 10, cat. nos 42, 92, 94a, 224), from their English patrons. It is these quickly executed, more economical styles, from a centre under English rule for a longer period, which had some impact in England, partly because the Fastolf Master was among the French who left Normandy.[6] He illuminated several Rouen and some English manuscripts, including the volume written in 1450 for Sir John Fastolf (see cat. no. 224). His linear style and emphatic surface pattern arguably influenced English illuminators like William Abell (cat. no. 20).

Calais remained English, facilitating trade and communications and offering potentially lucrative employment. Sir John Donne, patron of the Netherlandish painters Hans Memling and Simon Marmion, held various Calais offices from 1468 to 1497 (cat. nos 213, 214, 215). Sir Thomas More was there on royal business in 1517, when he received the gift of his Netherlandish friends, the scholars Erasmus and Pieter Gillis: a diptych with their portraits by Antwerp's leading painter, Quentin Massys (plate 48).[7] Diplomatic missions continued to take the English to France, as did military incursions and the brief occupations of Tournai and Boulogne. Nonetheless, greater isolation was inevitable as political and geographical boundaries approached coincidence at the Channel, which became a linguistic frontier

as French ceased to be a language of record and alternative vernacular.

In 1406, when the future King James I of Scotland was captured en route to France, Henry IV reportedly joked that he was saving the Scots trouble by teaching James French himself;[8] by 1445 the Earl of Shrewsbury thought Margaret of Anjou might forget her native tongue without his wedding present of French texts (plate 10, cat. no. 42). Although English had yet to match the quantity and variety of French literature, original works and translations were increasingly available. French offered access to other literatures – from the early thirteenth century, versions and translations of classical authors achieved great popularity – and some still chose to read in French. John Lydgate's *Fall of Princes*, elaborated in 1431–8 from the French expansion of Boccaccio's Latin *De casibus*, did not end demand for the French version: Edward IV commissioned a copy in Bruges as well as a French *Decameron*, taken from a Latin translation of Boccaccio's Italian.[9] Reading Petrarch's *Triumphs* in French needled Lord Morley into his English translation, since 'I beynge an Englishman myght do as well as the Frenche man', while the French evangelical reformers opened Lutheran teachings to Anne Boleyn's circle.[10] With the approved English Bibles (cat. no. 355) and English Litany of 1544, the church's universal language began following the

48   Diptych of Erasmus and Pieter Gillis, Quentin Massys, oil on panel, 1517 (Royal Collection and Private Collection)

fate of its universal authority, although Latin remained essential for educated communication, with French gaining ground in diplomacy.[11]

Despite Paris's reputation for illumination, the Netherlands was England's chief source of imported books until printing brought Germany, Italy and France into contention. Long before Gerard Freez settled in York, Netherlandish book craftsmen came to England – Herman Scheerre was possibly from Ypres – and Netherlandish styles predominated (cat. no. 103).[12] Production within the Netherlands centred on the great international market place of Bruges. In a recent exhibition, more than half the manuscripts selected to represent Bruges illumination from around 1380 to 1420 were made for the English market; exports continued to flourish into the sixteenth century.[13] This context helps explain why Bruges saw the first book printed in English, by the London mercer William Caxton, who subsequently brought his presses across the Channel to his market in 1475 or 1476 (cat. nos 173, 226). French book production was sufficiently vigorous to leave little room for imports but Netherlandish artists contributed crucially to the influential French court styles of c.1400, another route for Netherlandish developments to reach England. Netherlandish art and artists also permeated Spain and Germany, while in Italy Jan van Eyck (d. 1441) and Rogier van der Weyden (d. 1464) were repeatedly cited as the greatest painters of the age.[14] Netherlandish painting led Europe because of its compelling illusionism and manipulation of reality, achieved through superb draughtsmanship and brushwork, and especially through the new mastery of tone. Since painters dominated design, Netherlandish tapestries, embroideries, sculpture and stained glass also transmitted, and benefited from, the painters' achievements.

England was therefore fortunate in its two nearest continental neighbours, France as mediator of verbal culture and the artistically overmighty Netherlands as provider of material culture. Through Bruges and then Antwerp came not only Netherlandish products but also goods from the Mediterranean, the Baltic, the European hinterland and eventually Africa, India and America. European ships also sailed directly to English harbours and the Hanseatic League was represented in London and elsewhere. England's surplus of essential commodities (especially wool and one of Europe's rare supplies of tin), resulted in a generally favourable balance of trade, which did nothing to encourage native industries, already hampered by the depleted workforce left by the Black Death. Conversely, the densely urbanized Netherlands needed imports to feed its people and fuel the industries that provided the balancing exports – importing English wool and hides, for instance, and exporting cloth

and books on parchment. As England's own weaving industry developed, the Netherlanders increasingly concentrated on luxury textiles and other products now classed as art.[15]

Perceptions of quality, not just insufficient quantity, presumably made England so open to foreign competition in areas with long traditions of native production. Certainly illumination, the only form to survive adequately, rivalled the best continental achievements until the new Netherlandish developments in painting in the early fifteenth century.[16] How these reached England cannot be detailed. The well-travelled Jean Jouffroy stated in 1468 that all kings' courts were adorned by van der Weyden's paintings, which, like van Eyck's, could have been known through the Burgundian court – in 1413, for instance, John the Fearless gave Henry IV a panel painting.[17] Jan van Eyck was briefly in England in 1428; in 1432 his brother Lambert painted a much-copied portrait of Jacqueline of Bavaria, formerly Duchess of Gloucester.[18] No certainly English works are identifiable for Vewick and other Netherlanders like Henry Herperson from Holland in Southwark in 1436; a certain 'Hans' was sent to paint prospective brides for Henry VI in 1442; Hans Dutchman was employed for Henry VII's coronation in 1485; Gerard, Lucas and Susanna Horenbout were in Henry VIII's service from the 1520s and Levina Teerlinck, daughter of the famed illuminator Simon Bening, from 1546.[19]

Records reveal the presence, but not the appearance, of Netherlandish art such as the altarpiece 'of Flanders work' purchased for Carmarthen Castle in 1424–5.[20] 'Stained cloths', not dyed but painted in glue size, possibly with expensive pigments embellished with gold, were imported in huge quantities – around 2,500 were recorded from Antwerp between 1429 and 1481 alone – and caused deep resentment among the stainers, who in London formed a distinct craft within the Painter-Stainers Guild, as did the cloth painters in Bruges.[21] Since Netherlandish cloth paintings were often preferred, as by George Cely who ordered painted cloths in Antwerp in 1478 and a whole chamber of painted hangings in Bruges in 1482, quality and Netherlandish origin were presumably associated, as can be demonstrated for patrons of sculpture.[22] High quality is not, however, a characteristic of many Netherlandish panel paintings with English provenances, such as Sir Robert Tate's triptych wings (plate 56, cat. no. 136). When paintings by leading artists, like Petrus Christus (plate 23, cat. no. 161), Hans Memling (German by birth) (cat. no. 213) and the Master of the Magdalen Legend (plate 49, cat. no. 276), are known to have reached England, they contained portraits (perhaps explaining their survival) and so were made for patrons visiting the Netherlands, who were best placed

to judge and obtain superior work.[23] Inferior goods were frequently offloaded on foreign markets and inferior crafts-men forced abroad. Although Henry VIII secured the Horenbouts, many illuminators remaining in the Nether-lands surpassed the Caesar Master – his influence on Eng-lish illumination in around 1440–60 notwithstanding – or the Masters of the Dark Eyes (cat. no. 143).[24] Nonetheless, manuscripts reveal greater English discrimination than do the few surviving panels. English purchasers, not all trav-ellers to the Netherlands, obtained work by some of the greatest illuminators: the Beaufort Saints Master (cat. no. 223), Simon Marmion (cat. no. 215), Willem Vrelant, Philippe de Mazerolles, the exquisite Master of Mary of Bur-gundy and his contemporary, the Master of the Prayerbook of the Emperor Maximilian.[25]

Despite distinct regional styles, partly dependent on the availability of materials and skills, trade in finished goods required (and ensured) some underlying uniformity of demand. Hierarchies of visual display honouring God and man were recognizable across Europe. The ancient status

symbols of gold and silk reached Europe largely through Italy and silk weaving was virtually an Italian monopoly (cat. no. 201): Henry VII necessarily ordered cloth-of-gold vestments there (cat. no. 31). Woven tapestries, perhaps including silk and precious metal thread, were a much newer fashion (cat. nos 6, 153, 229, 230). Called *arras*, from their original centre of production, tapestries were often chosen as diplomatic gifts by the counts of Artois, also the dukes of Burgundy from 1384, possibly to stimulate foreign demand, which spread rapidly as people experienced the beauty and potential of this monumental, yet portable, art. Once the Paris industry had collapsed with the wars, only the Netherlands could supply large hangings requiring teams of highly trained weavers, such as the 11 pieces of the *Trojan War* series, each measuring at least 5 × 10 metres, bought by Henry VII from Tournai in 1488. In acquiring tapestry, Henry conformed to European taste – the rulers of the Netherlands, France, Milan, Urbino, Hungary and Scot-land owned *Trojan War* sets – and followed all his predeces-sors since Richard II.[26] By 1547 the English royal collection,

49 The Ashwellthorpe
Triptych (cat. no. 276)

50 The Dynham Tapestry
(cat. no. 154)

one of the greatest in Europe, numbered more than 2,000 pieces. Where kings led, others followed, so far as their purses and sense of decorum allowed: a piece with the royal arms is the surviving tapestry most closely related to Lord Dynham's hanging (plate 50, cat. no. 154).

Other crafts, initially only available as imports, were successfully transplanted because they required easily learned skills or fewer fully trained individuals. Brickmaking, another Netherlandish export, and printing are obvious examples, although paper, type and numerous printers still came from abroad. An English paper mill closed in 1510 because it could not match the price of imported paper. Foreign woodblocks were used for many book illustrations (cat. nos 225a, 310) and imported single-leaf woodcuts discouraged local competition: by 1509 'painted papers' were arriving from Antwerp in consignments of 10 and 12 gross. Engraving seems to have remained beyond English aspirations.[27] Some imported techniques continued to rely on aliens, as at the Almain Armoury, established by Henry VIII at Greenwich in 1515 with the Netherlandish makers of 'the Burgundian Bard' (cat. no. 56). Not all migrations were patron-led, since many craftsmen followed their products to England on their own initiative, like the uniquely skilled Murano glassblowers who settled in London by 1549 (cat. nos 75, 166).

For some arts, native craftsmen depended on imported materials.[28] France and the Netherlands supplied quality glass to the English artists who dominated stained-glass making until the sixteenth century, although already in 1474 more than 28 alien glaziers were reported in London. Brass came from the Meuse area for the popular memorial brasses, among other uses, and as finished products from various Netherlandish centres (cat. nos 243, 314). The commercial value of exclusive knowledge was well understood. Henry VI, anxious to glaze Eton and King's College (cat. no. 22), retained in 1449 a Fleming, John Utynam, to make coloured glass and give instruction in this and other arts new to England, although they could not be practised for 20 years without Utynam's consent. In 1455 three brass workers were imprisoned in Dinant to stop them taking their expertise to England, described in 1450 as the major contributor to Dinant's livelihood.[29] England likewise had specific materials and skills. The mining of tin permitted the trade in pewter, which by 1446–7 was the greatest manufactured export after cloth (cat. nos 196, 197). More significant for the dissemination of figurative art was 'Nottingham' alabaster, successfully traded since the fourteenth century all over Europe, including Iceland, as blocks and sculptures. The popularity of alabaster sculptures at home demonstrates that the desirable did not have to be foreign.[30]

Embroidery, once recognized as 'English work', was already in decline, with the Netherlands providing superior workmanship and design.

The English were alert to artistic excellence of any nationality, although inevitably this was often rooted in the Netherlandish tradition. John à Barrow in Antwerp in 1521 employed both Quentin Massys and the visiting Albrecht Dürer, whose European celebrity was largely disseminated through his prints.[31] The Reformation encouraged German contacts: pictures by Lucas Cranach, painter to the Lutheran electors of Saxony, are recognizable in Henry VIII's inventories.[32] Hans Holbein's portrait of Christina of Denmark was deemed 'very perffight' by Henry's ambassadors in 1538 in comparison with a 'sloberid' Netherlandish portrait.[33] English discernment, however, cannot be credited with bringing Holbein to London, since he first arrived on his own initiative, backed by the scholarly network of Erasmus and More, and on his return he relied initially on his countrymen, the Hanseatic merchants.

Recorded judgements of paintings were largely provoked by portraits, for which the English apparently had a longstanding and special liking. The determination of the poet and scribe Thomas Hoccleve to preserve Chaucer's appearance is a very early voicing of the value of representational portraiture.[34] The sculptor Pietro Torrigiano was probably first employed in England as a portraitist (cat. nos 7, 8, 9), and it was in England that Lucas Horenbout reportedly taught Holbein to paint portrait miniatures, known in the Netherlands by 1516 and popularized in France by another Netherlander, Jean Clouet.[35] Painted portraiture was where skills of lifelike representation, developed in the Netherlands, were most obviously required. In sending Master Hans to paint the Count of Armagnac's daughters, Henry VI was anxious for an accurate record of their appearance; More praised Massys's portraits of Erasmus and Gillis for their verisimilitude (plate 48).[36] More's emphasis on the successful imitation of his handwriting in the letter held by Gillis seems a simplistic response, however, conditioned by the limited criteria for assessing painting learned from classical authors, who concentrated on the faithful reproduction of the visible world.[37]

More, born in 1477–8, was of the first English generation to join the international scholarly community with a knowledge of Greek acquired at home. The new learning (termed humanism) took time to root in England, despite the church network that encouraged visiting scholars, led in

51 Miniature portrait of Jane Small, Hans Holbein (cat. no. 164)

1418 by Poggio Bracciolini, and the slowly growing numbers of English students in Italy.[38] The Italian Renaissance, the 'Rebirth' of the civilization of antiquity, was both cause and effect of the new linguistic and textual skills required for a more accurate knowledge of ancient Greece and Rome. For northern humanists, the re-creation of pagan antiquity

52 Tomb of Henry VII and Elizabeth of York, Westminster Abbey (cat. no. 29)

was never such an end in itself. Erasmus, encouraged by More, concentrated on the fundamental Christian texts; indeed, Massys showed him working on St Paul's Epistle to the Romans (plate 48). Although More collected antique coins, English scholarship did not share the interest in the visual forms of antiquity that in Italy accompanied the verbal exploration of the classical world. Apart from humanist script, gradually adopted from the 1440s, there was little repercussion from the Italian manuscripts of

Humphrey of Gloucester, whose investment in books – for himself and for the universities of Oxford and Cambridge – was matched by Sir John Tiptoft, Earl of Worcester, who studied in Italy in 1459–61. From the 1450s, supposedly classicizing white-vine decoration occasionally appears, but the more archaeologically-inspired Paduan manuscripts associated with Tiptoft were apparently ignored.[39] When *all'antica* illumination became fashionable, it was modelled less on Italian examples, such as Nagonius's panegyric to Henry VII (plate 16, cat. no. 48), than on French or Netherlandish patterns, as seen in Cardinal Wolsey's Lectionary (cat. no. 225). In 1518 the first printed classicizing frontispieces were copied from Basel books designed by Holbein among others.[40]

For all the scholarly contacts with Italy, the English seemingly only developed a taste for the antique style, giving familiar subjects a new appearance, when it arrived through their traditional artistic mentors. Although artistic leadership was eventually perceived to have passed from the Netherlands to Italy, England's experience of the new style still came largely through the Netherlands and France, with German developments made accessible and alluring through German mastery of the print. Printmaking, pioneered in the Rhineland, had already transformed the fusion of artistic traditions, and direct access to antique or Italian art seems to have been of little importance. Henry VIII did not purchase tapestries woven from Italian cartoons until the 1540s and did not respond to Francis I's offer in 1540 of moulds for casting from classical statues, which were acquired instead by the Governess of the Netherlands.[41] The Italianate dominated French taste, especially from 1494 when the French invaded Italy, and Henry VII possibly desired French prestige more than antique style when he followed Charles VIII in commissioning his tomb from Guido Mazzoni. Torrigiano, who eventually executed Henry's tomb (plate 52), apparently attracted his first documented English commission in 1511 through sheer ability, irrespective of style, because he was to follow Vewick's designs for Lady Margaret's monument (plate 55, cat. no. 29).

Subsequent commissions to Torrigiano and other Italian sculptors by Henry VIII and Wolsey demonstrate approval of antique references; unfortunately the style of the Neapolitan Vincente Volpe, Henry's painter by 1512, is unknown. Volpe was possibly encouraged north by the French conquest of Naples, since several Italians arrived via French service, notably Nicholas Bellin in 1537 from Francis I's chateau of Fontainebleau. Bellin, a stuccoist, and Giovanni da Maiano, producer of terracottas for Wolsey's Hampton Court by 1521, were foreigners offering both alien techniques, still known by their Italian names, and an alien, antique style.[42] In 1544 Antonio Toto, recruited to royal service by Torrigiano in Florence in 1518, became the first foreign Serjeant Painter. The following year, however, Henry wanted 'no more strangers' sent from Rome.[43]

In John Leland's poem praising images of various Italian women by 'one more famous among Italian painters', the images' Italian appearance seems the chief attraction, not some inevitable prestige associated with Italian art. These, whether illuminations, panel or cloth painting(s), had been given by the imperial postmaster Francis Taxis (d. 1517) to Henry VIII's postmaster, Sir Brian Tuke, a patron of Holbein, who owned another Italian painting commended by Leland. This was by Antonio de Solario, showing the death of a naval hero, probably Sir Thomas Knyvett, brother of the patron of the Master of the Magdalen Legend (plate 49, cat. no. 276), who was killed in 1512.[44] Solario, a competent Venetian follower of Giovanni Bellini and Vittore Carpaccio, was evidently in England by 1514 when he dated the triptych of the London merchant, Paul Withypool (cat. no. 135), who also knew earlier Netherlandish painting in the Beaufort Hours (cat. no. 223). The triptych format, half-length figures and soft tonalities, derived from familiar Netherlandish example, contrasts with the assertively new grotesque decoration on the reverse, a taste perhaps fostered by humanist scholarship. Withypool's own attainments are unknown, but his son was a Latin scholar and the epitaph of his daughter, who died in 1537, recorded that 'Latine and Spanish/and also Italian,/she spake, writ and read', that she could write in three different hands and knew arithmetic and music. Furthermore she was a talented embroideress, designing 'all Pictures artificiall,/Curious Knots or Trailes/ what fancy would devise,/Beasts, Birds or Flowers,/even as things naturall'.[45] Speaking Italian suggests contact with Italians, perhaps encouraging an unusually early combination of humanist aspirations with a taste for the visual forms of antiquity.

England's artistic dependence on the Continent, already well established when the antique became the rage, continued for centuries after 1547. The causes of such a long-lasting phenomenon were neither simple nor static. Alongside broad political, economic, religious and aesthetic considerations must be put individual choices and decisions, where More's friend, Sir Thomas Elyot, laid responsibility in *The Boke named the Governour* of 1531:

> For how many men be there whose sonnes in
> chyldehode are aptly disposed by nature to paynte, to
> kerve, or grave, to embrawder, or do other lyke thynges
> wherin is any arte commendable concernynge
> invention, which as sone as they espie it, be therwith

displeased and forthwith byndeth them to taylours, weyvers, towkers [cloth dressers], and sometyme to coblers. Which hath ben the inestimable losse of many good wittes and hath caused, that in the saide artes englisshmen be inferiours to all other people, and be constrayned, if we wyll have any thinge well paynted, kerved or embrawdred, to leave our own cuntraymen and resorte us unto straungers … [46]

Fear for their sons' future prosperity apparently conditioned men's dislike of artistic talent. When John Brown, Serjeant Painter to Henry VIII, became an Alderman of London in 1523, he had to join the Haberdashers because his own guild, the Painter-Stainers, was insufficient for the dignity of the post.[47] Robert Frevyll, a connection of the Withypools, made similar distinctions in 1521 when he provided for his eldest son to study law and his younger sons to be maintained in learning or 'good crafts'.[48]

The superiority of strangers does not seem new to Elyot, who wisely resorted to Holbein for portraits of himself and his wife, John à Barrow's sister.[49] Indeed, throughout the preceding century foreigners are found providing the more important or crucial elements of a work: miniatures for the Beaufort Hours (cat. no. 223); the finishing of the Warwick tomb figures to ensure their lifelike appearance (cat. no. 87); the frontispiece for the Luton Guild Book (plate 30, cat. no. 347); the tombs and altar in Henry VII's chapel (plates 52, 55, cat. nos 29, 117). What resulted from England's artistic indebtedness could be spectacular. The Bohemian Leo of Rozmital and his entourage, arriving from the Netherlands in 1465, found much to praise: the splendour of Edward IV's court, the numbers of goldsmiths, the tapestry collections, the elegant churches and, in Reading Abbey, 'an image of the Mother of God most beautifully executed. So much so that I have never seen its equal, nor shall I ever see one to compare with it if I progress to the ends of the earth. No image could be more lovely or more beautiful.'[50]

Whether or not it was English, the most beautiful image in the world was in England.

FURTHER READING

Particular aspects of this wide-ranging topic can be investigated through the works cited in the Notes, but additional contemporary writings are to be found in Windeatt 1985 (for experience of foreign pilgrimage and religious practice), Warner 1926 (for an analysis of trade), Davis 1971–6 (for the concerns and possessions of an English family and its connections), Radice 1993 (for Sir Thomas More, and pp.68–9 for national stereotypes), and Bull 1956 (for an Italian artist at the court of Francis I). For general surveys, see Barron and Saul 1995 and Mitchell and Moran 2000.

NOTES

1 Reynolds (C) 1994, p.311.

2 Davies 1868, pp.7–14; Duff 1912, pp.46–7; Armstrong 1979, p.281; for Vewick, see Campbell (L) 1985, p.xv.

3 For the book trades, see Hellinga and Trapp 1999; for sculpture, Woods 1988; for goldsmiths, Campbell (M) 1987; for glaziers, Marks 1993.

4 Stratford 1993, C90; Starkey 1998, no. 9035.

5 Reynolds 1993, p.113; McKendrick 1995, p.49; Starkey 1998, nos 13069 and 11969.

6 Reynolds 1989, 1993 and 1994; Griffiths 1981, pp.551–3.

7 Campbell et al., 1978.

8 Walsingham 1863, II, p.273.

9 BL, MSS Royal 14 E V and 19 E I; Branca 1999, III, pp.192–6, 243–4, 267–70.

10 Axton 2000, p.173; Carley 1998.

11 Russell 1992, pp.1–50.

12 Trio 1995, p.724; Scott 1996, I, pp.62–4 (arguably understating the Netherlandish influence on English illumination).

13 Of the 43 manuscripts, 24 were for England, two for Italy, one for Catalonia and two for presentation in France: Smeyers 1993, pp.1–137; Smeyers 1998, pp.186–9, 201–2, 467–9; Arnould and Massing 1993, pp.113–31.

14 Rohlmann 1994.

15 See, for instance, van Uytven 1992.

16 Alexander in Hellinga and Trapp 1999, pp.60–61.

17 Miglio 1975, p.141; de Laborde 1849–52, I, p.43.

18 Steppe 1983.

19 Campbell (L) 1998, p.227; Campbell 1990a, pp.155–97; Auerbach 1954, p.166; Campbell and Foister 1986; Campbell (L) 1985, p.xvi.

20 Colvin 1963, II, p.601.

21 Reynolds 2000.

22 Hanham 1985, p.216; Woods 1988.

23 For the Edward IV portrait, possibly by Memling, see Campbell (L) 1997, p.71.

24 Scott 1996, II, pp.277–9.

25 For the illuminators not exhibited, see the examples from the ex-Foyle collection, Christie's, London, 11 July 2000, lot 34; Los Angeles, J. Paul Getty Museum, MS Ludwig IX 8 (von Euw and Plotzek 1982, pp.142–59); Philadelphia Museum of Art, Philip S. Collins collection, MS 1945/65/2 (Philadelphia 2001, cat. no. 14); Madrid, Museo Lázaro-Galdiano, inv. no. 15503 (Lieftinck 1969, pp.109–25, figs 165–210); BL, MS Add. 54782 (Turner 1983).

26 McKendrick 1991, 1995 and 1987.

27 Asaert 1985; Smit 1928–50; Gras 1918, pp.562, 570; Hind 1952.

28 For English industries and their materials, see Blair and Ramsay 1991.

29 Muller 1983, pp.7–8; Thielemans 1966, p.245.

30 Foister 1981, pp.275–6; Cheetham 1984.

31 Levey 1971–2, pp.157–8; the portrait by Massys was recorded in 1737 (Vertue 1936, pp.115–16: reference generously supplied by Lorne Campbell).

32 Starkey 1998, nos. 10591, 10778, 15417–19; compare, for example, Friedländer and Rosenberg 1978, nos 290–91, 411–12, 338, and a wing panel in the Toledo (Ohio) Museum of Art (Christensen 1992, pp.69–71).

33 Chamberlain 1913, II, p.123.

34 Furnivall 1897, lines 4992–8; Alexander and Binski 1987, cat. no. 721.

35 Darr 1996; van Mander 1994, p.148; Campbell 1990a, pp.62–4.

36 Campbell 1990a, p.197.

37 Campbell et al., 1978, pp.716–17, 724.

38 Weiss 1967.

39 For the limited influence of Italian borders in Humphrey's circle, see Scott 1996, II, pp.239–41; for humanist script and Tiptoft, see de la Mare and Hunt 1970 and de la Mare and Gillam 1988.

40 Wells-Cole 1997, p.8.

41 Campbell (T) 1996a; Chamberlain 1913, I, p.284; Haskell and Penny 1981, pp.1–6.

42 For alien artists under the Tudors, see Chamberlain 1913, I, pp.263–87, II, pp.303–10; Auerbach 1954; Colvin 1975; Thurley 1993, pp.102–11; Hearn 1995; Lindley 1995, pp.31–46.

43 Wells-Cole 1997, p.9.

44 For the abstruse Latin poem, see Bradner 1956, pp.834–5, 828; for correspondences between its imagery and reality, and parallels in manuscripts, see Campbell 1990a, p.209 and Bologna 1989; for Leland's poems on Holbein and Lucas Horenbout, see Campbell and Foister 1986, pp.722–4, 727; for Tuke and Holbein, see Hand 1993, pp.91–7.

45 Moore Smith 1936; Bindoff 1982, III, pp.619–21.

46 Rude 1992, I, xiv, p.67.

47 Payne 1998, p.153.

48 Nicols 1826, II, p.575.

49 Roberts (J) 1993, nos 10 and 11.

50 Letts 1957, p.56.

VIII

PRODUCTION AND CONSUMPTION

CRAFTS
NIGEL RAMSAY

53 The Richmond Cup (cat. no. 134)

'Mason schulde never won other [one another] calle, Withynne the craft amongus hem alle, Ny soget [subject] ny servand.'[1] The word 'craft' was every bit as varied and nuanced in its meanings in late medieval England as it is today, but here, in the early fifteenth-century constitutions of the masons, it was used to indicate the masons' organization; this was defined in terms of the skill which they practised. A craft might alternatively mean the skill, occupation or even branch of learning by itself, like the craft of chasing (breaking or taming) horses, or 'the craft of Computacioun, To adde, dymynew, and to multiply'.[2] From the synonymous Anglo-Norman word 'mestier' (like the modern French *métier*) was derived the word 'mystery', which was almost equally wide in its range of meanings; only the word 'guild' (or 'gild') was limited to meaning an organization – originally, one that was supported by payments or contributions of some kind. Reasonably enough, historians use the words almost interchangeably.

The range of meanings of the words reflected the different ways in which the crafts' practitioners were organized, and these varied enormously in both time and place. In 1421–2 the clerk of the brewers' guild (or company) in London listed 111 crafts that were practised in his city;[3] he was probably indifferent as to whether he meant activities or guilds, since he and his readers would have known full well which were limited to a handful of specialists, like the bell-founders and marblers, and which were the names of major guilds, like the goldsmiths' company, or of middling guilds, like the pewterers'.

Outside London, divisions were less clear-cut. Guilds proliferated, but in even the larger towns and cities there might well be too few practitioners of a skill for it to be a viable proposition for them to form a guild. Guilds nonetheless flourished, because they served indispensable functions They benefited their members, by providing a clear administrative structure for the regulation of their activities; they were generally seen as being to the advantage of the town authorities, since they were a means by which these activities could be controlled and taxed; and they benefited the public, since they acted as a check on

shoddy workmanship. Major towns might have one to two dozen guilds, but their structure sometimes had to accommodate several rather disparate activities so as to provide a viable number of members. In Shrewsbury in 1525, the mercers' guild included cappers, goldsmiths, ironmongers and pewterers.[4]

The London guilds prospered increasingly in the fifteenth century, even when much of the rest of England was in economic recession in the second and third quarters (plate 53, cat. no. 134); the cause had little to do with the guilds themselves, being essentially the result of the growing strength of the cloth-making industry, the vast scale of its exports to the Continent, and the increasingly dominant position of London as the exporting port. London was responsible for roughly half the nation's cloth exports in the years 1400–30, two-thirds in c.1490 and five-sixths in c.1540.[5] English merchants prospered – even if they were shy of voyaging far, for none sailed even in the Mediterranean during this period – and so did London's luxury trades and their practitioners. The merchants' ships brought back from abroad what was most readily available or of high reputation – Italian silks (cat. no. 201), Flemish tapestries (cat. nos 6, 153, 154, 229, 230), Swedish iron, and so forth – and since London was the centre for English exports, it naturally acted as the centre for the distribution of imports. Provincial fairs were in serious decline even before the start of the fifteenth century: for anything other than food and basic clothing, the well-to-do looked to London. 'Fore-gete not to send me a kersche of cremelle [crimson kerchief] fore nekkerchys fore yowr syster Anne, fore … I can non gette in alle thys towne,' wrote an exasperated Margaret Paston in 1469 to her son in London – and yet she was in Norwich, a major city and quite a centre for the luxury textile trades.[6] Similarly, in 1448 the accounts of the newly founded King's College, Cambridge, show that it chose to pay for the carriage from London of candlesticks (presumably superior ones, made of some copper alloy or better, and perhaps imported from Flanders) and a great missal, rather than purchase these locally.[7]

Some English craft activities were dependent on raw materials that were obtainable only with difficulty. Cornish tin was the secret of the English pewterers' success (cat. nos 196, 197); more remarkable, because it was international, was the popularity of the alabaster carvings that were produced in enormous quantities – perhaps by the thousand annually – in the Midlands, for church altars or for people's private religious devotions (see, for example, cat. nos 278–9, 281–3). They were carved near to where they were quarried, principally in Staffordshire and Derbyshire, and were then marketed by specialist 'alabaster-

men' and other merchants, up and down England and abroad. The alabaster carvers may have prospered in part because their panels and figures of religious imagery undercut the prices of other countries' alternatives, but they are also a testimony that England's export trade was not limited to wool and cloths.

The dominance of London within England's art market was reinforced by the royal court being now more or less permanently based there: the crown's expenditure on works of art and architecture dwarfed that of all other patrons, and provided both employment and – no less important – artistic training, experience and influence for many of the most talented craftsmen. In London, too, English artists and craftsmen would intermesh with the workshops and communities of their foreign-born counterparts who were drawn to the capital by the prospect of work or sales there: the London guilds were hardly able to stop them, since they settled outside the city's jurisdictional controls and, sometimes, enjoyed the support of politically influential courtiers.

Arguably, at least, the greatest technical development of the later Middle Ages was one that may have been promoted by the concentration of artists and craftsmen in London, but which also, ultimately, was to lead them to national rather than court- or metropolis-based styles. This was the increasing reliance on drawn designs, and the resultant separation of design from execution (see, for example, plate 54, cat. no. 22). Artists and craftsmen had of course used drawn designs since before the thirteenth century – some of the drawings in the sketchbook of Villard de Honnecourt clearly reflect designs that had already been, and would continue to be, current in different parts of Europe for centuries. But the scale of the practice of using drawings seems to have been very significantly enlarged in England in the fifteenth and early sixteenth centuries: the increasing use of paper played a part in this, and so too, even more influentially, did the new technology of print (cat. no. 241).

Until well into the fifteenth century, pattern books (or rather, collections of drawn designs, probably not usually bound up as books) were still essentially the private creation and jealously guarded property of the leading artists and craftsmen. There is, however, a growing number of mentions of the use of patterns in contractual negotiations between private patrons and specialist craftsmen. In 1475 John Hobbs, a Gloucester mason, was contracted to construct a tomb and chapel for Sir John Beauchamp, Baron of Powick, according to 'the patroun of the portretor' (literally, 'pattern of the portraiture').[8] The pattern was perhaps not one that Hobbs had drawn; the cost of the work would certainly have been far less than that of the chapel and tomb made by London craftsmen, in 1439 and subsequently, for the remains of Richard Beauchamp, Earl of Warwick (cat. nos 86, 87).

Printing enabled this process to be taken much further: a collection of engraved ornamental patterns such as that of Thomas Geminus, *Morysse and Damashin renewed and encreased; very profitable for goldsmythes and embroderars* (London, 1548), enabled a touch of the exotic (moorish and

damascene) to be adapted and applied in the remotest corners of England by any craftsman or woman who could afford the book.[9]

FURTHER READING
Blair and Ramsay 1991; Harvey 1975; Palliser 2000.

54   Design for a monument to Henry VI (cat. no. 27)

THE COMMISSIONING PROCESS
PHILLIP LINDLEY

A unique insight into the commissioning process is provided by the records of a three-way lawsuit in 1498 between the abbots of the monasteries of Westminster and Chertsey and the Dean of Windsor, for possession of the remains of King Henry VI. Elderly witnesses gave oral depositions as to Henry's own choice of burial site in the crowded area around Edward the Confessor's shrine at Westminster Abbey. Their testimony revealed that Henry had contemplated various different locations on several visits, finally deciding on a spot between Henry III's tomb and the shrine. The precise dimensions were incised on the pavement by John Thirsk, the king's master mason, and the contract was given to the marbler John Essex and his partner Thomas Stephens. In the end, though, neither Henry VI's original plans nor those of Henry VII, to have a newly canonized Henry VI enshrined in the new Lady Chapel at Westminster, were realized, though the latter project is commemorated by a contemporary design for the unexecuted tomb/shrine (plate 54).

Royal commissions are of course in a wholly atypical category, but this episode highlights several issues of more general significance to the commissioning process in late medieval England. Henry's deliberations over his tomb's location are uniquely apprehensible through the witness depositions. Oral discussions are naturally ephemeral, but are sometimes recalled or anticipated, or their traces can be detected, in other lawsuits or written contracts of the period. Secondly, although the patron's role varied enormously, the most obvious way in which every patron shaped the production of a work was by initiating its commission. Thirdly, the failure of both projects reminds us that the patron's ability to fund the work and to ensure effective management of its production through to completion were essential. Some patrons, like Bishop Beckington of Bath and

Wells, took no chances and completed their monuments during their lifetimes: Beckington constructed his chantry chapel with double-decker tomb (cadaver below and effigy in full episcopal robes above) more than a decade before his death and consecrated his tomb in 1452, saying Mass at the chantry altar for his own soul.[10] The danger of leaving such a commission to your descendants was obvious. As one inscription in a London church complained:

> ... widows be slo[th]ful, and children beth unkynd,
> Executors beth covetos, and kep al yat yey fynd.[11]

This was not always the case. At Eton College, Bishop William Waynflete, one of Henry VI's executors, seems to have been largely responsible for ensuring the chapel's completion and decoration after Henry's deposition and death, in the face of hostility or indifference from Edward IV.

It was a major difficulty for all medieval patrons to know in advance what the finished product would look like. The citing of individual models, or parts of models, to be copied, amended or surpassed was one answer. In 1497–8, for instance, a mason undertook to build a west tower at Helmingham church, Suffolk, 60 feet (18 m) high, modelled on that of Framsden, but with some features (notably windows, buttresses and the western doorway with its flanking image niches) after the model of Brandeston.[12] Sometimes a wish to surpass the models is made explicit: a London joiner, John Fisher, agreed in 1486 to make a rood-loft for Merton College, Oxford, based on that of Magdalen College but with 'ferre better dorys' and with the upper part based on the rood-loft of St Mildred's in the Poultry, London, but 'better then it is there'.[13] Specific improvements were also indicated at St George's Chapel, Windsor, in 1506 (plate 70, cat. no. 25), when the choir vault bosses were to be modelled on those of the nave, but 'wrought more pendaunt and holower than the keyes or pendaunts of the body of the said' chapel.[14]

Another solution was the use of drawings. The 'portratura' or 'platt' – a drawn plan or design – of a royal work would generally be kept by the Clerk of the King's Works in the later Middle Ages.[15] These drawings will have been of many different types, including orthographic projections of proposed buildings and scale designs.[16] Drawings and designs were amongst the master masons' most useful tools and this could be reflected in their wills: Henry Smith, King Henry VIII's master mason at the Savoy, for instance, left 'all my Bokis of purtiturys' to a colleague in 1517.[17] Drawings constituted a visual repertoire for artists, could convey ideas to patrons or other artificers, and facilitated collaborative works such as buildings and complex tomb-projects.

In the late Middle Ages drawings were, for the first time,

widely employed in contracts to help guarantee the end result. Thus John Wastell contracted to make one of the corner turrets of King's College Chapel, Cambridge, 'after the best handelyng and fourme of good workmanshipp, accordyng to a platt therof made, remaynyng in the kepyng of the ... Surveyour'.[18] A manuscript of the executors' accounts for Margaret Beaufort's monument (plate 55) offers a glimpse into the pre-contractual evaluation by patrons of alternative designs. Three 'patrons in paper ... eche of theym diuerse facions' for the effigy and canopy were first shown to her executors. After one had been

55 Tomb of Lady Margaret Beaufort, Westminster Abbey (cat. no. 117)

selected, two identical patterns were painted on cloth by the artist Maynard Vewick, one for the executors and one for the sculptor Pietro Torrigiano, thus fixing the design. Torrigiano himself provided another 'patrone drawen and kerven in Tymbre' for the touchstone tomb-chest.[19] In one instance, in 1523, the process of consultation over a drawing became part of a fund-raising process.[20]

In stained-glass contracts a 'vidimus' might be used. A vidimus – literally a French rendition of the Latin *inspeximus*: 'we have seen' – was one of the two copies of a design for a stained-glass window that was agreed between patron and glazier (cat. nos 22, 295). This design might not be executed by the glazier or glaziers, but by a specialist artist. A set of vidimuses in Brussels contains, most remarkably, two versions of the Crucifixion, one with angels collecting the blood of Christ, one without. Hilary Wayment suggested that the designer evidently did not know, 'in an age racked by controversy about the Real Presence, which version the patron would favour'.[21]

The choice of iconography will often have been broadly indicated by the patron. Bishop Fox of Winchester was closely involved in the glazing scheme of King's College Chapel, Cambridge: a fairly detailed iconographic programme was decided and a series of vidimuses, drawing heavily on block-book illustrations of the *Biblia Pauperum* (cat. no. 241) and the *Speculum Humanae Salvationis*, was provided. Fox seems to have been regarded as something of an expert: in 1500 he had recommended the carpenter Humphrey Coke to Lord Darcy, stating that Coke 'is right cunnynge and diligente in his werkes … if ye take his advise … he shall advantage you large monee in the buldinge thereof, as well as in the devisinge as in the werkenge of yt'.[22] Informal contacts between patrons must frequently have been a means by which artists were selected, subjects emulated and artistic forms transferred. Edward IV's patronage of mammoth Flemish manuscripts (cat. no. 43) may well have been inspired by the library of Louis de Gruuthuyse in Bruges or by reports of the library of the dukes of Burgundy from the king's sister, Margaret of York, Charles the Bold's duchess, herself a distinguished collector of books.[23]

One issue that was always a concern was quality: both of the medium and the workmanship. The best-quality glass was specified in the mid fifteenth-century contracts for the Beauchamp Chapel, Warwick, signed by John Prudde (cat. no. 89); he was to use 'Glasse [from] beyond the Seas, and with no Glasse of England; and that in the finest wise, with the best, cleanest, and strongest glasse of beyond the Sea that may be had in England', the subject matter to be 'delivered and appointed by the … Executors by patterns in paper, afterwards to be newly traced and pictured by another Painter'.[24] In a legal case of 1443, Robert and Thomas Sutton and their associate John Chaloner were sued by Sir Thomas Cumberworth, who refused to accept the tomb-monument they produced because of their poor-quality workmanship and their use of flawed alabaster.[25] In another case, one frustrated patron tried to have a highly skilled but deceitful sculptor – James Hales – subpoenaed to complete an altarpiece he had abandoned: no other sculptor in the country could finish the work, the patron complained. It has recently been suggested that Hales was a Netherlandish carver.[26] Increasingly, in the late fifteenth century, many of the best artists to work in England seem to have come from the Netherlands. Many of them settled in Southwark, close to the patronage of king, court and merchants, but outside the jurisdiction of the city of London guilds, which fought a losing battle to control them.

FURTHER READING
Colvin 1975; Salzman 1967.

IMMIGRANT CRAFTSMEN AND IMPORTS
KIM WOODS

In 1517 the so-called 'Evil May Day Riots' broke out in London. A spokesman for the rioters claimed that 'strangers' (that is, foreigners) 'compass the city round about, in Southwark, in Westminster, Temple Bar, Holborn, Saint Martin's, Saint John's Gate, Aldgate, Tower Hill, Saint Katherine's, and forestall the market … which is the cause that Englishmen want and starve and they live abundantly in great pleasure … '[27] Among the goods allegedly suffering from foreign competition were wainscot, locks, baskets, cupboards, stools, tables, chests, saddles and painted cloths, 'so that if it were wrought here Englishmen might have some work and living by it'.

The allegations of foreign competition were well founded, and the Netherlands offered the strongest challenge. Wainscot and painted cloths do indeed feature prominently among imports to the port of London in 1480–81.[28] In 1483 the guild of cofferers complained that they were 'like to be undone' by Flemish imports.[29] A carved chest now in East Dereham church is probably a surviving example of the sixteenth-century 'Flemish chests' listed so often in English inventories. The 1509 Book of

Rates for the port of London included Flemish glass, gold or silver of Bruges and tapestry. Numerous images were also imported into London, including devotional images in pipeclay and wood (cat. nos 220, 221).[30]

The extent of immigration of foreign craftsmen, principally from France and the Low Countries, emerges in the denization records of 1544, when all foreigners resident in England were obliged to become subjects of the English crown or face expulsion.[31] Many foreign craftsmen had already been in the country for some years, integrated into small communities, like the joiner Philipp Arthus, aged 56, resident in rural Stratton for 26 years and 'stayed for his qualitie'. Others were in royal employment, like Paule Cauwe, a French joiner who had spent the last 20 years 'commonly wrought in the King's wourkes'. Significant numbers of alien craftsmen were concentrated in the London borough of Southwark, one of the many areas of liberty where, until now, citizenship had not been a requirement.[32] The celebrated glass painter Galyon Hone, denizen in 1535, lived in Southwark, as had his predecessor Barnard

Flower, glazier to the king by 1505 and almost certainly the overseer for the Fairford glazing (cat. no. 294).[33]

Foreign competition had clearly been an issue for many decades prior to the May Day riots. In 1521 Cardinal Wolsey received a petition from the 'stranger' joiners in which they complained of illegal imprisonment at the hands of the English joiners.[34] In one of a series of increasingly desperate measures by the glaziers in the early sixteenth century to stifle foreign competition, Hone was imprisoned for installing stained glass he had made within the City of London, and thus within the jurisdiction of the Glaziers' Company. In 1523 a parliamentary act forbade alien craftsmen, whether official citizens or not, from taking foreign apprentices and limited foreign servants (among whom might be classed journeymen) to two, specifying that aliens were not to work separately, but in such a way that the English could learn their craft secrets.[35]

The strength of foreign competition is probably to be explained by the superior levels of skill offered by foreign craftsmen and foreign imports alike. The recently published

56   Panels from a triptych commissioned by Sir Robert Tate (cat. no. 136)

documentation concerning the carved altarpiece commissioned in 1490–93 from James Hales for the Bridgettine abbey at Syon states that there was 'no werkman yn this land so well as the seid James', who was described as 'most expert in ymagery of eny oder in that land'. Significantly, whether English or not, Hales 'hath a grete part of his lif beyende the see in Flaunders' and the skills he offered were almost certainly acquired there.[36] Many such works of art were destroyed during the Reformation or the English Civil War, but the importance of continental art and artefacts in fifteenth- and early sixteenth-century England is clear both from documents and from surviving fragments such as the altarpiece shutters commissioned by Sir Robert Tate (plate 56).

As treasurer of Calais from 1517 until 1526, William Lord Sandys was well placed to secure the services of foreign craftsmen. From 1522 foreign glaziers were employed at his country house, The Vyne (Hampshire), and in the chapel of the Holy Ghost, Basingstoke.[37] He also owned Flemish furniture and chests. On 1 March 1536, acting on Sandys's behalf, prominent London mercer Thomas Leigh commissioned two stone tombs in Antwerp from the Amsterdam carver Arnoult Hermanssone, then resident in Aire in Artois.[38] It was probably from Antwerp that Sandys imported the Netherlandish floor tiles now in The Vyne's chapel (cat. no. 158).

Thomas Howard, 3rd Duke of Norfolk (1473–1554), evidently had a taste for continental art too. His tomb at Framlingham is thought to have been designed and partly made in the 1530s after Italian-derived French models (cat. no. 336). The duke's portrait was painted around 1539 (Windsor Castle, Royal Collection) by the most famous immigrant artist of all, the painter Hans Holbein, who settled in England for good in 1532. The 1551 inventory of his residence at Kenninghall (Suffolk) reveals that the sumptuous chapel contained a carved and gilded altarpiece of the Passion of Christ almost certainly imported from Brussels or Antwerp.[39] The Ashwellthorpe Triptych was owned by Christopher Knyvett, whose brother Thomas married the duke's sister (plate 49, cat. no. 276). The duke's daughter, the Duchess of Richmond, owned a 'flemyssh trussing cofre'.[40]

Imported goods such as altarpieces were often commissioned by the merchant classes. Robert Tate was a member of the Calais Staple as well as a mercer and London alderman. A carved altarpiece for the Mercers' Chapel in the church of the Holy Trinity, Hull, was brought from Zeeland in 1521, and a second was acquired from Flanders for the chapel of the merchants' guild almshouse.[41] The aforementioned Thomas Leigh ordered a carved altarpiece, including the unusual scene of the 'Raising of Lazarus', from Antwerp in 1535 on behalf of an unspecified (presumably English) client.[42] Leigh would already have been familiar with the Antwerp carved altarpiece commissioned in February 1523 from Walter Vandale for the princely sum of 90 Flemish pounds for the altar of the new Mercers' Chapel in London.[43] The chapel also featured a magnificent carved stone 'Dead Christ', probably dating from *c.*1500 and of continental craftsmanship (plate 57).[44]

Continental influences extended beyond imports and immigrant craftsmen to English art and artists. This is nowhere more apparent than in the Ripon choir stalls (cat. no. 240), in stained-glass windows like those in Tattershall (Lincolnshire) and East Anglian painted rood-screens, such as those at Tacolneston (Norfolk), where continental prints

57   Statue of the Dead Christ, limestone, *c.*1500 (The Worshipful Company of Mercers, London)

and the Netherlandish *Biblia Pauperum* (cat. no. 241) were used as models.[45] Where style was also imitated, the boundaries between what is continental and what is English craftsmanship become very difficult to draw, as the figural sculpture of Henry VII's Chapel, Westminster Abbey and elsewhere (cat. nos 28, 239) demonstrates.

FURTHER READING
Barron and Saul 1995; Mitchell and Moran 2000.

REGIONAL PRODUCTION
NICHOLAS ROGERS

In life and in death John Baret, merchant of Bury St Edmunds in Suffolk, was surrounded by works of art. His will details many of the contents of his house, from earthenware vessels to painted hangings, jewellery and books.[46] The complicated provisions for the welfare of his soul required painters, carvers and masons to work on the adornment of St Mary, Bury St Edmunds. Many of the objects he owned may have been, and some certainly were, made locally in Bury St Edmunds, which can be seen as a paradigm of regional artistic activity in late medieval England.

Although regional production, usually centred on a locus of major ecclesiastical or secular patronage, had long been a feature of English artistic activity, the increased importance of lesser patrons, chiefly burgesses and gentry, in the fifteenth century stimulated the establishment of artists in provincial towns. At Bury there was an important corporate patron, the Abbey of St Edmund, and a mercantile elite, and the prosperity of late medieval Suffolk ensured copious patronage, both communal and individual, in the surrounding villages. Baret's cadaver effigy (plate 58) is probably the work of a sculptor in the employ of Simon Clerk (*fl.* 1434–d. 1489?), master mason of Bury St Edmunds Abbey, to whom he refers in his will. Also named in his will are two painters. Baret specifies that certain work about his tomb should be carried out by Henry Peyntour, probably Henry Albreed (*fl.* 1453–d. 1492/3). He also refers to 'the ymage of oure lady that Robert Pygot peynted'. Pygot is identifiable as the artist of the St Etheldreda panels (cat. no. 319), which once formed part of her shrine at Ely.[47] Bury supported a population of at least seven painters and stainers in the fifteenth and early sixteenth centuries.[48] Despite the ravages of the Reformation, enough survives of late medieval panel painting to give a good idea of the range of skill available around the country. Much of what remains, such as the

Devon rood-screen panels (cat. no. 265) or the late fifteenth-century paintings in Hexham Priory (Northumberland), can at best be called crude and vigorous, the equivalent of modern folk art. East Anglian rood-screens show a wider range of quality, with some artists responsive to the latest artistic developments (cat. nos 264, 266, 277).[49] The altarpiece made for the nuns of Romsey (Hampshire) in the 1520s has links with early Renaissance work carried out under Bishop Fox at Winchester Cathedral. Similar work was produced in the vicinity of Chichester by Bishop Sherborne's 'court' painter, Lambert Barnard.[50] Wood carving has suffered even more than painting from iconoclastic destruction. Some idea of the quality of the lost devotional images is provided by architectural sculpture such as the wall post and hammer-beam figures of the nave roof in St Mary's, Bury St Edmunds (cat. no. 261).[51]

By the 1390s commercial book production was firmly centred on London – the usual, though not invariable, seat of the court and parliament, and the home of major sources of ecclesiastical, mercantile and legal patronage. Oxford and Cambridge required a constant supply of books, but the

58   Cadaver tomb of John Baret, St Mary's church, Bury St Edmunds (cat. no. 331)

stationers based in the university towns usually produced functional volumes, devoid of decoration. The fifteenth century saw the rise of the amateur illuminator, typically a scholar adding pen or wash drawings to a text compiled for his own use. Many medical, alchemical and heraldic manuscripts belong to this category. The particular liturgical requirements of the diocese of York helped sustain the York book trade.[52] However, most of the surviving figural illumination (cat. no. 141) is of poor calibre, especially when compared with contemporary York glass. The demand for de-luxe copies of the works of John Lydgate, monk of Bury, encouraged the growth of a local school of illuminators at Bury.[53] One of the finest products of this school is the presentation copy of the *Lives of Saints Edmund and Fremund*, made for Henry VI (plate 122, cat. no. 318), which shows an awareness of recent developments in Netherlandish art. Baret owned a copy of another Lydgate poem, the *Siege of Thebes*.[54] Monastic houses continued as focuses of local book production right into the age of printing. Three of the early presses outside London were associated with the Benedictine houses of Abingdon, St Albans and Tavistock.[55]

The bells that chimed *Requiem eternam* yearly for John Baret's soul were probably made in Bury.[56] There is evidence of bell-making in Bury from the twelfth century onwards, and between about 1450 and the 1530s there was a continuous workshop tradition, dominated by the Chirche family.[57] The practical advantages of casting close to the intended destination led to a proliferation of bell-foundries in late medieval England (cat. no. 313).[58]

The availability of the raw material often determined the place of production. Pottery and tiles were made in a large number of places for local sale, although earthenware goods were also transported long distances and even imported. Alabaster devotional panels and tomb-effigies were produced mostly in the Midland towns of Burton-on-Trent, Chellaston and Nottingham, close to the quarries. From there they were shipped as far afield as Iceland and Dalmatia.[59] There are also records of alabasterers at York between 1456 and 1525. The scenes from the life of St William of York that were found on the site of the House of the Holy Priests in 1957 may have been carved in the city.[60]

The continental origin of the latten used for monumental brasses was one of the factors which ensured that all but one (Coventry) of the workshops manufacturing brasses were situated in towns within easy reach of the east coast. Although the London workshops dominated production, the demand for this type of monument in late medieval England encouraged a proliferation of workshops, of varying degrees of permanence. Some 'workshops' appear to be no more than the entrepreneurial activity of one man. A series of brasses in Kent dating from between 1525 and 1545 can be assigned to an engraver operating in Canterbury.[61] The charming series of mostly small-scale brasses produced in Cambridge between about 1500 and 1541 may represent the work of one man.[62] Many of these regional series mimicked London models: the Fens 1 Series, probably originating in Boston, is based on patterns from the London C workshop.[63] Brasses had been engraved in York since the early fourteenth century, and from the 1380s to the beginning of the sixteenth century there was a continuous tradition of York design, manifesting a distinctive amalgam of London and continental motifs.[64] The most productive non-metropolitan centre was Norwich. At least six distinct workshop series, with different figure patterns and scripts, have been identified between about 1440 and 1550.[65] In regional centres links between the different media seem to have been closer than in London. The Norwich glazier William Heywood was probably involved in the designing of Norwich Series 3 brasses. One of the most important examples of this group, the brass of Joan, Lady Cromwell at Tattershall (Lincolnshire), engraved in about 1490 (plate 59), has also been compared with the screen paintings at Filby in Norfolk. Bury St Edmunds was the location of brass workshops between about 1470 and 1551.[66] The repertoire of designs suggests that this group is an offshoot of the Norwich brasses, but links can also be made with local painting. The kneeling figures of Jankyn Smith and his wife, in St Mary's, Bury, have their counterparts in contemporary Bury manuscripts. It has been suggested that this and related brasses were made by the bell-founder Reignold Chirche (d. 1499).[67]

The arrival of a distinctive artistic personality could shape the character of the arts locally. John Thornton of Coventry's work in York established the use by the city's glaziers of an International Gothic vocabulary which lasted into the third quarter of the fifteenth century.[68] Both York and Norwich sustained large communities of glaziers who were pre-eminent regionally.[69] But even a glazier based in a more obscure location could have a widespread clientele. The work of Richard Twygge of Malvern is to be found not only in Worcestershire, but also in Gloucestershire, Warwick-

59   Rubbing of brass of Joan, Lady Cromwell, Holy Trinity church, Tattershall (cat. no. 333)

shire, Tattershall in Lincolnshire and even in Westminster Abbey (cat. nos 37, 292).[70] It was Twygge's stylistic conservatism rather than his non-metropolitan work-base that was significant.

The presence of an artist locally did not in itself constitute a local style. An artist trained in London would, unless he came under some strong external influence, retain his metropolitan characteristics. Sidney Sussex College MS 80, illuminated in Bristol, is virtually indistinguishable from a manuscript of the same date illuminated in London.[71] But certain places, such as York, Norwich and Bury, developed distinctive artistic dialects. Discriminating patrons could often commission works of high quality locally. As the glass of John Thornton, the brass of Joan, Lady Cromwell, British Library Harley MS 2278 (cat. no. 318) or the Ranworth rood-screen in Norfolk demonstrate, a regional origin was not synonymous with 'provincial' quality in late medieval England.

FURTHER READING
Badham 1990; Friedman 1995a.

NOTES

1 Halliwell 1844, p.13.

2 Spindler 1927, line 1965.

3 Unwin 1963, pp.370–71 and illustration on p.167.

4 Palliser 2000, p.450.

5 Ibid., pp.417–18.

6 Davis 1971–6, I, p.339.

7 Cambridge, King's College Muniments, Mundum Books, vol. I, f.89v, f.137v.

8 Harvey 1984, p.146.

9 STC, no. 11718.4.

10 Stone 1972, p.214.

11 Weever 1631, p.19.

12 Salzman 1967, pp.547–8.

13 Hobhouse 1846.

14 St John Hope 1913a, II, p.461.

15 Colvin 1963, I, p.201.

16 Harvey 1953.

17 Harvey 1984, q.v.

18 Colvin 1975, p.191.

19 Cambridge, St John's College, MS D 91 24; Scott 1915.

20 Evans and Cook 1955, p.169.

21 Wayment 1991, p.119.

22 Harvey 1984, q.v.

23 Backhouse 1987, pp.25–6.

24 Dugdale 1730, I, p.446.

25 PRO, CP 40/729, m.287d.

26 Barron and Erler 2000; and see the essay by Kim Woods (pp.92–3).

27 Unwin 1948, p.248.

28 Cobb 1990; wainscot at this date almost certainly means wood as a raw material rather than panelling.

29 Chinnery 1979, p.354.

30 Gras 1918, pp.560–94, 694–705; Asaert 1985, p.83.

31 Shaw 1893, p.xxv.

32 Ibid., pp.vi, xli.

33 Marks 1993, p.217.

34 Brewer et al. 1862–1932, vol. 3/ii, no. 1530.

35 Ibid., no. 2956/4; Ransome 1969.

36 Barron and Erler 2000, p.324.

37 Wayment 1982; see also cat. no. 343 for sculpture from the same site.

38 Le Beffroi, IV, 1872–3, pp.202–4.

39 Foister 1981, p.276.

40 PRO, LR/2/225, f.37v.

41 Allison 1969, pp.201, 308; Harvey 1950, p.6.

42 De Smedt 1950, vol. 2, pp.410–11.

43 Lyell and Watney 1936, p.673.

44 Evans and Cook 1955.

45 Marks 1993, pp.68–9; Mitchell 2000b.

46 Tymms 1850, pp.15–44.

47 Fletcher 1974a and 1974b.

48 Rogers 1987, p.230.

49 Mitchell 2000b.

50 Croft-Murray 1957.

51 Tolhurst 1962.

52 Gee 2000.

53 Rogers 1987.

54 Tymms 1850, p.35.

55 Knowles 1959, pp.24–7.

56 Tymms 1850, p.28.

57 Raven 1890, pp.64–74.

58 Walters 1912, pp.193–208.

59 Cheetham 1984, pp.13–17.

60 Willmot 1957.

61 Norris 1977, pp.191–2.

62 Greenwood 1969.

63 Badham 1989b.

64 Badham 1989a.

65 Norris 1977, pp.179–86.

66 Badham 1980.

67 Badham and Blatchley 1988.

68 Marks 1993, pp.180–83, 199–200.

69 Knowles 1936, pp.222–53; Woodforde 1950, pp.9–15.

70 Marks 1993, pp.203–4.

71 Rogers 2001, p.198, pl. 39.

IX

'EXCELLENT, NEW AND UNIFORME': PERPENDICULAR ARCHITECTURE c.1400–1547

CHRISTOPHER WILSON

'Ther be 3 paroches chirches [in Notingham]; but the chirch of St Mary is excellent, new and uniforme yn work, and [hath] so many fair wyndowes yn it that no artificer can imagine to set mo[re] ther.'

Written in the early 1540s by the itinerating antiquary John Leland,[1] these words capture better than any earlier recorded comment two of the most distinctive qualities of Perpendicular Gothic architecture: its consistency of treatment and its emphasis on maximum fenestration (plate 60). But what seems at first sight even more striking about Leland's remarks is that they show him enthusing about the modernity of a building that was actually around 140 years old. Leland may or may not have realized that Perpendicular had already been current in England for 200 years when he was compiling his *Itinerary*, but his mistaken perception that St Mary's was new is entirely understandable, for Perpendicular changed relatively little in the course of its long lifespan and present-day scholars often find it difficult to deduce the date of individual examples from formal traits alone.[2] Leland's praise of St Mary's is just one among many expressions of approval for Perpendicular buildings in his *Itinerary*, where examples of older styles seldom elicit any aesthetic evaluation; and in being biased towards the idiom of his own day, Leland was only following a very long-standing medieval tendency to equate the contemporary with the excellent in architecture.[3]

PERPENDICULAR BEFORE 1400

Perpendicular architecture made its first appearances in the chapter house and cloister of St Paul's Cathedral, London (destroyed), and the remodelling of the Romanesque south transept of St Peter's Abbey, Gloucester (now Gloucester Cathedral).[4] Both buildings were begun in the early 1330s, and both will probably have seemed at the time to represent just two of the myriad styles thrown up in the previous 50 years, a period when the leading English architects were engaged in an almost frenetic pursuit of formal innovation, and when

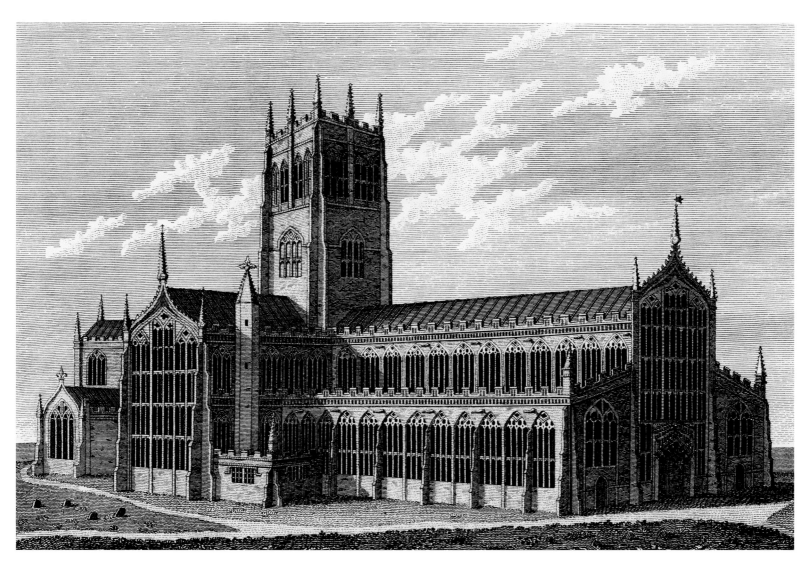

60 St Mary's church, Nottingham, exterior from the north-west, engraving after Wenceslaus Hollar, from R. Thoroton, *History of Nottinghamshire*, London, 1797, vol. II

much of that effort was channelled into devising the complex ornamental effects highlighted in the 'Decorated' label usually applied to this phase of Gothic. Yet there must have been something special about Perpendicular, for it supplanted all its rivals within a very few decades. No doubt mid-fourteenth-century architects and patrons appreciated that the long-standing English reliance on sophisticated and inventive decoration had given way to a new emphasis on the systematic and the unified, but the lack of any tradition of analytical writing on architecture during the Middle Ages means that there exists not a single contemporary comment on a change that is clearly recognizable from a modern perspective as an artistic revolution. The main factors in the rapid ascendance of Perpendicular are likely to have been the sheer novelty of its appearance and its capacity to be reduced to easily copied formulas.[5]

The second half of the fourteenth century saw the inno-

vations of the Gloucester south transept and the St Paul's cloister and chapter house consolidated in three outstanding works of ecclesiastical architecture, each of which was to exert great influence after 1400. In the first of these, the remodelling of the late eleventh-century choir[6] of Gloucester Abbey (begun after 1351), the two lower storeys of the massive Romanesque structure are mostly left in place, yet are masked from the view of anyone standing in the central vessel by tier upon tier of vertically linked 'panels' or upright arch-enclosing rectangles (plate 62). The panels are variously open, glazed or 'blind' (applied to solid masonry), and in the tracery at the heads of the windows the verticals defining the sides of the panels join directly on to the undersides of the enclosing arches in a way that was quite new and which nineteenth-century scholars identified as the touchstone of the Perpendicular style.[7] The immediate source of the panel motif is the earlier work in the south

61 Abbey church of La Trinité, Vendôme, detail of north clearstorey and triforium of the choir

62 Gloucester Abbey (now Cathedral), choir looking east

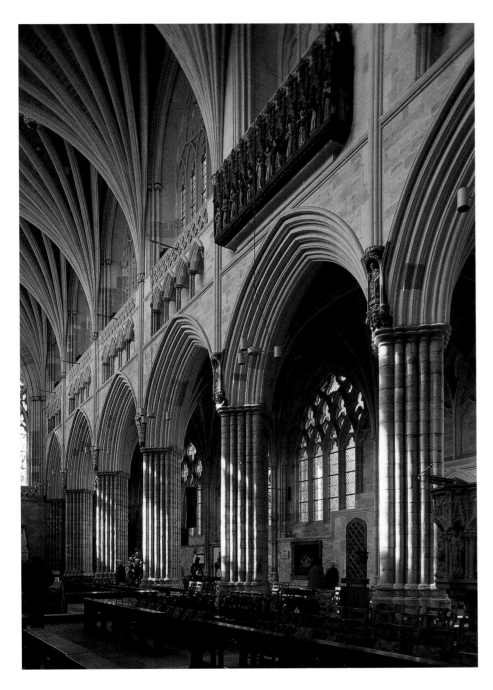

64 Exeter Cathedral, north side of the nave

63 Gloucester Abbey (now Cathedral), east walk of the cloister (left)

Exeter Cathedral (plate 64), a building whose construction overlapped with that of the Gloucester south transept. Exeter also illustrates the emphasis placed in earlier English Gothic on thick walls and on the decoration of the edges of the openings through those walls with complex and multi-layered moulding profiles.

In the cloister at Gloucester Abbey (begun after 1351) the concept of treating all visible surfaces as a system of tracery panels is taken an important stage further by being extended to the vault (plate 63). These earliest 'fan vaults' have nothing in common with the vault over the Gloucester choir, where a basic tunnel shape is overlaid by a dense mesh of ribs forming a pattern quite unrelated to that of the walls below. Technically too there is a great difference. Whereas the choir vault is built, like all rib vaults, out of two different kinds of masonry – carefully shaped freestone blocks for the ribs and irregular plaster-coated masonry for the interstices – the cloister vaults consist of shells made entirely of finely jointed blocks which encompass both tracery (the visual equivalent of ribs here) and plain 'background'. The three-dimensional form of the vault is no longer conceived as a by-product of the process of infilling the spaces between ribs, and has become instead a geometrically regular form, a half-conoid generated by rotating an arc about a vertical axis.[8] Since the horizontal mouldings that define the upper limits of the half-conoidal 'fans' are semicircles beginning and ending in the centres of the sides of each bay, it follows that the bays are all square in plan. Fitting fan vaults on to the rectangular-plan bays that were traditional in the central vessels of great churches inevitably compromised their geometrical regularity, and made heavy demands on the ingenuity and taste of the architect. Probably it was the latter factor which delayed and limited the dissemination of a vault type that may well have been regarded from the very moment of its invention as the Perpendicular optimum.[9]

The nave of Canterbury Cathedral (plate 118), unlike the Gloucester choir, was a completely new structure, a fact that accounts for many of the important differences between the two buildings. Probably because the concealing of retained Romanesque fabric was not a concern here, the panel motif is confined to the aisle windows and to the solid walling between the main arcades and clearstorey. The great height of the main arcades and the lowness of the clearstorey are almost an inversion of Gloucester's proportions, but in a sense they are a resemblance too, for the levels of the storeys follow those in pre-existing work, in this case the late twelfth-century choir. The heavy indebtedness of the piers to the far smaller vault responds in the cloister of St Paul's Cathedral[10] may have been something more than the result

transept, but it derives ultimately from the triforia (central storeys) of churches in the mid- and late thirteenth-century French Rayonnant style (plate 61). Equally French is the way in which the responds of the high vault extend without interruption between the floor and the capitals, although at Gloucester this feature is of particular value as a means of binding an elevation formed of multiple tiers of panelling into a single unified composition. The novelty of continuous responds in England can be appreciated by a comparison with the slight, bracketed-out shafts in the nave of

of studying an obvious source, for the St Paul's cloister was designed by William Ramsey (*fl.* 1323–49), first holder of the post of king's chief master mason, and the Canterbury nave is generally attributed to Henry Yevele (*fl.* 1353–1400), Ramsey's successor in that post from 1378.[11] Both Ramsey and Yevele were able to take on large amounts of work for wealthy non-royal patrons, in whose eyes they will have been of high standing on account of their royal appointments and, presumably, on account of the perceived merits of their designs. There can be no doubt that Ramsey and Yevele were each in his day the leading architect in southeast England, and their very extensive oeuvres, along with those of the architects they influenced, form a distinct strand of Perpendicular rivalling in importance Gloucester's remodelled south transept, choir and cloister. The services of royal architects continued to be in general demand in the period 1400–1540.

With only a couple of exceptions, late medieval English parish churches belong to an architectural type vastly less complex than the great church, the key distinction being the use of timber roofs rather than masonry vaults.[12] The lighter coverings of the parish churches gave rise to slight walls and arcades that possess their own distinctive style, and which also accord greater internal visibility to windows than do the thicker walls and supports of vaulted churches (plates 64, 65). By the early fourteenth century, prototypes of the major late medieval parish church existed in limited numbers in eastern England. They are characterized by very tall arcades incorporating slender four-shaft piers, relatively low clearstoreys forming a more or less continuous band of windows, and a roof of shallow pitch, which combines with the banded clearstoreys to produce a distinctive 'boxy' kind of space. In the second half of the century it was a straightforward matter to Perpendicularize this scheme by updating the detailing, and churches continued to be built on these lines until the end of the Middle Ages.

The simplicity of medieval secular buildings compared to churches embodies a notion which, even if it was never formally articulated, was undoubtedly fundamental to medieval thinking. This is the conviction that churches, as houses of God, must, whenever possible, be far more splendid than the abodes of earthly rulers. The latter usually consisted of informal assemblages of heterogeneous units built over an extended period, but there was a tradition of treating certain of these units as showpieces: typically, gatehouses, chapels and, above all, halls, whose communal dining function made them atavistic symbols of a lord's leadership of his war-band, the precursor of the medieval household. Since the thirteenth century it had been usual to light the side walls of halls by a series of tall, narrow win-

dows, but by *c.*1400 it was beginning to be common for the high table end of the hall to be equipped with one or two projecting bay windows. To design hall windows in the Perpendicular style was of course unproblematic, but by the mid-fourteenth century ways were being found to Perpendicularize the complex and varied roof structures that were more highly developed in England than anywhere else.

This process culminates in the roof of Westminster Hall (1393–99), by common consent the finest of all medieval timber roofs, where openwork tracery panels decorate the

65 Boston church, Lincolnshire, nave looking south-east

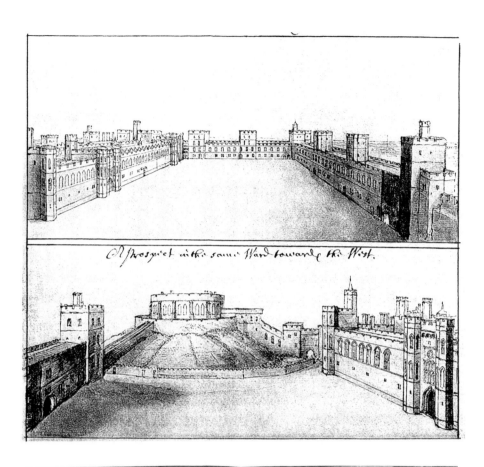

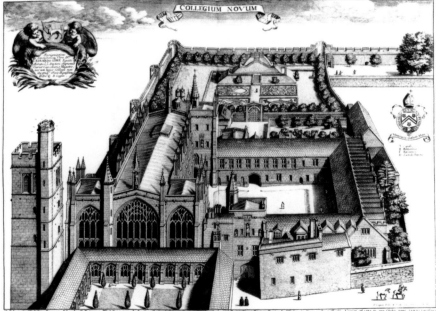

66 Windsor Castle, Upper Ward, looking east (above) and west (below), after a pen-and-wash drawing by Wenceslaus Hollar, probably 1650s or early 1660s, from St John Hope 1913a

67 New College, Oxford, engraving by David Loggan, *Oxonia Illustrata*, Oxford, 1675

interstices between the principal members (plate 25). The detailing of the roof, which differs from that employed by the architect of the hall's masonry parts, Henry Yevele, shows that the master carpenter Hugh Herland was himself fully capable of designing in the Perpendicular style. All major medieval buildings needed two architects – one for the stone parts and one for the timber parts – but whereas the work of the master carpenter is prominent in a hall or a parish church, in a vaulted church it is out of sight between the vault and the outer roof covering. Far less spectacular internally than Herland's carpentry, Yevele's contribution to Westminster Hall was to prove just as influential. Although the plain walling under the windows was an inheritance from the Romanesque hall on the site, it was perceived in the period *c*.1400–1540 not as an old-fashioned feature, but as an improvement on the long-windowed halls of the thirteenth and fourteenth centuries, in the sense that it provided far more scope for displaying the Netherlandish tapestries that were being imported in increasing numbers.[13]

Unified complexes of secular buildings erected in a single campaign were exceptional in late medieval England. The most important by far was the palace that Edward III built between 1357 and 1368 in the Upper Ward of Windsor Castle (plate 66). Its external elevations were treated with a uniformity fully in line with Perpendicular aesthetics – indeed, their consistency was so complete as to reveal absolutely nothing about the internal disposition of spaces on the main, first-floor level. Windsor exerted important influences on the design of castles and fortified manor houses, but in the long term its most important progeny was New College, Oxford, begun in 1380 by a patron and an architect intimately associated with the Windsor works. Yet New College also represents a critique of Windsor's extreme uniformity, for although the hall and chapel are set end-to-end, exactly as at Windsor, the windows that light these two rooms are clearly differentiated so as to underscore the higher status of the chapel. The other three ranges round the quadrangle at New College consist mostly of the Fellows' accommodation but, unlike the lodgings for household officers and guests that occupy the analogous ranges at Windsor, they are differentiated from the higher-status structures forming the north range by being treated far more simply (plate 67).[14] New College gave rise to a tradition of Oxford college architecture that endured to the end of the Middle Ages, and even beyond.

Without doubt, the second half of the fourteenth century was the heroic age of Perpendicular architecture. The Gloucester choir and cloister, the Canterbury nave, the Upper Ward at Windsor, Westminster Hall and New College are all buildings that were never surpassed as creative

achievements and which proved to be of enduring importance as influences on the subsequent development of Perpendicular. That the close of the fourteenth century was
also the end of an epoch in the history of Perpendicular is
evident from the disappearance around then of many of the
leading figures on the architectural scene. Richard II, a
young and discriminating patron of architecture and other
visual arts, was murdered in February 1400; the single greatest architectural patron, William of Wykeham, Bishop of
Winchester, died in 1404; and the two leading architects in
south-east England for many decades, Henry Yevele and
William Wynford, died in 1400 and 1405 respectively. The
new king, Henry IV, was not, and did not need to be, a great
builder, and all the signs are that, for the time being at least,
the demand for grand new buildings had slumped.

THE GREAT CHURCH

Most of the major ecclesiastical corporations that wished to
renew all or part of their churches during the late Middle
Ages had begun to do so well before 1400. Nevertheless, the
period 1400–1540 was very productive of what were often
conceived as the finishing touches to a great church, namely
towers. Not that tower-building was always a carefully pre-
planned activity. In 1407 the thirteenth-century crossing
tower of York Minster collapsed, apparently without warning. The Minster's architect Hugh Hedon was sacked and
replaced by the architect to Westminster Abbey, William
Colchester, who designed the majestic crossing tower that
still dominates the York skyline (cat. no. 231).[15] Colchester
almost certainly had a hand in the other most important
project of the early fifteenth century in the vicinity of York,
the completion of Beverley Minster's twin-tower west front
(plate 68), for this resembles the York tower in employing a
polished metropolitan manner quite different from the
more eclectic and robust version of Perpendicular hitherto
practised in York.

Another reason to replace old towers (besides accidental
damage) was their impairment by subsequent building
activity. The main examples of this are the crossing towers
of Canterbury Cathedral and Gloucester Abbey, whose
Romanesque predecessors had been encroached on by the
building of choirs much higher than the earlier structures
they replaced. At Canterbury new crossing arches were built
from 1433, but the tower itself was not begun until the 1490s.
At Gloucester, by contrast, the tower was brought to completion within a mere eight years during the 1450s (plate 69). All
the great church towers completed in the period 1400–1547
exemplify one of the peculiarities of Perpendicular vis-à-vis
both earlier English Gothic and contemporary Late Gothic

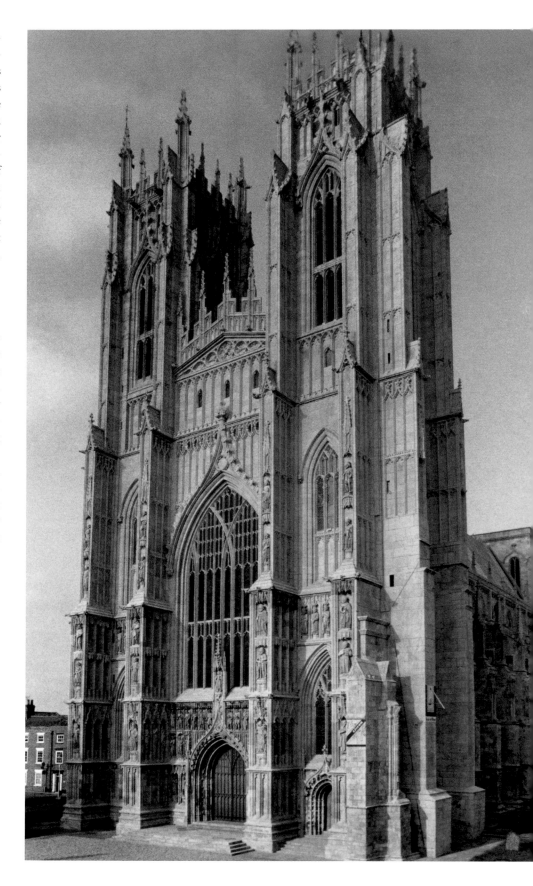

68 Beverley Minster,
East Yorkshire, west front

69 Gloucester Abbey
(now Cathedral), crossing
tower from the west

70 St George's Chapel,
Windsor, nave looking
north-west (cat. no. 25)

71 Sherborne Abbey, Dorset,
choir vault looking east

on the Continent, namely the omission of spires.[16] The simplest and perhaps most satisfactory explanation for this
phenomenon is that the Perpendicular stress on the motif of
the upright arch-enclosing rectangle was thought to
demand the elimination of all unequivocally vertical
accents. The only spires built at the great churches during
the fifteenth century – those at the cathedrals of Norwich
and Chichester – were masonry replacements for timber
spires on crossing towers of twelfth- and thirteenth-century
date respectively. In the Perpendicular period no cathedral
or major abbey church acquired a tower set axially at the
west end of the nave, where solid side walls would have

enabled it to rise to a greater height than any crossing tower.
The main reason why this arrangement was never employed
at the great churches is likely to have been a sense of rank,
the feeling that elite foundations ought not to follow a usage
that had been widely adopted by parish churches.

Out of the handful of partial or complete rebuildings of
the main bodies of great churches which are known to have
been undertaken in the early fifteenth century, the most
impressive is the choir of the Benedictine abbey and former
cathedral at Sherborne in Dorset (plate 71). Begun around
1425, the Sherborne choir has long held an important place
in the surveys of English Gothic as the first building to possess a fan-vaulted central vessel. However, if more had survived of the Gloucester-inspired remodelling of the choir at
Glastonbury Abbey (begun c.1360), Sherborne's niche in the
history of Perpendicular might well have been a less prominent one. Glastonbury's choir vault is unfortunately totally
lost, but enough of the elevations remains to show that their
combination of relatively low main arcades surmounted by
panelled wall surface and high clearstorey windows anticipated the choirs not only of Sherborne but of Great
Malvern Priory (begun c.1430?), Bath Abbey (begun 1501)
(cat. no. 237), and Christchurch Priory, Hampshire (after
1502). Roughly contemporary with Sherborne is the nave of
Crowland Abbey, Lincolnshire.[17] Now a ruin, this little-
known building retains tall, elegantly detailed arcades quite
unlike Sherborne's, as well as tierceron vaults and clearstorey
wall passages influenced by the early thirteenth-century
nave of Lincoln Cathedral. Crowland seems to have engendered no imitations. The one major opportunity to design a
great church elevation in northern England during the early
sixteenth century came when Christopher Scune was hired
to rebuild the nave of Ripon Minster from 1503. His old-
fashioned and aridly detailed design reveals only too clearly
how remote from the creative centres of Perpendicular
Yorkshire had become since the early fifteenth century.

Fifteenth-century England's most accomplished example of
the great church genre was commissioned not by a cathedral
or major monastery but by King Edward IV. In 1475 the
Oxford architect Henry Janyns began work on St George's
Chapel in Windsor Castle, a church which, though func-
tionally unique in being the permanent seat of a chivalric
order, was intended to be cathedral-like in almost every
respect except its scale (plate 70, cat. no. 25). When Janyns
drew up the designs, it is clear that he had become
acquainted with virtually all the outstanding exampl
the Perpendicular style. But St George's is far from
mere compilation of 'classics', and possesses a r
and clarity due in large measure to the
'Tudor' arches (four-centred arches

almost straight and of very low pitch). The resultant flatten-
ing out of vault surfaces enabled the blind tracery patterning applied to them to be both more readable and more
similar in treatment to the vertical surfaces of the interior
elevations.

The only sequel to St George's was the Lady Chapel begun
at the east end of Westminster Abbey in 1503 and usually
known as Henry VII's Chapel, after its builder (plates 72, 1,
cat. no. 28). Intended to house the shrine of the canonized
Henry VI, in close proximity to the tomb of Henry VII and
his queen, the chapel was conceived as nothing less than a
legitimization of Henry VII's rule in the eyes of God and of
posterity. Its architecture is frankly triumphalist in spirit,
surpassing in almost every respect the chapel begun at
Windsor by Henry's predecessor and father-in-law, whose
memory he had every reason to detest. The high vault is aesthetically and technically the most ambitious of all fan
vaults, the first large-scale example to incorporate pendants
and to be built strictly in accordance with the method enunciated 150 years earlier in the vault of the Gloucester cloister
(plate 63). The elevations of the main vessel also outdo
Windsor, most obviously in the substitution of bands of
images in niches for the panelling between the two storeys.
The lower and more visible part of the exterior (plate 72)
takes as its starting point the oddest features of St George's:
the transepts treated like bay windows and the 'onion'
domelets on the turrets of the east and west fronts. In place
of buttresses, there are domelet-crowned octagonal turrets,
and every window is a bay window of extravagantly complex
form. Yet another aspect of Perpendicular exploited here,
and in the interior as well, is the small-scale delicacy and
richness of the distinctively English and obviously relevant
genre of commemorative chantry chapel (cf. cat. no. 109).
Whether Henry VII actually demanded a building conceived
as the culmination of the entire Perpendicular tradition we
do not know, but that is assuredly what he received from
Robert Janyns, son of the first architect of St George's,
Windsor.

It is tempting to view the pre-eminence of St George's and
Henry VII's Chapel within the great church genre as a
symptom of the growing power of the crown and of decline
in the institutional church. But to argue thus would be to
take insufficient account of the English monarchy's long-
established and uniquely strong tradition of patronizing
church-building projects of exceptional scale and quality, a

72   Westminster Abbey, Henry VII's Chapel, south side (cat. no. 28)

tradition whose most important surviving product is Henry III's rebuilding of Westminster Abbey.[18] It would also entail ignoring the fundamental reason for the decline in the numbers of large-scale rebuildings by major ecclesiastical corporations: their evident satisfaction with the existing settings for their worship. Their enthusiasm for putting up grandiose towers remained strong in the years immediately before the Reformation, as is evident from the freestanding bell-tower built at Evesham by Clement Lichfield, abbot from 1513 to 1539, and from the new steeples going up around this time over the south-west angle of the nave at St Werburgh's Abbey in Chester (now Chester Cathedral), above the eastern chapel (the 'Corona') at Canterbury Cathedral, and on the crossing at St Augustine's Abbey in Canterbury. The cathedrals and major abbeys also continued to be very active in patronizing building types which may be thought of as ancillary to their churches, but whose architecture could often be complex and sophisticated: Lady Chapels, monumentally treated fittings, including tombs and chantry chapels, and additions to their precincts such as gatehouses, cloisters and residences for their institutional heads (cat. nos 150, 228, 109, 233).

THE PARISH CHURCH

The number of complete and partial rebuildings of parish churches undertaken in the fifteenth and early sixteenth centuries is almost beyond reckoning, and it is doubtless the sheer size of this body of work that has deterred architectural historians from giving it the attention it so obviously deserves.[19] St Mary's, Nottingham, with which this essay began, is a case in point, for no attempt has ever been made to analyse the sources of the design and hence of the expertise that created a magnificent building without precedent in its locality. Nottingham is the sort of regional centre where, from a general western European viewpoint, one would expect to find a grand and prominently placed parish church. What is peculiar to England is that so many of the best parish churches are sited in the country, a pattern due in part to the diffusion of cloth production far beyond the cities and large towns.

The pattern is most striking in East Anglia, where the greatest number of ambitious new parish churches was built in the late Middle Ages. The church of the small village of Salle, 20 km north-east of Norwich (plate 37, cat. no. 257), boasts the region's most impressive nave of c.1400, though it must be said that it does not exceed the levels of display already attained in the grandest East Anglian churches by the mid-fourteenth century. That situation had changed entirely by 1430 when work began on

rebuilding the nave and chancel of St Peter Mancroft in the heart of Norwich, a 25-year process that made this the largest and most impressive church of its time in East Anglia (cat. no. 120). The division of responsibility for the fabric between the rector (chancel) and the parishioners (nave) did not result here, as it so often did when the parish had high ambitions, in a church whose nave completely outshone the chancel. At St Peter's there is no structural division separating the two parts, and the boundary between them was marked only by an open-work wooden rood-screen (now removed). This rarely achieved spatial unity was undoubtedly the late medieval ideal, for it shows off to perfection the tall arcades and unbroken bands of clearstorey windows. The roof at St Peter's is novel in that its projecting hammerbeams are encased within fictive wooden vaults modelled on the sort of coving often employed under the lofts of rood-screens. A quest for distinction is also apparent in the unusual treatment of the spandrels of the main arcades – niches containing stone statuary, the latter now destroyed. The obvious means of enriching the main internal elevations would have been to borrow the panelling motif from great church elevations, but it appears that until c.1460 the only parish churches treated thus were in Coventry.[20] East Anglia's earliest example of a nave with panelled elevations was commissioned by the leading lights of the small cloth-producing town of Burwell in Cambridgeshire (plate 73). An indication of their ambition is the likely authorship of the design, to all appearances the work of Reginald Ely, first architect of King's College Chapel, Cambridge. Completed in 1464, Burwell was soon imitated at Long Melford in Suffolk, where, however, the effect is diluted by the retention of relatively low fourteenth-century arcades. Other economy-minded parishes got a more modern effect by heightening the piers of the existing arcades before a new clearstorey was added.

One of Reginald Ely's successors at King's College Chapel, John Wastell, was responsible in the years either side of 1500 for a group of churches which took the Burwell scheme a stage further. The finest of these are Great St Mary's in Cambridge, Saffron Walden in Essex, and Lavenham in Suffolk (cat. no. 258).[21] From 1493 or 1494 Wastell had been architect of the central tower at Canterbury Cathedral, and it can be no coincidence that his parish church designs incorporate enriched versions of the tracery in the spandrels of the main arcades of Canterbury's 100-year-old nave (plate 118). No previous innovation in the internal architecture of English parish churches achieved such instantaneous success, and within a very few years versions of this kind of elevation had appeared in places as far apart as Manchester, Beverley and Martock in Somerset. Of these the finest is Manchester's collegiate church (now the cathedral), where the transmission of the idea was probably due to the fact that the provost of the college, James Stanley, was also Bishop of Ely, the diocese in which Cambridge lies.[22] Its elegantly detailed elevations enabled Manchester to outclass all the many parish churches built around the same time in its own locality of South Lancashire and in the adjoining parts of Cheshire and North Wales.[23] East Anglia and the north-west typify England's wealthier and more architecturally active regions in that from *c*.1490 onwards they witnessed rapid growth both in the volume of new buildings begun and in the amount of decoration lavished on those buildings.

Regions of England highly productive of parish churches where the influence of Wastell's new type was not felt were the far south-west, the south-east and the Cotswolds. In Devon and Cornwall, where there was a high degree of standardization, the norm was the clearstorey-less church with wide aisles covered by wagon roofs (plate 34, cat. no. 260) – a lower version of a type evidently invented in neighbouring Somerset during the late fourteenth century. The picture in the south-east is dominated by London, where resources were spread among well over 100 churches, mostly on cramped sites. Many of these buildings were destroyed in the Great Fire of 1666, but it is clear that they were modest by national standards, possessing plain and rather low towers, tracery-less aisle and clearstorey windows, and arcades of no great height borne on four-shaft piers whose detailing was remarkably unvaried. The parish churches of London, like those of Devon and Cornwall, serve to make the point – easily lost sight of in an essay such as this, where the emphasis is on 'highlights' – that the Perpendicular period was one that produced much run-of-the-mill work in response to a greatly increased demand. One factor that could well have been critical in the emergence of the prosaic parish-church architecture of London and the south-east is the high cost of importing freestone into a region without good building stone. In the Cotswolds, by contrast, excellent stone was readily available and this, combined with the presence of concentrations of wealth generated by large-scale wool production, and the proximity of the architecturally active cities of Gloucester, Bristol, Oxford and Coventry, ensured that considerable numbers of high-quality parish churches were built. Unlike East Anglia, the region produced no predominant type of elevation, and in that situation the way lay open for the emergence of solutions that were independent from the 'mainstream'. The building most obviously in this category is the remarkable central vessel of the nave at Northleach, the gift of a rich wool merchant in the 1450s (cat. no. 259).

About half a century before the new main vessel of Northleach was put in hand, the nave had acquired a west tower, a south aisle and a south porch (plate 74). That the peripheral parts of a nave should have been rebuilt piecemeal around an older core, well before the core itself underwent renewal, was by no means unusual and the practice probably had to do with patrons' preference for projects of limited scope. The kind of patronage most favoured among local elites was to build a side chapel at the east end of the nave or chancel, where chantry masses could be celebrated

74 Northleach church, Gloucestershire, south porch

tions to onlookers to pray for the donors' souls indicate that a spiritual benefit was expected to accrue.[24] Another major influence on the decision to rebuild ambitiously – inter-communal rivalry – is particularly evident in Somerset, where competitive tower-building took hold of many parishes during the later fifteenth century.[25] The Somerset towers, like those of English parish churches generally, were normally placed at the west end, where they had the advantage over crossing towers that they could safely rise to a great height. From the 1460s the smartest towers in Somerset and the adjoining parts of Gloucestershire appropriated Gloucester Abbey's openwork parapets and turrets (plates 69, 75). In trying to visualize the effect of church towers in the cities and larger towns, it is important to remember the activities of the friars, who in many respects were in competition with the parish clergy. Although almost all their churches were demolished soon after the Reformation, it is clear that from the late thirteenth century onwards the friars' architectural signature was a distinctive kind of tower, which was tall, slender, polygonal in plan and set over the central part of a rectangular-plan crossing. The best surviving fifteenth-century representative of the type is that

75   St Mary Magdalene's church, Taunton, Somerset, west tower

76   Franciscan friary church, King's Lynn, Norfolk, crossing tower from the east

and tombs accommodated. Such chapels were not infrequently the grandest piece of architecture in the whole church (cat. no. 329). Sometimes it was evidently necessary to coax parishioners into participating in a general rebuilding, by having the names of individual donors inscribed on the parts of the structure they had funded. No doubt such inscriptions pandered to worldly pride, but their exhorta-

of the Franciscan church at King's Lynn (plate 76). Influence from these structures accounts for the considerable vogue at urban parish churches for polygonally planned top storeys (plate 111).

SECULAR AND UNIVERSITY BUILDING

As in the period before 1400, there were few opportunities to treat non-ecclesiastical buildings with any degree of monumentality. Nevertheless, the fifteenth and early sixteenth centuries witnessed a growing taste for the rich treatment of individual elements, particularly bay windows lighting the high-table ends of halls and great chambers. The trend is evident from a comparison of New College with Magdalen, the grandest college to be built at Oxford during the fifteenth century (plate 67, cat. no. 245). It is remarkable that Oxford's collegiate architecture should have inherited, via New College, so much more of the coherence and monumentality of Edward III's Upper Ward at Windsor than did the houses of the aristocracy. One of the finest houses surviving from the mid-fifteenth century, Lord Treasurer Cromwell's Wingfield Manor in Derbyshire (begun after 1439), illustrates the continuance of the informality that was traditional in major domestic buildings (cat. no. 145). Perhaps emulation of Windsor would have smacked of treasonable ambition, as the Duke of Buckingham's wholesale borrowings from Henry VII's palaces almost certainly did in the early 1520s (cat. no. 147). The influence of Henry V's favourite residence at Sheen in Surrey probably lies behind the finest fifteenth-century timber-framed house still surviving, Ockwells Manor in Berkshire, built *c*.1445–50 by one of the most favoured members of Henry VI's household (cat. no. 144). Ockwells exemplifies the ease with which it was possible to assimilate the Perpendicular panel motif to the grid formed by timber framing. By contrast, brick building, which was rapidly coming into fashion in the mid-fifteenth century, was barely able to encompass even the most elementary aspects of Perpendicular, although it soon evolved, under Netherlandish influence, a sophisticated ornamental vocabulary peculiar to itself (cat. no. 147).

At Ockwells, as at virtually every rich man's house built in the late Middle Ages, the hall is the largest and most prominent room. An attempt to make the internal architecture of halls conform more closely to Perpendicular aesthetics can be seen in the house of the London merchant Sir John Crosby (*c*.1468), where the roof structure is hidden by a panelled ceiling equipped with delicate masonry-derived pendants (plate 77). Henry VIII's hall at Hampton Court (1532–4) contrives to combine panelled ceilings and pendants with an open hammerbeam roof in the tradition of

Westminster Hall (cat. no. 4, plate 25). Although halls generally retained their architectural pre-eminence, their social importance declined, for the head of the household now preferred to dine and sup, often amid much ceremonial, in the largest of his own rooms, the first-floor great chamber. The grandest examples of great chambers could incorporate many of the same internal features as halls and could be treated as ambitiously (cat. no. 146). The external architecture of chambers reached a new peak – an isolated one, as it turned out – in Henry VII's palaces, where the abundant

77 Crosby Place, London, roof of hall, T. Garner and A. Stratton, *Domestic Architecture of England during the Tudor Period*, London, 1929, vol. 2, p.218, fig. 305

and richly treated fenestration of the royal lodgings marked them out from their surroundings (cat. no. 3). A feature found at Ockwells and increasingly favoured in gentry houses was the near-symmetry generated by setting two storeys of chambers at either end of the hall. It would be misleading to suggest that English late medieval domestic architecture was characterized by a concerted move towards symmetry, but in the later fifteenth and early sixteenth centuries approximate symmetry was undoubtedly coming to be thought a desirable attribute of the growing number of major houses erected in a single campaign of work (plate 6, cat. no. 149).

Oxford and Cambridge colleges housed communities of men who, despite the fact that they were in holy orders, had domestic needs very similar to those of a lord's household. The main difference from a great layman's house was the absence of elaborate accommodation for the warden or provost who, unlike any self-respecting lord or gentleman, adhered to the ancient tradition of dining regularly in hall.

In the two outstanding earlier fifteenth-century examples of collegiate architecture, All Souls, Oxford (1439–43) and Queens', Cambridge (1448–9), the tradition of integrated planning pioneered at New College, Oxford, was continued.[26] Far more ambitious were Henry VI's colleges, Eton and King's, Cambridge, neither of which was completed in accordance with the founder's original intentions. At each, a scheme begun in 1441 was superseded in 1448 by another even more grandly conceived. The most remarkable survival from the first Eton scheme is the Cloister Court, whose walks were integrated into the surrounding ranges (cat. no. 23). This arrangement was particularly fashionable in the mid-century decades, and later influenced Magdalen College, Oxford (cat. no. 245). Of the first scheme for King's there survives an entrance range whose lavishly treated gatehouse may have provoked the frequently cited passage in Henry VI's 1448 'will' (a detailed description of the second scheme) in which the king states that he requires his buildings to be 'in large fourme clene and substancial, settyng a parte superfluite of too gret curious werkes of entaille [i.e. carving] and besy moldyng'. These comments, along with similar criticisms of the levels of richness at the Oxford Divinity School (cat. no. 246) made around the same time, have been interpreted as evidence of a decisive shift in English architecture towards 'aesthetic puritanism' and of 'a clearly enunciated programme of artistic reform'.[27] In reality they are nothing of the sort. If they amount to more than symptoms of anxiety in a period of economic recession, they are surely assertions of the need to employ an architectural manner appropriate to educational buildings, and of the need to avoid the extreme elaboration evident in some of the other major works in hand at the time, works with which the king will have been familiar (plate 119, cat. nos 86, 228).

In the chapels of Henry VI's colleges, simplicity is apparent only in the ground plans. The choir elevations of Eton Chapel are monumental rather than plain (plate 93), and the small part of King's Chapel built under Henry VI incorporates bare walling, but also a number of richly treated elements. When Henry VII decided to complete King's Chapel in 1506 his aim was totally different: an unabashed display of magnificence appropriate to a royal foundation (cat. no. 19). What had originally been intended as simple panelling below the windows of the antechapel now acquired very large and boldly conceived carvings of the royal arms and supporters, and the comparatively simple vault planned by Henry VI's architect was superseded by one of the most skilfully designed and sumptuously decorated of all large-scale fan vaults (cat. no. 19). The controlled exuberance of King's Chapel and its royal fellows at Windsor and Westminster set the tone for the first 30 years of Henry VIII's reign, but

though stylistically distinctive, early Tudor architecture cannot reasonably be regarded as a phase distinct from Perpendicular. Except for one or two exotic and relatively rarely used motifs – most obviously onion domelets (plate 72, cat. no. 28) – its sources lay within the rich and diverse traditions built up over the 150 years during which the Perpendicular style had been in existence.[28]

ARCHITECTS AND PATRONS

The nature of the work done by architects c.1400–1547 did not differ importantly from what it had been in the preceding century or so. Master masons (the term normally applied to architects responsible for stone structures in the medieval period) were men of very different status from the working masons who cut stones at the bench or set them in place. They were always producers of designs and often supervisors of a large workforce, and their skills in those respects were acknowledged by their classification as esquires, the lowest rank of the gentry. Nevertheless, the training of architects was craft-based, and all will have started off as cutting masons. Training purely as a designer, like today's architects, was not an option, and neither was a Brunelleschi-style move sideways from another craft.[29] By the late thirteenth century the day-to-day running of a large site could be deputed to a 'warden', a fully trained mason capable of resolving any technical problems as they occurred. This meant that architects whose services were in demand could concentrate on designing, visiting each of 'their' sites only when necessary.

What made a sought-after architect? No contemporary source provides a direct answer to this question. In a period that saw few innovations in masonry construction,[30] technical virtuosity on its own is less likely to have been the key than an established reputation as an originator of fashionable and aesthetically compelling designs. Indeed, there is usually a close correspondence between the prestige and cost of a building and the merit of its design, as indicated by the amount of imitation it engendered. This is illustrated by Richard Winchcombe's Divinity School at Oxford (begun 1430), almost certainly the building that popularized 'Tudor' arches and vaults of the same flattened curvature (cat. no. 246). Those who recruited Winchcombe as architect of this very prestigious building may have done so on the strength of the chancel at Adderbury church, Oxfordshire, which he had built from 1408 for New College. Being expensively finished, the Adderbury chancel would have served effectively as a showcase for Winchcombe's rich and idiosyncratic detailing. In 1439, when his successor at Oxford was appointed, the university authorities condemned the Divinity School's 'superfluous curiosity'. But they must have known perfectly well that responsibility for the design's elaborate character lay squarely with their predecessors, for it is inconceivable that Winchcombe would have begun work before producing drawings to indicate what his intentions were. Most of the mere handful of architectural drawings to have survived from late medieval England will have been made to show a design to a patron, rather than to be used by the architect himself (cat. nos 27, 118).[31]

Of the non-visual language by which architects and patrons communicated even less is preserved, although a fragment survives in a letter of Bishop Oliver King, rebuilder of Bath Abbey, which reports that the brothers Robert and William Vertue had boasted of their design for the vaults that 'ther shal be noone so goodeley neither in england nor in france. And therof they make theym fast and sure' (cat. no. 237). The ability to better the buildings of competitor institutions, which the Vertues clearly felt confident was theirs, will also have been of the utmost significance for patrons, whose prestige was involved. When designs for a particularly important project were being drawn up, it would sometimes have been in a patron's own interest to underwrite the 'artistic education' of the architect, to the extent of sending him on a trip to inspect relevant exemplars at first hand. This process, which is attested from the fourteenth century onwards, probably lies behind the indebtedness of Henry Janyns's work at St George's, Windsor, to a large number of buildings, most of them relatively distant from his home town of Oxford.

Patrons of ambitious structures could and did influence the appearance of their buildings by indicating the size and general level of richness required. Input of this kind is represented by Henry VI's 'avyse', which describes the third and final scheme for Eton Chapel shortly before construction began in 1449. And yet this text, despite its wholly exceptional length, conveys no sense whatsoever of the architectural character of the work, and fails to mention certain key features, including the vaults and the number of bays. The initiative in the formulation of designs for important buildings probably always lay mainly with the architect. This is demonstrable in the case of John Smyth's internal elevations of Eton Chapel, which are dominated by vault responds of a bulkiness matched only by those in the nave of Canterbury Cathedral, the church at which Smyth had worked for a long time before moving to Eton (plates 93, 118).[32] For comparatively modest undertakings, contracts could be drawn up which specified that some already existing building was to be copied, but this procedure was never followed in commissioning complex and costly structures, when the

expectation would always have been that the design would be 'bespoke', a product of the individual designer's creative intelligence.[33] There can be little doubt but that elite English patrons of the period c.1400–1540 considered themselves well served by their architects, and it is telling that in the well-known passage bewailing the dearth of skilled English painters, sculptors and embroiderers in Sir Thomas Elyot's *Governour*, published in 1531, there is no reference to masons or carpenters.[34] In a sense, architects were fortunate, for unlike late medieval English figural artists, who will have been under constant pressure to keep up with continental innovations, they were exponents of an evolving indigenous tradition that faced no serious challenge from abroad.[35] Admittedly, the 1520s and 1530s saw growing numbers of patrons commissioning buildings decorated with Renaissance motifs such as putti and arabesques, but these never amounted to more than exotic flourishes on designs whose sources were otherwise English.[36] And, as the comments of John Leland quoted at the start of this essay clearly imply, Perpendicular could still be thought of as England's modern architecture in the early 1540s, even though the social order it had served for so long was fast disappearing.

FURTHER READING

Crossley 1939; Fawcett 1982; Harvey 1978; Harvey 1984; Woodman 1986.

NOTES

1 Toulmin Smith 1906–10, I, p.94.

2 Like all other medieval architectural styles, Perpendicular was not given a name until long after its demise. Dating Perpendicular buildings can often be complicated by revivals internal to the style. This is particularly evident in window tracery, and some buildings (generally of lesser importance) include tracery patterns of diverse form and origin which the architect has made no attempt to harmonize.

3 For example, the decision taken in 1215 by the Bishop of Auxerre in Burgundy to demolish the Romanesque cathedral and rebuild it in the Gothic style is reported in the following terms: 'When the bishop saw that his church of Auxerre laboured under the disadvantages of its antiquated and less than well-built structure, its roughness and its old age, while all around other cathedrals were raising their heads [i.e. east ends] in a wonderful kind of beauty, he determined to adorn his church with a new building and with the studied art of those skilled in the craft of masonry' (my translation, from 'Gesta Pontificum Autissiodorensium', in Duru 1850–64, I, p.474).

4 Harvey 1978, pp.72–96. The fullest account of early Perpendicular is Wilson 1980a.

5 It was presumably this aspect of Perpendicular that led Nikolaus Pevsner to write that 'once [Perpendicular] had been created … it brushed aside all the vagaries of Decorated and settled down to a long, none too adventurous development of plain-spoken idiom,

sober and wide-awake' (Pevsner 1963, p.128). Pevsner's great enthusiasm for Decorated clearly arose, even if he himself did not realize it, from what he perceived to be its relevance to German Late Gothic. His 'none too adventurous' jibe could equally well be applied to the majority of national Late Gothic traditions, for these were well established by c.1400 and continued without radical modification for more than a century. His description of Perpendicular as 'a plain-spoken idiom, sober and wide-awake' presumably refers to his curious teleological notion, expressed elsewhere in the same work, that the style was a sign of late medieval England's supposed predisposition to accept Protestantism.

6 Strictly speaking, the choir at Gloucester is the crossing, where the choir stalls stand and which was remodelled c.1337–51 to a design very like that of the following phase, the east arm. But the popular usage of applying the term choir to the east arm, followed here, dates back in England to the twelfth century.

7 On the history of the term 'Perpendicular', see the essay by Alexandrina Buchanan in this volume (pp.135–6).

8 Fan vaults grew out of a long English Gothic tradition of conoidal vaults, the most spectacular of which are those over the central piers of polygonal chapter houses.

9 The only self-contained treatment of the fan vault is Leedy 1980, but see also Wilson 1980a, pp.260–77.

10 Wilson 1980a, p.226, pls 401, 440.

11 The attribution of the Canterbury nave to Yevele has proved to be controversial, but the stylistic evidence, which is in my view entirely confirmatory of Yevele's authorship, has yet to be discussed in appropriate detail.

12 St Mary Redcliffe, Bristol, and the nave of Steeple Ashton, Wiltshire.

13 Wilson 1997, pp.45, 58.

14 Wilson 2002, pp.81–2.

15 Harvey 1984, pp.66–7, 133; Harvey 1977, pp.169–70, 190.

16 Harvey 1978, p.135.

17 Fulman 1684, pp.497, 515, 535–6, possibly indicating 1405–22 as the main building period, and certainly placing the vaults after 1427.

18 The uniqueness of this tradition has not been generally acknowledged, despite the obvious and easily ascertainable fact that no other European monarchy commissioned a series of major ecclesiastical buildings comparable to that which extends forwards from Edward the Confessor's reconstruction of Westminster Abbey.

19 Currently or recently active scholars who are honourable exceptions to this generalization include Richard Fawcett, John Goodall, Birkin Haward, Linda Monckton, Eileen Roberts and Francis Woodman. Nevertheless, the volume of publication on parish churches, as on Perpendicular generally, remains disappointingly small.

20 St John the Baptist and the nave of Holy Trinity, both poorly documented but belonging to the late fourteenth century, and St Michael, apparently mostly of the 1440s and 1450s.

21 Woodman 1986, p.200.

22 The central vessel of the Manchester nave is usually dated c.1465–81, but the main arcade spandrels (if they are not inventions of the Victorian restorer) indicate an early sixteenth-century date. A starting date of c.1500 for the central vessel of the choir is suggested by the fact that its splendid stalls were being made c.1506.

23 The nave at Mold in Flintshire (now Clwyd) is evidently modelled on Manchester. For parish-church building in this region, see Crossley 1939; Alexander and Crossley 1976, pp.68–99.

24 Among the more notable examples of parish churches bearing inscriptions requesting prayers for donors of specified features are Beverley, Cirencester, Lavenham and Long Melford.

25 The only recent survey of the subject is Wright 1981. See also Harvey 1982 and French 2001, passim.

26 Jacob 1933; RCHM 1939, pp.15–19; Willis and Clark 1886, II, pp.1–68; RCHM 1959, pp.167–78.

27 Harvey 1972, p.252; Harvey 1978, pp.174, 183. Harvey's over-interpretation of the references to rich detailing in Henry VI's 'will' and the Divinity School indenture grows out of the interpretation, based too narrowly on Oxford evidence, in Davis 1946–7, p.80. See also Colvin 1963, I, p.288. The text of Henry VI's 'wills' for Eton and King's and his 'avyse' for Eton Chapel are printed in Willis and Clark 1886, I, pp.352–7, 366–7, 368–70.

28 I am uncertain why John Harvey believed that Perpendicular after 1485 was not really Perpendicular at all, but rather 'a fresh style, largely fertilized from abroad' (Harvey 1978, p.162).

29 A handful of cases is known of masons and master masons who were also competent in carpentry.

30 The nearest thing to a technical invention – the construction of fan vaults from finely jointed freestone – is really little more than a specialized application of the French Rayonnant technique of building in large and more or less standardized blocks, which was introduced into England during the later thirteenth century.

31 No evidence is available from late medieval English sources to suggest that three-dimensional architectural models played any part in the design process or in informing patronal choices.

32 Harvey 1984, p.276. Except for another comparison with Canterbury Cathedral (Woodman 1986, p.131), the literature on Eton includes no discussion of the sources drawn on by John Smyth for the detailing of his design.

33 Perhaps the most important Perpendicular buildings to reproduce earlier works more or less exactly are the parish-church naves at Newark, Nottinghamshire (based on Holy Trinity, Hull) and Chipping Camden, Gloucestershire (based on Northleach).

34 Crofts 1883, I, pp.139–40.

35 The only foreign motifs that took hold were 'onion' domelets and tall brick chimneys with neo-Romanesque patterning, both of Netherlandish derivation.

36 The only definite instance of the use of an Italian building type during Henry VIII's reign is the 'ambulatory' or loggia of c.1527–9 in the garden of Horton Court, Gloucestershire. The design of this structure otherwise adheres to the Perpendicular idiom of the locality.

X

MUSIC SEEN AND MUSIC HEARD: MUSIC IN ENGLAND *c.*1400–1547

MARGARET BENT

Visitors to an exhibition may see musical manuscripts containing notated compositions, and they may hear discreet recorded background music designed to set atmosphere, music purporting to be from the period and perhaps from the manuscripts exhibited. Notated compositions are the literature of music; few people now read music silently, though in antiquity and the Middle Ages even the silent reading of verbal text was unusual. However much we know about old pronunciation, the actual sounds of spoken language cannot be recovered before the age of recording, and only then with constraints. The same applies to old music, which comes to us only in writing. Sound is central, music demands performance, but no efforts of reconstruction will bring back original sound. No amount of contextual or analytical knowledge can render 'authentic' any modern performance of music from whose living traditions we are severed, let alone produce the same effect on modern audiences.

Music – and drama – that was never written down, or of which no copy survives, has gone completely. Music that has come to us only in written form can be performed with skill and conviction, much as we do with Shakespeare's plays. But even a half-century of early music recordings demonstrates how each generation remakes music, applying to the bare written notes different tastes in performative rhetoric that may have little to do with those of its creators. For guidance we have only descriptions of the effect on listeners or the magnificence of an occasion; pedagogical and technical writings on the basics of musical grammar and performance practice; and written compositions that record the substance of musical thought, but not its sound.

Pictures can in principle be viewed at any time, but music must be activated, and paid for on each occasion. Notated music, moreover, was useful only to those who could read it, which made manuscripts additionally vulnerable after their day had passed. The problem is compounded by generational change and destruction; old music was lifeless once detached from the performing styles within which it was born.

The rites of the medieval church and its books can seem dauntingly complex but help is at hand.[1] Pre-Reformation English uses (the liturgies and rituals of the church) are dominated by

78 Old Hall manuscript,
Gloria by 'Roy Henry'
(Henry V) (cat. no. 14)

the Use of Salisbury (or Sarum), which differs somewhat from continental and monastic rites. Monophonic or single-line music, so-called Gregorian chant or plainsong, was the staple fare of Catholic church music from early times up to Vatican II (1962–5), composed over time but in a timeless tradition, a great treasury of unaccompanied melody to carry the sacred words. The priest's words and music for the Mass were contained in the missal (cat. nos 253, 308), for the Office in the breviary (cat. nos 72, 103). Books of Hours (see for example cat. nos 223–5), often beautifully illuminated, were reduced breviaries personalized for individual devotions. The choir's music for the Mass was found in a gradual, for the Office in an antiphonal (cat. no. 312). Although some central texts remained standard, the precise contents in each case could differ considerably to reflect local saints and local observances.

Very few books have remained in their original locations, but the provenance of others can sometimes be determined by localized contents and calendars. From about 1500, printing enabled easier reproduction of liturgical books, most easily of text alone (cat. nos 309, 310), but also of music. Printing also tended to curb local variation, even in the few decades that preceded the liturgical upheavals of the Reformation.

Most ordinary citizens in the Middle Ages would only ever have heard plainsong in their parish churches. In some larger establishments, part music, or polyphony, was composed to adorn the ritual, starting from about the year 1000 and reaching a remarkable flowering in England under Edward VI, shortly before a severe pruning at the Reformation.[2] Unlike the continuous but evolving tradition of plainsong, styles of polyphonic art-music changed rapidly by generation, subject to constant renewal and replacement. Whereas liturgical books containing plainchant follow standardized patterns, with local variation, each polyphonic manuscript is a uniquely compiled anthology with entirely unpredictable content. A single leaf surviving from a liturgical manuscript could be placed as, say, the Easter Office in the antiphonal (cat. no. 312); an isolated polyphonic leaf may reveal only that the pieces represented (incompletely) on each of its sides were adjacent.

No intact English polyphonic manuscripts survive between the Winchester Troper of *c.*1000 and the Old Hall manuscript of about 1415–25 (plate 78, cat. no. 14).[3] Even the Old Hall and Eton[4] Choirbooks lack some of their original contents (cat. no. 24). The Worcester Fragments of around 1300 consist of leaves from choirbooks dismembered long before the Reformation. Between Old Hall and the death of Henry VIII there are about a dozen substantially complete polyphonic manuscripts representing mostly liturgical genres, but also some secular song. Many more manuscripts are represented by fragments of just one to several leaves.

Although a significant increase over the preceding century, this relative dearth of fifteenth-century English manuscripts led earlier scholars to believe that English composers must have worked mainly on the Continent, where most of the known works survive. Recent discoveries of fragmentary sources everywhere show that losses are due largely to regular destruction and recycling, and are not confined to England. Almost nothing remains from the court of France, or of the copies made by the Burgundian court scribe Simon Mellet of dozens of works by Du Fay and his contemporaries. Copies of English and continental music are found in backwaters or on mountain trade routes that were not flushed out by regular repertorial renewal. The seven codices at Trent on the Brenner Pass are vast repositories containing sometimes disfigured but often unique versions of more than 1,800 pieces, including many English compositions; but that they are there at all attests to wide circulation, not that they were undervalued at home.

Some English composers did travel: the composer John Pyamour was a clerk in Henry V's chapel (see below, p.127, for the term), which accompanied the king in France from 1417 to 1421, and in 1427 he went there with John, Duke of Bedford, regent in France during the minority of Henry VI. The leading English composer John Dunstaple (d. 1453) was at different times in the service of Bedford, the dowager Queen Joan and Humphrey, Duke of Gloucester, and owned French lands;[5] Leonel Power may have travelled to France with Thomas, Duke of Clarence before 1421.[6] English musicians accompanied their patrons to church councils which,

like international conferences now, served as channels for employment and cultural exchange. The Council of Constance was a major conduit for the transmission of notated English music to the Continent, where it appears from about 1420. The Richental Chronicle reports that on St Thomas's Eve 1416 the English sent four sackbut players throughout Constance, and performed Vespers in the cathedral with sweet singing. The chronicler does not tell us whether they sang polyphony; organs are mentioned, but it is unclear whether they accompanied the singers.[7] Important continental guests also heard English music *in situ.* In August 1416 Henry V entertained the Emperor Sigismund; both attended a service of thanksgiving in Canterbury Cathedral for the Duke of Bedford's victory at Harfleur and the battle of the Seine, at which two motets by Dunstaple were evidently performed.[8] Gilles Binchois, demonstrably influenced by English music, was for a while in the service of the Duke of Suffolk, and Dunstaple's patron and obituarist, John Wheathampstead, Abbot of St Albans, entertained the circle of Humphrey, Duke of Gloucester, including Pietro del Monte and other humanists.

Many music manuscripts have been lost, as we know on the one hand from archives, payments, wills and inventories,[9] and on the other from surviving fragments. Some 250 leaves from dismembered English musical manuscripts for the period *c.*1400–1547 are all that remain of about 200 original manuscripts, some of which were large volumes of perhaps 100 or more folios.[10] Such loss was earlier attributed to the widespread destruction of popish manuscripts by Protestant reformers. It is now clear that many such manuscripts were dismembered much earlier, often within half a century of their original copying. Most of those leaves survive only because they were used in book-bindings, albeit further vulnerable to discarding when the books were rebound. Of the manuscripts cut up for lining or repairing houses, shoes and instruments, or used for sewing, baking and wrapping, almost nothing remains. Old music was like last week's newspapers, fit only for recycling. On the other hand, pieces occasionally survive in surprisingly late copies. Music by Dunstaple was still in circulation in the 1520s, and we learn from the index of the Eton Choirbook that it once contained a setting of his *Gaude flore virginali.* An anonymous composition fitting the index description, incomplete and unperformable, survives in a much-damaged paper manuscript (plate 79).[11]

The Old Hall manuscript includes a setting of the Gloria by Henry V (plate 78, cat. no. 14) and seems to have been prepared for the chapel of Thomas, Duke of Clarence,[12] before being taken over by the chaplains whom the infant Henry VI inherited from his father.[13] It is the first English

79 *Gaude flore virginali*, anon., Dunstaple?, incomplete (British Library Add. MS 54324, f.3v)

repertory, which found its way to the scrap pile of the early sixteenth-century Cambridge binder Nicholas Spierinck: two leaves are still in a Spierinck binding, two more demonstrably removed from one. Capitals at the heads of sections were evidently ornamented with royal beasts, including lions and a Lancastrian antelope.[14]

The normal layout for polyphonic music was in 'choirbook' format – that is, with the voice-parts copied separately (not vertically aligned as in modern scores). In the Gloria by Henry V (plate 78, cat. no. 14) the more elaborate and dominant topmost part, on the left-hand page, takes up twice as much space as each of the lower parts that go with it (contratenor and tenor), both placed on the right-hand page, though all parts are performed together and occupy the same amount of musical time. The whole piece is very compactly notated, without bar-lines, but takes up many pages of modern score, where the lower parts have to be spaced out to align graphically with the larger number of short notes in the top part. The singers of all three parts read from different areas of the open pages, but all can see their music at the same time (the chequered pattern at the end of the left-hand page simply fills up the blank stave). The three or four simultaneous voice parts normal in the austere style of the early fifteenth century gave way to a norm of five or six parts and more elaborate style by the end of the century. Compositions became not only richer in texture (more voices), but much longer, so that even with a larger format, a composition sometimes spreads over several manuscript openings. Despite its large format, Fayrfax's antiphon *Eterne laudis lilium* in Lambeth (cat. no. 311) required three manuscript openings (of which the exhibited opening, f.56v–57, is the first), so arranged that for all five parts the singers can turn the page at the same time. The same applies to Lambe's five-voice *Salve Regina* in Eton (cat. no. 24). In these later styles, each part occupies more nearly equal space on the page, reflecting more equal activity throughout the texture. Such music was evidently performed by voices alone, without organ or other instruments.[15]

The exhibited choirbooks reflect the progressively increasing size of manuscripts containing the most prestigious genres of sacred music from the early fifteenth to the early sixteenth century, from Old Hall at slightly less than A3 size to the Eton manuscript at more than twice that size, and the even larger Lambeth book.[16] None of this English sacred repertory was printed. Continental manuscripts rarely attain these latter proportions, and continental Masses and motets were published from soon after 1500. The illustrations to this essay complement the handsome books chosen for exhibition by including samples of more modest format and quality.

Smaller-scale compositions, whether liturgical works, secular songs or compositions for fewer voices, were usually

manuscript to name a significant number of composers, a striking change from the almost complete anonymity of the fourteenth century and even from some later manuscripts. Foremost in number and distinction of compositions is Leonel Power, who served in Clarence's chapel; pre-eminent is 'Roy Henry', now thought to be Henry V. Seventeen leaves recovered from book bindings have been identified as coming from a single dismembered royal choirbook some ten years younger than Old Hall, and with some overlap of

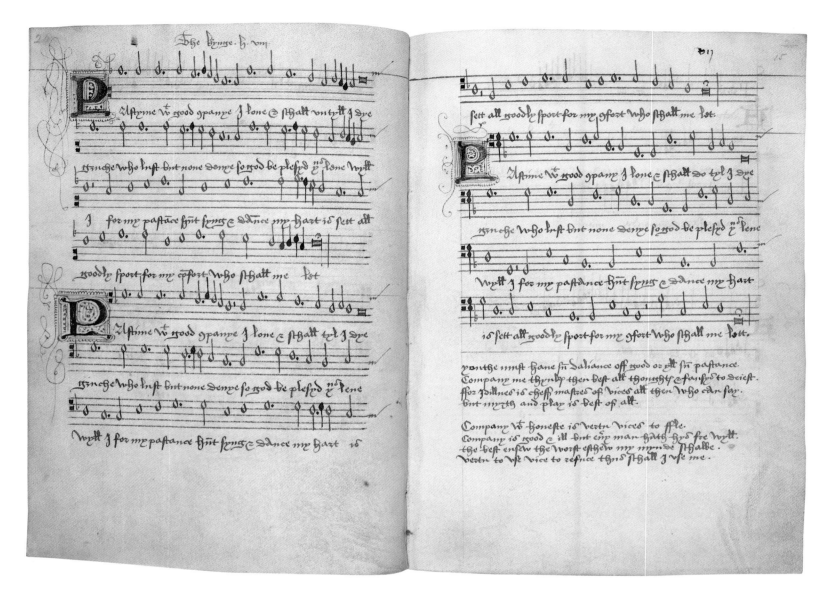

copied in manuscripts of smaller format (approximately A4 or letter size), such as the Egerton and Selden manuscripts, with carols and liturgical pieces, the Fayrfax manuscript from the reign of Henry VII, with more extended carols and songs, and the Henry VIII manuscript (plate 80 and see below, pp.126–7).

Some of these simpler genres are found, in England only, and even in de luxe manuscripts like Old Hall, in aligned score with the words under the lowest part and the parts one above the other. Most of the earlier English carols were laid out in this way, including the famous carol that narrates Henry V's triumphs in Normandy, naming Harfleur and Agincourt, shown here from a parchment carol roll (or scroll) in Trinity College, Cambridge (plate 81).[17] In this case, the notes are hollow or 'void', not filled in, as in the more formally notated manuscripts on display.

The great choirbooks now at Caius College, Cambridge, and Lambeth Palace (cat. no. 311) were copied by one scribe who also copied – albeit more roughly – another roll, containing a single voice-part, a separate performing part, also in void notation. Firmly anchored in archives at Arundel Castle (plate 82), it supports the hypothesis that both choirbooks were assembled for Arundel College, attesting to the repertory that flourished there under the mastership (from 1520) of Edward Higgins, previously in royal service.[18] Numerous other places enjoyed an equal level of musical cultivation and must have had similar books, now perished.

The separate copying of a single part points to another format for music copying which increased in popularity in the early sixteenth century: a set of part-books. Unlike the choirbooks discussed above, in this case each singer held a book containing just his own part for all the compositions

80 Henry VIII's manuscript, *Pastime with good company* by Henry VIII (cat. no. 15)

81 The Agincourt Carol, Trinity carol roll (Trinity College, Cambridge, MS O.3.58). The carol is at the top of the illustrated portion (*Deo gracias Anglia*)

82 Bass part of *Gaude flore virginali* by Nicholas Ludford, from a music roll copied by the scribe of the Lambeth Choirbook, cat. no. 311 (Arundel Castle Archives, MS A340)

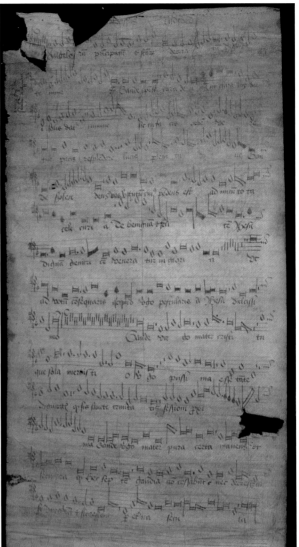

in the collection and, like a string quartet player today, his knowledge of and ability to coordinate with the other parts came more from listening than from looking at them. One of the earliest known part-books is a manuscript at Shrewsbury containing the third shepherd's part of a Christmas liturgical drama, also parts of two early Gospel passion settings (simple polyphonic passions are found earlier in England than anywhere else; others are in the Egerton manuscript and in fragmentary sources). There are just two important sets of pre-Reformation English part-books, complementing the copies of festal Masses and antiphons in the great choirbooks of the early sixteenth century: the Forrest-Heyther and the 'Henrician' Peterhouse set.[19] The Henrician set lacks one of its books, one entire 'horizontal' strand; some, but not all, of its contents can be completed from other copies in the choirbooks.

The Old Hall manuscript groups Mass movements of the same kind together, with separate sections devoted to Glorias in score, Glorias in choirbook layout, and Credos similarly, even after composers had begun to compose musically linked movements. Musically connected movements were often copied adjacent to each other in continental sources, and only later in English manuscripts, but copying habits changed by mid-century to recognize the musically unified Mass cycles initiated by Dunstaple and Power, continued by Walter Frye, and culminating in the great Masses by Taverner, Fayrfax and Ludford in the early sixteenth century.

At no time until the Beatles did English music again have such an impact outside its own country as in the early to mid fifteenth century. This statement is based partly on manuscript transmission and detectable compositional influence, and partly on famous sayings by two continental writers. The French poet Martin Le Franc's long poem *Le champion des dames* credits the leading Burgundian composers Du Fay and Binchois with finding 'a new way of making lively harmony in public and in chamber music (loud and soft), in the way they inflect and articulate it, and have adopted the *contenance angloise* (the English manner) following Dunstaple, wherefore wondrous pleasure renders their song joyful and noteworthy'. It seems that the 'English manner' relates to music as performed rather than as written, music of the present, and music within living memory. For us, music as written and music as sound are perforce separate, for we have the one but not the other, but the distinction would have seemed incomprehensible then. The other testimony is from the Franco-Flemish music theorist Johannes Tinctoris, writing for a different public in the 1470s. In the preface to his *Proportionale Musices* (1472–5) he refers to a new art arising among the English, of which Dunstaple was the origin and head: *caput, fons et origo*. Dunstaple's position as the leading composer of the first half of the fifteenth century is corroborated by the survival of some 50 works, mostly in continental manuscripts, closely followed in number by Leonel Power. They, together with a number of other less widely preserved composers, served various members of the royal family. The written compositions show many technically and stylistically distinctive features. The most audible ones – a tendency to full sonorities and to particular rhythmic and melodic patterns – must have been enhanced by a distinctively English performance style. In the same preface Tinctoris reported: *Hec eis Anglici nunc, licet vulgariter jubilare, Gallici vero cantare dicantur* ('The English are commonly said to jubilate, the French however to sing'). Similar statements recur in early sixteenth-century accounts, including a report of the Venetian ambassadors in 1516, judging that the King's choristers *non cantavano ma giubilavano* ('They didn't so much sing, as

jubilate') and praising the quality of English bass voices. This must refer as much to the performed effect as to the compositional technique of an increasingly rich and florid multi-voice style, whose wide range showed off the high trebles and low basses to fine effect.[20]

Almost without exception the surviving written music of the period, including all the exhibited items, was intended for performance by unaccompanied voices. Many churches had organs before the Reformation, either fixed or portable, but most were destroyed then and in the following century. Cardinal Wolsey had both a large and a small 'pair' of organs in his chapel at Hampton Court.[21] English organs did not yet have pedals, but they could play much of the surviving keyboard repertory for which the available keyboard instruments were largely interchangeable. Organs were not used to accompany polyphony, but for solo voluntaries, or to play (in alternation with verses sung in chant) 'organ verses', which often harmonized the chant. Three collections of keyboard music survive from the end of our period, mostly arrangements of vocal or ensemble pieces or elaborations of chant. Hugh Aston's famous 'Hornpipe' was not followed by other dances or character pieces until the following decades.

The *Mary Rose* shawm (plate 83) is one of a tiny number of surviving instruments. Even where we have a damaged or restored artefact, or where older pipework has been incorporated in a rebuilt organ, almost everything about pitch and timbre remains uncertain. Pictures are primary sources for what early instruments were like, literary and archival references for how they were used.

The classification of medieval instrumental music into *haut* and *bas*, loud (public instruments, such as trumpets, shawms and sackbuts) and soft (indoor, strings, recorders and lutes), reflects practical and acoustic considerations and a sense of decorum that no longer apply, with categories blurred by recordings and by interchangeable venues for music. But they were very real at the English court in the reigns of Henry VII and Henry VIII in the establishment of distinct instrumental groups to serve the public and private areas. Henry VIII assembled, by 1547, a huge band of 58 secular musicians, mostly instrumentalists.[22] His leading court and chapel musician was William Cornysh, who played a major role in the pageantry and entertainments ('revels') at the Field of Cloth of Gold in 1520.

Religious music overwhelmingly exceeds secular song in the period. Until the sixteenth century almost the only English vernacular texts set to music were carols, and a handful of courtly English songs (by Frye and Bedingham) preserved in foreign manuscripts. Courtly song came late to England, in the Tudor period.[23] The 'Fayrfax' manuscript is the first high-art manuscript of music with English texts, with 49 songs and carols, apparently for all-vocal performance, decidedly by professionals, not amateurs. The texts situate it in the reign of Henry VII, before the death of Prince Arthur. The prevailing mood is introspective and pessimistic, especially in the compositions by Henry's own musicians; the texts are largely characterized by religious devotion and melancholy, and by courtly love. Its sequel is very different in tone, with jollier English part-songs on courtly and chivalric themes: the 'Henry VIII Manuscript' (plate 80, cat. no.15), so called because it includes more than 30 compositions credited to 'the King Henry VIII'. Although Henry received musical training in childhood, played the keyboard and other instruments, his role and competence as a composer are uncertain: a version of one of these songs had been published in Venice in 1501.

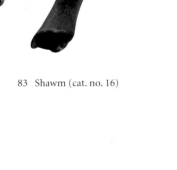

This manuscript contains the first purely instrumental pieces without text that must have been part of the repertory of Henry's enormous collection of instruments and instrumentalists; these may also have played arrangements of vocal polyphonic music, but probably did not perform together with voices. There are few signs of a notated instrumental repertory adequate to these forces, and we may assume that much of what they played was unwritten, though not necessarily spontaneous or improvised. Other survivals of English secular song are patchy and much less well documented than sacred genres. But secular songs account for three out of the four known examples of music (other than plainsong) printed in England before 1540, the exception being the Lutheran *Goostly Psalmes and Spiritual Songes* translated from German by Miles Coverdale in the mid-1530s. A new rich contextualization of these printed and manuscript song remnants relates them to items in the King Henry VIII manuscript.[24]

Throughout the later Middle Ages the Chapel Royal was not a place, but rather a peripatetic staff that travelled with the monarch, including a choir. Henry IV maintained the chapel at its existing strength of 24 gentlemen and four boys; Henry V enlarged it to the exceptional size of 32 gentlemen and 16 boys. For the rest of our period the numbers approached – but never exceeded – this size. In addition, other foundations associated with royal palaces had fixed staffs and became major centres of musical cultivation. Chief among these were the twin choral foundations of St Stephen's in the Palace of Westminster and St George's Chapel in Windsor Castle, the latter established by Edward III to pray for the souls of the king and his knights; its choir was now doubled in size. Choral establishments expanded in the fifteenth century and became more stable. Lady Chapel choirs were established and flourished at many major churches: Leonel Power

83 Shawm (cat. no. 16)

was probably the first director of such a choir at Canterbury.[25] This growth is reflected in the increase in the number of voice-parts from an average of three in Old Hall to five or more in Eton and Lambeth. Late-fifteenth-century statutes spell out the duties of choirmasters, giving some idea of pedagogy and education, and of unwritten and partly written practices – such as techniques of harmonizing chant, often by rule-of-thumb procedures (see also cat. no. 272)

Founded in 1438 by the septuagenarian Archbishop of Canterbury, Henry Chichele, and his teenage godson Henry VI, All Souls College, Oxford, is the first of an important series of royal collegiate educational foundations. Following the paired example of Winchester College and New College a century earlier, Henry VI went on to found Eton and King's colleges. Unlike these, All Souls was not a choral foundation, but the Fellows extensively cultivated polyphony around 1500, apparently including some of the Eton Choirbook repertory. The organ was dutifully destroyed at the Reformation and, unusually, was never replaced. The college statutes require prayer for the souls of Thomas, Duke of Clarence and his brother Henry V, the only two named dead among the general provision for the nameless dead of the Hundred Years War, a further echo of the Old Hall manuscript, and of the rich but sketchily preserved musical traditions spanning the period between two royal composers: Henry V and Henry VIII.

FURTHER READING

Bowers 1999; Harrison 1958; Grove 2001; Milsom 1997; Stevens 1961.

NOTES

1 Harper 1991.

2 Benham 1977, Strohm 1993.

3 Bent 1967–8.

4 Williamson 1995, 1997, 2000a, 2000b.

5 Bent 1981, Wathey 1986, 1989.

6 Bowers 1999.

7 Harrison 1958, p.243.

8 Bent 1981, p.8.

9 Wathey 1988.

10 Curtis and Wathey 1994; see also the Digital Image Archive of Medieval Music (DIAMM) at www.diamm.ac.uk, for images of many sources and examples of the virtual restoration of illegible items.

11 Bent 1969.

12 Bowers 1999.

13 Bent 1967–8.

14 Bent 1984.

15 Bowers 1999; Morehen 1995.

16 See cat. nos 14, 24 and 311 for the respective dimensions.

17 Over 200.7 cm long and just 17.8 cm wide.

18 Skinner 1997, 2002, 2003.

19 Sandon 1976–7.

20 Harrison 1958, pp.171, 258.

21 Bowers 1999.

22 Ashbee 1997, Kisby 1997a, and for Lady Margaret Beaufort, Kisby 1997b.

23 Stevens 1961.

24 Milsom 1997.

25 Bowers 1999, 2001; Kisby 1995.

XI

PERSPECTIVES OF THE PAST: PERCEPTIONS OF LATE GOTHIC ART IN ENGLAND

ALEXANDRINA BUCHANAN

'Now, our perception of former times, our historical organ, so to say, is more and more becoming visual. Most educated people of to-day owe their conception of Egypt, Greece, or the Middle Ages, much more to the sight of their monuments, either in the original or by reproductions, than to reading. The change of our ideas about the Middle Ages is due less to a weakening of the romantic sense than to the substitution of artistic for intellectual appreciation.'[1]

84 Christ Church, Oxford, hall staircase; vault *c.*1640 by 'Smith' of London, staircase 1805 by Wyatt

Starting from this insight, Johan Huizinga (1872–1945) created a work which has profoundly influenced both the perception of the late Middle Ages and the interpretation of culture. His book, originally written in Dutch and first translated into English as *The Waning of the Middle Ages* (though *The Autumn of the Middle Ages*, a later English title, might be preferable), encompassed an entire civilization, using artistic works as evidence for history, rather than using historical context to account for art.[2] This aim underpins many modern analyses of 'visual culture'. But Huizinga's work should not be seen purely in terms of present preoccupations. He believed that the culture of his time was more visually orientated than its predecessors – and this condition can only have been enhanced since his day by means of colour photography, film, television and IT. Yet Huizinga's generation was by no means the first to respond to the monuments of the late Middle Ages. These works had been a recurring source of fascination, both intellectual and artistic, throughout successive centuries. Moreover, changing perceptions were cumulative, continuing to affect the views of subsequent ages. When looking at the objects on display in the exhibition, we may feel that we are experiencing direct contact with their makers and users. This is a fiction, for we cannot entirely strip away the mentalities of our own era. Nevertheless, the palimpsest from which our own responses are formed should not be perceived as a screen, obscuring our view of the 'real' Middle Ages. It is instead an enrichment, a developing inheritance linking the present with the past.

Readers of Nikolaus Pevsner's *Buildings of England* series – indeed, of most works of architectural history – will be familiar with the identification of English late medieval architecture

as 'Perpendicular'. It is thus characterized by dominant verticals in its tracery, four-centred arches and all-over panelling.[3] We need not have read Thomas Rickman (1776–1841), who coined the term and its definition, for his insight to affect our interpretation. His seminal essay of 1817 identified the styles of English medieval architecture as Norman, Early English, Decorated and Perpendicular and thus created a 'periodic table' for medieval architecture.[4] Although his labels have stuck, Rickman was not the first to attempt the exercise: for over a century scholars had been attempting to create a system by which buildings could be dated by style. The methodology, with its promise of quasi-scientific accuracy, proved alluring. The pioneering studies of most types of medieval object, from stained glass to monumental brasses, have first sought to establish systems of classification.[5] It was through such structures that the late Middle Ages came to be identified as a distinct cultural era.

Although Rickman's scholarship had antecedents, their influence was limited. Before the nineteenth century, medieval art was generally perceived in its entirety as the 'other' to the norm of Classicism. The Middle Ages were both invented and pronounced dead, somewhat prematurely, in the fifteenth and sixteenth centuries, by Italian Renaissance humanists.[6] Meanwhile, in England, no one seemed concerned (or even aware) that the death-certificate had been signed, until the wholesale assault by the State on many of the fundamental aspects of medieval culture, otherwise known as the Reformation. Even then, only a few nostalgic conservatives seem to have mourned the passing of the medieval world until the Industrial Revolution ensured that from the later eighteenth century, in western Europe at least, its traditions were both dead and buried.

It was not merely the passage of time that served to de-familiarize the Middle Ages. Whilst the Reformation branded the Middle Ages with the taint of Popery, a Classical education served to make an Englishman feel at home among the ruins of ancient Rome. It also taught him to disparage more recent remains, associating them with the Goths, the barbaric destroyers of ancient civilization. For the Classical propagandist John Evelyn (1620–1706), Henry VII's Chapel (plate 89, cat. no. 28) was proof of the poor taste of Gothic, with its 'sharp *Angles*, *Jetties*, Narrow Lights, lame Statues, *Lace* and other *Cut-work* and *Crinkle-Crankle*', in comparison with the 'Majesty, and solemn Greatness' of Inigo Jones's Whitehall Banqueting House or Christopher Wren's work at St Paul's Cathedral.[7]

Yet the combined ideologies of Renaissance and Reformation could not entirely extinguish the allure of medieval objects. The indefatigable traveller Celia Fiennes (1662–1741) visited Warwick in 1697. Ignoring other aspects of

86 Arbury Hall, Nuneaton,
Warwickshire, dining hall;
Sir Roger Newdigate and
Henry Keene, 1769–73

85 Chalice and paten lid,
silver-gilt, English, 1640
(on loan to the V&A from
the National Trust, Staunton
Harold church, Leicestershire)

was presented with an alabaster figure of St Michael (similar to cat. no. 279), its iconography was apparently unknown to the author of the accessions register, 'the Book of Benefactors'. He described the statue simply as 'a figure in a coat of mail … holding a sword, still fully preserved, in its right hand and, in its left, a pair of scales'.[9]

During the eighteenth century a few individuals went beyond collecting medieval objects, to wanting to reproduce new ones in the same style. This desire was not wholly new. Architectural elements such as pinnacles topped with onion domes, fan vaults and hammerbeam roofs (all late medieval in origin) had been retained even into the seventeenth century to signify traditional building types: university colleges, great halls and chapels (plate 84).[10] In other art forms, too, practitioners continued to find inspiration in medieval precedent. A series of seventeenth-century chalices was clearly modelled on those of the late fifteenth and early sixteenth centuries, with their concave hexagonal feet and knops on the stems (plate 85, cat. no. 302). The iconography has changed – there is an image of the Good Shepherd on one side of the bowl and inscription in English on the other, but the foot is oriented so as to eliminate the flat frontal face where, in the Middle Ages, a Crucifixion usually appeared. Yet the deliberate revival of forms that had completely fallen from fashion speaks of an interest in the outward appearances, if not the doctrines, of the medieval church.[11]

Before the eighteenth century, the use of Gothic forms seems to have derived from their importance in signifying function. In the eighteenth century, whilst the overall superiority of Classical architecture was maintained, Gothic acquired its own aesthetic associations. It was believed to inspire emotions too deep for rational description: the awe of nature, the love of one's country, the melancholy of history.[12] Whigs, like Horace Walpole (1717–97) and Tories, like Sir Roger Newdigate (1719–1806) alike chose to express their sensibilities in newly-erected Gothic houses, based on medieval examples. The models they chose were primarily late medieval in date.[13] The gallery at Strawberry Hill and many of the interiors at Arbury Hall (plate 86) were based on Henry VII's Chapel (plate 1, cat. no. 28). Nevertheless, the borrowings show both a wider knowledge of late medieval forms and an ability to synthesize them into an aesthetic unity. Their visual appeal was enduring: as the novelist, George Eliot, who grew up at Arbury, wrote of the dining room, 'The room seemed less like a place to dine in than a piece of space enclosed simply for the sake of a beautiful outline.'[14]

The use of Late Gothic models continued into the nineteenth century, at least in part because they matched the requirements of the day, both structural and functional. The regular conoids of fan vaults were relatively easily reproduced

St Mary's church, she described the tombs in fascinated detail. She identified the figures around Richard Beauchamp's tomb chest (cat. no. 87) as members of his family and noted with Nonconformist disapproval what she mistook for religious habits 'which formerly in the tymes of Popery and superstition most persons coveted to dye in'. Nevertheless, she was full of praise for the naturalistic draperies.[8] Sepulchral monuments, of course, were one of the few forms of artistic production to have continued from the Middle Ages. Interest in medieval memorials – both tombs and stained glass – also continued, for they were associated with lineage and property. They were thus a focus of interest for professional heralds who, since the later Middle Ages, had scoured the country for evidence of pedigree. The genealogical preoccupations of the heralds and other antiquaries, however, meant that they rarely noted other imagery, and by the seventeenth century it was no longer generally understood.

Celia Fiennes's Protestant reading of the Beauchamp monument was standard. Medieval objects were widely collected as curiosities, but were rarely better comprehended than the exotic tribal artefacts alongside which they were displayed. When in 1693 the Ashmolean Museum in Oxford

in lath and plaster; obtuse arch forms combined a Gothic form with the widest and lowest possible opening, and panelled tracery was easily standardized and combined with opening windows. The use of medieval ornaments with a brick structure, or wide expanses of unadorned masonry in large blocks, frequently recalls the Perpendicular, in particular because the overall massing tends to remain Classical, with low-pitched roof and regular outline. Without developing a self-conscious philosophy of style, the early architects who specialized in the Gothic manner, from James Wyatt (1746–1813) and his nephew Wyatville (1766–1840) – as, for example, at Ashridge Park in Hertfordshire – to Edward Blore (1787–1879) at Lambeth Palace, produced an architecture whose overall impression, if not its details, is usually Perpendicular.

If Rickman's work prepared the field for the attack on such stylistic pluralism, the first salvo was fired by the young architect, Augustus Welby Northmore Pugin (1812–52). Immediately following his 1835 conversion to Catholicism, Pugin penned *Contrasts*.[15] This polemic opposed the social structure of fourteenth- and fifteenth-century England, perfectly expressed in its architecture, with the poverty and social divisions of modern Britain. The tract met with considerable (if perplexed) interest and a second edition was published in 1841. The differences between the two versions are instructive, for they reveal a general change in attitude towards Perpendicular architecture. In 1836, Pugin argued that buildings such as King's College Chapel in Cambridge (cat. no. 19), St George's Chapel, Windsor (cat. no. 25) and Henry VII's Chapel (cat. no. 28) were examples of the excellence achieved by English architecture on the eve of the Reformation, a perfection which he felt was shared by the glass-painting and manuscript illumination of the period. All this was brought to an abrupt end by the 'change in religion' wrought by Henry VIII and Edward VI. By 1841, however, Pugin had read the works of the French Catholic authors Montalembert and Rio and now believed that Protestantism, whilst it had been responsible for the destruction of Catholic art in England, was itself only a symptom of a wider decay. Having become disillusioned by nineteenth-century Catholicism, Pugin was prepared to suggest that medieval Catholics had fallen away from the ideals of their faith. They had revived pagan antiquity, which had paved the way for Protestantism, and they had colluded with Henry VIII in the Dissolution of the monasteries. On the Continent, post-medieval Catholicism had been responsible for much greater destruction and Pugin conceded that Anglican churches had preserved their medieval arrangements far better than those in Catholic Europe (he was also impressed by the Lutheran churches in Germany, but admitted that he had not visited Spain).

In the same year as the second edition of *Contrasts*, Pugin published *The True Principles of Pointed or Christian Architecture*. This condemned Late Gothic for falling away from the ideal, aspiring quality of pure Gothic. Before Rickman, Late Gothic had usually been described as 'Florid', or overladen with ornament.[16] A preference for the middle period of Gothic was already established.[17] This predilection was echoed by numerous influential authors of the 1830s and '40s and was shared, vociferously, by the members of the Cambridge Camden (later the Ecclesiological) Society.[18] Originally a body of like-minded undergraduates, the Camdenians soon became very influential. They aimed to revive

87 Legend of the fleurs-de-lis, the Bedford Hours, Bedford Master, *c*.1423 (British Library, Add. MS 18850, f.288v)

88 Legend of the fleurs-de-lis, Richard Gough, *An Account of The Rich Illuminated Missal Executed for John, Duke of Bedford*, London, 1794 (British Library, 676.f.17)

swept away in an attempt to return the building to a state of 'purity' and 'perfection'.

The architectural morality expounded by Pugin and the ecclesiologists was societal. Other interpretations also involved the individual morality of the architects and patrons. This argument had been used by John Britton (1771–1857), the author and publisher of a huge number of topographical works. Quoting Horace Walpole – who, as the champion of the innocence of Richard III, had particular reason to despise Henry VII – Britton argued that the first of the Tudors 'reigned as an attorney would have reigned; and he would have preferred a conveyancer to a Praxiteles'.[19] Henry VII was traditionally portrayed as a miser, so his patronage of such an obviously luxurious building as his burial chapel might have seemed something of a paradox. Walpole suggested that Henry must have been comforted by the thought that he would not be expected to enjoy it, or even pay for it, during his lifetime![20] The interest shown by Walpole and Britton in the great men of history was entirely typical of their time. The account of the medieval period in Walpole's *Anecdotes*, the first published account of English art, focused in particular on medieval portraits. Likewise, the earliest descriptions of manuscripts concentrated on those containing images of patrons and artists (plates 87, 88). As the introduction of portraiture was a late medieval phenomenon, the manuscripts discussed were therefore those of fifteenth- and sixteenth-century date, but this did not imply any aesthetic preference for their forms. Artistic judgement of the miniatures related solely to an evaluation of their accuracy, for their importance lay in their evidential value. It was not until the mid-nineteenth century that manuscripts in a medieval style began generally to be appreciated as works of art, rather than as illustrations of past customs.[21]

In line with the focus on powerful individuals, the early classifications of Gothic architecture were often based around the dates of monarchs. Thus the climax of Gothic was made to coincide with the Augustan reign of Edward III and the decline corresponded to the subsequent political chaos. The qualities attributed to Perpendicular were determined by those associated with its corresponding historical period – anarchy, debased feudalism and religious decadence. Obviously the characteristics assigned to any particular style depended also on the buildings identified as its exemplars, so the dating of individual monuments was of great importance. Rickman provided lists of dated buildings to corroborate his analysis of style, while in his series of monographs on cathedrals, Britton was publishing much of the documentary evidence for accurate dating of the most important monuments.[22] Although rivals, together they transformed the study of Gothic.

the forms of Gothic architecture and thereby to reform the contemporary Church of England. The association that Pugin had drawn between Gothic architecture and morality was vital to their project and thus they condemned the use of Late Gothic elements. Although, as Protestants, their championing of Gothic was controversial, they argued that the religion of the middle period was less tainted than that of the 'corrupt' late medieval church, which was ripe for Reformation. Their preferences also extended to the principles of restoration. Many a church which now appears as an authentic specimen of thirteenth- or fourteenth-century architecture does so at the expense of later Gothic features,

89 Palace of Westminster seen from the roof of Henry VII's Chapel; Barry and Pugin, 1837–67

90 Sts Catherine, Elizabeth, John and Agnes, stained-glass panels by Burlisson & Grylles, 1882 (St Stephen's Chapel, Holy Cross Convent, Haywards Heath, Sussex)

The stylistic origins of Perpendicular were first analysed by one of Rickman's disciples, a Cambridge professor, Robert Willis (1800–75). Although Britton (following the local antiquary, Thomas Rudge) had dated the crucial south transept of Gloucester Cathedral to the time of Abbot Wigmore (1329–37), it was still widely believed that Perpendicular had originated at Winchester Cathedral.[23] The importance of the famed William Wykeham, Bishop of Winchester and founder of New College, Oxford, as the putative architect of the nave and thus the inventor of Perpendicular, was celebrated by his inclusion as the token Gothic architect in sculptural programmes, including that on the Albert Memorial, of 1862–76. When Willis gave a lecture at Gloucester in 1860 and claimed it as the starting point of Perpendicular, he was therefore not original in his conclusions, but was arguing nonetheless against prevailing opinion.[24] More than 20 years later an eyewitness recalled the controversy: 'Many of his audience were then sceptical, but he carried those most capable of appreciating his genius with him, as he took them unerringly step by step to his point.'[25]

The carrying back of the date of the origin of Perpendicular to before 1350 allowed the development of an important theory, still current today, which associated its spread with the changed socio-economic conditions caused by the Black Death. The art critic John Ruskin (1819–1900) had been the first to transform Pugin's religio-cultural analysis of Gothic into a socio-cultural theory, connecting the heyday of Gothic with the freedom of the craftsman.[26] One of his followers, the socialist architect Edward Schroeder Prior (1852–1932), made the connection with the historical circumstances of the Black Death and the wars with France. Both factors aided the rise of the artisan and merchant classes, putting greater emphasis on the parish church as a site of architectural endeavour and giving rise to powerful guilds of specialist craftsmen. Prior saw the divorce of architecture from sculpture as the cause of the decline of both, though he did not utterly condemn Perpendicular, regarding it as the Indian summer of Gothic. Prior also argued that 'Its peculiarities lay in the root of the English character of art, and its fore-tokens can be seen in all the phases of our Gothic.'[27]

The idea that Perpendicular was a specifically English style was a long-standing one. Early beliefs that Gothic as a whole was of English origin were destined to demolition, but belief in the essential Englishness of Perpendicular lived on. It was given physical embodiment in the Palace of Westminster, which was rebuilt after a devastating fire in 1834 (plate 89). The new design was chosen by competition, the rules of which stated that the style should be Gothic or Elizabethan. The winning architect, Charles Barry (1795–1860), chose a Perpendicular style, with details (designed by Pugin) based

both on the fourteenth-century Westminster Hall (plate 25) and on the sixteenth-century chapel of Henry VII (plate 72). The associations of the building were therefore both general – the medieval origins of Parliament, the Englishness of parliamentary democracy – and local, relating it directly to its historical site.

As we have seen, by the date of his involvement with the Houses of Parliament, Pugin had moved away from his

championing of the Perpendicular and in terms of the Gothic Revival (by then in its Camdenian phase) the building was distinctly old-fashioned. A few authors continued to argue for the use of Late Gothic in modern buildings, just as the pioneering stained-glass scholar Charles Winston (1814–64) maintained that fifteenth- and sixteenth-century glass provided the most appropriate models for modern reproduction. Yet although the occasional 'rogue' architect, such as Edward Buckton Lamb (1806-69), found inspiration in Perpendicular forms, it was not until the 1870s and later that a more general move was made to re-explore the possibilities of Late Gothic. A pioneering lecture was given in 1880 by the architect John Dando Sedding (1838–91), who was apparently the first to employ the metaphor of autumn for the Perpendicular.[28] By then, it was clear to most observers that the Gothic Revival had become yet another architectural trend, shaped by aesthetics as much as by morality. Once the later phases of Gothic could be shown to have artistic merit, the arguments against their revival began to crumble. Further positive reasons could also be found. The inappropriateness of the Cambridge Camden Society's ideal of an early Decorated country church to meet the requirements of metropolitan parishes (where there was the greatest need for new churches) had been an important reason for the mid-century growth of interest in German and Italian brick churches. Subsequently, arguments were put forward that the larger, lighter and more open churches of English Late Gothic were both better suited to the liturgical needs of modern congregations and more representative of local architectural traditions. The art forms of Late Gothic, too, revealed a desire for naturalism shared by Victorian artists like Burlisson and Grylles, whose stained glass (plate 90) shows clear debts to examples such as the Beauchamp Chapel (cat. no. 89). Mid nineteenth-century revivalists had seen the copying of medieval specimens as the first stage in their desired project – the creation of a style appropriate for the Victorian age. For its supporters, the art and architecture of the fourteenth and fifteenth centuries were both best suited to modern requirements and represented the last period of purity before the polluting influence of the Renaissance. As one author put it, 'We are tempted to think that, but for this unfortunate foreign influence, we should shortly have developed a style which would have eclipsed everything preceding it'.[29]

The architectural supporters of English Late Gothic had a programme. They were largely associated with a controversial attempt by a body of churchmen to restore to Anglican services as many of the rites and ceremonies of the medieval church as were deemed consistent with reformed theology. Of all the architects associated with the liturgical revival, the forms and arrangements of the late medieval church are most closely reproduced in the early work of John Ninian Comper (1864–1960).[30] A church like St Cyprian's, Clarence Gate, Marylebone (plate 91) recalls the great East Anglian churches, such as Salle in Norfolk (plate 37, cat. no. 257), beloved of Comper, with a rood-screen based on Attleborough (plate 38, cat. no. 264) and the so-called 'English altar', complete with curtains suspended from riddel posts, can-

dles and a hanging pyx. When Comper used it as a model, the Attleborough screen was languishing at the west end of the church, removed from its place in the 1840s and whitewashed by a Victorian clergyman who was offended by its 'popish' imagery.[31] In 1847 a similar fate befell the wall-paintings of Eton College Chapel (cat. no. 320).[32] In 1930 the Attleborough screen was restored by the architect Frank Ernest Howard (1888–1934), another Perpendicular enthusiast.[33] Such arrangements proved very popular and the medieval appearance of many genuinely old churches has been enhanced by the introduction of similar fittings. Yet we should not be seduced by the apparent medievalism of Comper's vision into believing that we are experiencing the re-creation of a Gothic interior. What he and his associates were trying to revive was not the medieval church as such, but a reformed version, based on their interpretation of the ornaments rubric of the 1662 *Book of Common Prayer*, in the light of sometimes wishful historical thinking.[34] Comparing Comper's rood-screen with that of Attleborough, we see that while the medieval version provided for three nave altars, the Anglican version merely screened off the chancel and eastern chapels. The admittance of the rood itself was based on a belief that Marian reintroductions were actually medieval survivals. While St Cyprian's now holds two devotional images, complete with votive candles, they are later introductions and divorced from their medieval position at the altar. Medieval Salle, however, had at least nine additional images, placed throughout the church.[35]

The liturgical revival gave new purpose to the study of late medieval manuscripts and other art forms, which had hitherto been somewhat neglected in the adulation of all things thirteenth- and early fourteenth-century. The renewed interest in Englishness also encouraged the study of objects which had hitherto been dismissed, such as alabasters. From the 1890s, a considerable number of important exhibitions were mounted which – viewed as a series – both familiarized the interested public with medieval manuscripts, paintings and other objects and explored the contribution of the so-called 'English primitives' to native traditions.[36] In part, this was a deliberate attempt to counter a view, symbolized by the collections of the National Gallery, that art in England was of no interest before the eighteenth century. The later shows must also have been inspired by (though their contents could never hope to rival) the great exhibition *Les Primitifs flamands et l'art ancien* held in Bruges in 1902, which prompted similar exhibitions of national 'primitive' art traditions all over Europe.[37] In England the most significant exhibition of British primitive paintings was that held at the Royal Academy in 1923, initiated by Viscount Lee of Fareham, a founder of the Courtauld Institute of Art. Montague Rhodes James

91 St Cyprian's church, Clarence Gate, Marylebone, London, nave interior looking east; Bucknall and Comper, 1902–3

(1862–1936), Provost of Eton and the most important scholar of medieval manuscripts, used the occasion to unveil the remaining wall-paintings in the Eton College Chapel.[38] They were then displayed at the exhibition, in the form of watercolours by Professor Ernest William Tristram (1882–1952). For contemporary scholars their significance was that, as immovable fixtures, with a named (and apparently English) artist, their quality was sufficient to counter claims of English inferiority and to suggest that other major works might also have a native provenance.

The continuing importance of nationalism to the appreciation of medieval art is represented most strongly in the work of John Hooper Harvey (1911–97), arguably the most significant twentieth-century scholar of English late medieval art, especially architecture. Trained as an architect, he owed much to the work of the liturgical revivalists, without sharing their religious position. Like them, he sought a style to suit the age and felt that the architecture of the fourteenth century was most appropriate. Like Pugin, he believed that society could be renewed by a return to medieval values. His Golden Age was the late fourteenth century, but he felt there were lessons to be learned right up to the time of the introduction of Renaissance motifs. What he saw in this period was an England essentially independent from Europe, ruled by powerful monarchs, whose supremacy was expressed by the splendour of its culture. Such nationalism was more overt – and, to many modern eyes, offensive – than that of other British scholars at the time, but the difference was only one of degree. And in aiming to reawaken in his compatriots a zeal for his chosen period, he marshalled a formidable body of research.[39]

Harvey recognized that architecture was the central art form of the Middle Ages. His greatest interest, therefore, lay in recovering evidence of contemporary opinions about buildings and details of the masons responsible for their design. In opposition to the prevailing view of the anonymity of medieval masons, Harvey proved that their names could be identified in documents and that their individual careers and personal styles could be recovered. Like Huizinga, whose importance he recognized, Harvey sought to reconstruct an entire world, through painstaking analysis of contemporary sources, and to represent it in a manner more literary than that employed by conventional scholarship. He also used a series of seasonal metaphors in his analysis of the successive periods of late medieval culture. Like Huizinga too, he believed in moments of epiphany:

> Once, travelling in an express train between Nuneaton
> and Rugby, I glanced out to the west, and by some
> accident which had cleared the atmosphere, Coventry

appeared like a crystal city in the brilliant sunshine, set upon its hill, and dominating it, above its two attendant spires, soared the 300 feet of St Michael, portentous as its namesake's sword. It has never been my fortune to see it thus again, but the memory remains to prove that the possession of one masterpiece can make even Coventry glorious as the New Jerusalem.[40]

Harvey wrote this after the bombing of Coventry (plate 92). The ruins of St Michael's church, Coventry's former cathedral, now form a monument to the horrors of war.

Perhaps they stand, too, as an obituary to nationalistic scholarship. Late medieval scholarship today is as different from that of the pre-war era as Kenneth Branagh's *Henry V* (1989) is from Laurence Olivier's (1945). After the Second World War, Harvey continued to write in the same vein, though diluting his theories of English superiority, but a predominant tendency of post-war scholarship has been a growing internationalism. Our most prolific architectural historian, Nikolaus Pevsner (1902–83), was a German immigrant. Our national style, Perpendicular, has now been shown to have originated as an English reappraisal of a

92   *Interior of Coventry Cathedral, the morning after the Blitz*, John Piper, 1940, oil on canvas laid on board (Herbert Art Gallery & Museum, Coventry)

French architectural idiom.[41] Interpretations based on past moralities now seem irrelevant, for we have constructed our own moralities and our own interpretations. But, whether the period is seen in terms of Huizinga's autumn, or Harvey's pregnant winter and frozen spring, the late Middle Ages remains charged with possibilities for further study, and for building upon the researches of past scholars.

FURTHER READING

Brooks 1999; Frankl 1960; Hindman, Camille, Rowe and Watson 2001; Stamp 2002; Watkin 1980.

NOTES

1 Huizinga 1924, pp.222–3.

2 Haskell 1993, chapter 15.

3 See the essay on Perpendicular architecture by Christopher Wilson in this volume.

4 Rickman 1817. An earlier version of the essay was published in Smith 1815, I, pp.129–80.

5 For glass, see Winston 1847: his debt to Rickman is expressed on p.iii. For brasses, see Kent 1949.

6 de Beer 1948.

7 Evelyn 1706, p.10.

8 Morris 1949, p.115.

9 Translated from the Latin original in MacGregor et al. 2000, p.9. By the eighteenth century, however, there was a growing knowledge among collectors of medieval antiquities, who included Horace Walpole and William Stukeley (Williamson 1987, pp.9–10).

10 Colvin 1948.

11 Oman 1957, pp.205–10.

12 Discussed further in Sprague Allen 1937 and Robson-Scott 1965.

13 McCarthy 1987, pp.63–91, 117–20 and 128–39.

14 Eliot 1980, p.134.

15 Pugin 1836.

16 The term comes from Warton 1762, vol. 2, pp.191–3. Warton divided Late Gothic into 'Ornamental' (from 1390) and 'Florid' (from St George's Chapel, Windsor).

17 See, for example, Milner 1811. Milner's ideal 'Second Pointed' style nevertheless included works that we should class as Perpendicular, such as the naves of Winchester and Canterbury. He defined the 'decayed' Third Pointed by its obtusely pointed arches and dated the style to the late fifteenth century.

18 White 1962; Webster and Elliott 2000.

19 Britton 1807–20, II (1809), p.12.

20 Walpole 1762–71, I (1762), p.46.

21 Munby 1972.

22 See, in particular, Britton 1836.

23 Rudge 1815, p.296; Britton 1836, V, p.56.

24 Willis's unpublished lecture on Gloucester is discussed in Buchanan 1995, pp.178–82.

25 Hartshorne 1887.

26 Swenarton 1989, especially chapter 1.

27 Prior 1900, p.430.

28 'In brief, the Perpendicular period is the crown and culmination of a long series of effort. It is the harvest-time of all our mediaeval endeavour. For in English Gothic, as in nature, there are three phases of development – first the blade, then the ear, and afterwards the full corn in the ear': Sedding 1881–5.

29 Micklethwaite 1874, p.258.

30 Symondson 1988.

31 Barrett 1848, pp.141–3.

32 Maxwell-Lyte 1875, pp.431–2.

33 'The Screen in St Mary's Church, Attleborough, Norfolk', *Journal of the British Archaeological Association*, n.s. XXXVII, 1931–2, pp.184–8.

34 '… And the Chancels shall remain as they have done in times past. And here is to be noted, that such ornaments of the Church, and of the Ministers thereof, at all times of their Ministration, shall be retained, and be in use as were in the Church of England, by the authority of Parliament, in the second year of the reign of King Edward VI.' There was fierce controversy over the precise meaning of this clause, which formed the legal basis of the Anglican position on church furnishing.

35 Parsons 1937.

36 London 1890; London 1894; London 1896; Oxford 1904; London 1908; London 1909; London 1913; London 1924; London 1929; London 1930; London 1934a; London 1934b; Luton 1936; Birmingham 1936; London 1939.

37 Haskell 1993, pp.431–68.

38 Pfaff 1980, pp.353–8.

39 Of Harvey's many books and articles, the most important for Late Gothic are Harvey 1949, 1978 and 1984. A taste of the more controversial aspects of his work may be gained from Harvey 1940, discussed in Saint 1983, pp.43–7.

40 Harvey 1947, p.30.

41 See Christopher Wilson's essay in this volume; especially p.103.

THE CATALOGUE

1 ROYAL PATRONAGE OF THE VISUAL ARTS

CHRISTOPHER WILSON

In his treatise *The Governance of England,* written during the 1460s, the exiled pro-Lancastrian judge Sir John Fortescue was expressing a notion universally accepted in the Middle Ages when he declared that a king must be able to spend liberally on all the accoutrements of royal magnificence: new buildings, rich clothes, furs, fine linen, jewellery, rich hangings for his houses, plate and vestments for his chapel, and expensive horses and their trappings (Plummer 1885, p.125). Although much of this may seem to us less like art patronage than conspicuous consumption, in reality everything on Fortescue's list formed part of a single continuum, namely the 'dispendiousness' essential to maintaining the kingly estate. In a way that is perhaps difficult to grasp now, the correct order of society was thought to be threatened if the king's household did not *look* more important than the households of even the highest-ranking of his subjects. The parading of Henry VI through London to rally the city's support as Edward IV's army approached in April 1471 backfired because, as one observer wrote, it resembled a badly staged play, with the king surrounded by a very meagre entourage and clad in a gown that had seen better days (Thomas and Thornley 1938, p.215).

Of course to be a king amounted to much more than being the richest and most powerful man in the land: his anointing with chrism at his coronation transformed him into a *persona mixta,* a mortal man still, but with a potent aura of divinity about him. It was therefore apt that many royal ceremonies, and the most important of the buildings that housed them, should possess something of the heaven-evoking splendour of the church's sacred rituals and spaces. The effective assertion of the fundamentally different nature of the king's estate from that of his greatest subjects required that royal buildings be far larger, more elaborate and more numerous than those put up for dukes, marquises and earls, and it probably explains why royal patronage of the figural arts so frequently entailed recruiting foreign artists who were practitioners of internationally up-to-date styles not previously seen at home. The need for

93 Eton College Chapel, sanctuary looking north-east (vault mid-20th-century)

rulers to stand out from their subjects by employing visual modes that were 'strange' (meaning unfamiliar, foreign or even exotic) had been expounded in relation to dress in a treatise on good government compiled for an heir apparent to the English crown as long ago as 1326 (BL, Add. MS 47680, f.17v).

Besides deploying the luxury arts to glorify his household and court, a late medieval English king was obliged to create or improve one or more religious foundations, which would prosper his own soul, enhance the spiritual life of his kingdom and proclaim his status as the intermediary between God and the English people. Any king who cared to ponder the low survival-rate among the art-objects made for his predecessors will have realized that many of the costly and beautiful things made for his own and his household's use were likely to have a shorter lifespan than those that served his religious foundations. This has indeed proved to be the case – with a vengeance, for there is today astonishingly little to show for the vast expenditure of England's late medieval rulers, other than a good sample of the religious buildings erected for them. Admittedly there are substantial survivals from Henry VIII's work at Hampton Court and St James's Palace, but these represent only a very small proportion of the stupendous volume of building that he ordered at the royal residences; by contrast, the magnificent stained glass and woodwork he gave to complete his father's work at King's College Chapel, Cambridge – which are untypical of his patronage as a whole – have survived almost intact (cat. nos 19, 22).

That the patronage of England's late medieval kings should be represented today by little more than religious buildings is due to a formidable array of destructive forces: fires, financial stringency, iconoclasm and, not least, the contemptuous attitude of the Renaissance and Baroque periods towards the products of medieval culture. Yet the prominence of architecture in our perception of late medieval royal art patronage is arguably not entirely a distortion, for England's kings were peculiar in the degree of emphasis they placed on ambitious churches as a means of expressing their power and their piety. No other of medieval Christendom's monarchies could lay claim to a series of major church-building projects comparable in ambition and artistic importance to that which starts with Edward the Confessor's reconstruction of Westminster Abbey in the 1050s and culminates, almost half a millennium later, with the chapels of Henry VII. What must have been one of the most powerful factors sustaining this tradition in the late medieval period is revealed in a document drawn up in connection with the foundation of Eton College in 1440 (plate 93, cat. no. 23), in which the 17-year-old Henry VI effectively admitted that part of his motivation in creating the college was an awareness of the great achievements of his predecessors in founding religious houses and major churches (Williams 1872, II, pp.279–80). In France, by contrast, the only significant royal church-building project undertaken in the fifteenth century was Charles VII and Louis XI's church at Cléry near Orléans (1434–87), a handsome building unquestionably, but not one that can bear comparison with the chief works of those kings' English contemporaries: King's College Chapel, Cambridge, and St George's Chapel in Windsor Castle (cat. nos 19, 25). (For further discussion of English royal church-building, see the essay on Perpendicular architecture in this volume, pp. 109, 111, 113).

Palaces were rarely built or rebuilt in a single campaign of work before Henry VIII's reign. Exceptions are Henry V's Sheen, which was intended to be surrounded by three new monastic houses, and the replacement for Sheen built after its destruction by fire in 1497, which Henry VII renamed Richmond after the earldom he inherited from his father (cat. no. 147). Richmond is a good illustration of the exemplary role played by ambitious royal buildings, for the spectacular silhouette of its lodgings block gave rise to a vogue in Tudor architecture for domelets, ecclesiastical as well as domestic (plate 72, cat. no. 28), and its long and generously windowed first-floor galleries sparked enthusiasm for a feature that became indispensable in great houses for more than a century (cat. no. 148). In the later years of the reign of Henry VIII, when much of the vast wealth of the English church was passing through his hands, palace-building reached a volume unparalleled before or since. But with very few exceptions, Henry VIII's houses were not innovatory in their external architecture or their planning, and most were rambling and visually chaotic structures built piecemeal in response to the unpremeditated urgings of this most impulsive king. Renaissance architecture, albeit of a kind that would not pass muster in Italy, had made its debut in 1520 when the revels (the department responsible for pageants and other entertainments) created a temporary palace and other structures for the extravaganza staged outside Calais, which posterity knows as the Field of Cloth of Gold. Seven years later the same department erected a banqueting house at Greenwich for the signing of a treaty with France, whose main room incorporated a triumphal arch. Yet Henry VIII never saw fit to build permanent structures that conformed even approximately to the canons of Renaissance architecture, and it was only two relatively small buildings erected at Whitehall Palace in the mid-1540s – the gate over King Street and the loggia in the privy garden – that definitely made use of the classical Orders on their exteriors.

How early the interiors of Henry VIII's palaces incorporated Italian-derived Antique ornament is not known, but it was certainly present by the mid-1520s in the houses of Cardinal Wolsey, England's greatest architectural patron from 1515 until his downfall in 1529. Both English and Netherlandish artificers were involved in making this kind of work, which is now best represented by a ceiling at Hampton Court dating from 1537 or soon afterwards (cat. no. 5). Also in 1537 Henry VIII began to employ the Italian Nicholas Bellin, who had previously worked for Francis I at Fontainebleau, and it is likely that from this time onwards plasterwork incorporating the large nude figures and strap-work characteristic of Fontainebleau School Mannerism became predominant in Henry VIII's palaces. Its strangest application was at the aptly named Nonsuch (begun in 1538), the façades of whose inner court were covered with large Antique figures and other ornaments executed in *stucco duro* (cat. no. 352). If, as seems likely, the classical Orders were present here, their role must have been fairly minor, for the stuccoes were fitted into the grid of a traditionally conceived timber-frame structure. Henry VIII's espousal of the Fontainebleau style may well have been prompted by the royal need for the new and the exclusive; certainly by the late 1530s the style of decoration represented by the 1537 Hampton Court ceiling was being successfully imitated by other patrons. And Henry will not have forgotten that in 1506 his father had been the very first Englishman to commission an Italian to produce designs for a tomb in the Antique style.

The main monumental form of figural art deployed in the great houses of the late Middle Ages was Netherlandish tapestry. This had the capacity to transform the prosaic, essentially box-like character of most palace interiors into warm and luxurious chambers that were alive with brilliant colour and gleaming with gold and silver thread. Different qualities of tapestry could be used to underscore variations in status between rooms, though only a very few pieces will have been intended to hang always in the same place. Tapestries with religious and chivalric subjects seem often to have been displayed indiscriminately in secular and sacred spaces. There was no prejudice against acquiring tapestry second-hand, a process most notoriously instanced by Henry VIII's annexation *en bloc* of Cardinal Wolsey's huge collection (cat. no. 6) after the latter's fall from favour in 1529. Henry VII was only one of several purchasers of a ten-piece set of the *Great History of Troy*, but that he was also a patron of the most expensive and prestigious kind of tapestry manufacture – the specially woven 'one-off' – seems clear from documentary references to a 36-metre-long tapestry of the *comyng into*

Englonde of king henrye the vijth (Starkey 1998, p.273), a subject that will have entailed transmitting fairly detailed instructions to the Netherlandish artist who was responsible for drawing the cartoons.

Large-scale wall-painting began to appear alongside tapestry in English royal residences no later than 1532, when the French or Netherlandish painters Isaac Labrun and John Rauffe were at work on a very long mural of Henry VIII's coronation in a gallery in Whitehall Palace (Auerbach 1954, pp.160, 174, 182; Thurley 1999, p.51); and five years later Hans Holbein carried out the most celebrated commission of this kind, the dynastic portrait of Henry VIII, his queen and his parents in the Privy Chamber of the same palace (cat. no. 2). The sudden upsurge of interest in portrait miniatures in the mid-1520s (cat. nos 17–18) suggests that it was not until then that Henry VIII and his court began to grasp that painting had attained a level of sophistication unrivalled by any other form of figural art. Hitherto the most important contribution of painters at the royal court is likely to have been that of the serjeant painters and their assistants, who produced the colourful but ephemeral heraldic trappings of military campaigns and tournaments. Holbein found himself working alongside such men when he was engaged to produce paintings for the banqueting house and disguising house (theatre) put up at Greenwich in 1527, decorations that there is every reason to suppose were discarded after the conclusion of the festivities, which were their sole *raison d'être* (Starkey 1991, pp.54–93).

Apart from tapestry, precious metalwork was the art-form that best served to create an extravagantly luxurious ambience for the royal household and court. This was particularly apparent during feasts, when multi-stage buffets standing near the high table were decked with some of the king's choicest plate. Of the immense quantities of plate made for English kings between 1400 and 1547 nothing has survived except for a superb rock-crystal bowl with enamelled gold mounts stylistically akin to the designs for plate that Holbein made for Henry VIII in the 1530s (plate 94). Some idea of the kind of tableware in daily use by Henry VII may perhaps be got from the plate given by his mother, Lady Margaret Beaufort, to Christ's College, Cambridge (cat. nos 112–13). The smothering of the surfaces of some of these pieces with the personal devices of their owner was certainly a feature of Henry VII's patronage, although the idea of personalizing artefacts in this way (albeit more discreetly) had been current since the end of the fourteenth century. In the closets (oratories) opening off palace chapels, which were usually small and intimate spaces, the altars are likely to have been decorated, when the king was in residence, with a 'tablet' (miniaturized retable or altarpiece) in gold and enamel, and by great good fortune there has survived an example identifiable as Henry IV's from its incorporation of one of his personal devices, the forget-me-not (cat. no. 10). By Henry VII's reign, if not before, the retables of the high altars in the chapels of the main royal residences were made of jewel-encrusted gold or silver-gilt, but no details of their appearance are recorded. One of the most tantalizing glimpses of a king's valuables which documentary evidence

94 Bowl and cover from Henry VIII's plate; rock-crystal, gold, enamel, precious stones and pearls, probably late 1530s (Munich, Schatzkammer of Residenz)

gives us is the inventory of Henry V's plate and jewels drawn up after his death in 1422. The first item listed is a gold collar adorned with pearls and rubies and valued at the almost incredible sum of £5,162 13s. 4d. – more than 10 times what running a baron's household for a year was estimated to cost in Edward IV's reign (*Rot. Parl.*, IV, p.214; Myers 1959, p.103).

Medieval monarchy was most emphatically personal monarchy, and because the late medieval kings of England differed in their ambitions and predilections, it was inevitable that from reign to reign there would be wide variations in the nature and scope of the artworks and buildings they commissioned. But if the objects of royal patronage varied, the requirement that they be of the highest quality available was absolutely constant. When he drew up his will in April 1503, Henry VII knew that he would not live to oversee the equipping of the sumptuous burial chapel he had built for himself at the east end of Westminster Abbey, and in noting the need to obtain vestments and other equipment for all the altars there (cat. no. 31), he felt constrained to remind his executors that these items should 'bee of suche as apperteigne to the gifte of a Prince' (Astle 1775, p.35). For Henry VII, as for any king, the ultimate measure of quality was comparison with the patronage of other European rulers, but for us the dearth of artefactual evidence makes it impossible to assess how well English kings measured up to their continental peers in any field other than architecture.

The contemporaries best placed to make that kind of judgement were foreign diplomats, and among the most valuable evidence they have left is the diary of Gabriel Tetzel, a citizen of Nuremberg who accompanied a Bohemian ambassador visiting in turn all the major western European courts during the years 1465–7. Tetzel had no great liking for the English, but conceded that Edward IV was affable and very handsome, and had 'a court whose members were the most elegant that might be found in all of Christendom' (Schmeller 1844, p.155). Since Tetzel had recently been at the court of the Duke of Burgundy, which was then a byword for refinement and opulence, his praise of the English court is very telling. Early in 1466 he witnessed the churching of Queen Elizabeth after the birth of the royal couple's first child. The setting was Westminster, where the inherited splendours of the abbey and palace enabled the king to stage a courtly *Gesamtkunstwerk* in which architecture, liturgy, dress, tapestry, richly decorated furniture, plate, haute cuisine, song, instrumental music and dance all played their allotted roles faultlessly. Tetzel was clearly amazed by the formality of the three-hour-long feast held after the queen's return from church, during which no one spoke and all those involved in serving the queen (earls included) knelt before her while she ate. It is occasions such as this that we should try to keep in our minds when contemplating the scanty survivals from the immense profusion of artworks created for England's late medieval kings.

FURTHER READING

Colvin 1963, 1975; McKendrick 1995; Thurley 1993.

★ THESE ITEMS ARE NOT EXHIBITED.

1 The Evesham World Map★

*c.*1390–1415

Ink and colours on vellum; h. 94 cm, w. 46 cm
(on sheet h. 99cm, w. 44 cm)

Muniment Room, College of Arms, London (18/19)

The map has east at the top. Places of significance for
the history of mankind unfold in sequence from the
top, with a particular emphasis on biblical history
and the great successive imperial epochs of Babylon,
Persia, Macedonia and Rome. Starting with the
Garden of Eden at the top, with Adam and Eve and a
throne (modelled on the abbot's throne at Evesham)
alluding to God's authority, the viewer passes via the
Tower of Babel, Media and Persia, a magnificently
towered Jerusalem (with the Hebrews' crossing of the
Red Sea to the right), Troy and Olympus to a three-
spired tower representing Rome.

The lower part of the map, in contrast, reflects the
English world view during the Hundred Years War.
The realm over which the English kings held power
or exerted influence stretches from Scandinavia to the
Mediterranean. The tower representing Calais is
larger than that of Rome. Just as big is the tower indicating St-Denis, the burial place of the French kings.
By contrast, Paris is an insignificant little tower to its
left. Other towers represent England's commercial
partners, Bruges and Cologne, while Bordeaux is
named. The English place-names, scattered in
random fashion except for those in the vicinity of
Evesham, are those lining important routes that survive today as major roads. The exception is Taddi-
port, a minute settlement in Devon, which may have
been the scribe's home village.

The general form of the map, intended primarily
for didactic purposes, dates back to at least the late
eighth century, despite the dramatically contemporary content of its lower half. The map is probably
the *mappamundi* commissioned for six marks by
Nicholas Herford, prior of Evesham, in about 1390. It
was amended under Abbot Robert Yatton in about
1415, but between 1447 and 1452 the verso was
reused as the sixth sheet of the pedigree of Ralph
Boteler, Lord Sudeley.   PB

PROV. Evesham Abbey, Worcestershire; College of Arms.

LIT. London 1936, p.59 no. 68; Barber 1995; Pirovano 2001,
p.71, no. 33.

1

2 King Henry VII and King Henry VIII*

Hans Holbein the Younger, 1537

Ink and watercolour on paper; h. 257.8 cm, w. 137.2 cm

National Portrait Gallery, London (NPG 4027)

This life-size drawing is the left-hand portion of Holbein's preparatory cartoon for his great wall-painting in the Privy Chamber at Whitehall Palace, which perished when the palace was burned down in 1698. There is no record of the remainder of the cartoon, but a copy of the painting made for Charles II by Remigius van Leemput in 1667 shows on the right-hand side the full-length figures of Henry VII's wife Elizabeth of York and Henry VIII's third wife Jane Seymour. Between them was a stone tablet with a Latin inscription, also recorded by a visitor to Whitehall in 1600 (see also cat. no. 39).

The inscription makes clear the dynastic purpose of the painting, a celebration of the Tudor line. It is unlikely that such a painting would have been commissioned before Henry VIII was assured of a male successor. Jane Seymour died giving birth to the future Edward VI in October 1537. Holbein presumably made use of the drawing from life showing her in a different costume (Royal Collection) to create the image of the queen for the wall-painting.

The cartoon is made up of a number of separate sheets of paper pasted together, the head being a separate piece. The image of Henry differs from that shown in the van Leemput copy of the painting, and in the many early copies of Holbein's image (cat. no. 351), all of which show his face turned directly to confront the viewer. This change must have been made after the outlines of the cartoon had been transferred to the wall. This was effected by shaking charcoal dust directly through the tiny pricked holes still clearly visible in the cartoon itself, or by using a secondary cartoon for this purpose. Perhaps without needing a further sitting, Holbein then skilfully shifted the features of the king from the side to the front to create this stern and enduring image of Henry. SF

PROV. John, Lord Lumley by *c.*1590; by 1727 William Cavendish, 2nd Duke of Devonshire at Chatsworth House, and by descent; presented to the National Portrait Gallery in 1957 under the acceptance-in-lieu scheme.

LIT. Strong 1969, I, pp.153–5; Rowlands 1985, cat. no. L.14, pp.224–6, pls 195–8; Fairbrass and Holmes 1986.

2

Henry VII's tower after an engraving by F. Mackenzie, in J. Britton, *Architectural Antiquities of Great Britain*, London, 1835 (cat. no. 3)

3 Windsor Castle, Henry VII's Tower

*c.*1497

The households of English kings before Henry VII contained two domestic departments centred on the hall and the chamber. The latter was the more prestigious because it was concerned with the king's own living space, his lodging, and it was staffed by men of higher rank. In the mid-1490s Henry VII added a third department, the Privy Chamber, which, as its name suggests, was concerned with the king's life conducted beyond the outer chambers of his lodging. The servants here were of low rank, but were bound to the king by the closest bonds of trust.

From 1497 or 1498 Henry extended the existing mid-fourteenth-century king's lodging at Windsor by adding on a short range of building (not strictly a tower) to accommodate his Privy Chamber along with such ancillary spaces as a library and closet (oratory). The external architecture of this addition differed from the fourteenth-century work in being built of fine limestone from Taynton rather than rough grey heathstone, and in possessing oriel and bay windows of varied and unprecedentedly complex form. No convincing source for these windows has ever been identified, but they were immediately imitated in Henry VII's own rebuilding of Richmond Palace following a fire in December 1497 and, more surprisingly, in Henry VII's Chapel at Westminster (plate 72, cat. no. 28). During Henry VIII's reign, windows of this kind proliferated, not only in royal residences but in the houses of the great and the wealthy (cat. no. 147).   CW

LIT. Colvin 1975, pp.305–8; Wilson 1995, pp.135, 144–6.

4 Hampton Court Palace, Middlesex, hall

PLATE 114

1532–4

Hampton Court was totally rebuilt by Cardinal Thomas Wolsey from 1515, but around 1525, when it was substantially complete, he gave it to Henry VIII in exchange for Richmond. Like Wolsey, Henry was a compulsive builder, and this acquisition was not to be left alone for long. A new hall was begun in spring 1532 under the king's master mason John Multon and his master carpenter James Nedeham, and work proceeded so fast that by summer 1533 the roof could be leaded. In the following winter 'antik' decorations were being added: pendants by the London carver Richard Rigge and spandrels by Thomas Johnson, also of London but fairly certainly from the Netherlands.

In being covered by a hammerbeam roof, and lit by windows set high up in order to allow the hanging of tapestries, Hampton Court's hall was following a tradition inaugurated in the 1390s at Westminster Hall (plate 25) and continued in fifteenth-century halls such as that built for Edward IV at Eltham in the late 1470s. The roof differs from earlier hammerbeam structures in being ceiled with traceried panels, seemingly because the exposure of structural timbers was deemed inelegant or old-fashioned. Though clearly intending to follow the very ancient and particularly English tradition of making the hall the showpiece of a house, Henry VIII will have viewed this splendid room primarily as a vestibule to his own lodging. It was normally used for taking meals only by the lower ranks of the household, who ate here twice a day. Other traditional usages adhered to are the provision of a central hearth and louver (removed in 1663), a bay window opening off the dais, and storage of the household's drink in the cellars below.   CW

LIT. Colvin 1982, pp.133–4; Thurley 1993, p.120.

5 Hampton Court Palace, Middlesex, ceiling of 'Wolsey's Closet'

1537 or soon afterwards

The small Tudor-style room created around this ceiling when it was rediscovered in the 1880s was dubbed 'Wolsey's Closet' on account of its position on the first floor in the range that Cardinal Wolsey built between 1515 and 1526 on the east side of Fountain Court. Although it is in the right place to have been part of a 'closet' (oratory), the lodging to which this space belonged was built by Wolsey for the queen's use, and the ceiling's incorporation of the Prince of Wales's ostrich feathers dates it after October 1537, when Queen Jane Seymour gave birth in the palace to Prince Edward, the long-awaited male heir to the throne. This is the sole survivor of many richly decorated ceilings made for the inner chambers of the royal lodgings in Henry VIII's palaces during the 1530s. The craftsman most likely to have been responsible for the small-scale Renaissance motifs cast in leather *mâché* must be the Netherlandish or German 'molder of antik' Robert Skynke, who is documented working on ceilings in the royal lodgings at Hampton Court between 1534 and 1537.

The overall pattern of square and lozenge-shaped compartments has been thought to derive either from the ceiling of the *Camera dei Venti* in the Palazzo del Te at Mantua (1527–8) or from a plate in Sebastiano Serlio's *Fourth Book of Architecture* (1537), but whereas those designs incorporate coffering, this is a distinctively English late medieval type of ceiling decoration, a 'fretwork' formed of projecting battens and based on Gothic rib-vault designs. The same pattern combined with purely Gothic detailing was used in 1517 for the ceiling of a room adjoining the Star Chamber in Westminster Palace.   CW

LIT. Colvin 1982, pp.132–3, 288; Thurley 1993, pp.106, 110; Wells-Cole 1997, pp.11–12.

6

6 *The Triumph of Chastity over Love*

**Designer unknown, southern Netherlandish;
woven in an unknown workshop, Brussels, probably 1520**

**Wool and silk wefts on a woollen warp, 6–7 warp threads
per centimetre; h. 447 cm, w. 823 cm**

Victoria and Albert Museum, London (440–1883)

At the left of the scene, Chastity, riding a unicorn, reaches up to topple Cupid from his chariot. In the central carriage, bound Cupid sits at the feet of triumphant Chastity, preceded by virtuous maidens processing towards a statue of the chaste goddess Diana. This was originally the second from a six-piece tapestry set of the *Triumphs* of Petrarch.

The inventory of Henry VIII's splendid tapestry collection mentions at least two sets depicting Petrarch's poem *I Trionfi* (Campbell (T) 1998, p.151). The set from which this tapestry comes may have been specially commissioned either by Henry VIII or by Cardinal Wolsey, based on an existing set that Wolsey had obtained in 1523, adapted to include portraits of the king and cardinal (Campbell (T) 2002, p.155). The date 1507 included in the tapestry may indicate the date of the initial cartoon designs – the

date in the upper right corner, which may be read as 1510 or 1520, being that of this particular weaving. Like the group of *Triumphs* tapestries remaining at Hampton Court, this set probably also belonged to Wolsey (Campbell (T) 1996b, p.103), passing into Henry's collection at Wolsey's fall in 1529.

This tapestry reflects the taste in Henry VIII's court for humanist themes. From as early as 1512, Henry possessed two texts of Petrarch's *Trionfi*. Lord Morley dedicated his English translation of the *Triumphs* to Henry, emulating Baron d'Orpède's French version made for Francis I. The descriptive texts in this tapestry's borders come not from Petrarch but from a further French source, Jean II Robertet, suggesting that the original cartoons for this series were created for a French patron, perhaps Louis XII (Delmarcel 1989). By owning and displaying such a *Triumphs* set, Henry was aligning himself with the most fashionable courts of the day.   EC

PROV. Collection of G. B. Villa, Genoa, by 1868; collection of M. Leclanché, Paris, by 1878; collection of E. Lowengard, Paris, by 1880; purchased from Lowengard in 1883.

LIT. Wingfield Digby 1980, cat. no. 22; Campbell (T) 1998, pp.151–2; Campbell (T) 2002, pp.154–6.

7 Bust of Henry VII

PLATE 2

Pietro Torrigiano (1472–1528), *c*.1509–11

Painted terracotta; h. 60.5 cm, w. 68 cm, d. 35 cm

Victoria and Albert Museum, London (A.49–1935)

Pietro Torrigiano Torrigiani was trained in his native Florence and came to England via the Burgundian court of Margaret of Austria in Flanders. He was one of a number of Italian sculptors who worked at the English court, where he made a major contribution to artistic development, notably the great tombs in Westminster Abbey (cat. nos 29, 117).

The bust is first mentioned in a letter of 10 November 1779, when the antiquary Michael Tyson described 'three busts of Terra Cotta of Hen: VII, Bishop Fisher, and Hen: VIII aet. 19 ... taken out of the Room over the Holbien [*sic*] Gate Whitehall' (Remington 1936, pp.223–4; Pope-Hennessy 1964, p.399), which he had seen at Hatfield Peverel Priory in Essex. The three busts have since generally been accepted as a group, although their early history is unknown, Holbein Gate having been built in 1531–2, after Torrigiano's death. For the bust of 'Bishop Fisher' see the following entry.

The classically inspired portrait bust was revived in Florence in the mid-fifteenth century, initially as an image of status and power, but also with the purpose of expressing greater realism and personality. Torrigiano may also have made a bust of Mary Tudor (lost) for her proposed marriage of 1507–8 to Charles I (later Emperor Charles V).

Clay was an ideal medium for creating such works, due to its malleability and its potential for transformation into the more permanent material of terracotta (literally 'baked earth') through firing in a kiln. By comparison with measurements taken from the plaster and wood mask of the king's funerary effigy (Westminster Undercroft Museum), it appears that the face was created from a death-mask and applied to the modelled bust. The sunken features of the dead king were fleshed out before firing, and the terracotta painted to produce a realistic likeness of the monarch in his middle age. This posthumous image therefore dates to around 1509–11, shortly before Henry VIII commissioned the double tomb of Henry VII and Elizabeth of York from the same sculptor (cat. no. 29). It is not known who commissioned the present bust and the two companion portraits.

The bust had three layers of overpaint, one apparently applied by the English sculptor John Flaxman the Elder, or possibly even his young son John (1755–1826), during restoration work on all three busts in c.1769.

Recent removal of these layers has revealed the original polychromy, and details of the modelling, notably the ermine trim of the cloak, while Flaxman's painting has been partially retained and overpainted. PM

PROV. Reported as Holbein Gate, Whitehall; Mr Wright of Hatfield Peverel Priory (Essex) by 1779 (reportedly purchased from an iron dealer in Belton Street); purchased in 1928 by Mr Arthur Wilson-Filmer at Leeds Castle, Kent; acquired from his widow, Lady Baillie, in 1935.

LIT. Pope-Hennessy 1964, pp.399–401, cat. no. 417, with earlier lit.; Galvin and Lindley 1988; Chaney 1991; Darr 1992a, p.121 and n.55; Darr 1992b, p.136; Goronwy-Roberts 1992; Hepburn 2001.

8 Bust of an ecclesiastic (John Fisher?)

Pietro Torrigiano, *c*.1509–11

Painted terracotta (with later overpaint layers); h. 61.1 cm, w. 65.1 cm, d. 33.7 cm

Metropolitan Museum of Art, New York, Harris Brisbane Dick Fund, 19 (36.69)

The traditional identification of this bust as John Fisher, Bishop of Rochester (executed 1535), and those of Henry VII (cat. no. 7) and Henry VIII, has led to the suggestion that all three were commissioned by Fisher, who, as executor to Lady Margaret Beaufort, oversaw Torrigiano's commission for her tomb (cat. no. 117). However, while the 'Henry VII' is secure, the identities of this and the third bust ('Henry VIII', also now in the Metropolitan Museum) have been questioned, partly by comparison with drawn and painted portraits. The suggestion that the present bust represents Erasmus (Goronwy-Roberts) has received mixed responses. In any event, he must have been a churchman of high standing, closely associated – or wishing to be associated – with the dead king. PM

PROV. Reported as Holbein Gate, Whitehall; Mr Wright of Hatfield Peverel Priory (Essex) by 1779 (reportedly purchased from an iron dealer in Belton Street); purchased in 1928 by Mr Arthur Wilson-Filmer, Leeds Castle, Kent; bought by the Metropolitan Museum of Art from Seligmann and Rey, New York, 1936.

LIT. Remington 1936 (with earlier lit.); Galvin and Lindley 1988; Goronwy-Roberts 1992; Hepburn 2001.

9 Portrait relief of Sir Thomas Lovell

PLATE 13

Attributed to Pietro Torrigiano, *c*.1516–20

Bronze relief in modern painted wooden frame; diam. 67.3 cm

Inscr. with the motto: *hony coyt quy mal y pence* ('honi soit qui mal y pense': shame on him who thinks ill of it)

Dean and Chapter of Westminster, Westminster Abbey Museum

Sir Thomas Lovell (d. 1524) was a lawyer by training and an active patron of architecture. A staunch supporter of the Tudor cause, he fought alongside the future Henry VII at Bosworth in August 1485. As Chancellor of the Exchequer, knight of the king's body, and subsequently Speaker of the House of Commons, Lovell was a powerful and prominent figure, remaining so under Henry VIII (Archbold 1917). The significance of his knighthood, bestowed in 1503, is reflected in the way his likeness is framed by the Garter. The finely chiselled hair curled under an elaborate collar, the detailing of the 'woven' Garter, and particularly the strong modelling of the face, create the impression of a forceful personality.

The roundel is assumed to have been commissioned by Lovell for the gatehouse of the residence he built at East Harling Manor (Norfolk), where in the 1730s 'a Brass Bust of his own Likeness surrounded with the Garter' could still be seen along with his coat of arms. Like his arms, the bronze would have served to declare ownership, but more significantly his status. Despite the difference in scale and function, it is reminiscent of medallic art in its material, form and imagery. A medal of the Duke of Urbino, Federico da Montefeltro (1422–82), similarly framed by the Garter, has also been attributed to Pietro Torrigiano (Hill 1930, no. 1118; Hill and Pollard 1978, pp.83, 177, n.212). Lovell's role as executor to Henry VII and Dr Yonge, whose tombs were both made by Torrigiano (cat. no. 29), probably played a part in his choice of sculptor.   PM

PROV. Sir Thomas Lovell, East Harling Hall; Mr Angerstein of Weeting Hall (Norfolk); purchased by John Charles Robinson; presented by Robinson to Westminster Abbey, 1902.

LIT. Blomefield 1739, p.219, and 1805, I, pp. 322, 324–5, 326; Cust 1902; Cook 1903; Chaney 1991, p.235; Starkey 1991, cat. no. II.10, p.33 (entry by E. Chaney).

10 Reliquary of the Order of St-Esprit

*c.*1390–1410

Gold, enamelled *en ronde bosse*, set with pearls, rubies and sapphires, and enamelled flowers, unmarked; h. 44.5 cm, max. w. 15 cm

Musée du Louvre, Paris (MR 552)

An elaborately arcaded structure, standing on a rectangular base supported by four crenellated turrets with conical roofs, and decorated with flowers enamelled *en ronde bosse* (some or all restored), and a plaque with the arms of the French king Henry III (1574–89); 10 figures, all enamelled *en ronde bosse* (in red, white, blue and green) are arranged in four tiers, framed within Gothic arched niches.

The largest figure, placed centrally, is God the Father (of the Trinity), arms outstretched to hold the crucifix (now missing); above is the Virgin Mary, her arms also extended to hold perhaps a relic (now missing). At the summit stands the figure of Christ holding an orb and standard, symbols of his Resurrection. Six saints with their symbolic attributes flank these central figures. Flanking the Virgin are St Catherine and St Elizabeth of Hungary, below them four apostles: St Bartholomew and St Thomas on the left, St Peter and St Paul on the right. A seventh figure, St Barbara, is just above the base, below God the Father. The structure is lavishly adorned with sapphires, balas rubies and pearls. The sapphires and rubies are not cut, but simply polished and set in claw settings. The pearls are set in trios. The back of the reliquary is made of flat plaques engraved with stylized acanthus foliage, enriched with a few pearls (and the fixings for others, now missing).

This is one of a very few surviving examples of sumptuously bejewelled and enamelled *ymages,* made between about 1390 and 1410 (Eikelmann 1995) which would have been placed in private chapels. The devout and wealthy might own considerable numbers of images – generally incorporating relics – as did Charles VI of France and Richard II in the 1390s (Campbell (M) 1997, p.97) and John de Vere, Earl of Oxford, in 1513 (St John Hope 1914b, pp.332, 339).

The reliquary is a fine example of opaque enamelling *en ronde bosse*. This rich technique is thought to have been invented in Paris in around 1370 as a means of giving brilliant and permanent colour to three-dimensional goldsmiths' work, whether small jewels or larger pieces (Eikelmann 1995; Tait 1986, cat. no. 1). The technique was certainly known in England in the 1370s and practised by the 1390s, when Henry Bolingbroke (later Henry IV) commissioned the London-based goldsmiths Herman and Louis to enamel white hind brooches (Campbell (M) 1997, p.102). Richard II owned hart badges enamelled in white – as seen on the Wilton Diptych (plate 3) – and an elaborately enamelled and jewelled cross (*ibid*, p.113).

The reliquary is puzzling on various counts. Its iconography does not point to an obvious original owner – the Holy Trinity and the Virgin Mary were universally revered. Its style and origin are uncertain. Scholarly opinion differs as to whether the reliquary is one of the very earliest examples of Paris work (Tait 1986, cat. no. 1, pp.22–46, esp. p.42) or a late and possibly English piece of *c.*1410 (Kovacs 1981 and Eikelmann 1995, pp.114–15). Its architectural style seems closer to *c.*1380, and the technique of its enamelling somewhat tentative, very different from

such pieces as the *Goldenes Rössel* of 1404–5 (Baumstark 1995). The International Gothic style of the figures does not point unequivocally to England, but could be *c.*1380–1400. However, the figure style does resemble some English work (Scott 1996, ills 23, 26–7, 49, 89), and the engraved foliage has distinctly English traits (*ibid.*, ills 14, 16, 23, 195). What seems certain is that Henry IV's second queen, Joan of Navarre, sent it as a present to her son, John, via Arnel de Chasteaugiron, Marshal of Brittany, who visited England in 1412 (Kovacs 1981, p.251). Another lavish example of English enamelling was already in France: in 1402 Jean de Berry owned a large figure of the Virgin Mary *de l'ouvrage d'Angleterre,* seated on an enamelled rock within a castle wall, peopled with angels and other figures and set with gems (Guiffrey 1894, II, no. 361, pp.50–1). It is quite possible that the present reliquary was indeed made in England perhaps *c.*1390–1400, for Richard II, and was then given away by Henry IV's queen a few years later. Henry himself recycled quite a number of pieces inherited from Richard II (Campbell (M) 1997, pp.111–13, and nn.146, 153–7 on pp.307–8).   MLC

PROV. Given by Joan of Navarre, second wife of Henry IV, to the son of her first marriage, John, Duke of Brittany, *c.*1412; collections of the Dukes of Brittany and Kings of France; 1561 French royal inventory, listed as item no. 12; 1578 gift of Henry III of France to the treasury of the Order of St-Esprit; acquired by the Louvre with the treasury of the Order of St-Esprit, 1830.

LIT. Vienna 1962, cat. no. 468; Paris 1981, cat. no. 221; Kovacs 1981; Tait 1986, p.41; Campbell (M) 1991, pp.129–30; Eikelmann 1995, pp.114–15, 129, fig. 56.

◀10

11 Margaret of York's crown and case

*c.*1461–74

Crown: silver-gilt, enamels, precious stones and pearls; h. 13.2 cm, diam. 12.5 cm

Inscr: MARGARIT[A] DE [Y]O[R]K and the initials CM

Case: embossed leather with traces of gilding; h. 14.5 cm; w. 20 cm

Inscr: BIEN EN AVIENIR and the initials CM

Aachen Cathedral Treasury

The pearl-edged band of the crown is decorated with the inscription and white enamelled roses set with precious stones, including a diamond cross at the front; on the back are the arms of Burgundy. The CM initials are at the base of the smaller fleurons, which alternate with larger ones; enamelled white roses and stones embellish the fleurons. The case is decorated with scrolls and small dragons; with the arms of England and Burgundy, the motto and the CM initials are on the lid.

One of only two existing medieval crowns associated with the English monarchy, the crown of Edward IV's sister, Margaret of York, is among the most evocative objects of the period. It is also among the most problematic in respect of date, function, origin and condition and would repay more thorough study. Opinion is divided as to whether it was made for Margaret to wear at Edward's coronation in 1461 or as her bridal crown at her wedding to Charles the Bold, Duke of Burgundy, in 1468. The presence of Margaret and Charles's initials and the arms of Burgundy make the latter more likely. Another possibility is that it was from the outset a votive gift from Margaret to the fourteenth-century cult image of Our Lady of Aachen, on whose head the crown is still placed on major feast-days (for this image, see Christ and Minkenberg 1995; Hübner, Paradis-Vroon and Minkenberg 1996). Margaret's sole visit to Aachen, on pilgrimage in 1474, might have been the occasion for such an offering. The crown fits exactly the Virgin's head (see ill.). Unlike the crown in Munich recorded in England in 1399 (Alexander and Binski 1987, cat. no. 13, pp.202–3), Margaret's crown is not, as one might expect for a royal crown, of gold and is less lavish in its use of precious stones. The white roses could serve both as a Yorkist emblem and as a metaphor for the Virgin. Personalized *ex-voto* gifts to shrines and cult images were common from the

Middle Ages onwards. If the crown was made for the image, it was more likely to have been fashioned in the Netherlands than in England. The extent of the restoration in 1865 by the Aachen goldsmith Vogeno is uncertain (there are at least two hallmarks on the crown). The presence of Margaret's motto on the case (*Bien en Avienir*), in conjunction with the arms of England and Burgundy and the initials of herself and Charles the Bold, indicate that it was not made prior to their wedding; alternatively the case was associated with the votive donation. RM

LIT. Grimme 1972, no. 98, pp.111–12; Hammond 1984; Lepie 1990, p.54; van der Velden 2000, pp.215–17.

Margaret of York's crown on the head of the cult image of the Virgin at Aachen (see cat. no. 11)

11

12 Jane Seymour Cup design

Hans Holbein the Younger, 1536

Ink and chalk on paper, with grey and pink washes
and gold heightening; h. 37.6 cm, w. 15.5 cm

Inscribed: BOVND TO OBEY AND [SERVE] on the cover
and BOVND TO OBEY (twice) on the cup

Ashmolean Museum, Oxford, WA 1863.424

This is the final design for a magnificent cup evidently to be given by Henry VIII to Jane Seymour, the king's third wife; they married in May 1536 and she died in October the following year, after giving birth to the future Edward VI. A preliminary design by Holbein is in the British Museum (Rowlands with Bartrum 1993, cat. no. 326). A gold cup studded with diamonds and with pendant pearls, which matches the details of this design, is described in the inventory of Elizabeth I's plate taken in 1574 (Collins 1955, p.279, no. 47).

The design for the cup includes the queen's motto, 'bound to obey and serve', repeated on the lid and on the foot. The king's and queen's initials are intertwined with love knots, a motif also used at Hampton Court Palace. At the top of the elaborate lid, two putti hold a shield surmounted with the royal crown. In the middle of the cup are roundels with projecting busts of women in classical style. The surface is decorated with the arabesque designs fashionable during the Renaissance.

The cup was probably to be made by Hans of Antwerp, or Cornelis Hays, the royal goldsmith with whom Holbein had worked on a gilded statuette of Adam and Eve in 1533. One of a series of royal commissions to Holbein, including a table fountain given to Henry by Anne Boleyn in 1534, this is one of his most splendid surviving designs for goldsmiths' work. SF

PROV. Loggan; Douce; acquired by the Ashmolean Museum in 1863.

LIT. Parker 1938, pp.133–4; Starkey 1991, cat. no. IX.14, p.127.

13 'The Boleyn Cup'

London, 1535–6 (maker's mark: three flowers)

Silver-gilt; h. 31.4 cm

Church of St John the Baptist, Cirencester, Gloucestershire

The cup has a conical bowl, with foot and cover of ogee form. It is embossed with flutes and chased around the foot with acanthus foliage; the lip is engraved with naturalistic scrolling foliage and the finial is in the form of a crowned falcon above a tree trunk.

12

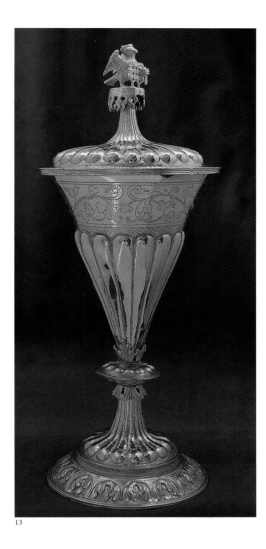

13

crowned falcon holding a sceptre and standing on a tree trunk from which grow roses. But the cup was made during the last year of her life and the falcon device is possibly not its original finial: it is attached to the cover by an iron screw, which is certainly not original and its tooling is less well executed than the chasing of the cup. TS

LIT. Jackson 1911, p.167; Oman 1978, p.33; Glanville 1990, p.237.

14 The Old Hall Manuscript

PLATE 78

c.1415–21, later additions

Parchment, ff.112; h. 41.6 cm, w. 27.6 cm

British Library, London (MS Add. 57950)

Displayed is a setting of the Gloria by 'Roy Henry' (f.12v–13r), who has variously been linked with all three early fifteenth-century kings of that name. Earlier attributions to Henry VI or Henry IV have been ruled out in favour of Henry V, who was king at the time of the manuscript's initial compilation, which took place between c.1415 and 1421, for the household chapel of the eldest of Henry V's younger brothers and heir apparent, Thomas Duke of Clarence. This hypothesis rests chiefly on evidence that from at least 1418 to the duke's death in 1421 Leonel Power, a principal composer in Old Hall, served as a singing-man and Instructor of the Choristers of the duke's chapel (Bowers 1975–6). It is then presumed that the manuscript passed to Henry V, and thereafter to the infant Henry VI. Additions were made, in various hands, after 1421, including compositions (some thought to be autograph) by the king's chaplains Thomas Damett, John Cooke and Nicholas Sturgeon.

The survival of English music manuscripts of this type is extremely rare, and Old Hall is the most important collection of English sacred music from the end of the fourteenth and early fifteenth centuries. Whereas in later manuscripts, such as the Lambeth Choirbook (cat. no. 311), music for the Mass is arranged in complete cycles (*Gloria, Credo Sanctus, Agnus Dei*), it was common practice in earlier manuscripts to place the movements together according to their liturgical order, such as is the case with Old Hall. Much of the music is for three voices, and the style ranges from homophonic to more complex and florid writing. DS

PROV. The college of St Edmund, Old Hall, near Ware (Hertfordshire), 1893–1973; British Museum, 1973.

LIT. Bent 1967–8; Hughes and Bent 1969–73; Bent 1984.

15 'The Henry VIII Manuscript'

PLATE 80

c.1518

Vellum, ff.128; h. c.30.5cm, w. 21 cm

British Library, London (MS Add. 31922)

'Pastime with good company', one of the 33 songs attributed to 'the king h.viii', is displayed here (f.14v–15r). The Henry VIII Manuscript, like the great ecclesiastical choirbooks on display (cat. nos 24, 311) is a rare survival and, in terms of secular music-making in the early years of the sixteenth century, is equalled in importance only by the so-called 'Fayrfax Manuscript' (British Library, MS Add. 5465), the chief monument of music at the court of the king's father, Henry VII.

The Henry VIII Manuscript is thought to date from around 1518. Certainly many of the works contained in the book describe the jollity, liveliness and passion of the early years of Henry's court, with themes of hunting, singing and dancing; also included are love songs that have 'a markedly erotic tone' (Stevens 1973), as well as a selection of carols and a small number of purely instrumental compositions. There is no evidence to suggest that the book ever belonged to the king, but with the inclusion of works by a number of Chapel Royal musicians (including Cornysh, Farthing, Lloyd and Fayrfax), it is likely that it at least circulated within courtly circles. The presence of compositions by foreign composers, such as Agricola, Heinrich Isaac and Compère, highlights the international musical influences at work in Henry's court.

Henry VIII was trained in the musical arts from an early age (Fallows 1993), and was noted to have been an accomplished musician on the organ, lute and virginals. He was also a competent singer and a great patron of music, having increased his private household of musicians (many of whom were foreign) to no fewer than 58 by 1547. Paradoxically, Henry was also responsible for shutting down the country's most lavish musical foundations when monastic and collegiate establishments were dissolved in the 1530s and 1540s. DS

PROV. Thomas Fuller, MD; Stephen Fuller, Bloomsbury, in 1762; Archibald, 11th Earl of Eglinton; Sir Charles Montolieu Lamb, Bt, Beauport Park, Sussex; passed in the mid-1880s to the British Museum.

LIT. Stevens 1979; Starkey 1991, pp.104–6, cat. no. XI.23.

The Boleyn Cup is a key piece in the assimilation of Renaissance ornament in English domestic, as opposed to courtly, silver. The basic shape is similar to that of *façon de Venise* glass, which was just starting to appear in England, and the acanthus foliage, flutes, knop and engraved flowers all reflect familiarity with contemporary continental ornament, such as in the *Kunstbüchlein* published by Hans Brosamer in Frankfurt am Main (see also cat. no. 358). That particular pattern book is thought to have been published around 1540, but the existence of the cup would suggest that it or similar designs must have been in circulation at an earlier date.

Elizabeth I's physician, Dr Richard Master, presented the cup to the church in 1563, having acquired the lands of Cirencester Abbey after the Dissolution of the monasteries. Traditionally it is said to have belonged to Queen Anne Boleyn (1507–36) and the finial is indeed in the form of her personal device, a

16 'Shawm' from the *Mary Rose**

PLATE 83

*c.*1530–45

Wood; overall l. 101.3 cm

The Mary Rose Trust, Portsmouth (80A0545)

The identity of this so-called 'shawm' has been a source of some confusion since it was recovered in 1982 with other musical instruments on Henry VIII's flagship, the *Mary Rose*. The most likely candidate seems to be a *douçaine*, or 'styll shawm' as it is called in the court records of Henry VIII. No contemporary examples of the still shawm now exist, although the theorist Johannes Tinctoris, writing in around 1487, describes the instrument as having a thumb-hole in addition to seven finger-holes; it was also said to be a quiet instrument with a limited range. As its name would suggest, the *douçaine* differed from 'loud' instruments (such as the shawm or crumhorn) in that it usually played in a 'soft' consort of lighter instruments such as the fiddle, lute and harp.

Musical instruments (other than organs) were not a regular feature in religious ceremonies, but were more prominent in courtly or private entertainments. Instrumental repertoire may have included those works now preserved in the Henry VIII Manuscript (cat. no. 15), and in other 'secular' music books of the period.   DS

PROV. Recovered from the *Mary Rose* in 1980.

LIT. Palmer 1983; Myers 1983.

17 Henry VIII

Attributed to Lucas Horenbout (*c.*1490/5–1544), *c.*1525–7

Watercolour and bodycolour on vellum laid on card; h. 5.3 cm, w. 4.8 cm

Inscr. in gold: '·HR·/·VIII·', centre left; '·ANº·/·XXXV·', centre right; 'HK', at top and bottom

Fitzwilliam Museum, Cambridge (PD.19–1949)

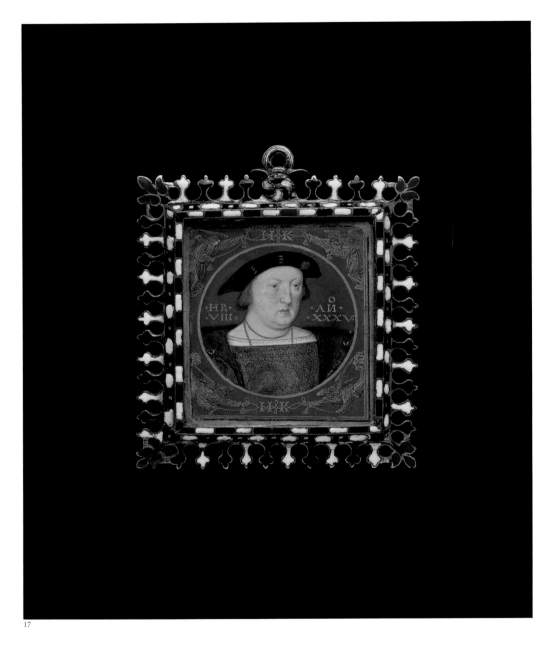

17

Henry VIII is depicted beardless, at the age of 34 or 35, framed by a thin gold circle and set against the deep-blue background that was to be conventional in miniature painting throughout the rest of the sixteenth century. The circular bust portrait is set within a red rectangle, decorated at each corner with golden angels holding cords that form the letters 'H' and 'K' for Henry and Catherine of Aragon. The enamelled frame is a modern imitation of a seventeenth-century reliquary frame.

This is one of the earliest detached portrait miniatures produced in England and, with its rectangular border decorated in gold, it provides a clear visual link between these kinds of objects and the traditions of manuscript illumination from which they derived. The miniature has been attributed persuasively to Lucas Horenbout, the son of the Ghent manuscript illuminator Gerard Horenbout, who is said to have taught Holbein miniature painting and is known to have worked for Henry VIII as 'King's Painter'. Five other versions of this portrait are known, attributed to Horenbout or his studio, and variously showing the king with and without a beard. Most were probably made as diplomatic or personal gifts; they exemplify the sophisticated development of art forms within the social and political context of Henry VIII's court.   CM

PROV. ?Horace Walpole, Strawberry Hill; collection of Hollingsworth Magniac, by 1862; his sale, Christie's, London, 4 July 1892, lot 183; purchased Colnaghi's; Duke of Buccleuch, from whom purchased in 1949 from the Spencer George Perceval Fund.

LIT. Bayne-Powell 1985, pp.128–30; Campbell and Foister 1986, pp.719–27; Hearn 1995, p.118.

18 Anne of Cleves

Hans Holbein the Younger, 1539

Gum on vellum in ivory case; diam. 4.6 cm

Victoria and Albert Museum, London (P.153:1, 2–1910)

Anne of Cleves became Henry VIII's fourth wife in 1540. Following the death of Jane Seymour in 1537, Holbein, the king's salaried painter, was sent abroad in 1538 and 1539 to take the likenesses of potential brides, a traditional duty for royal painters. In August 1539 Holbein was sent to Düren in Cleves to bring back portraits of the two daughters of the Duke of Cleves, Anne and Amelia. The full-face pose seen here would have ensured that any potential defects were visible; other portraits had been rejected, as 'but a parte of theyr faces' was displayed.

This miniature is one of two portraits of Anne of Cleves by Holbein that survive, the other a full-size painting (Paris, Louvre). Both portraits were presumably worked up from drawings on Holbein's return to court, rather than being produced on the spot: it has been established that the Louvre portrait, although also on easily transported vellum, was produced from a transferred pattern (Foucart 1985).

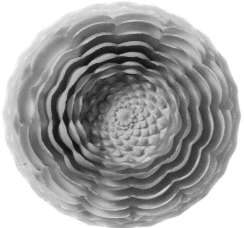

The miniature of Anne is painted with exceptional care and a lavishness in the use of precious pigments. Expensive ultramarine is used in the blue background, shading into cheaper azurite. The jewels on Anne's headdress are alternately ultramarine and azurite. The beautiful carved ivory case representing a rose may not be the original case for the miniature, as it is slightly trimmed to fit, but there can be no doubt that this was intended as a most precious object, fit for royal scrutiny. Conceivably its size allowed the king to have Anne's image constantly with him in anticipation of her arrival. However, Henry found Anne unalluring in the flesh and the marriage was annulled only a few months later.   SF

PROV. Apparently Mr Alexander 1720; Col James Seymour in 1732; Thomas Barret of Lee Priory, Kent, *c.*1739; sold by his son, Thomas Barret, in 1826; acquired by Francis Douce and bequeathed to Sir Samuel Rush Meyrick; Major General Meyrick, who bequeathed to Miss Eleanor Davies; George Salting Bequest, 1910.

LIT. Murdoch et al. 1981, p.37; Rowlands 1985, cat. no. M.6; Starkey 1991, pp.140–41, fig. 9; Hearn 1995, cat. no. 66, p.119.

19a

19 King's College Chapel, Cambridge

1448–1515

Henry VI's 'will and intent' of 1448 gives the key measurements and some other details of the chapel whose construction was about to start. It was to be aisleless, but the antechapel (nave) was to be flanked on each side by four closets (small chapels). The internal length was to be 288 feet (87.8 m), the height 90 feet (27.4 m) and the width 40 feet (12.2 m) – dimensions that put it in a different league from all earlier academic college chapels. Henry VI had envisaged spending £1,000 on the college's buildings for each of the 20 years following 1448, but as his government's power crumbled in the mid-1450s, his subventions dwindled. When work came to a standstill in 1461, the east parts of the choir had probably barely risen into the window zone. On the north side of the choir two closets (not envisaged in 1448) had been completed. The heavy influence on the detailing of these closets from early fourteenth-century (i.e. pre-Perpendicular) East Anglian sources reveals clearly the local origins of Reginald Ely, the first architect.

In the mid-1470s work resumed, albeit in a modest way. The easternmost north window, which existed by 1476–7, indicates that the second architect, John Wolriche, had reduced the internal height, and the spandrels above this window suggest that he intended to abandon the high vault in favour of a wooden roof. When Edward IV decided to support the work in 1480, another architect, Simon Clerk, was able to complete and roof over the five easternmost choir bays. He also revived the idea of building a masonry

vault. Unfortunately, this necessitated adding above the windows much solid walling, aesthetically the weakest feature of the chapel. Richard III supported the work, but after his death in 1485 building was suspended once more.

It took Henry VII 21 years to develop an interest in King's, but his commitment, once given, was unequivocal. Although a formal agreement between him and the college speaks of fulfilling Henry VI's intentions, in reality Lancastrian decorum had given way to Tudor ostentation. The determination to secure an excellent result accounts for the recruitment in 1508 of John Wastell, the most sought-after architect in East Anglia and the designer of the superb crossing tower of Canterbury Cathedral. Wastell made two outstandingly important contributions to the architecture of the chapel. The lower walls of the antechapel, always intended to be panelled, and therefore less severe than their counterparts in the choir, now acquired huge carvings of Henry VII's arms and badges, all very boldly conceived and executed (see fig. 19a). Wastell's other major contribution was the great fan vault spanning the central vessel. Its decoration contrives to be luxurious yet not oppressive, and the bay-disrupting potential of its tiered radiating panels is held firmly in check by the transverse arches continuing the strong bay divisions on each side wall.   CW

LIT. Colvin 1963, pp.268–78; Colvin 1975, pp.187–95; Leedy 1980, pp.24–9, 140–44 and *passim*; Harvey 1984, pp.56–9, 173–4, 316–23, 347–8; Woodman 1986.

19▶

20 Charter upon Act of Parliament for the foundation of King's College, Cambridge

16 March 1446

Vellum, five membranes, with pendant seal;
h. 72.5 cm, w. 99.5 cm, diam. of seal 14.5 cm

King's College, Cambridge (KC-18)

In 1447–8 the London illuminator William Abell was paid £1 6s. 8d. to illuminate the foundation charter of Eton College, an institution founded by the young King Henry VI for the education of poor boys in 1441. At the same time, Henry had founded King's College at Cambridge, with the intention that Etonians might continue their education at university. Both institutions retain charters, which record the Acts of Parliament that ratified the terms of their foundations in March 1446. Though no documentation survives linking Abell to the illumination of the King's charter, its style confirms that it was indeed executed by the same hand.

By the time he illuminated the Eton and King's charters, Abell was already established as a member of the Stationers' Guild. The survival of documents from subsequent years shows Abell to have been an involved member of his community, acting as surety, executor and churchwarden. In 1469 he took over the tenancy of a workshop in Paternoster Row, near London Bridge, and in the following years his business expanded into two neighbouring properties. Abell's widow maintained the properties for two years after his death in 1474. His business was successful, and his artistic style – perceived by Alexander to be a reaction against the prevailing International Gothic style – proved influential (cat. nos 91, 95, 131, 137, 172, 253).

The King's College charter expresses the importance of the foundation through its impressive size and the splendour of its illumination. Henry VI kneels inside a letterform that encloses him as though in a private chapel; he holds in his hand a charter from which dangles a seal. Behind him, in the left margin, members of the House of Lords and the House of Commons kneel in prayer. All gaze at the Virgin, placed in an aureola of light and encircled with angels, and the Trinity above her. Further angels hold the arms of Edward the Confessor and Edmund, King and Martyr, and the royal crown with the arms of England and France. St Nicholas, patron saint of the foundation, stands before the Virgin, interceding on behalf of the king, the Lords and the Commons.   AB

LIT. Saltmarsh 1933, p.87; Alexander 1972, no. 5; Scott 1996, II, pp.264–5, 267.

21 Seal matrix of King's College, Cambridge

Engraved in 1443, recut in 1449

Silver; diam. 7.3 cm

Inscr. in black-letter: *Sigillu*[m]: *co*[mun]*e: prepositi scolarium: collegii rigalis*(sic) *be*[ate] *marie z s*[an]*c*[t]*i nicholai de cantebr*[igie] (The common seal of the provost and scholars of the royal college of the blessed Mary and St Nicholas of Cambridge)

King's College, Cambridge

This circular seal shows in the centre the Virgin Mary, dressed as the Queen of Heaven. She ascends, amid clouds borne by six angels, three on each side, into the hands of God the Father, whose hands are outstretched ready to receive her. She is flanked by the founder Henry VI, praying, and St Nicholas, blessing. To the left an angel holds the shield of England and France quarterly, and to the right that of France alone, to symbolize that Henry VI was King of both England and France. Beneath are the arms of the college.

King's College was the major foundation of Henry VI. He founded his college of St Nicholas, his patron saint, in 1441, to complement 'King's College of Our Lady of Eton beside Windsor' (plate 93, cat. no. 23). The seals of King's College, Cambridge, and Eton College reflect his devotion to the Virgin Mary. In 1443 the king changed the title of the college to the College of the Blessed Mary and St Nicholas, and the present seal dates from that time.

The arms of the college on the seal, as first engraved in 1443, were two lily flowers, and in base a mitre pierced by a pastoral staff, with a chief per pale azure, a fleur-de-lis or and gules a lion of England. This combined the arms of the patron saints and the royal founder. On 1 January 1449 Henry VI authorized an entirely new shield for the college. The royal chief was retained, but the emblems of the patron

20

21

22

saints were changed into three roses on a black field, so that as the king himself said, 'our newly founded college, lasting for ages to come, whose perpetuity we wish to be signified by the stability of the black colour, may bring forth the brightest flowers, redolent of every kind of knowledge'; and he added: 'to which also that we may impart something of the royal nobility which may make the work truly royal and illustrious, we have appointed portions of the arms which by royal right belong to us in the kingdoms of England and France to be placed in the chief of the shield, parted per pale of azure with a flower of the French and of gules with a leopard passant'. The alteration of the arms was achieved by re-engraving the shield.

JC

LIT. Birch 1887–92, no. 4754; St John Hope 1883–5.

Stained-glass panel showing Sts Peter and John healing the Lame Man, King's College Chapel, Cambridge (see cat. no. 22)

22 Vidimus for stained glass in King's College Chapel, Cambridge

*c.*1535

Pen and brown ink and grey wash on paper; h. 16.7 cm, w. 17.5 cm

Bowdoin College Museum of Art, Brunswick, Maine, USA (1811.109)

A detailed design for six lights of windows 19 and 21 on the south side of the chapel, with the cusps for the tracery at the top and grid-lines representing the ferramenta (the supports for the glass). There are three subjects, each spread over two lights. Left: Christ appearing to the apostles; middle: Sts Peter and John healing the Lame Man; right: the death of Ananias.

The glazing of King's College Chapel is the best-preserved example of northern Renaissance glass-painting in England, and of a scale and magnificence befitting a royal commission. The overall iconographical scheme is typological – that is, the concordance between the Old and New Testaments (see cat. no. 241). The first windows were commissioned in 1515 and the glazing was not completed until at least 1535 (except for the west window). The leading glass-painters of the time were employed on the project, notably the immigrant craftsmen Barnard Flower and Galyon Hone. The vidimus, with its full-blown Renaissance architectural and ornamental details, monumental figures and complex pictorial narratives, belongs to the last phase of the work. The drawing and the painting of the Lame Man and other sections in the glass itself have been attributed to the Antwerp engraver Dierick Vellert, although no unequivocal documentary evidence of his presence in England has come to light.

During the later Middle Ages, vidimuses were an important feature of the commissioning process for all crafts that required individual designs, as they often formed the basis of the binding agreement between patron and craftsman. This and two other surviving vidimuses for King's College Chapel represent a later stage in the design process than the Edinburgh vidimus for Cardinal Wolsey (cat. no. 295). The grid-lines for the ferramenta suggest that they were not the original design drawings, but copies made after final approval had been given by the clients, and were intended for use as guides by the maker of the full-scale cartoons for the windows. The figure of St Paul in the exhibited drawing has been worked over in ink and appears to represent a touching-up by the glazier before delivering it to the cartoonist.

RM

PROV. Collection of the Hon. James Bowdoin III, Boston, Maine, USA; bequeathed 1811.

LIT. Boon 1964; Wayment 1979 and 1997.

23

23 Eton College, Berkshire, Cloister Court

1441–7 with later alterations

Cloister Court was begun in 1441 as the domestic quadrangle of Henry VI's collegiate foundation of St Mary at Eton. Work on it progressed briskly until 1448, when a series of proposals were put forward for the total redevelopment of the college on a gargantuan scale. But these miscarried and the incomplete court was finally patched together in the early sixteenth century. Since then it has undergone several alterations and been raised by a storey.

The court comprises three residential ranges and a great hall laid out on a regular plan. It encloses a cloister walk on two levels, the upper glazed and the lower open to the garth. A series of projecting square towers punctuate the crenellated exterior of the building, an unusual detail possibly modelled on the upper ward of neighbouring Windsor Castle. As the surviving accounts show, the Eton works employed a large, pressed-labour force and directly involved several courtiers. These circumstances contrived to make Eton hugely influential.

The most striking feature of the court is its use of brick. This material had been employed in English fine architecture from about 1400, but usually under the direction of foreign craftsmen and in designs of a distinctly continental style. But the designer of Eton, probably the mason Robert Westerley, used brick in lavish combination with stone. By doing so he created for the first time a brick building in an essentially English architectural idiom.

Three novel features of Cloister Court were to find favour in the English architectural mainstream into the seventeenth century: the lavish, combined use of stone and brick; an interest in patterning walls with vitrified bricks (so-called diaper); and window tracery without decorative cusping. Eton also served as the model for Queens' College, Cambridge, and, through this building, can claim to be the parent of the tradition of Cambridge collegiate design.   JG

LIT. Willis and Clark 1886, I, pp.380–464; Colvin 1963, pp.268 and 279–92; Goodall 2002.

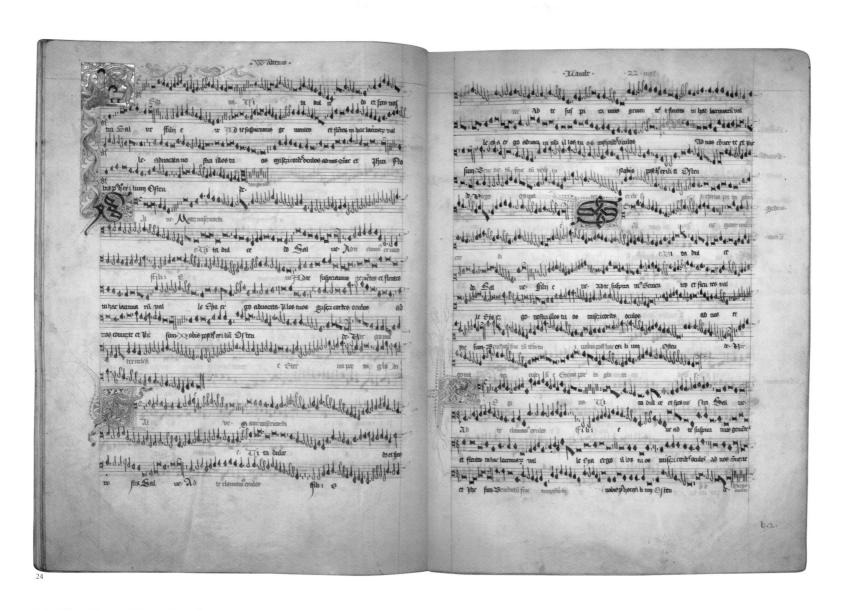

24

24 The Eton Choirbook

c.1505

Parchment, ff.126; h. *c*.42.5 cm, w. 29.7 cm

Eton College Library (MS 178)

During the reign of Edward IV, composed polyphony had undergone a major transformation since the time of the Old Hall Manuscript (cat. no. 14). The forces deployed for church music had been augmented to include boys' voices and a true bass line encompassing a range of up to 23 notes from the lowest to the highest voice, whereas previously overall vocal range rarely exceeded 16 notes (Bowers 1995). The result of this change was music conceived on a much broader canvas, with construction of symphonic proportions.

This explosion of activity reached its culmination in the last decades of the fifteenth century, as exemplified by the contents of the Eton Choirbook, our main source of English church music from this time. The book was compiled in *c*.1505 for use in the chapel of Eton College, containing music for the evening offices of Vespers and Compline, including 67 Latin antiphons and 24 settings of the Magnificat (many of these works are now missing or incomplete); also included is an extended setting of the St Matthew Passion, and the enigmatic 13-part canonical work *Jesus autem transiens*. Many of the composers represented were either employed at Eton or within its vicinity (St George's, Windsor), or their career patterns were such that they had close associations with the college; a number of compositions seem to have been acquired, via various networks, as far afield as London, Oxford, Cambridge, Winchester and Arundel.

Illustrated here (f.38v–39r) is the opening of a *Salve regina* by Walter Lambe, whose name is echoed in the legend '*ecce agnus*' (behold the Lamb [of God]) in the top left-hand illumination. After the Oxonian composer John Browne, more compositions are preserved by Lambe in Eton than by any other composer. Lambe, who had been a King's Scholar at Eton, was a singing-man of Arundel College and St George's, Windsor, intermittently between 1476 and 1504, and his music serves as a good example of the magnificence of compositional innovation in late fifteenth-century English church music.   DS

LIT. Harrison 1956–61; Williamson 1997 and 2000.

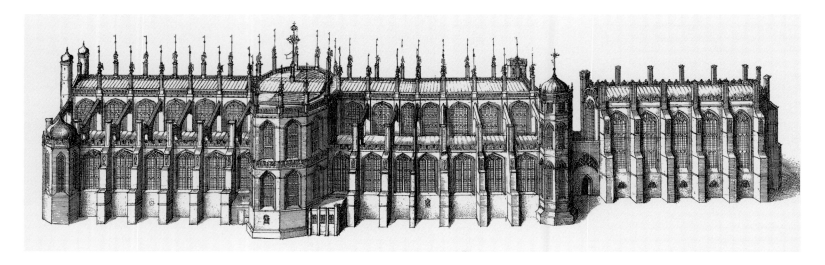

25 Windsor Castle, St George's Chapel

1475–1528

In building St George's Chapel, Edward IV had two main aims: the provision of a burial place for himself, and the creation of a chapel for the Order of the Garter, which would supersede the relatively small thirteenth-century building refitted by the Order's founder, Edward III (see also cat. no. 83). The reasoning behind the rejection of the conventional chapel format in favour of the curious concept of a miniaturized great church is not recorded, but one possibility is that Edward IV was attempting to evoke Camelot, seat of the prototype of all chivalric societies, which, in some versions of the Arthurian legend, is a minster rather than a mere chapel. There may also have been a desire to give St George's a measure of parity with Westminster Abbey, where the latest and largest royal monument was that of Henry V, the most illustrious member of the ousted Lancastrian dynasty. Edward IV's chantry, left unfinished in an act of posthumous revenge by Henry VII, occupied the privileged founder's position north of the high altar.

The design drawn up by the Oxford architect Henry Janyns in 1475 was little changed in Henry VII's reign, which saw the completion of the chapel except for the Lady Chapel vault and the lantern tower over the crossing – neither of which was ever to be built. Contemporaries would probably have been most impressed by the slenderness of the arcade piers and by the even greater constructional daring displayed in the raising of extremely low-pitched vaults over the wide central vessels (see plate 70).   CW

LIT. St John Hope 1913a, pp.375–477; Colvin 1963, pp.884–8; Colvin 1975, pp.311–15; Kidson 1975; Leedy 1980, pp.220–25 and *passim*; Wilson 1990, pp.217–21; Tatton-Brown 2001.

St George's Chapel, from the south, engraving by Wenceslaus Hollar, published 1672, from St John Hope 1913a (cat. no. 25)

26 Windsor Castle, St George's Chapel, gates enclosing the tomb of Edward IV

John Tresilian (attributed); *c*.1478–83

Wrought iron, previously gilded; total w., including gates and piers, 362 cm, h. of piers 241 cm

The gates and their half-hexagonal piers are built up from thousands of small openwork tracery plates, riveted in layers on to each other, and then pegged on to a light frame of iron bars. The result is a robust and delicate structure, like miniature architecture. Although each component is flat, the layered assembly creates canted bays, buttresses, lanterns, projecting canopies and an infinitely variegated surface. The work of two smiths can be detected: one producing the exquisitely refined details, and the other, using a coarser hammer, producing the main structural elements.

Their style is most closely paralleled in the Low Countries, although for technical virtuosity they are unmatched in England or abroad. The flamboyant tracery can be found in mid fifteenth-century iron and woodwork in Brabant. The structure resembles the wooden retable of Claudio de Villa, made in Brussels *c*.1470 (Derveaux-van Ussel 1977, pl. 4).

At the time Edward IV's tomb was commissioned, John Tresilian was engaged as 'principal smith' at Windsor, working there between 1477 and 1484. He was a clockmaker from Westminster, being paid for his services to the king in 1516. The precise technique of the Windsor gates reflects John's clockmaking skills.

Anthony Tresilian, presumably his son, continued as royal clockmaker, with payments up to 1529. Anthony's neighbours in Westminster included several Flemish and German metalworkers whose pattern books may have supplied designs for the Windsor gates.   JGe

PROV. Originally placed across the north side of the tomb bay, shifted to the south side in 1790.

LIT. St John Hope 1913a, II, pp.378, 399, 403, 406, 418–19, 428–9; Geddes 1999, pp.261–72, 386–7; Fehrmann 2002; Geddes 2002.

27 Drawing of a canopied funerary monument

PLATE 54

Probably by William Vertue, *c*.1515

Pen and grey-brown washes on vellum; h. 58 cm, w. 39 cm

Inscr. in early 17th-century (?) lettering: 'The Monument intended for Kinge Henry the sixte'

British Library, London (MS Cotton Augustus II 1)

The identification given in the inscription, which was presumably based on information available to Sir Robert Cotton when he acquired this drawing, is confirmed by the inclusion of features derived from the monument to Henry VI's father in Westminster Abbey. From 1498 onwards it was Henry VII's declared intention to move Henry VI's body from St George's Chapel, Windsor, to the new Lady Chapel at Westminster (Henry VII's Chapel, cat. no. 28), but it is almost certain that the translation was meant to take place only after Henry VI had been canonized, when the need would be not for a tomb (the class of object represented here), but for a shrine, a structure of quite different format (cf. cat. no. 316). By 1515 the plan to enshrine Henry VI at Westminster must have been

26

abandoned, for in that year Henry VII and his queen's monument was erected on the site originally allocated to the shrine. It may be suggested that the Cotton drawing shows an unexecuted project of *c*.1515 or later for a tomb over Henry VI's grave at Windsor.

The form of the canopy and its structural independence from the tomb-chest derive from the rear part of the chantry chapel of Henry V at Westminster. If, as seems certain, the broadly proportioned image niches at the centre of each long side were intended to resemble their Westminster counterparts in housing sculptures of the enthroned king, the aim will have been to celebrate Henry VI's status as the only English ruler ever to be crowned King of France. Details such as the bold cusping to the canopy arches and the polygonal shaft-buttresses surmounted by imbricated domelets illustrate a dependence on Henry VII's Chapel (cat. no. 28) which is common to virtually all complex masonry structures designed by royal architects in the period *c*.1510–35. The improvised perspective would have made the drawing more intelligible to non-expert viewers than a strictly architectural rendering employing only elevations and sections. The author of this superbly drafted drawing, and of the architectural design it represents, was probably William Vertue, king's chief master mason 1510–27.   CW

PROV. Collection of Sir Robert Cotton (1571–1631); acquired by the British Museum on its foundation in 1753.

LIT. Harvey 1953, p.100; Colvin 1975, pp.42 and n., 211, 219; Wilson 2003.

28 Henry VII's Chapel, Westminster Abbey

PLATES 1, 72

Begun 1503, consecrated 1516

In the 1490s Henry VII began to rebuild the Lady Chapel of St George's, Windsor, as a receptacle for his own tomb and the shrine of the as yet uncanonized Henry VI (cat. no. 25). He abandoned this scheme in 1497 when he became persuaded that Henry VI had intended to be buried in Westminster Abbey. In 1502 the thirteenth-century Lady Chapel at Westminster was demolished and in January 1503 the foundation stone of its successor was laid. The structure was probably complete by 1508, but the installation of its fittings (not fully in accordance with the founder's intentions) was completed only in 1515. Since Henry VI's canonization remained incomplete, his body was never transferred from Windsor (cat. no. 27).

The architecture of Henry VII's Chapel recalls the choir of a great church more than a Lady Chapel. This relationship and the inclusion of an apsidal east end indicate a desire to give Westminster's new saint parity with the existing one, Edward the Confessor, whose shrine stood in the thirteenth-century apse of the main church. The interior elevations are a much-enriched version of those of St George's, Windsor, but the most spectacular feature of the central vessel is the pendant fan vault (plate 1). Its design draws on sources in Oxford, home town of the original architect of St George's, Henry Janyns. The most important of these sources, the vault added c.1490 to the choir of St Frideswide's Abbey (now Oxford Cathedral), postdates the death of Henry Janyns, and the debt is most readily explained if one postulates that Henry's younger kinsman Robert designed the Westminster Chapel. The outstanding feature of the exceptionally richly treated exterior, the complex bay windows lighting the aisles and radiating chapels (plate 72), derive unmistakably from those of Henry VII's Tower at Windsor (cat. no. 3), a firmly documented work of Robert Janyns.   CW

LIT. Colvin 1975, pp.210–22; Leedy 1980, pp.214–17 and *passim*; Wilson et al. 1986, pp.70–78; Wilson 1995 and 2003.

29 Tomb monument of King Henry VII and Queen Elizabeth of York*

PLATE 52

Pietro Torrigiano; contract dated 26 October 1512

Touchstone, white marble, gilt-bronze, within bronze grate; l. c.275.5 cm, w. 154 cm, h. to cavetto 141 cm, h. to effigy 168 cm

Westminster Abbey, Henry VII's Chapel

An 'altar-tomb' on a white marble step; moulded plinth with gilt-bronze inset fillet of foliage, Tudor roses, fleurs-de-lis and separately cast male foliage masks at the corners. At the angles of the tomb-chest are gilt-bronze pilasters with Corinthian capitals and bases. The Beaufort portcullis and Tudor rose are included at the base and top respectively of the Renaissance vase and foliage decoration. The east end of the tomb has a crowned shield of arms of Henry VII and Queen Elizabeth suspended from ribbons held by two naked putti (these are also gilt-bronze). At the west end is a large crowned Tudor rose with a dragon and greyhound as supporters, again in gilt-bronze (the ribbons to the crown now largely lost). The north and south sides of the tomb-chest each have three gilt-bronze roundels enclosed in touch-stone wreaths, tied at the top with fringed ribbons. Each of the six tondi has a pair of saints: the north has (from the east) St Mary Magdalene and St Barbara; St Christopher and St Anne; and St Edward the Confessor and St Vincent. On the south side are St George and St Anthony; St John the Baptist and St John the Evangelist; and the Virgin and Child and St Michael. In the spandrels of the roundels are sprays of Tudor roses in gilded bronze (two lost) and between them are gilt-bronze pilasters. The entablature above contains the inscription poem, beginning '*Septimus hic situs est Henricus*', which has been plausibly ascribed to John Skelton. Above it is a large cavetto moulding of white marble, with gilt-bronze foliage at the corners, supporting a narrow slab of touchstone on which are the effigies of the king and queen. Four angels perch at the corners, originally holding royal banners or a sword and scales. The two at the east end (one missing wing) support a shield of the royal arms encircled by the Garter, all of gilt-bronze: Darr has shown that a similar shield was held by those at the west end (one missing both wings and his lower arm). In the middle of the cavetto moulding, which is carved with Renaissance ornament of foliage enclosing Tudor roses, and a pair of birds each side, is a gilt-bronze inscription plaque on each side, held by two naked putti, emerging from foliage.

The gilt-bronze effigy of Henry VII wears a long robe with flat-topped cap having lappets, feet on lion, head on two cushions (the tassels lost). The queen's effigy has a pedimental headdress, a fur-lined robe, with her feet also on a lion, and her head on two cushions (tassels also gone). Both effigies have their eyes open and their hands joined together in prayer.

The tomb of Henry VII (d. 1509) and Queen Elizabeth of York (d. 1503) is the most important work by Pietro Torrigiano Torrigiani (1472–1528), the great Florentine Renaissance sculptor who dominated the medium in England in the early years of Henry VIII (cat. nos 7–9). In 1512 it was contracted to cost £1,500 and probably took four years to complete. The saints represented on the tomb-chest are those specified in Henry VII's will of 1509 as his 'accustumed avoures', with the addition of the Virgin and Child, 'by whom I have … ever had my special comforte and relief', and St Christopher. The monument is housed within a bronze enclosure by 'Thomas the Dutchman', which was already complete by the time the tomb-monument was contracted. Work had already been started at Windsor for an earlier monument to the king and queen and two other plans are also known before Torrigiano's contract. He was responsible for both the design and execution of this monument, which omits some of the Gothic features – for example, the pinnacled canopy – found on his earlier monument to Margaret Beaufort (cat. no. 117); here, the Renaissance detailing is more prominent and for the first time in England a sarcophagus-type upper section is introduced.   PGL

LIT. Public Record Office MS SP1/18, pp.2–5; Astle 1775; Illingworth 1812; Higgins 1894, pp.134–42; Plenderleith and Maryon 1959; Colvin 1975, pp.220–21; Darr 1979 and 1980; Lindley 1995, pp.47–72.

30 Velvet chemise binding for Henry VII

1504

h. 82.5 cm, w. (chemise fully extended) 42 cm, d. 6.5 cm (not incl. bosses)

Public Record Office, London (E.33/1)

A set of four indentures between Henry VII and John Islip, Abbot of Westminster, the first concerning the foundation of Henry VII's Chapel, 16 July 1504.

Indentured wooden boards and text block, bound in a secondary chemise of crimson velvet lined with pink damask, possibly woven in Italy, edged with red and gold thread; three of the four red silk corner-tassels remain. There are four silver-gilt enamelled bosses with a portcullis and a central boss with the royal arms on each cover. Engraved silver-gilt clasps surmounted by an angel, attached to long embroidered straps, fasten on pins on the lower cover. The tail skirt of the chemise protects the five copies of the seal of the Abbot of Westminster in their gilt metal boxes.

Fine textiles were used to cover books as early as the eleventh and twelfth centuries. Embroidered textile bindings for sacred texts reappeared two centuries later. The lavish textile chemises and girdle books frequently depicted in medieval paintings are a display of ostentatious piety. Chemise bindings as symbols of veneration played a significant role in the religious life of medieval Europe, and during the late fourteenth century they became objects of luxury befitting the lifestyle of those who could afford them. Not only religious texts were thus adorned; the importance attached to other valuable books and official documents, such as those of the royal courts and Exchequer books, is often shown in their binding. English examples of such books in chemise bindings go back to the thirteenth and fourteenth centuries, but only a few velvet chemise bindings made in England before the Reformation have survived.   MF

PROV. Henry VII; Chapter House, Westminster Abbey.

LIT. Hobson 1929, pl. 41a; Nixon and Foot 1992, p.24, fig. 18; Bearman 1996, appendix I, nos 1–3; Foot 1998, pp.61–6.

31 Henry VII Cope with orphrey band, hood and morse

PLATE 11

Velvet cloth-of-gold, brocaded with loops of silver-gilt (?) and silver; Florence, 1499–1505

Orphrey and hood: embroidered on tabby linen in silver-gilt thread and coloured silks; English, c.1500

h. 163 cm, w. (top) 322 cm; hood: h. 54.2 cm, w. 45 cm; orphrey: w. 22.2 cm

Stonyhurst College, Lancashire, on loan to the Victoria and Albert Museum, London

The cope is woven to shape and brocaded with Henry VII's badges – the Beaufort portcullis and Tudor roses – with a Lancastrian collar of SS around the hem. The orphrey shows St Bartholomew, St Thomas, St Dorothy, Samson, an unidentified male and St Andrew, and four unidentified figures. On the hood, the Annunciation, with a scroll inscribed AVE MARIA P. The orphrey and hood are replacements, of contemporary work. The cloth-of-gold, which had been reduced at the top, has recently been restored to full height.

An outstanding example of Renaissance weaving, this cope comes from a set of 29 copes and Mass vestments bequeathed by Henry VII to Westminster Abbey in 1509. He had ordered them from Antonio

30

Corsi of Florence and the Buonvisi of Lucca, with English orphreys worked by nineteen 'orpherers' under the royal embroiderers, Morse and Robinet. In 1520, Henry VIII borrowed them to take to the 'Field of Cloth of Gold', his meeting with Francis I of France, where Hall described the cope-orphreys glittering with precious stones and pearls.

At the Dissolution, in 1540, Henry VIII took 14 of these copes from Westminster Abbey; more were taken under Edward VI in 1553, and others from the set were burned in 1643. Fortunately, c.1612, two of the Henry VII copes had been removed to the Jesuit college at St-Omer, moving with the college to Stonyhurst in the 1790s. This cope, together with a much-restored chasuble and chalice veil belonging to Stonyhurst, are the last surviving items from Henry VII's magnificent bequest.   LM

LIT. Hall 1809, p.606; London 1963, cat. no. 135, p.54; Mayer-Thurmann 1975, cat. no. 31, pp.113–14, pp.111, 115 (ills); Monnas 1989a; Knighton 1999–2000, pp.50, 51 (ill.).

2 IMAGES OF ROYALTY

ROSEMARY HORROX

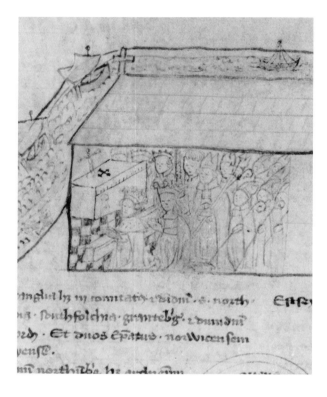

95 Henry VI venerating relics in Eton College chapel, *Polychronicon* (detail) (Eton College, ms 213, f.10.v)

For most people today, images of royalty are photographs or films of members of the royal family doing things, and doing them in real time. The immediacy of such images has largely eclipsed the power of formal portraits, which rarely now generate much public interest and are discussed, if at all, mainly in terms of their relationship to the sitter's 'real' appearance. The individual has triumphed over the ruler.

The individual, in that modern sense, was beginning to put in an appearance in the art of the late Middle Ages. We are all confident that we would recognize Henry VIII – certainly if he obligingly adopted the pose made familiar to us by Holbein (cat. nos 2, 351). But the king as individual, although emphatically a political reality, was still barely an artistic reality. What he looked liked remained less important than what he was: the king. Most representations of late medieval monarchs are specific – this is a *particular* king – without being portraits. Thus, in the drawing of Henry VI, accompanied by his queen, presenting relics to his foundation of Eton (plate 95 and Wolffe 1981, pl. 7a) the identity of the royal couple matters but their appearance does not.

One sees this clearly in the numerous late medieval representations of the English monarchs as a series, produced in a variety of media and contexts to assert the royal descent. Henry VII had a series made for his palace at Richmond, culminating with him (Howarth 1997, pp.78–9). His own picture could well have been a portrait, but its primary message was not 'this is what I look like', but 'here I am as king of England'. The choir screen at York, constructed in 1475–1505 and showing the English monarchs from William I to Henry VI, carried a similar message. The screen was probably planned by Henry VI's former secretary Richard Andrew, Dean of York from 1452 to 1477, as a memorial to his master. Revealingly, Andrew was in trouble in 1473 for erecting a statue of the king somewhere in the Minster, which had become a focus of veneration. The representation of Henry VI *could* have drawn on the memory of men who had known him, but this was not the point.

Worshippers were attracted by its evocation of Henry the martyred king, not by any verisimilitude as portraiture that it may or may not have possessed.

Representations of the king with his family, such as those in the stained glass of Canterbury Cathedral or Little Malvern (cat. nos 37–8), reveal the same priorities. They are not, in our sense of the word, family portraits. In a world of dynastic conflict they assert the existence of a lineage. It is thus important to know who the figures are, but there is no interest in them as individuals beyond that. Even in

96   Henry V initial, the Black Book of the Garter (detail) (St George's Chapel, Archives and Chapter Library, Windsor, DOC. 162C)

Holbein's 'Great Picture' – showing Henry VII and Elizabeth of York with Henry VIII and Jane Seymour – where what we are seeing is far closer to portraiture, the four figures stand round an explanatory inscription, barely even occupying the same space as each other (cat. no. 2). The closest parallel (in function at least) are the illustrated royal pedigrees that proliferated in this period.

Because it was the fact of kingship that mattered, artists rarely showed kings *doing* things. They are shown *being*. In formal representations they generally sit crowned in majesty. The iconography of the great seal (cat. no. 33), conveying the king's role of warrior as well as judge, is an exception, but it is significant that the king as warrior features hardly at all in other formal contexts, presumably because, important as that role was, it was not unique to the king. The royal arms might be carried in his funeral procession and hung over his tomb, but, unlike lords and knights, kings

were never shown in armour on their tombs. Instead they were generally depicted arrayed for coronation, as were their embalmed bodies in the grave.

What is striking about these formal images of majesty is the king's isolation and timelessness. Even the growing number of compositions that surround the king with other people do not generally locate them in any identifiable context or show the king responding. As the king kneels before God or the saints, in another standard image, so his subjects kneel respectfully before him. In BL Royal Ms 18D11 William Lord Herbert and his wife Anne kneel on both knees, with their raised hands apart in adoration before the enthroned Edward IV (Petre 1985, pl. 2). The representation of parliament petitioning Henry VI in the foundation charter of King's College, Cambridge shows the whole chain of petition (cat. no. 20): the king with his back to the peers and commons, petitioning heaven as they petition him (Horrox 1994, pl. 4).

Most representations of authors presenting their books to the king – the source of many of our surviving images of royalty – conform to the same model. The image is of majesty, not of an actual event. Of course this is not the whole story. There are what one might call narrative representations of the king doing things, and their numbers were growing. Illustrated chronicles show the king in battle, not as an image of monarchy but because he was there. The illuminations are not portraits, but they do locate an individual in real time.

Representations of royalty are thus a complex mix of what we would regard as the real and the fictive. At one extreme, the king could still be represented purely by symbols, as in the Tudor imagery in King's College Chapel (cat. no. 19). At the other, portraiture in the modern sense – the record of what somebody looked like as an end in itself – was arriving. The resulting representational complexity is well expressed in an illuminated initial in the Black Book of the Garter compiled in the reign of Henry VIII (Starkey 1991, p.95). This purports to show Henry V, but the figure is suspiciously like Henry VIII himself (plate 96). On one level this shows the importance of recognition – of portraiture in fact: viewers are expected to make the identification of the Tudor Henry with his warrior-predecessor. Meanwhile what Henry V actually looked like is an irrelevance. It is the idea of him that matters, just as it was the idea of the sainted Henry VI to which worshippers responded. It is a modern trait to be interested in images only for what they can tell us about what the king 'really' looked like.

FURTHER READING

Anglo 1992; Howarth 1997; Kipling 1998.

32 Coinage

In European terms, English coinage was distinctive. It was relatively simple, consisting of gold and fine silver, with no base-metal element. Its system of account was straightforward, using pounds, shillings and pence, plus the mark, which had a fixed relationship to £ s. d.: 1 mark = ⅔ pound. It had a reputation for stability and fine standards, and it made systematic use of the royal image in its designs.

In 1544 Henry VIII discarded the ancient English policy of a stable coinage of fine standards, by resorting to debasement for profit, making the coinage a vast fraud on the public. Henry's reputation suffered as a result of this disastrous policy (disastrous for the public; he made a huge short-term profit, to be spent on his last French war). Henry had inherited probably the most attractive and best-regarded coinage in Europe, but he left a currency in chaos and the most disreputable-looking money in English history. BC

a) Noble (6s. 8d.) of Henry V (1413–22), class B, London mint

Gold; diam. 3.2 cm, wt 6.91 g

Obv: king standing, facing, in ship; crowned and armoured, with sword in right hand and shield, quartered with the arms of England and France, in left

HENRIC DI GRA REX ANGL & FRANC DNS HYB (Henry by the grace of God king of England and France, lord of Ireland)

Rev: floriated cross with lis at end of limbs; central apartment containing initial H; lion and crown in each quarter; all within tressure of eight arches

+IHC AUTEM TRANSIENS PER MEDIUM ILLORUM IBAT (But Jesus, passing through the midst of them, went his way [Luke iv. 30])

British Museum, London (CM 1900-11-3-3 and E4534)

LIT. Brooke 1950, p.144; North 1991, p.69; Woodhead 1996, pp.23–5, pls 21–3.

b) Quarter-noble (1s. 6d.) of Henry V, class G, London mint

Gold; diam. 2 cm, wt 1.72 g

Obv: shield quartered with arms of England and France, within tressure of eight arches

+HENRIC DI GRA REX ANGL (Henry by the grace of God king of England)

Rev: floriated cross with lis at the end of each limb; lion in each angle; all within tressure of eight arches

+EXALTABITUR IN GLORIA (He shall be exalted in glory [cf. Psalms cxii. 9])

British Museum, London (CM 1935-4-1-6147 and E4538)

LIT. Brooke 1950, p.144; North 1991, p.70; Woodhead 1996, pp.23–5, pls 2 6.

c) Groat (4d.) of Henry VI, Annulet issue (1422–7/30), Calais mint

Silver; diam. 26 mm, wt 3.8 g

Obv: crowned, beardless bust facing, within tressure of arches

+HENRIC DI GRA REX ANGL & FRANC (Henry by the grace of God king of England and France)

Rev: legends in two concentric circles divided by long cross pattée; three pellets in each angle

+POSUI DEUM ADIUTORE MEUM (I have made God my helper [cf. Psalms liv. 4])

VILLA CALISIE (town of Calais)

British Museum, London (CM 1935-4-1-6712, T. B. Clarke-Thornhill Bequest, and 1871-8-4-169)

LIT. Whitton 1938–41, pp.62–70; North 1991, p.74; Woodhead 1996, pp.80–84.

d) Salut (= 22½ sous tournois) of Henry VI, Rouen mint, issued 1423–c.1449

Gold; diam. 2.6 cm, wt 3.44 g

Obv: Annunciation scene of Archangel Gabriel and Virgin, between them AVE written upwards on scroll, surmounted by five-rayed sun; before them shields of France (to the left, in front of Mary) and England (in front of Gabriel)

HENRICUS DEI GRA FRACORU & AGLIE REX (Henry by the grace of God king of the French and England)

Rev: Latin cross over letter H, French fleur-de-lis to left, English leopard to right, inside tressure of 10 double arches

XPC VINCIT XPC REGNAT XPC IMPERAT (Christ conquers, Christ reigns, Christ commands)

The legends on both sides begin with the mint mark leopard, indicating Rouen mint.

British Museum, London (CM 1922-12-17-16 and E3727)

LIT. Elias 1984, pp.242–3; Cook 2001, pp.302–7.

e) Grand blanc aux écus (= 10 deniers tournois) of Henry VI, Paris mint

Silver; diam. 2.8 cm, wt 3.13 g

Obv: the shields of France and England side by side under the king's name, HERICUS

FRANCORUM ET ANGLIE REX (Henry king of the French and England)

Rev: Latin cross between lis to left and leopard to right, over the king's name, HERICUS, on a line

SIT NOMEN DNI BENEDICTU (Blessed be the name of the Lord)

British Museum, London (CM 1840-7-14-55 and 1935-4-1-6692, T. B. Clarke-Thornhill Bequest)

LIT. Elias 1984, pp.246–7.

f) Rose noble, or ryal (10s.), of Edward IV, first reign, light coinage, initial mark sun (1465–6), Coventry mint

Gold; diam. 3.5 cm, wt 7.69 g

Obv: similar to noble (a. above), with king standing, facing in ship; but with rose on ship's side; banner inscribed E at the stern; and, in the temporary recoinage mints, the initial of the mint, C for Coventry in this case

EDWARD DI GRA REX ANGL & FRANC DNS HYB (Edward by the grace of God king of England and France, lord of Ireland)

Rev: design similar to noble, but with rose upon radiate sun over centre of cross

(Sun)IHC AUT TRANSIENS PER MEDIUM ILLORUM IBAT (But Jesus, passing through the midst of them, went his way [Luke iv. 30])

British Museum, London (CM 1896-6-9-173 and 1935-4-1-6425, T. B. Clarke-Thornhill Bequest)

LIT. Blunt and Whitton 1945–9; North 1991, p.85; Woodhead 1996, pp.32–5, pl. 41.

g) Angel (6s. 8d.) of Edward IV, second reign, initial mark annulet (1472–3), London mint

Gold; diam. 2.9 cm, wt 5.15 g

Obv: the Archangel Michael, piercing the devil as a dragon with his spear (from the Book of Revelations)

EDWARD DEI GRA REX ANGLI & FRANC (Edward by the grace of God king of England and France)

Rev: ship at sea, with large cross as mast, from which hangs royal shield, letter E to left of cross, and rose to right

PER CRUCEM TUA SALVA NOS XPC REDEMPTOR (By thy cross save us, O Christ our redeemer)

British Museum, London (CM 1915-5-7-608 and 1886-4-1-4)

LIT. Blunt and Whitton 1945–8, p.307; Webb Ware 1985, pp.109–16; North 1991, p.92; Woodhead 1996, pp.38–9, pls 43–4.

h) Sovereign (£1) of Henry VII, initial mark lis/crosslet, London mint, c.1489–90

Gold; diam. 4.2 cm, wt 15.48 g

Obv: king, wearing closed, imperial crown, enthroned holding orb and sceptre; portcullis at his feet

HENRICUS DEI GRACIA REX ANGLIE ET FRANC DNS HIB (Henry by the grace of God king of England and France, lord of Ireland)

Rev: royal shield in the centre of Tudor rose

IHESUS AUTEM TRANSIENS PER MEDIUM ILLORUM IBAT (But Jesus, passing through the midst of them, went his way [Luke iv. 30])

British Museum, London (CM 1935-4-1-816 and 1935-4-1-817).

32 obverses

32 reverses

LIT. Grierson 1964; Metcalf 1976, pp.xxvi–xxx, pl. 90; North 1991, pp.100–1; Cook 1995, pp.4–5; Woodhead 1996, pp.43–7, pls 51–2.

i) Testoon (shilling, or 12d.) of Henry VII, c.1504

Silver; diam. 2.8 cm, wt 8.9 g

Obv: portrait bust of king to right, wearing closed crown

HENRIC DI GRA REX ANGLIE & FRAN
(Henry by the grace of God king of England and France)

Rev: royal shield over cross fourchée

POSUI DEUM ADIUTORE MEU
(I have made God my helper)

British Museum, London (CM Bank M86 and 1935-4-1-1559, T. B. Clarke-Thornhill Bequest)

LIT. Potter and Winstanley 1962, pp.109–12; Grierson 1972; North 1991, p.104.

j) George noble (6s. 8d.) of Henry VIII, Second Coinage (1527–44), London mint

Gold; diam. 2.6 cm, wt 4.52 g

Obv: ship with a rose on the mast, the initials H K at its sides (for Henry and Catherine)

HENRIC D G R AGL & FRANC DNS HIBERNI
(Henry by the grace of God king of England and France, lord of Ireland)

Rev: St George as an armoured knight on horseback, with the cross of St George on his chest, slaying the dragon

TALI DICA SIGNO MES FLUCTUARI NEQUIT
(Consecrated by such a sign, the mind cannot waver)

British Museum, London (CM 1915-5-7-640 and 1935-4-1-932, T. B. Clarke-Thornhill Bequest)

LIT. Whitton 1949–51, p.186; Kent 1981; North 1991, pp.110–11; Woodhead 1996, pp. 53–4, pl. 54.

k) Crown of the double rose (5s.) of Henry VIII, Second Coinage, initial mark rose (1526–9), London mint

Gold; diam. 2.6 cm, wt 3.64 g

Obv: double (Tudor) rose crowned, with the crowned initials H and K (for Henry and Catherine) at its sides

HENRIC VIII RUTILANS ROSA SINE SPINA (Henry VIII, a dazzling rose without a thorn)

Rev: royal shield crowned, with crowned initials H and K at its sides

DEI G R AGLIE FRANC DNS HIBERNIE (By the grace of God king of England, France, lord of Ireland)

British Museum, London (CM E0041 and Grueber 407)

LIT. Whitton 1949–51, pp.172–3; Challis 1978, pp.68–70; North 1991, p.111; Woodhead 1996, pp.53–4, pls 54–5.

l) Groat (4d.) of Henry VIII, Second Coinage, York mint under Thomas Wolsey, initial mark voided cross (1526–30)

Silver; diam. 2.4 cm, wt 2.62 g

Obv: crowned portrait of Henry VIII, facing right

HENRIC VIII D G R AGL & FRANC (Henry VIII by the grace of God king of England and France)

Rev: royal shield over long cross fourchée, with T W (for Thomas Wolsey) beside shield, and cardinal's hat below

CIVITAS EBORACI (City of York)

British Museum, London (CM 1935-4-1-1164; and 1935-4-1-1161, T. B. Clarke-Thornhill Bequest)

LIT. Whitton 1949–51, pp.203–4; Challis 1975, pp.96–8; Challis 1978, p.77; North 1991, pp.111–12.

m) Sovereign of Henry VIII, Third Coinage (1544–7)

Gold; diam. 3.8 cm, wt 12.91 g

Obv: Henry VIII, holding orb and sceptre, seated on elaborate throne, with rose at his feet

HENRICUS DI GRA ANGLIE FRANC & HIBERNIE REX (Henry by the grace of God king of England, France and Ireland)

Rev: crowned royal shield with lion and dragon supporters, H R monogram below

IHS AUTEM TRANSIENS PER MEDIUM ILLORUM IBAT (But Jesus, passing through the midst of them, went his way [Luke iv. 30])

British Museum, London (CM 1935-4-1-823 and E0007)

LIT. Whitton 1949–51, pp.74–8; North 1991, p.113; Woodhead 1996, pp.54–5, pls 56–7.

n) Testoon of Henry VIII, Third Coinage, London mint

Base silver; diam. 3 cm, wt 7.87 g

Obv: crowned, bearded bust facing

HENRIC VIII DI GRA AGL FRA & HIB REX (Henry by the grace of God king of England, France and Ireland)

Rev: crowned Tudor rose with crowned H and R (for *Henricus Rex*) at sides

POSUI DEUM ADIUTOREM MEUM (I have made God my helper)

British Museum, London (CM Bank M93 and E0059)

LIT. Whitton 1949–51, pp.292–3; Challis 1978, pp.81–112; North 1991, p.114.

33 The Second Great Seal of Henry IV*

a) Obverse

The seal matrix was engraved between 1406 and 1408; applied to form the wax seal on this document at Westminster in 1410

Parchment and beeswax; diam. 12 cm

Inscr. in black-letter: *Henricus dei gr*[ati]*a rex Anglie E .Francie et D*[omi]*n*[u]*s Hibernie* (Henry by the Grace of God king of England and France and lord of Ireland)

Public Record Office, London (PRO DL 10/373)

Henry IV ordered the engraving of a new matrix for the Great Seal sometime between 1406 and 1408 (Heenan 1968–9). Very different from the Great Seals of his predecessors, it presents an impressive statement of the authority and right of the first Lancastrian King of England. Within an elaborate series of receding niches and canopies, the king is seated with crown and sceptre and orb, surrounded by the defenders of his realm, both temporal and spiritual. Above are the Virgin and Child. To his left and right are four saints – St Michael and St George, King Edward the Confessor and King Edmund the Martyr. These royal saints are there in recognition of the

descent of Henry IV from Henry III, since Henry IV stated that his claim to the throne was of the right blood royal coming from King Henry III. Outside this saintly protection, two men-at-arms hold standards with the arms of the kingdom of England and those of England alone. Beneath the king are the arms of Wales, Cornwall and Chester.

The seal was certainly engraved by 1408, and this use of the seal dates from 1410. In design it has been considered the greatest of all the medieval Great Seals of England, combining the vigour and variety of detail with a perfect sense of vertical balance and harmony.

LIT. Wyon 1883, pp.157–8.

b) Reverse

PLATE 40

Applied to form the wax seal on this document in 1411

Brown beeswax; diam. 12.3 cm

Inscr. in black-letter with the same legend as for the obverse (a)

British Library, London (Add. Ch. 11, 158)

This fine impression of the reverse of the Second Great Seal shows the position of the pins by which

33a

the two sides of the matrix were secured. On a background filled with delicate fronds, the king in armour decorated with the royal arms, bearing a shield with the arms of France and England, holding a raised chained sword, gallops to the right on a horse, whose caparisons are decorated heraldically with the royal arms and with a lion crest on his head.

The design follows the traditional equestrian obverse of the Great Seal that goes back to William I. It is a particularly vigorous and energetic depiction of the equestrian king, and provided a model for other seals such as that of Henry, Prince of Wales for the Lordship of Carmarthen (cat. no. 34) and also that of the town of Wallingford, Berkshire. JC

LIT. Birch 1887–92, no. 259; Wyon 1887, no. 80A, pl. XIIIA.

34

34 Seal matrix of Henry, Prince of Wales (later Henry V), for the Lordship of Carmarthen

1408–13

Copper alloy; diam. 7.1 cm

Inscr. in black-letter: *S*[igillum] *Henr*[ici] *principis Wall*[iae] *duc*[is] *acquit*[anie] *lancastr*[ie] *et cornub*[ie] *comes cestr*[ie] *de d*[o]*m*[in]*io de kermedyne* (Seal of Henry, Prince of Wales, Duke of Aquitaine, Lancaster and Cornwall and Earl of Chester for the Lordship of Carmarthen)

British Museum, London (MME 1987, 4-4, 1)

This copper-alloy matrix is for the reverse of the seal, and the obverse would have been positioned above it

by the use of pins through the four projecting lugs. The design shows an equestrian figure, with sword raised, galloping across the ground against a background of foliage. On his helmet there is a lion, and on his shield and on the trappings of his horse are the English royal arms of France modern quartering England with a label of three points. The inclusion of France modern indicates that the seal must date from after 1406–8 (Heenan 1968–9). The arms and the legend indicate that this is the seal of Henry of Monmouth, later to become Henry V, for the Lordship of Carmarthen.

Carmarthen was the administrative centre of the Prince of Wales for south-west Wales. This seal would have been used for the appointment of local officials, granting lands, holding inquisitions and issuing local writs. The revolt of Owen Glendower collapsed in 1408, and the seal was probably engraved as part of the prince's reassertion of his control over the country. This seal was replaced by the engraving of seals for the principality of north and south Wales in 1413 by John Bernes, a prominent London goldsmith. He was warden of the Goldsmiths' Company in 1407 and 1408, and was later known to have engraved seals for Henry V. It is likely that he engraved this seal five years earlier. JC

PROV. Mr Richard Green, Lichfield, in 1786; acquired by the British Museum in 1987.

LIT. Jenkinson 1936; Cherry 1990.

35 Canterbury Cathedral, statue of St Ethelbert from choir-screen*

c.1450

Caen stone; h. 172 cm

The Canterbury choir-screen was built c.1455 to the designs of Richard Beke, master mason successively of London Bridge (1417–35) and Canterbury Cathedral (1435–58). The figures of kings occupying the three large niches on either side of the portal were originally accompanied by 48 much smaller figures (over and above the 13 surviving shield-bearing busts of angels on the cornice), whose explicitly religious iconography was doubtless the cause of their removal in the sixteenth century (plate 119).

The figure illustrated is the only one whose identity is clear: in this context, a king carrying a miniaturized church must be St Ethelbert, King of Kent (d. 616), supporter of St Augustine's mission in 597 and founder of Canterbury Cathedral. Of the three sculptors responsible for the Canterbury kings, the carver of the St Ethelbert is arguably the most accom-

35

plished; certainly the level of finish is far higher, especially in respect of the detailed surface naturalism of the face and hair. The overall design relates closely to that of another founder figure, the King Sebert on Henry V's chantry in Westminster Abbey (c.1441–9). The right hand and sceptre are early nineteenth-century restorations. At least five earlier English choir-screens bore statues of English rulers. CW

LIT. Carter 1780, p.56; Cotton 1935; Woodman 1981, pp.188–96.

36

36 Henry VI

Probably by John Massingham, *c.*1438–42

Limestone (Taynton stone), with slight traces of paint; h. 183 cm

All Souls College, Oxford

The College of All Souls was founded by Archbishop Henry Chichele in 1438, partly as a war memorial for those who had 'drunk the cup of bitter death' in the wars with France. Associated with him in the foundation was the young King Henry VI. His statue, together with that of his of co-founder (cat. no. 99), lodged formerly in niches in the gate-tower, below an image of Christ in Judgement (destroyed in 1642) with the resurrected dead (replaced in 1826–7). A similar grouping of images is on the original seal of the college (cat. no. 100). These sculptures were replaced on the gate-tower by modern copies in 1939–40 (Jones 1954, p.187).

Henry is shown in parliament robes, and his crown is adorned with crosses alternating with foliage. The teenaged king is an idealized figure, but realistic in its presentation, showing an awareness of recent developments in Netherlandish sculpture. It is probably the work of John Massingham (*fl.* 1409–50), the chief sculptor at the college. He was one of the team who worked on the tomb effigy of Richard Beauchamp, Earl of Warwick, started in 1447–8, and there are links with the Beauchamp effigy in the treatment of the eyes and mouth (cat. no. 87). However, in view of the repair of the statue in 1633 and 1826–7, it would be unwise to place too much reliance on the present appearance of facial details. The heavy folds of drapery around the king's neck are reminiscent of figures in Henry V's chantry chapel, Westminster Abbey. NR

LIT. Gardner 1951, p.235, fig. 458; Stone 1972, p.206; Colvin and Simmons 1989, p.6.

37 The children of Edward IV and Queen Elizabeth (Woodeville)

PLATE 19

1480–82

Stained and painted glass; each light h. 173 cm, w. 41 cm (approx.)

Church of St Mary and St Michael, Little Malvern, Worcestershire (former Benedictine priory church of St Giles)

These panels occupy two lights below the chancel east window transom and depict Edward, Prince of Wales (later Edward V) and four of his sisters kneeling in prayer before desks bearing books, set on richly brocaded grounds and under elaborate canopies of estate.

Originally these panels were accompanied by Edward IV, Queen Elizabeth (partly surviving), their other son Richard, Duke of York, and John Alcock, Bishop of Worcester. The last was responsible for the moral and material reform of Little Malvern Priory between July 1480 and October 1482. The richness of the glazing contrasts with the architectural modesty of the choir and reflects the regal subject-matter and the prominence of the patron. A lost inscription in the window mentioned Alcock's offices of Chancellor of England and president of the royal council; the window can be read as an affirmation of his loyalty to Edward IV. Like its Canterbury counterpart (cat. no. 38), the Little Malvern window is an example of a late fifteenth-century predilection for prominent representation of the royal family in sacred spaces; no doubt the Little Malvern monastic community would have included Edward IV's family as well as Bishop Alcock in their prayers.

The iconography of the royal family at Little Malvern is similar to that in the Canterbury 'Royal Window', but the execution is very different. The Little Malvern glass can be attributed to the local workshop of Richard Twygge and Thomas Wodshawe, which was responsible for the Seven Sacraments and Seven Works of Mercy windows at Tattershall (cat. no. 292). RM

LIT. Marks 1984a, pp.79–81.

38 Princess Cecily (1469–1507)

*c.*1482–7

Stained and painted glass; h. 40.2 cm, w. 31 cm

Burrell Collection, Glasgow Museums (45.75)

A rectangular panel depicting the now half-length figure of the princess, who is dressed in a tight-fitting, richly ermine-trimmed brocade bodice. It has been cracked and edge-bonded in several places and is now plated. Blue fragments have been stopped into the damask background top left and bottom right.

Princess Cecily, second surviving daughter of King Edward IV, was originally represented in the row of kneeling 'donor' figures in 'The Royal Window' of Canterbury Cathedral, which included her father, her mother Elizabeth Woodeville, her two brothers, Edward, Prince of Wales, and Richard, Duke of York, and her four sisters, Anne, Catherine, Bridget and Elizabeth (see ill.). Angel figures supported their shields of arms. The royal figures flanked an image of the Crucifixion, while in the register above the Joys of the Virgin Mary were depicted. These scenes, together with the large image of St Thomas Becket, made the window a target of Puritan iconoclasm in December 1642.

A lost inscription described Cecily as '*Domina Cecilia secunda filia*'. Cecily was actually Edward IV's

38

'The Royal Window',
Canterbury Cathedral
(see cat. no. 38)

third daughter, her sister Mary having pre-deceased her in May 1482, helping to date the conception of the window. It was probably made before the death of the king in April 1483, when the children accompanied their mother into exile. In 1487 Cecily married John, Viscount Wells.

The royal family was represented kneeling before prayer desks, in a mode derived from Flemish panel-painting, and the window has been compared to the work of Hugo van der Goes and his associates. The figures display elements of portraiture, comparable to Hugo's images of James III of Scotland and his family on the altarpiece commissioned by Edward Bonkil of Edinburgh, c.1478–9. The window was painted by at least two groups of glass-painters. Those entrusted with the main lights worked in a style described as 'dramatically innovative' and whose commissions were all associated with court or highly placed ecclesiastical patrons. It was in the reign of Edward IV that

the subtly modelled, realistic styles associated with Netherlandish immigrant craftsmen began to make their mark on English glass-painting. The figure of Cecily is characterized by its soft stipple shading and delicate stick-work highlights.

It is likely that this window influenced the later Magnificat window in the north-west transept of Great Malvern Priory, c.1509, which contains a similar combination of royal figures (including the Princess Elizabeth, by now Henry VII's queen) and the Joys of the Virgin Mary.   SB

PROV. Canterbury Cathedral, north-west transept, window N.XXVIII, 'The Royal Window', until 1789; A. L. Radford; F. W. Bruce; Roy Grosvenor Thomas and Wilfred Drake; bought by Sir William Burrell, Hutton Castle, in 1939.

LIT. Wells 1965, no. 84, p.28; Tudor-Craig 1973, cat. no. 32, pp.18–19; Caviness 1981, pp.251–67, 316, fig. 464; Marks 1993, p.206, pl. XXV.

39 Henry VII and Elizabeth of York

PLATE 18

*c.*1537–40

Stained and painted glass; h. 182 cm, w. 50 cm

Church of St Nicholas, Stanford on Avon,
Northamptonshire, chancel east window

The left panel depicts the standing figure of Henry
VII with his arm resting on a draped pedestal embellished with Renaissance ornamentation; the right
panel shows Elizabeth of York standing at the other
end of the pedestal and with the black-letter label
'/Elizabetha R/'. Both figures are set below crocketed
and gabled canopies; on the damascened ground are
diagonal scrolls bearing the royal motto '/Dieu et mon
droit/'. The label and ground behind Henry VII, his
head and that of Elizabeth are restored. Conserved by
Barley Studio, 1987–97.

The panels are a Gothicized version of Holbein the
Younger's famous lost mural of 1537 in the Privy
Chamber of Whitehall Palace (cat. no. 2). His cartoon
shows only Henry VII and Henry VIII and, apart
from a copy of the entire mural made in 1667 by
Remigius van Leemput, the Stanford representation
is the only one to include Elizabeth of York. It also
shows details of the pedestal, which appear neither in
Holbein's cartoon nor van Leemput's copy.

The history of the panels is unknown before their
discovery at Stanford Hall in the 1880s. Possibly they
were installed in one of Henry VIII's residences; if so,
their composition and royal imagery are more appropriate to a secular space than to a chapel or oratory. If
the window from which they came included, like the
Whitehall mural, Henry VIII and Jane Seymour, it must
have been a substantial one of at least five lights.   RM

PROV. Stanford Hall, 1880s; Stanford church since 1932.

LIT. Marks 1998a, pp.185–6, 190; Marks 2000.

40 Sword of State of a Prince of Wales as Earl of Chester

*c.*1473–83

Steel, copper alloy (latten?), champlevé enamel and lead;
l. 182.3 cm

British Museum, London (MME Sloane 17537)

Of exceptionally large size, this sword has a broad,
double-edged blade (German, made in Passau or
Sollingen) of flat-hexagonal section, with, on each
face of the forte, a double fuller changing to a single
one, and, on one face, two small running wolf marks
inlaid in copper alloy. The cruciform hilt is entirely of
copper alloy, originally gilt, decorated throughout
with pounced scrollwork, and engraved foliage and
inscriptions in Gothic letters (much rubbed); the few
words that have been deciphered appear to be invoca-
tions to the Virgin in Latin and Low German. It comprises: a slightly arched cross of diamond section
tapering to beak-like tips; lead-filled octagonal
pommel, with a circular recess within a slightly raised
moulding on each face, one filled with a copper disc
enamelled with the cross of St George, the other now
empty; grip, tapering towards each end and formed
of two riveted scales of plano-convex section sandwiching the tang, each inlaid with two copper panels

enamelled with shields of arms, three a side, arranged
to be viewed when the sword is point upwards. They
are, from top to bottom: *Side 1*. A Prince of Wales
(under a crown and supported by kneeling angels, all
engraved), the ancient kingdom of North Wales
(according to English heralds), the Duchy of Cornwall. *Side 2*. The Earldom of March, the Earldom of
Chester, unidentified (silver a chief azure).

The combination of identified arms indicates that
the sword could only have belonged to one or other
of two Princes of Wales, both named Edward: the
eldest son (1471–83) of Edward IV, and his successor
as Edward V, given the title with that of Earl of
Chester in 1473; and the son (1473–84) of Richard
III, who received them in 1483. Since their only enti-
tlement to a sword of state was as rulers of the Palatinate of Chester, this sword must have a connection
with it: it is most likely to have been the one that
would have been carried before the elder Edward in
1475 when, according to Ormerod, he 'came to
Chester in great pompe'.   CB

PROV. Hans Sloane Collection

LIT. Gough 1786, p.cxlviii; Ormerod 1835; Laking 1920–22,
II, pp.331–2; Tudor-Craig 1973, p.8 and pl. 54; Marks and
Payne 1978, pp.111–12, no. 214.

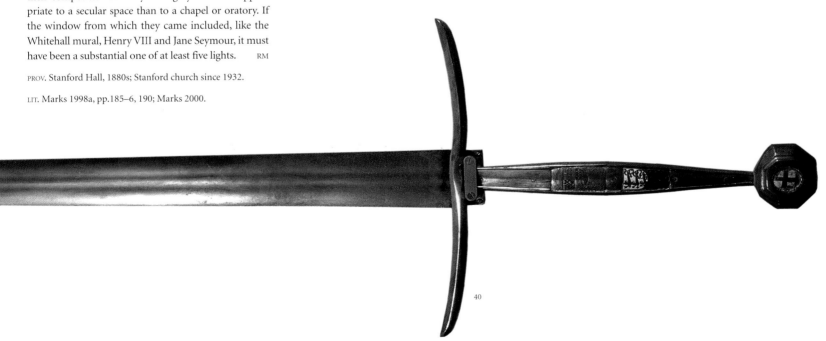

40

3 ROYAL BOOKS

JENNY STRATFORD

97 Marriage of King David and
Michal, Psalter and Hours of John,
Duke of Bedford (cat. no. 73)

How much can we know about the books and reading of English kings and queens, princes and princesses, in the years between the accession of Henry IV in 1399 and the death of Henry VIII in 1547? This may seem an odd question, given the number of exceptional royal books on display in different sections of this exhibition and the many others for which no room could be found. Yet untold numbers more are lost, while a peculiarity of English royal accounting means that there are no formal inventories of the king's books until the Tudor period. The earliest inventory of an English king's books is the brief list of 143 manuscripts and printed works seen at Richmond Palace by a French visitor in 1535 – and these were the books in just one of the 50 or so palaces and houses occupied by Henry VIII during his lifetime (Stratford 1999, pp.255–6; Carley 1999, p.274; Carley 2000, especially pp.lxiii–lxvi, 3–29). Nevertheless, scattered evidence from written sources suggests that there were indeed much earlier royal libraries in England, although they may not have had a continuous existence. Building accounts reveal, for example, that Henry IV constructed a new study at Eltham Palace soon after his accession. It was lit by seven magnificent stained-glass windows and furnished with two reading desks. The larger was fitted out to store the king's books, but there is no record of what these were (Colvin 1963, p.935; Salzman 1929–30, pp.26–7, no. 59; Marks 1993, pp.48, 94–5; Stratford 1999, pp.260–61).

All the sons and daughters of Henry IV were 'wel boked', as the poet John Gower put it (Macaulay 1900–1, ii, p.242). Henry V, depicted as Prince of Wales in Thomas Hoccleve's *Regimen of Princes* (cat. no. 41), seems by his death in 1422 to have acquired a considerable library by inheritance, gift, purchase, conquest and confiscation. In his last will of 1421 and its codicils of 1422 he made clear his intentions for his books. His legal and scholastic books were to go to Oxford University (they had not been sent by 1437) and his books for sermons and for meditation to his two new religious foundations, the Charterhouse at Sheen and the double monastery of the Bridgettines at Syon. But his other books were to be preserved within the household for his baby son, Henry VI, 'for his library' (Harriss 1972, pp.232–8; Strong and Strong 1981, pp.93–4, 96, 99–100; Stratford 1999, pp.260–61).

Henry V's next brother, Thomas, Duke of Clarence (d. 1420), is especially remembered for the music of his chapel (Bowers 1975–6, pp.103–12) (cat. no. 14). His two younger brothers, John, Duke of Bedford, and Humphrey, Duke of Gloucester, the patron of humanist learning and a founder of the Bodleian Library, were both outstanding bibliophiles (Weiss 1964, pp.161–70; Sammut 1980; Oxford 1988; Rundle 1998; Saygin 2002). About 12 manuscripts made for Bedford are known today (Stratford 1987 and 1993, pp.91–6, 119–23). The superb Psalter and Hours of around 1420 (cat. no. 73) was decorated by Herman Scheerre and his associates, the leading group of craftsmen of their day in London, the artists also of the Chichele Breviary (cat. no. 103) and the Hours later owned by Richard III (cat. no. 44).

Other exquisite liturgical books were ordered in Paris for Bedford after 1422, as Regent of France. They were the work of illuminators who were termed after these books 'the Bedford master' or 'the Bedford workshop' (Reynolds 1996, pp.624–6). The Bedford Hours (plate 87) was adapted, rather than ordered, for Bedford and his first wife, Anne, sister of Duke Philip the Good of Burgundy. The famous portraits of the duke and duchess were among the leaves added for them. Bedford kneels before St George, who is dressed in the Garter robes; in the borders are his arms and heraldic supporters, the eagle and the yale (an heraldic antelope), and the root badge that he adopted as regent (Backhouse 1981 and 1990; Stratford 1993, p.114). The Salisbury Breviary (cat. no. 72) was begun after about 1424. Its decorative programme of large miniatures, full-page borders and marginal roundels, many framed by the regent's root badge, was immensely ambitious and it was never completed. These books, together with sumptuous textiles and rich plate (now lost and known only from inventories), evoke the magnificence of the regent's household and chapel. By 1424 Bedford also owned one of the largest secular libraries in medieval Europe; he bought the great Louvre Library of Charles V and Charles VI of France, consisting of 843 volumes. This went via Rouen to London, only to be dispersed after Bedford's death in 1435. About a hundred volumes survive today (Stratford 1993).

Henry VI sent many of the scholarly books left to him by his father to Oxford and Cambridge colleges. Very little is known about what other books he owned. John Lydgate's *Life of St Edmund and St Fremund* (cat. no. 318) was begun on the abbot's orders after Henry's stay in 1433 in the monastery at Bury St Edmunds. Henry is depicted as a boy, kneeling before the shrine of St Edmund. The charters recording his foundations of Eton and King's College, Cambridge were commissioned from the London citizen and stationer, William Abell (see cat. no. 20). Margaret of Anjou, Henry VI's queen and daughter of a great French bibliophile, King René of Anjou, received on her marriage in 1445 the collection of poems and romances commissioned by John Talbot, Earl of Shrewsbury (cat. no. 42), and still among the royal manuscripts. This is an important reminder that queens and princesses (as well as other women) were often highly literate and owned secular works as well as the Books of Hours for their private devotions which have more often survived, such as the Hours of Katharine de Valois, Henry's mother (BL, MS Add. 65100).

With the accession of Edward IV the royal library emerges somewhat from obscurity. A group of very large volumes, most still among the royal manuscripts in the British Library, were ordered for Edward from Flanders. Some are decorated with his arms alone, others with those of his sons, the princes in the Tower (Backhouse 1987, 1995 and 1999b; McKendrick 1990 and 1994). The *Chemin de Vaillance*, in French verse, combining moral and didactic instruction in palatable narrative form and well illustrated, could have been ordered to instruct Edward's sons and was most probably read aloud from a lectern (cat. no. 43). Even more massive is the set of six chronicle volumes commissioned by Sir Thomas Thwaytes, treasurer of Calais, in around 1487–90 and presented to Henry VII. The frontispiece miniature to BL, Royal MS 20 E. i (cat. no. 46) depicts Childebert and Clothaire before Saragossa. In the initial is Henry's portcullis and in the full-page border with its cast shadows are his arms and Tudor roses. Something is known about Henry VII's librarian, Quintin Poulet, and about the printed books as well as manuscripts ordered for the king (cat. nos 47, 48). Yet more than 60 years after the invention of printing, around 1509, Henry VIII still had illuminated manuscripts presented to him by leading scholars and humanists, as well as acquiring a growing collection of printed books (Carley 2000, pp.xlvi–li).

FURTHER READING

Backhouse 1987; Carley 1999; Stratford 1993 and 1999.

41 Thomas Hoccleve, *The Regimen of Princes*

PLATE 15

*c.*1413

Vellum, ff.99; h. 29 cm, w. 18.5 cm

British Library, London (Arundel MS 38)

Hoccleve's lengthy English poem, offering advice on conduct to a potential ruler, mentions events that took place in 1411 and is addressed to Henry V as Prince of Wales. It must therefore have been composed before Henry's accession to the throne in March 1413. The work achieved a considerable circulation and numerous copies survive. This particular manuscript includes a presentation miniature of exceptional quality (f.37) which has generally been taken to indicate that it was made for Henry himself. The miniature is placed, not at the beginning of the volume, but at the point in the text where Hoccleve addresses the prince directly. It is unclear who is the donor and who the recipient in the composition, or whether indeed an actual gift of this specific manuscript is truly implied.

Coats of arms enclosed in the book's main initials have been identified as relating to the young John Mowbray, Lord Mowbray and Segrave, hereditary Earl Marshal of England, who later became 2nd Duke of Norfolk. As their main arms, the Mowbrays bore a differenced form of the old royal arms of England, through their descent from Thomas of Brotherton, Earl of Norfolk, fifth son of Edward I. This charge appears in the first initial and has been wrongly but consistently interpreted as the arms of Prince Henry. The arms below the miniature are the earlier Mowbray Arms. John Mowbray was close to Henry and his brothers, having been a ward of their grandmother, Countess Joan of Hereford. At the time of Henry's accession, he was summoned to parliament as Earl Marshal. Later in 1413 he formally came of age and into his landed inheritance. The manuscript may have been commissioned or presented to him to mark his enhanced status in the new reign.   JMB

PROV. John Mowbray, 2nd Duke of Norfolk (1392–1432); Thomas Howard, Earl of Arundel (1585–1646); Henry Howard, 6th Duke of Norfolk (1628–84); Royal Society, 1666; British Museum, 1831.

LIT. Harris 1984; Scott 1996, no. 50.

42 The Shrewsbury Book

PLATE 10

Rouen, 1444–5

Vellum, ff.440; h. 47 cm, w. 34 cm

British Library, London (Royal MS 15 E.vi)

This richly decorated volume of French romances and works on chivalry was written and illuminated in Rouen for John Talbot, Earl of Shrewsbury, to present to Margaret of Anjou on her marriage to Henry VI. Talbot was among those appointed to escort Margaret to England, and probably bestowed his wedding gift in Rouen in late March 1445 when the embassy stayed there en route for home. The volume opens with a striking double-page frontispiece.

On the left-hand page (f.2v), a miniature above the verse dedication shows the earl, in Garter robes and collar of SS, accompanied by his Talbot dog, kneeling to present his book to the queen. In the lower border are the arms of England impaling Anjou, which are repeated on the facing page on a banner supported by the Lancastrian badge of an heraldic antelope. The earl's own arms appear within the Garter in the lower margin beside his verse motto on a scroll and a badge of daisies (marguerites); the flowers, an allusion to Margaret's name, are used in profusion throughout the border decoration.

On the right (f.3) is a genealogical table, in the form of a fleur-de-lis, showing French and English royal descents from St Louis uniting in the figure of Henry VI of England. This is a version of a picture commissioned in about 1423 by Henry's uncle, the Duke of Bedford, Regent of France, who had it posted up with an accompanying poem in Notre-Dame in Paris as part of a propaganda campaign for King Henry VI's claim to the French throne. Both the genealogy and the dedication verse express Talbot's hopes for a peaceful union of the two countries under the rule of the royal couple and their heirs. Most of the book, however, concerns not peace, but the themes of chivalry and martial prowess. The Order of the

Garter, the embodiment of chivalric ideals for Talbot the war veteran, is given particular emphasis.

As many as four artists contributed miniatures to the Shrewsbury Book, but the predominant style is that of the Talbot Master, named from this manuscript and from two Books of Hours made for the earl and countess (see cat. no. 94a). Unlike his contemporary, the Master of Sir John Fastolf (cat. nos 92, 224), the Talbot Master did not follow his English patrons across the Channel, but remained in Rouen after the expulsion of the English in 1449, working with members of the same team of scribes and illuminators for the *échevinage* (city council).   AP

PROV. Royal Library (1535 Richmond inventory; Carley 2000, H1, no. 91); passed to British Museum in 1757.

LIT. Avril and Reynaud 1993, pp.168–72; Reynolds (C) 1993, pp.109–16; Reynolds (C) 1994, pp.305–6.

43 Jean de Courcy,
Le Chemin de Vaillance

Southern Netherlands, *c*.1479

Vellum, ff.345; h. 47 cm, w. 34 cm

British Library, London (Royal MS 14 E. ii)

This massive volume of 345 leaves is typical of the many prestigious secular library books that Edward IV ordered from the professional workshops of Flanders in and around 1479. Its custom-designed decoration incorporates the arms of the English king, together with the Yorkist badge of the white rose in a sunburst, set against the livery colours of blue and murrey and surrounded by the Garter motto, '*Honi soit qui mal y pense*'. Elsewhere in the book, the arms of his two sons and the arms traditionally assigned to the two sainted English kings – Edmund King and Martyr and Edward the Confessor – are also featured.

Jean de Courcy was a Norman knight who turned

to authorship towards the end of a long and active life. This lengthy allegorical poem, of which Edward's is the only known copy, dates from about 1426. It is here punctuated by four large and nine small miniatures, in which the characters are shown attired in the high fashion of the late 1470s. In the exhibited illustration (f.194), the author is seen leaving the Forest of Temptation, accompanied by the Virtues. The manuscript includes four shorter works, one of which is a French version of the *Book of the Order of Chivalry* by the Catalan author Ramon Lull (1235–1315). This was soon afterwards to feature as one of the earliest books printed in England, published in or about 1484 in an English translation by William Caxton.   JMB

PROV. Edward IV; Royal Library; passed to British Museum in 1757.

LIT. Warner and Gilson 1921, II, pp.139–40; Backhouse 1987, pp.25, 39; Dubuc 1994; Carley 2000, pp.12–13.

44 Hours of Richard III

***c*.1420**

Vellum, ff.186; h. 19.5 cm, w. 13.5 cm

Lambeth Palace Library, London (MS 474)

During his brief reign of little more than two years, Richard III apparently used this relatively modest and clearly second-hand manuscript as his manual of personal devotion. The anniversary of his birth is noted in its calendar on 2 October, possibly in his own hand, and a long prayer for private use is added at the end of the volume. Attempts have been made to equate its petitions with Richard's personal circumstances, but versions of this text were in fact in widespread use throughout Europe. In both additions Richard is mentioned by name and as king.

The manuscript itself was made well over 60 years before Richard's accession in 1483, probably in a professional London workshop. The original owner is not known. The very conventional illumination, though of good quality, is restricted to decorated initials and borders at significant divisions of the text. Only the opening pages of the Hours of the Virgin (f.15), the Penitential Psalms (f.55, now missing) and the vigils of the Dead (f.72, shown here) are distinguished by historiated initials.

After Richard's death at Bosworth, the manuscript apparently passed through the hands of Lady Margaret Beaufort and was inscribed: 'In the honour of god and Sainte Edmonde, pray for Margarete Richmonde'.   JMB

PROV. Richard III (d. 1485); Lady Margaret Beaufort (d. 1509); Cambridge University Library, 1647–54; Lambeth Palace Library, late 17th century.

LIT. Tudor-Craig 1973, no. 51; Sutton and Visser-Fuchs 1990; Scott 1996, no. 52.

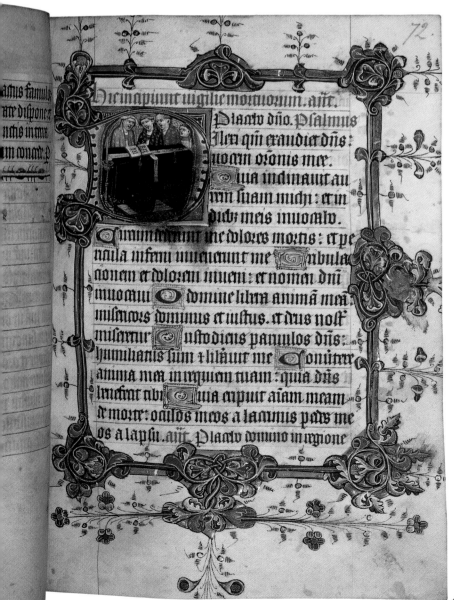

44

45 Hours inscribed by Henry VII to his daughter Margaret

Southern Netherlands, *c*.1500

Vellum, ff.187; h. 20.5 cm, w. 14 cm

Devonshire Collection, Chatsworth

This Book of Hours, of Sarum use, is one of many works by Flemish illuminators of the Ghent–Bruges school designed for the English market in the late fifteenth and early sixteenth centuries. More than one hand may be distinguished, though the style is basically that associated with the anonymous artist known as the Master of the Prayerbooks. In addition to major miniatures introducing the principal elements of text traditionally found in a Book of Hours, the manuscript offers miniatures of 12 individual saints, a calendar and a large number of historiated initials, including a series of scenes of the Passion.

Two very personal autograph inscriptions, addressed by Henry VII to one of his children, give this otherwise unpersonalized book a special poignancy. They read: 'Remembre yor kynde and lovyng fader in yor prayers. Henry Ky' (f.14) and 'Pray for your lovyng fader that gave you thys book and I geve you att all tymes godds blessy(n)g and Myne. Henry Ky' (f.32v). The child is not named, but is identifiable as Henry's elder daughter, Margaret, Queen of Scots, because the manuscript also contains an inscription (f.186v) by Lady Margaret Douglas (1515–78), the daughter of her second marriage to the Earl of Angus, presenting it to the Archbishop of

St Andrews. In the summer of 1503, some months short of her 14th birthday, Margaret left England for her long-anticipated marriage to James IV of Scotland. She took leave of her father at Collyweston in Northamptonshire, home of her grandmother, Lady Margaret Beaufort. The Hours may well have been given to her on this occasion.

The miniature of St Anne teaching the Virgin to read in a homely domestic setting (f.35v) is characteristic of the contents of this manuscript. It is high-quality work, but not in the same class as the magnificent Hours that James IV himself commissioned to mark his marriage to Margaret (Vienna, Österreichische Nationalbibliothek, cod. 1897). JMB

45

46

46 *Chroniques de France*

*c.*1487

Vellum, ff.225; h. 55 cm, w. 37 cm

British Library, London (Royal MS 20 E.i)

This is the first in a set of six enormous matching volumes of French chronicles, work on which was never finished. Some of the content is bound out of order and the planned programme of illustration is far from complete. The scribe is named in a colophon in the third volume, dated 14 October 1487, as Hugues de Lembourg, native of Paris, '*povre clerc et humble serviteur domestique*' to Sir Thomas Thwaytes, Treasurer of Calais (for comparable script, see cat. no. 214). Thwaytes, himself a book lover, had been Edward IV's Chancellor of the Exchequer and was among those dispatched to Calais to ensure its loyalty after the king's death in 1483. He was one of those servants of the crown who contrived to survive the political turmoil of the next few years, retaining his Calais post until 1490. The lavish use of Henry VII's arms and devices in the decoration of the *Chroniques* suggests that it may have been designed as a political offering to the Tudor king, in a taste perhaps more appropriate to Edward IV.

The only large miniature in this volume shows Childebert and Clothaire outside the walls of Saragossa (f.47). A procession with the relics of St Vincent is emerging from the town. It is the work of a Flemish or Flemish-taught artist, although other illustrations in the series are accompanied by English instructions and appear to be by English hands.   JMB

47

47 *Le grant boece, de consolacion* (Boethius, *Consolation of Philosophy*)

Printed in Paris for Antoine Vérard, 19 August 1494; illuminated *c.*1494

Vellum, ff.156; h. 34.5 cm, w. 24.5 cm

British Library, London (C.22.f.8)

Henry VII's library contained a group of printed books published by Antoine Vérard, the notable Paris bookseller. Most were illuminated. Vérard's publishing strategy was governed by his relations with the French king, Charles VIII, as the choice of texts and prefaces makes clear. Henry's collecting thus echoed that of Charles.

This copy of the 1494 Boethius was 'customized' for Henry VII. The presentation miniature is one of the most refined works of the prolific Paris illuminator, the Jacques de Besançon Master, who regularly worked for Vérard. The miniature is delicately painted, but with no concessions to the new conventions of Renaissance style. Charles VIII's name in the preface was erased and Henry's name substituted in manuscript. The king portrayed, however, was French: the address, '*Au roi tres chretien*', was that for the Kings of

France; in the miniature, the king wears a fleur-de-lis gown and the collar of the Order of St Michel – this was the French equivalent of the Order of the Garter, with similar nationalist overtones. Henry is not known to have been a member of this Order. Though magnificent illuminated volumes were added to the royal library under Henry VII, his interest in it as part of a coherent cultural programme seems incidental. Books from Vérard were certainly being bought for the library in 1502, though the Boethius may have been acquired earlier (the date, 1494, is erased).   RW

PROV. Royal Library; passed to British Museum in 1757.

LIT. Macfarlane 1900, no. 37; BMC, VIII, 84; Courcelle 1967, pp.95–6, figs 60–61, 83–4, 95–6, 104–5; Avril and Reynaud 1993, pp.256–62; Winn 1997, pp.138–53, 314–25.

48 Nagonius, Latin poems

PLATE 16

Between 1496 and 1502

Vellum, ff.76; h. 22.5 cm, w. 14.5 cm

York Minster Library (MS XVI. N. 2)

Among the secular manuscripts acquired by Henry VII are a number of works addressed to him by itinerant Italian poets and scholars, who moved between the courts of Europe in quest of patronage. Johannes Michael Nagonius, who describes himself as a citizen of Rome and a poet laureate, was recommended to the English king by Cardinal Francesco Piccolomini, who became Pope Pius III in 1503. In the course of his career Nagonius also addressed poems to the Emperor Maximilian, Louis XII of France, Alfonso of Aragon and Pope Julius II. A reference to him in the royal accounts shows that he was personally in England in 1496 (Wormald 1951).

The manuscript, which is of Italian workmanship, must be close to that date. The principal poem includes a reference to the papal gift to Henry of a sword and a cap of maintenance in November 1496. There are also verses addressed to his heir, Prince Arthur, who died in 1502. The frontispiece shows Henry riding in a triumphal car of a kind familiar from illustrations to Petrarch's *Trionfi*. The accompanying decoration is typical of Italian manuscripts of the period, featuring stylized floral motifs, together with antique arms and trophies. The English royal arms, supported by putti, are placed on a Tudor rose in an arrangement that is probably derived from contemporary English coinage.   JMB

PROV. Henry VII (d. 1509); York Minster Library.

LIT. Gwynne 1984; Ker and Piper 1992, pp.746–7; Backhouse 1995, pp.178–9.

49 Embroidered velvet binding for Queen Catherine Parr

c.1546

h. 21.5 cm, w. 14.8 cm, d. 3.4 cm

British Library, London (C.27.e.19)

The binding covers *Il Petrarcha con l'espositione d'Alessandro Vellutello*, Venice, Gabriel Giolito, 1544, rebound with the original covers retained. Purple velvet with appliqué work in variously coloured silks,

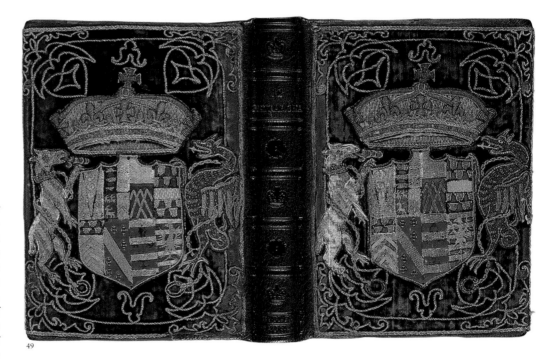

49

embroidered with coloured silks and gold and silver thread to a bold design of decorative fleuron- and leaf-shapes in the corners, and a fleuron above and below the large crowned coat of arms of Catherine Parr between two supporters, a greyhound and a wyvern, both gorged. The edges of the leaves are gilt and gauffered.

Embroidered bindings in velvet, silk or canvas were popular in England during the reigns of the Tudors and Stuarts. They are often found on Bibles and prayer books; many were worked by professional embroiderers, some by amateur needlewomen. Many, but by no means all, were made for women. Queen Elizabeth I is said to have preferred her books to be bound in velvet. The suggestion that Catherine Parr made the embroidery for this binding has not been substantiated.   MF

PROV. Royal Library; passed to British Museum in 1757.

LIT. Davenport 1896, fig. 5; Davenport 1899, pl. 17.

4 THE ARCHITECTURE OF WAR

JOHN A. A. GOODALL

On 15 February 1538 Henry, Earl of Cumberland was surveying Knaresborough Castle for the king. The survey he produced records in dry, business-like prose the desolation of this castle, but for one significant moment its official manner lapses. Confronted by the decaying fourteenth-century donjon or great tower of the castle, there is a sudden outburst of enthusiasm:

> The dungeon is a marvelous house of strength, the walls thereof four yards thick or more; and is of fine hewn stone, clean polished within and without; and strongly fortified with work and man's ingenuity to abide all assault; and hath but one stair upward and that is fortified with three gates and three portcullises – albeit they be but of timber – and also above the vault an open vent to make war downwards.
> (PRO E36 159, folio 6r)

Cumberland's response reflects a late medieval admiration for, and fascination with, the architecture of war. As functioning defences or fantastical ornament, the architectural trappings of fortification – such as crenellations, arrow loops and turrets – were features of every kind of building in this period, from great houses to churches. Clearly understood to convey status, they were rich with chivalric and knightly associations (Coulson 1979).

In the context of domestic building, this interest in the architecture of war has received a bad scholarly press. Most late medieval castles, although richly adorned with crenellations, appear considerably less defensible than their predecessors. And as a direct consequence the whole castle-building tradition in this period has been characterized as being in decline (most notably and influentially in Brown 1976, pp.128–53). There are good reasons for rethinking this received judgement about castles. In the first place there are the buildings themselves. These are simply so spectacular as to make any accusations of architectural decline seem ridiculous. Moreover, if buildings called 'castles' were still being constructed well into the sixteenth century, who are we to judge them as being better or worse than their forebears? In fact, the catholic use of the term throughout the Middle Ages can be easily explained. The word 'castle' was not – as modern scholars have treated it – a technical term, but an honorific applied to great houses built in a fortified style. Castles clearly remained the most prestigious kinds of residence for the nobility up to 1547 and far beyond. A peer without a castle (old or new) among his houses was like a knight without a horse.

It was in consequence of this that a steady flow of major castles continued to be erected by figures with outstanding political pretensions into the sixteenth century and beyond. These castles are closely allied architecturally to the mainstream of domestic design and can only be understood in the wider context of developments in this tradition (Thompson 1987). New castles typically took one of two time-honoured forms. The more common might be termed the enclosure castle, which comprised one or more courtyards faced externally with multiple towers and dominated

by a gatehouse. This form of castle had a long architectural pedigree stretching back to the late twelfth century, but it enjoyed wide popularity in the later Middle Ages through the medium of Edward III's palace in the upper ward at Windsor (plate 66). This building, which boxed all the necessary elements of a palace into a regular plan, proved hugely influential in every sphere of domestic architecture, from collegiate planning to castle design (see the essay by Christopher Wilson in this volume, and Wilson 2002).

Edward III's palace at Windsor was directly to influence the mainstream of late fourteenth-century castle architecture. But in the early fifteenth century the regularized, enclosure form which distinguished the design of Windsor was brilliantly reworked in the castle-like designs of the neighbouring college at Eton built by Henry VI (cat. no. 23). Begun in 1441, the Eton domestic quadrangle was a seminal work of brick architecture, which inspired the design of numerous houses and castles, including Ewelme Manor (begun in 1444) and Herstmonceux Castle (licensed in

98 Herstmonceux Castle, Sussex (cat. no. 51)

1441, plate 98). A large number of brick buildings – including Kirby Muxloe Castle (begun in 1480) and the castle-like Hengrave (begun in 1525, cat. no. 149) and Oxborough Halls (licensed in 1482) – can also trace their descent back to the designs of Eton and Windsor. Stone castles were also erected in this enclosure form, as at Sudeley Castle (complete by 1458, cat. no. 146).

The standard alternative design to the enclosure castle – but by no means an exclusive one – was of an architectural composition dominated by a massive keep or donjon

(Dixon and Lott 1993). Particularly celebrated in this respect is the great tower at Warkworth, a highly complex domestic design of *c*.1380 informed by a local tradition of tower-house architecture. Most great towers were rather simpler structures, however, as is the case with the keeps erected by two Lord Treasurers Cromwell and Hastings at their family castles of Tattershall (under construction in 1446, plate 99) and Ashby de la Zouch (licensed in 1474) respectively.

It is tempting to see these great towers as modern evocations of the twelfth-century donjon tradition. Certainly, Romanesque great towers remained prestigious buildings even into the seventeenth century. At Dover, for example, Henry II's keep was extensively remodelled by Edward IV and continued to serve as the royal lodgings in the castle, even until Charles I's reign (Colvin 1975, pp.247–8). This conservatism is partly to be explained by the fact that most of the greatest English castles of the late Middle Ages were also the most ancient, from Windsor to Fotheringhay, from Framlingham to Pontefract. A new castle was a rarity, but when one was built it aimed to stand architectural comparison with its established peers.

As a whole, the period between 1400 and 1547 is one of remarkable continuity in castle-building. But Henry VIII's reign undoubtedly witnessed a turning point in the architecture of war. Cannon fortifications, which had previously been integrated within castle defences, began to be separately developed as fort emplacements. Perhaps the most celebrated of these are the connected series at Deal, Walmer and Sandown on the South Downs (begun in 1539, cat. no. 52). Although the long-term impact of cannon on castle-building was to be profound, much more immediately important was Henry VIII's personality and style of government. His political jealousy made castle-building by subjects a positively dangerous exercise, as the unfinished state of the unfortunate Duke of Buckingham's magnificent castle at Thornbury testifies (begun *c*.1511, cat. no. 147). And his cupidity made him possessor of more castles than he could possibly maintain. Arguably the ruin of Knaresborough in 1538 has less to do with the natural decline of the castle than with Tudor tyranny.

FURTHER READING

Emery 1996–2000; Saunders 1989; Thompson 1987.

99   Tattershall Castle, Lincolnshire
(cat. no. 50)

50 Tattershall Castle, Lincolnshire

PLATE 99

1430s and '40s

The great tower of Tattershall Castle still dominates the surrounding Lincolnshire Levels. It was built by Ralph, Lord Cromwell, Treasurer of England between 1433 and 1443, as part of the remodelling of his family seat during the 1430s and '40s. During this protracted operation he erected magnificent new residential buildings within the thirteenth-century castle enclosure (now largely destroyed) and encircled the site by a second moat to create an outer bailey. The operations – which also extended to the improvement of the estate and its working buildings – made extensive use of locally produced brick, then a material in high architectural fashion.

Four accounts relating to Cromwell's building operations at Tattershall survive. The first two relate respectively to 1434–5 and 1438–9 and indicate that work was under way on an impressive scale. But in the next account for 1439–40 there is a new intensity apparent in the operations, with more than two million bricks being used on site. This surge in activity corresponded with the foundation of a college of priests – a hallmark of the greatest contemporary residences – to serve Tattershall parish church, and it is possible that these circumstances indicate a new departure in the work. One element of the castle possibly planned at this moment – and certainly begun after 1440 – is the great tower. This is mentioned as being under construction in the last surviving account of 1445–6.

The great tower is massively conceived on a rectangular plan and built of brick with stone detailing. It stands five storeys high and is divided internally into four floors, each more richly appointed than that beneath. The building is crowned by a machicolated parapet (now rebuilt) and its four corner turrets were formerly capped by small spires. Contrary to what is sometimes asserted, the form and detailing of the building suggest an English provenance for the design.   JG

LIT. Curzon and Tipping 1929; Simpson 1960; Emery 2000, pp.308–16.

51 Herstmonceux Castle, Sussex

PLATE 98

1441–c.1448

Reflected in the water of its moat, the embattled circuit of Herstmonceux answers every popular expectation of a great castle. It was built by Sir Roger Fiennes, Treasurer of the Household from 1439 to 1448, and is representative of the vastly ambitious architectural projects undertaken by several prominent courtiers in Henry VI's reign.

As it was originally constructed, the domestic buildings were arranged around four internal courtyards. But these were destroyed in 1777 and all that now survives of the medieval fabric is the outer shell of walls and towers. The moat, enlarged in the 1930s, is the sole remnant of a substantial system of medieval ponds around the castle.

Sir Roger was licensed in February 1441 to 'furnish with towers and battlements his manor house at Herstmonceux' and to extend the park there. Crucially, 1441 was also the year in which Henry VI began constructing his new college at Eton (cat. no. 23) and Sir Roger helped oversee this royal project. He even loaned 'brickmen' to the Eton works, including a certain John Roweland, from Malines in Belgium, possibly a prominent figure in the Herstmonceux workforce. Given these connections, it can be no coincidence that Herstmonceux compares closely in design with Eton and is built in the same combination of brick and stone.

The exterior is of particular interest on two counts. Rather than regular towers on a square plan (as at Eton), those at Herstmonceux are polygonal and alternately large and small. And they frame the main gatehouse – a building essentially in a traditional English form – within a distinctive and unprecedented symmetrical façade composition. This composition (tower, turret, gatehouse, turret, tower) subsequently became a staple of grand English design, from Thornbury Castle (cat. no. 147) to Burghley House (remodelled in the 1570s and '80s). Second, the towers are pierced on several faces by rectangular windows, a detail that – in the context of other brick buildings of the 1440s – can be understood to look forward to the great projecting oriels of Jacobethan palaces.

Some modern authorities have asserted that Herstmonceux is not a 'real' castle, on the basis that its fortifications are largely theatrical. But to view the defensive qualities of Herstmonceux – or those of any other late medieval castle – as an index of its status is completely to miss the point. The technical use of the word 'castle' is a modern phenomenon. To a medieval audience, a residence of this ambition, made magnificent through the trappings of fortification, clearly deserved the honorific title of a 'castle', whatever its real military strength.   JG

LIT. Venables 1851; Tipping 1937; VCH 1937, pp.131–4.

52 *Plat* (design) for a Henrician castle on the Downs*

1539

Ink and paint on parchment; approx. h. 47.5 cm, w. 55.5 cm

Inscr.: *Castle in the Downes*

British Library, London (Cotton MS Augustus, I.i, f.20)

This bird's-eye view of an artillery castle with its canons blazing is one of a pair of *plats* or designs associated with the fortifications begun by Henry VIII along the Downs anchorage during the invasion scare of 1539. These comprised three artillery castles with overlapping arcs of fire – Walmer, Deal and Sandown – connected by ditches and earth and timber bulwarks. The project was undertaken by craftsmen seconded from Hampton Court and this drawing probably comes from their office of works. It appears to be a draft design for Deal, the principal castle in the series (Coad 1998).

The castle is countersunk in a deep moat and concentrically planned with its inner fortifications overlooking the outer. There are two walled lines of defence laid out on a circular plan, each comprising six hollow, lobed bastions. These are set on different axes so that the bastions do not align. At the centre of the castle stands a tall, drum-shaped tower. The cannon in the castle are mounted on the walls between protective wicker gabions, but there is also a lower tier of guns in the outer bastions to command the moat. Entrance to the building is across a timber bridge and through an internal barbican within the central bastion.

Henry VIII's known interest in fortification and the involvement of craftsmen from the royal works probably explain the idiosyncratic nature of this design, with its relatively high outline and thin walls. These features, as well as the use of semicircular bastions – by this date outmoded in Europe – suggest that the source for the design lay in the tradition of artillery fortification which had been developing in England since the mid-fourteenth century.   JG

LIT. Colvin 1982, pp.455–65; Saunders 1989, pp.34–52.

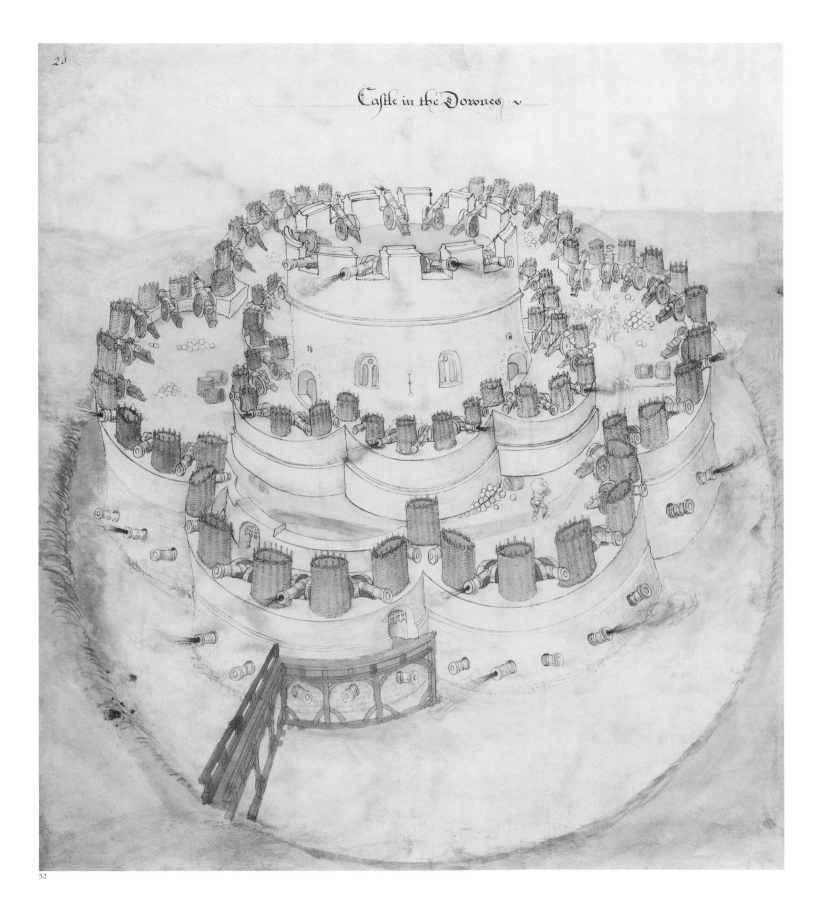

5 THE ARTS OF COMBAT

KAREN WATTS

100 Rubbing of brass of Thomas, Baron Camoys and Lady Camoys, Trotton church, Sussex (cat. no. 53)

I n 1473 Martin Rondelle, a Bruges armourer of the Bastard of Burgundy, wrote to Sir John Paston:

… Moreover, I have heard that you would like to have a full armour. As I recently took your measurements when you were in this town of Bruges, you know that I still have them for all pieces. For this reason, if you would like me to make it for you, I will do it willingly and all the elements that you would like made. With regard to the price, I shall ensure that you will be satisfied with me. So, when you know which pieces you would like to have and the style and the day you would like to receive them through someone with whom I can deal in your name and who will pay me a deposit, I will work so well that, God willing, you will praise me.

(translated from the French, in Gairdner 1904, III, pp.95–6)

This extract reveals some interesting details concerning the acquisition of bespoke armour from the Continent and concerning the versatility of supplying 'all pieces' for a full armour, presumably for war and tournament, as required. No price is quoted, but in an earlier letter of about 1468 Paston states that he has recently bought an armour for £20 (Gairdner 1904, V, p.699). The correspondence also reveals that it was not the prerogative of senior nobility to own quality armour. But perhaps the most interesting feature is that Rondelle is offering to make the armour in whatever style (*la faisson* [sic]) is required.

In the light of Rondelle's comments, can there be said to be a distinct and identifiable style of English armour? English armourers are known by name – Thomas Parker and John Smyth, for example – and the London Armourers' Company had existed since the fourteenth century, but no single surviving piece of armour has been associated with a particular English maker (Wiedemer 1967, pp.62–4). The reference to a pair of gauntlets of English style (*à la façon d'Angleterre*) suggests that there was a distinctive English style of armour (Laborde 1849, p.360, no. 1243), and the Black Prince's helm at Canterbury Cathedral, Henry V's helm at Westminster Abbey (cat. no. 54a) and the Warwick Shaffron (Royal Armouries VI.446), together with some Italianate helmets in English churches, are probably of English origin. Much armour, however, was imported from Italy, Germany and Flanders, from armourers like Rondelle who were capable of making it to the specifications of the client.

In general, English armour for the mounted man-at-arms, as portrayed on effigies and brasses, is Italianate, with variations (Blair 1958, pp.79–92, 107–8). Funerary monuments are an important source, as very little armour for the limbs and torso has survived for the fifteenth century. This period saw the arrival of steel-plate armour joined together as an homogeneous suit with articulating rivets and leathers. The brass of Thomas Camoys (d. 1421, plate 100) shows the characteristic deep fauld (skirt) of hooped lames (metal plates), small pauldrons (shoulder-defences), pendant besagews (rondels protecting the armpits) and the great bacinet. The latter helmet continued to be popular in England (seen under the head of the Thomas Reynes brass of 1451 in Marston Mortaine church, Bedfordshire), but gradually became part of the specialist equipment of the foot combats in tournaments (cat. no. 79). This followed the path of the great helm, which by 1400 was used almost exclusively for the joust. Instead, versatile open helmets were preferred for war, especially the sallet (plate 101). The new, and more expensive, Italian enclosed armet helmet (cat. no. 338) was less popular in England. One of the finest examples of a mid-century armour can be seen in the Beauchamp effigy (cat. no. 87). Every lame, embossed rib, rivet and strap is carefully depicted. The armour has become more complex and, while Italianate in aspect, has characteristic English fluting. A comparison with the Camoys armour shows developments, as for example in the large spade tassets

101 Sallet (cat. no. 59)

(thigh-plates) hanging from the shortened fauld, large pauldrons with reinforces and distinctive couters (elbow-defences) and cuisses (thigh-defences).

When Henry VIII became king he found that there were no armourers in England who could make the finest armours that he required for tournament and parade. After importing armourers to work for him in London, he finally set up Martin van Royne as the first master armourer of a new 'Almain Armoury' in 1515 (see cat. no. 56). Initially manned by Germans and Dutch, it came to be staffed entirely by Englishmen, all working exclusively for the monarch at the Royal Workshops at Greenwich. The armours produced were of the highest and finest quality ever seen in England.

Armour was versatile and adapted itself to requirements for foot soldiers. Brigandines were an alternative (but not cheap) body defence of small plates and textile covering, while jacks were composed of textile padding. The indigenous armouries of Helmingham and Mendlesham contain elements of fine quality and simple armours (cat. no. 60), including rare examples of flexible arm defences (splints), which incorporated ingeniously simple hand-defences.

Weapons encompassed swords, staff-weapons, bows and firearms. The sword was chiefly used as a cutting weapon and had a broad flat blade. The hand-and-a-half (bastard) sword used for dismounted fighting was larger and could be gripped with both hands (cat. no. 61). The pollaxe was a favoured staff-weapon for fighting within an enclosure in foot combats (cat. no. 57). The longbow was over 2 metres in length and, in the hands of skilled men, could be discharged quicker than the contemporary crossbow (cat. no. 63). It maintained its superiority of range and accuracy over firearms well into the sixteenth century. Handguns had the advantage, however, of needing less training and strength (Blair 1962, pp.1–41, and cat. no. 65).

Weapons and armour were not solely associated with war and tournament. Daggers known as baselards, for example, were commonly carried for self-defence (cat. no. 203). One of the most intriguing developments was the military weapon becoming a symbol of authority, and changing shape and function. This is clearly seen in civic swords and maces. A civic sword could be old but modified (cat. nos 82, 127), or even impractical for use. As a weapon, the mace had been carried with the war-head upwards, but in its civic use this was reversed to favour the other end, bearing the coat of arms (cat. no. 128). These objects were thus identified with corporate rather than individual power.

FURTHER READING

Blair 1958; Blair 1962; Wiedemer 1967.

53 Brass rubbing of Thomas, Baron Camoys, and Lady Camoys

PLATE 100

*c.*1421

h. 262 cm, w. 118 cm; l. of figure of Baron Camoys 147 cm

Inscr. in *textura*: *Orate p*[ro] *a*[n]*i*[m]*ab*[us] *Thome Camoys & Elizabeth eius Consortis qui quond*[am] *erat d*[omi]*n*[u]*s de Camoys baro & p*[ro]*uidus Consul Regis & regni Anglie ac Strenuus Miles de Gartero suu*[m] *fine*[m] *co*[m]*mendauit* [Christo] *xxviij° die mens*[is] *Marcii A*[nn]*o d*[omi]*ni M°CCCC°xix° quor*[um] *a*[n]*i*[m]*ab*[us] *p*[ro]*piciet*[ur] *de*[us] *ame*[n]. (Pray for the souls of **Thomas Camoys and his wife Elizabeth. He was formerly Lord Camoys, a baron and prudent counsellor of the King and realm of England, and a valiant Knight of the Garter. He commended his end to Christ on the 28th day of March in the year of our Lord 1419** [*sic*, for **1421]. On whose souls may God have mercy, Amen.)**

Derrick Chivers Esq. (original in St George's church, Trotton, West Sussex)

This brass, on a table tomb in the chancel of Trotton church, has been nominated as 'the finest English brass of the fifteenth century'. Lord Camoys is depicted in plate armour, with fan-shaped besagews, holding the hand of his wife, who wears a sideless cote, a mantle and a *crespine* headdress, with the hair in square network cauls. At her feet stands a boy, probably their son Roger (b. *c.*1406). Both Lord and Lady Camoys wear the Lancastrian livery collar of SS, and he wears the Garter below his left knee. The Garter also encircles the Camoys arms above the double canopy, an early example of this practice (Begent and Chesshyre 1999, p.194). Thomas commanded the English left wing at Agincourt, and was one of several commanders installed as Knights of the Garter on St George's Day 1416. Elizabeth, Thomas's second wife who died in 1417, was the daughter of Edmund Mortimer, Earl of March, and the widow of Sir Henry Percy (the Harry Hotspur of Shakespeare's *I Henry IV*). The brass was produced by the London D workshop, which is characterized by its attention to decorative details, such as the trefoil patterning on the armour. At the bottom of the left-hand canopy-shaft is a stamped mark, almost certainly that of the supplier of the latten plate.   NR

LIT. Davidson-Houston 1939, pp.124–6; Norris 1977, pp.76, 78, 94.

54 Helm, shield and sword associated with the funeral of King Henry V on 6 November 1422

Dean and Chapter of Westminster, Westminster Abbey Museum

a) Helm

Early 15th century

Iron or steel and copper alloy; h. 42.5 cm

The basic form is that of a tall oval-section cylinder that tapers from eye level upwards to form a crown of truncated conical shape, and with a turned lower edge that follows a concave curve on either side to meet at front and back in a blunt point; riveted over each point is a small rectangular iron plate carrying a loose tongueless buckle, for attachment to straps on the wearer's chest and back. It comprises three main parts: a single rear plate that extends halfway round the sides and, overlapping it, two plates that form respectively the front of the crown and the lower part of the helm; a horizontal gap between them forms a sight, while at the apex is a small egg-shaped opening filled with another plate. A low medial ridge runs from front to rear. A riveted reinforce covers the whole of the left side and half of the right side of the front below the sight. The lower edge is bordered throughout by an applied, riveted copper-alloy (latten?) strip engraved with a design of repeated quatrefoil flowers between zigzag and dotted borders; the plate of the front buckle is covered with a similar strip engraved with two oak leaves (another at the rear is missing). The crown contains various holes for attaching a lining and a crest, while at the back of the neck is a flat fixed hook by which it would have been secured to a support in a funerary display. It is of English (almost certainly London) make.

This represents the final development of the medieval 'great' helm, worn in battle over a visorless bacinet (the reason for the high crown), though the fact that it is fitted with a reinforce suggests that it was actually intended for the joust. It can be compared with two helms in Cobham Church, Kent, probably associated with burials of 1405 and 1407, which suggests that it was not new in 1422: the king's funeral accounts in fact refer only to the painting of a helm. They also mention a leopard crest with a rich textile mantling. The ornamental copper-alloy border, which was probably originally gilded, can be compared to the borders depicted on some English alabaster military effigies (for example, Spilsby, Lincolnshire; Cheadle, Cheshire; Christchurch, Hampshire).

54a

b) Shield

Probably late 14th century

Wood (lime or poplar?) and textile; h. 61 cm

This shield is heater-shaped and concave towards the body. The exterior face, which would originally have borne heraldic charges, painted and probably moulded in relief, now retains only some layers of bast fibres, chalk and glue, and minute traces of colour. The interior retains much of its lining of pale-blue figured oriental silk, displaying a pattern of tiny leaves, sown with fleurs-de-lis in couched gold thread, and a crimson velvet arm-pad stuffed with raw wool dyed blue. This last is embellished with a charbocle formed of strips of parchment decorated with couched gold thread. The braces and guige are missing.

The charbocle formed part of the arms of Joan of Navarre, Henry IV's second wife, whom he married in 1403. It had no direct connection with Henry V, so the shield must have belonged originally to his father. It is probably the shield painted with the king's arms mentioned in the funeral accounts. It is presumably of English make.

c) Sword

15th century

Steel, iron and wood; l. 89.5 cm (blade 73 cm)

A cruciform fighting sword, probably English, of fine quality with a straight, double-edged, leaf-shaped blade of flattened hollow-diamond section, tapering to a sharp point, and struck on one face with a 'twig' mark. The arched cross curves down in the centre on the blade side to form a low point with a central dart-shaped flute, and terminates in small buttons formed of inward scrolls. The wheel-shaped pommel is possibly made of three discs brazed together, each of the outer ones with a raised central feature encircled by a hollow moulding and with a circular central recess containing a painted red cross; the button of flattened pyramid shape formed from the tip of the tang of the blade. The circular-section wooden grip tapers towards the ends. The metal parts of the hilt and the base of the blade retain traces of gilding.

The sword was found in 1869 in the triforium of Westminster Abbey. There is no certainty that it came from Henry V's achievements, though they would undoubtedly have included a sword. It could date from anywhere in the fifteenth and early sixteenth centuries, and might have belonged to any of a number of burials in the abbey, including that of Henry VII.

The remains of an early fifteenth-century saddle

54b

(not shown) have also long been displayed in the abbey as part of Henry V's achievements. It is unlikely that it was, since no other English instance of horse-equipment being used for this purpose is recorded, though it was almost certainly used in the funeral. The only pieces that we can be certain were suspended over the king's tomb are the shield and helm, since they are illustrated in this position in a work published in 1707, together with a crest (now missing) like that of the Black Prince in Canterbury Cathedral. CB

LIT. St John Hope 1914a; Laking 1920–22, II, pp.99–105, 230–34, 262, 265, III, pp.156–60, V, pp.196, 211; Tanner 1930; Mann 1931, pp.405–7; Oakeshott 1952; Monnas forthcoming.

54c

55

55 Tournament armour for the foot combat of King Henry VIII

Flemish and Italian craftsmen working in England, 1520

Steel, etched and formerly gilt; h. 188 cm

Her Majesty the Queen, on loan to the Royal Armouries, Leeds (II.7)

This armour was made for Henry VIII to fight in at the Field of Cloth of Gold tournament in June 1520. It is distinguished by a tonlet (deep skirt) and a great bacinet (helmet). The armour shows signs of being hastily assembled – because Francis I of France changed the rules governing the type of armour to be worn – using elements from several earlier armours drawn from store. The bacinet, for example, bears the marks of the Italian Missaglia family, while the leg harness has spur slots at the heel for cavalry use. Henry and his opponent would fight in an enclosure with a variety of weapons that could include spears, swords, axes, daggers or staff-weapons. Each had a prescribed number of blows. The etched decoration includes the Tudor rose, St George, the Virgin and Child, the Garter and the Garter collar.   KW

PROV. In the armoury of Henry VIII and subsequently in the Royal Armouries collection; the leg harness was purchased with the assistance of the National Art Collections Fund in 1971 from the Dymoke Estate at Scrivelsby House.

LIT. Starkey 1991, cat. no. IV.2; Eaves 1993; Blair 1995; Richardson 2002, pp.18–22.

56

56 Horse armour of King Henry VIII

Flemish, by the armourer Martin van Royne and the decorator Paul van Vrelant, *c*.1511–14

Steel, embossed, engraved and formerly gilt; h. 140 cm, l. 254 cm, w. 99 cm

Her Majesty the Queen, on loan to the Royal Armouries, Leeds (VI.6–12)

Known as the 'Burgundian Bard', this horse armour was probably a gift from the Emperor Maximilian I to Henry VIII to mark his marriage to Catherine of Aragon in 1509. The bard is embossed with a trailing design of pomegranates, the badge of Catherine, and the firesteels and raguly crosses of the Burgundian Order of the Golden Fleece, which Henry had received in 1505. The crupper (rear defence) is stamped with the armourer's mark: a letter 'M' surmounted by a crescent. This is now thought to be the mark of Martin van Royne, who later became the first master armourer of the royal workshops at Greenwich. The whole armour was engraved and gilded by Paul van Vrelant, who is first recorded working in Brussels for Philip the Fair, son of Maximilian I. By 1514 he was working for Henry VIII.   KW

PROV. In the armoury of Henry VIII and subsequently in the Royal Armouries collection.

LIT. Blair 1965; Starkey 1991, cat. no. III.1; Richardson 2002, p.11.

57 Pollaxe

English?, 1500–40

Copper alloy and iron, wooden haft; l. of head 37.5 cm, wt 4.2 kg

University Museum of Archaeology and Anthropology, Cambridge (1948.1708); on long-term loan to the Royal Armouries, Leeds (AL.101 1)

The head is mostly of cast copper alloy (probably originally gilt) with cast relief, punched and incised decoration. Half the rear fluke and top spike have partly exposed iron cores (the latter restored in wood). Lions' masks support the hammer head and fluke. The shortened haft (restored to approximately its original length) is strengthened by four straps (langets) decorated with applied fleurs-de-lis (some missing).

Pollaxes (the term denotes weapons with both axe blades and hammer heads) were much used for set foot-combat in the ring (Anglo 2000, pp.151–9). The crowned rose with putti supporters on the socket suggests English royal associations. Similar devices are found on two weapons owned by Henry VIII (Royal Armouries XII.1, XIX.17) and a very similar – though not quite identical – pollaxe is described in the 1547 inventory of Henry's possessions (Starkey 1998, p.104, no. 3860). The present weapon belongs to a group of copper-alloy mounted pollaxes (see Borg 1975; a few others have since come to light), one of which, in the Musée de l'Armée in Paris (K.84), is decorated with the rose within a sunburst device, which was used by Henry VIII among others. The association of the present pollaxe with Henry may be strengthened by the incised decoration on the base of the rear fluke resembling a pomegranate, the device of his first wife Catherine of Aragon, which, if accepted, would date the weapon to between 1509 and about 1530. While heavy and robust, the construction indicates parade use. If not made for Henry personally, it may have been intended for an officer of one of his royal guards, or for a gift.   PJL

PROV. Acquired by Richard Neville, 3rd Lord Braybrooke, in about 1847 from Sir Francis Vincent, Debden Hall, Essex; presented to the University Museum by Lord Braybrooke in 1948, from the Neville family collection at Audley End, Essex.

LIT. Borg 1975.

57

58 St George and the Dragon

Third decade of the 16th century (1528?)

Polychromed wood, iron, leather, textiles and horse-hair; h. (excluding sword) 84.5 cm

The Worshipful Company of Armourers and Brasiers of London

A group, made of two main parts: an oval wooden base, carved and coloured to represent grass-covered ground and supporting a rearing white horse with a horse-hair tail, which tramples on a partly recumbent dragon, mainly green in colour, all made from a single piece of oak; and, mounted on the horse, a wooden mannequin representing the saint, with carved face and hands, the right one holding a sword above his head. The broken end of the saint's spear is represented as passing through the dragon's neck, while the rest of it lies, in two pieces, beside him.

The saint and horse are both dressed in miniature iron armour that differs from the real thing only in having most of the articulated parts made solid, with the articulations indicated by engraved or raised lines; considerable traces of fire-bluing survive beneath the brow-plate of the helmet, suggesting that all the surfaces were once similarly treated. The remains of the original polychrome were repainted, and a few missing pieces of armour and the sword replaced, in 1975–6.

The saint's armour comprises: a visored armet with cusped brow-reinforce, a rondel at the rear, and a separate reinforcing-bevor; breastplate and backplate each of a single piece, the former rounded with a low medial ridge, and a lance-rest on the right; laminated skirt carrying a pair of one-piece pointed tassets (modern); pauldrons extending well over the back where they are decorated with shallow radiating ribs, the front of the left one completely covered by a reinforcing-piece with a large haute-piece and a central rivet with an elongated pyramidal head; complete vambraces with shell-shaped cowters, the left one with a small haute-piece at the shoulder; mitten gauntlets with long pointed cuffs; complete leg harness with poleyns with large, fan-shaped, fluted side wings, square-toed sabatons and, held by rivets, rowel spurs with straight necks.

The horse's bard is made of large riveted plates, and has the main external edges turned and with plain recessed borders. It comprises: a three-piece peytral with large circular bosses on each side; a four-piece crupper completely enveloping the hindquarters; large shaffron and crinet, the latter completely enclosing the neck, and the former with a large rondel carrying a prominent spike on the brow.

Saddle with high bow and cantle faced with plate, that on the latter probably an old replacement. Near the right edge of the peytral is what might be the remains of a maker's mark, but is more probably a flaw in the metal.

The style of armour on the figures, which is of the Italian-inspired type current in western Europe (including England) at the time, indicates a date in the third decade of the sixteenth century. This date, and the English origins of the group, were confirmed by a dendrochronological examination of the base, carried out in 1975 by the Oxford Research Laboratory for Archaeology and the History of Art, which concluded that it is English oak from a tree felled during the period 1515–30, and probably grown in the Home Counties. There thus seems to be good reason, given that the group incorporates armourer's work, for identifying it with a record in the Armourers' Company's *Memorandum Book* (f.119) of the gift by William Vinyard (or Vinzard) in July 1528 of (in modern spelling) 'the George that stands in the Hall next the high table … at his proper cost and charge he made it and gave it … ' That this was of portable size is established by a description of how, on 4 January 1539/40, 'we [the Company] went to Greenwich aboat with our banners, targets, & our George standing over ye rails' to greet the king and Anne of Cleves when they came to the palace (*Court Minute Book*, p.26). Vinyard (d. 1535) was three times master of the company, and the husband of the lady who bequeathed the owl pot (cat. no. 193) to it. The armour for the group was almost certainly made by him.

The group not only provides a unique representation in the metal of armour used and made in England in the early sixteenth century (other than by the royal workshops at Greenwich), otherwise known only from other media (e.g. Stone 1972, pl. 192); it is also a unique example of the kind of patronal figure, with appropriate craft accessories, that must once have existed in many of the halls of the craft guilds – St George is the Armourers' patron. The pose is very similar to that of the well-known fifteenth-century carved wooden St George and Dragon group from St Mary's Hall, Coventry (cat. no. 284).   CB

PROV. Francis Charles Bullock of Slater Street, Liverpool; Alfred Miller of West Didsbury, Manchester; acquired by the Worshipful Company of Armourers and Brasiers of London, 1975.

LIT. Richardson 2002, pp.6–7, ill.

58

59 Sallet

PLATE 101

*c.*1460–90

Steel and copper alloy (latten?); h. 28 cm

The Herbert Art Gallery and Museum, Coventry (1962/54)

This helmet has a high pointed skull, forged from a single piece, with an arched face-opening and a short pointed tail; it is encircled by a row of iron and copper-alloy lining-rivets (some replaced), has a pair of holes for the chin-strap (missing) on each side, and a cusped triangular brow-reinforce. A bluntly pointed half-visor projects beyond the line of the brow and incorporates the flanged lower edge of a vision slit, of which the top is formed by the front edge of the skull. The external edges, except for the sides of the face-opening, are flanged slightly outwards and bordered by turns. A pronounced keel-like medial ridge runs from front to rear, and is flanked at the summit by a pair of short, low side ridges. Struck on the right rear of the skull is a triple mark of Italian type, comprising the crowned Gothic minuscules *ro* above two split crosses straddling the same letters.

From the old municipal armoury in St Mary's Hall, Coventry, most of which was dispersed in the eighteenth century. The helmet survives because, traditionally, it belonged originally to Peeping Tom, who spied on Lady Godiva, and was worn by a figure representing him in the triannual Godiva procession (a later plume-pipe riveted to the apex for this purpose was removed at the V&A in 1967). It is a version of the type of helmet, probably introduced in *c.*1415–20, that from the 1430s was the most commonly used in Europe, except in Italy, though it was made there for export. It was commonly accompanied by a separate chin-defence (bevor). The most popular form has a rounded skull with a low comb, but other pointed examples are known, both from illustrations and from a few surviving examples (Thomas and Gamber 1976, no. A 2334). Among the latter is an exactly similar skull to that of the present helmet, bearing the remains of what are clearly the same marks, incorporated in a seventeenth-century funerary helmet in Harefield Church, Middlesex. The letters in the mark are either the first two of the maker's surname or his full initials. An obvious identification of him is Martin Rondelle, armourer to the Bastard of Burgundy: a Milanese armourer working in Bruges, he corresponded with John Paston in 1473 about armour with which he was supplying him (see pp.192–3; Barnes 1932 and 1935–6; Richardson 2001, pp.18–19).   CB

LIT. Laking 1920–22, II, pp.23–6.

60 'Almain Rivet' Armour

Flemish or German, 1510–20

Steel and leather; h. 66 cm, w. 44 cm

Church of St Mary the Virgin, Mendlesham, Suffolk

This is a rare survival of a light half-armour worn by English infantry. In 1512 Guido Portinari, a Florentine merchant, supplied Henry VIII with '2000 complete harnesse called Almayne Ryvettes … accounting always a salet, a gorjet, a breastplate, a backplate and a pair of splints for every complete harness' at 16 shillings a set (Brewer, et al., 1862–1932, I, p.415). This almain rivet is missing the sallet (open helmet, probably resembling a skull-cap), the gorget (collar) and the backplate.

The splints (arm-defences) are the most distinctive feature. Simple curved plates, connected by internal leathers, protect the outside of the arm. An ingeniously simple design – a slider in a slot in each wrist-plate extending plates to protect the hand as desired – replaces gauntlets.   KW

LIT. Blair 1958, p.119.

60

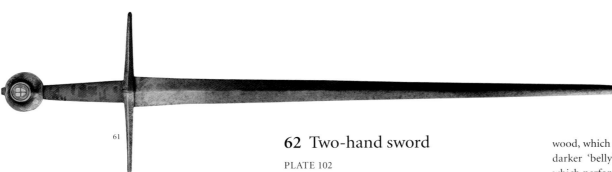

61

61 The Battle Abbey Sword

1417–37

Steel, silver-gilt and wood; l. 105.5 cm

Royal Museum of Scotland, Edinburgh (reg. no. 1905-633)

A hand-and-a-half fighting sword with a broad, straight, double-edged blade (much worn), struck with an indecipherable mark. The silvered and gilt iron hilt is engraved with running rose tendrils and a chequered diaper containing quatrefoils. It comprises a long, straight cross tapering towards the ends, a wheel-shaped pommel with a truncated pyramid-shaped button, and prominent 'hubs'. Each of these has a circular central recess containing a shield bearing the arms – probably originally enamelled – of Battle Abbey, Sussex, within olive (?) sprays, and flanked by the Gothic minuscule letters t and l, the initials of Thomas de Ludlow, abbot between 1417 and 1437. The modern wooden grip is covered with green velvet.

William the Conqueror, when founding Battle Abbey, granted the abbot for the time being sole jurisdiction, including the administration of justice, within his own lands and certain other areas. The sword – which itself provides the only known evidence for the association of such a weapon with the abbey – was presumably used as a bearing-sword to symbolize this (Eden 1930). Rather surprisingly, if this is correct, the shields of arms and initials are designed to be viewed when it is point-downwards.   CB

PROV. Battle Abbey; Sir John Gage (1479–1556), one of Henry VIII's commissioners for the suppression of religious houses, and his successors down to the 4th Viscount Gage (1791–1877); Llewellyn and Samuel Meyrick; Sir Noël Paton; the Royal Scottish Museum, 1905.

LIT. Meyrick 1826; Laking 1920–22, II, pp.261–5; Norman 1972, p.19, no. 20.

62 Two-hand sword

PLATE 102

Second quarter of the 15th century

Steel and wood; l. 135.8 cm

Museum of London (39.142)

A fighting sword, with a straight double-edged, sharply tapering blade of flattened hexagonal section; a long straight cross of circular section, with a pair of small ribs in the centre of each face, and tapering towards the tips, which swell into hemispherical knobs; a 'fishtail' pommel; and a grip formed of two wooden scales of lenticular section sandwiching the tang.

This sword belongs to a large group of fifteenth-century swords, mostly with English associations. A very similar one (Royal Armouries, IX.1787) was part of a large find of swords made in the River Dordogne not far from the site of the Anglo-French battle of Castillon (July 1453), with which it has been tentatively associated, while another (now mutilated) is represented on the effigy of William, Lord Bardolph (d. 1441) in Dennington church, Suffolk (see also cat. no. 127).   CB

PROV. Said to have been found in the River Thames at Syon Reach; H. G. Keaseby (sale, New York, December 1924, lot 82); Clarence H. MacKay (sale, London, July 1939, lot 27).

LIT. Laking 1920–22, II, pp.252–3; London Museum 1940, pp.36–7; Melville 2001, pp.20–21.

63 Longbow and arrows

1545

Yew and poplar; l. of bow 202 cm; l. of arrows 76 cm, 76 cm, 76.5 cm, 77 cm, 77 cm, 78.5 cm

The Mary Rose Trust, Portsmouth (81A1607, 80A0764/269-274)

As with all of the 170 examples recovered from the *Mary Rose*, this longbow is made from a single piece of yew, retaining the natural laminate characteristics of the wood. The lighter-coloured flat 'back' is sap-wood, which operates better under tension, while the darker 'belly' that faced the archer is heartwood, which performs better under compression. Each bow would have had a horn nock at either end to take the bowstring. This has a replica fitted at its lower end to show how they would have looked. The bow has an arrow-pass mark of three V-shaped incisions, some 103 cm from the nock. Experimental work indicates that it had a draw weight of 172 lb (78.08 kg) at 28 inches (71.12 cm).

The arrows are poplar, but examples of alder, ash, birch and walnut have also been identified among the 4,000 recovered from the ship. The notches for the bowstring were reinforced with a sliver of horn. Only microscopic traces of the flights remained, identified as goose or swan feathers. These were held in place with glue and red silk thread. The greenish tinge to the glue is caused by the presence of copper, used as a fungicide to protect the arrows during storage. The steel tips have corroded away.

During the medieval period the longbow was in its ascendancy and the bowmen of England (and Wales) were famed and feared. Fine bodkin-tipped arrows could pierce chain mail at 200 yards (*c.*180 metres) or even plate armour up to 100 yards (*c.*90 metres) away. Driving deep into the body, arrows could inflict serious damage to major organs and penetrate bone, from which they were difficult to extract.

Although aware of the advance of the handgun, Henry VIII encouraged the use of the longbow. It was cheap, reliable and, in skilled hands, deadly. The law dictated ownership and regular practice. However, despite its success, by the middle of the sixteenth century the longbow was being superseded. Ongoing improvements in armour and firearms eventually rendered it obsolete as a weapon of war.

A contemporary inventory for the *Mary Rose* records her as carrying 250 longbows, 9,600 arrows and 50 handguns.   AE

PROV. Recovered in 1980 (b) and 1981 (a) from King Henry VIII's warship the *Mary Rose*, which was sunk in 1545.

LIT. Rule 1990, p.180 (ill.); Hardy 2000, pp.210 (ill.), 213–16.

63a

63b

64

64 Bracer for an archer*

Early 16th century

Leather; h. 12.5 cm

British Museum, London (MME 1922, 4-1, 1)

When shooting a longbow, the string sometimes strikes the inside of the left forearm when the arrow is loosed. To prevent injury or damage to clothing, it was normal to wear a bracer that presented a smooth surface to the string. This bracer of hardened leather was fastened in place by laces originally threaded through five holes along each edge. Some lace-holes have broken and extra holes have been created to extend the life of the bracer.

The part worn on the outer forearm has gilt punched decoration with incised detail on a stippled ground, comprising oak-leaves and acorns beneath an inscription '*ihc helpe*' (Jesus help) enclosing a crowned Tudor rose. The Tudor *emblemata* and the fine gilt decoration indicate that the bracer was worn by a court archer. KW

PROV. Purchased from H. J. Ellis, 1922.

LIT. Dalton 1922.

65 Breech-loading gun belonging to Henry VIII

Dated 1537

Wooden stock, iron barrel and lock; overall l. 97.5 cm, l. of barrel 65 cm, weight 4.22 kg

Her Majesty the Queen, on loan to the Royal Armouries, Leeds (XII.1)

The large match lock is a restoration, probably of the nineteenth century; this gun would originally have been fitted with a wheel-lock mechanism. The large iron trigger guard and the trigger itself are also restorations. The stock originally extended to the muzzle, but has been shortened. Beneath the forward end of the lock plate is a boss carved with acanthus foliage, perhaps intended as a handgrip for the shooter. Behind the lock plate, the right side of the stock is incised twice with the letters GT, the identification of which has not been established. The butt is cut with one recess on the right side and a smaller one on the underside, for shooting necessaries such as the spanner for the wheel lock, but the sliding lids for both recesses are missing. The left side of the stock originally had an upholstered

cheek pad, probably of velvet, but now only its brass securing nails survive.

The barrel is formed in the manner of an architectural column. The muzzle has a raised circular moulding, and the forward portion of the barrel is chiselled with longitudinal flutes above a panel of three columns framing two medallion heads and surmounted by the letters HR. The square section breech portion of the barrel is chiselled with a crowned Tudor rose with lion supporters, and engraved with the initials WH and the date 1537. An iron pin passes horizontally through this section, locking into place a hinged breech piece. Removing the pin enabled the breech piece to be opened to the left, allowing a reloadable iron cartridge containing a charge of gunpowder and a lead ball to be inserted into the rear end of the barrel. Closing the breech piece and replacing the pin secured the cartridge and held it firmly in the barrel during firing.

Breech-loading handguns were rare in the mid-sixteenth century. Their relative complexity meant that their cost compared to that of simpler muzzle-loading firearms must have been considerable. This gun is the smaller of two made for Henry VIII that still survive in the Royal Armouries collections: at the time of his death in 1547 there were 139 breech-loading guns in his possession.

The initials on the breech of this piece are thought to be those of William Hunt, one of Henry's English gunmakers, who in 1538 was appointed Keeper of the King's Handguns and Demi-Hawks. GR

PROV. Tudor Royal Collections; in the collections of the Armouries at the Tower of London probably since 1599, and certainly since 1691.

LIT. Ffoulkes 1916, p.331, pl. XXXIII; Norman and Wilson 1982, pp.73–4, ill.; Starkey 1991, cat. no. XI.39, p.166; Rimer 2001, p.15, ill.; Richardson 2002, pp.25–6, ill.

65

66 Saker

Dated 1529

Bronze; l. 222.2 cm; calibre 95 mm

Royal Armouries, Fort Nelson (XIX.165)

The tapered barrel is divided into two main sections by a prominent moulding in front of the trunnions. The muzzle terminates in a bold moulding. Inscribed in rear of this is the founder's name FRANCISCUS * ARCANUS and a band of foliage decoration. The reinforce bears the Tudor badge in relief consisting of a crowned rose surrounded by the Garter, below which is inscribed POUR * DEFENDRE / HENRI-CUS VIII * ANGLIE / ET * FRANCIE * REX * FIDEI / DEFENSOR * ET * DNS * HIB / ERNIE * A*D M * CCCCCXXIX. In front of the bold base ring mould-ing is the vent amid relief scroll decoration. The cas-cabel button is of the plain cylindrical form sometimes seen on earlier guns. Known as a saker after the bird of prey, this type was widely used on land and sea. Characterized by having a long barrel in relation to calibre, sakers nevertheless displayed wide variations. This example is a smaller version of the type, but in calibre corresponds to that of the ordi-nary saker listed later in the sixteenth century (Black-more 1976, p.393).

Francesco Arcana was a member of the Italian gun-founding family from Cesena who came to Eng-land in 1523. The family established a foundry in London at Salisbury Place. Henry VIII found it neces-sary to import foreign craftsmen to satisfy his requirements for large quantities of good-quality arms and armour (cat. no. 55). As in the case of armour making, the settling of foreign founders had a beneficial effect on English gun-founding.

This saker would have fired a cast-iron ball of about 3½ inches diameter (9 cm), weighing about 6 lb (2.72 kg). Its effective range would have been about 360 yards (330 metres).   NH

PROV. Transferred in 1930 from the Rotunda Museum, Woolwich.

LIT. Blackmore 1976, cat. no. 27, p.58.

67 Yorkist and other roundels*

PLATE 44

*c.*1480–82

Stained and painted glass; h. 52 cm, w. 62 cm

Holy Trinity church, Tattershall, Lincolnshire (former collegiate church of the Holy Trinity, the Virgin and Sts Peter, John the Baptist and John the Evangelist)

Of the nine roundels, five depict badges associated with the house of York: a white rose, two white roses *en soleil* (for Edward IV), a falcon in a fetterlock (for the Duke of York) and a falcon displayed. Two have a purse suspended from a plant cutting, with the purse representing Ralph, Lord Cromwell's office of Lord Treasurer and the plant (a gromwell) a pun on his name. The last two roundels display the evange-list symbol of St Mark (a winged lion) and a Eucharistic emblem (a chalice and Host). Currently

in the chancel east window, these roundels were originally distributed over the numerous transept and nave windows. They were conserved by Barley Studio in 1988–9.

Tattershall College was founded by Ralph, Lord Cromwell (d. 1456) in 1439, but construction of the church did not begin until *c.*1470, and the nave and transept windows were still being glazed in the early 1480s. It is perhaps surprising to find Yorkist badges in an establishment whose purpose was to pray for the soul of Henry VI as well as Lord Cromwell (for long a loyal servant to this king) and his family. Their presence is probably due to the leading role played by one of Cromwell's executors, William Waynflete (d. 1486), Bishop of Winchester, in estab-lishing the foundation. The locally born Waynflete was one of Cromwell's executors and served Edward IV well (see also cat. no. 245).   RM

LIT. Marks, 1984a, pp.178–81, 274–5; Hebgin-Barnes 1996, p.312.

66

68a 68b 68c 68d

68 Heraldic livery badges

All 15th century

Livery badges identified the wearer as a person who was attached to a magnate or the king and who therefore enjoyed his lord's protection. They marked the wearer's secular allegiance, just as wearing a pilgrim's badge proclaimed devotion to a particular cult. Beginning in the reign of Edward III (1327–77), they were in general use until the early sixteenth century. Livery took other forms of cloth (dress), and hoods as well as badges. Badges were simpler to recognize than elaborate coats of arms and were produced in large numbers. Lead badges were probably worn by supporters outside the lord's household and less important members of such households. The grander members would have worn examples of silver or gilded bronze. JC

a) Swan badge

Lead; h. 4.8 cm

British Museum, London (MME 1904, 7-20, 19)

The swan was the livery badge of the house of Lancaster and, more particularly, of the Prince of Wales. This is a poor man's version of the Dunstable Swan Jewel (cat. no. 70).

LIT. Cherry 1969, p.53, pl. XXV, 4.

b) Badge with arms of St George in collar of SS

Lead; h. 5.6 cm

British Museum, London (MME 1856, 7-1, 2124)

The collar of SS was another Lancastrian badge, and it appears on the alabaster effigies of many Lancas-trian knights. The badge is a very much cheaper version of the silver SS collar (cat. no. 71), and combines this with a representation of the arms of St George.

PROV. From London.

c) Badge of the bear and ragged staff

Lead; h. 4.3 cm

British Museum, London (MME 1904, 7-20, 23)

This badge combines two badges of the Earls of Warwick, a title held by the Beauchamp and Neville families (see cat. nos 89, 92, 97).

LIT. Smith 1957; Marks and Payne 1978, cat. no. 60.

d) Badge of seated talbot

Lead; h. 4.4 cm

Inscr. in black-letter, on the collar of the dog: *ta*

British Museum, London (MME 1933, 3-8, 3)

The talbot had hanging ears, powerful jaws and a tail that curled into a complete circle. He was naturally a symbol of the Talbot family, one of the most famous members of which in the fifteenth century was John Talbot, 1st Earl of Shrewsbury (d. 1453) (cat. nos 42, 94), who was referred to as 'Talbott our good dogge' in a poem of *c.*1449 on the French Wars. Of Sir Gilbert Talbot, his great-nephew, who was one of Henry Tudor's captains at Bosworth, it was said 'the Talbott he bitt wonderous sore'. This particular example has a collar inscribed with the two letters *ta*, thus proving that he is a talbot.

PROV. Found in Bristol harbour.

LIT. Barnard 1925, pp.81–2; Marks and Payne 1978, cat. no. 55.

e) Badge with rose in fetterlock

Lead; h. 4.4 cm

British Museum, London (MME 56, 6-27, 116)

The rose within the fetterlock combines two Yorkist badges (see cat. no. 67). These were produced in different sizes (Spencer 1998, nos 290c, d, e).

PROV. From London.

LIT. Ellis 1814; Marks and Payne 1978, cat. no. 56.

f) Badge with a mulberry

Lead; h. 3.4 cm

Inscr. in black-letter, underneath the leaves: *mullberi*

British Museum, London (MME 56, 7-1, 2111)

The mulberry was a punning device favoured by the Mowbray Dukes of Norfolk. Thomas, the 1st Duke, had the crimson trapper of his horse decorated with mulberry trees and white lions for his proposed combat with Bolingbroke in 1398.

PROV. From the Thames, August 1844.

g) Badge with elephant and castle

Lead; h. 4 cm

British Museum, London (MME 56, 7-1, 2152)

The elephant and castle was a badge of William, Viscount Beaumont (1438–1507). An active supporter of Henry VI, he was on the losing side at both Towton (1461) and Barnet (1471) and spent the remaining years of Yorkist rule in exile or prison.

PROV. From London.

LIT. Spencer 1998, p.103, no. 177.

68e

68f

68g

69 The boar badge of Richard III

15th century

Copper alloy, gilded; h. 3.6 cm, w. 5.8 cm

English Heritage, on loan to York Museums Trust
(Yorkshire Museum)

Since it was found at Middleham Castle, this badge can be clearly interpreted as one worn by a retainer of Richard III. The badge of Richard appears in a collection of drawings of mainly Yorkist badges made in about 1466–70. 'A boar argent, armed, bristled and membered or' was used by Richard as a supporter. His association with the white boar is often referred to in contemporary literature.

The rhyme put up on the door of St Paul's Cathedral by William Collingburne on 18 July 1484 referred to Richard as 'the Hog':

The Cat, the Rat and Lovell our Dog
Rule all England under the Hog.

William Catesby, Sir Richard Ratcliffe and
Viscount Lovell
Rule all England under Richard III.

In September 1483, Richard ordered the Keeper of the Wardrobe in London to supply 13,000 costume

69

badges of the white boar to distribute just before his son Edward was invested as Prince of Wales at York Minster. While this is not one of those badges, it shows the large scale on which these livery badges were made.

Examples of livery badges of the boar are known in silver. One has recently been found in Sussex and others, such as that found at the Steelyard on the Thames in 1994, are known in lead (Spencer 1998, p.289, no. 281h). The interest of this copper alloy example, with a stud at the back, possibly to affix it to leather, was that it was worn by a retainer at Richard's favourite castle.   JC

PROV. Found on the north side of the bank of the moat at Middleham Castle, Yorkshire, in December 1930.

LIT. Barnard 1925, p.11; Marks and Payne 1978, p.37; Cherry 1994, p.38, ill.

70 The Dunstable Swan Jewel

PLATE 116

c.1400

Gold with white, black and red enamel; h. 3.3 cm,
w. 2.5 cm, l. of chain 8.3 cm

British Museum, London (MME 1966, 7-3, 1)

This is one of a group of gold enamelled objects covered with opaque white enamel, a technique known as *émail en ronde bosse*. The technique may be seen on the Reliquary of the St-Esprit (cat. no. 10). The finest productions of this Parisian technique of white enamel over gold, such as the *Goldenes Rössel* in Altötting and the Holy Thorn Reliquary in the Waddesdon Bequest at the British Museum, are closely connected with the French court at the beginning of

the fifteenth century. The gold and enamel are modelled to give a lively impression of a mute swan.

Given the find place and the associations of the swan with the house of Lancaster, the jewel may have been produced in London. The swan was the badge of the Bohun family and was adopted by Henry of Lancaster, son of John of Gaunt, who married Mary de Bohun in 1380. The jewel provides an excellent example of the richest form of livery badge, which may be seen in the White Hart jewel worn by Richard and the angels surrounding the Virgin on the Wilton Diptych, painted after 1395 (see plate 3).

After the accession of Henry IV to the throne, the swan was adopted as the livery of the Prince of Wales, Henry of Monmouth. It appears on the tomb of Henry V as king in Westminster Abbey. The swan was also used as the badge of Henry, Prince of Wales, the son of Henry VI and Margaret of Anjou, and it is recorded that in 1459 Margaret made him give out the livery of swans to all the gentlemen of Cheshire in order to quash rumours that he was not her child. We do not whether this livery was of gold, silver or lead (cat. no. 68a); they may not have been of metal at all, but of silk or cloth.   JC

PROV. Found during excavations by the Manshead Archaeological Society on the site of the Dominican Friary at Dunstable, Bedfordshire, in 1965; acquired by the British Museum with the help of the National Art Collections Fund, the Pilgrim Trust and the Worshipful Company of Goldsmiths, 1966.

LIT. Cherry 1969; Marks and Payne 1978, cat. no. 53; Alexander and Binski 1987, cat. no. 659; Baumstark 1995, cat. no. 18.

71a

71a Collar of SS

First half of the 15th century

Silver; l. *c*.73 cm

Museum of London (84.80)

This comprises 41 S-shaped links, cast and set with small curls of applied wire, joined by pairs of simple ring links; for the terminals there is a pair of decorative, oval-framed pseudo-buckles, which are in turn attached to a trefoil tiret, from which hangs a circular torse of plain bands alternating with rows of pellets; both buckles, to give the impression of functioning, have strap-like additions, each consisting of two rectangular plates (joined in the same way as the S links) – the more prominent of these in each pair having a granular field and acting as a form of strap-end. One link at the centre of the main length has a hook at the back to secure the collar against slippage while being worn. The silver, at *c*.91 per cent pure, is comparable with the standard used for coins.

The collar of SS perhaps originated as the livery of John of Gaunt, Duke of Lancaster, in the late fourteenth century, but by the middle of the next century 'a collar with the letters S made of gold or silver' was given by the king to newly ennobled men (plate 23, cat. no. 161). After disfavour under the Yorkist Edward IV, the collar of SS was revived by Henry VII. Spencer notes that versions in silver were likely to be intended for men of the rank of esquire. He assigns this collar to the middle years of Henry VI's first reign

(1422–61) as the popularity of this Lancastrian symbol declined soon afterwards, while Lightbown favours an early fifteenth-century date.

The exact significance of the SS motif has been much debated. Lightbown gives several possibilities: *souverayne* (sovereign), *souveignez* (remember) or a combination of *sainteté, sagesse, sapience* and *seigneurie* (sanctity, wisdom, learning and lordship). GE

PROV. Found in 1983 on the Thames foreshore at Kennets Wharf, City of London.

LIT. Spencer 1985, pp.449–51; Gough 1988, pp.56–7; Murdoch 1991, p.130, cat. no. 301; Lightbown 1992, p.249, pl. 91; Cherry 1994, pp.12–13, ill.; Fletcher 1997.

71b

71b Pewter collar

Probably late 15th century

Lead/tin; surviving overall l. 31.5 cm; each link l. 4.1 cm, w. 0.15 cm

Museum of London (VHA89 site acc. no. 854)

This collar has crude, openwork links in the form of rectangular panels, each with a central quatrefoil in a lozenge, flanked by opposed, tripartite leaves, all in corded borders with terminal loops; each link is joined to the next by a plain ring. Parts comprising almost eight complete links were recovered together.

The fashion for collars in the fifteenth and early sixteenth centuries is here evident in one of the very few survivals in base metal. This pewter example and a handful in copper alloy, some of intricately wound and knotted wire, are all that are left apart from small fragments of once-plentiful lower-class versions that imitated the courtly ones. GE

PROV. Found in 1989–91 on the Thames foreshore at Vintry, City of London, during archaeological excavation within a coffer dam.

LIT. Egan and Forsyth 1997, p.230.

72 Breviary of John, Duke of Bedford (The Salisbury Breviary)

PLATE 47

Paris, 1424–*c*.1460

Parchment, ff.712; h. 25.5 cm, w. 17.5 cm

Bibliothèque nationale de France, Paris (MS lat. 17294)

The Duke of Bedford commissioned this Breviary of Sarum Use presumably in 1424, the first date in the Easter tables, with illuminations by the Parisian

workshop named after him. He had probably already ordered from the Bedford Workshop additions to, and perhaps the completion of, the Bedford Hours (plate 87) and would order a Benedictional (burned in 1871) and an Hours and Psalter (British Library, MS Add. 74754). The incomplete Breviary remained in Paris after Bedford's death in 1435 and the huge and intricate decorative programme was finally abandoned after some 25 years' further work.

The exhibited opening (ff.105v–106) shows the Adoration of the Kings, with Isaiah bearing the opening words of the lesson below; the border medallions illustrate further quotations from the Epiphany offices with (top left) Bedford kneeling before a hanging with his root badge. Except for the shield painted after his second marriage to Jacquetta of Luxembourg in 1433, the illumination dates from the 1420s. CR

PROV. Pierre de Morvilliers, Chancellor of France (d. 1476); given by M. de St Germain in 1625 to Claude de Neufville, subsequently Archbishop of Lyon (1606–98); Jesuits of Lyon; Duc de La Vallière's sale, 1784.

LIT. Leroquais 1934, III, pp.271–348; Avril and Reynaud 1994, pp.22–4; Reynolds forthcoming.

73 Bedford Hours and Psalter

PLATE 97

Between 1414 and 1422

Vellum, ff.iv + 240; h. 43 cm, w. 26.5 cm

British Library, London (Additional MS 42131)

Distinctly reminiscent of the impressive psalters produced in England during the previous century, this manuscript was clearly intended for display rather than for intimate personal use. Entirely unknown before 1928, it was written and illuminated for Henry V's second brother, John, after he had been given the title of Duke of Bedford in May 1414 (mentioned in an inscription in a line-ending) and almost certainly before his appointment as Regent of France for his infant nephew, Henry VI, in 1422. As regent, Bedford was later to commission manuscripts from the leading workshops of France (cat. no. 72). The image of the marriage of King David and Michal, daughter of Saul (f.166v) may be intended to reflect the marriage of Henry V to Katharine, daughter of Charles VI of France, in 1420.

It is clear that several hands were involved in the

magnificent decoration of this book. Further inscriptions in line-endings mention the name 'herman', suggesting an association with the workshop of the immigrant illuminator Herman Scheerre (cat. nos 74, 103, 223). Of special interest are the smaller initials, almost 300 in number, enclosing tiny, lifelike portrait heads. One of these is labelled with the name of the poet John Gower (d. 1408), and attempts have recently been made to identify others as leading personalities of the period. The arms added at the foot of each of the main illuminated pages are those of Richard III's councillor, William Catesby (d. 1485), who is known to have owned the manuscript in 1484.   JMB

PROV. John, Duke of Bedford (d. 1435); probably his widow, Jacquetta of Luxembourg (d. 1472) and her son, Anthony Wydeville, Earl Rivers (d. 1483); William Catesby (d. 1485); the Weld family of Lulworth, Dorset, 18th century to 1929; British Museum, 1929.

LIT. Turner 1962; Wright 1992; Scott 1996, no. 54; Fisher 2001.

74 Prayer book of Charles of Orleans

After 1415

Vellum, ff.ii + 557; h. 21.5 cm, w. 16 cm

Bibliothèque nationale de France, Paris (MS lat. 1196)

Captured at Agincourt while still only 20 years old, the poet-prince Charles of Orleans, nephew of Charles VI of France, spent a quarter of a century as a prisoner-of-war in England awaiting ransom. During this long period he lived in various parts of the country, placed in the households of a succession of keepers. This anthology of prayers, identified by the inclusion of his arms, is one of a number of manuscripts made for or by him in England. The style of decoration suggests a date not later than the beginning of the 1420s, although attempts have been made to place the book substantially later on textual and historical grounds.

The decoration of the manuscript, though luxurious, is comparatively restrained, confined to historiated initials and partial borders. Four miniature painters can be distinguished, one of whom has been identified as Herman Scheerre (cat. nos 73, 103, 223), who was active until about 1420. There are some 11 border painters, linking the volume with several other major books, including the Hours of Elizabeth the Queen, and the Cambridge *Troilus and Criseyde* (cat. nos 93, 171).   JMB

PROV. Charles of Orleans; Royal Library at Blois.

LIT. McCleod 1969, pp.347–50; Avril and Stirnemann 1987, no. 220; Scott 1996, no. 57; Ouy 2000.

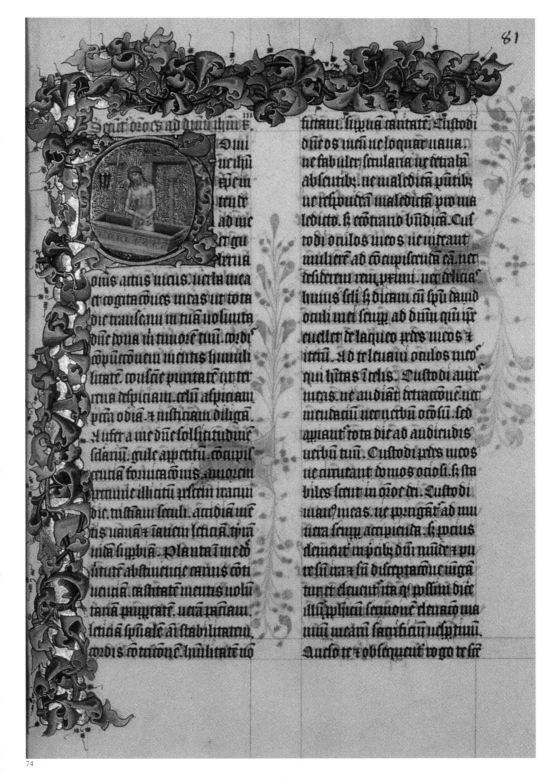

74

75 The Weoley Cup

Italy (Venice), *c.*1500 (the glass); London, 1547 (the foot)

Colourless glass, blown, tooled, enamelled and gilt; silver-gilt foot, with hallmarks for London and 1547; h. 23.2 cm (incl. foot), diam. 13.5 cm

The Worshipful Company of Founders, London

By the early sixteenth century Venetian glass had become a sought-after luxury commodity throughout the western world. The Venetian state had carefully developed the industry, which was organized and protected by the Guild of Glassmakers. The guild tightly regulated quality and quantity of production and encouraged technical innovation.

The Weoley Cup is made of colourless *cristallo* glass of extraordinary purity, a Venetian innovation of about 1450. The use of scratched gold-leaf in combination with painted enamel, applied to the finished object and subsequently fired on, was developed around the same time. This was particularly suitable for simple dot-and-scale pattern, as we can see on the rim of the cup. Figural groups, often including sea-creatures and sea-gods, were usually taken from contemporary prints. The decoration on the Weoley Cup – showing a king and two naked youths riding sea-horses and separated by flaming candelabra and skulls – is close to northern Italian decorative prints of about 1500. The quality of the enamelling is particularly fine, with details in gold paint, as for instance on the king's mantle.

In 1642–3 Richard Weoley presented this glass cup to the Founders' Company in London, of which he had been Master in 1631–2 and 1640–41. According to Weoley, he had purchased the cup from a family whose ancestors had brought it back from 'Bullen' (Boulogne) at the time it surrendered to Henry VIII in 1546. This story is given credibility through the London hallmarks on the silver-gilt foot, which can be dated to 1547 and thus provide the glass with an exceptionally early provenance. According to Weoley's wish, the cup is still used once a year by the Master of the Founders at the annual election ceremony.   RL

LIT. Hadley 1976, pp.92–3, col. ill. opposite p.92; Charleston 1984, p.45, n.10, pl. 9a.

75

6 IDEALS OF CHIVALRY, REALITIES OF CONFLICT

C. S. L. DAVIES

Chivalry can be defined as the ethos appropriate to the mounted warrior of 'gentle' or noble status, the knight. A series of qualities is commonly listed: prowess (courage and proficiency), 'largesse' or generosity, courtesy, and 'franchise' (which implies an independent spirit likely to be found in those of gentle birth and adequate means). The knight was expected to uphold justice, protect the weak, show courage and rise above a calculating and self-interested attitude to life. There is plenty of scope to argue about the details of the formula – on the respective importance of birth and virtue, for instance. But in broad terms the concept of a 'parfit gentle knight' is clear. Found in romances such as Sir Thomas Malory's *Morte d'Arthur* (cat. no. 174), the same ethos penetrated conduct books and histories.

War, it needs hardly be said, differed greatly from the ideal. It is worth looking at examples from both ends of the period covered by the exhibition: the French wars of Henry V, and those of Henry VIII. Henry V's campaign was essentially a war of conquest, first of Normandy, then of northern France generally. It involved carefully conducted sieges of towns: organization, discipline and patience were of the essence. There were plenty of opportunities for the display of courage, but few for other chivalric qualities. Henry's march from Harfleur to Calais, which resulted in the battle of Agincourt in 1415 (plate 12), may have been audacious – even foolhardy; but victory in the battle was due to the disciplined steadiness and fire power of the English archers, deployed in conjunction with dismounted knights fighting as heavy infantry. Sieges necessarily involved non-combatants. Towns were summoned to acknowledge Henry's 'right' to dominion; refusal justified what could be, in the case of Rouen, a six-month siege until starvation led to surrender. Henry certainly kept good discipline in his ranks; violence was to be used exclusively in his own, allegedly God-given, purpose. He was determined to prevent the licentious indiscipline of the 'free companies' who were given free reign by his predecessors and his opponents; such mayhem was condemned by the commentators, and was generally ascribed to the lowly origins of the perpetrators. The assertion of royal control meant, however, a curbing of the individualism which was itself part of the chivalric ethos. In particular, it replaced the obligation to seek justice by that of obedience to constituted authority. As Shakespeare noted, it was not for Henry's soldiers to debate the justice of his cause: 'if his cause be wrong, our obedience to the king wipes the crime of it from us'. But the converse was also true: 'if the cause be not good the king himself hath a heavy reckoning to make; when all those legs and arms, chopped off in a battle, shall join together at the latter day, and cry all, "we died at such a place" … ' (*Henry V*, Act IV, Scene 1). Henry was acutely aware that he was heir to a usurper; as such, his adoption of the 'legitimist' claim of his great-grandfather Edward III to the French crown hardly carried moral conviction.

Henry VIII's French wars actually gave more opportunity for cavalry warfare than Henry V's had done, but not in the form of classic battles. The French tactic was to avoid battle with the English, saving their effort for more spectacular campaigns in Italy. In 1522 and 1523 the English raided deep into French territory, torching and plundering farms, villages and towns in the hope of provoking the French to fight a battle. The French resisted the temptation, and the English armies broke up ignominiously (Potter 1993, chapter 6). By 1544 Henry was more cautious; a massive and well-equipped army besieged and captured Boulogne. In the process, the countryside was reduced to starvation; a begging countrywoman refused money and asked for bread – 'and only a little of that so we can eat it now' – rather than be beaten up by 'wild men' robbing her (*ibid*., p.212, quoting the Calais soldier Ellis Gruffydd). Any sense that such suffering was justified by the righteousness of Henry's cause was negated by his frequent change of alliance, his readiness for ostentatious (if short-lived) friendship with the French king, as in the case of the 1520 Field of Cloth of Gold, and his inclination to trade in his 'title' to France for an annual monetary payment.

There were other fields of conflict. There was fairly continuous border warfare with Scotland, largely a matter of small-scale raids, but sometimes escalating, as at Flodden in 1513, into a massive battle. Again, however, burning and devastation were the order of the day; Henry VIII's commander in 1544 was ordered to burn Edinburgh and any other Scottish towns in his way, 'putting man, woman and child to fire and sword without exception' if there was resistance (Bain 1890–92, II, p.326). The Wars of the Roses, too, saw heavy fighting. The battle of Towton in 1461, fought all day in a snowstorm, saw thousands killed – among them,

apparently, defeated soldiers killed in cold blood and crammed into a grave-pit (Fiorato, Boyston and Knusel 2001). It is notable how little the chronicles of the period record feats of chivalry.

Chivalry was a myth. War was, inevitably, brutal. Non-combatants were victims, and chivalric courtesy hardly extended beyond the relationship between the well-born on both sides. Infantry and artillery challenged the primacy of cavalry on the battlefield. Discipline and order, rather than prowess, determined the outcome of campaigns. Wars might be undertaken for *raison d'état*, but hardly for justice. In spite of academic attempts to define 'just war', rulers had little difficulty in adapting the criteria to suit their own ambitions. Yet the chivalric ideal was not totally divorced from military reality. Training for tournaments developed physical skills, the art of handling weapons, horsemanship, hardiness – all still indispensable in the field. Courage remained the most conspicuous of military virtues, often accompanied by a careless brutality. The splendour of banners, the mystique of heraldry, the celebration of ancestry, the memorialization of heroism in literature and stone, all contributed to make war glorious. Art and religion were persuasive recruiters. While we enjoy the beauty that chivalry created, we should at least remind ourselves of the death and destruction that represented the other side of the coin.

FURTHER READING
Anglo 1990; Kaeuper 1999; Keen 1990.

102 Two-hand sword
(cat. no. 62)

76 The Great Tournament Roll of Westminster

1511

Vellum (36 membranes); h. 37 cm, w. 17.85 metres

The College of Arms, London

The tournament recorded in this lavishly illuminated roll was held by Henry VIII to celebrate the birth of a son, Prince Henry, to Catherine of Aragon on New Year's Day, 1511. Jousting and festivities in honour of the short-lived prince continued over two days on 12 and 13 February at a cost of more than £4,000. Following the Burgundian fashion, the tournament centred on an elaborate allegorical conceit, with the king and three courtiers playing the part of 'Challengers', undertaking feats of arms on behalf of the queen of the imaginary realm of *Cuere Noble*. The roll also reflects a narrative element, depicting three scenes from the tournament: the entry procession to the lists on the second day; the king tilting, watched by Queen Catherine and members of the court from an ornate tilt-gallery; and finally the procession returning from the lists.

Part of the purpose of the roll – as of the event – was to laud the princely magnificence of King Henry, and in the exhibited view of him jousting he is seen breaking a lance on the helm of one of the 'Answerers' to his challenge. Surviving score-cheques show this to be artistic flattery. Beyond the knights waiting to joust come six trumpeters announcing the closing procession (the black trumpeter in the second row is known from contemporary accounts to have been called John Blanke). Attention to the details of costume and accoutrements throughout the Tournament Roll suggests that it was not just a striking review of the pageantry of February 1511, glorifying the role of Henry as a great European prince. Almost certainly the product of the heraldic studio of Sir Thomas Wriothesley, Garter King of Arms, it was intended also as a pictorial record for reference and precedent in the organizing of state ceremonial. As far as is known, it has always remained in the possession of the heralds.   AP

PROV. Sir Thomas Wriothesley, Garter (d. 1534); College of Arms (item 1 in first cat., 1618).

LIT. London 1936, cat. no. 23 (ills); Anglo 1968; Marks and Payne 1978, cat. no. 74 (col. pl.).

76

77 The Military Roll of Arms in Sir Thomas Holme's Book

Before 1448

Paper; h. 39 cm, w. 29 cm

British Library, London (Harley MS 4205, ff.9–40v)

In the Military Roll, coloured drawings of pairs of horsemen, tilting with lances or engaged in sword-combat, are used as models to display the arms painted on their tabards, shields and horse trappers. Of the 41 known leaves of the Roll, 31 are bound in a volume of heraldic material that takes its title from one of its earliest owners, Sir Thomas Holme, Clarenceux King

of Arms (d. 1493). Holme bequeathed his books of arms to those who followed him as Clarenceux, and this manuscript has been identified (see Wagner 1967, pp.271–3) in the 1534 inventory of one of his successors, Thomas Benolt, as the 'Visitation of many shires' made by Roger Legh, Clarenceux 1435–60. County headings on a number of pages – for Suffolk, Norfolk, Essex, Kent and Sussex – confirm the original arrangement to have been according to locality.

The arms (Quarterly or and azure on a bend gules 3 crosses crosslet of the first) displayed by the unnamed knight at the top left of the exhibited pages (ff.36v–37) identify him as Sir John Fastolf, KG; he is jousting with a member of the Timperley family. This

type of pictorial roll of arms with equestrian figures was known also on the Continent, where examples include armorials of the *Toison d'Or* and *El libro de la cofradia de Santiago de Burgos*. AP

PROV. Roger Legh, Clarenceux (d. 1460); Sir Thomas Holme, Clarenceux (d. 1493); inventory mark for Thomas Benolt, Clarenceux (d. 1534); bought from Christopher Bateman, bookseller, by Robert Harley, 1st Earl of Oxford, 27 May 1720; acquired by the British Museum in 1753.

LIT. Wright 1973, pp.4, 9–11 (col. pl.); Marks and Payne 1978, cat. no. 70 (col. pl.); Scott 1996, no. 85 (ills 334–8).

77

78 Ordinances of Armoury, etc.*

Mid-15th century

Vellum, ff.320; h. 24.5 cm, w. 17 cm

Pierpont Morgan Library, New York (MS M. 775)

This miscellany of predominantly military and chivalric texts was owned and at least partly commissioned by Sir John Astley (d. 1486), an accomplished knight and jouster, whose famous deeds of arms in single combat are commemorated by two items included in the collection (ff.275–9). Brief texts record the challenge and rules of combat for John Astley's mounted joust against Pierre de Massy, which took place in Paris in 1438, and a general challenge from Philippe de Boyle, a knight of Aragon. Boyle's challenge was successfully taken up at Smithfield before Henry VI on 30 January 1442 by Astley – then an esquire – whom the king instantly honoured with a knighthood and a grant of 100 marks for life. In both cases the challenges are preceded by tinted pen-and-ink drawings of the events.

The illustrated picture (f.277v) shows the 1442 contest. The joust, fought on foot with axes, was held on the open ground in Smithfield market – enclosed for the occasion by lists erected at a cost of more than £50. Astley and Boyle, identifiable by the arms on their surcoats, stand ready to fight with pollaxes (cat. no. 57) before the king, who is seated on a raised throne. In the background on the left can be seen the illustrator's version of St Bartholomew's church. The drawing is a rare example of a record of an actual event made under the supervision of one of the participants. The artist is unknown outside this manuscript. AP

PROV. Sir John Astley (acquired before he was made KG, 1461); Thomas Fitzhugh; Bryan Tunstall; Thomas Tunstall; R. Page (?); bound for Edward VI (d. 1553), before his accession in 1547; restored to and descended in the Astley family; bought at Sotheby's sale (Sir A. E. D. Astley, 21st Lord Hastings), London, 20 July 1931, lot 7.

LIT. Dillon 1901; Lester 1985, pp.95–7; Scott 1996, no. 105 (ills 395–7, col. pl. 14).

79 Bacinet of Sir Giles Capel

Early 16th century

Steel and copper alloy; h. 44.45 cm, w. 28.6 cm

The Metropolitan Museum of Art, New York
(Rogers Fund, 1904, 04.3.274).

This bacinet is made in three pieces – skull, bevor and visor – joined at ear level on each side by a pivot-pin. The skull and bevor narrow at the neck and then extend down over the chest, where they are pierced for attachment to a cuirass, and are encircled and bordered by rivets for the missing lining, of which the upper part was secured by adjustable laces passed through pairs of holes with copper-alloy grommets in the sides of the skull. The latter is rounded and has a low central comb on top, pierced at the apex for a crest-attachment, and continued as a low medial ridge at front and rear, including down the visor and bevor. The visor, which is almost hemispherical, is linked to the pivots by concealed hinges with removable pins, and is pierced with many small rectangular slots that serve both for vision and ventilation; a spring locking-catch is missing from the right.

This belongs to a group of late fifteenth- and early sixteenth-century tournament-helms – called *bacinets* in the sixteenth century – equipped with interchangeable visors appropriate for different forms of combat, in this example foot-combat (cat. no. 78). A number are associated with funerary-achievements in English churches (Laking 1920–22, II, pp.146–51), and so were once all thought to be English. Others, however, are associated with the Habsburg Burgundian court in Brussels, and it is now clear that many, if not all, were imported from the Continent (Blair 1998; Thomas and Gamber 1976, pp.183–4, no. B33, 195–6, nos B 23 and 152). This bacinet belonged to Sir Giles Capel (1485–1556) of Rayne Hall, Essex. Capel was a prominent figure at the court of Henry VIII and a famous jouster. In accordance with his will that 'my beste Helmett and my Armyng Sworde be sett over my funerall', the bacinet was displayed over his tomb in Rayne church.   CB

PROV. Rayne church, Essex, until 1840; W. Parmenter, Bocking, Essex; Miss Courtauld (later Mme Arendrup); Baron Charles Alexander de Cosson; bought by the Metropolitan Museum of Art, 1904.

LIT. Cosson 1883; Hills 1937; Blair (C) 1987.

80 William Bruges's Garter Book

*c.*1440–50

Pen-and-ink and watercolour on paper, ff.15;
h. 38.5 cm, w. 28.7 cm

British Library, London (Stowe MS 594)

A pictorial roll of arms of the Order of the Garter, executed for William Bruges (d. 1450), first Garter King of Arms. Full-page coloured drawings show, as a frontispiece, Garter King of Arms kneeling before St George, followed by Edward III and 25 founder knights who formed the Order at its institution in 1348. The knights wear blue Garter mantles over plate armour and surcoats with their personal arms; framed tablets display painted arms of successors in their Garter stalls at St George's Chapel, Windsor.

On the exhibited pages (ff.18v–19) are Sir Neel Loryng (d. 1386) and Sir James Daudele [Audley] (d. 1369), both of whom fought at Poitiers. The last shield of arms given for Sir James's stall is that of John Talbot (d. 1453), Earl of Shrewsbury (cat. nos 42, 94); names identifying these shields are in the hand of a later owner, John Writhe, third Garter King of Arms 1478–1504.

Bruges's Garter Book is the first armorial for the Order of the Garter and an early instance of the fifteenth-century fashion for heraldic records employing painted figures to display arms. Other examples include the Aldermen of London (cat. no. 130) and the Military Roll (cat. no. 77).   AP

PROV. William Bruges, Garter; John Writhe, Garter; Sir Thomas Wriothesley, Garter (d. 1534); Elias Ashmole, Windsor Herald (d. 1692) [belonged *c.*1665]; John Anstis, Garter (d. 1744); William Bayntun, FSA (d. 1785); John Meyrick (d. 1805); John Townley (d. 1816) (bookplate); Duke of Buckingham and Chandos (d. 1839), collector of the Stowe MSS; bought by the 4th Earl of Ashburnham, 1839; bought from the 5th Earl of Ashburnham for the British Museum, 1883.

LIT. Wagner 1950, pp.83–6, pl. VII; Wagner 1967, p.271; London (H.S.) 1970, pp.41–56, frontispiece; Marks and Payne 1978, cat. no. 237; Scott 1996, no. 84 (ills 330–32, col. pl. 13).

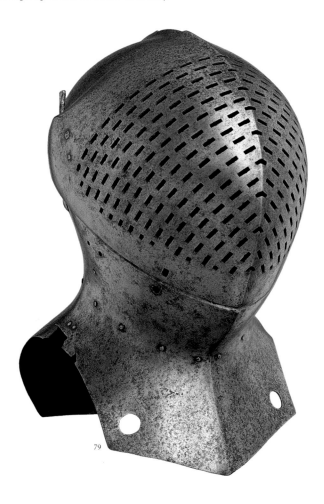

79

80

81 Garter of Maximilian I, King of the Romans (1459–1519)

*c.*1490

**Silk, embroidered with silver-gilt thread, with buckle
and applied ornament of gold, enamelled; l. 54 cm**

The National Trust (Anglesey Abbey, Cambridgeshire)

The blue silk garter has six gold Tudor roses, enamelled red upon white, barbed with green. The roses
are set between the words '*honi coit quy mal y pence*',
embroidered in gold thread. The embroidered silk is
a replacement, although the form of the motto suggests a faithful copy of a fifteenth-century garter. The

backplate is engraved with the arms of Maximilian I
as King of the Romans (elected king in 1486, emperor
in 1493). Maximilian was created a Stranger Knight
by Henry VII in 1489. He was first invested with the
insignia in 1490, and then again in 1503. Henry VII's
instructions to Norroy, King of Arms, delivering the
insignia in 1503, illustrate the importance attached to
chivalric ornaments as indicators of political affinity.
Norroy was to observe closely not only the manner of
the emperor's acceptance, but, afterwards, whether
and how often Maximilian wore any Garter ornaments – and report to the king.

Garter insignia were normally returned to the
Crown upon a knight's death. However, a new mantle

was prepared for Maximilian in the Great Wardrobe
in 1502–3 and, possibly, a second garter. This might
explain why a 'spare' lingered in imperial possession,
passing eventually to the Counts Festetics of Hungary, who served the Habsburg court.   LM

PROV. The Counts Festetics, Hungary; entered the collection
of Lord Fairhaven, Anglesey Abbey, between 1918 and 1939.

LIT. Anstis 1724, II, p.85; Gairdner 1861–3, I, pp.417–18;
Beard 1953; Marks and Payne 1978, p.127; Starkey 1991, cat.
no. VI.6, p.98; Begent and Chesshyre 1999, pp.157(ill.), 161;
Jefferson 2002, p.33, n.23.

81

82 Bearing sword of the City of York with scabbard

English?, *c.*1416 and later

Steel, copper alloy and other materials; l. (sword) 132 cm

Inscr.: *SiGiSMVNDI . IMPERAT*[ORIS] . *DAT*[US] . *M*[AIORI] . [ET] *C*[OMMUNITI(?)] . *EB*[ORACO] . *1439; ORNAT*[US] . *HENRi* [CO] . *MAY . MAiOR*[E] . *1586* ([The sword] of the Emperor Sigismund given to the Mayor and Communalty(?) of York 1439; embellished by Henry May, Mayor 1586)

The Lord Mayor of York and the City of York Council

This is an exceptionally heavy hand-and-a-half sword with a cruciform hilt of copper alloy, originally gilt. A tapering two-edged blade of flattened diamond section bearing a maker's mark, a crowned Lombardic H or I, inlaid in copper alloy; etched and gilt, with the arms of the City of York, of England quartering France and the above inscription, all against a blued ground. Wooden grip bound with modern silver wire and encircled by a silver ring. Later wooden scabbard covered with red velvet: the silver-gilt mounts include six dragons (one replaced), the device of the knightly Society of the Dragon (founded by the Holy Roman Emperor Sigismund in 1408), applied to one side.

According to an account in the York City Memorandum Book (York City Archives, B/Y, ff.88v–89r), the sword was originally hung over Sigismund's stall in St George's Chapel, Windsor, when he was created a Knight of the Garter in May 1416. On his death it became the property of the Dean and Canons of St George's. It was acquired by one of the latter, a Yorkshireman named Henry Hanslap, who presented it to the City of York on 5 May 1439 to be used, as it still is, as a civic sword. The dragons on the scabbard are described in the Memorandum Book as being made of red silk, so the present silver ones are presumably copies – probably made, like the grip-ring, in 1586, when it was refurbished and the blade etched. CB & PJL

LIT. Jewitt and St John Hope 1895, II, pp.446–51; London 1967, cat. no. 182, p.77 (ill.); Blair and Delamer 1988, pp.109 (ill.), 110.

83 Windsor Castle, St George's Chapel, choir-stalls

1477–83

Oak; l. (east to west) 32.7 m, w. (max.) 7.24 m

There were originally 50 back stalls (eight returns and 42 lateral stalls) and two blocks of substalls each side with 10 seats in each, traversing the first four and a half bays of the choir. In the late eighteenth century

82

83

the medieval pulpitum to the west was removed and replaced by one in Coade stone. Also at this time, among other alterations, the desking of the return stalls was run together in a single line instead of being in two sections, and two new stalls at the east end were added, so as to close off the fifth bay from the west altogether. Many poppy heads were replaced, and a low tester for the monarch's stall provided below its medieval canopy.

The stalls were intended from the start to accommodate the knights-companions and canons of the Order of the Garter, the seats at the west end being

designed for the monarch (south) and the Prince of Wales (north). Originally seats in the back row of the lateral stalls were provided alternately for canons and knights. The former's consisted of spired two-tier canopies, but the latter's were considerably grander, with a bigger circular second tier and an open-traceried 'stool' above, on which to hang the helms and crests of the knights, with their swords hanging in front. In the late eighteenth century, due to an enlargement of the Order, most of the canons' canopies were suppressed in favour of those for the knights.

In spite of its distinctly Flemish appearance, the furniture is recorded as having been made by English craftsmen, and can be shown stylistically to be largely a native product. A William Berkeley was the master carver, and the other artists mentioned in the surviving accounts are Robert Ellis and John Filles in connection with the canopy work, and William Ipswich, Hugh Gregory and William Crue for making and carving 10 great gablets. The canopies were subcontracted to Ellis and Filles in London, and were transported to Windsor by river.

The principle of telescoping towers, one on top of another, and the use of angle-turrets, external squinches and traceried parapets, can be seen in the urban landscapes of early fifteenth-century Flemish panel paintings. In real architecture, many of the features of the main stall canopies at Windsor can be found on the west front at St Peter's, Leuven (Belgium). In the wing screens one is confronted by a decorative aesthetic typically found on the façades of Netherlandish town halls and great churches.　CT

LIT. St John Hope 1913a, II, pp.429–36; Tracy 1990, pp.47–51, 54–8, 160 (ills), 162–74 (ills), 185–96 (ills).

84 St George and the Dragon

*c.*1400–20

Alabaster group, painted and gilded; h. 81.5 cm, w. 60.5 cm, d. 20.5 cm

National Gallery of Art, Washington (Kress Collection, inv. no. K1377)

Apparently unique among existing English alabasters, this group is carved entirely in the round. St George, on horseback and fully armoured, plunges his lance into the stomach of the dragon, caught under the hooves of the horse. In front, the kneeling princess holds the end of her girdle, which encircles the dragon's neck (for the full account of this episode in *The Golden Legend,* see Ryan 1993, I, pp.238–40). Much of the original paint survives, and although there are significant losses to the group, the surface is in good condition. The right forearm of St George, much of his lance and the blade of his sword are missing, as is the head of the princess.

The popularity of St George in late medieval society is easy to explain. As the personification of bravery and chivalric virtue, his image and story appealed strongly to knights and those engaged in warfare, and his adoption as the patron saint of England and the Order of the Garter further enhanced his standing (see Riches 2000, pp.101–39, for an overview). After the battle of Agincourt in 1415, when St George was called upon by Henry V for support, Archbishop Chichele raised his feast-day in rank to one of the principal feasts of the year. Sculptures and painted representations of the saint of course abounded in England in the fifteenth and sixteenth centuries (cat. nos 58, 284, 297), but this alabaster group is undoubtedly one of the finest surviving. St George was also popular on the Continent, and many English alabasters of the saint may have been made for export, including the present example and a similar but standing figure of St George, probably from an altarpiece, now in the Castle Museum in Nottingham but originally in Barcelona (Cheetham 1973, pp.52–3); two complete altarpieces with scenes from his legend are to be found in Borbjerg in Jutland, and La Selle in Normandy (Riches 2000, pp.78–84, figs 3.11, 3.12, and Rouen-Evreux 1998, pp.89–98). On the basis of the armour and a *terminus post quem* of 1374 provided by the foundation date of the convent at Quejana, its presumed first home, a date in the early years of the fifteenth century is probable.   PW

PROV. Dominican Convent of San Juan, Quejana (Alava, Spain), until 1907; Benoit Oppenheim, Berlin; Lionel Harris, London; Goldschmidt Galleries, New York; Otto H. Kahn, New York; Mogmar Art Foundation, New York; Duveen and Co., New York; acquired in 1944.

LIT. Stone 1972, p.191, pl. 148A; Middeldorf 1976, pp.118–19, fig. 200 (entry by Charles Avery, with earlier lit.); Lahoz 1996, pp.202–3; Franco Mata 1999, p.124, fig. 120; Marks forthcoming (a), chapter 4.

85 Richard Beauchamp dubbed a knight of the Bath; from *The Pageants of Richard Beauchamp, Earl of Warwick*

After 1483

Vellum, ff.28; h. 27.5 cm, w. 20.8 cm (f.2)

British Library, London (Cotton MS Julius E. iv, art. 6, f.2)

In this series of 53 pen-and-ink drawings, each accompanied by an explanatory text in English, the life of Richard Beauchamp, Earl of Warwick (d. 1439), is told through his 'noble actes' – his accomplishments, honours and chivalric exploits (cat. no. 90 and pp.219–20). Here, Henry IV creates the 17-year-old Richard a knight of the Bath in a ceremony held at the Tower of London on the eve of the king's coronation, 13 October 1399. It was the elaborate ritual followed in such special ceremonies, including vigil and ceremonial bathing, which distinguished those initiated to knighthood on these occasions as knights of the Bath.

The manuscript of the *Beauchamp Pageants* is a rare example of an illustrated narrative eulogizing an historical figure of the recent past. It was probably made under the direct patronage of one of the earl's descendants, and the suggestion that Richard's daughter Anne, Countess of Warwick, commissioned the *Pageants* receives some support from her prominence in the two Beauchamp genealogies, decorated with half-length effigies and (unfinished) shields of arms, which end the series (ff.27v, 28).

The drawings have been attributed to the Caxton Master, an anonymous artist from the Low Countries working in England from the 1480s (Scott 1976, pp.55–66). The text, although different in style, suggests close connection with the work of the Warwick family historian, John Rous (cat. no. 96).   AP

PROV. (?) Made for Anne, Countess of Warwick, or other member of the family of the Earls of Warwick; Sir Robert Cotton (d. 1631); acquired by the British Museum, 1753.

LIT. Sanna 1991; Scott 1996, cat. no. 137, ills 495–9; Brindley 2001, pl. III; Sinclair 2003.

84

7 THE BEAUCHAMPS AND THE NEVILLES

ANN PAYNE

85

Even among the most mighty families of late medieval England, the Beauchamps and the Nevilles were conspicuous for their wealth and power. For much of the fifteenth century these closely related dynasties were dominated by two great magnates: Richard Beauchamp (1382–1439), Earl of Warwick, and his yet more famous son-in-law, Richard Neville (1428–71), the 'Kingmaker', who succeeded to the earldom of Warwick and the rich Beauchamp estates through his wife Anne, Richard's daughter by his second marriage.

Richard Beauchamp, 13th Earl of Warwick, military leader and diplomat, with a claimed descent from the legendary Guy of Warwick of Anglo-Norman romance, was himself a natural candidate for the role of chivalric hero – as much an inspiration for the arts as a patron of them. The seventeenth-century antiquary William Dugdale maintained that in this respect Richard enjoyed an advantage over his ancestors, in those who were on hand to record his triumphs for posterity (Dugdale 1656, I, p.405). He named in particular the celebrated John Rous, a chantry priest who served for most of his life at Guy's Cliff, near Warwick, in the chapel endowed especially by Earl Richard 'that God wold send hym Eyre male'. Dugdale ascribed to Rous (an attribution not universally accepted), the elegantly illustrated life known as *The Pageants of Richard Beauchamp, Earl of Warwick* (cat. nos 85, 90). The *Beauchamp Pageants* portray episodes in Richard's life from cradle to grave (Brindley 2001, pls I–LV). They highlight his exploits at the tournament and in battle, show him in statesman-like guise as tutor and mentor to the young Henry VI, follow him to the General Council of the Church at Constance and as a pilgrim to the Holy Land. The Emperor Sigismund is reported in the *Pageants* to have dubbed Richard 'the father of courtesy'. It is a title that occurs again in the illustrated roll-chronicles made by John Rous to commemorate the Earls of Warwick (cat. no. 96).

The *Beauchamp Pageants* and the *Rous Rolls* were not compiled for Richard himself, but in the 1480s for his descendants, in both cases with underlying political considerations. Much is made in the *Pageants* of Earl Richard's devoted service to the Lancastrian crown. Loyalty to the throne and the parade of Beauchamp family achievement were here, as in other artistic endeavours, dominant themes. The most likely patron for such a propaganda campaign was Richard's youngest daughter Anne Neville. As legitimate successor to her brother, Duke Henry (the prayed-for son and heir, but the last of the male line), and as widow of the Kingmaker, Anne struggled over many years to regain her Beauchamp inheritance and restore the honour of the family name. John Rous's roll-chronicle gives an affectionate biographical picture of this 'semly and bewteus' countess (Ross 1980, no. 56). It may have been to excite sympathy on her behalf that he compiled his *Roll* (Lowry 1988, p.337), although the intention has been more commonly attributed to a straightforward desire to please and impress the current Lords of Warwick, Richard III and his queen consort, the countess Anne's daughter, Queen Anne Neville (Ross 1980).

Within Richard Beauchamp's immediate retinue were others well placed to extol the Warwick tradition. His secretary, the scribe and translator John Shirley (d. 1456), is a telling witness to the literary patronage of the Beauchamps (Connolly 1998, *passim*); he even gives us an example of the earl's own literary efforts, a love poem addressed to his second wife Isabel Despenser. Could John Shirley, thought to have accompanied Richard on his travels, be the scribe with pen and parchment roll pictured in the *Beauchamp Pageants*, making a record of the occasion when Henry V appointed the earl his ambassador to the Council of Constance (British Library, Cotton MS Julius E. iv, f.16v; Brindley 2001, pl. XXXII)? Shirley's manuscripts include poems by John Lydgate, who counted Earl Richard and his family among his noble patrons. Two copies were preserved by Shirley of Lydgate's *Guy of Warwick*, the poem commissioned in the mid-1440s by Richard's eldest daughter Margaret, the wife of John, Lord Talbot, Earl of Shrewsbury, to do honour, no doubt, to her family's association with the legendary Guy 'of whos blode she is lynially descendid' (Richmond 1996, pp.123–7).

Another source within Richard's household confirms that he shared the enthusiasm of the wealthy – and he was one of the two richest noblemen in the country – for building. In his *Itineraries,* William Worcestre quotes from a work of Master John Brewster, Richard's receiver general, listing the building projects that the earl undertook to improve his various residences (Harvey 1969, pp.215–21). The centre for this activity was Warwick: castle, town and collegiate church of St Mary's (already home of much ecclesiastical patronage from Beauchamp forebears). In his will, made two years before his death in Rouen, Richard maintained this focus on his principal seat of power. Most importantly, he directed his executors to construct in St Mary's Warwick 'a Chappell of our Lady, well, faire and goodly built' in which his tomb could be housed and masses sung daily for his soul. In the fulfilment of this commission, Richard's executors did him proud. The Beauchamp Chapel and the tomb-chest and effigy that it contains form one of the finest monuments of fifteenth-century England (cat. nos 86–7).

Whether or not Richard Beauchamp was thinking primarily of 'his soul's advantage' when he made his will, the spectacular memorial chapel, some 20 years in the making, also delivers a powerful statement about his worldly status and lineage. The sheer scale and grandeur of the undertaking tell us as much about the intentions – and patronage – of Richard's heirs and executors as they do about those of the founder himself (see Marks forthcoming (b)). One undoubted aim was to proclaim the high estate of the Beauchamp Earls of Warwick through homage to their most illustrious representative. Both chapel and tomb are rich in heraldic splendour. Richard's effigy, for example, although dramatically portrayed as the simple *miles Christi*, hands raised in supplication to Mary, is nevertheless supported by the heraldic beasts that most reflect his dynastic might: at the head a Beauchamp swan, marking a supposed descent from the Swan Knight of legend; and at the feet the muzzled bear of Warwick and the griffin of the Despensers. On the tomb-chest below, enamelled armorial shields identifying the 14 mourners – mainly the children of the deceased with their spouses – provide an opportunity for further dynastic display, both for Beauchamp and for Neville. Such is the close connection between the families that over half of these shields include the arms of Neville.

That Richard Neville, Warwick the Kingmaker, more than matched the pride of his predecessors in the Warwick title and the traditions to which he found himself heir is well attested (Hicks 1998, pp.53–63). He expressed it in conspicuous use of the badge of the bear and ragged staff (see cat. no. 68c). He continued to support the benefactions of his parents-in-law at the Despenser mausoleum of Tewkesbury Abbey and at Warwick. He would have been consulted closely by Earl Richard's executors (men who remained in Neville's own service) during the protracted construction of the Beauchamp Chapel. According to Rous, Neville wished to be buried there himself. In the event he was to be interred at Bisham Priory in Berkshire, the foundation and burial place of his mother's family, the Montagu Earls of Salisbury. It was to Bisham in 1463, on the death of his mother and his succession to the Salisbury earldom, that he transferred the bodies of his father and brother, slain three years before, to lie alongside his mother and the previous Earls of Salisbury. It was a funeral ceremony

103 Lady Joan Beaufort and her daughters, Neville Hours (Bibliothèque nationale de France, MS. lat. 1158, f.34v)

of the Kingmaker's father, Richard, to the heiress of the Salisbury earldom, are celebrated in the Neville Book of Hours (Reynolds (C) 1994, pp.300–3, pls 20, 21). Two miniatures inserted in this French manuscript show Earl Ralph and his second countess, Joan Beaufort, with their family at prayer; the roll of arms beneath proudly registers on the shields of the married daughters their excellent matches (plate 103).

The interest which the Beauchamps, Nevilles and their circle took in books, secular and religious, has been frequently discussed as part of the pattern of medieval book ownership (e.g. Lowry 1988; Griffiths and Pearsall 1989, pp.163–238 *passim*). Richard Beauchamp and his first wife, Elizabeth (and indeed their daughter, Margaret), followed a tradition set by Elizabeth's father, Lord Berkeley, a noted literary patron, in commissioning literary texts. That these secular works were sometimes illuminated is shown by a volume of John Trevisa's *Polychronicon* (translated for Lord Berkeley) bearing Richard Beauchamp's arms (Connolly 2000, pp.114–15). Other stray survivals are an illuminated collection of Froissart's poetry owned by Richard Beauchamp, and a luxury copy of *L'enseignement de vraie noblesse* obtained from Flanders by Richard Neville (Hicks 1998, pl. 19).

Members of the Beauchamp and Neville families were among those who retained lands and houses across the Channel during the military occupation of English Normandy, and they had ample opportunity to acquire manuscripts from French artists. It was from the thriving book trade of Rouen that John Talbot, Earl of Shrewsbury, and his wife, Margaret Beauchamp, commissioned their near-matching Books of Hours (cat. no. 94) and the sumptuous presentation volume of French romances intended for Margaret of Anjou (cat. no. 42). Talbot's magnificent gift to Margaret was itself in part a vehicle for promotion of his own family connections. The fleur-de-lis genealogy at the front of the book recalls Lydgate's commission from Talbot's father-in-law, Richard Beauchamp, to translate the poem justifying Henry VI's title to the French throne, composed to accompany just such picture genealogies. Its use by Talbot underlines the family's long support for the Lancastrian throne and the notion of dual monarchy. Talbot no doubt also intended that the French versions of the Guy of Warwick and Swan Knight romances included in his book should make plain to the new queen the ranking of the great house of Warwick among the leading dynasties of Europe. Artistic patronage always offered a powerful medium for Beauchamp and Neville family pride.

so grand that it became the model for the burying of an earl, and was probably the inspiration for the fine pictorial roll of arms created to glorify the Kingmaker's Salisbury ancestors and Bisham as their spiritual home (cat. no. 95).

Although laying claim to a venerable pedigree, the Nevilles came to real prominence through Ralph Neville, 1st Earl of Westmorland (d. 1425), Warwick the Kingmaker's grandfather. Earl Ralph had 22 children by two wives and, in the admiring words of a later herald, 'he maried his children gretly'. These glittering alliances, which included the marriage

FURTHER READING

Hicks 1998; Macfarlane 1973.

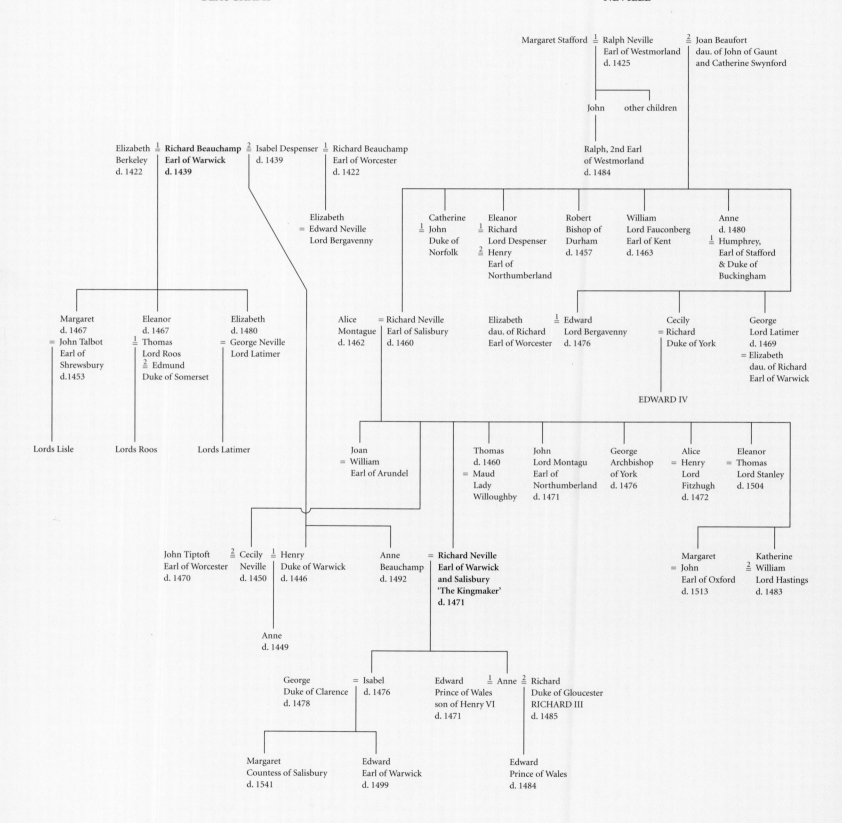

BEAUCHAMP   NEVILLE

Margaret Stafford ⁼¹ Ralph Neville   ²⁼ Joan Beaufort
Earl of Westmorland   dau. of John of Gaunt
d. 1425   and Catherine Swynford

John   other children

Ralph, 2nd Earl
of Westmorland
d. 1484

Elizabeth ⁼¹ **Richard Beauchamp** ²⁼ Isabel Despenser ⁼¹ Richard Beauchamp
Berkeley   **Earl of Warwick**   d. 1439   Earl of Worcester
d. 1422   **d. 1439**   d. 1422

Elizabeth
= Edward Neville
Lord Bergavenny

Catherine   Eleanor   Robert   William   Anne
⁼¹ John   ⁼¹ Richard   Bishop of   Lord Fauconberg   d. 1480
Duke of   Lord Despenser   Durham   Earl of Kent   ⁼¹ Humphrey,
Norfolk   ²⁼ Henry   d. 1457   d. 1463   Earl of Stafford
   Earl of   & Duke of
   Northumberland   Buckingham

Margaret   Eleanor   Elizabeth   Alice   = Richard Neville   Elizabeth   ⁼¹ Edward   Cecily   George
d. 1467   d. 1467   d. 1480   Montague   Earl of Salisbury   dau. of Richard   Lord Bergavenny   = Richard   Lord Latimer
= John Talbot   ¹ Thomas   = George Neville   d. 1462   d. 1460   Earl of Worcester   d. 1476   Duke of York   d. 1469
Earl of   Lord Roos   Lord Latimer   = Elizabeth
Shrewsbury   ²⁼ Edmund   dau. of Richard
d.1453   Duke of Somerset   Earl of Warwick

EDWARD IV

Lords Lisle   Lords Roos   Lords Latimer   Joan   Thomas   John   George   Alice   Eleanor
                                          = William   d. 1460   Lord Montagu   Archbishop   = Henry   = Thomas
                                          Earl of Arundel   = Maud   Earl of   of York   Lord   Lord Stanley
                                                Lady   Northumberland   d. 1476   Fitzhugh   d. 1504
                                                Willoughby   d. 1471   d. 1472

John Tiptoft ²⁼ Cecily ⁼¹ Henry   Anne   = **Richard Neville**   Margaret   Katherine
Earl of Worcester   Neville   Duke of Warwick   Beauchamp   **Earl of Warwick**   = John   ²⁼ William
d. 1470   d. 1450   d. 1446   d. 1492   **and Salisbury**   Earl of Oxford   Lord Hastings
                                         'The Kingmaker'   d. 1513   d. 1483
                                         d. 1471

Anne
d. 1449

George   = Isabel   Edward   ⁼¹ Anne   ²⁼ Richard
Duke of Clarence   d. 1476   Prince of Wales   Duke of Gloucester
d. 1478   son of Henry VI   RICHARD III
                       d. 1471   d. 1485

Margaret   Edward   Edward
Countess of Salisbury   Earl of Warwick   Prince of Wales
d. 1541   d. 1499   d. 1484

86 The Beauchamp Chapel, St Mary's church, Warwick

1443–63

The foundation stone for the elaborately conceived burial place for Richard Beauchamp was laid in 1443, four years after his death. Constructed in accordance with the earl's will, the project was overseen by his executors, being finished 20 years later after a total expenditure of £2,481 4s. 7d., a spectacular sum. The site chosen, to the south of the chancel of St Mary's, a collegiate foundation long in the patronage of the Beauchamp family, was already occupied by the Deanery. Its demolition along with the construction of a new Deanery elsewhere was the first task for the executors.

Of the chapel's three bays, the easternmost houses the vestry, the altar platform and the remarkable survival of two wooden prayer desks fitted into the building. Centrally located is the founder's tomb (cat. no. 87), with the Beauchamp arms carved into the vault above. The western bay houses the stalls and the door from the church's south transept, above which a Doom scene was painted (repainted in the seventeenth century).

The chapel is as rich architecturally as its various fittings. Slender, multi-shafted responds support the unique lierne vault and all surfaces receive panelling on the interior and exterior of the chapel. Precedents for specific details, especially in the West Country, can be found: for example, the finely detailed responds have a precise parallel in St Mary Redcliffe, Bristol, the wealthy merchant church constructed 50 years earlier and located within a manor held by the Beauchamp family.

The chapel, with its documents and the degree of survival of its fittings and glass, provides a clear indicator that architecture was not seen in isolation; that the various aspects of the chapel were part of an ensemble, rather than separately conceived. Through their detailed directions, Richard Beauchamp's executors aimed not to emulate a single architectural source, but instead to surpass all precedents and expectations.   LAM

LIT. Dugdale 1730, I, pp.445–7; VCH 1969, p.417.

86

OPPOSITE 104 Genealogy of the Beauchamp and Neville families in the 15th century

87 Effigy of Richard Beauchamp, Earl of Warwick (d. 1439)

1447–50

Gilt-bronze; l. of figure 183 cm; tomb-chest, l. 257 cm, w. 111 cm, h. 138.8 cm (from step to flat top)

The Beauchamp Chapel in the collegiate church of St Mary, Warwick

The tomb is inscribed, in English, on gilt-bronze, in two separate lines, punctuated by the Beauchamp badges of the bear and ragged staff and a floral motif. The inscription (Chatwin 1921, p.63) identifies Richard Beauchamp by his full titles, describes how his corpse was brought back from Rouen Castle to Warwick after his death in 1439, and cites the authority of his will for the chapel's construction and for his entombment in a vault beneath the monument.

The gilt-bronze (latten) effigy of Richard Beauchamp lies with his head on a tilting helmet, on which is his crest, a swan's head on an earl's coronet. He has his hair cropped in a pudding-bowl style and is clean-shaven. He wears full Milanese armour and is shown with his hands raised slightly apart in an attitude of prayer. At his right foot is a muzzled bear, his badge, and his left rests on a griffin, the badge of Isabel Despenser, his second wife. The effigy lies on a latten plate below a curving hearse of carriage design.

The figure is uniquely important as the sole surviving English example of a gilt-bronze effigy for anyone other than a member of the royal family. It is, indeed, quasi-royal in its magnificence, reflecting Beauchamp's great status as a warrior knight and as Henry VI's 'Lieutenant General and Governer of the Roialme of Fraunce and of the Duchie of Normandie' – to quote the tomb's inscription. A team of London-based artists was responsible for the monument. The founder, William Austen of London, contracted to cast the effigy and its ancillaries in latten, according to patterns supplied to him. These wooden patterns were carved by the London sculptor John Massingham, following painted designs by an artist named Clare. Austen's contract is dated 1450; the effigy was already 'in making' the previous year and the design stages took place in 1447–8. The finished effigy was chased, polished and

87

gilt by Bartholomew Lambspring, a Dutch goldsmith resident in London, his high pay demonstrating the importance attached to the appearance of the gilt surfaces. Austen, with John Essex, marbler, and Thomas Stevyns, coppersmith, also of London, contracted to produce the latten plate on which the effigy lies, the inscription and the hearse above the effigy.

The Purbeck marble tomb-chest was carved by John Bourde of Corfe, who covenanted 'to make a Tombe of marble … of a good and fine Marble, as well coloured as may be had in England … and … fourteen principall housings [niches for the weepers] and under every principall housing a goodly quarter for a Scutcheon of copper and gilt, to be set in'. Bourde worked to a 'portraiture' or model delivered to him, perhaps by Austen. Bourde also paved the whole chapel in Purbeck marble.

At the waist, where the two parts of the body were joined, the upper part was slightly sunk to allow the lower part to fit into it, with a tenon and mortise arrangement and an 18 cm-long pin hammered up from the back. The main part of the body was made from seven different castings: the two parts of the body, the head, the arms and the legs. Where the shoulders and hips touch the top of the tomb there are lugs with slots through which a pin could be placed, to hold the effigy onto the tomb. At the feet, the effigy was held in place by the heraldic bear; a projecting pin in its shoulder fitted into the sole of the right foot and prevented any movement. The monument was restored in the seventeenth century: Nicholas Paris cast a new wing for the griffin and some other details, re-enamelled eight escutcheons and replaced five of them and regilded the statue (Dugdale 1956, pp.15ff.). Restoration of the hearse took place in the early eighteenth century. The sword-belt and dagger were already missing when Charles Stothard made his drawings in 1813. The effigy was conserved in the 1920s and again in 1972.   PGL

LIT. Dugdale 1656, pp.354–6; Nichols 1838; Stothard 1876, pp.164–75; Chatwin 1921 and 1926; Dugdale 1956; Stone 1972, pp.207–10; Blair 1979b; White 1988; Morganstern 2000, pp.133–41; Munby 2002.

88 St Catherine and the Avenging Angel

1443–7

Painted and gilded stone; St Catherine: h. approx. 91.5 cm; angel: h. approx. 53.5 cm

The Beauchamp Chapel in the collegiate church of St Mary, Warwick

The Beauchamp Chapel, dedicated to Our Lady, was built in accordance with the will of Richard Beauchamp, Earl of Warwick, who died at Rouen Castle in 1439, aged 58. His will, dated 1435, required the construction of a Lady Chapel in a space he had chosen, in which his tomb would be placed. Licence was granted to Beauchamp's executors to grant in mortmain possessions to the value of £40 p.a. to the dean and chapter of St Mary's, Warwick, in September 1439. The commission to John Mayell, Thomas Kerver and John Skynner of Warwick to build the chantry chapel dates to July 1441. It was built as a separate structure to the east of the south transept of St Mary's church, attached to the chancel (built by his grandfather) by a narrow vaulted chapel. The chapel was consecrated in 1475, when the earl's body was translated to the tomb (Cook 1963, p.198).

Both these freestone figures come from the great east window: the double rows of canopied niches in the jambs, on the window arch and on the major mullions all house images. The central figure, carved on the window's apex, is the Almighty; below are the nine orders of the heavenly Hierarchy of Angels, four angels holding coats of arms and, in the outer jambs, four larger-scale female saints. Thirty figures represent the Hierarchies of Angels: 14 are on the jambs and 16 on the mullions. Many of the representations are unusual. This is certainly the case with the figure first identified by Chatwin as the Angel of the Expulsion. He comes from the inner angle of the northern window jamb. The angel is entirely feathered, with a cloud and flower-studded girdle and a plain band of ornament at his neck; he wears a diadem. He carries a large sword in his right hand (the tip is broken off) and an apple tree in his left hand. The background behind his legs and feet is also covered with sprays of apple foliage and fruit.

St Catherine is placed beneath St Barbara in the northern window jamb, balancing Sts Mary Magdalene and Margaret on the opposite jamb. She is shown with a dress cut low at the neck, holding her mantle in her right hand. She wears a crown and has long hair; she holds a sword in her right hand and an open book in her left, but lacks her customary attribute of the wheel.

It is difficult to separate out the costs of the freestone sculpture in the extracts from the lost original accounts, but the figures seem to date from the late 1440s when the stained glass (cat. no. 89) and desking were certainly being ordered. All the figures that stand vertically in the jambs or mullions are independently carved and hooked in place: a groove in the back acts as a guide and keeps the figure straight. It is likely that they come from the workshop of John Massingham, who was responsible for the wooden model of the earl from which his tomb effigy was cast (cat. no. 87). Massingham was the leading English sculptor of his period.

The figures may originally have been painted by Christian Colebourne, a painter trained in the Netherlands or western Germany, who contracted to paint the lost images (perhaps from the reredos and flanking niches) of the Annunciation, St Anne and St George. All the east-window figures were repainted in 1824, and an inscription written in gold on the sword of this angel records that it was regilded in October of that year (Chatwin 1928, p.328).   PGL

LIT. Dugdale 1730, I, pp.445–7; Nichols 1838; Chatwin 1928a and 1928b; Stone 1972, pp.207–8, pl. 166; Sutton 1982; White 1988.

88

89 St Thomas Becket and two seraphim holding musical scrolls

1447–*c*.1449

Stained and painted glass; Becket: h. 134 cm, w. 53 cm; each angel: h. 72 cm, w. 23 cm

The Beauchamp Chapel in the collegiate church of St Mary, Warwick

These panels are *in situ*, with the seraphim occupying the lower row of tracery lights above St Thomas Becket on the left side of the east window. Becket (identified in antiquarian sources), is vested in full pontificals with an archiepiscopal cross-staff, and stands against a repeated design of a bear and ragged staff. The seraphim, set on a ground speckled with stars, have identical red bodies with white scarves and stand on wheels; both hold scrolls with musical notation and the words '/Glorificamu[s] te/ and /Gracias agimu[s] tibi'. All the glass is well preserved, with very minor restorations.

The glazing of the Beauchamp Chapel is of a sumptuousness and quality matching that of the earl's tomb and sculpture and represents the peak of insular glass-painting of its time. It was commissioned from John Prudde, the King's Glazier, in 1447 at a cost of two shillings per square foot, making it the most expensive glazing scheme known in the fifteenth century. It is notable for the quantity of coloured glass and for the prolific use of inserts in imitation of jewels, especially on the Becket figure. This, together with three other figures in the east window, represents British saints for whom Earl Richard had particular veneration; they also were associated particularly with the Lancastrian dynasty served so loyally by the earl. Their association with him is emphasized by the bear and ragged-staff family devices that surround them (see also cat. nos 68c, 92, 97). The texts held by the seraphim (part of a set of eight) are from the antiphon *Gloria in excelsis,* as found in the Sarum Gradual; the unusual inclusion of the musical notation here and in the side windows reflects the particular concern for musical provision expressed in the earl's will.   RM

LIT. Winston 1865, pp.326–41; Hardy 1909; Marks forthcoming (b).

89

90 Marriage of Henry V and Katharine of Valois, 1420, and (verso) the birth of Henry VI, 1421; from *The Pageants of Richard Beauchamp, Earl of Warwick*

PLATE 20

After 1483

Vellum, ff.28; h. 27.5 cm, w. 20.8 cm (f.22)

British Library, London (Cotton MS Julius E. iv, art. 6, f.22 recto and verso)

This drawing from the *Beauchamp Pageants* (see also cat. no. 85) shows the wedding of Henry V and Katharine, daughter of the French king Charles VI, which took place in Troyes Cathedral on 2 June 1420. According to the Treaty of Troyes, sealed by this marriage, children of the union would be heirs to the thrones of both England and France. On the reverse of the leaf (Brindley 2001, pl. XLIV), Katharine is seen in bed at Windsor Castle after the birth of Henry VI, both mother and swaddled new-born infant wearing crowns. The inclusion of major royal events in the *Beauchamp Pageants,* such as those shown here, served to emphasize Richard Beauchamp's role at the centre of national life and his close identity with the Lancastrian cause.   AP

PROV. (?) Made for Anne, Countess of Warwick, or other member of the family of the Earls of Warwick; Sir Robert Cotton (d. 1631); acquired by British Museum, 1753.

LIT. Scott 1996, cat. no. 137, ills 495–9; Brindley 2001, pls XLIII–XLIV; Sinclair 2003.

91 Psalter and Hours of Henry Beauchamp, Duke of Warwick

*c.*1430–45

Vellum, ff.261; h. 27.1 cm, w. 18.5 cm

Pierpont Morgan Library, New York (MS M. 893)

The signature and motto of Henry Beauchamp, Duke of Warwick (1425–46), are inscribed on f.12 of this psalter and Book of Hours, but the manuscript may originally have been commissioned by his father, Richard Beauchamp. An image of the Mass of St Gregory (f.106r), in which Christ miraculously appears before Pope Gregory the Great, includes two kneeling men, one young and the other more mature. These figures could represent Richard, who died in 1439, and Henry. At his father's death, Henry, aged 14, inherited the dukedom; he was to die only seven years later, aged 21.

In the Rous Roll (cat. no. 96), John Rous described Henry Beauchamp's special devotion to the psalter: he recited it daily, and knew it by heart. By the time this manuscript was produced, Psalter-Hours manuscripts were comparatively uncommon: the two books generally circulated independently. Henry's special devotion to the psalter may, in part, have been stimulated by this manuscript, which is illuminated with 22 half-page miniatures and historiated borders.

The Psalter-Hours is part of the substantial oeuvre attributed by Alexander to the London illuminator William Abell (e.g. cat. no. 20), but this identification has been disputed by Scott, who identified two hands at work in the miniatures. Localized to London on the basis of style, these miniatures can probably be seen as representing the style from which Abell developed in the earlier stages of his career.   AB

PROV. Henry Beauchamp, Earl of Warwick (d. 1446); possibly John Tiptoft and Cecily Neville, widow of Beauchamp (d. 1450); probably in northern Italy by the late 15th century; Colonel Malcolm of Polltalloch, *c.*1896; in the library of C. W. Dyson Perrins by 1908; Dyson Perrins sale (Sotheby's, London, Part I, 9 December 1958, lot 19); Pierpont Morgan Library, 1958.

LIT. Warner 1920, no. 18; Alexander 1972, pp.166, 169; Scott 1996, no. 88.

91

92 Prayer roll of Henry Beauchamp, Duke of Warwick

*c.*1440

Parchment; h. 143.5 cm, w. 12.5 cm

Museum Catharijneconvent, Utrecht (MS. ABM h4a)

The miniature of the Crucifixion, with Mary and St John standing under the Cross, is painted at the beginning of a prayer to the crucified Christ. Its historiated initial contains a portrait of the man for whom this prayer roll was made, Henry Beauchamp, Earl (later Duke) of Warwick. Further down, a hymn to the Virgin is preceded by a miniature of the Nativity. The texts are in Latin, but the first prayer is interspersed with directions to the devotee in French.

Warwick's identity is established by the inclusion of his Christian name in the final supplication at the end of the prayers to Christ, and by his badge of the ragged staff, with which the piece of cloth over his prie-dieu is decorated. The ragged staff, a trunk with lopped branches, was used by the Beauchamp Earls of Warwick from at least the late fourteenth century (see cat. nos 68c, 89, 97). The miniatures are attributed to the Fastolf Master (cat. no. 224), who was active in Rouen at the time when the Beauchamps were present in that city. Henry Beauchamp had accompanied his father there when the latter was appointed Lieutenant-General of France in 1437, but Henry's use of the Warwick badge suggests that the prayer roll was only commissioned after Richard's death in Rouen, in 1439. Although prayer rolls of this kind were typical of English late medieval devotional practice, relatively few have survived. The Beauchamp roll is the most lavish example that has come down to us.   HvV

PROV. Gift of J. H. Mol, before 1923.

LIT. Korteweg 2002, p.166; van der Velden forthcoming; Wüstefeld forthcoming.

92

93 'Hours of Elizabeth the Queen'

*c.*1420–30

Vellum, ff.154; h. 28 cm, w. 15 cm

British Library, London (Additional MS 50001)

The so-called 'Hours of Elizabeth the Queen' has been described as the finest English illuminated manuscript of its time. It boasts well over 400 historiated initials, in addition to the 18 large miniatures marking major divisions of the text. The majority of these, all accompanied by luxurious marginal decoration, are devoted to scenes of Christ's Passion. The representation of the Agony in the Garden (f.10v) is typical of the richness of the principal artist's work, strongly influenced by the miniature painting of contemporary France and Flanders and distinguished by a taste for an unusually wide range of brilliant pigments. Most of the initials feature exquisitely painted portrait heads, some identifiable as saints or biblical characters, others purely imaginary. It is likely that the manuscript was written and illuminated in a London workshop.

The volume takes its name from a signature of Elizabeth of York, queen of Henry VII (d. 1502), below the miniature of the Crucifixion (f.22), but there is nothing to prove that she ever actually owned it. The signature of Edward Stafford, 3rd Duke of Buckingham (d. 1521), also occurs. The earliest of the added inscriptions asks for prayers for the soul of Cecily Neville, sister of 'the Kingmaker', wife of Henry Beauchamp, 1st Duke of Warwick (d. 1446), and afterwards of John Tiptoft, Earl of Worcester (d. 1470), who died in 1450. She was too young to have been the original owner of the manuscript, but a book so grand could well have been commissioned within the Beauchamp and Neville family circles. JMB

PROV. Bertram, 4th Earl of Ashburnham (1797–1878); Henry Yates Thompson (d. 1928); C. W. Dyson Perrins (d. 1958); British Museum, 1958.

LIT. Warner 1920, no. IX; Scott 1996, no. 55.

93

94 Books of Hours of John Talbot and Margaret Beauchamp, Earl and Countess of Shrewsbury

Rouen, *c*.1444

Vellum, ff.144, 102; h. 27.5 cm, w. 11 cm; h. 22 cm, w. 11 cm

Fitzwilliam Museum, Cambridge (MS. 40–1950, MS. 41–1950)

These two manuscripts, made in a tall, narrow format very unusual for Books of Hours, were apparently commissioned by John Talbot, Earl of Shrewsbury, and his second wife, Margaret Beauchamp, whom he married in 1425. In each book the dedication miniatures (ff.7v, 2v respectively) show the earl in a tabard of the Talbot arms, with his countess, kneeling before the Virgin and Child, accompanied by their patron saints George and Margaret. The larger book (a) displays armorial banners of Talbot (left) and Beauchamp (right), and beneath, within Garters, the Talbot badge of a white talbot with a gold staff and the Warwick bear with a ragged staff. On scrolls between the banners and badges a partially erased inscription begins with the words '*Mon seul desir …*', recalling the verse motto in the Shrewsbury Book, John Talbot's celebrated wedding present for Margaret of Anjou (cat. no. 42). English verses added to the text include John

94a

94b

Lydgate's prayer to St Alban (f.135), a favoured Lancastrian saint and of special importance to Margaret's father, Richard Beauchamp, Earl of Warwick.

In the smaller book (b), the banners have had the arms erased, but sufficient shading remains to show that they bore the same Talbot and Beauchamp arms (reversed). The Garters here enclose the daisy or marguerite badge in compliment to Margaret, and marguerites are again prominent throughout the border decoration. At the foot of both dedication pages are crowned monograms for Jehan and Marguerite.

The manuscripts were written and illuminated in Rouen, the larger with miniatures by the so-called Talbot Master, who takes his name primarily from his work on the Shrewsbury Book, and the smaller, in a different style, by a follower of the Bedford Master, who also contributed to the Shrewsbury Book. Another Talbot Book of Hours, smaller still in size but with the same unusual tall, narrow format (22.4 × 9 cm), containing miniatures by the Talbot Master and a similar frontispiece depicting the earl and countess kneeling, belongs to Blairs College, Aberdeen (National Library of Scotland, MS Deposit 221/1; see Paul 1892, no. 689, pl. xliv; Ker 1977, pp.111–18).

The supposition that the two Cambridge Books of Hours formed a pair presented by John and Margaret to each other on their marriage, current since the two books came together in the Yates Thompson collection more than a century ago, cannot now be supported. The commissions are certainly of a later date, probably contemporary with the Shrewsbury Book made at Rouen in 1444–5, which the decoration so closely resembles.   JMB & AP

PROV. John Talbot, 1st Earl of Shrewsbury (d. 1453) and Margaret Beauchamp, Countess of Shrewsbury (d. 1467);

bought by T. H. Riches in Yates Thompson sale, Sotheby's, London, 3 June 1919, lots 6–7, and bequeathed to the Fitzwilliam Museum, 1935.

LIT. James 1902, nos 83, 84, pp.218–38, and *Henry Yates Thompson Illustrations*, I, 1907, pls xxvi–xxviii; Wormald and Giles 1982, pp.441–53 (pls 48–53); Reynolds 1993, p.113; Reynolds (C) 1994, pp.305–6.

95 Bisham Priory church from The Earldom of Salisbury Roll

*c.*1463

Vellum roll (extract); h. 27.7 cm, w. 99.3 cm (p.188)

The Duke of Buccleuch and Queensberry, KT

This picture of Bisham Priory church, Berkshire, flanked by its founder (in 1337), William Montagu, Earl of Salisbury, and his wife, comes from a painted vellum roll made to honour the lineage of the Salisbury earls and Bisham as their family mausoleum. The roll (now cut up and bound into a composite volume known as Writhe's Garter Book at pp.176–225) contains 50 full-length figures of successive Earls of Salisbury and their kin. Beginning with Richard I and his illegitimate half-brother William Longespée, Earl of Salisbury, the roll traces the descent of the Monthermer and Montagu branches of the family and ends with the generation of Richard Neville, the 'Kingmaker'. The Kingmaker's family pride, demonstrated in the lavish reburial ceremonies held for his father and brother at Bisham in February 1463, soon after his inheritance of the earldom from his mother, offers a powerful incentive for the making of the roll (see pp.220–1).

Most of the figures on the roll process in pairs, man and wife linked by a tasselled cord, a conceit inspired by the pageantry of courtly love associated with the tournament. The men are in armour with tabards of their arms, accompanied by crested helms, shields, banners and pennons of arms. The women display their arms on heraldic mantles. The form derives from heraldic rolls of arms, which by this date sometimes employed human figures for armorial display instead of shields or written blazons (e.g. cat. no. 77). The picture of the church and the delicate painting of the faces and other details on the figures differ from the flat heraldic colouring, and it has been suggested that the London artist, William Abell (see cat. no. 20), or an associate, may have been responsible for this part of the work (Alexander 1972, p.168; Scott 1996).

Included in Writhe's Garter Book are seven of the 11 extant leaves from a later, coarsely executed copy of the Salisbury Roll, updating it with pictures of Richard III and Queen Anne Neville; the copy is part of the heraldic record-making of John Writhe, Garter King of Arms (d. 1504), from whom the volume takes its name.   AP

PROV. (?) Richard Neville, Earl of Warwick and Salisbury (d. 1471); Robert Cooke, Clarenceux King of Arms (1593 inventory, no. 109); in the possession of John, 2nd Duke of Montagu (d. 1749) by September 1737 (although not acquired as part of Writhe's Garter Book); by family descent to the Dukes of Buccleuch.

LIT. Payne 1987; Wagner, Barker and Payne 1993 (col. facsimile); Scott 1996, no. 96 (ills 371–2).

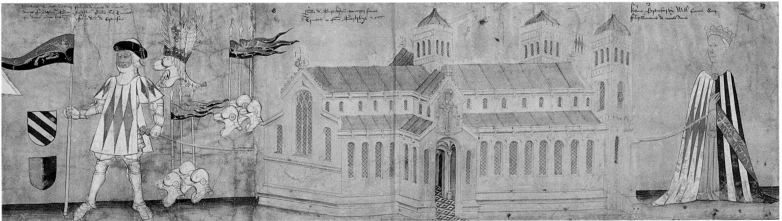

95

96

97

97 Ring with bear and ragged staff

Mid-15th century

Gold; external diam. 2.6 cm

Inscr. in black-letter: *soulement une* (only one), on the bezel; on the outside of the hoop, *be goddis faire foote* (by God's fair foot)

National Museums and Galleries on Merseyside, Liverpool Museum (53-114-292)

The oval bezel of this massive ring is engraved with a bear chained to a staff. This was the badge of the Earls of Warwick in the fifteenth century (cat. nos 68c, 89, 92). The motto behind the bear and the oath on the exterior of the ring are not otherwise associated with the Earls of Warwick. There is no written record of the finding of the ring on the body of the Earl of Warwick at the battle of Barnet (see PROV. below) before the eighteenth century.

The inscription around the hoop is not magical, but an example of swearing by parts of the deity, which was very popular in the later Middle Ages. Chaucer, Langland and others all refer to the injury done to our Lord by blasphemy. The wall-painting in Broughton church (Buckinghamshire) showing the Virgin with the dead and mutilated body of Christ, surrounded by fashionably dressed youths holding parts of the dismembered corpus, is clearly a reference to the ill fashion of swearing by parts of God's body (cat. no. 298).   JC

PROV. Said to have been discovered on the body of Richard Neville (1428–71), Earl of Warwick (the Kingmaker), after the battle of Barnet, 14 April 1471; collections of George IV, Miss Craven, General Johnson, Sir John Evans, F. Harman Oates, H. Gordon Bois, and Philip Nelson; acquired in 1953.

LIT. Jones 1877, p.265; Nelson 1949; Tudor-Craig 1973, cat. no. 165; Oman 1974, no. 103, pl. 40E; Taylor and Scarisbrick 1978, no. 344, p.53; Ward et al. 1981, no. 165.

96 The Rous Roll

1483–5

Vellum roll (8 membranes); h. 33.5 cm, w. 7 metres

British Library, London (Additional MS 48976)

One of two illustrated roll-chronicles compiled by John Rous (d. 1491), chantry priest of Guy's Cliff, Warwickshire, to commemorate the benefactors of Warwick and to celebrate the deeds of his patrons, holders of the Warwick earldom. This is the English form of Rous's roll; the other (College of Arms), in Latin, appears to be the earlier version, but was altered after the accession of Henry VII in 1485 to give a more acceptably Lancastrian flavour.

Sixty-four figures are drawn in pen-and-ink, each with a biographical notice beneath and coats of arms painted on banners or shields above. The roll begins with mythical, royal and historical benefactors of Warwick (including Edward IV and Richard III) and then traces the direct descent of the earls through the legendary Guy of Warwick to the Beauchamps and Nevilles; it concludes with the figures of Queen Anne

(Neville), Richard III and their son Edward, who is named as Prince of Wales (created September 1483, died April 1484). The use of colour is confined to the coats of arms and to highlighting the wealth of heraldic detail (shields, surcoats, badges and crests, etc.), a prominent feature of the roll.

The illustrated section shows Anne Beauchamp, daughter of Richard Beauchamp, Earl of Warwick (d. 1439), with her husband Richard Neville, Earl of Warwick (the Kingmaker) and their daughter Isabel de Spencer. Rough genealogical descents inserted between the figures trace the connections of the Warwick family to the royal houses of both France and England. The handwriting of these genealogies is thought to be that of Rous himself.   AP

PROV. Family of the Earls of Warwick (?); Robert Cooke, Clarenceux King of Arms (no. 110 in his inventory, 1593); London, College of Arms, 1640; Dukes of Manchester, Kimbolton Castle, before 1768 until after 1869; bought from Messrs Robinson, Pall Mall, by the British Museum, 1955.

LIT. Marks and Payne 1978, cat. no. 39, with pl.; Ross 1980; Lowry 1988; Scott 1996, no. 138 (ills 500–1).

98 The Middleham Jewel

Mid-15th century

Gold, set with a sapphire and the inscription originally enamelled blue; h. 6.4 cm, w. 4.8 cm

Inscr. on the obverse (sapphire side) and around the edge, in black-letter: *Ecce agnus dei qui tollis peccata mundi miserere nobis tetragrammaton ananyzapta* (Behold the Lamb of God that takest away the sins of the world, have mercy on us …)

York Museums Trust, Yorkshire Museum
(YORYM 1991.43)

The jewel is a gold lozenge-shaped pendant designed for use as a container. On the front there is a sapphire above a depiction of the Trinity, with an inscription that consists of the well-known passage from the Gospel of St John (I, 29) followed by two magical words. The first, '*tetragrammaton*', literally derived from four letters, is used to indicate the unwritable name of God; '*ananyzapta*' is a magical word that was used as a charm against epilepsy or the falling sickness (Jones and Olsan 2000, pp.260–8, 287–90; see also cat. no. 211). On the reverse is the Nativity of Christ surrounded by 15 saints in the border. When discovered in 1985, the jewel was opened by sliding out the panel with the Nativity, and was found to contain three and a half roundels of silk thread wound around with gold foil, although this may not have been the original contents. The jewel was certainly an aid to private devotion, and the iconographic programme centred on redemption.

Made in the mid-fifteenth century, it is not known when this jewel was lost. Its relationship with Middleham and the Nevilles – if any – is uncertain. Richard, Duke of Gloucester, later Richard III, and his household certainly lived at Middleham for much of the third quarter of the fifteenth century, but after 1485 the castle was no longer the centre of a Yorkist retinue. If it was lost after 1485, the jewel may have had nothing to do with the owners of the castle in the fifteenth century.

It has been suggested that it was made for an aristocratic lady 'concerned about her pregnancies, health and most of all about her religious devotion and the redemption of her soul' (Cherry 1994, p.34). If the jewel was a container for an *Agnus Dei* (a wax roundel made from the Paschal Candle at Rome and often thought to be efficacious in childbirth), then it might have belonged to a number of ladies of the Neville family. An obvious candidate would be Cecily Neville. Born in 1415, a daughter of Ralph Neville, the first Earl of Westmorland who owned Middleham Castle, she was a lady of great piety. Her will of 1495 mentions many of the items of gold and silver jewellery that were used as aids to prayer and devotion, such as the *Agnus Dei* and the rosary (see also cat. no.

222). She left a great *Agnus* of gold with the Trinity, St Erasmus and the Salutation of our Lady to Richard Brocas and his wife Jane, and all the other *Agnuses* unbequeathed (all with the Trinity) to Anne Pinchbeck. While Cecily provides an excellent example of the type of person who would have owned the Middleham Jewel, it is unlikely that it actually belonged to her.   JC

PROV. Found near Middleham Castle, Yorkshire, in 1985; Sotheby's, London, 11 December 1986; private collection; purchased with the aid of the National Art Collections Fund, 1991.

LIT. Cherry 1994; Husband 1992; Jones and Olsan 2000.

98

8 TWO ECCLESIASTICAL PATRONS:
ARCHBISHOP HENRY CHICHELE OF CANTERBURY (1414–43)
AND BISHOP RICHARD FOX OF WINCHESTER (1501–28)

BARRIE DOBSON

According to one of the most fundamental precepts of the corpus of medieval canon law, '*scire debes Episcopum in ecclesia esse, et ecclesiam in episcopo, et si quis cum episcopo non sit, in ecclesia non esse*: You are to know that the bishop is within the Church, and the Church within the bishop; and so if there is no bishop there can be no Church' (Friedberg 1879–81, I, c.7 q.1, c.9). Although in Britain, as throughout western Europe, the political power of fifteenth-century bishops had been increasingly eroded at the hands of secular governments, the 21 men who constituted the English and Welsh episcopal bench from the 1130s to the 1540s were always formidable and awe-inspiring figures. As the prelates who presided over the ramshackle engines of both the late medieval state as well as the Church, they were all the more powerful founts of patronage because there were comparatively so few of them. Indeed, no fewer than 12 of the 40 richest bishops in the whole of medieval Christendom were holders of English sees (Lander 1980, p.120). Of these, the most fabulously wealthy was the Bishop of Winchester, who enjoyed an annual income of more than £4,000 towards the end of the Middle Ages and therefore had more liquid capital at his disposal than all but the king and one or two of the richest lay magnates in the country. Only slightly less well endowed was the Archbishop of Canterbury, normally to be found at his London palace of Lambeth or at one or other of his Kent manor houses (Knowles and Hadcock 1971, p.447).

What artistic or other causes did these spectacularly wealthy members of the English episcopal bench support? Although it can be extremely difficult to recapture the individual priorities of men who often seem positively 'faceless' (Hamilton Thompson 1947, pp.2–16), there seems no doubt that their two greatest passions were building on a lavish scale and the promotion of higher education. For the wealthiest and most well-connected bishops in the land the optimum objective was therefore to combine both ambitions in one project and fund the establishment of a new university college. Over five centuries later it is clear that a new academic college could indeed prove an exceptionally shrewd spiritual as well as educational investment. To this very day, prayers for the soul of Archbishop Henry Chichele are being offered more or less continually at his foundation of All Souls College (1438); while Bishop Richard Fox is still remembered more fervently at his own Corpus Christi College (1513) than anywhere else. In establishing new colleges at Oxford, Chichele and Fox were also following that long tradition whereby the majority of Oxford's medieval colleges tended to be episcopal foundations, whereas after 1441 an increasing number of Cambridge colleges were created

became extremely prosperous members of the Grocers' Company in the City of London – seems to have been of yeoman descent and was certainly born and bred in Higham Ferrers, Northamptonshire, where the archbishop founded a chantry college of some distinction for eight secular canons, eight clerks and six choristers in 1422. If anything, the social origins of Richard Fox (plate 106), a native of Ropley near Grantham, are even more obscure. What is clear is that both clerks owed their initial success – and their important early contacts with members of the ecclesiastical and royal

105   Tomb effigy of Archbishop Chichele, Canterbury Cathedral, completed by 1426

by members of the royal family (Rashdall 1936, III, pp.191–235, pp.315–22).

Although Henry Chichele (born in or about 1362) and Richard Fox (born nearly 90 years later in about 1448) were men of very different generations, they both exemplify an English ecclesiastical career structure that changed little in its fundamentals from the twelfth to the early sixteenth century. Their rise from comparative obscurity to the highest offices in the kingdom testifies to the fact that the Church was one of the few careers in late medieval England that was genuinely open to talent. In the mournful inscription placed round his cadaver-tomb at Canterbury Cathedral, Henry Chichele went out of his way to state that '*Pauper eram natus*: I was born poor' (Stone 1972, p.213). In fact Chichele – whose two brothers, William and Robert,

bureaucracy – to their academic prowess at university. Chichele had graduated from Oxford with the degree of Doctor of Civil Law by 1397, when he was practising as an advocate in the London Court of Arches (Jacob and Johnson 1937–47, I, pp.xvii–xxv). By contrast, and as befitted the most influential clerical patron of English humanism in the age of Erasmus, Richard Fox obtained his canon law degrees at Louvain (Leuven) and Paris: indeed, it was while studying in the French capital in 1484 that he caught the attention of the exiled Henry Tudor and entered his service for ever (Mallet 1924–7, II, pp.20–21).

It can go without saying that both prelates owed their prominence, and the speed with which they were promoted to the highest prizes of the English Church, to royal favour. Chichele was appointed Bishop of St David's as early as

1407; but it was to Henry V that he owed his translation to the archbishopric of Canterbury in 1414, where he remained as the 'primate of all England' until his death nearly 30 years later, in April 1443. Fox was quite as indebted to the first Tudor king; and it was as Henry VII's favourite clerk and keeper of the privy seal (1487–1516) that he became in quick succession Bishop of Exeter in 1487, of Bath and Wells in 1492, of Durham in 1494, and of Winchester for 27 years – from 1501 until his death as a blind old man in 1528 (Emden 1957–9, I, pp.410–12; II, pp.715–19).

Their extremely stylish chantry chapels, tombs and funeral effigies, both of cadaver design, still survive in their respective cathedrals (plate 105, cat. no. 109). However, Fox was much more involved in sponsoring building at Winchester than was Chichele at Canterbury more than half a century earlier. Recent analysis of the unique series of early Renaissance screens, chests and his chantry chapel constructed at Winchester Cathedral soon after Fox became bishop there in 1501 has suggested that his 'taste was conservative, preferring the Gothic to the new Franco-Italian manner' (Crook 1993a, p.275; see also Smith 1988 and Lindley 1988). Similarly, the remarkable collection of Bishop Fox's surviving plate, especially his crosier and salt (cat. nos 104, 108), seems to look back to the fifteenth century – to the age of the giant salt at All Souls traditionally associated with Henry Chichele (Ellory, Clifford and Rogers 1999, pp.47–73, 129–73; see cat. no. 179). With the exception of Cardinal Wolsey, Fox was also one of the last great episcopal builders in pre-Reformation England. From his substantial modifications to Durham and Norham Castles in the 1490s to his role in commissioning the first stained-glass windows at King's College Chapel, Cambridge 20 years later, he was indefatigable in the repair and adornment of the buildings under his care (Emden 1957–9, II, p.716).

Both Henry Chichele and Richard Fox were alike in being very experienced administrators with an especially high reputation as royal envoys and diplomats; but there is no doubt that Chichele was much the more conservative intellect of the two. By contrast, Fox was a radical religious reformer, thoroughly committed to the new Italianate learning: the books he gave to Corpus Christi College before his death may well have been the most impressive collection of classical texts in England for their date (Emden 1957–9, II, pp.717–19). Not surprisingly, the differences between the religious attitudes of the two prelates led to two very different collegiate foundations at Oxford. Henry Chichele's 'college of the Souls of all the faithful departed' was primarily a great prayer house or chantry foundation designed to pray for the soul of Henry V, the Duke of Clarence and other Englishmen who had fallen at

106   *Bishop Richard Fox*, Johannes Corvus, oil on panel, 1529–33 (Corpus Christi College, Oxford)

the battle of Agincourt or some other battle in the recent French wars. Before he died in 1443, Chichele just had time to inspect his new college, notable for its large and sumptuous chapel and for its elegant frontage on the High Street: it was here that 'the Oxford collegiate façade achieved its classic form, imitated again and again down to modern times' (Tyack 1998, pp.58–9). By contrast, Bishop Fox's college of Corpus Christi – often called the first Renaissance college in England because of the founder's establishment of public lectures in Greek and Latin there – was less majestic. Here again, however, the most outstanding master masons of the day were responsible for the fabric of the new college, which was probably complete by 1517. Even more important than the contributions of William Vertue and William East, both masons associated with Henry VIII's Office of Works, was that of Humphrey Coke, a royal carpenter who constructed the splendid hammerbeam roof at Corpus Christi. To cite Fox's own words about Coke, 'he is righte cunnynge and diligente in his werkes' (Harvey 1984, p.64). Despite the bad press which the prelates of medieval England have so often enjoyed since the Reformation, Henry Chichele and Richard Fox deserve no less a tribute.

FURTHER READING

Crook 1993a; Ellory, Clifford and Rogers 1999; Jacob 1967.

99

99 Archbishop Chichele

*c.*1438–42

Limestone (Taynton stone), with slight traces of paint; h.190 cm

All Souls College, Oxford

This statue, with that of Chichele's co-founder Henry VI (cat. no. 36), formerly adorned the college gate-tower, below an image of Christ in Judgement with the resurrected dead. Chichele is in academic dress and wears a jewelled mitre. The statues are the work of the same sculptor, probably John Massingham (*fl.* 1409–50), who was certainly responsible for the images on the chapel reredos (destroyed in 1548). NR

LIT. Gardner 1951, p.235, fig. 459; Stone 1972, p.206; Colvin and Simmons 1989, p.6, fig. 2.

100 Seal matrix of All Souls College, Oxford (with modern wax impression)

1443

Silver; diam. 7 cm

Inscr. in black-letter: *Sigillu*[m] *commune collegii animar*[um] *o*[mn]*ium fidelium defunctorum de Oxonia* (The common seal of the college in Oxford of all the souls of the faithful departed)

All Souls College, Oxford

In the centre, under an elaborate canopy, Christ is seated in Judgement with hands raised, showing his wounds. Beneath him seven souls arise from the ground. On the left, King Henry VI, kneeling in prayer and facing towards Christ, is presented by St Ambrose with St Gregory behind. To the right, Henry Chichele, Archbishop of Canterbury, kneels facing Christ, with St Jerome behind and St Augustine, who places his hand on Chichele's shoulder. Beneath the king are the royal arms of England, and beneath Chichele are his arms as Archbishop of Canterbury (1414–43).

The seal reflects the dedication of the college that Chichele founded. It was to be a place of prayer for (besides the two co-founders) the souls of Henry V, Thomas, Duke of Clarence, and the English captains and other subjects who had died in the French wars, as well as for all the souls of the faithful departed. Planned by Chichele, the foundation charter was granted by Henry VI on 20 May 1438 and, at the archbishop's request, Henry accepted the title of co-founder. The confirmation of the charter of foundation and donation of lands took place on 28 January

1443. It is likely that the seal was engraved shortly afterwards. It is therefore almost contemporary with the seal of King's College, Cambridge (cat. no. 21) and, like that, is probably the product of a London goldsmith.

The role of faith and orthodoxy is emphasized by the presentation of the co-founders to Christ by the Four Fathers of the Church (Alexander 1994). Chichele had a special devotion to the Latin Fathers,

100

and the earliest book lists of the college library illustrate the archbishop's predilection for the writings of Jerome, Augustine and Gregory the Great. The chapel in the college is dedicated to the four Latin Fathers and within, in the north antechapel window, are the figures of the four Latin Fathers seated with the symbols of the Evangelists (originally in the Old Library) (Hutchinson 1949, pp.54–9). JC

LIT. Birch 1887–92, no. 5278; VCH 1954, p.182.

101 Pair of wine flagons or bottles

Paris, c.1400–40

Silver-gilt, each marked three times (twice on the body and once on the foot) with a crowned fleur-de-lis with an indistinct letter (the hallmark for Paris, 1379–1493); h. 40.7 cm

All Souls College, Oxford

The body of each flagon has a broad, flat profile, simply decorated with spiral lobes, on an oval foot also lobed, its base decorated with a repeated stamped pattern of flowers and leaves. The two handles on each bottle are formed by the heads and necks of swans, to which heavy link-chains are attached. These link with lighter chains, which are attached to the trefoil-shaped handles of the screw stoppers.

These handsome and very heavy bottles would have been used for wine, and displayed on a sideboard during the meal. The superb craftsmanship of the bottles attests to the skill of medieval Parisian goldsmiths, whose work was admired throughout Europe. They are the sole survivors from medieval Europe of a type of plate well known from inventory descriptions and manuscript illustrations (Lightbown 1978, pp.28–9; Versailles 1994, pp.22, 25). These bottles – known as flagons to contemporaries – appear to be a type of plate invented in the Middle Ages, to enable wine to be decanted from the cask and brought to the table (Blair 1983, p.9). The king had a 'yeoman of Bottles' (Kurath 1956–99: *Botel*, p.1067) in charge of these, and his chief servant was the 'Botler' – hence butler – in charge of wine and ale. Aristocratic households would have followed suit.

The swan motifs of the handles are highly decorative, but also have a clear heraldic message, as Archbishop Chichele used swans as the supporters to his coat of arms, a fact hitherto oddly ignored. The noblest of birds, the swan was used as a badge by various prominent contemporaries of Chichele: Jean de Berry (d. 1416), Henry IV and Henry V (Cherry 1969, pp.40, 42, 48; see also cat. nos 68a, 70). It is not known how Chichele acquired the bottles: he frequently visited France on diplomatic business and might have commissioned them in Paris. He might equally well have been given them after an occasion such as the coronation in Westminster Abbey of Henry V's queen, Katharine, who was the daughter of Charles VI of France. One of the earliest college inventories, before 1462, includes 19 silver and silver-gilt bottles, but without descriptions (Gutch 1781, II, no. XV, p.258). MLC

PROV. All Souls College, gift of the founder, Archbishop Chichele (d. 1443).

LIT. Moffat 1906, p.88 and pl. XLIV; London 1953, cat. no. 49; Lightbown 1978, pp.28–9; Campbell (M) 2002, p.138.

◀ 101

102 Mazer of Thomas Ballard

Before 1437

Maple wood mounted with silver; h. 20.5 cm, diam. of bowl 19.5 cm

Inscr. with Lombardic letters TB above the arms on the print

All Souls College, Oxford, on loan to the Ashmolean Museum, Oxford

Mazers are so called from the maple tree (*maserle*), the wood from which they were made. They were common in the inventories of great houses.

This mazer is of interest as the print (the circular piece in the bottom of the mazer) has a shield of arms of the Ballard family, over which are the letters TB, for Thomas Ballard (d. 1465), Sheriff of Kent in 1452. One of the Ballards of Horton, he married Philippa, daughter of Thomas Walsingham of Chiselhurst. He and his wife appear on the leaf of a service book with a list of benefactors preserved at All Souls College (Martin 1877, p.396), and his seal matrix is preserved in the Ashmolean Museum. He gave the mazer to the college as early as 1437, since it appears in the college inventories of the same year as '*i magna murra coop'ta cum armis thome Ballard armigeri in fundo qui thomas dedit eandem coll.anim*' (one large mazer covered with the arms of Thomas Ballard in the base, which Thomas gave to All Souls College). The mazer was a very early gift to the college. JC

LIT. St John Hope 1887, pp.150–51; Jackson 1911, p.613; Cripps 1914, p.301; Campbell (M) 2002, p.12, pl. 19.

102

103 Breviary of Archbishop Chichele

*c.*1414

Vellum, ff.iii+414+iv; h. 34 cm, w. 23 cm

Lambeth Palace, London (MS 69)

Both in size and scale of decoration, with 29 histori-ated initials, this Sarum breviary proclaims the status of its owner. The lavish opening folio incorporates the royal arms in the form in use after 1406 (top), Canter-bury impaling Chichele (left), Chichele (right) and a differenced form of the Chichele arms, perhaps for one of his brothers, either Robert, Mayor of London 1411–21, or William (bottom). These imply that the book was made for Henry Chichele after 1414, when he became Archbishop of Canterbury, but the arms have been added over the border decoration. The bishop is shown, vested in a blue cope, instructing his canons. He is not attended by a cross-bearer, unlike Archbishop Arundel in Bodleian MS Laud. Misc. 165. St David is included in the calendar. All this suggests that the book was produced between 1408 and 1414, while Chichele was Bishop of St David's. During this period he was largely non-resident, being much employed on diplomatic missions and serving as a delegate at the Council of Pisa in 1409.

The miniature on f.1 is a signed work by the minia-turist Herman Scheerre. The background incorpo-rates a micrographic inscription: '*Si quis amat: non laborat quo*[d] *herman*'. Scheerre was the foremost of a group of Netherlandish artists working in London in the first quarter of the fifteenth century who trans-formed English illumination (cat. nos 73–4, 223). His style, with its distinctive beady eyes, delicate figures and bright, harmonious palette, indicates a familiarity with recent developments in Flemish illumination. Scheerre collaborated in the Chichele Breviary with another miniaturist of Netherlandish origin, the artist of the Lapworth Missal (Corpus Christi College, Oxford, MS 394).   NR

PROV. Henry Chichele, Archbishop of Canterbury (d. 1443).

LIT. James and Jenkins 1930–32, pp.109–12; Scott 1996, no. 30, ills 127–33, col. pl. 5.

103

104 Bishop Fox's crosier

Probably beginning of 16th century

Silver-gilt and enamel; l. 181 cm

Corpus Christi College, Oxford

One of only three surviving English late medieval silver crosiers, this impressively architectural example was made for Bishop Richard Fox (*c.*1448–1528) and is decorated on the upper knop and the crook in black enamel with his personal badge, the pelican in its piety.

Despite the renewal of its gilding, probably done during the nineteenth century, the crosier is in remarkably good condition. It is, however, difficult to date with certainty. It has no marks or inscribed date and stylistically could have been made at any time during the late fifteenth or early sixteenth centuries. Its most telling feature is perhaps the series of 12 apostle figures around the architectural part of the crosier, but these come from the same casting patterns as the finials of early sixteenth-century apostle spoons, many of which continued in production over several decades (cat. no. 195). The sees of Exeter and Winchester are both dedicated to St Peter, whose seated figure appears prominently within the curved crook, and on that basis the crosier could have been made either between 1487 and 1491, when Fox was Bishop of Exeter, or after 1501, when he was appointed to Winchester. But he appears to have delegated his episcopal duties in Exeter, and Winchester – as the richest see in England – is more likely to have provided the means for such a lavish commission.

There is no firm documentary evidence for the crosier being at Corpus Christi College before the eighteenth century, but it was almost certainly bequeathed by the founder. Although Fox may be assumed to have made certain gifts to the college at the time of its foundation, such a symbol of his episcopal authority is likely to have remained with him until his death.   TS

LIT. Jackson 1911, pp.137–8; Ellory, Clifford and Rogers 1999, pp.51–73 (T. Wilson).

104

105

105 Chalice and paten

London, 1507–8

Gold, each marked with the London date letter for
1507–8, and a maker's mark of a fleur-de-lis (?) within
a shield; h. 15.2 cm, diam. of paten 12.7 cm

Corpus Christi College, Oxford

The bowl of the chalice is slightly conical on a hexagonal stem, with a large central knop, pierced with
Gothic tracery and set with six diamond-shaped
plaques, each enamelled with a stylized flower and
leaves, in a brilliant translucent red and green. The
splayed six-lobed foot has a vertically hatched edge.
Each compartment is engraved with cusped tracery in
a flamboyant style, within which are respectively the
Crucifixion, the Virgin and Child, St Mary Magdalene
with her attribute (a pot of ointment), St Jerome with
a lion, St Margaret with the dragon, and St Augustine
with an arrow. The paten, a circular plate, is engraved
in the centre with the head of Christ within a roundel,
and a 'cross pattée' on the rim.

The chalice and paten, from Bishop Fox's chapel
plate, are the only surviving examples of pre-Reformation English gold plate, and are amongst the finest
pieces of English medieval goldsmiths' work. Chapel

plate was essential for a bishop, and gold chalices are
mentioned quite frequently in the wills of medieval
bishops (Oman 1957, p.34).

The simple form of the chalice is given richness by
the enamelling and the complex engraving, the quality of which is notably competent. In certain aspects,
the costume of the fashionably dressed female saints
and the style of the architectural tracery suggest
either a German or Flemish artist, or one steeped in
the vocabulary of artists from the German cultural
area. Although the elaborate scheme of engraved
designs on the chalice has no extant English parallel,
the scenes and saints depicted are commonplace. Yet
none of these saints appears to be of particular significance to Fox, and it seems likely that he did not himself commission the chalice, but was perhaps given it,
or simply bought it. It is possible, although unprov-
able, that the chalice was given to Fox by Lady Margaret Beaufort, whose name-saint it depicts, and who
named him as one of her executors.   MLC

PROV. Presumed gift of Bishop Richard Fox.

LIT. Moffat 1906, no. LXII; Oman 1957, pp.34, 45; Oman
1978, pp.27–8; Ellory, Clifford and Rogers 1999, pp.75–110
(M. Campbell).

106 Pair of ablutions basins

London, 1493–4 (maker's mark a horseshoe) and 1514–15
(maker's mark an orb and cross)

Silver-gilt and enamel; diam. 42 cm and 43 cm

Corpus Christi College, Oxford

The circular basins are embossed in the centre with a
pattern of sunrays on matted ground surrounding an
enamelled coat of arms. Each is stamped around the
rim with a slightly differing band of foliage, and the
1514 basin (b) has an aperture in the left side, on the
outside of which is a small spout in the form of an
animal's head.

The coat of arms is that of Richard Fox (c.1448–
1528) as Bishop of Winchester. Since he was not
appointed to that see until 1501, the arms on the
earlier dish (a) must have been replaced, presumably
around the time that the second was made, as the two
are extremely similar.

Pairs of ablutions basins were an important item of
pre-Reformation church plate and were used for the
ritual cleansing of the priest's hands before the consecration during Mass. Their most distinctive feature is

106a

the small spout under the rim of one of the dishes,
through which water was poured from one basin into
the other. This was one of many aspects of Roman
Catholic worship excised from the mid-sixteenth-
century Protestant liturgy; most such basins were
melted down, although a few were preserved as alms
dishes.

106b

107 Two rings

Early 16th century

a) Gold, set with a faceted sapphire, the shoulders engraved with a foliate design against a translucent green enamel; diam. 2.2 cm

b) Gold, on reverse of bezel, London goldsmith's mark of a heart; diam. 2 cm

Corpus Christi College, Oxford

The first ring (a) is almost certainly the sapphire ring that is referred to in the will of John Claymond, the first President of the College, who bequeathed to his successors *'quodam anulo cui impactus est Lapis Saphyrus'* (that ring which was set with a sapphire stone). This identification has been challenged, since this ring with a faceted sapphire is not the sapphire ring shown in the Corvus portrait of Bishop Fox (plate 106). The sapphire is cut into lozenge facets and it has been suggested that this was not possible in the late fifteenth or early sixteenth centuries. However, a hundred years before, the inventories of the Duc de Berry refer to a *'dymant fait a petits losanges'* (diamond cut into little lozenges). Cutting a sapphire in this manner would always have been restricted. The parallels are mostly from the courts of Burgundy or Paris, and the interest of this ring is that it was probably imported or possibly a gift to Bishop Fox.

The gold signet ring with the Pelican in its Piety (b) is first recorded in the college in the Plate Book for 1835. It has been suggested from the other uses of the heart goldsmith's mark that the ring should be dated before 1527. Fox certainly used a signet ring with the Pelican in its Piety on his letter and will, but it was not this one. The ring with the Pelican depicted on the Corvus portrait is also different, and there is no evidence that Fox actually possessed the present ring. A number of other gold rings with this device are known and it would appear that it was a type quite common in the early sixteenth century. JC

LIT. Taylor and Scarisbrick 1978, p.92, no. 945; Cherry 1981–2; Ellory, Clifford and Rogers 1999, pp.113–27 (J. Cherry).

The Fox basins, one of which was regilded in the nineteenth century, have no religious decoration and were not necessarily made for church use. Several apparently similar examples, decorated with 'beamys in the bothom' (beams in the bottom) or with 'a starre chased in the Bothoms' appear in the royal inventory of 1521 and are listed among the secular plate. They were, however, almost certainly made for ceremonial use of one sort or another, such as that described in the Venetian ambassador's report of a meeting between Henry VIII and the Emperor Charles V at Canterbury in 1520. The ceremonial washing of hands before a banquet was an elaborate ritual and clearly involved a basin very like these (Brown 1867, item 50):

> The Duke of Suffolk brought a large gold basin with a cover bearing a crown … The Marquis of Brandenburg's brother … took off the cover,

holding it under the basin bourne by the Duke of Suffolk; whereupon … [he] poured the water from his basin, *which had an aperture or mouth at the side*, over the hands of the sovereigns.

TS

PROV. Presumed gift of Bishop Richard Fox.

LIT. Jackson 1911, p.574; Glanville 1990, p.151; Ellory, Clifford and Rogers 1999, pp.179–94 (P. Glanville).

107a

107b

108

108 Bishop Fox's salt

*c.*1494–1501

Silver-gilt, with a crystal, pearls and enamel; unmarked; h. 30.8 cm

Corpus Christi College, Oxford

This salt is hexagonal, in the shape of an hourglass, with a prominent knop. The body of the salt is decorated with 12 similar cast panels, with figures of hares and hounds amid foliage, and a single pelican, all against a gilt ground. The cover is decorated with six more of these. The knop is embellished with six identical images of the Coronation of the Virgin against a translucent green enamel ground; in between each is a cast lion rampant. The large openwork finial is set with a faceted crystal and pendant pearls, and is supported by three cast pelicans. Around both the base of the salt and its cover is a narrow band stamped with a pelican between the letters R d (for *Ricardus Dunelm*, Richard Fox's title as Bishop of Durham).

This is the most spectacular and one of the earliest of the typically English hourglass-shaped salts to survive (see cat. nos 113, 181). It would originally have had a more colourful appearance, with blue enamel behind the openwork panels throwing them into decorative relief. Traces of the enamel survived into the nineteenth century, when restoration and regilding removed it. The salt was evidently commissioned while Fox was Bishop of Durham, as indicated by his initials, 'R d', much repeated, and by the rampant lions on the knop, which were prominently incorporated in his episcopal arms. As Bishop of Durham, Fox was also Prince Palatinate of the region, a powerful and wealthy figure, bound to entertain to proclaim his status.

The size of the salt belied the small amount of salt it held, for its prime purpose was symbolic. The great or standing salt was one of the principal pieces of medieval domestic plate and indicated the wealth and status of its owner, as much as it marked out the place of honour at a feast.   MLC

PROV. Presumed gift of Bishop Richard Fox.

LIT. Moffat 1906, no. LXV; London 1953, cat. no. 39; Campbell (M) 1987, p.46 and pl. 3; Ellory, Clifford and Rogers 1999, pp.130–73 (M. Campbell).

109 Winchester Cathedral, Chantry Chapel of Bishop Richard Fox

*c.*1513–18

Not long after his appointment as Bishop of Winchester in 1501, Fox rebuilt the aisles of the presbytery of his cathedral. His chantry, called 'newly built' in 1518, stands at the east end of the south aisle, and together with the renewed aisles, was no doubt intended to be seen as his personal contribution to the beautification of his church. A concern to appear humble is evident from the placing of a cadaver effigy in a recess near the centre of the chapel's most visible side.

Fox's chantry belongs to a genre unknown outside late medieval England: the self-contained chapel for soul-masses created by screening off part of the interior space of a major church. Some earlier Bishops of Winchester had embellished their cathedral with chantries that are some of the finest ever built – as befitted occupants of Europe's richest see. The architecture of Fox's chantry is notable for its combination of overall clarity with minutely and exquisitely realized detailing. The design has been ascribed to William Vertue, king's chief master mason 1510–27 and designer of the stonework of Fox's foundation of Corpus Christi College, Oxford. The attribution is strengthened by the presence here of several very specific borrowings from the late fifteenth-century architecture and fittings of St George's Chapel, Windsor (whose completion had been Vertue's responsibility since 1508), although Fox's chantry resembles all Vertue's ecclesiastical works in showing him to have been an exponent of the early sixteenth-century 'court style' stemming from Henry VII's Chapel at Westminster (cat. nos 25, 28). The classical volutes inside the chapel are not, as has sometimes been claimed, original features.

A part-elevation of the chapel's south front owned by the Elizabethan architect John Smythson has been interpreted as an original design (RIBA/SOS/A/15). In reality a none-too-accurate topographical record of the chapel's image-shorn, post-Reformation state, it is vastly less accomplished than cat. no. 27, the only extant design for a complex Gothic structure definitely originating within the early Tudor royal works organization.   CW

LIT. Girouard 1956; Lindley 1988; Smith 1988; Lindley 1993b, p.115; Biddle 1993, p.259.

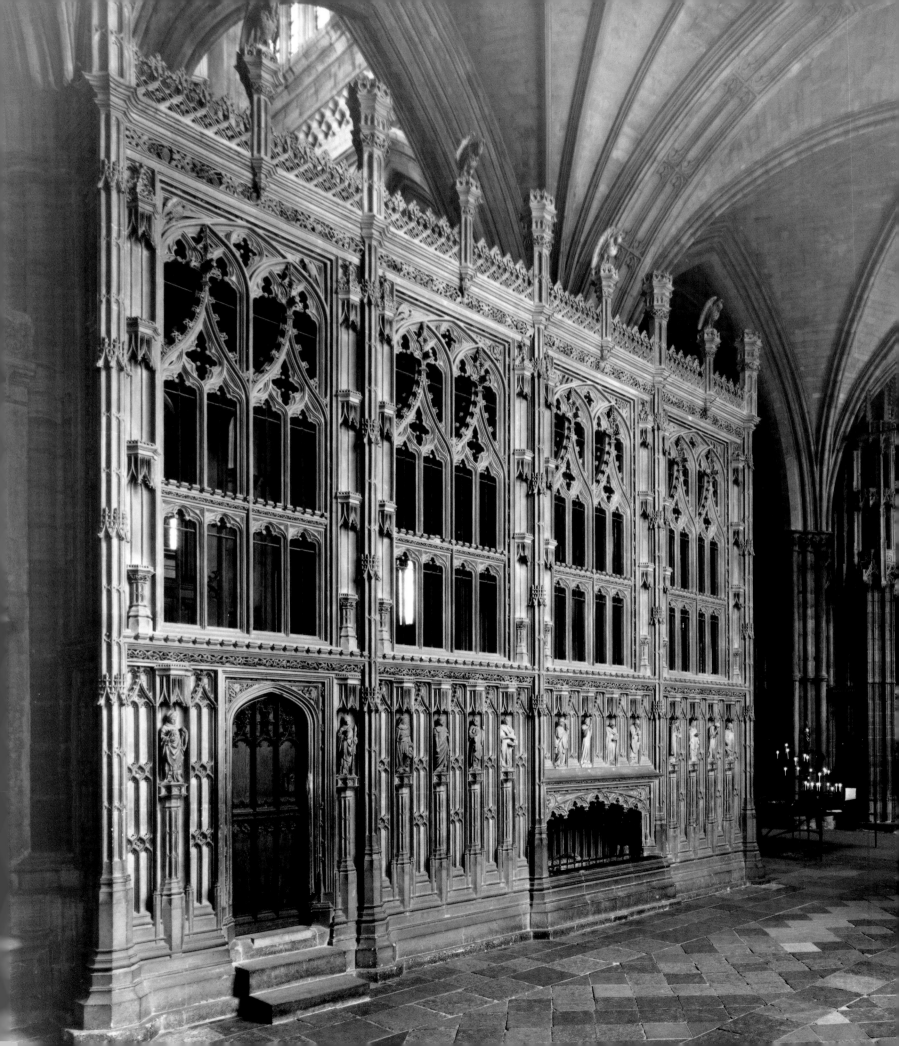

9 LADY MARGARET BEAUFORT

JANET BACKHOUSE

107 Gatehouse, Christ's College, Cambridge

Lady Margaret Beaufort (1443–1509), Countess of Richmond and Derby, mother of Henry VII and, by her direct descent from Edward III through John of Gaunt's alliance with Katherine Swynford, source of the Tudor claim to the English crown, enjoys a formidable personal reputation as a patron of scholarship and the arts. This is reflected in comprehensive documentary evidence, as well as in surviving works both large and small (Jones and Underwood 1992, *passim*), and was concentrated largely in the later years of her life, certainly after Henry's accession to the throne in 1485, when she was acting independently as a major landowner and local administrator, notably in the north-east Midlands and East Anglia. Her possible input into works carried out by her second and third husbands, Sir Henry Stafford (d. 1471) and Thomas Stanley, Earl of Derby (d. 1504), should not, however, be overlooked, especially as the latter is associated with the building of Lathom House (Lewis 1999). Her vigorous support for her royal son's works at Windsor and afterwards at Westminster Abbey, bound up with the campaign for Henry VI's canonization, should also be appreciated (Jones and Underwood 1992, pp.206–8).

Lady Margaret's personal appearance is familiar from a lengthy series of closely related images, which includes Pietro Torrigiano's tomb figure at Westminster, contracted in 1511 (cat. no. 117), and a miniature attributed to Lucas Horenbout and painted *c*.1530 (Hepburn 1992). All show a woman in old age, in the severe, quasi-religious garb appropriate to a widow and vowess. No surviving version can be dated within her lifetime, though Henry VII's painter, Maynard Vewick, may well have taken her likeness along with those of other members of the royal family (plate 108).

Margaret's scholarly benefactions, embracing endowments both for individuals and for communities, were wide-ranging but concentrated in particular on the university of Cambridge. The original parts of Christ's College, incorporating a suite of rooms designed for her own use, offer the most complete and eloquent surviving witness to her building activities in general (Jones and Underwood 1992, pp.224–6). On gatehouse, oriel and chimneypiece, heraldic decoration incorporating references to family badges and symbols underlines the dynastic identity of the foundress (plate 107). This is mirrored at her second major foundation, St John's, though there posthumous development was entrusted to her executors. Similar dynastic displays are known to have appeared at her personal residences, notably at the Coldharbour in London and at Collyweston in Northamptonshire, where extensive building works were carried out in 1502 in readiness for the visit of Henry VII

108 Portrait of Lady Margaret Beaufort (cat. no. 110)

and his elder daughter, Margaret, on her wedding journey to Scotland in the summer of the latter year (Jones 1987).

The richness with which houses, chapels and foundations were furnished is clear from accounts and inventories, and from successive versions of Lady Margaret's will, though almost all material goods have long since vanished. Vestments and other textiles are described in profusion, as are service books. So too are items of plate, a substantial quantity of which was willed to Christ's College in 1509. The college still treasures a handful of vessels (cat. nos 112–13), including a great beaker ornamented with the portcullis of Beaufort, the rose of Tudor and Margaret's own daisy badge (Jones and Underwood 1992, pls 10–12). Mention should also be made of the music in the countess's household chapel, where the establishment was said to rival that of the king himself.

Lady Margaret's interest in books and her endorsement of the printing trade, introduced into England only in 1476 and still at a relatively early stage of development even at the time of her death in 1509, has been much studied (Powell 1998). She commissioned books from William Caxton, Richard Pynson and Wynkyn de Worde, including her own translations from the French of the fourth book of the *Imitation of Christ* (cat. no. 116) and of the *Mirror of Gold for the Sinful Soul*, often buying in large numbers for distribution. Although the great majority of these books were of a devotional kind, one of her earliest commissions was Caxton's 1488 translation of *Blanchardin and Eglantine*, for which she herself provided a manuscript copy of the French original. This was only one of a number of secular works that she is known to have owned, though it is not possible to tell from the records which of them was newly made for her and which acquired second-hand.

Several illuminated books of private devotion can be linked to her, including the Hours of Richard III at Lambeth Palace (cat. no. 44). She seems to have made a habit of passing on second-hand manuscripts of this kind to members of her circle (Backhouse 1995, pp.185–7). Four substantial contemporary illuminated books are distinguished by the display of her arms and devices. Of these, one – the 1505 Letters Patent for the foundation of Christ's College (cat. no. 111) – may probably be regarded as reflecting her personal taste. The remainder – a magnificent Parisian Book of Hours (cat. no. 115), a prayer book now at Westminster (cat. no. 114) and an Italian copy of the Office and Mass for the Feast of the Holy Name of Jesus, commissioned for her by Giovanni Gigli (Backhouse 2002) – probably show her as an appreciative recipient rather than a personal patron.

FURTHER READING

Jones and Underwood 1992; Powell 1998.

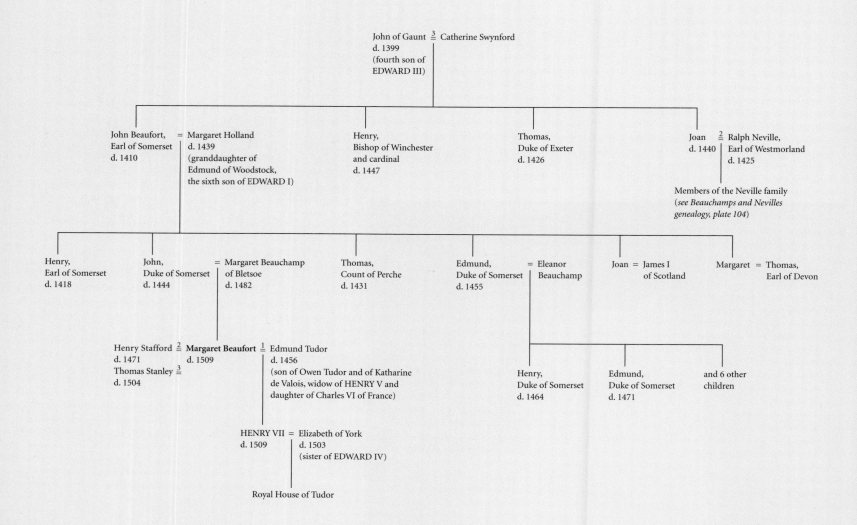

John of Gaunt ⦴³ Catherine Swynford
d. 1399
(fourth son of
EDWARD III)

John Beaufort, = Margaret Holland
Earl of Somerset   d. 1439
d. 1410   (granddaughter of
                   Edmund of Woodstock,
                   the sixth son of EDWARD I)

Henry,
Bishop of Winchester
and cardinal
d. 1447

Thomas,
Duke of Exeter
d. 1426

Joan ⦴² Ralph Neville,
d. 1440   Earl of Westmorland
          d. 1425

Members of the Neville family
(*see Beauchamps and Nevilles
genealogy, plate 104*)

Henry,
Earl of Somerset
d. 1418

John,
Duke of Somerset
d. 1444

= Margaret Beauchamp
of Bletsoe
d. 1482

Thomas,
Count of Perche
d. 1431

Edmund,
Duke of Somerset
d. 1455

= Eleanor
Beauchamp

Joan = James I
of Scotland

Margaret = Thomas,
Earl of Devon

Henry Stafford ⦴² **Margaret Beaufort** ⦴¹ Edmund Tudor
d. 1471   d. 1509   d. 1456
Thomas Stanley ⦴³   (son of Owen Tudor and of Katharine
d. 1504   de Valois, widow of HENRY V and
                                             daughter of Charles VI of France)

Henry,
Duke of Somerset
d. 1464

Edmund,
Duke of Somerset
d. 1471

and 6 other
children

HENRY VII = Elizabeth of York
d. 1509   d. 1503
            (sister of EDWARD IV)

Royal House of Tudor

110 Portrait of Lady Margaret Beaufort, Countess of Richmond and Derby

PLATE 108

Probably after Maynard Vewick (*fl.* 1502–25), early 16th century

Oil on panel; h. 50.5 cm, w. 35.9 cm

Christ's College, Cambridge

Dressed in the costume of a widow or vowess, with a white gable headdress, white chin *barbe* and black mantle, Lady Margaret is appropriately shown holding a small devotional book. There are no known contemporary images of Lady Margaret; this is probably the earliest of a number of surviving paintings depicting her. These oil portraits and a miniature attributed to Lucas Horenbout all have the same facial type and may well derive from a posthumous painting by Maynard Vewick (for other versions, see Strong 1969, pp.18–21; Jones and Underwood 1992, pp.293–5). Vewick's portrait, now lost, was commissioned by Lady Margaret's executors for Christ's College in 1510–13. It may itself have been based on an earlier painting, or perhaps a death-mask. A full-length oil belonging to Christ's was once thought to be Vewick's work, but is now considered to be later in date.

Maynard Vewick (Wewyck) was clearly a highly regarded artist in his day, and in addition to his portraits of Lady Margaret and other royals, he produced designs for Lady Margaret's tomb in Westminster Abbey (cat. no. 117). Torrigiano's effigy on this tomb is closely related to the extant paintings. Vewick may have been the first of the many Netherlandish artists who were to be employed in the service of Henry VII and his descendants. First recorded as 'maynard the kings payntor' in 1502, he continued to work for Henry VIII, and is last recorded in a salary payment of 1525 (Campbell (L) 1985, p.xv).   CM

PROV. Sotheby's sale, London, 25 February 1925, lot 62; purchased by Leggatt for Sir Arthur Shipley, Master of Christ's College; bequeathed (?), 1927.

LIT. Cooper 1874, pp.186, 198, 200–1; Goodison 1985, pp.34–8; Hepburn 1992.

111 Letters Patent for the foundation of Christ's College, Cambridge

1505

Vellum, ff.34; h. 35.8 cm, w. 26.6 cm

Christ's College, Cambridge

The Letters Patent of 1 May 1505, whereby Henry VII gave formal leave to his mother to set up Christ's College in place of the medieval God's House, is written out in book form on fine, well-prepared vellum, by a professional scribe signing himself, in one of the penwork initials, Paulus Cooke. Like the foundation documents for Henry VII's chapel at Westminster (cat. no. 30), the manuscript retains its original chemise binding of silk velvet over wooden boards, with ornamental clasps. One half of the skippet that originally contained the Great Seal remains, attached by a cord in the Tudor livery colours of green and white.

The opening page of the document is illuminated to a very high standard. Its border incorporates the Beaufort portcullis badge, the red rose of the house of Lancaster and the daisy (marguerite), which was Margaret's personal emblem. Close scrutiny of the panels of scrolling golden foliage reveals the foreparts of Henry's heraldic supporters, the dragon and the greyhound. The technique of these panels in particular suggests that the work is attributable to the London workshop of the Dutch immigrant Masters of the Dark Eyes (cat. nos 114, 143).   JMB

PROV. Christ's College, Cambridge, from 1505.

LIT. Lloyd 1934, pp.289–91; Backhouse 1997.

111

113

112 The Foundress's Beaker

1507–8

Silver-gilt, marked on both the cup and lid with the hallmarks for London 1507–8, and the maker's mark of a fish; h. 24.2 cm

Christ's College, Cambridge

Both cup and cover are entirely covered with an engraved diaper design, filled with Tudor roses, portcullises and fleurs-de-lis, with daisies (marguerites) at each section, all badges of Lady Margaret Beaufort. The tapering body of the beaker is set into a deep base, embossed in the shape of a Tudor rose in outline, with a battlemented top and stamped bands of roses below. A regular series of holes around the base indicates the presence originally of jewelled ornaments, perhaps pearls or enamels. The cover has an outsized finial, a cast hexagon incorporating portcullises, daises and a Tudor rose, set onto a double rose. Inside the beaker at the bottom is another Tudor rose. The gilding on both pieces has probably been renewed.

To both her foundations of Christ's College and St John's College, Lady Margaret Beaufort gave and bequeathed quantities of plate, much of it ecclesiastical – images, crosses and chalices especially (Cooper 1874, pp.129–36). Only a few secular pieces survive, and only at Christ's College (Campbell (M) 2002, pp.133–4). Many pieces were adorned with her heraldic badges, as on the beaker. This density of ornament was clearly popular: a similar contemporary example given to the Mercers' Company by Sir Thomas Leigh, a covered cup of 1513, is entirely covered with the Mercers' Company badges set within a diaper framework (Jackson 1911, I, pp.144–5).

The beaker shape seems to have become fashionable in Europe in the fourteenth century (Fritz 1982, pls 372–6 and nos 621–36) and continued into the eighteenth century. It was used for wine, sometimes specified as 'sweet' (Kurath 1956–99, *s.n. biker*). MLC

PROV. Christ's College, given by the foundress, Lady Margaret Beaufort.

LIT. Foster and Atkinson 1896, cat. no. 1b; Jones 1910, p.71, pl. LXXVII; London 1959, cat. no. 114; Crighton 1975, cat. no. B2; Campbell (M) 2002, p.133, pl. 21.

◄112

113 Three standing salts

a) Standing salt

1507–8

Silver-gilt, marked with the London mark for 1507–8 and a maker's mark of a fish; h. 20.8 cm

b) Pair of standing salts

c.1500 (the lid of one a 19th-century replacement)

Silver-gilt, marked twice with a single maker's mark (indecipherable: perhaps a horseshoe) on the body and cover; each h. 23.5 cm

Christ's College, Cambridge

The single salt and cover (a) are of hourglass shape. The base consists of six rounded compartments alternately plain or engraved with a Tudor rose, portcullis and fleur-de-lis on a matted ground. The large central knop is of sexfoil form, as is the disc, domed in the centre, which tops the tower. The gilding is worn and possibly original.

The dominant decorative motifs on the salt are the badges of Lady Margaret Beaufort and its shape aptly underlines this heraldic theme, being a stylized rose in profile. This was evidently a fashionable shape, and very similar salts survive in the Ironmongers' Com-

pany of London, dated 1518 and 1522 (Jackson 1911, pp.148, 155, ill.). Its unknown maker – his mark a fish – also created the Foundress's Beaker (cat. no. 112).

The pair of standing salts (b) are also of hourglass form, each of which is divided into six rounded compartments, alternately plain and embossed with a large Tudor rose in relief, on a matted surface. Base, cover and salt receptacle all have an outline of a six-petalled flower, and are stamped with a border of crosses. A Tudor rose in relief decorates the disc on top of each cover. The central knop is elaborately pinnacled, and of apparently identical design to the finial on the lid of the Foundress's Cup, of c.1440 (Jones 1910, p.70, pl. LXXV).

Like the single salt, the pair are of the classic English shape for a ceremonial salt, and are also heraldically decorated. But the dominance here of the Tudor rose – the royal badge *par excellence* – and the absence of badges more personal to Lady Margaret, may indicate that they were given to her by her son, Henry VII. MLC

PROV. Christ's College, given by the foundress, Lady Margaret Beaufort.

LIT. Foster and Atkinson 1896, cat. nos 9–10, 17; Jones 1910, pp.70–1, pl. LXXVI; London 1959, cat. nos 112–13; Crighton 1975, cat. nos S51–2; Campbell (M) 2002, p.133.

114 Prayer book of Lady Margaret Beaufort

*c.*1500 (probably before 1504)

Vellum, ff.119; h. 22 cm, w. 15 cm

Dean and Chapter of Westminster, Westminster Abbey Muniments Room (MS 39)

The opening page of this anthology of private prayers displays the arms of Beaufort surmounted by a coronet, the distinguishing bordure somewhat eccentrically detached into the shape of a livery collar, perhaps to underline the basic royalness of the arms. The Beaufort portcullis and Lady Margaret's daisies are included in the border and the eagle-leg badge of her third husband, Thomas Stanley, Earl of Derby (d. 1504), is enclosed in the initial. Both eagle leg and portcullis occur throughout the volume. The masculine form of some of the prayers has been taken to suggest that Lady Margaret ordered the book for her husband. This is not, however, conclusive and it may equally well have been ordered by Stanley for his wife, with whom he remained on close terms even after Margaret took her vow of chastity and set up her separate household in 1499.

The text of the book includes a number of devotions in honour of the Holy Name of Jesus, a cult enthusiastically promoted by Lady Margaret, in whose favour a papal bull was issued in 1494, granting an indulgence and naming her as patron (see cat. no. 116). The style of its decoration associates the manuscript with the London workshop of the Dutch Masters of the Dark Eyes (cat. nos 111, 143). An image of the Christ Child (f.38v) prefaces the prayer of St Bernard in honour of the Holy Name.   JMB

PROV. Lady Margaret Beaufort (d. 1509); members of the Stanley family, 16th century; Arthur, Viscount Dillon (d. 1892); Harold, Viscount Dillon (d. 1932), by whom presented to Westminster Abbey in 1923.

LIT. Dillon 1877; Ker 1969, pp.411–15; Tudor-Craig 1973, no. 123.

115 The Lady Margaret Beaufort Hours

Paris, *c.*1500

Vellum, ff.219; h. 23 cm, w. 16 cm

The Duke of Northumberland, Alnwick Castle (MS 498)

The unique decorative programme of this richly illuminated Book of Hours combines miniatures celebrating the sanctity of the Mother of Christ with dynastic heraldry demonstrating the royal lineage of

114

Lady Margaret Beaufort, through which her only son, Henry VII, derived his claim to the English crown. Lady Margaret's paternal grandparents, John Beaufort, Earl of Somerset, and Margaret Holland, afterwards Duchess of Clarence, were both of royal blood. Their arms appear below a miniature of the Tree of Jesse, which illustrates the descent of the Virgin from the royal house of David (f.13). Elsewhere in the manuscript the arms of Lady Margaret's parents, the arms of Lady Margaret herself with those of her husband, Edmund Tudor, and the arms of Henry VII and his queen, Elizabeth of York, all feature in conjunction with appropriately symbolic imagery.

The Hours, which is of Sarum Use, was written and illuminated to order in Paris, in the workshop of a fashionable but still anonymous book painter who has recently been renamed the Master of the *Chronique scandaleuse* (Avril and Reynaud 1993, pp.274–7). His commissions included work for a number of other European royal and noble clients, among them Charles VIII of France and the Archduchess Margaret of Austria, Regent of the Netherlands. His style is also recognizable in the decoration of contemporary Parisian printed books of the luxury type favoured by Henry VII as purchases for the English Royal Library.

The first Duchess of Northumberland bought this manuscript in 1773 in the belief that it had belonged

to Henry VII's elder daughter Margaret (cat. no. 45), in whom the Percy family had a special interest after entertaining her on her marriage journey to Scotland in 1503. While it is not impossible that she once owned it, there is no supporting evidence.   JMB

PROV. Lady Margaret Beaufort (d. 1509); James West, 1735; Elizabeth, 1st Duchess of Northumberland, 1773; by descent in the Percy family.

LIT. Backhouse 2000.

116 *A ful devout and gostely treatyse of the Imytacyon … of … cryste*

Printed by Richard Pynson, Fleet Street, London, 1503–4

Paper, ff.116; cropped to h. 19.5 cm, w. 13 cm

British Library, London (C.21.c.5)

Through printing, as well as through her endowments of colleges and chantries, Margaret Beaufort promoted in evangelical fashion the contemplative

115

spirituality and disciplined devotional exercises fostered by the Carthusian, Friars Observant and Bridgettine orders. She herself translated into English works in this vein that circulated in continental Europe. Caxton, Wynkyn de Worde and Pynson were among the printers whom she patronized.

Pynson was chosen as printer for the English edition of Thomas à Kempis's *Imitation of Christ*, the first three parts published on 27 June 1503 and the fourth in 1504. Margaret had commissioned William Atkinson, fellow of Jesus College, Cambridge, to translate the first three books while she herself translated the fourth from the French. This was a work that encouraged mystical contemplation of the Sacrament: 'It behoves thee to keep thee from too curious inquisition of the right profound sacrament if thou willt not be confounded in thy proper vice and drowned in the depth of opinions.' Margaret distributed the work widely. For her own household alone, she had 76 copies bound; the '100 printed books' carried to her palace at Collyweston, Northamptonshire, at the end of 1503 may have been the same work.

Pynson's book includes woodcuts of the Beaufort portcullis, with the arms of England supported by two angels; a frontispiece added to the portcullis the Tudor rose and the letters IHC, a reference to the Name of Jesus cult favoured by Margaret and put under her protection by Pope Alexander VI in 1494 (see cat. no. 114).

RW

PROV. James West (1704–73); William Herbert (1718–95); John Towneley (1740?–1813); George Spencer, Marquess of Blandford (1766–1840); Whiteknights sale 1819; Richard Heber (1773–1833); acquired by the British Museum after 1833.

LIT. de Backer 1864, no. 2285; STC, no. 23954.7; Jones and Underwood 1992, pp.184–5; Powell 1998.

117 Tomb monument of Lady Margaret Beaufort*

PLATE 55

Pietro Torrigiano; contract dated 23 November 1511

Westminster Abbey, south aisle of Henry VII's Chapel

An 'altar-tomb' carved from touchstone, with moulded base, standing on a step, and moulded upper slab. The slab has the gilt-bronze inscription, which reads from the north-west, written by Erasmus – he received £1 for the task – on an inset fillet. The tomb is divided into three bays by fluted composite pilasters, each bay and each end containing a gilt-bronze coat of arms enclosed within a wreath of bay leaves, tied at the top with ribbons, and with Tudor

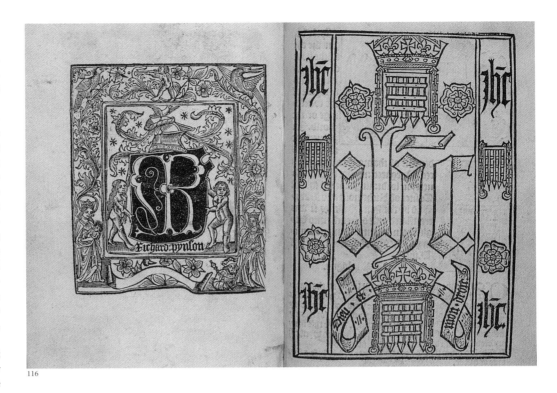

116

roses and foliage in the spandrels. The arms commemorate Margaret Beaufort's parents and grandparents, two of her husbands (Edmund Tudor and Thomas Stanley), Henry V and Katharine de Valois, Henry VIII and Catherine of Aragon (in the north-west bay, now missing) and Arthur, Prince of Wales.

The gilt-bronze effigy shows the countess in gabled coif and long cloak, head on two cushions, ornamented with Tudor badges, her feet resting on the yale of Kendal. On the north side are the remains of a thin, flat bronze plate engraved with portcullises. The canopy is openwork, traceried, and with flanking pinnacles, diagonally turned, embattled cresting and corbelled bases. The use of paint on the effigy (for her face, hands, cuffs, wimple and cloak lining) is unprecedented on gilt-bronze effigies in England.

Pietro Torrigiano Torrigiani (1472–1528) contracted in 1511 to make 'or cause to be made' this tomb, following his timber model for the tomb-chest, and a pattern drawn on cloth by the painter Maynard Vewick for the effigy and tabernacle. The executors furnished Torrigiano with the designs for the escutcheons and Erasmus's text for the inscription. The tomb was to cost £400, with Torrigiano supplying the materials. This prestigious monument, which introduced Italian Renaissance forms into English sculpture, was of critical importance for Torrigiano's career in England. The quality of his carving and fash-

ionable classical vocabulary were clearly of importance, as was his ability to execute all parts of the commission: previously in England the masonry and metalwork had been the responsibility of separate craftsmen. For this tomb, though, Torrigiano was constrained to follow the design of a painter, Maynard Vewick, for the effigy and Gothic tabernacle (see cat. no. 110). Important elements are missing from the pinnacles and canopy superstructure, most importantly the front section, which joined to the pinnacles and would have made the canopy even more elaborate.

PGL

LIT. Higgins 1894, pp.134–42; Scott 1915 (not entirely reliable as to the accounts held at St John's College, Cambridge); Plenderleith and Maryon 1959; Colvin 1975, pp.220–21; Darr 1979 and 1980; Lindley 1995, pp.47–72.

10 THE URBAN LANDSCAPE

JANE GRENVILLE

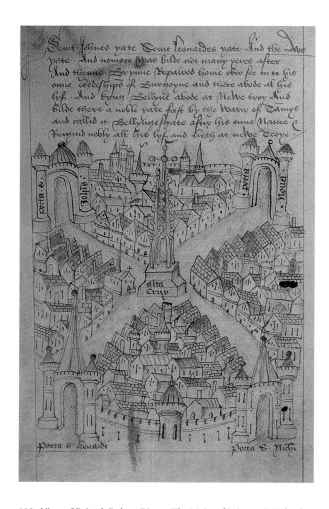

110 View of Bristol, Robert Ricart, *The Maire of Bristowe is Kalendar*, 1479–1898 (Bristol Record Office, BRO 0472 [1]a) (cat. no. 124)

By 1400 the main elements of the morphology and topography of the larger provincial towns were well established (for surveys, see Reynolds 1977, Schofield and Vince 1994, Swanson 1999, Palliser 2000 and Lilley 2002). Castles, cathedrals, churches and monastic precincts were all in place, as we can clearly see from almost any example, be it York, Oxford, Bristol or Norwich. Furthermore, it would appear that a sense of urban identity had also developed: while the circuits of walls formed defensive and economic barriers, it seems that they were also understood as means of self-identification for urban communities. Towns were seen as different from their hinterlands, and those differences were expressed in terms of independent civic government and the distinctive social and economic characteristics of non-agrarian communities: trade specialization and occupational zoning, collective government and civic ceremonial. All of this was expressed in the built environment, not least in the urban thoroughfare of streets and market places, whose functions differed from their rural counterparts, in that they operated as a 'stage' for the acting out of urban identity (cat. no. 118).

There are strong suggestions in the patterning of streets of deliberate planning for aesthetic as well as functional purposes – not surprising, perhaps, given the fact that the street was the principal backdrop for civic ceremonies and religious processions, epitomized by the Corpus Christi plays. Even in their function as the location for commercial activity, streets may have been the subject of a degree of social engineering. We can find both documentary and archaeological evidence for the zoning of activities and the construction of specific reputations for different neighbourhoods: for instance, the location of tanners away from the centre of York, in North Street, where their noxious trade would not cause distress to their fellow-citizens (Goldberg 1992); and through modern names we can identify specific streets with specific trades or functions, as at Coppergate, York (taking its name from the coopers who lived and worked there), Mercury Row, Otley (where the mercers had their centre of activity) and Cheapside, London (a main market place). The subdivision of plots into long narrow strips, or burgage plots, is often seen as characteristic of the urban environment. This is often explained as a response to constraints of space: in a walled area, where space is physically limited, long thin strips allow the maximum number of commercial frontages on to the street, while maintaining sufficient space behind for the house, yard, garden and service buildings (Platt 1976). Yet the long, narrow form is also observable in many village layouts, where constraints of space cannot be invoked. Some of these are failed market

111 St Botolph's church, Boston, Lincolnshire

towns, but others are not, and the question of the origins of this distinctive form of plot division would reward further research.

By the end of the period, often seen as one of general economic decline and urban decay, it becomes much more difficult to generalize about towns and their appearance (Britnell 1993; Dyer 1995; Postan 1975). Those heavily dependent on the wool trade had indeed seen a collapse in their fortunes: Boston, the fifth-wealthiest town in England in the lay subsidy list of 1334, had collapsed to 26th in the league table by the time of the subsidy of 1524–5, while others maintained their position. Over the same period Bristol slipped only from second to third position, and although York appears to have slid from third to 11th, it may well be that its citizens were canny about their tax returns and that the true situation in 1525 was better than the documentation suggests. Yet if we look at the evidence of the buildings, there is an abundance in York of merchant housing of the fifteenth and sixteenth centuries, and at Boston building continued on the magnificent tower of the church of St Botolph (plate 111) long after the economic decline had set in, while the guildhall dates from as late as 1450 (Slater and Rosser 1998; Giles 2000; RCHM 1981). Archaeological evidence, below and above ground, suggests little deceleration in development in the period, whether civic, commercial, ecclesiastical or domestic. A likely explanation is that in times of economic or political stress, major building campaigns can serve to boost confidence and fuel a recovery, a phenomenon that would prefigure the theories lying behind the Keynesian economics of the mid-twentieth century. Furthermore, competitive emulation between institutions could lead to major building campaigns, such as the construction of new aisles to churches and of guildhalls (cat. no. 123). One could extend the argument to the domestic sphere by noting that, even in periods of stress, individuals may be doing very well and a depressed housing market can offer favourable opportunities to the few who are continuing to prosper. The grander houses of York, such as Mulberry Hall, might be best understood in this way. The same individuals seem also to have been investing in movables, fixtures and fittings inside their buildings, as the essay by Geoff Egan in this volume shows.

But the story of towns in the fifteenth and early sixteenth centuries cannot be understood through a consideration of individual buildings alone, or even through groups of structures. We need to understand the development of urban topography and the polarization of society that is reflected in such phenomena as the zoning of towns and the expulsion of unpleasant trades to their margins. Much attention has been paid recently to these liminal areas in which, it has been suggested, it was possible to control and observe stigmatized groups such as the poor, the sick and the criminal. Thus, in the areas immediately inside the city walls, around the gateways and on extramural land, we find the housing of the poor, hospitals for the aged and infirm, while prisons were often located within city gateways. It was to such disadvantaged sectors of society that the newly arrived orders of friars sought to minister, and the location of their houses in the outer areas of the town may reflect the removal of social undesirables to liminal areas, as much as the more traditionally invoked explanation that city-centre land was already occupied (plate 76). The status of this marginal land persisted after the Reformation and it should scarcely surprise us that the buildings chosen by early modern civic authorities as houses of correction should so often have been former religious institutions such as guildhalls or hospitals.

This last point must lead us to consider the impact of the Reformation on the urban landscape. The release of prime land and building stock on to the property market in the mid-sixteenth century had a major effect on town centres: the demolition of monastic buildings and the removal of precincts as distinctive enclaves within the townscape opened up opportunities that were readily seized by civic and secular institutions and by enterprising individuals. The decline of the Church as a political player on the urban stage signals the end of our period – one that may have been more subject to the influences of deliberate planning, both topographical and social, than is generally acknowledged.

FURTHER READING

Lilley 2002; Palliser 2000; Schofield and Vince 1994.

118 Design for a street frontage*

*c.*1520–40

Ink and lead on parchment; h. *c.*38 cm, w. 106 cm

Worcester Diocese, BA 2648/9 (1) ref. b7 16.093
(kept at Worcester Record Office)

This unfinished architectural drawing of a timber-frame street frontage survives on a vellum sheet used to bind the episcopal register of Geronimo Ghinucci, Bishop of Worcester between 1522 and 1535. The design is executed on both sides of the sheet: the illustrated side shows the main façade of the building, and the reverse (now badly worn) an elevation of the jettied gable to the right of the drawing. These two drawings have been precisely set out so that their structural elements correspond through the sheet – conclusive evidence that they depict the same building.

Along the lowest register of the drawing are a series of doors and large windows, presumably a set of shop fronts. Given the number of doors depicted, one might have opened onto a passage running through to the back of the building. The form of the upper storeys is difficult to determine. To the left of the sheet the building had two upper floors. As the stylized rendering of perspective makes clear, these were both lit with projecting windows. But the gable drawing on the reverse shows that to the right the frontage had only one upper floor. At what point the change in the number of storeys occurred is not clear. Another curiosity of the design is that only the right gable end is jettied. Presumably, therefore, a forward-facing gable capped the left extreme of the façade and the street frontage extended beyond it.

118

There are several contracts for the construction of medieval timber-frame buildings that make reference to drawings. This was presumably prepared for such a contract, though nothing is known about the details, date or circumstances of the commission, nor why the drawing was abandoned. The annotations do not relate to the drawing, but suggest that the register was bound with this sheet by 1546, a useful terminal dating for the design. JG

LIT. Charles and Down 1970–72.

119 Glastonbury, Somerset, George Inn

*c.*1470

The George Inn is a splendid surviving example of a late fifteenth-century hostelry. First documented in the town's parish-church accounts of 1489, it was probably built in the preceding decade by the Abbot of Glastonbury, John Selwood.

The stone façade is crowned by a battlemented parapet and defined within the street frontage by two buttresses, one of which is capped by a stone canopy – possibly for a bell. It comprises three unequal storeys, each defined externally by a heavy string-course and faced with panelling. In typical Perpendicular fashion, this pronounced decorative grid forms the framework for the fenestration of the building. It also serves visually to impose regularity on this asymmetrical and varied façade.

Rising through the full height of the building to the left of the façade is a projecting oriel. To the right of this is the main door, which swells imposingly outside the constraints of the façade grid. It is ornamented with coats of arms, including Edward IV's. The left jamb of the door stands roughly on the central axis of the façade. This formerly supported a large projecting beam, presumably the fixing for a sign or for a statue of St George. There were also statues in the niches above the door and figures peering between the battlements.

Early drawings show three distinct window types within the building. At ground level there were rectangular, mullion windows (now replaced) and, in the zone of the façade above the door, windows with flattened-arch heads. Each of the remaining window heads was decorated with ogee arches flanked by quatrefoil falchions. Such variation in detail is commonly used in medieval design to express the relative importance of different floors and chambers. The tracery patterns are typical of the south-west region.

Claims that the George Inn was a hostelry intended primarily for pilgrims or to make money for the neighbouring abbey are not supported by

historical evidence. However, inns such as this did increase in numbers in the late Middle Ages, providing accommodation for travellers and acting as a focus for urban communal life. JG

LIT. Warner 1826, pp.lvii–lx; Wood 1965, pp.192–3.

119

120 Norwich, church of St Peter Mancroft, nave and chancel

*c.*1430–55

To judge from references in wills, the renewal of the nave was under way by *c.*1430. In 1441 the institutional rector consented to the rebuilding of the chancel, and by 1445 its north aisle was up, although its east wall, which is of one build with the south aisle, had yet to be begun. Some scholars think that the chancel alone was dedicated in 1455 and that the nave was started only after that event. It seems preferable to take literally the record that the *church* was dedicated in 1455 and to interpret bequests to the font in 1463 and to the rood-screen in 1479 as indications that in 1455 the structures of both nave and chancel were newly completed and that much work remained to be done on their fittings (see cat. no. 289).

Always the main parish church in Norwich, St Peter's faces the market-place broadside on. Its long flanks impress by virtue of their uninterrupted clear-storey fenestration and by their being faced with imported Ancaster stone rather than the knapped or rendered flint generally used in Norfolk. The equally unified interior elevations incorporate strikingly slender arcades and shafts linked to the roof's wall-posts, features that indicate a knowledge of St Mary's at Bury St Edmunds (begun *c.*1424, see cat. no. 261). The image niches in the spandrels recall the other grandest

early fifteenth-century church in East Anglia, St Nicholas at King's Lynn (rebuilt by 1419). Almost certainly an innovation was the encasing of the hammer-beams of the main roof within fictive vaulting. This feature was still being imitated in the region many decades afterwards.   CW

LIT. Woodman 1995.

121 Figure of St Peter

Probably *c.*1500

Oak, painted; h. 1.97 m

Exeter City Museums (1/1988)

Dressed in gown and tunic, the bearded figure of St Peter tramples a diminutive male figure (replaced *c.*1900) beneath his feet. He holds in his right hand a church and his crossed keys (formerly iron, now replaced); in his left is a book. The sculpture formed the corner post of the ground floor of a house at the junction of High Street and North Street, Exeter, supporting the jettied upper storeys (see ill.). St Peter is the patron saint of Exeter Cathedral.

The figure displays the sharply angular drapery characteristic of the late fifteenth and early sixteenth centuries. Although external wooden imagery was not uncommon in late medieval England (see cat. no. 157), the Exeter figure is a rare – and very large – survival

of religious 'street iconography'. Since no local tradition of large wooden sculpture is known, the possibility arises that this is the work of an immigrant craftsman. The Low Countries or Germany are perhaps the most obvious origins for such an individual, but a third possibility could be France, where broadly comparable figures stand on house façades, for example at Morlaix. Exeter city documents of the early sixteenth century record a sizeable immigrant community, including people from all these areas.   JA

PROV. No. 187 High Street, Exeter; removed 1986.

LIT. Norris 1867.

High Street, Exeter, Samuel Prout (1783–1852), watercolour, showing the figure of St Peter *in situ* after 1804, before 1819 (Exeter City Museums) (see cat. no. 121)

◀ 120

121

122 Statue of Discipline or Temperance

*c.*1430

Stone; h. *c.*108 cm

Museum of London (2002.117/1)

This statue is one in a set of four female figures from the demolished porch façade of the London Guildhall. Work began on the porch in, or soon after, 1426 and the statues were probably carved at about this time.

Antiquarian drawings show that the statues were originally set in niches flanking the main door of the porch. Each is distinctively dressed and shown trampling a miniature figure. This latter detail would serve to confirm the received identification of the statues as personifications of virtues standing triumphant over vices. Their specific titles of Justice, Fortitude, Temperance and Discipline are derived from a mid-sixteenth-century poem by William Elderton. His inclusion of Discipline in the list is a little odd, and a more conventional grouping with Prudence as the fourth personification has also been suggested. In niches above these figures were sculptures of Moses and Aaron – described by Elderton as figures of law and learning – and a statue of Christ.

Of the virtues listed by Elderton, this statue probably represents Discipline: she is dressed in a manner reminiscent of a nun, a vowess or a widow in weeds. The figure is clothed in a long, flowing undergarment and full-length cloak. Over her head she wears a veil and beneath this a wimple, crimped across the throat. The rim cut around the head indicates that the figure once wore a crown, probably of metal. Whether this was a medieval detail or later addition is unclear. The arms and the features of the figure beneath her feet have been smashed away.

Sculpted decorative programmes for entrances are a commonplace of both secular and ecclesiastical medieval architecture across Europe. But the form of this particular display – for the most ambitious of all English guildhalls – perhaps best compares with such important works as the north doorway of Westminster Hall and its sculpted display of kings.   JG

PROV. Acquired from Soughton Hall, Flintshire, in 1972.

LIT. Barron 1974, pp.26–7 (ill.); Wilson 1976.

123

123 Lavenham, Suffolk, Corpus Christi Guildhall

*c.*1529

The Guildhall at Lavenham is a fine example of late medieval East Anglian timber-frame construction. It was built in the 1520s by the Corpus Christi guild, probably at the time of its incorporation by charter in 1529. The guild was then one of four religious fraternities in this prosperous wool town, and the prominent location of the hall on the market place reflects the wealth and influence of its brotherhood.

Built over a cellar and on a brick foundation, the guildhall is a two-storey building with pitched roofs.

Rather than incorporate a central hall rising the full height of the building in the traditional English domestic fashion, it is divided throughout into two floors, the upper jettied out over the lower. It comprises three principal carpentry elements: two gabled ranges set at right angles to one another – an arrangement that conforms to the site of the building on a street corner – and a projecting porch. This is set asymmetrically within the market-place façade and highlights the position of the hall within the jumbled street frontage.

In the manner typical of high-quality construction in the region, the carpentry frame is dense with timbers. The rectilinear pattern of the frame and its

design with numerous windows reflect the Perpendicular interest in creating architectural grids with a high ratio of glass to wall surface area. Throughout, the frame is cut with mouldings and decorative patterns. The porch and prominent outer angle of the building are particularly rich in such ornament.

It is not clear what function the rooms within the building originally served. The principal chamber was on the ground floor and was entered directly through the porch. It presumably served as the common hall of the fraternity and was formerly panelled. JG

LIT. Corder 1891.

11 CIVIC INSTITUTIONS

DEREK KEENE

Late medieval England was a country of small towns, perhaps 650 of them, of which only about 50 had populations of more than 2,000. Some had no more than a few hundred inhabitants. Only London, with some 50,000 inhabitants after the Black Death and overshadowing other English towns to an increasing degree, had a significant standing among European cities (plate 9). London practices served as models for elsewhere and its citizens were able to ensure that their rights overrode those of others. Most English towns were smaller than they had been in 1300, and remained so until well after 1500. Physical contraction reduced the resources of many towns, promoting a discourse of urban decline. Nevertheless, a redistribution of wealth towards peasants, craftsmen and distributive traders, plus an increasing circulation of people and goods, brought new types of prosperity to many towns. Some long-established provincial centres lost ground and showed obvious signs of decay, but even they reflected new developments in urban culture.

English urban institutions, including distinctive customs, courts, forms of collective association and bureaucracies, were well established before the Norman Conquest. They developed further during the twelfth and thirteenth centuries, when the idea of urban liberty – associated with some capacity for self-administration under the Crown or some other superior lord – took hold, but not to the extent that it did in more urbanized parts of Europe. Late medieval English urban institutions were relatively weak. Indeed, many places that clearly functioned as towns lacked legal or administrative definition of that status, although their inhabitants (as in many villages) found ways of collectively managing their affairs. Even major towns such as Salisbury might lack that quintessential figure of urban collective identity, the mayor, who was first instituted in London in the 1190s and stood at the head of a community of citizens or freemen. Norwich did not acquire a mayor until 1404. In many towns a significant part of the urban area lay outside the control of the community or principal lord. At Winchester, for example, the bishop had effectively claimed about one-third of the built-up area, although that did not include the wealthier commercial districts, which the mayor and citizens held directly from the king. Even in London there were important suburbs not controlled by the city authorities. Most larger towns contained religious precincts outside the rule of the secular authorities, and by 1500 those precincts often contained numerous lay households.

By the fourteenth century, in the larger towns, the community of freemen (and sometimes women) perhaps represented no more than a quarter of heads of household. Decision-making, order and concord were promoted through hierarchies of courts and councils and by neighbourhood systems of watch and ward. Among many other concerns, urban governments regulated building, sanitary affairs, trade and the transmission of property. They raised funds for a multitude of purposes, including payments due to the king and gifts to buy the favour of local magnates. They supervised public institutions and works such as hospitals, water supplies and defences. Town walls and gates had for long been signs of identity for the larger towns, but in the later fourteenth century they received special attention on account both of the threat from the French and of a new urban consciousness. In collective governance the economic reputation of the town and the interests of merchants, craftsmen and shopkeepers were major concerns. Guilds and fraternities provided an almost infinitely variable means of articulating neighbourhood, economic and religious interests. Guild membership was one in which urban communities could enlist the support of powerful outsiders, including landed magnates or influential figures at court, who might further the interests of a town or simply wish to formalize their everyday relations with it.

Urban social or political groups, which nominally (or initially) came together for one purpose, might assume other roles. At Winchester the citizens came to be equated with the members of the guild of merchants, which had a separate origin and privileges and contained several 'houses' representing different quarters of the city. Members of the guild were recruited from lesser bodies representing the crafts. The citizens assembled periodically at the civic hospital of St John the Baptist, where important archives were kept and where in the fourteenth century the city's tailors established a fraternity dedicated to the saint. This fraternity became the principal focus of the city's social and ceremonial life, with a membership virtually identical to that of the citizen community. Other towns had similar or even more complex arrangements. Urban landscapes thus included numerous guildhalls, courthouses and other meeting places, while guilds often met in churches or in private houses.

London lacked a merchant guild, although the physical heart of its governance was the Guildhall (cat. no. 122), but its separate guilds or companies collectively played a similar role in civic government and in regulating trades. Their origins were diverse. Weavers, tanners, saddlers and others could trace their origins to the twelfth century, when at least one of them had a guildhall. The Drapers' Company began in the fourteenth century as a fraternity at the church of St Mary-le-Bow, to which practitioners of several trades belonged, although the neighbourhood had long been frequented by drapers. Later the drapers' fraternity became more exclusive. After more than a century at St Mary-le-Bow, it moved to St Michael Cornhill and later established Drapers' Hall.

In many late medieval towns there was less pressure on space than there had been before the Black Death. This, together with the new distribution of wealth and an increasing interest in expressing local and neighbourhood identities, facilitated a new wave of investment in institutional building. The parish became a stronger focus of community interest and administrative activity, and even in towns where redundant parish churches were being pulled down, those that remained were enlarged and beautified (cat. no. 120). Urban government itself commonly became more elaborated and defined, with a more visible hierarchy of officials and clerks. There was a renewed interest – common to municipal, guild and parish administrations – in defining constitutions, in codifying rules and memoranda, and in adopting systematic forms of record keeping, especially for finance. Statutory innovations, and legal notions such as that of the body corporate, clarified the legal capacity of urban collectives, regularizing practices that had existed for some centuries. Towns increasingly acted as trustees for charities and chantries, and thereby extended their property holdings. Monarchs formally enhanced the status and identity of some provincial cities by making them counties in their own right. Guildhalls and other civic buildings were enlarged, elaborated and built anew. The city of London's projects, including the chapel (1384–97) and drawbridge tower (1426) on London Bridge, Guildhall (1411 onwards) and the granary, market, chapel, college and school at Leadenhall (1440s), were especially impressive, but could be matched on a smaller scale in many other towns. Through a variety of institutions that they controlled, town dwellers became more wide-ranging patrons of architecture, the decorative arts, music and liturgy than they had previously been.

The enhancement of English urban culture (in its widest sense), drew – both directly and indirectly – on ideas and examples from elsewhere, including Italy. It was also reflected in the elaboration of civic ceremonial and in the increased status and authority of the leading officers, especially the mayor (cat. no. 124). The mayors of London and York came to be known as 'Lord Mayor' and acquired retinues of attendants, including sword-bearers. Much civic regalia – including common seals, maces and moot (meeting) horns – dated from the twelfth and thirteenth centuries and remained in use, but mayors and other officials subsequently acquired their own seals, along with additional regalia such as swords, collars and jewels (cat. nos 82, 127–9).

Processions gained a new significance in ceremonial, emphasizing the unity and hierarchy of social and political elements in the town, both drawing on and incorporated in a much older Christian urban liturgy. That civic liturgy was seasonal, and at many places the Corpus Christi procession came to play a major part in collective life. Such processions, along with royal entries into towns, were sometimes accompanied by plays and pageants, in a tradition that extended back to the thirteenth century, if not earlier. A number of towns had St George's Day processions with images of the saint, the dragon and the maiden, symbolizing national identity, urban order and perhaps fertility. Urban strength was also expressed by images of giants at the city gates and elsewhere. These seem to have been a late medieval innovation, perhaps associated with a new, more widespread interest in urban identity, origins and myth, expressed in public imagery and inscriptions as well as in books.

FURTHER READING

Jewitt and Hope 1895; Palliser 2000; Reynolds 1977.

124

124 Robert Ricart,
*The Maire of Bristowe is Kalendar**

1479–1898

Paper and vellum, ff.140; h. 28 cm, w. 21 cm

Bristol Record Office (MS 04720 (1))

This collection of materials on history, customs, laws, liberties and privileges relating to Bristol was begun in 1479 at the behest of the then mayor, William Spencer. It was initially compiled by Robert Ricart, town clerk, and additions were still being made as late as 1898. The volume, made up of a combination of vellum and paper leaves and written by a variety of different scribes, includes a number of illustrations, mainly coloured drawings, also attributable to more than one hand (see also plate 110).

Of special interest is a large and fully coloured miniature representing the swearing-in of a new mayor (f.152). The ceremony, fully described in the text, traditionally took place on the feast of St Michael the Archangel (29 September) in the Guildhall, here depicted with blue hangings below glass on which are emblazoned the cross of St George, the royal arms and the arms of Bristol itself. The outgoing mayor offers his successor the book on which to take his oath. His official sword and hat are borne by an attendant wearing, like other participants, a formal livery of blue and murrey rayed with red. Mayors and aldermen are dressed in scarlet and portrayed on a larger scale than the watching citizens crowded into the foreground. On a green-covered table separating the two groups appear a small parchment scroll, a pen case and inkpot, a money bag and a container perhaps intended to protect a book, though possibly representing the casket for the various seals of office mentioned in the accompanying text.   JMB

PROV. Bristol City Records, from the 15th century.

LIT. Smith 1872; Scott 1996, no. 134.

125 Charter of Henry V
to the Borough of Colchester

1413

Vellum; h. 45.5 cm, w. 69 cm

Colchester Museums (COLEM: 2002.174)

The citizens of Colchester secured a renewal of their royal charter less than four months after Henry V's accession to the throne (see cat. no. 126). It was issued at Westminster on 7 July 1413, written out and signed by a clerk named John Roderham, and provided with an elegant illuminated initial, protected by a piece of contemporary silk and accompanied by suitable marginal decoration. The cost to the town was £16. The initial, commissioned from a professional illuminator possibly in London, encloses a figure of St Helena, the True Cross at her left hand linking her to a marginal figure of the Emperor Constantine (see also cat. no. 291). An accompanying scroll reads: '*Sancta Elena nata fuit in Colcestria / Mater Constantini fuit / Sanctam Crucem invenit Elena*' (St Helen was born in Colchester / She was the mother of Constantine / Helen discovered the Holy Cross).

Below the initial is the earliest surviving example of Colchester's arms in full blazon. Of particular interest is the heraldic cross, shown here in the proper colour green (vert) rather than in the silver (argent) of sixteenth-century and later versions, and with its two components firmly dovetailed rather than overlaid. The three crowns, perhaps reflecting Helena's supposed connection with the relics of the Three Kings rather than the traditional arms of East Anglia, are affixed to its arms by the three nails of the Crucifixion, discovered by her together with the True Cross.   JMB

PROV. Borough of Colchester, from 1413.

LIT. Round 1895; Benham 1900 and 1907.

125

126 The Colchester town seal matrix, with modern wax impression

Probably *c.*1413

Gilded copper alloy; diam. 9 cm

Inscr. on obverse: **:sigillu[m]: commune : ballivoru[m]: &: communitatis : ville : domini : regis: colcestrie* (Seal of the community of the bailiffs and community of the king's town of Colchester); on reverse (beginning at the bottom to the left of the steps): *:intravit: ihc': in : quoddam : castellum: et : mulier : quedam : excepit : illum* (Jesus entered into a certain castle, and a certain woman received him)

Colchester Borough Council, Essex

This double seal matrix of Colchester replaced an earlier thirteenth-century double seal matrix. St Helena was believed to have been born in Colchester and this accounts for her presence on the seals of the town (see also cat. no. 125). The obverse (a) of the seal shows, within elaborate niches and canopies, the Empress Helena clasping in her arms a large cross and three nails (see cat. no. 291). Beneath the topmost canopy is a half-length figure of Our Lord, blessing, and in the base of the seal a shield of the borough arms – a cross raguly between two crowns in chief and passing through a third in base – supported by a lion dexter and a raven sinister. On either side of the canopy is a smaller niche, richly canopied, with dexter an angel holding a shield of St George, sinister angel with a shield of France modern and England quarterly. At each side is an elaborately panelled and pinnacled buttress. The use of France modern in the English royal arms indicates that it dates from after 1406–8.

The reverse of the seal (b) has an attractive view of the medieval town of Colchester, which shows a town wall with four round towers surrounded by a river, over which there leads a flight of steps, starting from the edge of the seal. Inside the town is Colchester castle. On either side of the town are two lions with scrolls, with flowers above them. The inscription on the reverse is taken from Luke X, 38, where it refers to Martha rather than Helen. The engraving is deeply cut, especially for the doors and windows, giving the scene a well-modelled architectural quality.

Although it has been suggested that the seal was engraved in the time of Edward IV, it is more likely that it dates from the time of the renewal of the charter in 1413. JC

LIT. Perceval 1883–5; St John Hope 1893–5, pp.445–7; Jewitt and St John Hope 1895, pp.197–8; Pedrick 1904, pp.55–8, pl. XXXVIII.

127 The 'Pearl' bearing-sword of the Lord Mayor of Bristol

Late 14th century (before 1399), with later additions

Steel and silver-gilt; l. 122 cm

Lord Mayor and Corporation of Bristol

In design a two-hand fighting sword, but with its arms and inscriptions arranged to be viewed when it is point upwards, it has a straight double-edged blade, much ground down. The hilt, of silver-gilt, probably over an iron core, comprises a long straight cross of rectangular section tapering towards the tips, a pommel of flattened pear shape with a low medial ridge on each face, and a grip of rounded section, tapering towards the pommel, with a central double moulding. The front of the grip has a shield applied at each end and is engraved in Gothic letters with *'Jon wellis of london groc' & meyr to bristow gave this swerd feir'*; each face of the pommel is similarly engraved, but in a different hand, with Wells's motto, *'mercy and grace'*, on a scroll, and the back with the name *'w. cleve'*. The lower shield, which overlaps the base of the pommel – suggesting that it is a replacement – is engraved with the arms of Bristol, and the upper one with those of Richard II (incorporating France modern).

John de Wells (d. 1442) was a prominent London merchant and politician, master of the Grocers' Company for six years, and mayor in 1431–2. It is not known why he gave the sword to Bristol, but it must have been in or after 1431–2, since he is described as mayor (of London) on it. The arms of Richard II (deposed 1399) indicate that it must have been already old when given. It may have been used by one of Wells's predecessors as the London mayoral sword, with the arms of that city where those of Bristol now are. Its name is said to derive from the fact that its original scabbard, which does not survive, was sown with pearls. Nothing certain is known of W. Cleve. The sword is presumably of English make. CB

LIT. Jewitt and St John Hope 1895, I, p.237; Laking 1920–22, II, p.321; Hayward 1956.

126a

126b

128 The Hedon Civic Mace

Early 15th century

Iron and silver-gilt; h. 63 cm

Hedon Town Council, East Riding of Yorkshire

Hedon was an ancient municipal borough and parish close to Hull. It was incorporated by a charter of Edward III in 1348, under which the town was self-governed by a mayor, bailiffs and aldermen. The silver-gilt mace, one of three belonging to the town, is one of the earliest civic maces now remaining in England. It has been associated with the granting of a later charter by Henry V in 1415.

This civic mace is particularly interesting as it shows the transitional development from war to civic use. The silver shaft encloses an iron core that terminates in a usable weapon-head with six solid iron flanges. But this use is now subsumed, as the other end is carried upwards as an emblem of office. The conical head terminates in a circular plate (originally enamelled), with the royal arms of France and England quartered, between the letters *hh*. The decoration also includes lions rampant and strawberry leaves.

The crown of four crocketed arches terminating in an orb, and originally also a cross, is a later addition, probably of the late sixteenth century. KW

LIT. Jewitt and St John Hope 1895, II, p.511; London 1930, cat. no. 429; Garvey 1979, pp.6–8; Garvey 2000, pp.5–6.

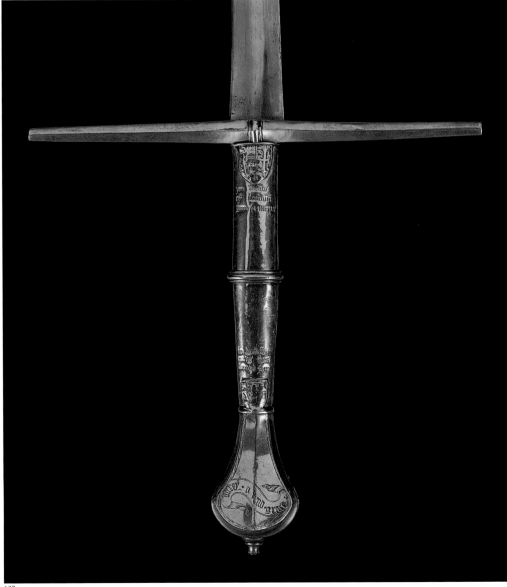

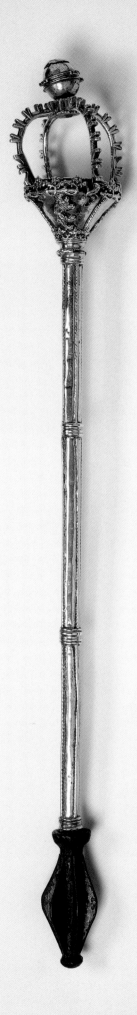

129 One of the four Waits' Chains of Exeter

Probably *c.*1476

Silver; l. 122 cm

Exeter City Council, Devon

This silver chain – one of four – has 40 links. It displays within circles alternately the letters X and R – pre-sumably for Exeter – joined to each other by loops attached to projecting rings on each circle. The chains end in a trefoil from which hangs a silver shield, engraved with a castle, the symbol of the city, which also appears on the city seal. These chains are believed to be those recorded in 1476–7, when 14 shillings was spent by the city in remaking the 'colors' (collars) with shields for the Waits (the city's paid musicians). They were repeatedly repaired after that date.

The chains are remarkable survivals. The term 'wait' probably derives from the musicians' duty to accompany those who kept watch or wait in the period between Hallowe'en (31 October) and Can-dlemas (2 February). The first reference to a Wait is in 1362–3. Robes were provided in the early fifteenth century and 45s. 4d. was spent in 1429–30 on three silver 'skugyns' (escutcheons or shields), weighing 16 ounces, for the Waits. There were three by the 1420s and four by the 1520s. Of the four chains that sur-vive, one is exhibited.

It was not until the sixteenth century that there was mention of the instruments that the Waits played; these were 'A Doble Curtall [probably a kind of bassoon], a Lyserden [probably a serpent], two tenor Hoyboyes [Oboes], a treble Hoyboyes, a cornet and a sett or case of ffower Recorders [a kind of flute or flageolet]'. The occasions on which the Waits were required to play were before the watch, when they went about the city at Midsummer and St Peter's night, at the election of the new mayor and when he took his oath, and on Christmas Day and Easter Sunday. The most onerous duty was to play in the winter from Hallowe'en until Candlemas every morning from 3 a.m. until they had gone through the whole city, except on Sundays, holidays and Fridays.

These chains, with their lettered devices, recall the importance of music in civic ceremonial during the period. Replicas of the chains are still worn by the Sergeants-at-Mace of Exeter.   JC

LIT. Lloyd Parry 1936; Allan and Timms 1996, pp.38–9, no. 14.

130 Aldermen of London

1446–50

Pen-and-ink and watercolour on paper; h. 36.4 cm, w. 25 cm

Guildhall Library, Print Room, London (K1306480)

Two of a series of 26 coloured drawings representing aldermen of London during the mayoralty (1446–7) of mercer John Olney. Each figure, identified on the scroll above, holds a shield of his own arms and rests his left hand on a framed tablet designed to display the arms of successors in his ward. In com-position and design, the aldermen drawings are closely related to the figures of Garter knights in William Bruges's Garter Book (cat. no. 80), and form a similar illustrated roll of arms. As with Bruges's Book, their exact purpose is unknown. The

129

130a

130b

outline of each figure is identical, reproduced by the medieval method of 'pouncing', making clear that these were not portraits but primarily models for the heraldry. Every alderman wears a pink cloak with plaid lining, seemingly the formal mantle of office at this period.

The drawings have been attributed to Roger Legh, Clarenceux King of Arms 1435–60 (Wagner 1967, p.273) and their later provenance shows that they remained among the heralds' records. They date, however, from an active building period for the Guildhall, home of the Court of Aldermen. In October 1444 the rebuilding of the Guildhall chapel was marked with a ceremony of dedication, even though

it was unfinished and work was to continue until the 1450s. The drawings depict the 25 aldermen (and one unidentified figure) who were in office at the 'founding' of their new chapel and perhaps relate to a scheme for stall plates or other furnishings.

The aldermen shown are (a) John Sutton, goldsmith, alderman for Aldersgate (1437–50), who was killed defending the city during Jack Cade's rebellion in 1450, and (b) John Derby (d. 1479), draper, alderman for Candlewick ward (1444–54). The chronicler Fabyan relates that in later life Derby was fined £50 by the Court of Aldermen for failing to remove a dead dog from his door and for the consequent 'unfyttynge langage which he gave unto the mayre'.   AP

PROV. Roger Legh, Clarenceux (d. 1460) (?); Sir Thomas Wriothesley, Garter (d. 1534) (?); William Smith, rector of Melsonby, 1718; detached from the Wriothesley collections (BL, Add. 45133), presented to the British Museum by Viscount Wakefield of Hythe in 1938, and with the agreement of the donor transferred to be reunited with three leaves already in the Guildhall (presented by Alexander Sefi, London, 1932).

LIT. Beaven 1908–13, II, pp.8, 164; Wagner 1950, pp.92, 96–7; Wagner 1967, p.273; Goodall 1959–61; Barron 1974, pp.35–9; Scott 1996, no. 86 (ill. 333).

131

131 Letters Patent of Henry VI to the Leathersellers' Company

1444

Vellum; h. 36 cm, w. 58 cm

The Worshipful Company of Leathersellers, London (MS 1)

The letters patent, dated 19 August 1444, confirms ordinances of Richard Whittington of 1398, which initially incorporated the Leathersellers' Company. It goes on to set out the methods by which the company's wardens should be selected, to prohibit fraudulent practices, to note fines for shoddy goods, and to describe how the company should enforce standards nationally.

The letter opens with a large illuminated initial in which the figure of Henry VI is depicted enthroned, holding in his right hand a likeness of the letter itself, with its pendant seal dangling from it. The original seal is now lost. Below the image of

Henry, in the left margin of the document, kneel members of the company, who are arranged in five registers. Scrolls over their heads read '*Domine salvum fac regem*' ('God save the king'). Stags, hinds and goats in the opposite margin bear the same inscription, and probably represent the animals from which the Leathersellers produced their wares.

The decoration of the letters patent belongs in the stylistic milieu of the London illuminator William Abell, whose atelier occupied properties near London Bridge. He executed royal documents for Henry VI's foundations of Eton and King's College (cat. no. 20). On the basis of style, it seems likely that Abell or one of his assistants was responsible for the Leathersellers' document. The grand style of the letters patent reflects the ambitions of the Leathersellers within the burgeoning economy of fifteenth-century London.   AB

LIT. Black 1871, pp.26–9, ill.

132 Seal matrix of the Shearmen and Fullers of the Guild of the Nativity of our Lord of Coventry

PLATE 26

Probably 1439

Copper alloy; diam. 4.8 cm

Inscr. in black-letter: *Sigillu co[mmun]e scissor[is] et ffulloni ffrat[er]nitat[is] gilde nativat[is] d[omi]ni de Coventre* (The common seal of the fraternity of the Shearmen and Fullers of the Guild of the Nativity of our Lord of Coventry).

British Museum, London (MME 1989, 6-4, 1)

The design and engraving of this seal matrix is of a remarkably high quality. It reflects the discerning patronage of the socially important Midland town guilds of the later Middle Ages, and emphasizes the legal independence of the guild. It may well have been engraved in Coventry. Coventry was prosperous in the fifteenth century, and of the 108 metal-workers recorded in deeds in the late fourteenth and early fifteenth centuries, 12 were goldsmiths (VCH 1969, pp.331–2).

The central image shows the enthroned Virgin and Child, with the Child reaching out with his right hand to receive the chalice-shaped gift presented to him by the leading king. The two kings behind bear their presents in their left hands and gesture with their right. The whole design is admirably adapted to the shape of the seal. At the bottom, on a shield, the heraldic bearings of the guild are shown. They are the shearmens' shears, handles uppermost so that the blades encompass a fuller's bat.

The seal matrix, which has a hinged-shaped handle at the back, was most probably engraved in 1439. In that year Henry VI granted the Shearers and Fullers the privilege of using a common seal as a body corporate. The journeymen guilds at Coventry, of which this was only one, were interested in protecting the interests of the minor crafts of the woollen industry against the interest of the rich drapers and mercers. The guilds at Coventry made a rich and substantial contribution to the cultural life of the city. Apart from feasting, they presented pageants, particularly at the feast of Corpus Christi. The Three Kings of Cologne formed part of the pageant exhibited before Prince Edward in Cross Cheaping in 1474. The manuscript of the Shearmans' and Fullers' play *The Nativity* was preserved in Coventry until it was burned in 1879.　　　　　　　　　　　　　　　　　　JC

LIT. Fretton 1879, pp.22–3.

133　Book of the Fraternity of Our Lady's Assumption

PLATE 32

*c.*1441–1689

Vellum, ff.v + 124; h. 41 cm, w. 28.5 cm

The Worshipful Company of Skinners, on loan to the Guildhall Library, London (MS 31692)

In London, the Worshipful Company of Skinners supported two confraternities, dedicated respectively to Corpus Christi and to the Assumption of the Blessed Virgin Mary. The register of the latter, begun in or around 1441 with a fair copy of earlier records, runs up to the end of the seventeenth century. It includes a miniature of the Assumption (f.41), painted in the late fifteenth century and inserted between the lists of the members enrolled in 1491 and 1492. The Virgin, supported by bands of angels displaying a monogram of the name Maria and the ermine cap used as a badge by the

company, wears a mantle lined with ermine and a regal robe with a deep band of ermine at the hem. The company employed ermine, the richest of furs, as its principal symbol. It is prominently featured in the apparel of two royal patronesses of the confraternity, Elizabeth Wydvile (Woodeville), queen of Edward IV, and Margaret of Anjou, widow of Henry VI, who are portrayed elsewhere in the manuscript. A number of references to gifts of plate record the use of a pattern of powdered ermine tails in their decoration.

The figure kneeling below the image is unidentified, but at his belt a pen case and an inkwell are suggestive of the profession of scribe. The register's lists show that the membership of the confraternity was not confined to members of the company nor to London residents.　　　　　　　　　　　　　　　JMB

PROV. The Worshipful Company of Skinners.

LIT. Meale 1989, pp.212–13; Scott 1996, no. 130.

134　The Richmond Cup

PLATE 53

*c.*1520–50

Silver-gilt, marked only with the maker's mark of a sunflower or daisy; h. 31.7 cm

The Worshipful Company of Armourers and Brasiers of London

The cup, cover, foot and finial are embossed with lobes. Around the edge of the cover runs a cast decorative band of Gothic foliage sprays, and three large roundels, engraved with a rose (perhaps once enamelled). The form of the cup is highly distinctive and resembles the columbine flower. The body and lid of the cup are finely pounced (engraved) with inscriptions asking for prayers for John Richmond and his two wives Amy and Isabel.

The cup was given by John Richmond, to be used at the choosing of each new Master of the Armourers Company and it remains in use, by each master, who pledges his successor with it on election. The decorative band around the lid is almost identical to those on the Warham Bowl and the Eton coconut cup (cat. nos 188, 190). Although it is wholly medieval in style, the cup probably dates from *c.*1520–50, since there are four other pieces known by this maker, the latest of 1556. The same maker's mark appears on a chalice of 1543–4 and three Edwardian communion cups dating between 1552 and 1556.

One of the most beautiful of English Late Gothic cups, this is the only surviving example shaped as a columbine. These flowers were popular as motifs engraved or enamelled on silver, also inspiring goldsmiths to emulate their shape. The earliest known

English reference is in a will of 1436 to 'a standynge cuppe gilt shapp of a columbyn' (Kurath 1956–99, *s.n. columbine*). So-called columbine cups were quite commonly made in fifteenth- and sixteenth-century Germany, where Nuremberg goldsmiths were required to make one as part of their qualification to become a master goldsmith (New York 1986, cat. no. 80), but they differ markedly in appearance from the Richmond Cup.

It seems likely that two different visual traditions were at work, inspired perhaps by the common belief in the medicinal properties of the columbine. Drinking the seed of the plant was believed to be a cure for a sore throat in *c.*1450, and in 1500 the seed drunk with stale ale was credited with curing quinsy (inflammation of the throat) (Leach 1959–62, II, *s.n. columbine*).　　　　　　　　　　　　　　　　MLC

PROV. Presented in 1557 to the Armourers and Brasiers' Company by John Richmond (d. 1559), thrice master.

LIT. Ellis 1892, pp.9–10; London 1951, cat. no. 3; Cooper 1977, p.412; Blair 1983, cat. no. 14.

12 MERCHANTS

JENNY KERMODE

'There was a merchant with a forking beard
And motley dress; high on his horse he sat
Upon his head a Flemish beaver hat
And on his feet daintily buckled boots.'

Thus, at the opening of the fifteenth century, Chaucer described his typical merchant: an ambitious man promoting an image of success through his stylish foreign clothes and lofty mount. This was a man knowledgeable about international affairs, quick-witted, literate, and often in debt (*Canterbury Tales*, Prologue).

Merchants depended for their livelihood on investing in the goods produced by others. They were prominent in urban society, accumulating more wealth and power than most other townsfolk. The number of merchants, their status and disposable income increased as the scale and value of England's overseas trade expanded after 1300, so that by 1547 diverting commercial profits into personal and public display and consumption was commonplace. Through their dominance of town government, and their spending on charity, on civic works and on religious observance, merchants thus played an important part in shaping attitudes and influencing cultural and political life.

The commercial world of English merchants extended throughout Europe, from Iceland to North Africa and the Middle East. They associated with the nobility, farmers, craftsmen, clerks, lawyers and ship masters. Some invested in ships themselves, often as part-owners in cogs and hulks. William Canynges owned a fleet of 11 ships, employing 800 men in mid-century Bristol (Sherborne 1985, p.11). Venturing into long-distance trade required confidence and flexibility, and merchants had to acquire sophisticated skills to rival those of a modern entrepreneur: negotiating prices in several currencies, establishing credit-worthiness, spreading investments to reduce risk in an age of shifting diplomatic alliances and piracy (Hanham 1985, pp.109–223). Success could bring extraordinary wealth from exporting wool and cloth and importing wine, augmented by an increasing

112 Paycocke's House,
Coggeshall, Essex

Wealth drew merchants into regional and national events as financial and political supporters in aristocratic conflicts. During the Wars of the Roses, the mayor and Member of Parliament for Hull, Richard Anson, was killed fighting at the battle of Wakefield. Knighthoods, as royal thanks for all manner of services, were granted to merchants and they began to enjoy other titles, such as 'master' and 'lord' mayor, a reflection of the status that wealth and politics could achieve (Thrupp 1962, p.277). Material comfort was another signal of commercial success and distinguished prosperous merchants from their neighbours. Though all social levels intermingled in medieval towns, merchants tended to cluster in the expensive central streets, close to the markets. The less successful might share a house with other families, but some merchants could afford to build elaborate residences. William Canynges built himself a hall, chapel and impressive stone house in Bristol, overlooking the River Avon (Sherborne 1985, p.15), whereas the Essex clothier Thomas Paycocke later opted for a fashionable, early Tudor timber house on the main street at Coggeshall (plate 112), which was elaborately decorated with his own merchant mark: an ermine tail (Power 1963, p.158). Business was never far away though, and such houses often included a 'counting house' and warehousing within the expanded domestic space.

Merchants' wills document an increasingly comfortable lifestyle surrounded by cushions, feather beds, bolsters, pewterware, silver and gilt dishes, silver and gold spoons, imported tapestries and religious images. Domestic comfort was matched by personal adornment. Gold rings, bracelets and decorated girdles were itemized in wills, alongside bequests of scarlet, violet and blue gowns, often with lamb or fur collars. Merchants displayed a similar attention to public ceremonies, when each category of civic official was dressed in a different colour to reflect their rank: aldermen invariably claiming the most expensive scarlet for themselves (Attreed 1991, p.584).

Apprentice merchants learned through practice. Numeracy was essential at every level of commerce, but literacy was not. Merchants used individual marks, as well as signatures, to seal documents and to identify their goods en route for distant markets. A mark became a visual representation of the individual in many contexts: John Browne put his on the clasps of his Book of Hours and Thomas Paycocke in the decoration of his house. There is evidence, though, to suggest that increasing numbers were becoming literate (Thrupp 1962, pp.156–8). Bequests towards the university education of relatives and friends appeared in wills, together with gifts of books – generally psalters and other works of religious devotion. Elegantly bound books were intrinsically valuable and were prized as much for their social cachet as for their devotional

variety of goods such as straw hats, kettles, silk, damask, spices, liquorice, almonds, fish, soap, paper and combs (Bolton 1980, pp.287–305; Kermode 1998, pp.168–89).

Londoners gradually came to dominate overseas trade during the fifteenth century, though some provincial merchants continued to make substantial fortunes. Wool staplers like John Bolton of York and John Browne of Stamford (cat. nos 139–41), and general merchants like William Canynges of Bristol, were the millionaires of their time. At their most successful, merchants achieved high office as aldermen, mayors and Members of Parliament, mingling with local gentry, churchmen and royal servants, sometimes as members of the same religious guilds. The York Corpus Christi Guild was one such, offering social as well as spiritual advantages to its members (Tillott 1961, p.111). Not all gentlemen accepted those 'comen up lightly', but marriages between gentry and mercantile families were not unusual. Proud merchant aldermen competed equally with minor gentry in wealth, though their political influence was limited outside the towns (Kermode 1998, pp.25–69).

use. Overseas travel cultivated expensive and refined tastes and, although merchants were generally conventional in their religious observance, there were rare instances of merchants commissioning elaborate aids to private contemplation. One such is John Browne of Stamford's Book of Hours, an ornate and expensive Flemish creation, prominently 'signed' with his name and merchant-mark (plate 113). Of different quality was the Bolton Book of Hours, an early fifteenth-century compilation drawn in a crude provincial style (cat. no. 141). It was commissioned for the same combination of purposes – conspicuous devotion and display – probably for use in one of York's prominent merchant families, the Blackburn, Bolton and Ormeshead group (Rees-Jones and Riddy 2002; Kermode 1998, pp.82–3).

With more disposable income than most townsfolk, merchants could choose many ways to invest in their salvation. Parish churches were popular beneficiaries and merchants left embroidered chasubles, cloth of gold and silverware. They commissioned decorative windows and, as in the example of London alderman Robert Tate, an elaborate, imported triptych (cat. no. 136). Munificent gifts of this sort were often 'signed', to keep the donor's name in the prayers of the faithful. Monumental brasses, also intended to achieve perpetual commemoration, were more direct in their statement, asserting the centrality of the nuclear family to lay society (cat. no. 334) (Kermode 1998, pp.123–41).

Salvation was won in other ways. Charitable benevolence in all its forms – feeding and clothing the poor, caring for the sick and infirm – could be accomplished collectively by endowing almshouses. They were often founded by one wealthy merchant anticipating gifts from successive generations, as William Browne did at Stamford (Newton 1966, pp.283–6). Life was uncertain and mercantile dynasties were not common in England. Families were also disrupted by migration. Robert Tate made his fortune after moving to London from Coventry, an increasingly common pattern as the metropolis gained commercial ascendancy (Thrupp 1962, pp.200–4, 225).

Much was changing in fifteenth-century England. Merchants played an active role in this, contributing to the commercial transformation of the country and bringing an important wider perspective, informed by experience of other cultures and driven by their own ambitions.

FURTHER READING

Kermode 1998; Sutton 1994; Thrupp 1962.

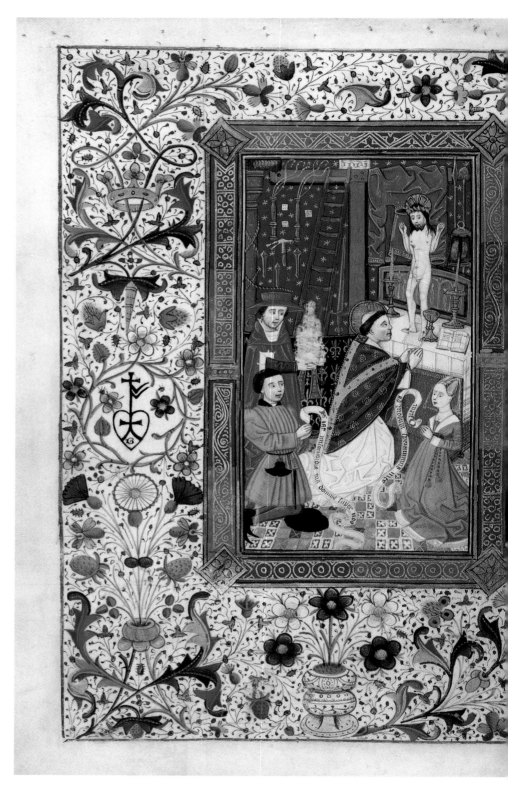

113 John and Agnes Browne kneeling at the Mass of St Gregory, Browne Hours (cat. no. 140)

135

135 Withypool Altarpiece

Antonio da Solario, 1514 (frame is modern)

Centre: canvas on oak panel; h. 77.4 cm, w. 89.5 cm;
shutters: oil on oak, each h. 84 cm, w. 40 cm

Inscr.: on the central panel: *Antonius Desolario, Venetus
1514*; on the reverse of St Catherine: AVE GRACIA PLENA/
DOMINVS TECVM (Hail [Mary] full of Grace, the Lord
be with you); on St John's scroll: ECCE AGNVS DEI
(Behold the Lamb of God); on the reverse of St Ursula:
BENEDICTA TV INTER/MVLIERES ET BENEDICTVS
F[RVTVS] V[ENTRIS] T[VI] (Blessed art thou amongst
women, and blessed is the fruit of thy womb)

Central panel: Bristol Museums and Art Gallery
(K 1394; L77/163); shutters: National Gallery, London
(NG 646 [St Catherine], NG 647 [St Ursula])

The triptych is signed by the Venetian artist Antonio
da Solario, who may have worked in England, since
other works by him in English collections are mentioned in poems by the humanist and antiquarian
John Leland (Bradner 1956; Foister 2002). On the
outer faces of the shutters of the triptych are coats of
arms that identify the merchant Paul Withypool as
the donor figure shown in the centre panel kneeling
before the Virgin and Child and an angel.

The inner faces of the shutters show Sts Catherine
and Ursula. The outer faces are a very early English
example of the decoration with motifs inspired by
ancient Roman decoration called 'antique work':
putti support medallions with St John the Baptist and
St Paul, Withypool's name-saint. St John the Baptist
was the patron saint of the London guild of Merchant
Taylors. The three panels have been set into a modern
frame.

Although the donor's family had West Country
connections, Withypool himself was London-based.
He sat as Member of Parliament for the City of
London in the Reformation Parliament from 1529 to
1536, served on commissions in the 1530s as a trusted
supporter of royal policies and in the 1540s acquired
property at Walthamstow. Withypool had dealings
with Italian merchants, and possibly these contacts
provided Solario's entrée into England.

The relatively small size of the triptych indicates
that it might have been a domestic altarpiece. It has
been suggested that it was painted for a chapel in a
Bristol church, but there is no evidence to support
this, and a location in or near London is more likely.
Withypool's will (PRO PROB 11/31) does not refer to
the triptych.   SF

PROV. Central panel: Duke of St Albans; bought 1937.
Shutters: bought by the National Gallery with the Edmond
Beaucousin Collection, Paris, in 1860.

LIT. Falcke 1936; Davies 1957, pp.492–4.

136 Four panels from a triptych of the Adoration of the Magi

PLATE 56

Southern Netherlands, c.1500

Oil painting on oak; each panel: h. 79 cm, w. 31 cm

All-Hallows-by-the-Tower church, London

From left to right: kneeling king with St Robert and St Ambrose (originally left wing interior and exterior), St Jerome and St Joseph (originally right wing, exterior and interior). St Joseph's panel contains the coat of arms of Sir Robert Tate, an alderman of London, and his wife Margaret Wood of Coventry. The kneeling king in the left panel may refer to Robert Tate, as St Robert acts as the king's servant and patron saint, although his face is mod-elled on that of St Ambrose. The altarpiece was made for the Chapel of St Mary of Barking near the church of All-Hallows-by-the-Tower, the former housing a famous Marian cult image, before which Tate desired burial.

The panels are in the tradition of Rogier van der Weyden and Hans Memling, and can be associated with the style of Jan Provost, who became a citizen of Bruges in 1494. The types of faces can be compared with those of the saints in his altarpiece showing the enthroned Virgin at Hampton Court.   CG

PROV. Disappeared after 1547, reappearing in the 18th century without its central panel; Horace Walpole, Strawberry Hill; after 1945 loaned and then given to All-Hallows by Messrs Tate and Lyle, one of whose partners was descended from Robert Tate.

LIT. Grössinger 1992, cat. no. 33, pp.131–3, figs 111–12.

137 Ordinances of Richard Whittington's Almshouse

1442

Vellum, ff.20; h. 21 cm, w. 14.8 cm

The Worshipful Company of Mercers, London

In his will of 1421, the legendary Dick Whittington, thrice Mayor of London, fabulously wealthy mercer and benefactor of the poor, established an almshouse and college of priests. After his death in 1424, his executors drew up ordinances to govern the administration of the foundation. Originally drafted in Latin, the ordinances were translated into English in or before 1442, when the present manuscript was made.

The ordinances begin with an image of Richard Whittington on his death-bed, surrounded by his executors and the residents of the almshouse. At the back of the group, a physician examines urine in a flask. His executors – John Coventre, John Carpenter and William Grove – are identified with inscriptions. Whittington is shown in the surroundings of a wealthy man, with bolsters supporting his emaciated frame, and handsome striped curtains hanging from the canopy. The imminence of his death is implied by his grey complexion and his fragile, bony form, which contrasts sharply with the rosy complexions of the men at his bedside.

The style of the miniature led Alexander to attribute it to the hand of the London limner William Abell (e.g. cat. no. 20). Though Scott did not retain the ordinances in Abell's oeuvre, there is nevertheless reason to maintain the association between Abell (or, more probably, his atelier) with the ordinances. The angular modelling of the faces, with a clear preference for three-quarter profiles, is characteristic of Abell's work, as are the finely modelled eyes, with white catchlights next to dark, unmodelled irises.   AB

LIT. Imray 1968; Alexander 1972, no. 1; Christianson 1990, pp.59–60.

137

138 Set of Richard Whittington's spoons and case

c.1410

Silver, unmarked, gilt knops; each l. 18.4 cm;
the case cuir bouilli (boiled leather)

The Worshipful Company of Mercers, London

This set of four spoons has hexagonal knops, faceted stems and fig-shaped bowls; engraved on the back of each bowl is a shield with Whittington's arms.

These plain spoons are all that remain of Richard Whittington's rich collections of plate and jewellery. These included a gold rosary with beads enamelled in white and red enamel, a collar of SS, many silver cups, bowls and at least three different seals. One of these showed a classical bust, a design more typical of Italian Renaissance than of medieval English taste, and quite exceptional among merchants' seals of this date. Another included a variation of Whittington's arms just as on the spoons. Both have the Whittington arms without those of his wife Alice Fitzwaryn (d. before 1414), which suggests that she may have been dead by the time they were made. The shape of the armorial shields on the spoons indicates a date of *c*.1410.

As in this example, cases for plate and jewellery were generally made of a durable, specially heated leather, sometimes decorated with the owner's arms, initials or other motifs. MLC

PROV. Whittington College (?) (mentioned in MS inventories, 1511, 1582); Mercers' Company by 1759 or earlier.

LIT. London 1951, cat. no. 1; How 1952–7, I, pp.78–80; Alexander and Binski 1987, cat. no. 216 (with earlier lit.).

139 Brass rubbing of John and Agnes Browne

c.1476

l. of figures 91 cm; inscription h. 17 cm, w. 73 cm

Inscr. in *textura*: *Te p*[re]*cor O* [Christe] *matris q*[ue] *p*[at]*ris miserere; No*[n] *sim deiectus uos om*[n]*es claudito celis./ Est m*[ih]*i nome*[n] *idem q*[ue] *p*[at]*ri labor vn*[us] *vt*[ri]*q*[ue]*; Milleno C quat*[er] *sexageno simul xv/ Vita*[m] *mutaui Februar*[ii] *me*[n]*sis q*[ue] *trideno; Huc ades o*

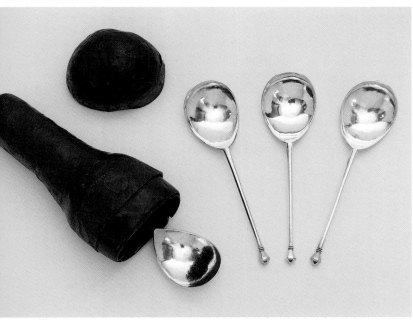

138

co[n]*iunx Agnes m*[ihi] *cara fuisti. Du*[m] *mu*[n]*do vixi, post me sis sponsa q*[ue] [Christi]*; Anno milleno C quat*[er] [blank]/ *Mensis* [blank]*; Mundu*[m] *liquisti celestia regna petisti.* (I beseech thee O Christ have mercy on my mother and father. May I not be cast down from heaven in which you are all included. My name is the same as my father's and our occupation the same. I went to another life in 1475 on the thirteenth of February; Come to this place, O Agnes my wife, you were dear to me while I lived in this life. After me may you be a bride of Christ. In the year 14 [blank] in the month of [blank] you passed away from this world and sought the heavenly realms.)

Derrick Chivers, Esq. (original in All Saints' church, Stamford, Lincolnshire)

John Browne the Younger, draper of Stamford, for whom the Widener Hours (cat. no. 140) was made, is shown wearing an alderman's mantle over a fur-lined gown, with a large metal-framed purse suspended from his belt (see also cat. no. 204). His wife Agnes is depicted as a widow, wearing veil, barbe and mantle. The brass is modelled on that of John Browne the Elder (d. 1442), also a draper and merchant of the Staple of Calais, in the same church. John Browne the Younger's brother William was the founder of Browne's Hospital, Stamford. The Browne family were benefactors of All Saints' church.

The brass is an example of the 'Sub-B' group of brasses, probably produced by craftsmen associated with the workshop formerly headed by the London marbler John Essex (d. 1465). Their work has been characterized as 'a strange mixture of new influences and sheer incompetence' (Emmerson 1978b, p.323). NR

LIT. Emmerson 1978b, p.323, pl. III.

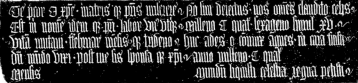

139

140 The Hours of John Browne

PLATE 113

Southern Netherlands (Bruges), 1460s

Vellum, ff.153; h. 23 cm, w. 17 cm

Free Library of Philadelphia (Widener MS 3)

Between the 1390s and the beginning of the sixteenth century a significant proportion of the Sarum Books of Hours in use in England were produced in ateliers in the Low Countries. Despite widespread destruction during the Reformation, more than 250 of these imports have survived. Flemish miniaturists sometimes executed special commissions for English clients; the Hours of John Donne of Kidwelly (cat. no. 215) is an example. But for the most part they are stock items, intended for speculative sale, with standardized contents, usually illustrated by full-page inserted miniatures, which enabled a book to be assembled more quickly.

This manuscript, with its gaudy miniatures by two mediocre Bruges miniaturists of the 1460s, is a typical imported Book of Hours. Where the present book is exceptional is in the survival in good condition of its original blind-stamped calf binding by the Bruges binder Anthonis van Gavere (*fl.* 1458–d. 1505). This has silver-gilt clasps with miniatures of the Virgin and Child and St Veronica set under crystal, and is engraved on the reverse with the name and merchant's mark of John Browne. He is depicted with his wife in a prefatory miniature, kneeling before a representation of the Mass of St Gregory at which Christ appeared miraculously. In the border is John Browne's merchant's mark. Facing this is a prayer, added in England, with an attached indulgence, erased at the Reformation, as was St Gregory's tiara. The initial *memoriae* of saints are standard but for the inclusion of St Agnes, and the calendar includes Lincoln diocesan feasts. This confirms that the book was personalized for John Browne the Younger of Stamford (d. 1476), who is buried with his wife Agnes in All Saints, Stamford (cat. no. 139).   NR

PROV. John Browne the Younger (d. 1476); given by Margaret, Lady Ayloffe to John Topham (1746–1803), 1782; Sir Henry St John Mildmay of Dogmersfield, Hampshire; Sotheby's, London, 18 April 1907; Quaritch, London, 1907; P. A. B. Widener; Joseph E. Widener, 1915; given to the Free Library of Philadelphia, 1944.

LIT. Philadelphia 2001, cat. no. 33; Rogers 2002, pp.1167, 1173, 1177, 1178.

141 The Bolton Hours

PLATE 33

1410–20

Vellum, ff.210; h. 15 cm, w. 11 cm

York Minster Library (MS Add. 2)

Several English political victims were venerated unofficially as saints. Following his irregular execution in a field outside York on 8 June 1405, after his involvement in the failed Percy Rebellion, Richard Scrope, Archbishop of York, attracted devotees. At first efforts were made by Henry IV to impede pilgrims to his tomb, but as early as the second decade of the fifteenth century a window depicting him as a saint was installed in York Minster, and eventually devotion to 'St Richard' became a staple element of Yorkshire piety (McKenna 1970). There was an element of rivalry with Canterbury; one prayer in this Book of Hours refers to him as co-equal to the most glorious martyr Thomas. The miniature on display is one of two in the book depicting Richard Scrope. In the other he is shown holding a windmill. This is one of a remarkably extensive series (for a Book of Hours) of 47 full-page miniatures, mostly of saints, including Sitha, Peter Martyr, Bridget and possibly John of Bridlington (f.185).

The manuscript was made for the woman depicted on ff.40v, 100v and 123v, evidently connected with the Bolton family of York. On f.33 she is shown with her family adoring the Trinity. It has recently been proposed that this is Margaret Blackburn, the mother of Alice Bolton (d. 1472), into whose family the book passed (Cullum and Goldberg 2000). Alice's husband, John Bolton (d. 1445), was an eminent mercer and served as Sheriff of York in 1419 and 1420, as Member of Parliament in 1419–20 and as the city's Lord Mayor in 1431.

The provision of books for the liturgical use of York was one of the factors which ensured that the book trade flourished in York. The Bolton Hours, like most of the products of the York illuminators, is unsophisticated and stylistically conservative. The two closely related artists work in a mode derived from London miniaturists of the 1390s. A date of 1410–20 is suggested by costume details.   NR

PROV. Bolton family, York; lent by Thomas Fairfax of London to Dr George Harbin, 1715; Sotheby's, London, 12 April 1927; Quaritch, London, 1931; bought by the Dean and Chapter of York, 1943.

LIT. Ker and Piper 1992, pp.786–91; Friedman 1995a, pp.xv, xxi, 9, 17–18, 85–6 and *passim*, ills 40, 41, 45; Scott 1996, no. 33, ills 138–41, 147; Osborne 2000; Rees-Jones and Riddy 2002.

142

142 Binding for law book of Thomas Segden

The Scales binder, *c*.1457

h. 28.5 cm, w. 21 cm, d. 8 cm

Guildhall Library, London (MS 208)

The binding covers a copy of the *Abbreviationes placitorum, etc.* (in French), English MS, written by J. Luke for Thomas Segden of Furnival's Inn, 1457. Brown calf tooled in blind with lines and small hand tools; on the lower cover, the name 'T Segden' has been incised.

The Inns of Court, as well as parliament, provided good custom for the bookbinders. Law books, books of statutes, legally binding deeds and other legal documents often occur in bindings of note. The earliest binder in England to have revived the craft of blind tooling on leather in the mid-fifteenth century, the Scales binder, worked for the lawyers. He was active in London from the 1450s until after 1481. He used 36 decorative tools, from one of which – a pair of scales – he gets his name; 20 bindings from his shop are known, 13 dating from before 1465 and seven between 1466 (or later) and 1481. The most characteristic feature of his work is that he practised the technique of cutting the leather with a knife to effect part of the design, a habit otherwise unknown in England, but much used (especially during the fifteenth century) in German-speaking countries.   MF

PROV. Thomas Segden of Furnival's Inn; C. Griffith, 1845; Henry Alworth Merewether; Guildhall, 25 July 1846.

LIT. Barker 1972, pp.365–6, no. 13, pl. VII; Foot 1989, p.68; Nixon and Foot, 1992, pp.8–9; Foot 1993b, pp.121–2.

143 Epistle Lectionary*

*c.*1508

Vellum, ff.30; h. 30.5 cm, w. 20 cm

British Library, London (Royal MS 2 B. XII)

One of a pair of complementary volumes containing the Epistle and Gospel readings for use at Mass on the most important festivals throughout the liturgical year. They were presented to the London city church of St Mary Aldermanbury in 1508 by Stephen Jenyns and his wife Margaret during his term of office as Lord Mayor. Both manuscripts retain their original bindings of heavy oak boards, the upper covers recessed to contain panels of decorative metalwork, which were no doubt removed at the Reformation. The marginal ornament of the illuminated pages is typical of English work of the period, but the miniatures – of which the image of St John the Baptist (f.19v) is representative – are in the style associated with a group of Dutch book painters known as the Masters of the Dark Eyes (Utrecht 1989, pp.285ff.), at least one of whom seems to have settled in London in about 1500. The same style appears in manuscripts associated with Lady Margaret Beaufort (cat. nos 111, 114).

Stephen Jenyns had been Master of the Merchant Taylors' Company in 1489–90 and was the first of their number to become Lord Mayor. His term of office coincided with the death of Henry VII and he was knighted at the coronation of Henry VIII.   JMB

PROV. Church of St Mary Aldermanbury, 1508; Royal Library; passed to British Museum in 1757.

LIT. Wordsworth and Littlehales 1904, pp.195–6 and pl.; Warner and Gilson 1921, I, pp.48–9.

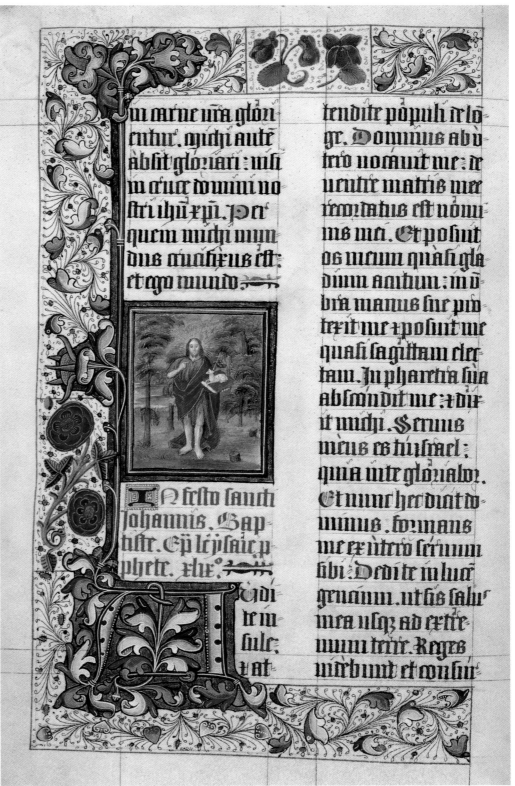

143

13 DOMESTIC SPACE: DAILY LIVING IN THE HOME

GEOFF EGAN

While much in the late medieval home would be familiar to modern visitors, if transported back in time they would soon find themselves running foul of a series of social conventions that were second nature to the inhabitants. These unwritten social rules, which determined who had access to particular rooms and areas in them, and what they were able to do there, might be compared to conventions of precedence and other matters widespread in offices today.

Most of the housing stock at any one time in medieval England was not new, and while some, particularly at the upper end of the social scale, conformed to what can now be regarded as ideals for their period, others were the eccentric results of lack of money, available space or of design far removed from any mainstream. Within this framework the diverse practicalities of domestic life went on in towns and the countryside, in the palaces of the court circle, the houses of the gentry and successful merchants, and in the urban slum or peasant hovel. Surviving buildings and the fixtures, furnishings and other objects used in them (kept for generations or recovered during archaeological excavations), along with contemporary illustrations and documentary evidence such as inventories listing significant chattels, illuminate the intimate lifestyles of those to whom these were familiar homes.

The essentials were a main room – the hall – with the table where the head of the house habitually ate close to the principal fireplace, all of which was normally divided from service areas by a passage containing the main entrance/exit door of the property. The messy practicalities of food preparation in the kitchen area were thus (like the lavatory today) kept as remote as possible from the rituals of consumption. This form of house is exemplified by Barley Hall in York, a building now restored and furnished to its state in 1482 (Grenville 1997, p.89) and by Bayleaf farmhouse (Zeuner 1990; the building is reconstructed to its state in c.1540 at the Weald and Downland Open Air Museum,

114 Great Hall, Hampton Court Palace (cat. no. 4)

Singleton, West Sussex). This basic bipartite division in plan was reflected in many smaller rural longhouses, where the passage marked off a dairy and livestock shelter from the owners' living quarters. The pattern is apparent from excavated evidence at the remote Yorkshire-wolds village of Wharram Percy (Beresford and Hurst 1990) and in a cottage from Hangleton in Sussex (Clarke 1984, pp.38–43; this building is also reconstructed at Singleton).

The most elaborate homes, most notably royal palaces, had a huge series of rooms dedicated to a variety of specific purposes, both highly ceremonial (like the Great Hall for the reception and entertainment of foreign and other dignitaries, plate 114) and mundane (like a coal store). The most fully developed domestic scheme of all in this period was arguably Henry VIII's Hampton Court, where as well as a tennis court, there were separate, corresponding sets of private apartments in which the king and queen slept and were dressed; there were similar parallel arrangements at Whitehall Palace (Thurley 1993 and 1999, pp.4–64). The fashions in lifestyle set in these sumptuous dwellings were of course widely emulated.

The scene of Richard Whittington's death-bed, with the successful plutocrat's extensive retinue in attendance (cat. no. 137) along with his doctor, emphasizes the crucial role in society of patronage by the rich, as well as countering today's notions of dying as a very private, family affair. The unbridgeable social distance that separated the head of an aristocratic house and his immediate retinue from a humble tenant or a homeless beggar seeking alms at the door was maintained with the help of a series of servants or guards. The closer one was in rank to the head of the household, the further through successive doorways and rooms one might progress, before reaching the socially acceptable limit (Schofield 1994a, pp.61–93, and 1994b). Locks for doors (and also chests and cupboards) are among the most complex everyday objects to have come down to us from the Middle Ages, though most actually have very simple – and easily picked – mechanisms inside elaborate cases that were designed to look as robust and secure as possible (Egan 1998). Seating position and precedence at the dining table or tables, including exactly who served whom, was also strictly arranged according to the social hierarchy.

Almshouses, a particularly fashionable form of charity in the fifteenth century, brought a limited number of selected poor deemed worthy of sustained support into sheltered accommodation, in return for prayers for the souls of the benefactors (for whom these accumulating deposits of merit would provide an essential character reference at the Final Judgement). At Ewelme in Oxford, founded in the mid-fifteenth century, 13 poor men each had a personal chamber around a quadrangle, which also included dwellings for two priests, a kitchen, common dining hall and a covered passage leading directly into the adjoining church, where a prescribed routine of lengthy prayer was undertaken daily (Goodall 2001). This privileged access to a far higher standard of living than could otherwise be contemplated brought a small number of ordinary folk not into their benefactor's home but into a highly structured, relatively modest and completely separated reflection of it, furnished with some essential comforts.

The introduction in the late fifteenth century of the continental invention of large stoves to heat one or more core rooms in the winter was one manifestation of a new appreciation of European Renaissance culture and comforts (Gaimster 1988). This imported fashion has left a readily recognizable legacy at the sites of several gentry houses in London and the south-east, in the form of the highly decorated glazed tiles that helped radiate the heat. The earliest are in the Gothic tradition, but most have Renaissance motifs or patriotic royal arms along with the monarch's initials.

Furniture was far more sparse than is customary today. A table with enough chairs or benches to cater for the main members of the household and a chest to keep stored goods clean (or less commonly a cupboard, perhaps providing for display) in the hall were adequate for comfortable living, perhaps supplemented by a stool and bench for work and accounting in a different chamber (cat. no. 178). An assemblage of metal and ceramic food-preparation equipment that survived a conflagration of domestic dwellings in Norwich in 1507 (Margeson and Goodall 1993, pp.86–94, 118–19) provides a vivid illustration of everyday urban provision to supplement a few aristocratic survivals and inventory references. A wider variety of artefacts, mainly of ordinary domestic fixtures, fittings and tablewares excavated in London, has been analysed, showing trends in consumption of a variety of domestic goods (Egan 1998 and forthcoming). Base-metal wares can now more readily be compared with the upper-class items discussed in the essay by Marian Campbell in this volume. Candle holders of various everyday materials seem to cater for marginally larger candles during the late medieval period, presumably as this basic amenity became more affordable throughout society. Mass-produced religious figurines of pipeclay and occasionally pewter for the ordinary home were becoming popular in the generations just before the Reformation, following the devotional paintings and sculptures in the dwellings of the rich (cat. no. 221).

Business and light manufacturing were habitually undertaken within the home. Commercial interests were provided for in affluent urban properties by a solar – an inner chamber set aside for the reception of customers or accountancy and for the storage of expensive stock. A shop on the street frontage is evident in many records (cat. no. 118), and one with a folding wooden counter survives at Lavenham in Suffolk. Despite all the conventions of room use, children would probably have managed to get almost everywhere. Their presence in houses, playing in familiar ways, is obliquely suggested by rare finds of toys – knights, dolls and miniature vessels of pewter (Egan 1996 and cat. nos 176–7). Although there are obvious differences with the passing of half a millennium, the discernible continuities between many aspects of late medieval domestic spatial usage and today's are remarkably striking.

FURTHER READING

Egan 1998; Grenville 1997.

144

144 Ockwells Manor House, Berkshire

Probably later 1440s

The main front of Ockwells faced on to a court whose other buildings, now largely gone, may have offset somewhat the present impression of carefully contrived near-symmetry. Normal usage would have been to put the kitchen at the low end of the hall, on the left, but Ockwells has in this position a high-status first-floor chamber, which almost exactly mirrors the great chamber in the conventional place next to the dais end of the hall. This sort of composition is foreshadowed in earlier aristocratic residences (e.g. Ludlow Castle, late thirteenth century) and occasionally occurs later (e.g. Great Chalfield Manor, Wiltshire, c.1470). Directly behind the hall lies a small court surrounded on three sides by a two-storey cloister, whose lower level links the kitchen to the hall and whose upper level connects the first-floor chambers at opposite ends of the hall. This neat piece of integrated planning is not known to have had any exact counterpart elsewhere. In the late nineteenth century Ockwells underwent a careful restoration, which entailed adding (or perhaps re-creating on the basis of original remains) the oriel over the porch and the two-storey bay windows to the chamber flanking the hall.

The builder of Ockwells was the courtier John Norreys, whose career peaked in the mid and late 1440s. His royal service almost certainly explains the exceptional refinement of the architecture and decoration of his house. During the early 1440s one of Henry VI's favourite residences, Sheen in Surrey, was acquiring new chambers that resembled the Ockwells hall in being timber-framed and lit by low and long clearstories designed to facilitate the hanging of tapestry; and the references in the Sheen building accounts to windows glazed by the king's glazier John Prudde read almost like descriptions of the celebrated armorial glass in Norreys's hall. Among other features that may reflect influence from buildings erected in the 1440s for the Suffolk affinity then dominant at court are the two-storey cloister (cf. Herstmonceux Castle, cat. no. 51) and the brick nogging and richly traceried bargeboards (cf. God's House at Ewelme, Oxfordshire).   CW

LIT. Kerry 1861, pp.116–20; Hussey 1924.

145

145 South Wingfield Manor, Derbyshire

1439–c.1450

Set magnificently on a hill, the rambling outline of South Wingfield Manor, busy with chimneys, battlements and a great tower, is indistinguishable from that of many late medieval castles. This great residence was erected by Ralph, Lord Cromwell – who also built at Tattershall Castle (cat. no. 50) – when he gained possession of the property in 1439. Slighted in 1646 after two sieges, the ruined buildings nevertheless constitute an important example of grand fifteenth-century domestic architecture.

Wingfield is planned around two rectangular courts, divided by a cross-range. At the western extreme of the cross-range is the great tower. Visitors entered the residence through the outer or 'base' court – comprising ancillary buildings – and passed through a gatehouse in the cross-range to reach the main domestic buildings. Facing them across the inner court as they came in was the principal façade of the house, now badly damaged.

Central to this façade was the two-storey porch, which still survives, ornamented with crenellations, sculpture and coats of arms. To its right extends the great hall. Except for its oriel window – with tracery distinctive of 1440s' court-connected design – the inner face of the hall is now lost. Opening off the hall and closing the inner court to the right were the principal withdrawing apartments. These appear to have been arranged within a massive tower-like structure, now completely destroyed. The kitchen, buttery and pantry occupy the ground level of the range to the left of the porch. Above these are a second series of

withdrawing chambers on first-floor level, clearly identified by elaborately traceried windows.

The double courtyard arrangement of Wingfield and the essential disposition of its elements have a long pedigree in English domestic design. What is remarkable about this building is its sheer scale and its rapid construction.   JG

LIT. Blore 1793; Emery and Binney 1982; Emery 1985.

146 Sudeley Castle, Gloucestershire, great chamber

c.1473–8 or c.1485–95

Sudeley Castle – in reality not a castle, but a grandly castellated manor house – was rebuilt in the 1440s for one of Henry VI's leading courtiers, Ralph Boteler. It had two courtyards, the outer with a hall facing the entrance gate, the inner with chambers ranged around two of its sides. After Boteler's death in 1473, Sudely passed to Edward IV, who gave it to his brother Richard, Duke of Gloucester, the future Richard III. In 1478 Gloucester surrendered it to the king, but Henry VII granted it to his uncle Jasper Tudor. The Sudeley great chamber is usually credited to Gloucester, but there must be a possibility that Tudor was the builder. It has often been called a hall, but that identification is unsatisfactory, since the much lower ground-floor room beneath it was clearly for high-status occupation and must have been a parlour, a private living room for the owner's personal use. Parlours were routinely placed below great chambers and could be used for taking meals when there was no occasion for the ceremonial that went with dining and supping in the great chamber.

In its original state, the Sudeley great chamber would have been an extremely impressive and elegant room. It combines enormous windows with masonry details that bespeak great refinement and luxury. Particularly sophisticated are the miniature fan vaults in

146

the bay window, the stone 'false ceilings' concealing the structural arches over the parlour windows, and the contriving of a window above the great chamber fireplace, where one anticipates that the presence of flues would dictate that the wall be solid. CW

LIT. Kingsley 1989, pp.183–6.

147 Thornbury Castle, Gloucestershire, lodgings range

c.1511–21

As an inscription on the gatehouse to the inner court proclaims, Edward Stafford, 3rd Duke of Buckingham, began to rebuild Thornbury in 1511. Work was halted by financial problems caused by the duke's

147

enormous outlay on royal festivities in 1519 and 1520, and had not been resumed in 1521 when Buckingham was summoned to London by Henry VIII, tried for treason and executed.

Buckingham had aroused the king's mistrust on account of several ill-judged actions, including over-emphasizing his own royal descent. His situation would not have been helped if, as seems likely, Henry was aware that the lodgings range at Thornbury bore a strong resemblance to the royal lodgings at Richmond, his father's finest new residence and still in 1521 the most impressive house in the possession of the Crown (see ill.). Perhaps the most blatant borrowing from Richmond was the series of fantastic and varied bay windows on the south side (see also cat. no. 3), but the no less extraordinary brick chimney-stacks will have been recognized as deriving from the same source, for Richmond had more elaborate chimneys, and more of them, than any earlier building. The south front looked on to a garden surrounded on the other three sides by a two-storey timber-framed gallery – all just as at Richmond. Richmond was probably also the source for the placing of the lodgings with the taller first-floor rooms of the duke over the duchess's lower-ceilinged ground-floor rooms. Such planning had a long history in French royal residences and was intended to signify the higher standing of the king vis-à-vis the queen. The only part of Thornbury Castle to deploy castle imagery is the heavily towered range between the inner and outer courts. This, like all Buckingham's work at Thornbury except the lodgings range, remains incomplete. CW

LIT. Hawkyard 1978; Kingsley 1989, pp.186–9; Thurley 1993, pp.42–3.

Richmond Palace from the west,
Antonis van Wyngaerde, mid 16th-century
(Ashmolean Museum, Oxford) (see cat. no. 147)

147

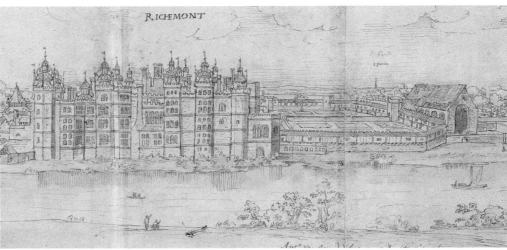

148 The Vyne, Hampshire, long gallery

1526–8

Galleries connecting first-floor spaces larger and more important than themselves had a very long medieval history, but it was apparently only in late fourteenth-century France that such structures began to be valued on account of the opportunities they gave for admiring gardens, and strolling, especially in bad weather. In early Tudor England galleries proliferated, fairly certainly under the influence of Henry VII's rebuilding of Richmond Palace from 1498, where they surrounded gardens, but also gave access to a newly founded Observant Franciscan friary (see cat. no. 147). At The Vyne the gallery probably also fulfilled a link-ing role, that of connecting the king's and queen's lodgings. Like the lodgings, the gallery belonged to a rebuilding undertaken after 1526 when The Vyne's owner William Sandys became Henry VIII's Lord Chamberlain.

The lost ceiling of the gallery will doubtless have been a 'fretwork' of wooden ribs similar to those still surviving at Hampton Court and in Sandys's chapel in The Vyne. The main decoration has always been linenfold panelling, which contemporary sources indicate was thought of as an alternative to tapestry, and indeed an inventory of The Vyne taken in 1541 reveals that the gallery was sparsely furnished and contained neither tapestry nor pictures. Linenfold was a Netherlandish invention, and by the late fif-teenth century it was being imported into England by the boatload. Sandys's custom-made panelling bears his own badges as well as those of the king and queen, Cardinal Wolsey and various relations and associates. Integral to the same campaign of work is an overdoor carved with the royal arms flanked by putti, the whole closely based on the end panels of Pietro Torrigiano's tomb of Henry VII in Westmin-ster Abbey (cat. no. 29). CW

LIT. Howard 2000, pp.34–5, 44–7; Howard and Wilson 2003.

149 Hengrave Hall, Suffolk

PLATE 6

1525–38

Hengrave Hall was built between 1525 and 1538 by Thomas Kytson, a successful London merchant. As originally constructed, the house was encircled by a moat and approached through an outer court of ser-vice buildings. The body of the house, which still sur-vives largely intact, is arranged around a courtyard and comprises a great hall and three residential ranges. An enclosed, two-storey cloister runs around three faces of the courtyard.

Several contracts for the construction of Hengrave survive and these identify all the principal craftsmen involved in the project. The house is built in a combi-nation of locally made grey bricks and cut stone. Its outline is crowned with crenellations, gables, domes and chimneys, and well reflects the medieval love for fantastical complexity. The chimneys are constructed in red brick to add colour to the design.

148

A series of towers punctuates the exterior walls of the court, but these were arranged regularly only on the main façade. Before it was remodelled in 1775, this was symmetrically designed, the present right half of the building almost mirroring that on the left. At the centre of the façade is the great gatehouse with its magnificent tripartite oriel window. The detailing of this is exceptionally rich and unusual. It combines miniature architectural, heraldic and Renaissance decoration and an inscription.

In both plan and detail, Hengrave is closely comparable to Thornbury Castle (cat. no. 147). So close, it should be observed, that to distinguish between one as a 'castle' and the other as a 'hall' on architectural terms alone would be difficult. Given this similarity, it must be significant that Kytson actually bought Hengrave from the Duke of Buckingham, the builder of Thornbury. But this connection should not obscure the fact that both Thornbury and Hengrave are themselves deeply indebted to the 1440s designs of Eton and Herstmonceux Castle (cat. nos 23, 51). JG

LIT. Gage 1822; Tipping 1926.

150 Wenlock Priory, Shropshire, prior's lodging

Probably *c*.1500

Like the heads of many other late medieval religious houses, the priors of Wenlock sought to discharge their duty of hospitality by rebuilding their own house to a high standard – high enough indeed to ensure its survival as a private house after the Dissolution. The most likely moment for the replacement of the earlier lodging on the site was after 1494, when the priory secured its independence from the Cluniac order. Dendrochronological examination of the roof timbers has apparently indicated a date of *c*.1430, an historically and stylistically improbable dating for the masonry.

Perhaps more completely than any other piece of late medieval domestic architecture, the west front of the Wenlock prior's lodging appropriates the monumentality of ecclesiastical Perpendicular. In fact the concept of the all-embracing tracery grid could be realized here only because the spaces immediately behind the front are two corridors giving access to all

Much Wenlock prior's lodging, west front, from Parker and Turner 1859, part 1, plate opp. p.145 (see cat. no. 150)

ground- and first-floor rooms. From at least the thirteenth century, royal and other major residences had had two-storey corridors enabling long sequences of chambers to be accessed and serviced efficiently, but because these structures were almost invariably timber-built, hardly any have survived. Near the centre of the prior's lodgings, the first-floor hall is linked to the kitchen underneath by one of the rare English late medieval examples of a double-spiral stair. Its value here would have been as a means of separating servants bringing food upstairs from those descending to the kitchen. CW

LIT. Parker 1859, pp.366–71; Cranage 1922; Emery 2000, pp.589–94.

151 Screen panels

Early 16th century

Oak; h. 187 cm, w. 97.5 cm, d. 6.2 cm

**Victoria and Albert Museum, London
(1974 and 1974A–1900)**

Two portions of panelling, carved in pierced work, with three fields of flamboyant tracery carved on both sides, the framework moulded.

Sutton Place, Guildford (Surrey), from where these panels are supposed to have come, was built in the mid-1520s by Sir Richard Weston (Harrison 1888). He was a faithful officer of Henry VIII, and is distinguished by having retained the king's affections throughout his reign. In 1518 he was appointed as one of the embassy sent to France, and in 1520 he took part at the meeting with Francis I, known as the Field of Cloth of Gold. In 1523 he served in the French War under the Duke of Suffolk. Two years later he was made treasurer of the town and marches of Calais. Weston's eclectic continental taste is evident in the architecture of his house.

From the style of these panels, it is clear that they were either imported or made by a denizened foreign craftsman. The tracery is French, rather than Flemish, and can be seen in muted form on French chests in England (Tracy 2001, pls 122–3). Adapted to a different medium, it recalls the flickering incandescence of the northern French Flamboyant style, as typified by the early sixteenth-century central portion of the west front of Rouen Cathedral.   CT

PROV. Purchased in 1900.

LIT. Tracy 1988, cat. no. 286.

152 Heraldic glass from Fawsley Hall, Northamptonshire

c.1537–42

Stained and painted glass; shield of Sir Edmund Knightley: h. 80 cm, w. 50.1 cm; shield of De Vere impaling De Quincy: diam. 45 cm

The Burrell Collection, Glasgow Museums (45/332, 330)

The arms of Sir Edmund Knightley (d. 1542) impaling De Vere, both with numerous quarterings; elaborate mantling, buck's head crest and supporters (a); the shield of De Vere impaling De Quincy is set within a circular wreath border (b).

These two shields form part of an extensive series originally in the great hall of Fawsley, glazed (and probably built) by Sir Edmund Knightley; until the early twentieth century the large achievement occupied the apex of the oriel window, with the second shield just below it (see ill.). These shields show how the later medieval gentry and nobility used the more public areas of their houses to display their lineage and connections, a practice unaffected by the Reformation. The Fawsley series stressed not only Sir Edmund Knightley's own ancestry, but also the more aristocratic pedigree of his wife Ursula, sister and co-heiress of John de Vere, 14th Earl of Oxford. The second shield represents the marriage of Hugh, 4th Earl of Oxford (d. *c.*1263) and Hawise, daughter of Saher de Quincy, 1st Earl of Winchester. Heraldic glass of this quality, detail and complexity demanded the highest skills of glass-painters.   RM

PROV. Acquired 1950.

LIT. Wells 1962, nos 122, 117; Marks 1998a, pp.lxxiii, 64–71.

152a

152b

Interior of the great hall with
heraldic glass *in situ*, Fawsley
Hall, Northamptonshire
(see cat. no. 152)

153

153 Tapestry, *The Boar and Bear Hunt*

Southern Netherlands, *c*.1425–30

Wool warp and weft; h. 406.5 cm, w. 1021.1 cm

Victoria and Albert Museum, London (T.204–1957)

The *Boar and Bear Hunt* tapestry is one of four large hunting tapestries in the V&A, which are of similar dates and styles but not from the same original set. The tapestry retains elements of the International Gothic style in its predominantly red and blue tones, the limpid forms of the figures and details of the costumes.

South Netherlandish tapestries with hunting scenes were much favoured throughout the fifteenth century, as recorded in contemporary inventories. Hunting was pursued with passion by rulers and the nobility, and Henry VIII is known to have owned more than 200 tapestries with scenes of hunting and hawking. The hunting scenes, based on contemporary treatises on the subject, are accurately portrayed, but the nobles wear the exotic fashions of the Burgundian courts, totally inappropriate for the chase.

Tapestries were immensely important in making large and draughty rooms more habitable and often entirely covered the walls, abutting each other to form a 'tapestry chamber'. This had the twofold effect of providing insulation and an unbroken series of colourful and powerful images with which the household and visitors could identify.

It has been suggested that the tapestry (with the other three mentioned above) belonged to George Talbot, 6th Earl of Shrewsbury. He was Elizabeth, Countess of Shrewsbury's fourth husband and may have given them to her to furnish Hardwick Hall, but there is no documentary evidence of this. Related pieces in the Burrell Collection in Glasgow show part of a *Boar Hunt* and a small fragment of a *Bear Hunt*.   LW

PROV. Hardwick Hall, Derbyshire; acquired in 1957.

LIT. Wingfield Digby 1971; Wingfield Digby 1980, cat. no. 3, pp.12–14, pls 2A, 4–5; Woolley 2002.

154 Tapestry with the arms and badges of Lord Dynham

PLATE 50

Southern Netherlands, 1488–1501

Wool warp and wefts, with a few silk wefts; h. 386 cm, w. 368 cm

The Metropolitan Museum of Art, The Cloisters Collection, New York (60.127.1)

The heraldic motifs on a millefleurs background relate to the life of John, Lord Dynham. He had a distinguished career, chiefly as naval commander in the Channel and later as Captain of Calais.

The principal badge has a shield with the arms of the Dynhams of Devonshire encircled by the emblem of the Order of the Garter (with the motto '*honi soit qui mal y pense*'), to which John Dynham was elevated in 1487 or 1488. Two other coats of arms with emblems of the Order of the Garter are seen above with 11 examples of Dynham's personal badge, showing the topcastle of a warship, broken at the mast, and a pennant with

155 The Buxton Achievement

*c.*1470

Glue size on linen cloth; h. 142 cm, w. 112 cm

Inscr.: *dies* [day] *nox* [night] *vita* [life] *laetetur homo in bonis diebus* [let a man rejoice in good times] *mors* [death] *recordetur dies tenebrarum* [let the day of darkness be remembered] *Clotho vitae stamen/Lachesis fortunam/Atropos finem dat* (Clotho gives the thread of life, Lachesis the fortune, Atropos the end)

Norfolk Museums Service (Strangers' Hall, Norwich) (143.929)

This is a rare surviving example of a type of inexpensive painting or wall-hanging frequently mentioned in fifteenth- and sixteenth-century domestic English inventories, and also common in northern Europe at this period. Such paintings were not made to last, and the condition of the Buxton picture, which is faded and has lost some of its painted surface, reflects this.

The secular, heraldic subject matter of the painting is also a rare survival. At the top in the centre is the half-length image of a member of the Buxton family, traditionally identified as Peter de Buckton, Constable of Bordeaux under Richard II. However, the coat

155

the cross of St George. Part of the tapestry below the stags' hooves is missing. This would have included a repeat of the devices seen above the main coat of arms.

Millefleurs tapestries with heraldic patterns, woven in the southern Netherlands, were fashionable in the second half of the fifteenth and early sixteenth centuries. A similar tapestry with the royal arms is in Haddon Hall (Derbyshire) and a *Verdure* of 1466 in Berne shows the armorial devices of Philip the Good (Rapp-Buri and Stucky-Schürer 2001, pp.115–43).

Tapestry hangings were acquired in large numbers by rich and powerful individuals and families to add colour, decoration and comfort to their rooms. They could also, as in this example, make a conspicuous display of the owner's social position and achievements. It is almost certain that this hanging belonged with others to make up a series of furnishings for a grand room. LW

PROV. Appleby Castle, Westmorland; Spanish Art Gallery, London, before 1929; Collection of Mr and Mrs Myron C. Taylor, New York; acquired by the Metropolitan Museum of Art at Parke Bernet sale, New York, 11–12 November 1960, lot 1019.

LIT. Young 1961–2; Cavallo 1993, cat. no. 16, pp.273–7 (with earlier lit.); Delmarcel 1999, fig. on p.34.

of arms in the centre is not his, and the subject may be William Buckton, in command of Lisieux in northern France in 1438. The costumes indicate a date of around 1470.

The scrolls on either side of the figure at the top originally read in Latin 'whatever you undertake, do it as well as you can'. To the left is a figure representing day, and on the right is the figure of night. Supporting the coat of arms are the figures of life on the left and death on the right. Below are the three fates spinning the thread of life, each with a figure representing a stage of life: a small boy, a young man and an old man.

It has been suggested that the Buxton Achievement might have been displayed in church when members of the family were the subject of marriages or funerals. It may have been made to boost the claims of the Buxton family to a coat of arms to which they may have been doubtfully entitled, and probably survived because of the importance attached to it in bolstering their claim. SF

PROV. Presented to the Norwich Museums by Mrs Maud Buxton, 1929.

LIT. Moore and Crawley 1992, cat. no. 2, pp. 66–8.

156 The Dacre Beasts

*c.*1520

Painted oak; h. Bull 206 cm, Gryphon 189 cm, Ram 185 cm, Dolphin 205 cm

Victoria and Albert Museum, London (W.6-9–2000)

The beasts represent different members of the Dacre family. The Red Bull is the crest of Thomas, Lord Dacre (1467–1525), who commissioned the set. His wife Elizabeth de Greystoke (1471–1516), with whom he eloped in 1488, is represented by the Dolphin. The Black Gryphon stands for Lord Dacre's forebears, the Dacres of Gilsland. The White Ram is the supporter of the coat of arms of the de Multon family; Margaret de Multon was the wife of Ranulph de Dacre, who was licensed to crenellate Naworth Castle in 1335.

These four giant beasts are rare survivors of a tradition of heraldic ornament. They stood in the largest Great Hall in Cumbria, at Naworth Castle, until 1999. Close to the Scottish border, Naworth was the seat of the Dacre family from 1317. In 1577 Lord William Howard (1563–1640), third son of the Duke of Norfolk, married the heiress Elizabeth Dacre, and

156a

156b

Naworth passed into the ownership of the Earls of Carlisle. An account of the fire that ravaged the castle in 1844 lists 'the four large wooden crests' as being among the property rescued from the flames. Their original location is still open to question, however, and it has been suggested that they were actually made for the Great Hall at Kirkoswald, another Dacre castle in Cumbria, now ruined (Chappell 2002, pp.24–5, 32–41).

Dendrochronology shows that the Dacre Beasts were carved from the trunk of the same oak tree, felled in the early sixteenth century. Although they were repainted after the 1844 fire, traces of earlier pigment have been found on the Bull, the Ram and the Dolphin.

The scale and grandeur of the Dacre Beasts reflects royal custom. In 1520, during preparations for the Field of Cloth of Gold, Charles Brandon, Duke of Suffolk, was asked to send 'divers of the Kynges arms and bestes cast in moldes, which wold do great ease and furtheraunce to the Kynges busyness' (Brewer et al., 1862–1932, III/1, no. 750; see also Colvin 1975, III/2, p.287, for other early sixteenth-century examples in wood). Such an heraldic statement was an important status symbol and the significance of such badges was easily understood.   TM

PROV. Kirkoswald Castle, Cumbria (?); Naworth Castle, Cumbria, until 1999; Sotheby's, London, 15 December 1999, lot 35; acquired in lieu of inheritance tax by HM Government and allocated to the V&A, with additional funding from the National Heritage Memorial Fund, the National Art Collections Fund, the Friends of the Victoria and Albert Museum, and others, 2000.

LIT. Murdoch 2000a and 2000b; Chappell 2002.

156c

156d

157 Corbel bracket or corner post

*c.*1500

Oak; h. 127 cm, w. 21.9 cm, d. 36.8 cm

Victoria and Albert Museum, London (W.6–1928)

The corbel bracket is carved with a full-length bowed figure of a wild man or 'woodwose' with hairy body, wearing high boots and holding a knotted club in his hands. He stands against a background of foliage, his feet on a monster's mask (half of which is a restoration). His head supports a moulded capital. Part of one of his boots and a corner scroll are modern replacements. The sculpture has been mounted on a new base, and the monster's head is detached from the main figure.

As well as maximizing floor space on a congested frontage, the jettying-out of medieval timber-framed houses allowed the freest possible flow of people and carts at street level. The buildings were supported at the corners by a substantial bracket, which provided an opportunity for the display of carving (see also cat. no. 121). These brackets, or corbels, were often decorated with low-relief tracery. This wild-man figure was clearly intended to make a considerable impression.

In contemporary pageantry the woodwose was often represented, and the London Chronicles for 1505 describe a procession in which 'cam In therle [the Earl] of Essex … wyth a woodhous precedyng and bering a Sere Tre'. In 1780 John Carter illustrated a wild-man corner post 'against a house at the place where East gate stood, (the house being without the gate)' at Bury St Edmunds, Suffolk. It was life-size, nearly two metres high (Carter 1780, I, tipped in between pp.58–9). The placement of the wild man in this position was probably seen as a means of protection for the household.   CT

PROV. Given by Mr Frank Surgey, through the National Art Collections Fund, in 1928.

LIT. Tracy 1988, cat. no. 240.

157

158 Floor tiles at The Vyne, Hampshire*

Antwerp, early 16th century

Tin-glazed earthenware (maiolica)

The National Trust (The Vyne, Hampshire)

Detail of a pavement showing four hexagonal maiolica tiles with blue, orange, yellow and green foliate decoration, enclosing a square tile decorated in blue and green with a winged monster and a dolphin.

The polychrome mosaic pavement at The Vyne is painted with a range of Renaissance motifs, such as portrait busts in both classical and contemporary dress. Tiles from similar pavements are known from a number of high-status sites in England, many associated with royalty and the nobility, dating from the 1520s to the 1540s. They reflect the fashion for the new Renaissance style in English interiors of the first half of the sixteenth century (Gaimster and Nenk 1997).

The tiles are now laid in the chapel; their original position is unknown. They are traditionally considered to have been laid during the rebuilding of The Vyne by William, Lord Sandys (now dated to 1526–8), although this is uncertain. They are thought to be products of the Antwerp workshop of Guido Andries, a potter of Italian descent (Dumortier 1999). They are similar, although not identical, to other tiled pavements, such as that at Herckenrode Abbey (Belgium) of the early 1530s, also produced in Antwerp.   BN

LIT. Rackham 1926; Hurst 1999; Blanchett 2000; Graves 2002, pp.57–8, fig. 3.14.

159 Floor tiles from Acton Court, near Bristol*

Late 15th century

Glazed earthenware; each tile 12–12.8 cm square, d. 2.4–3.2 cm

Bristol Museums and Art Gallery (Q1590 b, c, d & f; Q1591 a, c, h & l; Q1592 c, d, e & g; Q1593 a, c & d, and 36/1989/467)

A 16-tile panel of floor tiles, reconstructed to consist of four repeating designs, forming four lions between two concentric bands pierced with rosettes, an eight-petalled rose in the centre and foliage in the corners.

Acton Court, a moated manor house near Bristol, was the seat of the Poyntz family. The tiles, among many discovered during excavations on the site, were not found in their original position. The date at which they were laid is uncertain. They were probably installed by Sir Robert Poyntz, the owner of Acton Court from 1471 until his death in 1520, possibly during a refurbishment prior to a visit by Henry VII in 1486 (Bell 1991, p.120). They were discarded during the late 1540s and 1550s, by which time some had become very worn.

The tiles are thought to be the products of a commercial tile industry based in or near Bristol, and are comparable with the tiled pavement discovered in Canynges' House, Redcliffe Street, Bristol, in 1820. They are thus known as the Canynges/Bristol group. Some of the designs were derived from, or influenced by, the Great Malvern tilers (cat. no. 242). The Canynges pavement, dated to between 1481 and 1515, is thought to have paved the private chamber of the owner. The tiles were laid diagonally to the walls, within a border of plain tiles, and with each decorated panel separated by plain tiles; the tiles at Acton Court may have been laid in a similar arrangement.   BN

PROV. Acton Court, Iron Acton, Avon.

LIT. Williams 1979; Eames 1980, pp.236–54; Williams forthcoming.

158

159

160 Three roundels of the Labours of the Months

*c.*1480–1500

Stained and painted glass; (a) diam. 25 cm,
(b) diam. 25.5 cm, (c) diam. 29.2 cm

a) The Burrell Collection, Glasgow Museums (45.83)

b, c) Victoria and Albert Museum, London
(C.133, 134–1931)

a) January or February. A warmly-dressed man in blue and yellow stain sits indoors holding out his hands and one foot towards a hearth, where a pot sits on the fire. The roundel is complete, but has cracks and repair leads.

b) September. A man gathers grapes in a vineyard. With a knife he cuts a bunch from a vine tied to a stake; behind him is a basket of grapes. There are some repair leads and one small intrusion in the background.

c) October. A man sows seed, scattering it from a basket on his arm. Part of the background is intruded glass (restored 2002). This roundel has a coloured border with cloud pattern and stars.

These roundels, together with another from the V&A showing a man gathering fruit (August, C.135–1931), were seen in 1851 in the south window of the entrance hall of the old parsonage of the church of St Michael-at-Coslany in Norwich. Labours roundels

(and quarries) appear in domestic glazing from the mid-fifteenth century onwards, and parts of five sets made in Norwich from *c.*1450 to *c.*1510 are extant. This one is closest in style to the Life of St John window in St Peter Mancroft, Norwich, dated to *c.*1480–1500.   DK

PROV. (a) Philip Nelson Collection; purchased by Sir William Burrell through Wilfred Drake, 1944; formerly Hutton Castle. (b, c) St Michael's School, Coslany, Norwich; purchased 1931.

LIT. Woodforde 1950, p.153; Wells 1965, cat. no. 127; Lasko and Morgan 1973, cat. no. 96; Marks 1993, p.97; Ayre 2002, cat. nos 174, 293–4; Williamson 2003, no. 41.

161 Portrait of Edward Grimston

PLATE 23

Petrus Christus, 1446

Oil (?) on oak panel, painted surface; h. 32.5 cm, w. 24 cm

Inscr. on reverse, repainted: PETRUS XPI / ME FECIT. A° 1446, with heart device

Earl of Verulam, Gorhambury, on loan to the National Gallery, London (L3)

The sitter, displaying a Lancastrian SS collar (cat. no. 71), is flanked by the Grimston arms, which presumably once also bore the spot ermine seen on the shield on the reverse – pictures were not routinely hung on walls and often had painted backs. This

mark of difference identifies him as Edward Grimston of Rishangles, Suffolk, sent to the Netherlands in 1446 to negotiate for Henry VI. A minor diplomat, he shows that the taste for portraiture and Netherlandish painting extended beyond great nobles. Petrus Christus, Bruges's leading painter from 1444, probably painted at least one other English sitter (Berlin, Gemäldegalerie) and his works were found throughout Italy.

Netherlandish portraitists were masters of manipulation. The invented room's lines and curves counterpoint the figure in a design typical of Christus's sense of geometry, taut without rigidity. Seeing through continual eye movements, we expect to see mobile faces, experiences re-created by Christus as Grimston's features are seen from different viewpoints. Although the original effect is distorted by discoloured varnishes and repaint, some awkwardness seems intentional, as Grimston faces our right, yet directs his gaze uncomfortably to our left.

Apparently passing down his family, the portrait fulfilled its presumed primary function of preserving his likeness: how he looked and who he was, patron of some of the most desired art in Europe.   CR

PROV. Presumably by descent to the Earls of Verulam; recorded at Gorhambury in 1782; on loan to the National Gallery since 1927.

LIT. Thoms, Franks and Scharf 1866; Ainsworth and Martens 1994, pp.49–53, figs 64–5; Campbell 1995.

160a

160b

160c

162

162 A Lady with a Squirrel and a Starling

Hans Holbein the Younger, 1526–8

Oil on oak panel; h. 56 cm, w. 38.8 cm

National Gallery, London (NG 6540)

The red squirrel seated on the sitter's arm, nibbling a nut, wears a silver-grey metal chain around its neck and is therefore a pet. On the left-hand side perches a starling, perhaps also a pet. It is conceivable that either or both animal and bird may have featured in the sitter's coat of arms or may allude to her name in some other way. However, the squirrel was evidently a late addition to the composition: the sitter's right arm was slightly raised and her left hand altered in order to accommodate the presence of the animal.

The lady has not been identified, but she wears fine clothes: she has a hat of white ermine and her black dress is trimmed with velvet. Holbein's sitters on his first visit to England were drawn from the influential and educated court circles to whom he was recommended by the humanist Erasmus, and the lady is likely to be among them.

The portrait's arresting design, with the sitter shown against foliage scrolling across an intensely blue background, is paralleled by other English portraits by Holbein, and suggests a date during his first visit to England in 1526–8. The extraordinary quality of the painting demonstrates the allure that Holbein's skills as a painter must have had for his English patrons.   SF

PROV. Thomas Howard, Earl of Arundel (1585–1646); Jan Six (1618–1700); Pieter Six (1655–1703); his widow Ammerentia Deymans (1664–1727); Willem Six (1662–1773); Pieter Six (1686–1755); G. van Slingelande sale, The Hague, 1752; Sir William Hamilton sale, 20 February 1761, lot 75 ; bought by George, 3rd Earl of Cholmondeley, thence by descent to the Marquess of Cholmondeley; bought by the National Gallery in 1992 with the assistance of the National Art Collections Fund, the National Heritage Memorial Fund and the American Friends of the National Gallery.

LIT. Ganz 1925; 46; Strong 1980, p.40, no. 54 (ill.); Rowlands 1985, pp.72, 134, no. 28, col. pl. 14, pls 57, 60; Foister 1992; Foister, Wyld and Roy 1994.

163 Margaret Roper and William Roper

Hans Holbein the Younger, *c*.1536

Bodycolour on vellum mounted on card; both h. 4.5 cm

Inscr.: William Roper: ANᴼ AETATIS SVAE XLII; Margaret Roper: Aᴼ AETATIS XXX

Metropolitan Museum of Art, New York, Rogers Fund, 1950 (50.69.1 and 2)

Margaret More (1505–44), the eldest child of Sir Thomas More, Holbein's first English patron, married William Roper (1495–1578) on 2 July 1521. They had five children. Like More's other daughters, Margaret was a highly educated woman and was close to her father. She is said to have been charged by the king's council after the execution of her father in 1535 with keeping his head as well as his papers, but was released.

William Roper, from a gentry family in Kent, entered More's household when he was studying law at Lincoln's Inn in 1518; he later became a bencher, governor and pronotary. In 1529, 1554, 1555 and 1557–8 he served as a Member of Parliament. He was

an early enthusiast for Luther, but was persuaded to change his mind. Although he remained a Catholic, unlike his father-in-law Sir Thomas More he was prepared to take the oath of supremacy and acknowledge Henry VIII as head of the church.

Margaret Roper is shown full-length in Holbein's lost life-size painting of the family of Sir Thomas More of 1526–8, which did not include the husbands of his daughters. The likeness here – showing her at the age of 30 – appears to have been based on a separate sitting, after More's execution. She holds a book (possibly a prayer book) and wears a medallion, which may show a devotional image. The details of her headdress, which are picked out with gold, the fine blackwork embroidery at her neck and the texture of the fur pelts she wears are all rendered with Holbein's characteristic vivid accuracy. SF

PROV. Roper family; Lord Rothschild; Lord Carnarvon; Mrs H. Goldman, New York; bought by the Metropolitan Museum of Art in 1950.

LIT. Trapp and Schulte-Herbrüggen 1977, cat. no. 174; Rowlands 1985, cat. nos M3, M4.

164 Mrs Nicholas Small

PLATE 51

Hans Holbein the Younger, *c*.1540

Bodycolour on vellum; diam. 5.3 cm

Inscr.: ANNO.AETATIS SVAE 23

Victoria and Albert Museum, London (P.40–1935)

The young woman in this exquisitely painted portrait miniature was formerly known as a Mrs Pemberton, but has now been correctly identified through the coat of arms kept with the portrait; this bears the date 1556, but is probably a seventeenth-century or later copy of a coat of arms once attached to the miniature's original setting. This coat of arms allows the sitter to be identified as Jane Pemberton, wife of Nicholas Small, a City of London cloth merchant who held office on several occasions in the Clothworkers' Company, and who lived in the parish of All Hallows the Great. She married secondly after 1565/6 another cloth merchant, Nicholas Parkinson, and died in 1602.

Mrs Small holds a green leaf, and at her bosom is a red carnation, perhaps a reference to her betrothal, which is likely to have taken place in about 1540, and which may have been the occasion for the portrait commission. Her costume, with its white cap and shawl and black dress, is relatively simple, reflecting her social status. Jane Small's father, Christopher Pemberton, was a Northamptonshire gentleman. Her husband Nicholas Small was not a courtier, but Holbein's portraiture might have come to their attention via their links with Robert Cheseman, painted by Holbein in 1533 (The Hague, Mauritshuis), who had court connections: his cousin Emma, widow of a prosperous fishmonger, was godmother to their daughter. SF

PROV. John Heywood Hawkins by 1865; J. Pierpont Morgan, 1904; sold to Messrs Duveen in 1935 and acquired by the V&A with the assistance of the National Art Collections Fund.

LIT. Campbell (L) 1987 and 1990b.

163a

163b

165 The Bainbridge Snuffers

Probably Italy, c.1512–14, no marks

Silver, parcel-gilt, translucent enamel; l. 16 cm

British Museum, London (MME 78,12-30,633)

These are among the earliest known silver snuffers. Snuffers are used for extinguishing candles and for trimming their wicks to prevent the flame from guttering. Their scissor-like form was largely dictated by their function and changed little in basic design over 300 years. They are decorated in translucent enamel with the royal arms and the personal arms of Cardinal Christopher Bainbridge (c.1464–1514). All the other decorative features of the snuffers – the squirrel terminals to the handles, the engraved and gilded axe,

165

the squirrel and star to the sides and even the star-shaped pivot of the handles – are taken from his coat of arms.

Bainbridge was a typical prelate of the pre-Reformation period and was an important figure on the international stage during the early years of Henry VIII. Educated at Queen's College, Oxford, he rose rapidly through the ranks of the church, being appointed Dean of Windsor in 1505, Bishop of Durham in 1507 and Archbishop of York the following year. In 1509 he was sent to Rome as ambassador to Pope Julius II and was soon to become a pivotal figure in papal politics, when France invaded Italy later in the same year and Julius formed the Holy League against Louis XII. His loyalty was rewarded and in January 1512 Bainbridge was appointed cardinal to strengthen the pope's hand against a faction within the Curia; at the same time he was given command of the papal forces at Ferrara. Such success inevitably made him enemies and Bainbridge was poisoned in Rome by one of his own chaplains, allegedly on the orders of Sylvester de Giglis, Bishop of Worcester.

Although made for an English patron, the snuffers are much more likely to have been made in Italy than in England. Bainbridge probably never returned to England after he became a cardinal, and the royal arms would be more appropriate to his role as ambassador than they would have been at home. His tomb in the English College in Rome is carved with his personal arms and the royal arms, in exactly the same way as on the snuffers.   TS

PROV. Cardinal Christopher Bainbridge; bequeathed to the British Museum by John Henderson, 1878.

LIT. Marks and Payne 1978, cat. no. 130; Glanville 1990, pp.363, 474.

166 Vase with a portrait of a king, probably Henry VII

Italy (Venice), 1504–9

Opaque white glass, blown, tooled, enamelled and gilt; h. 19.8 cm

British Museum, London (MME 1979, 41-1)

The profile head, and particularly the crown with orb and cross, resemble the portrait of Henry VII on coins struck between 1504 and 1509, while the portcullis on the back of the bottle was frequently used as a badge by the Tudors, especially by Henry VII and his mother. The identification is confirmed through the publication in 1897 of a similar vase (now lost) of emerald-green glass, bearing the same

portrait in combination with the royal arms of England. The collection of Venetian glass built up by the Tudors must have been substantial. The inventory of Henry VIII of about 1547 lists more than 600 glasses, some described as 'paynted', including 'a cruse wth ii covers painted blewe wth A kinge crowned on the side'.

The shape of the 'Henry VII vase', with a tall neck and two small loop handles, is not typical of Venetian glass, but does occur in Netherlandish tin-glazed earthenware known from excavations in Holland and London.

Relatively small numbers of *lattimo* or milk-glass objects have survived, all attributable to a relatively narrow period around 1500. Various documents from c.1490–1512 relate to the production of enamelled *lattimo* glass: most interestingly, on 7 August 1490, a certain Bernardino Ferro was reported for having illegally fired for the painter Maria Obizzo 'more than a thousand pieces of lattimo and other colours, all gilt and enamelled', the blanks having been provided by a member of the prominent Barovier family (Clarke 1974, p.23).   RL

PROV. Private collection in London 1951–79; acquired by the British Museum in 1979.

LIT. Clarke 1974, pp.38–41, 51; Charleston 1984, p.46; Starkey 1991, cat. no. II.14 (entry by H. Tait).

167 Maiolica vase with the royal arms of England

Italy (probably Tuscany), 1480–1510

Tin-glazed earthenware, painted in cobalt blue; h. 18.2 cm

Victoria and Albert Museum, London (C.298–1938)

Once thought to be an early example of Netherlandish maiolica, this vase has been identified by recent research as originating in Italy. During the last quarter of the fifteenth century, Italian galleys from Genoa and Venice exported novelty-luxury wares in ceramic and glass to northern Europe, including England, where they found their way to the courts, and other wealthy patrons. Such rare imports were treasured possessions, and vessels of similar shape and decoration, often containing flowers and peacock feathers, are depicted in various contemporary images, including the Book of Hours of Engelbert of Nassau of 1477–90.

The vase is said to have been excavated in Mark Lane in the City of London. Its original foot is missing and the modern replacement was based on a vase of almost identical size and shape, and with identical tournament shield and arms, excavated from the moat of the Tower of London (Historic Royal Palaces

Agency; Gaimster 1999b, pls 2–3). The arms and the find-site of this second vase suggest a courtly provenance for the two vases. The fact that both show an unusual version of the English royal coat of arms, in which the conventional quarterings are reversed and slightly different beasts featured, could be explained as a misinterpretation by the Italian potters.

Stylistically the two vases are close to the wares produced at Pesaro in the Marches, but chemical analysis of the ceramic bodies has indicated that the vases were most likely made in Tuscany.   RL

PROV. See above; William Ridout Collection, London and Toronto; acquired in 1938.

LIT. Honey 1934, pp.37–8, pl. XLIV, 1; Blake 1999, pp.42–3; Gaimster 1999b, pp.141–3, col. pls 2–3.

166

167

168 Swan Roll of the Broadland area of Norfolk

*c.*1500

Vellum roll; 5 membranes; h. 82 cm, w. 11.4 cm (exhibited membrane)

Norfolk Record Office, Norwich (MC 2044)

The Broadland Swan Roll contains a pictorial register of swan owners' marks for an area that includes the Norfolk Broads and the rivers Wensum, Yare and Waveney. Instead of recording the swan-marks diagrammatically, as in most such rolls (more than 60 are known to survive), this roll displays the distinctive ownership marks on the beaks of swans' heads drawn in black and red ink, with owners' names written above. At the annual 'swan-upping' these marks – some similar to merchants' marks or even quasi-heraldic in character – would have been cut or branded on the beaks of the birds themselves.

Swan Rolls illustrate the prestige and high value accorded to these royal birds, which were the property of the crown by prerogative right. Only persons of sufficient status would be granted a licence to own a 'game' or flock of swans. Licensing became more strictly regulated by an 'Act for Swans' of 1482, and was controlled by the King's Swan-Master and his regional deputies (see Ticehurst 1957).

Beginning with the king and the Dukes of Norfolk and Suffolk, the Broadland roll includes among 99 owners the Bishop of Norwich, Sir William Bullen (Boleyn) of Blickling, John Coke, Mayor of Norwich, and institutions such as the hospitals of Norwich and three Norfolk parish churches. Despite its decorative appearance, this is a working document, and would have been made for a deputy Swan-Master and probably passed down to his successors, who kept it current. It is the earliest known roll for Norfolk. AP

PROV. (?) Hobart family (Sir Henry Hobart, deputy Swan-Master for East Norfolk and Suffolk, 1625); Lawrence of Crewkerne auctioneers, 10 December 1998; Christie's, London, 2 June 1999 (lot 32); bought from Sam Fogg Rare Books and Manuscripts, London, 1999.

LIT. DCMS 1999–2000, case 1, pp.17–19, pl. III.

169 Folding calendar almanac

Before 1521

Parchment; h. 76.5 cm, w. 12 cm

Magdalene College, Cambridge (F.4.42)

The first surviving printed almanacs date from the 1460s. Apart from a calendar and related tables, almanacs might include prognostications (to identify, for example, days for letting blood or harvesting), and

medical information such as details of planets and signs of the zodiac thought to govern parts of the body (see Capp 1979; Friedman 1995; Mooney 1997; Jones 1999).

This copy was folded to make a square of *c.*6 cm. The format imitates fifteenth-century manuscript examples (e.g. British Library, Egerton 2474). The woodcut edition has lettering in red added in manuscript. Illustrations of the labours of the months are paired with diagrams that indicate the number of daylight hours. On the verso is a Sarum calendar with small pictures to represent major feasts (Thomas Becket, written in red and not erased, has the image of a mitred bust), after which comes a list of significant dates in world history, beginning with '6700 years from the origin of the world'. Some are completed in manuscript, among them '1539 from the incarnation of Christ' (dates in other copies range from 1521 to 1554) and '49 years from the coronation of the king' – this last and other dates led a seventeenth-century annotator to dub them 'clearly ridiculous'.

Many of the surviving copies are coloured in a very similar fashion, suggesting they were illuminated by a publisher. Most copies are stamped with the letters M.S. reserved in a black circle, possibly the initials of the maker or publisher; this copy has only the letter M. RW

PROV. Found loose in a press of the Pepys Library; bequeathed to Magdalene College in 1703.

LIT. Bosanquet 1917, A II; STC, no. 388.

170 Two treatises on falconry*

Late 1430s

Vellum, ff.79; h. 25 cm, w. 15 cm

HRH The Duke of Gloucester (9437)

A staple feature of late medieval gentry libraries were tracts on practical subjects, such as law, heraldry or hunting, often bound together. This volume consists of two treatises on falconry, the first in the form of a dialogue between Ypocras (Hippocrates) and Cosma, a Roman senator, and the second attributed to one Symmachus.

The illustrated opening (ff.31v–32) shows the miniature at the end of the first treatise, depicting Ypocras, in academic dress, writing, and a group of three falconers with hawks and beaters' sticks. The tower at the top left may be intended as a mews. In the right-hand border, at the beginning of the second treatise, is the quintessential English sporting image of fox and hounds. Elsewhere in the book, the borders include such motifs as a retriever, peafowl and hawks with their prey.

The arms of Kerdeston occur throughout the

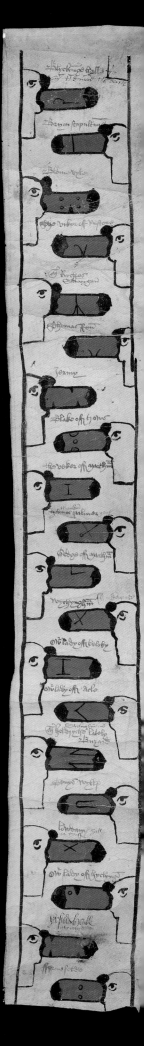

168

169

book. On f.79v they are also shown impaling de la Pole and Wingfield quarterly. Unless these are commemorative in function, this would indicate that the book was made for Sir Thomas Kerdeston of Claxton, Norfolk (d. 1446), before the death in April 1440 of his first wife Elizabeth, daughter of Michael de la Pole, 2nd Duke of Suffolk. Though there are links with books illuminated in Bury St Edmunds (e.g. cat. no. 318), the style of the miniatures, with their sombre facial shading, is closest to British Library Arundel MS 302, a Sarum Book of Hours made for a

Hamelden of Holton St Peter, in north-east Suffolk (Scott 1996, no. 92). This, and Kerdeston patronage of Norwich churches, suggests that this book was produced in Norwich. NR

PROV. Sir Thomas Kerdeston (d. 1446); Robert Regn ... , late 17th century; Robinson Bros; bought by HRH Henry, Duke of Gloucester (d. 1974), York House; HRH Richard, Duke of Gloucester.

LIT. Scott 1996, no. 91, ills 357–9; Keiser 1998, pp.3698, 3913.

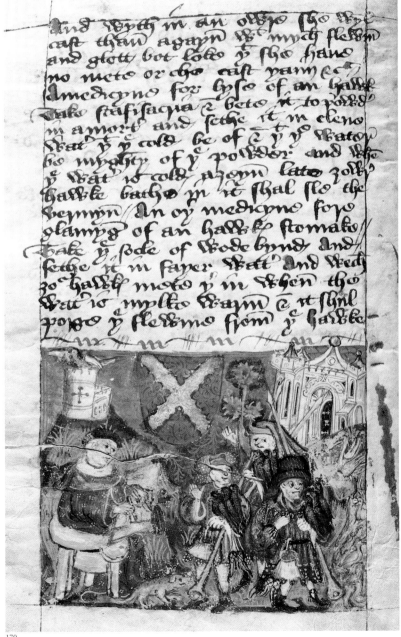

170

171 Geoffrey Chaucer, *Troilus and Criseyde*

c. 1415–25

Vellum, ff.151 + 2; h. 31.5 cm, w. 22 cm

Corpus Christi College, Cambridge (MS 61)

171

Although this copy of *Troilus and Criseyde* was designed to include approximately 90 miniatures, only the introductory image (f.1v) was ever painted. Accompanying the prologue, it shows the poet declaiming his work to a courtly gathering. In the upper register we are shown a scene from the poem, of Criseyde leaving Troy to be handed over to the Greeks. This could be meant as a reflection of a con-temporary political alliance, the marriage of Henry V to Katharine of France, which took place in 1420 but had been proposed as early as 1413. Both the miniature and its typically English borders are finished to the highest standard, including tooled decoration on the gilded surfaces. Very little related work has been identified. The style has frequently been compared with French work from the artistic circle of Jean de Berry. Italian influence has also been noted and recently a strong case has been made for associating the miniature with illumination produced for members of the Visconti family. It is perhaps worth remembering that the widowed Countess of Kent (d. 1424) was a Visconti (Bradley 1994). Several possible patrons have been suggested, most recently the captive Charles of Orleans (cat. no. 74), whose mother was also a Visconti.

The remainder of the book lacks not only the miniatures for which spaces were allocated, but also any hint of decorative initials and borders. *Troilus* is one of the tales of Troy that were popular all over Europe and attracted lengthy picture cycles. In England, Lydgate's *Troy Book*, commissioned by Henry V as Prince of Wales, survives in a number of illustrated copies (cat. no. 172). The provision of a cycle of the extent required here would nonetheless have presented a challenge. JMB

PROV. Inscribed by Chaucer scholar John Shirley (d. 1456); given by William Carye (?) to Stephen Batman, 1570; Archbishop Matthew Parker (d. 1575); bequeathed to Corpus Christi College.

LIT. Parkes and Salter 1978; Scott 1996, no. 58; Hardman 1997; Harris 2000; Scott 2000b; Schmidt 2001.

172 John Lydgate, *Troy Book*

Late 1440s

Vellum, ff.174; h. 45 cm, w. 33 cm

John Rylands University Library, Manchester (MS Eng. 1)

One of the most widely read poets in fifteenth-century England was the Benedictine monk John Lydgate (1370?–1449). On several occasions he worked closely with artists. He composed verses to accompany the Dance of Death in the Pardon Churchyard at St Paul's, and paintings of the legend of St George in the Armourers' Hall, London. Many of his longer poems seem to have been envisioned as illustrated works, and he may have exercised author-ial control over the imagery, especially in copies pro-duced in Bury St Edmunds (e.g. cat. no. 318).

The *Troy Book* was commissioned by the future Henry V in 1412 and completed in 1420. It is a rework-ing, in 30,112 lines, of the thirteenth-century prose *Historia Destructionis Troiae* by Guido delle Colonne.

In addition to recounting the Trojan War, various other Greek legends (such as that of Jason and Medea) are included. The Rylands *Troy Book* is remarkable for the way in which the illustrations, by a London illuminator working in a style related to that of William Abell (e.g. cat. no. 20), are presented as tableaux in the margins. The elaborate landscape settings are reminiscent of tapestries. The exhibited opening (ff.22v–23)

depicts Jason returning with the Golden Fleece to King Cethes, on the left, and Jason and Medea sailing away from Colchis, on the right.   NR

PROV. Carent family; Sir Humphrey Talbot (d. 1494); Thomas Booth; Sir John Mundy (d. 1537); given to Vincent Mundy, 1535; Adrian Mundy; Francis Mundy, 1615; Hugh Morgan of Monmouth; ?John, Baron Somers (d. 1716);

Thomas Barrett of Lee, Kent, 1786; Longmans, 1818; Henry Perkins (d. 1855); Algernon Perkins (d. 1873); Earl of Crawford and Balcarres, 1882; John Rylands Library, 1901.

LIT. Bergen 1906–35, IV, pp.29–36; Scott 1996, no. 93, ills 363–6, 385, col. pl. 12.

172

173

173 Geoffrey Chaucer, *The Canterbury Tales*, 2nd edition

Printed by William Caxton, Westminster, *c*.1483

Paper, ff.314; h. 26.5 cm, w. 21 cm

British Library, Department of Printed Books (G. 11586)

Chaucer's *Canterbury Tales*, written mainly in the last decade of the fourteenth century, already had many readers when it circulated in manuscript among the cultured and educated who formed his own social background. This was also its audience when it first appeared in print in 1476, one of the first books printed in England. Its appeal was that in the *Tales* people of all social classes, speaking in their own voices, were united in their pilgrimage to Canterbury, an undertaking that became emblematic of their journeys through life.

The comments received by the printer, William Caxton, on this first venture led to improvements when seven years later he launched a second edition. He made some textual adjustments, but it was the addition of woodcut portraits of the pilgrims riding throughout the book that made the work much more accessible.

The illustrations guide the reader through the framework of the collection of tales by indicating who is speaking, and strengthen the concept of the different voices, each revealing in their tale an individual character, sometimes cruelly so. In the General Prologue, however, only the narrator (Chaucer himself) speaks, as he joins the pilgrims in the inn at Southwark. He introduces each member of the company with a description of their appearance on first acquaintance. Here (ff. a.4v, a.5r) we see the Squire, son of the Knight, a dashing and fashion-conscious young man, who will embark on an elaborate chivalric tale so boring that he is not allowed to finish it. On the following page rides his servant, the Yeoman, dressed as a gamekeeper, but armed to the teeth with bow and arrows, dagger, shield and sword; he is due to remain silent.

Chaucer, who in his public functions was used to dealing with people in many walks of life, did not write this collection as tales for the people. The early printed editions helped it on its way to an ever-widening popularity that continues to this day. LH

PROV. Thomas Grenville; bequeathed to the British Museum in 1846.

LIT: Duff 1917, no. 88. Hodnett 1973, pp.214–26; STC, no. 5083; Benson 1987.

174 Thomas Malory, *Morte Darthur*, 2nd edition

Printed by Wynkyn de Worde, Westminster, 1498

Paper, ff.326; h. 26.5 cm, w. 20 cm

John Rylands University Library, Manchester (15396)

The *Morte Darthur* is an apotheosis of the age of chivalry, but, written when the qualities of knighthood began to lose their overriding value, it is also a work of nostalgia for a mythical golden age set in England.

Nothing can illustrate this better than the life of its author, Sir Thomas Malory, a knight of Newbold Revel in Warwickshire, about whom we now know with certainty that he was a prisoner in Newgate in 1469, where he died in 1471. Initially a respectable MP, he had from 1450 been in and out of jail for attempted murder, rape and extortion, among

174

other misdeeds. Imprisonment gave this gangster-knight the leisure to read widely and to absorb most of the romances of King Arthur, the Knights of the Round Table and the Holy Grail, in English and in particular in French. Out of these varied sources he adapted and compiled the *Morte Darthur* as one continuous history. His preference was more for the military elements in the stories than for that other aspect of chivalry, love and romance.

Malory's compilation hardly circulated in manuscript, but it was brought to the notice of William Caxton, who printed it in 1485 after dividing the lengthy text into short chapters. In this form the *Morte Darthur* found readers among Caxton's wide circle of acquaintances and clients, both gentry and well-to-do merchants. When his successor Wynkyn de Worde reprinted the text in 1498, he added 20 woodcuts that made it even easier for readers to find their way in the convoluted stories. Here (f. c2v) we see the damsel who has challenged King Arthur and his knights to unsheathe the sword – Excalibur – that she is carrying. Where Arthur and the knights have failed, the poor knight Balyn (just released from prison) succeeds with a flourish.   LH

PROV. William Herbert; the Duke of Roxburgh; the Althorp Library, sold by George John, 2nd Earl Spencer to Mrs John Rylands in 1892.

LIT. Dibdin 1814–15, vol. 4, pp.403–9; Duff 1917, no. 284; Hodnett 1973, no. 1266; STC, no. 802; Archibald and Edwards 1996; Sutton 2000, pp.243–51.

175 John Holt, *Lac puerorum. Mylke for chyldren* (Latin grammar)*

Printed by Wynkyn de Worde, London, 1508

Paper, ff.48; h. 18.7 cm, w. 12 cm

British Library, Department of Printed Books (C.33.b.47)

Latin grammar was central to the proper educational programme of young gentlemen, allowing participation in the international world of educated discourse. John Holt had taught at Magdalen Grammar School in Oxford, in the Archbishop of Canterbury's household at Lambeth Palace and in the Chichester prebendal school, before becoming tutor to the young Henry VIII just before his death in 1504. The *Lac puerorum* was written when Holt was at Lambeth, in 1496–1500 (no copies of this date survive), and was dedicated to Archbishop Morton (d. 1500); it included an introductory epigram by Thomas More, who had been a page in Morton's household when Holt taught there.

School books were printed in England only

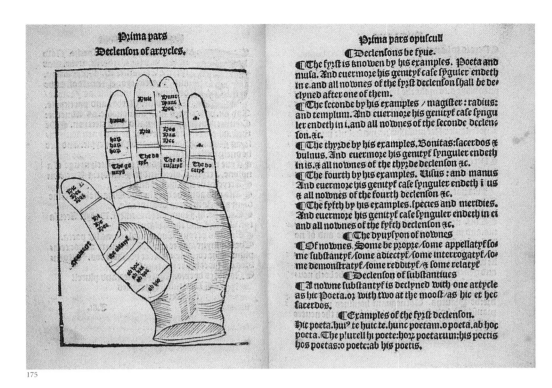

175

sporadically, in Oxford and London, until just before 1500. At this point, several prominent teachers, Holt among them, influenced pupils beyond their classrooms by getting their methods and examples printed in little textbooks. This book opens with the image of a schoolmaster, rod in hand, lecturing to three children holding books. Such images had been used for school books by printers in Germany. The woodcut of Wynkyn de Worde's version was first used by Gotfried de Os in Gouda in 1486. Holt's book used traditional visual aids of a kind found, for instance, in devotional pamphlets: the fingers of a hand listed what was to be memorized (here, the declensions of the demonstrative pronoun, *hic, hec, hoc*). Holt followed the modernizing tendency of his day in using classical texts (including Cicero and Virgil) as examples. Gothic founts were to be used to print schoolbooks for many generations.   LH & RW

PROV. Machell Stace Collection; Richard Heber (1773–1833); bought by the British Museum in 1885.

LIT. Proctor 1895; Nelson 1943, pp.341–5; McConica 1965, p.50; STC, no. 13604; Hellinga 1995, pp.342–59; Orme 1996; Hellinga and Trapp 1999, pp.449–69.

176 Toys

Miniature playthings for children had been mass-produced in pewter since the thirteenth century, so these items from the late fifteenth to the early sixteenth century are by no means the first of their kind in England. There seems from the start to have been a basic division – tableware and display vessels for girls and mounted knights for boys. No complete example of the latter is yet known from the period considered here. Both branches of this sideline of early pewter workers kept up with the latest fashions. London is the main find-spot for early toys in England, and all of the following items were discovered there. A few medieval playthings are known from other towns and rural areas.   GE

a) Flagon

*c.*1500–50

Lead/tin; h. 5.4 cm, diam. at base 2.1 cm

Museum of London (98.2/154)

Fluted, baluster form with a base probably originally more flared than at present; the rod handle is recurved at the base and the separate, fluted lid can

176a–d

be opened. The vessel contained a cherry stone when found.

This is a fairly close copy of contemporary full-size vessels. If the dating indications of the associated material are correct, this is an early version of this particular type of flagon. It is similar in form to some shown as prizes on a London lottery ticket of 1567 (Glanville 1987, p.36), but no surviving full-size piece has been traced.

PROV. Found on the Thames foreshore, Dockhead (Southwark), along with early to mid-16th-century items.

LIT. Egan 1996, fig. inside front cover; Forsyth and Egan forthcoming.

b) Mazer

*c.*1500

Lead/tin; h. 2.9 cm, diam. at top 2.7 cm, at base 2.2 cm

Museum of London (98.2/179)

PROV. Found on the Thames foreshore in London.

LIT. Egan 1996, fig. 13; Orme 2001, p.4, fig. 2; Forsyth and Egan forthcoming.

c) Two plates

*c.*1500

Lead/tin; diam. 3.1 and 3.5 cm

Museum of London (98.2/258 and 256)

The first has rim decoration of alternately plain and hatched triangles, with two concentric rings in the well; the second has similar rim decoration, and in the well a cross with trilobe-terminal arms and pellets in the angles.

Toy plates, which seem to have come into fashion along with their full-size counterparts, first appeared in the fifteenth century. The simple rim design with triangles is known on finds in Paris and Amsterdam as well as in England. The place or places of origin for what appear, from very close matches in different parts of northern Europe, to have been internationally traded playthings, remain to be clarified. Continuing into the post-medieval era (with a tradition of manufacture that in Nuremberg lasts to the present day), plates are the most common category of pewter toys through the sixteenth and seventeenth centuries.

PROV. Found on the Thames foreshore, London.

LIT. Both items: Egan 1996, fig. 15; Forsyth and Egan forthcoming.

d) Plate with *ihs*

Early 16th century

Lead/tin; diam. 2.7 cm

Museum of London (98.2/266)

Plain, except for black-letter *Ihs* in the well; probably a representation of a paten.

This seems from a modern viewpoint an unlikely category for a toy, but religious paraphernalia forms a significant category among miniature artefacts found in the Low Countries and thought to be for children's play (Willemsen 1998, pp.102–4). The present item is the only one from before the Reformation so far even provisionally recognized in England.

PROV. Found on the Thames foreshore, London.

LIT. Egan 1996, fig. 15; Blake et al. forthcoming; Forsyth and Egan forthcoming.

177 Toy chest front

Early 16th century

Lead/tin (one component from a composite miniature) h. 1.6 cm, w. 4.1 cm

Museum of London (excavation archive ABO92, no. 400)

Openwork in the form of applied (imitation turned) columns, with angled arches; a mounted lock plate is accurately shown. The opposed triangles with hatching or pellets are conventional pewter-makers' ornamentation. A series of tabs along the edges on the back may have been folded through corresponding slots in the other components – the sides, base and lid – to secure them in place, making the whole composite piece. Alternatively, the tabs may have retained a foil of gold-coloured copper-alloy sheeting to contrast with the openwork: a piece is retained in what may be a curved lid from a later version (Egan 1996, lower right ill., inside front cover).

Parts of somewhat rougher, less detailed versions are known, showing that this was a popular plaything.   GE

PROV. Museum of London excavation, Abbots Lane site, Bermondsey (Southwark); date of context early 16th century.

LIT. Egan 1996, fig. 21; Egan forthcoming, no. 601; Forsyth and Egan forthcoming.

177

14 THE TABLE AND FEASTING

MARIAN CAMPBELL

Splendid feasts were an indispensable expression of the power of medieval monarchs, noblemen and gentry. Gold and silver plate, often embellished with gems and coloured enamel, was displayed on tiered 'buffets' or cupboards (boards to hold cups). Dazzling quantities of food and drink – including much roast meat, wine and ale – would be served to all, the leftovers being collected and given as alms to the poor. Public displays of wealth and generosity were vital indicators of status in a society which greatly valued Christian charity – attitudes that were reflected in contemporary books of etiquette (Myers 1959). Gold and silver were at the top of the hierarchy of materials used for tableware. Lower down came pewter, pottery, wood and leather, while kitchen equipment was largely made of copper alloys, pottery and iron (Cherry 1987; Weinstein 1988). Because all metals were valuable, vessels were melted down to provide ready cash, or recycled into more fashionable forms. Little has survived, so all studies must rely heavily on contemporary documentary sources (Campbell 1991).

A large household, like the royal court, required spoons, knives and vessels for everyday dining. Inventories from Richard II's reign list dozens of silver dishes, spoons and saucers, decorated simply with the royal arms of England or a leopard's head (probably the sterling mark, and the earliest English hallmark); the spoons indicated their ownership by the mark of a crowned R. The only surviving silver saucer of this date, from Shrewsbury Abbey, is unadorned save for a leopard's head (cat. no. 194). Royal households also used pottery, leather and wooden vessels at table well into the reign of Henry VIII (Myers 1959, p.183).

Function partly governed vessel types and shapes. The food eaten by the peasantry and urban poor – the majority of the population – was very different from that of the aristocracy, gentry and merchant class. Throughout medieval Europe, diet was determined more by social class than by region (Dyer 1983; Mennell 1985, chapter 3). The poor ate pottages made from cereal grains and pulses, with herbs and garden vegetables – cheap foods, simmered in a pot over the fire

(Cherry 1987; Weinstein 1988). Dairy products, saltfish and eggs were occasional extras, meat a rarity. Bread and ale, though staple foods, were by no means affordable to all, certainly not in *c.*1400. Increasing prosperity and good harvests from *c.*1440 to 1520 notably improved the diet of peasants and the urban poor (Dyer 1983 and 1994; Carlin 1998) – more meat and ale were consumed and fewer dairy products.

The nobility and gentry ate plentifully, if monotonously, including quantities of wheat bread, meat and fish – favouring costly freshwater fish – with ale and wine. Expensive, imported spices added flavour. Fresh vegetables and dairy produce were avoided, except by children and the infirm (Dyer 1983; Henisch 1976). Imported sugar, regarded as medicinal as well as delicious, was often used in savoury foods, and in 'subtleties'. These sculptural creations, made of sugar paste or marzipan, were the highlights of each course at a feast. One, made for the feast marking William of Warham's enthronement as Archbishop of Canterbury in 1505, showed a miniature abbey interior, complete with altars (Sim 1997, p.9; Wilson 1991).

Even in the greatest households, feasts were relative rarities and one of the excitements of medieval life, being occasions of spectacle as well as gastronomy (Mennell 1985, chapter 3; Henisch 1976, chapter 5). They were held to mark special occasions and at certain times in the church year: at Easter, after the six-week-long Lent fast, and at Epiphany. Feasts were dominated by roasts and complicated savoury and sweet made-up dishes, with elaborate sauces. Costly ingredients were transformed – roast swans and peacocks gilded or clad in their own feathers, pork pies painted yellow with saffron, jellied broths bedecked with colourful heraldic shields (Henisch 1976, chapter 5). Two or three courses were served, each consisting of up to 30 savoury and sweet dishes.

The feast concluded with hippocras – spiced sweetened wine – served with wafers and 'spices' (dried fruits and comfits). By about 1520 this had evolved into a separate course or 'banquet', with conserves, fresh fruit and sugar confections, eaten in a separate room, in summer perhaps in a garden 'banqueting house' (Wilson 1991, pp.1–10). Details of royal festive dishes survive, the earliest being in a manuscript compiled for Richard II, *The Forme of Curye* of *c.*1390; the first English printed cookbook is of 1500, *The Boke of Cokery* 'for a Princys household' (Hieatt 1998).

Seating at a feast showed one's place in the social hierarchy, proximity to the host being an indication of status. On important occasions the great hall was still used (Girouard 1978), with the host and principal guests seated at a 'high' table set on a platform above the hall and eating the choicest food. Those seated in the hall below would eat a different menu, according to their rank. To a modern eye, if the food was lavish, the implements and vessels on the table were few, and the manners strange. The principal table would be covered with several linen cloths, removed one by one as the meal progressed. Square trenchers (from the French *trancher*: to cut) made from four-day-old stale bread (or from wood, silver or pewter) served as plates for individuals. Just such trenchers are illustrated in use at private Garter investiture feasts in 1503 and 1523 (plate 115).

Knives, spoons and fingers were used to eat with, since forks were not yet employed, except for serving sweetmeats like green ginger. Knives needed to be pointed to facilitate spearing food morsels. Spoons and knives would probably

be provided by the host for his principal guests, but most diners would bring their own. Spoons, so essential for eating sauces, pottages and sweets, are the most numerous tablewares to survive from this date. Made of wood (although few survive in this material), pewter, copper and silver, with mostly fig-shaped bowls (cat. no. 138), the bowl or stem often carries an initial or symbol, either representing the owner's or maker's name or sometimes the metal standard. The focus for decoration is the finial, and some forms – acorns and 'diamond' points – are common to most materials (Jackson 1893). Others survive in only one example, such as the woman in a fashionable horned headdress, in pewter (Weinstein 1989, cat. no. 33), or the wildman in silver (How 1952–7, I, p.108).

Sets of silver spoons with finials showing the 12 Apostles and Christ, documented as early as 1380 (*ibid.*, II, p.42), became popular during the early sixteenth century. Numbers survive (cat. no. 195). Their decoration perhaps

115 A private feast in Nuremberg on 8 December 1523, celebrating the investiture with the Order of the Garter of Ferdinand, Archduke of Austria. With him are those sent out from England to invest him, Lord Morley and Sir William Hussey on his right, and Sir Thomas Wriothesley, Garter King of Arms, and Edward Lee, Archdeacon of Colchester, on his left. The plate depicted is distinctively English (Prince Arthur's book, College of Arms Ms. Vincent 152, f.178)

reflects the popularity of the cult of saints, especially the Apostles (Duffy 1992, pp.158–9). It is not known if they had a specific use.

The important symbolic role of the ceremonial salt-cellar – set to the right of the host in front of the principal guest – is reflected in the size and ornateness of surviving examples (Campbell in Ellory, Clifford and Rogers 1999, pp.135–7). The hourglass salt was a distinctively English form, the most ornate surviving example being that made in the 1490s for Richard Fox as Bishop of Durham (cat. no. 108). Records tell of still more lavish or exotic salts: shaped as ships, as owned by Richard II (Oman 1963, p.7); castles, as owned by Sir John Fastolf; and the splendid elephant and castle, made of gold, set with hundreds of rubies, diamonds, sapphires and pearls, owned by Edward IV in 1468 (Campbell 1991, p.156).

Drinking cups were generally shared, and surviving silver and wood examples are capacious. By around 1500 the fashion for imported drinking glasses – of smaller capacity – suggests that manners may have started to change. Various forms of drinking vessel were in use, made of wood, pottery, leather, pewter, silver and gold. Rates of survival today do not reflect usage at the time. Several dozen drinking vessels exist in ancient foundations – Oxford and Cambridge colleges and London City companies – while excavations of the last 30 years have uncovered fragments of many more. Though once common, wood survivals are now the rarest and take the form of wide shallow bowls, made of ash, elder and beech (Keene 1990; Keys in Egan 1998, pp.196–216). Maple bowls, known as mazers, were often mounted with silver and inset with a roundel, depicting a favourite saint or coat of arms (cat. no. 102). By about 1500, mazers, like horns, were going out of fashion (Glanville 1990, chapter 11), but they survived as heirlooms, as in the case of the Pusey Horn of c.1400 (cat. no. 182), mounted in silver-gilt, with an English inscription.

Throughout the Middle Ages prestige lay in gold and silver drinking vessels. They took the form of a bowl, with a foot and often a cover. Grace cups were used for ceremonial toasts and thanksgiving on formal occasions, and consisted of large covered standing cups (cat. nos 186, 189). The 1523 manuscript illustrates wide-bowled standing cups with embossed, lobed decoration characteristic of the fifteenth century; also 'flatpeces', now known as font cups, a new shape of cup which appears around 1500 (cat. no. 186). Exotic fruit-shaped cups – of apple, pear or pineapple form – appear in English records from the 1440s (Campbell 1991, p.156), possibly the work of German goldsmiths. Inscriptions, in Latin or English, are generally pious ('Glory be to God alone': Campion Cup, V&A (M.249–1924)), but sometimes superstitious – the three kings named on the mazer at Corpus Christi College, Cambridge were invoked to ward off epilepsy.

In the sixteenth century the distinctively rounded earthenware cup form first appears, with a dark metallic glaze (Hurst 1968, p.111, fig. 326). But recent archaeological and documentary analysis has demonstrated the growth in wares connected with eating, drinking and preparing food imported to England from c.1400 (Harding 1998), and especially after c.1500. German stoneware Raeren jugs and tankards are notable (Gaimster 1997); and the owl-shaped example (cat. no. 193) – the head removable to serve as a cup – is an appropriate if unusual form, the owl being associated with drinking and greed (Blair 1983, cat. no. 21). Colourful maiolica dishes and jugs came from the Netherlands, Italy and the Iberian peninsula (Gaimster and Redknap 1992), wine glasses from Venice (Charleston 1984, pp.42–50), brass jugs and pots from the Netherlands (Blair and Blair 1991). Prosperity probably drove material changes around 1500. Metal cooking pots replaced pottery ones (Cherry 1987), and farmers were substituting pewter for wooden dishes and vessels (Pinto 1969, p.67). From about 1500 perhaps the most desirable drinking vessels were the coloured or milky white glasses from Venice (cat. no. 166), fragments of which have been found in Southampton and London (Charleston 1984; Egan 1998, pp.224–35).

By about 1580 drinking vessels of glass – much of whose value lay in their workmanship – had ousted precious metal from pride of place on the wealthy English dining table. The high status of Venetian glass inspired new shapes in silver, such as the London-made 'Boleyn' wine cup of 1535 (cat. no. 15). Innovative in ornament too, its 'Antique' style, including Italianate acanthus, symmetrical foliage and putti, became popular in English court circles from the 1520s, although Gothic forms also persisted until c.1540 (cat. no. 134).

FURTHER READING

Carlin and Rosenthal 1998; Henisch 1976; Mead 1931.

178 Trestle-type table

Early 16th century

Oak; h. 83.5 cm, w. 249.3 cm, d. 90.1 cm

The Burrell Collection, Glasgow Museums (14/312)

The top consists of two folded boards, which allow the table to be doubled in length. The hinges, by which they are joined, are strengthened by adjacent nailed iron straps, applied to the board edges on either side. Each section is made up from two longitudinal panels in the centre, with four cleats around the outside. To extend the table, the hinged end is pushed towards the centre along a channel protected by guard rails inside the superstructure. From this position the boards can then be unfolded. They rest on a continuous joined trestle-cum-armoire, 37 cm deep, and fronted by linen-fold-type panels on each side, which are divided by flat moulded buttresses. Two of the panels are designed as access doors without handles, and are provided with primitive-type peg-hinges carved in the solid. When opened, these doors give access to the double-compartment storage space inside. Although both door panels look remarkably convincing, one was reported by the vendor of the table to be an early nineteenth-century copy (Burrell Collection archives). The other was commissioned from the dealer Frank Surgey in 1952.

The linenfold panels, corbelled ends and clawed feet are convincingly late-medieval in appearance. However, the contrasting colour of the table top and sill feet is a puzzle. It is perhaps tempting to date these elements to a later remodelling. A joined construction of table boards is practically unheard of in England before 1600, but it did occur as early as the fifteenth century in Flanders. This table seems to be of a type with no direct comparisons in England, and probably very few indeed in Belgium. In Flemish paintings dining tables are invariably supported on separate trestles of the simplest design. Possibly the Burrell Collection's table was originally of purely domestic type with armoire combined, and was converted at an early date into its present much grander dining form. CT

PROV. Durham Cathedral Deanery kitchen, *c*.1780; Edward Greatorex, Durham chapter librarian (1859–62, 1866–73); purchased by Sir William Burrell from John Hunt, 1952.

LIT. Eames 1977, pp.215–27; Marks 1984c, p.14.

179 Archbishop Chichele's salt

c.1420–40

Silver, partially gilt and painted, with rock crystal; total h. 43.8 cm, h. of main figure 30.5 cm

All Souls College, Oxford

The salt shows a bearded man who stands on a low, circular, crenellated base encircled by eight crenellated turrets with conical roofs. On his head, supported by his right hand, is the crystal salt-receptacle and cover. Both these are mounted in silver-gilt, decorated in a similar manner to the base, but without the turrets and with the addition of scalloped edges and cross-bands. The cover has a large leafy finial. The figure is made hollow, and is attached to the base by two bolts soldered to the soles of the man's feet, which pass through corresponding holes in the base and are secured by nuts underneath.

The figure has aquiline features, and is bare-headed, with a short, forked beard and a moustache. He wears a girdled shirt-like garment. The legs are covered by plain hose, and the feet by pointed ankle-boots. Suspended over the man's left hip on a narrow sword-belt is a falchion, on the hilt of which he rests his left hand. It has a broad curved blade, which widens towards the clipped-back point.

The man stands on an undulating ground made from a separate circular plate that fits inside the top of the base and is held in position by the same two bolts and nuts as he is. This seems more roughly made than the rest of the ensemble, and is set with a series of tiny, crudely modelled and cast silver figures of animals and men, of which all but one are soldered in position. The exception, the tallest figure at 3.6 cm high, is secured in the same manner as the salt-bearer, but by a single nut and bolt. It represents a bagpiper wearing a short doublet, a pair of full breeches with a prominent codpiece or pouch, hose, round-toed shoes and small hemispherical hat with a very narrow brim. Other figures include: two boars, two seated hounds, two running hares, a hound pursuing a stag, two men blowing large horns, and another hound pursuing a stag.

There are considerable traces of pigment in addition to the green ground on which the figures stand, all of which appear to have been applied over an undercoat that was itself applied over gilding. The salt has suffered from wear and use, but also has an inherent flaw in its design, rendering it very top-heavy. Visible damage now includes a large split on the line of the man's girdle and a large, ragged hole on the top of his

178

head. Past repairs include crude soldering with lead and an intermediate screw-threaded support, in an attempt to secure the crystal cup to the huntsman's head. Both crystal salt and cover have numerous ancient breaks, and several small sections are missing altogether. The paint now covering the base of the salt seems to be a restoration of irreparably damaged enamel. Other restorations to the base, probably of c.1550–1600, include all the cast figures and possibly the ground-plate too. The identification of these figures as later replacements invalidates the theory that the main figure represents a giant or a huntsman.

The salt is one of the most important survivals of medieval plate in England, and is of unique design. A rare comparable piece is described in the inventory of John de Vere, Earl of Oxford (d. 1513), as 'a salt of berall [crystal] standing with an ymage of a Morion [Moor] under the berall [crystal] bering up the Salt with a cover silver gilt' (St John Hope 1914b, p.328). The traces of paint visible on the huntsman's face, neck and hands are notable, and unusual – compare, for example, that on the gold reliquary of Charles the Bold (Flemish, 1467), now in Liège Cathedral, Belgium. At this date colour was achieved on gold and silver figure sculpture usually by enamelling, or more rarely by painting. Very few examples of the latter technique survive, and little research has yet been done into the pigments involved.

The salt has in the past been ascribed to both English and German goldsmiths, and dated generally to the later fifteenth century. Certainly the zigzag assay marks under the base are typical of German (but not of English) workmanship. The floral knop on the cover is also a decorative feature often found on German late medieval cups (Fritz 1982, pl. 644), but also seen on the English Election Cup at Winchester College (cat. no. 185). The castellation is a universal European feature, and the turreted base is found on such pieces as a French salt in the Louvre (Lightbown 1978, pl. LXXVII) and the St-Esprit reliquary of c.1390–1410 (cat. no. 10). The modelling of the figure, especially that of the face, suggests a date in the first half of the fifteenth century. The salt may have been a diplomatic gift to Chichele, but may equally have been made in London by an alien goldsmith, c.1420–40.   CB & MLC

PROV. Bequeathed to All Souls College in 1799 by Mrs Catherine Griffith, widow of Christopher Griffith, whose first wife Anne was a collateral descendant of the founder, Archbishop Henry Chichele.

LIT. Moffat 1906, p.86, pl. XLIII; London 1953, cat. no. 37; Hayward 1976, p.63; Lightbown 1978, pp.100–1, pl. LXXIVa; Campbell (M) 2002, pp.138–40, pl. 23.

180 The Ape Salt

*c.*1450–1500, with 18th–19th-century restorations

Silver-gilt, the bowl of crystal; h. 26.1 cm

New College, Oxford

A hemispherical bowl (now badly cracked) intended for the salt rests on the head of a seated ape, which steadies it with one paw. At the bottom of the bowl is a lion's head in cast silver-gilt. The ape is made of embossed silver, engraved to simulate fur, with tiny

180

red crystal (?) eyes. The tasselled cushion on which he sits rests on a band of interlaced and quatrefoil decoration (the band a later restoration). Below this is a circular base, decorated with branches and leaves, a band of stamped flowers and a cast battlemented cresting. The whole rests on small cast figures of three hairy wildmen, holding clubs and seated on cushions.

This sumptuous but playful piece is a type of goldsmiths' sculpture incorporating a 'Babewyn', as apes were called in the Middle Ages. Barbary apes (found in Spain and North Africa) were the only kind of simians then known. They were extremely popular as motifs to decorate the margins of manuscripts, woodwork, glass and enamel from the fourteenth century

onwards, although to philosophers and moralists apes often represented evil (Janson 1952, pp.163–98; New York 1975, cat. no. 269). *Vanitas*, or the love of finery, was also attributed to apes, which were sometimes associated with the work of goldsmiths (Janson 1952, p.191); both ideas may underlie this piece.

The salt is an extremely rare survival in the context of European silver: the only other medieval figural salt extant is the Chichele Salt (cat. no. 179). The present salt originally had a cover: this is mentioned in a college inventory of 1516, as is the donor, William Warham (Oman 1979, p.297).

The crystal, used as the salt container, had the practical quality that it was impervious to the corrosive power of salt. It was also believed to have the power to reveal the presence of poison, when it would change colour. The hairy wildmen that support the base are commonly found on German cups of the fifteenth century (Husband 1980, cat. nos 51–2), but also on English spoons. Warham was a generous benefactor to New and All Souls Colleges (cat. nos 180, 188). He was not only Archbishop of Canterbury, but a prominent statesman, in his time Chancellor, ambassador and patron of Erasmus, and obliged to entertain lavishly.   MLC

LIT. Moffat 1906, no. XXXIII; Oman 1979, p.297; Campbell (M) 2002, p.138.

181 Warden Hill's salt

*c.*1475–94, with 19th-century restorations

Silver-gilt and gilded glass, unmarked; total h. 37 cm, max. diam. 13.5 cm

Inscr.: *Super W A montes T E R stabunt H I L aque M'* ('The waters shall stand above the hills')

New College, Oxford

The salt is of hourglass form, composed of ridged volutes with intermediate ribs, also ridged and deeply engraved, ascending and descending to double rows of ridged lobes. A central knop is decorated with scrolled leaves of Gothic design. The flanged foot supports an openwork cresting, and the edge is incised to represent a riband. On the flange is engraved the inscription in black-letter and Lombardic characters on a crosshatched ground. The receptacle for salt is a shallow bowl. The cover is decorated with a moulded vertical band, bearing an openwork crown of leaves with intermediate berries intended to represent pearls. Above this is a hexagonal pyramid with circular buttresses connected by a minute cresting with crocketed ribs. The panels are filled with purple-red glass, decorated with a gilt diaper pattern (three restored). The finial (partly restored) is formed by leaves surmounted by a seeded berry.

181

This is the classic form of an English late medieval hourglass-shaped ceremonial salt. The size of the piece and its elaborate decoration far outweigh its function, and indeed the receptacle for the salt is rather small. Such salts formed the focal point of the high table (raised on a platform) at a feast, and were placed in front of the guest of honour, on the right-hand side of the host. Tables for less important guests were not on a platform and so the guests were 'below the salt'.

This salt is remarkable in two ways. It was clearly commissioned by Walter Hill, warden of New College from 1475 to 1494, as indicated by the punning inscription on it, which alludes to him through a quotation from Psalm 104, 6. It was first recorded in a college inventory of 1508. The goldsmith who made the salt is not known, but the elaborately embossed style is strongly reminiscent of contemporary German work, and may indicate that the goldsmith was from the German cultural area, working perhaps in London. The decorative embellishment of coloured and gilded glass in the cover is a unique feature in a medieval piece of silver tableware. Glass of this sort was a great rarity at the time, and generally a Venetian speciality, which may indicate that the glass panels were imported.   MLC

PROV. Gift of Warden Hill to New College, Oxford.

LIT. Moffat 1906, no. XXXII; Oxford 1928, cat. no. 69; Oman 1979, pp.295–6; Ellory, Clifford and Rogers 1999, pp.137, 152 (M. Campbell).

182 The Pusey Horn

*c.*1400–50

Ox horn, mounted in silver-gilt, unmarked; h. 25.5 cm, l. 45 cm

Inscr. in black-letter: *I Kynge knowde geve wyllyam pecote/thys horne to holde by thy lond* [land]

Victoria and Albert Museum, London (M.220–1938)

The horn stands on two legs with claw feet and is mounted with three bands of silver-gilt, the tip also decorated with a sheep's head with glass eyes. The central band of silver is engraved in black-letter, with stylized acanthus between the words. More acanthus engraving decorates a band near the tip. Both legs have been broken and repaired, and the band near the tip is split.

This drinking horn is of a type that was in general use in Anglo-Saxon times, but which by the late medieval period had become rare. Such horns tended to be regarded as heirlooms (Alexander and Binski 1987, cat. nos 545–6). The Pusey Horn has the additional unique interest that links it both with an ancient family and its legendary part in King Canute's campaigns, and with the feudal legal system. The Puseys held their land and the manor of Pusey, in Berkshire, by the right of cornage, which involved the liability to produce the horn itself in court as evidence of this right, as was last done in 1684 before Lord Chancellor Jeffries. Feudal tenures of this sort were abolished only in 1922 by the Law of Property Act (Cherry 1989, pp.114–16).

The late medieval decoration of the horn may replace something else, indicated by various marks on the horn itself. The inscription alludes to the tradition that the horn was given by Canute to William Pusey (the name misspelled by the goldsmith), one of the king's officers, who warned him of an impending Anglo-Saxon attack, having entered the enemy camp disguised as a shepherd. The sheep's head forming the tip is a jocular allusion to this episode, the sort of visual pun favoured by medieval goldsmiths and their clients (Alexander and Binski 1987, cat. no. 545).   MLC

PROV. Supposedly the gift of King Canute (d. 1035) to the Pusey family of Berkshire, and in the family by descent; sold at Sotheby's, London, 30 May 1935, lot 168; William Randolph Hearst Collection, sold at Christie's, London, 14 December 1938, lot 120; bought by Mrs Lucy Violet Bouverie-Pusey (widow of Philip Bouverie-Pusey) and given to the V&A in 1938 in memory of her husband.

LIT. Pegge 1786; Jackson 1911, II, pp.589, 593–4; Oman 1944, pp.22–3; Oman 1947, pp.1–2; Oman 1978, pp.30–31; Cherry 1989, pp.114–16.

183 The Studley Bowl

*c.*1400

Silver, parcel-gilt; h. 14.5 cm, diam. of bowl 14.3 cm, wt 25½ troy oz

Victoria and Albert Museum, London (M.1–1914)

The bowl stands on a heavy foot-ring. The lid has a rim punched with pellets, and a knop engraved with the letter *a* in black-letter (textura). Both cover and bowl are gilt on the outside (except for the inscription), inside the lid and under the foot. Each is engraved with an identical inscription in black-letter in two rows, separated by leafy wreaths. The inscription begins with a cross, followed by the alphabet (lacking letters *j*, *w*), the symbol for *et*, the word *est*, a tittle (the line drawn over an abridged word) and the symbol for *con*.

The letter *x* resembles the *y* beside it, but although its form is close to that of the Anglo-Saxon runic letter thorn (*p* = th) still used at this date – and found on the Pusey Horn (cat. no. 182) – its position in the letter sequence here makes such an interpretation unlikely. The symbols following the alphabet are part of a set of common abbreviations that conclude alphabets in primers, which were for children to learn. The child crossed himself or herself before starting the primer, an act symbolized in the cross with which it, like the bowl's inscription, begins, giving rise to the name crisscross (Christ cross) row.

The bowl is beautiful and of unique form. It may have been made for a rich or noble child to eat from, and a similar-sounding vessel, 'a silver bowl with the ABC on the cover', was bequeathed by John Morton of York in 1431.   MLC

PROV. Lady Ripon (d. 1907), said to have been inherited; given to Aldfield cum Studley church, near Ripon, for use as an alms basin, in *c.*1872; sold by the church in 1913; bought by C. J. Jackson; bought by Harvey Hadden as a gift for the V&A in 1914.

LIT. Alexander and Binski 1987, cat. no. 728 (with earlier lit.).

182

183

184 Cup and cover

*c.*1430–50

Silver, partially gilt, unmarked; h. 35 cm

**St Cyriac's church, Lacock, Wiltshire,
on loan to the British Museum, London**

A plain conical cover sits on the simple hemispherical bowl, which is supported on a trumpet-shaped foot. Cast and gilt crestings of Gothic foliage with twisted ropework decorate the top and base of the foot and the rim of the cover, which is surmounted by a large spherical finial. This is decorated with gilt twisted ropework; the protruding stalk is probably a modern replacement.

The elegant simplicity of this cup makes it one of the most beautiful pieces of medieval plate. It is of a type now extremely rare, but which was probably one of the most common forms in the Late Gothic period. Known as a 'chalice-shaped' cup from its resemblance to a chalice, the form of the bowl probably varied little from the thirteenth century onwards, but the exaggerated lid, finial and foot are typically fifteenth-century features. Although it is difficult to date precisely, its form resembles a drawing of 1429, showing a gold cup presented by Henry VI to the Lord Mayor at his coronation (Blair 1979a, pp.372–3). MLC

PROV. Lacock church, Wiltshire; on loan to the British Museum since 1962.

LIT. London 1955, cat. no. 2; Vienna 1962, cat. no. 460, pl. 28; Blair 1979a, p.373, fig. 56; Campbell 1991, p.157, fig. 75.

185 The Winchester Election Cup

Third quarter of 15th century, unmarked

Silver-gilt, with applied pastes; h. 44.5 cm

Winchester College, Hampshire

The cup stands on a high-stemmed domed foot and has a gourd-shaped bowl and ogee cover with large hemispherical finial. The foot, bowl and cover are embossed with leaves on matted ground and the edges are applied with an openwork cresting of Gothic foliage above stamped dentils. The foot and cover rims are set with precious stones and the finial, which was originally surmounted by a figure or other decorative motif, has traces of enamel.

The cup was presented in 1555 by Bishop John White of Lincoln, Warden of Winchester College, and

described by its donor as 'thys pore cownterfetyd cuppe, which I desire maye remayne as an ymplemente of The electyon'. In early sixteenth-century usage 'counterfeit' meant 'wrought', while White's description of it as 'poor' was probably meant in the sense of lacking elements or being damaged. At the time of its presentation the cup was already some 70 or 80 years old, and it is possible that the enamel and crowning motif of the finial had already been lost. The jewelled settings are possibly a later addition, perhaps from around the time of its presentation.

Very few standing cups of this size or importance have survived from the late Middle Ages and, in the absence of marks, it is difficult to date this example with any precision, since there was relatively little formal development in their design between about 1450 and 1510. The absence of marks, however, would suggest that it was made before 1478, when an ordinance of the Goldsmiths' Company required that all plate be marked before being 'put to sale'. This ordinance seems to have been widely complied with, no less in the case of important special commissions than of ordinary domestic wares. The most closely related object to the Election Cup is probably the so-called Warden's Grace Cup, coincidentally at Winchester's sister foundation, New College, Oxford. The latter, also unmarked, has closely similar decorative and constructional features and relates in turn to a third cup at Pembroke College, Cambridge, which is hallmarked for 1481. TS

LIT. Jackson 1911, p.653; Oman 1962b, p.27, fig. 3; Oman 1979, p.295, pl. 69; Glanville 1990, p.248.

186 The Cressener Cup

London, 1503–4 (maker's mark: a cross bow)

Silver-gilt, enamel and rock-crystal; h. 16.5 cm

The Worshipful Company of Goldsmiths, London

The plain cup stands on a spreading foot and low stem; the shallow bowl has straight sides and the ogee cover is surmounted by a large hemispherical finial incorporating an enamelled coat of arms beneath a rock-crystal disc. The arms are those of Sir John Cressener, who was knighted by Henry VIII after the siege of Tournai in 1513 and died in 1536. They are displayed with those of the powerful families of Mortimer and Ferrers, with whom the Cresseners were allied by marriage. Unlike most substantial early

184

Tudor plate, which has survived in church or institutional ownership, this cup is exceptional in having descended until the last century through the family for which it was made.

The cup is thought to be the earliest surviving English covered cup of this kind. Its straight-sided form is of a type commonly known today as 'font-shaped', but which would probably have been called a 'flat cup' or standing bowl in the sixteenth century. It is unusual in being almost completely plain, although the profile of the cup and the distinctive form of its finial are shared by many cups of the early sixteenth century. Far from being a utilitarian piece, the presence of a cover marks it out as a prestigious object that would have conferred a sense of status on its owner or user.

The Cressener Cup is in remarkably good condition, although in common with most surviving pieces of this period, the gilding has been renewed at some stage; the rock-crystal disc covering the coat of arms has almost certainly also been replaced, since there are losses to the underlying enamel.   TS

PROV. Sir John Cressener (d. 1536); by descent to Col William Nevill Tufnell of Langleys, near Chelmsford, Essex; acquired by the Goldsmiths' Company in 1908.

LIT. Jackson 1911, p.689; Carrington and Hughes 1926, pp.22–4.

185

186

187

187 The Howard Grace Cup

The mounts London, 1525–6, the cup possibly 12th-century

Silver-gilt, elephant ivory, garnets and pearls; h. 27.3 cm, diam. 10.5 cm

Inscr.: VINUM TUUM BIBE CUM GAUDIO (Drink thy wine with joy) on lip mount, chased inscription ESTOTE SOBRII (Be sober) divided by mitre between TB and pomegranates on cover and +FERARE GOD on chased ring beneath finial

Victoria and Albert Museum, London (M.2680–1931)

The turned ivory cup is supported by a silver-gilt mount set with rubies, garnets and pearls. The ivory cover has a silver-gilt lip mount culminating in a figure of St George. The Renaissance flavour of the mounts and lettering is at variance with the medieval profile of the cup. The motif in the cast cresting is taken from engraved ornament by the Renaissance artist Hans Burgkmair (1473–1531), whereas the cast trefoil band around the foot of the cup is more sug-gestive of Gothic design.

Traditionally described as a 'grace cup', used for communal drinking at the end of a meal, this cup in fact may have been used for display on a buffet or cupboard because of the fragile nature of its gem-set decoration.

It has been suggested that the ivory cup was a relic of St Thomas Becket (1118–70), which Sir Edward Howard left to Catherine of Aragon at his death in 1513, although no documentation survives. Catherine possibly added the mounts, chased with her pome-granate badge and the initials of Thomas Becket, as a courtly gift. It is next mentioned in the inventory of Henry Howard, Earl of Northampton, in 1614 as 'one Ivory cupp garnished with pearles and precious stones', which passed to his nephew Lord William Howard of Naworth (d. 1640) (see also cat. nos 218, 222b). It was the only item of plate selected by William Howard from his uncle's extensive inventory, even though by 1614 it would have been old-fashioned. The Howards were recusants, retaining their Catholic loyalties, who would have valued the Becket association. When the cup was examined at the Society of Antiquaries in 1768, a label tacked to the cup referred to the Becket connection, and this, with the initials TB and the bishop's mitre, has been taken to support the long-standing tradition of ownership.   RC

PROV. See above and detailed provenance given in Glanville 1990, p.397. Passed by descent through the Howard family; Duke of Norfolk by 1808; Christie's, London, 12 May 1931, lot 66; acquired by Lord Wakefield and presented by him to the V&A, through the National Art Collections Fund.

LIT. Glanville 1990, cat. no. 7, pp.394–7 (with earlier lit.).

188 Mounted bowl

Chinese, c.1400–50 (the bowl); English, c.1500–30 (the mounts)

Green glazed porcelain, decorated with silver-gilt mounts, unmarked; h. 12.1 cm, max. diam. 16.2 cm

Inscr. under the base of the bowl, scratched in Gothic minuscule: W. WARHM CANTUA

New College, Oxford

The bowl is of celadon porcelain carved on the outside with a pattern of lotus petals and on the inside base with a tiny flower, under a grey-green glaze, the surface of which is abraded in places. A deep silver rim-mount is attached to three hinged bands, decorated above and below with a crown-like motif. These mounts, of cast Gothic foliage, are attached to a deep band decorated with pellets, which covers and encircles the base of the bowl. The bowl has four discoloured cracks.

The mounts appear to fit the bowl rather loosely, especially around the lip. However, this may be because the lip of the porcelain bowl flares outwards more than the goldsmith had allowed for. It is possi-ble that the mounts were originally made for some-thing else – such as a mazer – which got broken, or that the original mounts were damaged and remade.

The bowl is unique in an English context – the only complete piece and the earliest surviving medieval example of porcelain brought to England soon after it was made. It is one of only two or three extant pieces in Europe. Porcelain was of extreme rarity in medieval Europe, and was prized for its craftsmanship and curiosity as well as for the therapeutic powers it was believed to possess: celadon vessels were thought to be able to reveal the presence of poison in any sub-stance placed in them (Whitehouse 1972, pp.63–5). Although Chinese silks and bronzes were known to the Romans, there is no record of Chinese porcelain in Europe before c.1300, and even after 1400 it was rare. Only in the sixteenth century did it become more available, after the Portuguese had opened up trading stations in the Indian Ocean. In the four-teenth and fifteenth centuries the few owners known from inventories were exclusively royal or noble (Whitehouse, *passim*); their collections included porcelain unmounted, like in that of Charles V of France, or both mounted and unmounted, like Jean de Berry's (Lightbown 1978, p.57).

The European tradition of mounting oriental porcelain in silver, gold or gilt bronze continued well into the nineteenth century. Because of its rarity, the bowl might simply have been used for display. However, the diagnostic properties that celadon was thought to have may have dictated its use – perhaps as a drinking bowl, although drinking bowls were unfashionable by the late fifteenth century (Fritz 1982, pls 377–83), or for fruit, like those in the possession of the Duc d'Anjou (Lightbown 1978, p.57). There seems no reason to doubt that it was given by William Warham (d. 1532), Archbishop of Canterbury and warden of the college, to which he was a generous donor of plate and books (cat. no. 180). However, a 1516 inventory description is not unambiguous, and describes a cup made like a mazer (which this is), with a stone of variegated colour (which this is not), and with a base and straps of silver-gilt (which again this is). It is most likely that this cup is not the one listed, but did belong to Warham. The scratched inscription, perhaps of *c.*1600, supports this tradition. The solid silver straps are almost identical in design to those on the Eton coconut cup of *c.*1500–20 and on the Richmond Cup of *c.*1520–50 (cat. nos 134, 190).   MLC

LIT. Moffat 1906, no. XXXIV; Oman 1979, pp.297–8; Campbell (M) 2002, p.138.

189

188

189 Tazza

London, 1528–9 (maker's mark: a star over a crescent); the cover 1532–3 (maker's mark: a covered cup)

Silver-gilt; diam. 21.5 cm

British Museum, London (MME 1971, 5–2, 1–2)

The tazza, or 'flat cup', has a broad foot and low stem and is embossed on foot, stem and cover with gadroons and scalework. The cover has a disc-shaped finial above two ropework rings, and the inside of the bowl is embossed with a honeycomb pattern and engraved around the lip with a Latin inscription reading *Benedicamus Patrem et Filium cum Sancto Spiritu* (Let us bless the Father and the Son together with the Holy Spirit).

This exceptionally rare object is one of a pair (the other lacks its cover), known from their inscriptions as 'grace cups'. They probably belonged originally to a monastic foundation, and the 1593 *Rites of Durham*, describing pre-Reformation monastic life, mentions 'the Grace-cup … which did service to the monks every day, after grace was said to drink in round the table'. They almost certainly owe their survival to having been adapted at an early date for use as communion cups.

They are recorded at Rochester Cathedral in *c.*1670 and it is likely that they were there a good deal earlier, possibly from soon after the Reformation. The replacement of the original heraldic device on the finial of the cover by a later Tudor rose, however, means that their original provenance will probably never be known.

The cup and its companion evidently belonged originally to a larger set that was assembled over several years, and the surviving cover is of a different year and by a different maker from either of the two cups. The owners of the makers' marks are unlikely ever to be identified, but there is some reason to suppose that the maker of this cup was responsible for initiating the set, since the same mark is found on two other pieces, a covered cup of 1524 at Christ's College, Cambridge, and a cup of the same year at Charlecote Park, Warwickshire. Both have very similar and distinctive stylistic features, including chased scalework and pronounced raised gadroons.   TS

PROV. Rochester Cathedral (from at least *c.*1670); acquired by the British Museum in 1971.

LIT. Hayward 1976, p.366, pls 297–8; Cherry 1988, pp.7–8; Schroder 1988, p.24.

190 Coconut cup

*c.*1500–20

A coconut shell, mounted in silver gilt; unmarked;
h. 20.3 cm; diam. of foot, 10.2 cm

Inscr. (around the lip) in *pointillé: ex dono mri Johis
edmonds theologie professoris quondam socii hui coll[e]gii*

Eton College, Berkshire

The silver lip is plain, with a moulded edge; the
mount on the shoulder and on the lower part of the
cup is hatched with V-shaped ornament; the nut is

supported by three jointed straps of cast foliage, in
the centre of which are small circular medallions
engraved with stylized pinks, originally enamelled.
The stem is embossed with plain lobes, below which
is a narrow beaded band; the foot is plain, with a
moulded edge. The foot is split in places and has a
large silver patch over two lobes.

In the Middle Ages coconuts were exotic rarities,
imported from the Middle East and known as Indian
nuts. They were believed to have medicinal and
aphrodisiac qualities (Fritz 1983, pp.8–24) and were

generally mounted with silver for use as drinking
cups (although the earliest extant medieval coconut
is a reliquary of *c.*1250 in Münster Cathedral: see
Washington 1991, cat. no. 11). Kings, popes and the
wealthy owned coconuts mounted in precious metal
– Jean de Berry (d. 1416), brother of the French king
and one of the wealthiest connoisseurs of his day, was
given in 1402 two coconut vases with silver-gilt necks,
which had been brought from Constantinople
(Guiffrey 1894, I, p.46). But by the early sixteenth
century, with the opening up of the Indian Ocean by
Portuguese traders and the discovery of the Ameri-
cas, coconuts became more common. Of the 11
medieval surviving coconut cups with English
mounts (Jackson 1911, pp.650–52), all but one are
from the fifteenth and early sixteenth centuries.

According to the inscription on it, this cup was
given by John Edmonds, who was elected fellow of
Eton in 1491, and died *c.*1526 (Oman 1971, p.104).
The cup is first recorded in a college inventory of secular plate in 1550 (*ibid.*, p.101). The spiky-leafed strap-
work decoration of the cup mounts is very similar
indeed to those on the New College celadon bowl (cat.
no. 188) and on the rim of the lid to the Richmond
Cup (cat. no. 134): all the goldsmiths were evidently
using related moulds (Cooper, 1977, p.412). Notably
pious, Henry VI provided more generously for his new
college chapels than for their halls (Campbell (M)
2002, p.32, n.27). Even so, in 1456 Eton owned 200
silver spoons, 12 silver cups and just one coconut cup
and one mazer (Oman 1971, pp.100–4).   MLC

LIT. Jackson 1911, II, p.650, fig. 862; Jones 1938, cat. no. 1, ill.;
Oman 1971; Fritz 1983, cat. no. 28, pl. 16f.

190

191 Bowl

*c.*1480–1510

Silver, parcel-gilt, unmarked; diam. 17.2 cm

Inscr.: stippled on the rim 'St Michaell Bristoll 1684'; underneath are several scratched merchants' marks

St Stephen's church, Bristol, on loan to Bristol Museums and Art Gallery

The curved sides of the bowl are embossed with spiral lobes, the prominently domed centre embossed with sun rays on a matted ground, and set with a roundel engraved with stylized carnations, which contemporaries called gillyflowers. These were originally decorated with translucent enamel, of which traces remain. The foot is stamped with a running band of flowers and foliage.

The bowl may be the same as one listed – without description – in a church inventory of 1575: 'item one boulle of silver pcell gilt weainge 13 ounces'. It was given to the church for use as a communion cup. Shallow bowls in wood, or precious metal, were commonly used for drinking throughout the Middle Ages (Andersson 1983; Lightbown 1978, p.20). The lobed decoration on the Bristol bowl can be paralleled by other late medieval pieces, notably the Fox ablution basins (cat. no. 106). The merchants' marks on the base have not been identified. It was fairly common for silver to be stamped with an owner's mark, whether an initial – crowned, if that of the king – or a badge. MLC

PROV. In the church of St Michael, Bristol, by 1684 and perhaps by 1575; ownership transferred to St Stephen's church, Bristol, in 2002; since *c.*1972 on loan to Bristol Museums and Art Gallery.

LIT. London 1955, cat. no. 4; Ellory, Clifford and Rogers 1999, pp.180–81, 191 (P. Glanville).

192 Wine cup

1493

Silver parcel-gilt, with the hallmarks for London (a leopard's head crowned), the date letter Q for 1493 (the maker's mark, a scallop shell below a baton); h. 14 cm, diam. of bowl 8.1 cm

The Worshipful Company of Goldsmiths, London

The cup has a broad foot and a short stem. Both bowl and foot are gadrooned – a form of decoration that contemporaries would have called 'writhen', and which seems to have been very common on English plate throughout the fifteenth century (Blair 1979a, pp.370–71).

Apart from spoons, this is one of the earliest pieces of fully marked plate (that is, including a date-letter), and would have been made for retail sale. It is a unique survival of a type of cup probably once common, and was long mistaken for an eggcup. It closely resembles the cups that are shown in a drawing of *c.*1480–1500 of the Goldsmiths' Company arms (Reddaway and Walker 1975, pl. I (i) and p.162) and, like them, would probably originally have had a cover. Its small capacity suggests that it would have been used by one individual. The goldsmith has made a mistake that is not at once obvious, miscalculating the number of embossed lobes: there are 15 on the cup, but only 14 on the foot. MLC

PROV. St Andrew's church, Middleton-on-the-Wolds, near Pickering, Yorkshire, until 1976; bought by the Goldsmiths' Company.

LIT. Wallis 1975–6; London 1978, cat. no. 13; Blair 1983, cat. no. 11.

191

192

193 Owl cup and cover

Cologne, *c.*1530–37

Brown iron-dipped salt-glazed stoneware, the basic shape
of pot and lid thrown on the wheel, with details hand-
modelled and moulded feathers individually applied;
the silver mounts unmarked; h. 19.7 cm

The Worshipful Company of Armourers and Brasiers
of London

The company's records for 1537 state: 'This year the
26 day of Aug. Julyan late the wife of William Vinyard
alias Seger deceased and gave to the Hall a stone Pot
like an Owl with certain silver about it gilt the value
of 26s. 8d.' (see also cat. no. 58). The extremely high
value may well reflect the rarity of such imported
novelty vessels, which combined the functions of decorative work of art and ceremonial drinking pot. No
other examples survive in Britain, although part of a
bear jug from the same workshop has been excavated
at Barnard Castle, County Durham.

A complete and almost identical owl, now in the
Kunstgewerbemuseum in Cologne, together with
sherds of lion and bear pots, was recovered from the
site of the Maximinenstrasse workshop in Cologne,
which operated in about 1520–40 (Reineking-von
Bock 1976, cat. no. 314). Although these anthropomorphic stoneware pots were almost certainly used for
drinking (like the eighteenth-century Nottingham
stoneware bears and Staffordshire slipware owls with
detachable heads), it has been convincingly argued
that a parallel series of owl pots from workshops in
Austria or the Tyrol, similar in form but of painted tin-
glazed earthenware with armorials and dates between
1540 and 1561, were made as prestigious prizes for
archery competitions (Honey 1936). Not only is one of
these painted with the story of William Tell, but there
is contemporary evidence that the target for archery
took the form of a stuffed owl.   RH

193

194

194 detail

194 Saucer

*c.*1400

Silver, punched on the rim with a leopard's head, the sterling mark; diam. 13.3 cm, wt 2.6 troy oz

The Strategic Rail Authority, on loan to Shrewsbury Museum and Art Gallery (Rowley's House)

This undecorated bowl is hammered from a single sheet of metal. It is circular, with a plain edge, and with a moulding above the rim and a prominently domed base. The contemporary sterling mark (see ill.) is on its rim, indicating that the silver content was of the legal sterling standard of 92.5 per cent – this has been confirmed by metal analysis.

Since the saucer was found in a datable archaeological context, the mark on it is the only secure pre-1478 English hallmark – all other such marks being found on spoons, which lack a provenance. The saucer is the only known medieval survival in silver of a type certainly once very common, although a few saucers in pewter survive. Such pieces would have been essential at any meal at which sauces were served. These were popular as the accompaniment to both meat and fish dishes in the Middle Ages.　MLC

PROV. Excavated on the site of Shrewsbury Abbey, 1986, in a medieval rubbish pit of before *c.*1400; British Rail; the Strategic Rail Authority, 2002.

LIT. Campbell 1988; Campbell 1991, p.143, fig. 66.

195 Apostle spoons

London, 1536–7 (maker's mark indistinct)

Silver, parcel-gilt; l. (of each spoon) 19.5 cm

British Museum, London (MME 1981, 7-1, 13)

Apparent references to silver spoons with finials in the form of the apostles occur at least as early as the mid-fifteenth century, when a set was mentioned in the will of Sir John Fastolf (d. 1459). They were made in sets of 13, the thirteenth usually being surmounted by the figure of Christ, and were found in both personal and institutional ownership. The earliest surviving spoons of this type date from the second half of the fifteenth century, but by around 1500 they were relatively common, both as sets and individual spoons, and remained so for well over a hundred years.

The present set, known as the Astor spoons, from their ownership throughout most of the twentieth century, is unique in having the figure of the Virgin Mary rather than Christ as its centrepiece. The spoons are engraved on the back of the bowls with the crest of the Bruges family, which dates from the nineteenth century and appears to be engraved over an erased feature. The Sacred Monogram (*IHS*, for *Iesus Hominum Salvator*, 'Jesus, the Saviour of Man') is engraved in the bowls.

The figural models for apostle spoons were seldom – if ever – unique and the same casting patterns, often with separately made and attached emblems, were used repeatedly by specialist spoon makers over several decades. A number of the figures on this set are damaged and several have lost their individually identifying emblems, but the spoons are of great interest in being one of the earliest complete sets to survive; the apostle figures of this set are also exceptionally well modelled. But the castings were not new at the time the spoons were made and several of them appear on Bishop Fox's crosier, made about 30 years before (cat. no. 104).　TS

PROV. (Probably) Henry Long of Whaddon, Wiltshire (d. 1611); by descent to Katherine Long (d. 1814); Thomas Bruges of Seend, Wiltshire (d. 1835); by descent to Richard Heald Ludlow-Bruges (sale, Christie's, 16 July 1903); Viscount Astor of Hever; sale, Christie's, London, 24 June 1981, lot 104.

LIT. How and How 1952–7, pp.102–17; Wilson 1984; Schroder 1988, p.48.

195

196

196 Flagon

*c.*1500

Cast pewter; h. 29.2 cm

Incised under the foot with the date 1620

Private collection

The body is of bulbous form with a waisted upper section and moulded lip; broad trumpet-shaped foot with moulding at the base; domed lid with raised central boss and twin ball and wedge thumb-piece, narrow scrolling strap handle with 'attention' finial. Inside the lid is a copper medallion with stamped fleur-de-lis.

This rare survival is one of four known examples of similar form. One was found in the *Mary Rose*, another (missing its lid) is in Letchworth Museum (Hertfordshire) and a further example with a different thumb-piece is in a church in Somerset. The consistent English provenance of the pieces strongly implies that they are all of indigenous manufacture.   AN

LIT. Homer 1995.

197 Dish

PLATE 27

*c.*1500

Cast pewter; diam. 34 cm

The Worshipful Company of Pewterers, London (51/104)

A plain circular dish with a prominent rim and slightly domed centre. The front of the rim bears a stamped badge of a crowned feather.

This is one of a series of pewter dishes from various sources, all bearing crowned feather marks. The largest number, including one in the Victoria and Albert Museum (M.39–1945), were dug up in 1899 when excavations were being made for an extension to Guy's Hospital. Two more were recovered in 1978 from excavations near the river at Hampton Court. Another was discovered in 1984 bearing the crowned feather and other marks, including armorial devices used by Anne of Cleves, wife of Henry VIII.

For many years these dishes have been associated with Arthur, Prince of Wales (1486–1502), eldest son of Henry VII. It has been suggested that all these crowned feather dishes once formed part of a pewter service made for the coronation of Henry VIII in 1509, and subsequently dispersed. It has also been argued that the Guy's Hospital group of dishes may have belonged to an inn named the Prince of Wales. However, no inn bearing this name is known from that site.   AN

LIT. Read 1899–1901; Law 1985; Homer 1989.

198 Chafing dish

The Netherlands, *c.*1490

Cast and turned copper alloy; h.10.5 cm, w. 18.3 cm

Bristol Museums and Art Gallery (G1437)

A shallow bowl supported on a hollow skirted foot. Cast into the top of the rim are three flanges. Attached through lugs at each side are two trefoil openwork handles. The interior and exterior are decorated with a series of shallow turned mouldings. The damage to the foot implies a very brittle alloy used in its manufacture, perhaps with a high tin content.

Chafing dishes were widely used at table in the fifteenth and sixteenth centuries and frequently appear in contemporary paintings. Hot coals were put in the bowl, and a dish placed above was kept clear of the coals by the three flanges set in the rim. These vessels were produced in large quantities in Germany and the Low Countries in the later Middle Ages and were widely exported.

This chafing dish can be related to a series in English collections, including three in the British Museum, an example in the Victoria and Albert Museum and one in a private collection (Lyons 1907–9). On stylistic grounds this last example can be attributed to the same workshop as the Bristol chafing dish. The occurrence of two virtually identical chafing dishes, both with West Country provenance, can possibly be explained if they were part of a batch supplied by one merchant, probably located in Bristol.   AN

PROV. Excavated in Bristol.

198

199 Mug or jug

Cologne, c.1510–25

Brown salt-glazed stoneware with applied moulded and hand-modelled decoration; h. 20 cm

Victoria and Albert Museum, London (C.9–2002)

Essentially functional, the multi-purpose tough stoneware pots of the Rhineland were widely exported and provided northern Europe with ale mugs, serving jugs and vast numbers of storage bottles (Hurst et al. 1986; Gaimster 1997). The bearded mask and trailing oak or rose decoration made their appearance on Cologne wares – known as Bartmann jugs – in the early years of the sixteenth century and soon became standard features. The title IHESUS on a bottle of this type in the Kunstgewerbemuseum,

Cologne (Reineking-von Bock 1976, cat. no. 256), as well as the frequent rendering of the trailed decoration as the Tree of Jesse (symbolizing the ancestry of Christ), suggest piety as the potters' original inspiration.

This pot was recovered by a diver in around 1840 from the wreck of the *Mary Rose*, Henry VIII's flagship, which capsized in a sudden squall in 1545 while engaging a French fleet off Spithead (see also cat. nos 16, 63). Although of a type securely datable to the first quarter of the sixteenth century, and possibly therefore part of the original equipment of the ship, which was built in 1509–11, the evidence recently salvaged from the vessel indicates that the crew used wood for their mugs and plates, while the officers used pewter plates and – we may suppose – imported

stoneware pots for the ale that formed such an important dietary supplement for fighting men in the Tudor period. RH

PROV. The *Mary Rose* until c.1840; Alfred Everitt, Portsmouth, 1916; on loan to the V&A 1916–2002 (at Southsea Castle 1959–97); acquired 2002.

LIT. Townsend 1984, p.34, ill.

200 Surrey ware jug

PLATE 29

Late 15th/early 16th century

Earthenware, partially glazed; h. 28.5 cm

Museum of London (A22817)

A 'Tudor Green', baluster-form jug, with a globular body, flared base and strap handle. The top half, with the rudimentary slit eyes, pinched ears and beard of applied clay, and the almost right-angled, applied lines of thumbing (intended for arms held with the hands not quite meeting across an ample stomach), was dipped in green glaze, leaving the bare fabric in the lower part. This is the only complete jug known from the 'Tudor Green' industry.

This vestigially anthropomorphic vessel was described by Rackham as 'barbaric', the eyes 'staring in a gaze of almost imbecile fixity'. Standing right at the end of a centuries-old line of ceramic jugs with humanoid characteristics, the loss of the inspiration evident at an earlier time is all too clear. This is the perfunctory product of a maker continuing to manufacture a form already being overtaken as a status symbol by different vessels in pewter or silver. The weariness of this ceramic tradition is reflected in the semi-comatose appearance of the jug itself: appropriate, perhaps, for the latest of an outmoded line, left behind as fashion moved on. GE

PROV. Found at the Aldwych, London.

LIT. London Museum 1940, p.227, fig. 75, no. 1; Rackham 1972, p.21, pl. 48; Pearce and Vince 1988, pp.787–9, no. 584, figs 37, 126.

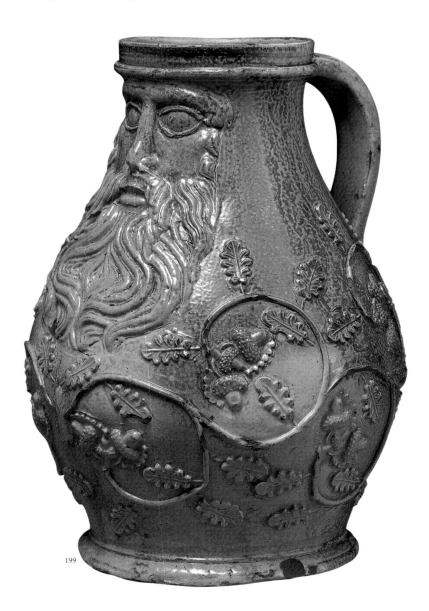

199

15 DRESS AND ADORNMENT

JOHN CHERRY

In the absence of surviving clothes, our knowledge of dress is seen through manuscript illuminations, sculpture, stained glass or the depiction of people on brasses and effigies. While these show how people were seen, they represent the upper levels of society and were rarely intended to provide realistic depictions. The best recent review of the sources for late medieval costume, the raw material, the means of acquisition, the dress of different classes (especially the working classes) and their significance is for France rather than England (Mane 1989; Piponnier and Mane 1997).

Fragments of textile from excavations survive in museums (Crowfoot et al. 1996). Wool was the basic textile, and the fineness of English wool was much remarked on. English cloth was still exported. When Richard Beauchamp, Earl of Warwick, set out for the Holy Land in 1408, he loaded his ship with (among other things) 'Englissh [sic] clothe', some of which he gave to the sultan's lieutenant and his men, 'to array them in his livere after their degrees' (Carus-Wilson 1954, p.xvii).

The two most attractive, sumptuous and luxurious materials were silk and furs. Silk was not produced in England, but was imported from Italy and parts further east. There was an increased import of silk brocaded with gold thread in the fifteenth century. Henry VI was the first English monarch to wear a velvet cloth brocaded with loops of gold thread. In 1429 one of the robes for his coronation (at the age of eight) was a knee-length toga with open sleeves of 'crimson velvet upon velvet', furred with sables (Monnas 1989b).

There was also a complete change in the use of furs and their status. While fine northern squirrel skins had been fashionable earlier, they were now replaced by the more valuable northern variety of marten fur known as sable, by skins of pine marten, and by the black lambskins from south-west Europe known as budge. The increase in the use of these skins is shown by the royal accounts of Henry V and Henry VI, in whose reigns marten rather than squirrel was worn by the king (Veale 1966, pp.133–41).

Late Gothic clothes represent a sense of finery, display and status. Display is most clearly seen in women's clothes and the striving after status shown in the extensive sumptuary legislation, which attempted to regulate clothes and adornment (Hunt 1996). Such laws appear to have been widely disregarded, but their existence coloured the outlook of the period as well as writings on dress. Thomas Hoccleve, writing in *c.*1413 in a poem to Prince Henry, complains about contemporary fashions in male attire, with their wide furred gowns and long, full sleeves (cat. no. 41); and Peter Idley, between

116 Dunstable Swan Jewel (cat. no. 70)

1445 and 1450, criticizes men's short gowns and doublets 'cutted on the buttok even aboue the rumpe', which are 'conducive to immorality because, by revealing the shape of the male body, they inflame women with lecherous desires' (Scattergood 1987, p.266). Such fashions were not only socially dangerous, but also deleterious to the economy. In the words of the Sumptuary Act passed in England in 1463, they contributed to the 'impoverishing of this realm of England and the enriching of other strange Realms and Countries to the final destruction of the Husbandry of this said Realm'.

Of such strange countries, Burgundy and its dukes led fashion in northern Europe. Their lavish expenditure on clothes helped to produce scenes of great splendour and magnificence (Evans 1952, pp.38–58). A notable example was the marriage in Bruges of Margaret of York to Charles the Bold, Duke of Burgundy, in July 1468. John Paston III wrote to his mother on 8 July that 'she was received as worshipfully as all the world could devise, as with procession with ladies and lords best beseen of any people that ever I saw or heard of' (Davis 1983, p.165).

Alabaster effigies (Gardner 1940), brasses (Druitt 1906) and incised effigial slabs (Greenhill 1976) provide useful evidence for dress. The organization of brass engraving has enabled us to understand the repetitive nature of the workshops and the use of drawings (patrons) for designs (Kent 1949, Badham 1990).

In the fifteenth century the most extravagant headdresses are found, often following French court fashion (for continental examples, the best study is Mireille 1995). Examples are the horned headdress, the chimney pot, the mitre, the butterfly and the bourrellet (horseshoe-shaped headdress). Fantastic headdresses are shown on the tombs of the Duchesses of Arundel, at the Fitzalan Chapel at Arundel (Brodrick and Darrah 1986). Between 1485 and 1490 a radical change took place. The extravagance was swept away, except for the frontlet, which was retained and developed into the pedimental (or gable) headdress. The peaked frontlet, stiffened with wires, often had a jewelled border that matched the one around the edge of the square-cut dress.

The collar was a major item of masculine court adornment (Boulton 1987). The collar of SS (plate 23, cat. no. 71a), associated with John of Gaunt, Duke of Lancaster, was taken up by Henry IV as the official livery collar of the Lancastrians (the swan being the Prince of Wales's badge). Some collars were of elaborately bejewelled gold (Lightbown 1992, p.249), but others were simpler, such as that from the Thames (cat. no. 71b). The Yorkists had their collar of suns and roses, shown in the painting of Sir John Donne and his wife (cat. no. 213). From their collars hangs the lion of March, painted as if it were white enamel on gold (Campbell (L) 1998, pp.374–91). This rich technique, derived from Parisian goldsmiths, appears on the earlier Dunstable Swan Jewel (plate 116). Such jewels were the finest examples of the livery badge. Many of these were sewn onto jackets. Those that have survived are the lead badges that showed family devices or heraldic animals, such as the bear and ragged staff of the Earls of Warwick or the talbot of the Earls of Shrewsbury (cat. nos 68c–d).

The feminine counterpart of the collar was the necklace, often ornate and set with jewels. Necklaces are shown on brasses such as that of Joyce Tiptoft at Enfield, engraved *c.*1475, or that of Agnes Yelverton at Rougham, Norfolk, of 1472. Necklaces often had pendants, which were frequently religious and sometimes used as containers for relics or other precious objects. The Middleham Jewel (cat. no. 98) provides a most remarkable example of such a pendant. Not only is it large, still set with a sapphire and originally embellished with a border of pearls, having scenes of the Nativity and the Trinity engraved on the faces, but it was also capable of being opened, so that the protective contents could be contemplated or changed.

Sometimes chains were worn around the neck, linked to other jewels such as locks or lockets (see the example from the Fishpool hoard, cat. no. 206e) or the *Agnus Dei* (a container for a circular wax stamped with the Lamb of God). These combined ornament with the devotional and amuletic function of jewellery (Cherry 2001).

The rosary was worn by both men and women. At its most elaborate it was of gold, sometimes decorated with white enamel. The Langdale rosary (cat. no. 222b) is a fine example of gold engraved with a whole litany of saints. More commonly rosaries were of less precious metal or wood (cat. no. 222a). Sometimes they were worn from girdles, which are mentioned in wills and inventories and are well represented on brasses (cat. no. 334).

Cecily, Duchess of York, provides a remarkable example of extravagant expenditure on both dress and adornment. In 1443–4 nearly £608 was spent in London on purchases for the duchess and the greatest single item was the making of 'an open surcote, a mantle and a cope hoode', all of crimson velvet lined with ermine. Made by John Legge, a tailor of the king's wardrobe, it involved the purchase of 60 yards (55 metres) of velvet, 325 pearls (30 of them very costly at £6 each) and 8½ oz (240 g) of gold (Pugh 1986). In her will of August 1495 she left a large amount of expensive jewellery, including girdles and demi ceints, and a collection of *Agnus Dei* containers – of which the most magnificent was 'a great agnus of gold with the Trinity, Saint Erasmus and the Salutation of our Lady, rosaries, one, of white amber, having six large gauds [large beads] of gold, partly enamelled' (Nichols and Bruce 1862–3, pp.1–6; Armstrong 1942). Few women in England before Queen Elizabeth represent the luxury and ostentation of dress and adornment in the fifteenth century as well as Cecily Neville, Duchess of York and mother of the King of England.

FURTHER READING

Lightbown 1992; Piponnier and Mane 1997; Scott 1980.

201

202

203

201 Panel of fabric

Italy, c.1475

Crimson velvet cloth-of-gold, with weft loops
of silver-gilt thread; h. 183 cm, w. 60 cm

Victoria and Albert Museum, London (81–1892)

This costly fabric, woven with undulating stems bearing stylized pomegranates, is typical of the fine textiles
imported into England from Italy under licences stip-
ulating that the monarch should have 'first sight and
choice' of them. Costing £2–£11 per yard, when some
royal craftsmen earned 12d. per day, under Henry VIII
the use of gold-looped fabrics, termed 'cloth of gold
of tissue', was restricted by law to the king and his
immediate relatives (with notable exemptions). This
panel does not, however, represent the finest quality.
The Fayrey pall (cat. no. 349) incorporates a finer
cloth-of-gold, and the textile of the Henry VII cope
(cat. no. 31) is richer still.

'Tissues' with this particular design were popular
for noble dress and furnishings from the 1470s into
the early sixteenth century, as may be seen in the
cloth of estate depicted in the Donne Triptych (cat.
no. 213). Although versions were woven into the seventeenth century, by the 1540s their popularity as
dress fabric had waned, and at the court of Henry
VIII, where they were dubbed 'churchwork', they were
mainly relegated to his chapel. Too valuable to dis-
card, Henry VIII's churchwork hangings were still
listed in the Commonwealth sale of 1649.   LM

PROV. Bardini Collection, Florence; acquired in 1892.

LIT. Monnas 1998, p.66 (ill.).

202 Belt with mounts

Early 15th century

Leather, silk and copper alloys: l. c.77 cm, w. 3.4 cm

Museum of London (89.65)

This elaborate strap is of suitable size for a sword belt,
but it lacks specific provision for attachment of a
weapon. It is of leather with the remains of plain-
woven silk, probably dyed red or pink, originally covering both front and back; 142 riveted and pinned sheet
copper-alloy mounts survive, all but one of either of
two forms. The most prolific mounts are four-armed,
cruciform ones set in pairs flanking composite circular
ones (the central domes of which retain traces of silver
coating). Those of the latter form comprise two different copper alloys, giving a gold-coloured, brassy surround to the coated centre (the alloys used respectively
contain greater and smaller additions of zinc). The proliferation of the two basic shapes of mount, regularly
repeated, makes an overall pattern in which the individual elements blend into the whole.

A single, rectangular mount with tooled ornament,
set at one surviving end, probably secured the missing buckle.

Assigned, by comparison with similar items found
in datable deposits, to the early fifteenth century.   GE

PROV. Found on the Thames foreshore, Bankside, Southwark.

LIT. Egan and Pritchard 1991, pp.23, 245, pls 5E and F;
Murdoch 1991, p.109, cat. no. 203.

203 Short sword (baselard)

Late 14th–early 15th century

Steel and wood; l. 78 cm

Museum of London (80.34)

The broad, tapering, single-edged blade is inlaid in
one face with a copper-alloy (latten?) mark, a 'Y' on
its side and a saltire. The one-piece hilt is of characteristic 'I' shape, the grip of flattened octagonal section, and the top of the pommel and the underside of
the guard are each reinforced with an iron plate. The
pommel, instead of being symmetrical, as on the
normal double-edged baselard, is slightly curtailed
on the side in line with the back of the blade.

This is an example of a weapon very widely used in
the second half of the fourteenth and first half of the
fifteenth centuries, in England mainly by civilians: a
fifteenth-century poem comments, 'Ther is non man
worth a leke… But he bere a baselard'. It is depicted on
many effigies and brasses, and the three pairs of crossed
swords in the coat of arms of the London Cutlers'
Company are all baselards on their earliest surviving
seal, which must date from 1476, when it was granted
to them. The name is derived from the city of Basel,
where the weapon apparently originated (Blair 1984).
This example is presumably of English make.   CB

PROV. Excavated at Bull Wharf, London, 1979.

LIT. Alexander and Binski 1987, no. 175.

204 Purse frame

The Netherlands, c.1450

Copper alloy; h. 20.5 cm, w. 11 cm

British Museum, London (MME 1998,10-1,1)

This metal frame consists of two loops from which
the textile fabric would have hung and a bar from
which hang two panels, elaborately decorated with
openwork tracery, consisting of windows on each
side of a circle with a sixfold flowing pattern. This is
reminiscent of French Flamboyant tracery. From this
bar there arise two towers (originally four were
intended). At the centre of the bar is an elaborate

tower with a swivel, which would have attached it to
a belt.

Comparisons of the openwork panels with those
on a Burgundian clock (Victoria and Albert Museum,
M.11–1940, now on display in the British Museum),
and of the shape and type of the frame with examples
in paintings, such as the *Portrait of a Young Man* by
Petrus Christus in the National Gallery (Campbell
(L) 1998, pp.104–9), suggest that the purse frame was
made abroad, perhaps in the Low Countries, and
imported into England.

Such a purse frame may have belonged to a rich
merchant and, rather than being a purse for coins
alone, it probably contained all that he needed for
negotiating a business deal. A purse of similar type,
though lacking the towers, is shown on the memorial
brass of John Browne (d. 1475) (cat. no. 139).   JC

PROV. Found in the Thames near Cannon Street station;
Morgan Collection; purchased with the aid of the British
Museum Society, Mr Sam Fogg, and the National
Art Collections Fund, 1998.

LIT. Cherry 1998 and 1999.

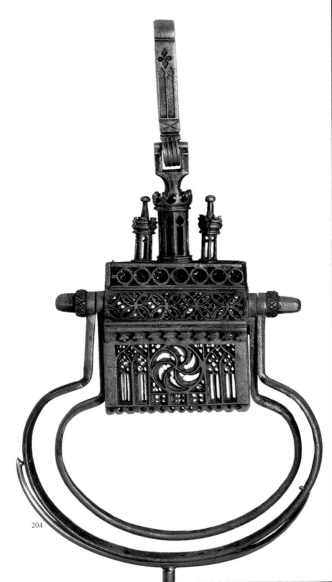

204

205 Everyday coinage

Ordinary people in the mid-fifteenth century would rarely use and handle gold coins. Daily transactions involved the lesser silver denominations, from the half-groat down to the tiny farthing. The English policy of maintaining fine silver throughout the system, and not resorting to 'black money' – coins of very base silver – as most of her neighbours did, left people struggling with these tiny coins. Despite its small size, however, even the farthing's purchasing power was significant, and accounts might be kept in subdivisions of the farthing that never existed as coins. Penny production was left largely to the ecclesiastical mints, Durham and York. The coins in use at this level of the currency were very mixed in nature. Since there had been no full recoinage since 1279, much older coin still circulated, now very worn and sometimes clipped down to, or beyond, the current weight standard. While the London mint retained the monopoly on halfpennies and farthings, these were in short supply, due to the economics of minting: it was more cost-effective to coin a pound's worth of silver into 60 groats than into 960 farthings. Parliamentary petitions and governmental instructions sought to remedy this, in the interests of alms-giving and the aid of the poor, but to little effect, compounding an overall European shortage of coin caused by limited bullion supplies in the first half of the fifteenth century. Credit, barter and the offsetting of small debts were all means by which ordinary people surmounted the limitations of their currency.   BC

LIT. Britnell 1996, pp.181–96; Dyer 1997.

a) Penny of Henry V (1413–22), class G, York mint

Silver; diam. 1.6 cm, wt 0.79 g

Obv.: crowned bust facing, with mullet to left of crown and trefoil to right

HENRIC REX ANGLIE (Henry king of England)

Rev.: long cross pattée dividing legend; quatrefoil in centre; three pellets in each angle

CIVITAS EBORACI (City of York)

British Museum, London (CM 1993-4-23-287)

LIT. North 1991, p.71.

b) Coins of Henry VI, Leaf-Pellet issue (1445–54)

i. Silver half-groat, London mint

diam. 2.3 cm, wt 1.97 g

Obv.: crowned bust facing; two pellets by the crown; leaf on bust

HENRIC DI GRA REX ANGLI & FRAN (Henry by the grace of God king of England and France)

Rev.: long cross pattée dividing legend; three pellets in each angle

POSUI DEU ADIUTORE MEUM (I have made God my helper)

British Museum, London (CM 1866-3-22-13)

ii. Silver penny, York mint

diam. 1.6 cm, wt 0.8 g

Obv.: crowned bust facing, two pellets by the crown

HENRIC REX ANGLIE (Henry king of England)

British Museum, London (CM 1839-3-21-1)

Rev.: long cross pattée dividing legend; quatrefoil in centre; three pellets in each angle

CIVITAS EBORACI (City of York)

British Museum, London (CM 1839-3-21-26)

iii. Silver halfpenny, London mint

diam. 1.3 cm, wt 0.45 g

Obv.: crowned bust facing, two pellets by the crown

HENRIC REX ANGLI (Henry king of England)

Rev.: long cross pattée dividing legend; three pellets in each angle

CIVITAS LONDON (City of London)

British Museum, London (CM 1840-5-9-21)

iv. Silver farthing, London mint

diam. 1 cm, wt. 0.23 g

Obv.: crowned bust facing, two pellets by the crown

HENRIC REX ANGLI (Henry king of England)

Rev.: long cross pattée dividing legend; three pellets in each angle

CIVITAS LONDON (City of London)

British Museum, London (CM 1848-6-22-1)

LIT. North 1991, p.80.

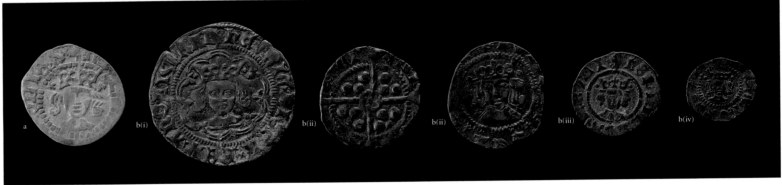

205

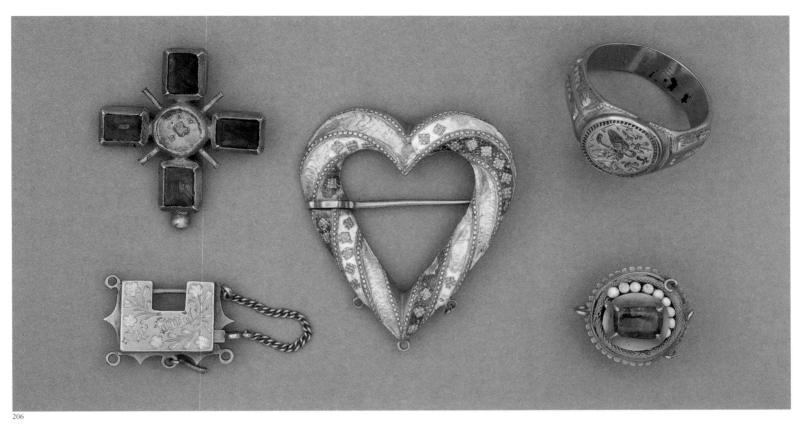

206

206 Jewellery from the Fishpool Hoard

Deposited in spring 1464

a) Signet ring

Gold; diam. 2.5 cm

Inscr. in black-letter: *de bon coer* (of good heart), inside the hoop, the letter *t* engraved on the bezel

British Museum, London (MME, 1967, 12-8, 4)

b) Cross

Gold, set with a ruby on one side and four amethysts on the other; h. 3.1 cm, w. 2.6 cm

British Museum, London (MME, 1967, 12-8, 7)

c) Heart-shaped brooch

Gold, with blue and white enamel; h. 4 cm, w. 4.3 cm

Inscr. in black-letter on reverse: *Je suy vostre sans de partier* (I am yours for ever)

British Museum, London (MME, 1967, 12-8, 8)

d) Roundel

Gold, with beads of white enamel and a sapphire; diam. 1.7 cm

British Museum, London (MME, 1967, 12-8, 9)

e) Padlock locket

Gold, engraved and with white enamel; h. 1.6 cm, w. 1.2 cm

Inscr. in black-letter: on one side *de tout* (with all); on the other: *mon cuer* (my heart)

British Museum, London (MME, 1967, 12-8, 6)

This hoard shows the jewellery that would have been worn by a leading noble or gentleman on important social occasions. The large number of coins (1,237) found in the hoard reveals that it was hidden in spring 1464, around the time of the battle of Hexham (May 1464), which ended the Lancastrian resistance in the North of England. The hoard was unusual since it was entirely of gold. The presence of the latest issues of the coins suggests they may not have been far removed from the royal treasury. The coins may have been carried by a prominent member of one of the opposing factions in the Wars of the Roses. The value would have been around £400, a very considerable sum.

The principal pieces are shown here. The bullion value was just under £6 in terms of the late fifteenth century. All the pieces are different. The presence of the signet ring suggests that a man owned the jewellery and rings. If the device on the signet ring (a) could be understood, then he might be identified, since the ring would have been used for sealing letters and instructions. The signet bears the device of a hawk's lure with the wings bound with cords, above which is the letter *t*, fleurs-de-lis on each side and flowers on each side of the lure. The hawk's lure is a rare charge in fifteenth-century heraldry and is associated with the families of Fitzpaine, Seymour, Wakering and Aldington. It was also used as a crest by the Sacheverell family of Kirkby-in-Ashfield in Nottinghamshire, near to where the hoard was discovered.

Just as a substantial proportion of the coin (18 per cent) comes from abroad, so there are possible foreign influences to be seen in the jewellery. Much could have been made in England, and the French inscriptions were in standard use on English jewellery. Whether any of the jewellery pieces were imports, or were made in London by goldsmiths (either English or alien) in a continental style, remains open to question.   JC

PROV. Found at Fishpool, near Blidworth, Nottinghamshire, in March 1966; acquired by the British Museum, 1967.

LIT. Archibald 1967; Cherry 1973; Ward et al. 1981, no. 163.

207 Brooch

Early 15th century

**Gold, with white enamel set with a tourmaline;
h. 5 cm, w. 4.1 cm**

**All Souls College, Oxford, on loan
to the British Museum, London**

A brooch in the form of a white flower with five petals, at the centre of which is an elongated tourmaline surrounded by cut gold to give the impression of stamens. The *ronde-bosse* white enamelling on gold is similar to that on the Dunstable Swan Jewel and the Reliquary of St-Esprit (cat. nos 70, 10). It is probable that this, like the other *ronde-bosse* white enamels, was made in Paris. Although it is tempting to associate it with the use of the white rose by the Yorkists, this jewel probably dates to the early part of the fifteenth century, when the flower form was widely used as a motif for the setting of a prized stone. The stone is a pink tourmaline, a very unusual stone in jewellery before the seventeenth century, and this may be the earliest known example of a mounted tourmaline. It is likely that the stone came from the East, perhaps Sri Lanka, and so the setting indicates the highly prized nature of the stone. JC

PROV. Already in the possession of All Souls College in the time of John Stokes, the fifth Warden (1466–94).

LIT. Lightbown 1992, p.175, pl. 73; Stratford 1997; Bowman and Stapleton 1998.

208 Pendant cross

*c.*1475–1500

Gold with black enamel; h. with suspension loop 3.6 cm, w. 2.8 cm

Norfolk Museums Service (Castle Museum, Norwich) (NCM 76.94 (432))

The cross was designed as a case for the inclusion of a relic, with a high rim running around the back of the front plate. On the front Christ hangs on the cross between St John the Baptist holding the Lamb, on his left, and an unidentified bishop saint holding a crosier on the right. Described as 'wonderfully elegant with its dark pathos' (Lightbown 1992, p.204), an effect created by the framing of the central figures of the Crucifixion scene with flowers and leaves in

207

208

black enamel, this reliquary jewel is in the shape of a tau-shaped cross.

Such crosses were often known as St Anthony crosses from their association with that saint, the patron of the Order of the Hospitallers of St Antoine-de-Viennois; the purpose of the order was the healing of the sick and especially those suffering from the disease of 'St Anthony's Fire'. This was a disease known to modern medicine as ergotism, which was caused by the consumption of grain that had been contaminated with the mould *Claviceps purpurea* (Husband 1992).

Other fifteenth-century tau-crosses are known, notably from Bridlington (Yorkshire), which has the Annunciation, and Winteringham in Lincolnshire (now in The Cloisters, New York), which has the Trinity on one side and the Virgin and Child on the other. Together with the occurrence of references to such crosses in inventories, it suggests that they were often used for personal devotion and as protection against illness among prosperous and devout households. JC

PROV. Found at Matlask, Norfolk, before 1852.

LIT. Fitch 1852; Husband 1992, fig. 17; Lightbown 1992, pl. 64.

209 The Clare Reliquary Cross

PLATE 7

Mid-15th century

Gold, set with pearls and originally enamelled; h. 3.1 cm, w. 2.7 cm, l. of chain 60 cm

Inscr. with the titulus *Inri* (Iesus Nazarenus Rex Iudeorum) above the cross and the individual letters I N R I pounced on the front arms of the cross

Her Majesty the Queen, on loan to the British Museum, London

Suspended by two rings from a twisted wire chain, the front of the cross is engraved with a panel on which a crucifix figure is reserved against a cross-shaped area, which was once keyed for enamel (all now missing). Beyond the enamelled area are pounced the individual letters I N R I in black enamel. The back is pounced with a design of leaves in a scrolling pattern. Behind the enamelled cross there is a cavity where minute fragments of wood and stone were found when the cross was discovered, indicating that it was a reliquary cross. The pouncing recalls the work on the Royal Gold Cup

210

211

212

in the British Museum (Paris 1981, cat. no. 213) and it may be that this technique is an example of the influence of French goldsmiths' techniques on London goldsmiths. The chain enabled the reliquary cross to be worn for personal devotion and display. JC

PROV. Found during the construction of the railway station on the site of Clare Castle, Suffolk, in 1866 (Clare belonged to the Mortimer family, Earls of March, in the fifteenth century; passed to Richard, Duke of York, on the death of Edmund, Earl of March, in 1425, and later granted by Edward IV to his mother Cecily, Duchess of York, who remained in possession until her death in 1495).

LIT. Way 1868; Tait 1976, cat. no. 366; Husband 1992, fig. 6; Lightbown 1992, p.203, pl. 61.

210 Ring

Early 15th century

Gold; diam. 2 cm, bezel h. 1 cm, w. 0.9 cm

Inscr. on the hoop in black-letter: *a vous ma gre*
(to you my accord)

Ipswich Borough Council Museums and Galleries
(R.1997.16)

A very similar inscription, *'prens en gre'*, is known from a fifteenth-century dagger hilt found in Norfolk before 1858 (Way 1858, p. 275). The inscription is essentially secular and this ring shows the combination of a non-religious inscription with a devotional scene. The finger ring is of the type known as 'iconographic' from the engraving of saints on panels on the bezel. This example has a finely engraved scene of the Annunciation in two panels, originally with an enamelled background. The

cabled hoop has foliate details bearing quatrefoil and cinquefoil flowers. The delicately pounced workmanship can be compared with the pouncing on the back of the Clare Cross (cat. no. 209). JC

PROV. Found on the beach at Covehithe, Suffolk; acquired in 1997 with the assistance of the National Art Collections Fund.

LIT. Plunkett 1997.

211 The Coventry Ring

Late 15th century

Gold, originally with black enamel in the inscriptions and red enamel in the wounds and drops of blood; diam. 2.7 cm, d. 1.55 cm

Inscr. on exterior in black-letter: *the well of pitty, the well of merci, the well of confort, the well of gracy, the well of ewerlastingh lyffe;* and on the interior: *Vulnera quinq[ue] dei sunt medicina mei pia / crux et passio xpi sunt medicina michi iaspar / melchior baltasar ananyzapta tetragrammaton* (The five wounds of God are my medicine, the holy cross and passion of Christ are my medicine, Caspar Melchior Baltazar ananyzapta tetragrammaton)

British Museum, London (MME AF 897)

The ring consists of a thick broad band, the exterior of which is engraved with Christ standing in the tomb, with the Cross and the Instruments of the Passion behind him. The five wounds of Christ are engraved at intervals around the hoop, the largest ('the well of everlasting life') next to Christ and the others in pairs one above the other, with their descriptions beside them. The devotion to the five wounds, so clearly displayed on the outside, is

reflected by the inscription on the inside. The interior inscription adds the names of the Three Kings and the magical words *'ananyzapta'* and *'tetragrammaton'* (see cat. no. 98).

The will of Sir Edmund Shaw, an important London goldsmith of the second half of the fifteenth century, refers to the making of 16 such rings, to be distributed to those close to him. They were to be made 'of fyne gold' and 'graven with the well of petey, the well of mercy and the well of everlasting lyff'. JC

PROV. Found near the town wall in Coventry Park, Coventry, in 1802.

LIT. Dalton 1912, no. 718; Gray 1963, p.165; Ward et al. 1981, no. 189; London 2000, cat. no. 63, pp.162–3 (entry by G. Finaldi); Cherry 2001, pp.169–71.

212 Ring

c.1400–50

Pewter; external diam. 1.5 cm, internal diam. 1.3 cm

Museum of London (BWB83 5810)

This ring, cast in a three-piece mould, serves as an example of a type of ring that would have been produced in large numbers. With a slender hoop of flat section, it is decorated on the outside with a chevron pattern, and has a bezel in the form of a mitred head. This has provoked the suggestion that it was worn in the manner of a pilgrim badge, and that the mitred head could represent Thomas Becket. JC

PROV. Found among material from Billingsgate Market, London, 1983.

LIT. Egan and Pritchard 1991, p.334, no. 1642, fig. 218.

16 PRIVATE DEVOTION

SUSAN FOISTER

On New Year's Day 1535 Sir Thomas More sent to his fellow-prisoner Bishop John Fisher 'an image of the Epiphany', a representation of the infant Christ worshipped by the Magi, an event to be celebrated by the Christian church a few days later on 6 January (Brewer et al. 1862–1932, VIII, 856[9]). The record of his gift gives a fleeting glimpse of the role played by small portable images as the focus for private prayer and meditation during this period. Private devotion is an elusive pastime, by its nature hard to document. It requires no priest, no building, no special equipment or even a physical image, only the mind's ability to visualize the object of devotion: the crucified Christ, perhaps, or the Virgin offering the breast to the Christ Child. Texts such as the fourteenth-century *Meditationes Vitae Christi*, attributed to the Italian St Bonaventura – which, in the fifteenth-century English translation by the Carthusian Nicholas Love, was 'probably the most popular vernacular book of the fifteenth century' (Duffy 1992, p.235) – and Ludolph of Saxony's *Vita Christi*, as well as the works of English followers, Margery Kempe and Richard Rolle, emphasized the importance of imagery for private devotion. They presented the life and, especially, the sufferings of Christ and the Virgin to their readers as a series of images over which the devout were to linger in meditation and use as the focus for their prayers. For those without the mystic's powers of concentration, the availability of a physical image would serve to sharpen and intensify the experience: imagery and images were inseparable from the devotional process.

There is much evidence that acts of private devotion using images took place in England as they did throughout Europe in this period. Many of the images survive, though later attitudes to them have helped to ensure that fewer remain than accidents of time alone would have allowed. More are recorded in household inventories and other documents: their evidence emphasizes the common nature of religious devotion in England and the rest of Europe. The images in use were often universal – Christ displaying his wounds (Duffy 1992, pp.243–5) or the Virgin holding the Christ Child – but there were also reflections of local saints, as well as images promoted by specific orders of monks and friars and those associated with indulgences, notably the Gregorian Man of Sorrows (*ibid.*, p.109).

Although in sixteenth-century Europe the advent of Protestantism was associated with disapproval and even destruction of religious imagery in the public domain, private devotion was hard to police. In the England of Henry VIII, throughout the 1530s, the imagery of private devotion still permeated court and country alike. In many of the portrait drawings and paintings of Hans Holbein the Younger, Henry's courtiers and their wives wear hat badges or medallions with images of the Virgin and Child or saints, and sim-

ilar devotional imagery is reflected in many small drawings for jewellery (Parker 1983; Rowlands 1993). The inventories of Henry VIII and of his queens and daughter similarly show that they owned many such small jewels and other images (Starkey 1998).

Prayer and meditation could take place without the use of images, but in practice many different types of small portable images were used, from illuminated Books of Hours and primers, sometimes with separately inserted images (Duffy 1992, pp.243–5; cat. no. 326), to single painted or printed sheets; from folding images with painted or sculpted imagery to single images, such as sculpted wooden figures (cat. no. 220) and small medallions that could be worn on the person; from pilgrim badges to pendants

117 Alabaster head of St John the Baptist in a painted tabernacle (cat. no. 219)

(cat. nos 98, 208–9, 324). The range of types of object and material is far greater than modern categories for works of art suggest. Some, neglected today, were evidently of great importance for private devotion during this period. Alabaster heads of the decapitated St John the Baptist, for example, were seemingly very popular in England (plate 117). Many images feature in domestic inventories; they appear to have been cheap and are sometimes recorded covered with a cloth of precious material of greater value than the image itself (Foister 1981; Cheetham 1984). In the London house of Sir Henry Guildford, Comptroller of the Household of Henry VIII, four devotional images were listed in 1532 in the bedchamber, only one of which appears to have been a painting, and one 'a tablet of oure lady of paynted lether set in woode sore worne'. There were also four religious images in the chapel, two of the Virgin, one of which was a 'stayned' panel, one an embroidery and one a glass panel depicting the beheading of St John (Foister 1981).

A chapel for private devotion was a feature of some of the grander households of the period (Howard 1987). Here permission – known as an indult – could be obtained for an altar to be set up so that a priest could officiate at Mass, but smaller spaces might also be used for informal devotion. Sir John and Lady Donne had an indult to establish a private altar, but there were many locations where they might have had their triptych by Memling (cat. no. 213) and it may have been placed in houses with no altar and no chapel. The triptych owned by Paul Withypool (cat. no. 135) may also have travelled with him. Domestic images are sometimes recorded in chests and bags, indicating their portability. Inventories record religious images in many different spaces, including bedchambers such as that of the Guildfords. Thomas Cromwell's living rooms included a number of images with religious subjects that could have been used for devotion (Foister 1981), although in sixteenth-century Europe the production of paintings with ostensibly religious subjects – such as St Jerome and St Mary Magdalene – in which landscapes or nudity were prominent motifs, suggests ambiguity surrounding the function of some of these images.

How were devotional images acquired? Painted folding images of great quality, such as the Donne Triptych or the Withypool Altarpiece, were usually the result of direct commissions from the artist, although the extent to which patrons were selecting personalized variants on a theme well established in the artist's workshop should not be underestimated; it appears to have been common practice for workshops in the Low Countries to produce stock images to which shutters with personalized coats of arms could be attached (Campbell 1976). A great many of the devotional images in use in England as well as in Europe at this time must have been mass-produced, from sources ranging from paintings and sculpture (including alabaster) to prints and illuminated books. Many of those in use in England were probably imported especially from the Low Countries (see the essays by Catherine Reynolds and Kim Woods in this volume).

It is easy to underestimate today the extent of the use of this devotional material and its significance in fifteenth- and early sixteenth-century English life. A few objects produced for the wealthiest consumers were of the great quality that would ensure that they qualified for preservation over future centuries as 'works of art', but many others – well used, well worn and bearing 'Popish' imagery – have inevitably been lost, and with them a sense of the intensity, individuality and everyday nature of private devotion in England in this period.

FURTHER READING

London 2000; Nuremberg 2000; van Os 1994.

213

213 The Donne Triptych

Hans Memling, 1478

Oil on oak panels; centre: h. 72.3 cm, w. 71.6 cm;
wings: h. 72 cm, w. 31.1 cm (modern frames)

National Gallery, London (NG 6275)

The closed wings, with Sts Christopher and Anthony Abbot in monochrome, open dramatically to the richly coloured Virgin and Child between angels with musical instruments, emblems of praise, and an apple, symbol of Christ as the second Adam; Sts Catherine and Barbara present the owners, the Welshman Sir John Donne (d. 1503) and his wife Elizabeth (d. 1506/7), sister of Lord Hastings, with their daughter. High in Edward IV's favour, they wear his livery collars (see cat. no. 71). Their shields of arms appear in the capitals and glass of the fictive loggia, which extends into the wings containing Sir John's name-saints, the Baptist, perhaps with a Donne retainer behind, and the Evangelist.

Often in Calais and on Netherlandish embassies, Donne was a knowledgeable patron (cat. nos 214–15), who commissioned his triptych from the German Hans Memling, who settled in Bruges in 1465. It shows all the Memling characteristics that were imitated across Europe: religious feeling expressed through idealized beauty, apparently effortless composition and illusionistic effects of landscapes, portraits and still life. Originally dated 1478, as shown by copies, it seems a personalized variant of the centre panel of Memling's large St John's Hospital Triptych, signed and dated 1479, but in progress earlier (Bruges, Sint-Janshospitaal). The smaller size may mean that it was intended not for a specific location, such as Horsenden (Buckinghamshire), Donne's principal residence, but for moving with his household, as an altarpiece or other devotional focus.   CR

PROV. Richard Boyle, 3rd Earl of Burlington (1694–1753); the Dukes of Devonshire by descent; acquired 1957.

LIT. Campbell (L) 1998, pp.374–91.

214

214 Legends of Saints*

Southern Netherlands, *c.*1475–80

Vellum, ff.80; h. 26 cm, w. 17 cm

British Library, London (Royal MS 20 B. II)

Sir John Donne acquired secular as well as devotional works from the craftsmen of Flanders. One of the manuscripts in which his arms appear is this collection of stories from the lives of saints. It contains an account of the miraculous events surrounding the death and assumption of the Virgin Mary, a life of St John the Evangelist – to which is appended the story of the loss and return of the ring of Edward the Confessor – and a much romanticized life of St Mary Magdalene. Although this material is of a religious nature, it is to be classed with books for the library rather than books intended for the chapel.

The illustrations, beginning with a major miniature of the Virgin, supported by angels, rising into heaven before the assembled apostles (f.1), are attributable to the popular and well-patronized illuminator known as the Master of the Dresden Prayerbook, who also painted many of the miniatures in Donne's Book of Hours (cat. no. 215). This must be among his earliest work. The distinctive bold and angular script is very similar to that in the *Chroniques de France* (cat. no. 46), which suggests that the volume may have been written out in Calais, where Donne served Edward IV under the leadership of his brother-in-law, William Lord Hastings, and was eventually himself Lieutenant under Henry VII.   JMB

PROV. Sir John Donne (d. 1503); Royal Library, before 1542; passed to British Museum in 1757.

LIT. Backhouse 1987, pp.30–31; Backhouse 1994, pp. 51–3; Brinkmann 1997, pp.85–7, 369; Carley 2000, p.175.

215 Hours of Sir John Donne (formerly the Louthe Hours)

Southern Netherlands, *c.*1480

Vellum, ff.118; h. 15 cm, w. 11 cm

Université catholique de Louvain, Louvain-la-Neuve (MS A.2)

Only very recently has it been established that this richly decorated Flemish Book of Hours, of Sarum Use and thus unquestionably intended for an English client, was made for Sir John Donne of Kidwelly, patron of the Memling triptych (cat. no. 213). The coat of arms that accompanies two of its miniatures, both featuring the figure of the owner, was formerly identified as that of the Louthe family of Lincolnshire. It now appears that the black pigment on these shields covers the blue appropriate to the very similar arms of Donne. The new identification is confirmed by the unusual crest of knotted snakes that surmounts the helm, alongside the image of the patron with his guardian angel (f.100v), echoed by the inclusion of spotted snakes among the grapevines in the marginal decoration. The use of a knotted snake crest by Donne's elder son is documented in the sixteenth century.

The manuscript contains an exceptionally lengthy series of miniatures of individual saints, including the very rare St Thomas of Hereford, whose appearance is probably due to Donne's connections with Wales and the Marches, as well as the more conventional illustrations for the components of a typical Book of Hours. It is the work of three main illuminators, two of whom – Simon Marmion of Valenciennes and the anonymous Master of the Dresden Prayerbook (cat. no. 214) – were among the outstanding book painters of the period. The manuscript is of key importance for any study of Marmion's work, as it has given the name 'Louthe Master' to a putative second hand working in his style. Most scholars are now satisfied that this distinction is unjustified and that all work in this artistic idiom, seen in the miniature of Donne and his guardian angel, should be associated with a single hand.   JMB

PROV. Sir John Donne of Kidwelly (d. 1503); Université catholique de Louvain.

LIT. De Schryver 1992; Clark 1992; Brinkmann 1997, pp.153–9, pls 20–21, 24, figs 135–45; Campbell (L) 1998, p.382; Backhouse 2001, pp.158–9.

215

216 Altar frontal

*c.*1500

Figures, fleurs-de-lis and coat of arms embroidered in coloured silks and *filé* metal thread on linen, with some details on tabby silk, applied to a ground of crimson silk velvet; h. 82 cm, w. 277 cm

The National Trust (Cotehele House, St Dominick, Cornwall)

Thirteen figures standing beneath castellated canopies represent (from the left) Sts Philip, Thomas, Matthew, James the Less, John the Evangelist and Peter; Christ; Sts Paul, Andrew, Bartholomew, James the Greater, Simon and Jude. There are fleurs-de-lis above and below the figures.

Beneath Christ is a shield bearing the arms of Edgcumbe, gules a bend sable cotized gold, with three boars' heads silver upon the bend, impaling Durnford, sable a ram's head silver with horns of gold. These are the arms of Sir Piers Edgcumbe (1472–1539) after his marriage, in 1493, to Joan Durnford (d. 1525), and before his second marriage in 1530.

The Edgcumbes owned Cotehele House for 600 years, from 1353 until it passed to the National Trust in 1947. The chapel was rebuilt during the late fifteenth century under Sir Richard Edgcumbe (d. 1489) and his son Sir Piers, as part of their major rebuilding of Cotehele. The frontal is a rare survival of a pre-Reformation liturgical furnishing preserved in the domestic chapel of the family for whom it was made. Conserved in the 1990s, with silk, crepeline and nylon net.   LM

LIT. Mallon 1894, pp.189, 190, ill.; St John Hope 1913b; Cotehele 1998, pp.14, 34, ill.

216

217

217 The Annunciation to the Virgin Mary

*c.*1420–35

Stained and painted glass; h. 81 cm, w. 48.7 cm

Inscr. in black-letter: *A/ve gracia /plena d(omi)n(u)s tecu(m)*

The Burrell Collection, Glasgow Museums (45.389)

The archangel Gabriel, depicted as a seraph with peacock-feather wings, kneels before the Virgin Mary and offers her the Annunciation salutation on a scroll. The Virgin, who has been disturbed while reading at a richly canopied prie-dieu, raises her hands in surprise. The scene is watched by God the Father.

The panel is one of a pair in the Burrell Collection devoted to Marian subjects, the other depicting the Assumption of the Virgin. The panels were probably originally part of a larger series depicting the Joys of the Virgin.

The Joys of the Virgin Mary – commonly five, but sometimes seven, nine or even 15 – have their origins in the thirteenth century, but became popular in the fourteenth century, appearing in both the visual arts and in the popular lyrics of the day (cat. no. 275). They depicted the joyful events of the Nativity, together with the Resurrection and Ascension of Christ, and usually culminated in her own assumption and coronation in heaven. It was one of the first formalized meditative exercises to be widely adopted by religious and lay people alike. Prayers concerning her joys appear in a large number of English manuscripts, particularly in Books of Hours, intended for personal and private devotions. Both literary and visual sources encouraged an emotional response from the devotee, who meditated on the Blessed Virgin's own emotional response to the joyous events of the biblical narrative (Woolf 1968, pp.114–58, 274–308).

The Joys of the Virgin were an ideal subject for the glazing of a private chapel. Indeed, the Virgin herself is shown kneeling at her devotions, reading from a small devotional work, probably a Book of Hours. In 1434 Sir Roland Lenthall was granted licence to crenellate his house, Hampton Court (then known as Hampton Richard), and the chapel may have been built at this time. It has been suggested, however, that the glazing may not originally have been made for the chapel (for the other panels, all but one now dispersed, see Caviness 1970 and 1997). The panel is of the highest quality, characterized by richly textured and decorated surfaces, and has been compared with work in the St William window of York Minster of *c.*1414 (cat. nos 232, 317).   SB

PROV. East window of the domestic chapel of Hampton Court, near Leominster, Hereford and Worcester, until 1924; Roy Grosvenor Thomas and Wilfred Drake; private collection, New York, 1927–60; Parke-Bernet Galleries sale, New York, 12 November 1960, lot 880; Dirk de Leur, Switzerland, 1960–79; Sotheby's sale, London, 29 March 1979, lot 136, acquired by the Burrell Collection.

LIT. Caviness 1970; Marks 1993, pp.96, 183, fig. 149; Caviness 1997, pp. x–xi, chapter XV.

218 The Bedingfeld Chalice and Paten

London hallmark 1518–19 (maker's mark: a fish)

Parcel-gilt silver, engraved and enamelled; h. 15.2 cm (chalice), diam. 13.1 cm (paten)

Inscr. on the foot: the sacred monograms *IHS*, *CPS* (in black-letter) and, in a later style, the initials *EH* joined by a knot

Victoria and Albert Museum, London (M.76&a–1947)

The design of the set conforms to standard late medieval form; the chalice has an engraved six-lobed foot, a polygonal knop and a hemispherical bowl. The paten is enamelled in the centre with the head of Christ (the Vernicle) surrounded by an engraved sunburst design within six engraved lobes. The high quality of this chalice and paten, and its good condition, make it unusual among surviving sets.

This silver chalice and paten are rare examples of pre-Reformation English church plate. Most English church plate was confiscated by the Crown during the Reformation. Many chalices that survived were subsequently altered in the late sixteenth century to resemble Protestant communion cups. The few that remain intact tend to be from private chapels or remote parishes. The quality and condition of this set, along with its known provenance, suggest that it was made for an aristocratic patron and was subsequently retained in a private chapel.

Until 1905 the chalice and paten were owned by a recusant family, the Bedingfelds of Oxburgh Hall, Norfolk. Academic interest in the chalice has focused on this family and the identification of the initials EH, which were engraved three times on the foot of the chalice between *c.*1550 and *c.*1650. The initials could refer to either Elizabeth Howard of Naworth (d. *c.*1607) or Elizabeth Houghton, the first and second wives of Sir Henry Bedingfeld (1586–1656). As the letters appear to be joined with a love knot, they could stand for Henry and either Elizabeth. A further possibility is that the initials are those of Elizabeth Howard's mother, also Elizabeth (née Dacre), wife of Lord William Howard (1564–1640; see also cat. nos 187, 222b). AW

PROV. The Bedingfeld family of Oxburgh Hall, Norfolk until 1905; Swaythling Collection; Prince Duleep Singh; loan to Norwich Castle Museum, 1936–47; purchased at Christies's, London, 29 October 1947 (lot 120), with the aid of a contribution from the National Art Collections Fund.

LIT. Oman 1948, p.1077; Oman 1957, pp.45, 67, pls 19, 30; Glanville 1990, p.133.

219 Tabernacle with Head of St John the Baptist and saints

PLATE 117

Probably *c.*1470–85

Two alabaster reliefs, painted and gilded, set in a contemporary painted oak box; h. 42.7 cm, w. 53.3 cm (incl. box, with wings open)

The Burrell Collection, Glasgow Museums (reg. no. 1/34; inv. 23)

The Head of St John the Baptist is shown on a round plate at the centre of the composition. The personification of the Baptist's soul – in a mandorla, held by two angels – emerges from his skull, and below Christ as Man of Sorrows is shown in the sepulchre. The Head is flanked by three standing figures on each side. The upper two are identified by inscriptions on the wings as Sts James and Catherine on the left and Sts Anthony (the head now missing) and Margaret on the right. The foremost figures, however, are not singled out by inscription: that on the left is certainly St Peter, holding the keys in his right hand, but the bishop saint cannot be conclusively identified. It has been suggested that he could be St William of York, and that the tabernacle was made for a York patron (see Stone 1972, pp.216–17; Tudor-Craig 1973, cat. no. 21). The canopy, consisting of three four-light windows, is made from a separate piece of alabaster.

Alabaster Heads of St John the Baptist were made in large numbers in the last decades of the fifteenth century, mostly for private devotion (see especially St John Hope 1890 and Cheetham 1984, pp.28–30). There were clearly different versions available, from the modest to the more ambitious, as is evident from the reference made in the action brought in October 1491 by Nicholas Hill of Nottingham – the image-maker – against a salesman, William Bott, who had failed to pay him for 'fifty-eight heads of St John the Baptist, part of them in tabernacles and in niches . . .' (Cheetham 1984, p.30; for a selection of St John's Heads of varying size and quality, see Cheetham 1984, pp.317–32, and Boldrick, Park and Williamson 2002, cat. nos 7–8). They occur frequently in English household inventories of *c.*1480–1540, which usually confirm that they were kept either in a private chapel or in one of the main living rooms (Foister 1981, pp.275–6, 278, 280–82). PW

PROV. Bought by Sir William Burrell by 1920; formerly with Grosvenor Thomas, London, and said to have come 'from an old house in Ipswich'.

LIT. Nelson 1920, pp.213–15, pl. II; Tudor-Craig 1973, cat. no. 21; London 1977, cat. no. 176; Marks et al. 1983, p.117, fig. 4; Cheetham 1984, p.54, fig. 33; Boldrick, Park and Williamson 2002, fig. 9, p.32.

218

220

220 St Anne with the Virgin and Child

Malines (Mechelen), 1500–20

Walnut, painted and gilded; h. 36.5 cm

Victoria and Albert Museum, London (487–1895)

The standing St Anne, wearing veil and wimple, supports the young Virgin on her right arm, who in turn holds the Christ Child on her knees. The Child reaches forward to play with the pages of the book in St Anne's left hand. The group has been repainted, but traces of the original polychromy, including gilding, remain visible in places. The Virgin's head has been cut back to take a crown, now missing. The separately made base is lost. Small devotional images of this type were common in the houses and private chapels of the late Middle Ages. The triple group of St Anne with the Virgin and Child – known as an *Anna Selbdritt* in Germany, *Anna-te-Drieën* in the Netherlands and *Sainte-Filiation* in France – was one of the most popular of these, celebrating as it did the role of motherhood and domestic virtue (see Ashley and Sheingorn 1990 and Uden 1992). Such statuettes were imported into England in good numbers in the late fifteenth and early sixteenth centuries, to be sold on the open market. Customs records probably refer to these imports when listing the contents of a ship docking in London in 1509, which included a basket containing 14 wooden images and a further 15 small wooden images (Gras 1918, pp.562, 567, 575; see also Woods 1988, p.92). They provided an alternative to the home-produced alabaster products and, being relatively inexpensive, would have been snapped up by the burgeoning merchant class. PW

PROV. Emile Peyre Collection, Paris; acquired by the V&A in 1895.

LIT. Borchgrave d'Altena 1959, p.59; Williamson 2002, no. 39, pp.128–9.

221 Bronze mould and pipeclay figure of the Virgin Mary

a) Mould

Netherlands, 1500–50

Bronze; h. 12.6 cm, w. 3.1 cm

British Museum, London (MME 1905,12-29,1)

The two-part, bronze mould is finely engraved with a standing figure of the Virgin and Child. The Virgin wears a high, closed crown and supports the Christ-child with her left arm. He sits upright and holds an orb. The front has three pins for fixing to the other half of the mould: one top centre, one bottom left and one bottom right. The back has holes in the same positions to receive the pins.

PROV. Gift of Max Rosenheim, 1905.

LIT. BM 1924, p.264.

221a

221b

b) Figure

15th century

Pipeclay; h. 10.2 cm; w. 2.7 cm

Museum of London (4970)

This pipeclay figure was probably produced by a similar mould to (a). This is a livelier representation as the child seems to wriggle naturalistically, placing his right hand on the covered breast of the Virgin. Traces of red paint remain on her robes, while a small hole in the top of her crown may indicate how the figure was removed from its mould. Such figures were cheaply made and simply produced for the mass-market. Operating as aids to devotion, their sale was undoubtedly (though not exclusively) associated with shrines relating to the Virgin (Williamson 2002, cat. no. 31). Sixteenth-century imports of pipeclay figures in different forms are known from the Netherlands and Germany, but the moulds themselves may also have been imported for use in local production centres in England (Gaimster and Weinstein 1989).　　JR

PROV. Found at Great Winchester Street, London.

LIT. Guildhall Museum 1908, p.156; Gaimster forthcoming.

222　Two rosaries

a)　Rosary

*c.*1500

Beads of turned wood on a modern string; l. 15 cm

Museum of London (5079)

PROV. Excavated, Worship Street, London, 1890.

LIT. Guildhall Museum 1908, no. 5079.

b)　The Langdale rosary

*c.*1500, two additional beads added probably *c.*1600

Gold, engraved and enamelled; l. 40.5 cm

Inscr. : each bead engraved with the title of the scene or saint depicted, in black-letter script on the rim; the two later beads have italic inscriptions

Victoria and Albert Museum, London (M.30–1934)

PROV. Possibly Lord William Howard (1564–1640) of Naworth Hall, Cumbria; by descent (from Ann Howard, the great-grand-daughter of William Howard, who married Marmaduke Langdale of Houghton) in the Langdale family, Houghton Hall, Sancton, Yorkshire; purchased in 1934.

LIT. Maclagan and Oman 1935; Oman 1948, p.1076; Lightbown 1992, cat. no. 81, pp.526–8, col. pls 144, 144a, 144b; Cherry 1994, p.20, ill.

Rosaries were in use from the thirteenth century onwards and came in a great variety of forms. During the fifteenth century their form gradually standardized into groups of 10 beads for reciting the *Ave Maria* prayer, separated by one for the *Paternoster*. They were a regular feature of private devotion at all levels of society. The rosary from the Museum of London (a), made from 27 plain turned wood beads, illustrates a type that would have been readily available in fifteenth-century England. Due to their close association with the cult of the Virgin, rosaries were frowned upon by reformers and they were forbidden by the Church of England in 1547.

As the only gold English rosary known to have survived from the Middle Ages, the Langdale rosary (b) is an exceptional piece consisting of 50 oval *Ave* beads, six lozenge-shaped *Pater* beads and a large rounded knop. Each bead is enamelled either with a saint or with a Christological scene. The later beads feature three St Williams (of Norwich, Maleval and either Rochester or Aquitaine) and St Endelient, a little-known Cornish saint. This choice of saints suggests a link with both Lord William Howard, who became a Catholic in 1584, and his friend Nicholas Roscarrock (*c.*1550–1634). The latter was a Cornish recusant, who wrote the only known Life of St Endelient. It is likely that the rosary was owned by Lord William Howard, and the new beads added at his request (see also cat. nos 187, 218).　　AW

222a

222b

223

224

Margaret Beauchamp of Bletsoe, married first to Sir Oliver St John and then (*c.*1442) to John Beaufort, 1st Duke of Somerset. His death in 1444 and Lady Margaret's birth in 1443 are noted in the calendar. The donors in the Annunciation miniature were for many years identified as Lady Margaret's paternal grandparents, John Beaufort, Earl of Somerset (d. 1410), and his wife, Margaret Holland, afterwards Duchess of Clarence, but current thinking seems to place the miniature too late for them. Evidence of Lady Margaret's own ownership of the manuscript is far from conclusive and requires further investigation.   JMB

PROV. Margaret Beauchamp, Duchess of Somerset (d. 1482); possibly Lady Margaret Beaufort (d. 1509); Royal Library; passed to British Museum in 1757.

LIT. Rickert 1962; Marks and Morgan 1981, pls 31–2; Smeyers 1993, nos 14, 15; Scott 1996, no. 37.

223 Beaufort/Beauchamp Hours

*c.*1410–20 and *c.*1430–40

Vellum, ff.242; h. 20.5 cm, w. 15 cm

British Library, London (Royal MS 2 A. XVIII)

Of exceptional refinement and delicacy, this miniature of the Annunciation, flanked by kneeling donors (f.23v), is one of 13 images with accompanying prayers now attached to a Book of Hours written and illuminated some 20 years later. The inscription on the Virgin's prayer desk, beginning '*Omnia levia sunt amanti*', appears elsewhere in manuscripts associated

with the immigrant book painter Herman Scheerre, though this miniature is of finer quality than his signed work (cat. nos 73, 103). The remaining miniatures, all of individual saints, are by a different and basically Flemish hand, named the Master of the Beaufort Saints in honour of this book, and were apparently transferred from a contemporary English psalter now in Rennes (MS 22), in which three related images remain. The series includes St John of Bridlington, canonized only in 1401.

The Hours to which the miniatures are now attached probably belonged to Lady Margaret Beaufort's mother,

224 Book of Hours, Use of Sarum*

1440s

Parchment, ff.191; h. 17.5 cm, w. 12.5 cm

British Library, London (Harley MS 2915)

The chief illuminator is named from a manuscript (Oxford, Bod. Lib. MS Laud misc. 570) completed for Sir John Fastolf in 1450 by the scribe Ricardus Franciscus, also credited with this Book of Hours. The

Fastolf Master (see also cat. no. 92) moved from Rouen to England in *c*.1440; the structure and isolated marginal scenes here are English in character, although the acanthus borders derive from Parisian patterns. The semi-monochrome austerity of the extensive illumination may reflect the Netherlandish spiritual movement of the *Devotio moderna*, which popularized the Hours of Eternal Wisdom, found in this book but not common in England. Gold is severely restricted: typically in *Christ before Pilate*, for Prime of the Hours of the Passion, f.163, Pilate's wife's gold headdress offsets Christ's white halo.

The original owner is unknown. A prayer composed for the Duke of Bedford (ff.97–101; BL, MS Add. 74754, ff.385v–391) is appropriate for a royal owner entrusted with governing parts of the kingdom; other prayers reveal a soldier, engaged in great undertakings and menaced by someone more powerful. Obvious candidates are Richard, Duke of York, and John and Edmund Beaufort. Bedford's petitions for children would become less urgent for York and Edmund, whose wives regularly gave birth from 1439 and *c*.1436 respectively; John married in *c*.1442 and fathered Lady Margaret before dying in 1444. Added prayers are for a woman.   CR

PROV. Harley Collection.

LIT. Backhouse 1997, p.175; Scott 1996, I, p.77, II, pp.296–9, 318–20; Stratford and Reynolds forthcoming.

225 Books of Hours

a) *Horae beate marie secundum usum Sarum*

Printed by Wynkyn de Worde, Westminster, 1493

Paper, ff.85 (imperfect); h. 21 cm, w. 15 cm; binding: calf on wooden boards, late 15th century

British Library, London (IA.55169)

PROV. Purchased in 1856.

LIT. Duff 1917, no. 183; Hodnett 1973, no. 378; STC, no. 15876; Foot 1993a, pp.106–8.

b) *Horae . . . ad usum Sarum*

Printed by Philippe Pigouchet for the bookseller Simon Vostre, Paris, 16 May 1498

Vellum, ff.128; h. 17.5 cm, w. 11.5 cm

British Library, London (IA.40335)

PROV. Obituary notes of members of the Arundel family in the calendar; Henry Fitzalan, Earl of Arundel; his son-in-law Lord Lumley; sold to King James I for Henry, Prince of Wales; became part of the Royal Library; passed to British Museum in 1757.

LIT. Duff 1917, no. 195; BMC, VIII, 1949, p.119; STC, no. 15887; Avril and Reynaud 1993, no. 147.

225a

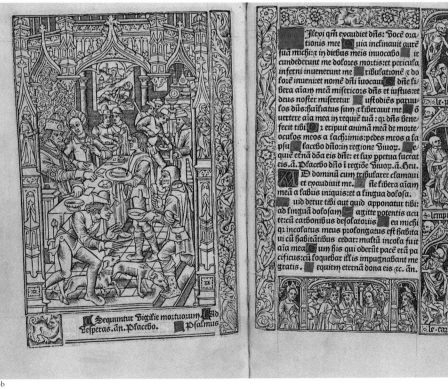

225b

225c

c) *Horae beatissime marie ad legitimum Sarisburiensis ecclesie ritum**

Printed by François Regnault, Paris, 1526

Paper, ff.188 (incomplete); h. 24 cm, w. 17 cm

Victoria and Albert Museum, London (L.1730–1887 (RC.H.10))

PROV. Purchased in 1887.

LIT. STC, no. 15944; Duff 1905, pp.133–4; Erler 1984; Duffy 1992, pp.229–32.

On Books of Hours generally, see de Hamel 1994, pp.168–99; Erler 1999.

Once exclusive to the propertied classes, Books of Hours were probably the most commonly owned book by the late fifteenth century. They contained cycles of prayers for devotions carried out according to the canonical hours, mostly in domestic environments. The prayers were considered necessary for personal and collective safety in this life and for salvation in the next. Early printed versions lacked extensive ornament, but by the end of the 1480s Paris had become the centre of an enormous production of printed Hours that were illustrated, inundating northern Europe with decoration and images. The density of images was unprecedented; as an edition of 1489–90 put it, text and image together allowed 'everyone to have clear knowledge of the mysteries of God through pictures from the Old and New Testaments'.

Many were for a common liturgical 'use' such as that of Paris or Rome, but local uses were also covered (often by the replacement of just a few sections into the standard core of text); booksellers in cities in France and neighbouring regions commissioned editions from Paris to sell locally, and from 1488 printers in Paris and Rouen began to produce Hours in the English Use of Sarum (Salisbury). Books of Hours formed a substantial part of the books imported into England.

English printers had produced Books of Hours from an early date. Caxton printed at least five editions, c.1475 in Bruges and c.1480 and later in Westminster, all sparsely decorated. In 1493 Wynkyn de Worde produced illustrated versions that began to rival the Paris products. He used woodcuts from a series that Caxton had commissioned from the Continent a few years before his death. The edition displayed here (a), in a binding by a binder who worked regularly for Caxton and de Worde, includes a magnificent image of three death-figures confronting horsemen out hunting (the falcon has flown up with its lead trailing) to remind them of their mortality; this was a standard image for the Office of the Dead and the composition suggests a French origin.

Pigouchet emerged as an outstanding printer in the late 1480s, supplying Books of Hours for many regions of France using metal plates set with type for the images. His first works for the English market date from 1494. The Book of Hours of 1498 displayed here (b) includes a list of contents in English (though the text referred to was in Latin). In the early 1490s Pigouchet had updated his set of illustrations, commissioning designs from a major artist, the Master of the 'Très Petites Heures' of Anne de Bretagne, an illuminator who provided designs for tapestries as well as printed images and manuscripts. These were included in the works destined for English customers, who thus had widespread access to the most accomplished versions of French ornament and graphics. The Office of the Dead is heralded by the image of Dives and Lazarus, a representation of a wealthy man enjoying all possible comforts of the rich household and ejecting the beggar Lazarus; in the border, a death-figure seizes dignitaries, one of a series that demonstrates the capricious intrusion of death at all levels of society.

François Regnault was a Parisian printer and bookseller who had been active in London since the last years of the fifteenth century. From his presses in Paris, he invested massively after 1519 in service books for the English market, and from 1525 produced densely decorated Books of Hours that had substantial text and rubrics in English. These dominated the market until 1536–8. Most bear signs that government instructions to delete references to Thomas Becket and popes were respected, but their content ensured that they had no role in the new Anglican church, driving Regnault towards bankruptcy. The title-page of Regnault's 1526 Hours (c) had a prefatory image of the Virgin Mary flanked by two popes receiving the Holy Ghost represented as a dove – not likely to commend the work to those suspicious of Marian idolatry. The ornamental elements were copied (not always happily) from designs circulating in the Paris book trade. The image of the Presentation of Christ in the Temple, standard for the Office of None, is faced by the prayer known as the 'Five joys of the Virgin', the recital of which, according to the rubric, allows 40 days remission of time spent in Purgatory after death.   LH & RW

226 *The Golden Legend*

Printed by William Caxton, Westminster, c.1483

Paper, ff.449; h. 36 cm, w. 25.7 cm

Private collection

The Golden Legend is a collection of lives of the saints to be read on their feast-days. The original version is the *Legenda Aurea*, written in the thirteenth century in Genoa by the Dominican friar Jacobus de Voragine. It was often adapted according to local veneration of saints in places far from its origin and translated into vernacular languages.

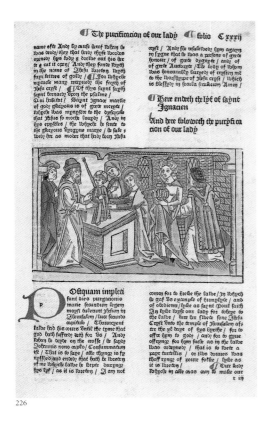

226

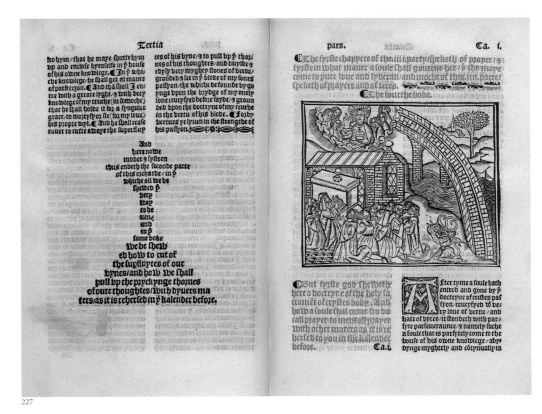

227

Caxton's version, his largest book, is an unusual cultural amalgam at the end of a chain of traditions. He translated a northern French version, the *Légende dorée*, which included many French and Flemish legends, but he added translations from the Latin and inserted 17 legends of English saints. The result was an extensive collection that was frequently reprinted down to the Reformation.

The page shown (f.132 r) relates to a feast-day of the Virgin Mary, celebrated on 2 February and known variously as the Purification, the Presentation of Christ in the Temple, the Meeting of Mary and Simeon, and Candlemas Day. The woodcut depicts the Jewish ritual of Purification and the Presentation; 40 days after giving birth, the mother makes a sacrificial offer, two turtle-doves being the traditional offering of the poor. Through the hands of the priest, Mary presents her son to his heavenly Father.

Caxton's book was commissioned by the Earl of Arundel, who rewarded his work with 'a buck in summer and a doe in winter' and, more crucially for a publisher, undertook to take a 'reasonable' number of copies. The book, printed for use in noble households, was also destined for less exalted homes. Its execution is simple. The red initials were probably provided by the printing house, as they are very similar in most surviving copies. The colouring of the woodcuts is contemporary. LH

PROV. Robert Hedrington, 1577; Beriah Botfield (1807–63); bequeathed by him to the Thynne family, into whose possession it came in 1911 on the death of Botfield's widow; transferred in 1946 by the 5th Marquess of Bath from Botfield's home, Norton Hall, to Longleat; sold at auction, Christie's, London, 13 June 2002, lot 41.

LIT. Duff 1917, no. 408; MME, II, pp.436–9; STC, no. 24873; Blake 1973, pp.88–96; Hodnett 1973, pp.237–305; Hamer 1998.

227 St Catherine of Siena, *The Orchard of Syon*

Printed by Wynkyn de Worde, London, 1519

Paper, ff.175; h. 28.3 cm, w. 20.4 cm

Lambeth Palace Library (ARC L.40.4/98)

The *Orchard of Syon* is the title of the printed English version of St Catherine of Siena's mystical visions. St Catherine's text is a dialogue with God, which she dictated in her native Tuscan to one of her disciples. The *Dialogo*, completed in 1378, was widely circulated and was introduced into England in a Latin translation. Some 50 years later an English translation was written for the Bridgettine nuns of Syon Abbey, founded in 1415 by Henry V. The text had a special meaning to them as St Catherine

and St Birgitta of Sweden had similar mystical experiences.

Its allegorical framework is that of paths through an orchard, along which the sisters walk as the spirit may guide them. As they wander along in contemplation, readers are led to St Catherine's heavenly visions.

At the end of the book the printer writes that the steward of Syon Abbey, Richard Sutton, found the English text in a corner, apparently forgotten after some hundred years. In 1519 he commissioned the book to be printed 'at greate coste, trustinge that moche fruyte shall come thereof', for the nuns but also for lay readers. The cost must have included the design and execution of eight woodcuts. Shown here (ff.14 v, 15 r) is the narrow bridge to heaven as a symbolic presentation of Christ. Those who join St Catherine in prayer may cross, while only the man who turns away from her will be received by the devil in the foreground, who appears to expect him. The printer participated in the spirit of the text by creating in his typesetting on the facing page an even narrower bridge and celebrating with a larger typeface once the expanses of heaven are reached. His typographical sophistication is also shown off in red printing, a woodcut initial and decorative line-fillers. LH

PROV. Sion College, London.

LIT. Hodgson and Liegey 1966; MME, IX, p.xxiii (74); Hodnett 1973, p.867; STC, no. 4815; Driver 1986 and 1995.

17

THE ARTS OF
THE GREAT CHURCH

CHRISTOPHER WILSON

The attacks on traditional religion mounted by the agents of the crown in the 1530s and 1540s left the architectural structure of many of England's great churches more or less unscathed, yet the contents of those buildings were in every case irretrievably wrecked. The tens of thousands of works in precious metals that they housed in 1538 were reduced to bullion, while vast quantities of sculptured images were removed from their settings and destroyed. Two-dimensional imagery, being made from materials that were of little or no intrinsic value, and being somewhat less obnoxious to Protestants than 'graven images', was assaulted less systematically, yet by the 1560s few if any panel or wall-paintings will have remained un-defaced and free of whitewash. Stained glass, which was ini-tially protected by its practical functions and by a general reluctance to pay for replacing it with plain glazing, eventu-ally succumbed in the mid-seventeenth century to the onslaughts of indiscriminately iconophobic Puritans.

For present-day visitors to the great churches, the impact of successive waves of iconoclasm is softened a little by the work of the Victorian restorers, who set about repopulating the stripped interiors with neo-medieval imagery. At Winchester Cathedral, for example, the mid-fifteenth-century screen that towers over the high altar now houses in its many niches a series of unpainted stone figures introduced between 1888 and 1899 (cat. no. 233); but if we could see this ensemble as it was before 1538, we should find that its present subfusc guise has little to do with its makers' intentions. We would be con-fronted by an array of images – saints, angels and kings – whose stone surfaces were completely concealed under bril-liant and highly naturalistic polychromy (cat. no. 234), a gold frontal to the altar, an embroidered and pearl-encrusted dossal immediately above the altar, a silver-gilt and jewelled retable with figures of Christ and the Apostles above the dossal and, in pride of place at the centre of the screen, large images of Christ crucified, the Virgin Mary and St John the Evangelist, all three wrought in gold and studded with gems (Brewer et al. 1862–1932, XIII, pt ii (1538), p.402).

118 Canterbury Cathedral, nave looking north-east

Winchester's high altar screen stands in a part of the church considerably older than itself and exemplifies a widely favoured strategy for modernizing great churches without rebuilding them: the replacement of imagery and fittings at the liturgical core. That the retable of the Winchester screen was made partly from the silver of a retable given for the high altar little more than a hundred years earlier (Greatrex 1978, pp.102–4; Quirk 1955) illustrates the strength of the late medieval imperative that artworks occupying key positions be up-to-date in style. Parallel to this renewal at the centre of the great church was the extensive development of the periphery, typically by the building or rebuilding of a Lady Chapel (cat. no. 228) and by the insertion of chantry chapels commemorating the heads of the community into whatever spaces that community was prepared to make available for the purpose (cat. no. 109). All these ways of embellishing a great church share one important feature: their architectural structuring. The insistently compartmentalized character of Perpendicular architecture ensured that most imagery, whether two- or three-dimensional, consisted of ensembles of single figures standing under elaborate canopies rather than narrative compositions. By comparison with continental Late Gothic art, which was beginning to emancipate itself from niches and other small-scale architectural settings well before 1400, much of what little has survived of the late medieval imagery of English great churches is apt to seem, despite its naturalism, constrained and formal.

The Winchester screen was only a particularly splendid example of a type of fitting introduced into virtually all of England's great churches between the early fourteenth and early sixteenth centuries. The aesthetic delight and competitive pride felt in the institutions that commissioned altarpieces of this kind are well conveyed by an entry in the Book of Benefactors of St Albans Abbey, recording that Abbot William Wallingford (1476–92) lavished 1,100 marks (£733 6s. 8d.) on a tall 'front' for the high altar, which 'greatly beautifies the church, gladdens the eyes of beholders and seems to all who see it the most divine spectacle in the kingdom' (Lindley 2001, p.256). It would be interesting to know whether any controversy attended the introduction of very tall screens into those churches where, as at St Albans and Winchester, the shrine of the principal house saint was installed in the area immediately to the east of the high altar, for this change meant that the *feretrum* (the elevated reliquary coffin containing the saint's relics) became invisible to anyone standing in the sanctuary or the choir. No doubt all screens of this kind automatically incorporated figures of the saints whose shrines they were blocking from view, but their central images were probably always Christological, and it is difficult not to see in that an important sign of the

growing Christ-centredness of late medieval religion. Even so, there are no good grounds for supposing that the English were generally less enthusiastic about their native saints in the fifteenth and early sixteenth centuries than they had been in earlier times.

The *feretrum* enclosing all or most of the relics of a principal house saint would normally be the single most valuable artwork that a great church possessed, and the sumptuousness of the metalwork and jewels of such objects astounded foreign visitors to England during the late Middle Ages (Letts 1957, pp.43–4, 50–2; Sneyd 1847, p.30; Thysius 1651, p.23). A *feretrum* was invariably fixed on top of a high marble base whose sides were hollowed out as prayer niches for pilgrims, the two elements together constituting a shrine. Most English shrines pre-dated 1400, but that of St William in York Minster acquired a new base in 1470–71 (cat. no. 316), and complete new shrines were made for St Swithun at Winchester Cathedral and St Osmund in Salisbury Cathedral in 1451–76 and 1471–94 respectively (Wilson 1977, pp.19–21; Crook 1993b, pp.64–6; Nilson 1998, pp.22–3). In 1538 Henry VIII ordered the general destruction of shrines and the transfer of their precious materials into his own coffers, with the result that nothing now survives of the fifteenth-century shrines, except parts of the bases of those of St Swithun and St William.

Like high altar screens, choir-stalls could function very effectively as a means of deflecting attention from the old-fashioned architecture of their immediate settings, although their unpainted wood would have made them appear sober by comparison with altar screens. In northern England the choir-stalls of great churches were invariably surmounted by tall, spire-shaped canopies of a type apparently first used in the 1370s at Lincoln Cathedral. The finest fifteenth-century choir-stalls of this type, and the only ones known to have existed in southern England, are the London-made set at St George's Chapel, Windsor, begun in 1477 (cat no. 83). The architecture of the stalls made for northern great churches during the final decades of the fifteenth century and the first two of the sixteenth century continued to adhere to the Lincoln tradition, but the sets made for the minsters of Ripon and Beverley by William Bromflet (Brownfleet) are innovatory in that the iconography of their misericords draws heavily on German and Netherlandish prints (Purvis 1935; Grössinger 1989; see cat. no. 240). A totally different approach to the decoration of choirs, and one becoming common on the Continent, was to hang tapestries above the stalls. This was not a practical proposition where the stalls were surmounted by complex canopies, but at Canterbury Cathedral, where the stalls of *c.*1300 lacked canopies altogether, a set of Netherlandish tapestries devoted mainly to

the life of Christ, the dedicatee of the cathedral, was acquired for this position in 1511 (cat. no. 229).

Although the introduction of a large-scale narrative cycle into the choir at Canterbury seems to have had no English sequels, narrative art could sometimes exert such a strong appeal that a patron would demand its use in settings where it might have been wiser to adhere to the obvious alternative: ranks of standing figures. A case in point is the stained glass that John Thornton of Coventry contracted to make for the east window of York Minster in 1405, a work whose superb quality it is all but impossible to appreciate without binoculars (plate 5). The subject matter, the Apocalypse and Old Testament scenes including the Creation, is of obvious universality, and the same is true of the other fifteenth-century glazing to have survived from the east window of a great church, that at Great Malvern Priory showing Christ's

Passion, of c.1423–39 (O'Connor 1995; Rushforth 1936, pp.47–104). Narratives of more local interest are found at York in two further giant windows, those in the end walls of the eastern transepts, which flanked the site of the shrine of St William. The window on the more honorific north side, of c.1415 and evidently also by John Thornton, shows the story of St William (cat. nos 232, 317), whereas that of c.1440 on the south side is dedicated to St Cuthbert of Durham – a pairing clearly designed to shed some much-needed lustre on the cult of York's own saint. House history (or legend) makes a fairly modest appearance in one window of the choir clearstorey at Great Malvern (Rushforth 1936, pp.120–36), and it is striking that the much larger cycles of this kind that are known to have existed at Durham and Worcester Cathedrals and Peterborough Abbey (now the cathedral) were sited in the cloisters rather

119 Canterbury Cathedral, choir-screen (see cat. no. 35)

than the churches (Marks 1993, pp.73, 90). There is no obvious way of knowing whether this was done because such subjects were thought to be of small interest to lay people or because an extended cycle was best displayed in a long sequence of windows that were set low down and close together.

Compared to stained glass, other forms of painting seem to have played a comparatively minor part in the fitting out of great churches. An exception is the extensive work carried out by the Netherlandish artist Lambert Barnard at Chichester Cathedral in the 1530s and early 1540s (Croft-Murray 1957, pp.110–18; Fines 1994, p.54; Brighton 1994, pp.80–84). The Dutch-style floral decoration which he added to the simple late twelfth-century vaults, and his painting of the Crucifixion on cloth [canvas?] fixed to the wooden high altar screen, were doubtless effective enough as works of modernization, but to anyone who had seen Chichester's vastly richer neighbour, Winchester Cathedral, Barnard's work is likely to have seemed in the nature of a 'cheap and cheerful' sprucing-up operation. Nevertheless, it is Winchester that furnishes the main instance of the choice of wall-painting where some other form of display might have been expected: the series of Miracles of the Virgin painted c.1500 in grisaille on the side walls of the newly remodelled Lady Chapel (James and Tristram 1928–9, pp.13–37). The decision to introduce wall-paintings, and also their style, are clearly consequences of the fact that an earlier Bishop of Winchester, William Waynflete, had ordered closely related paintings for Eton College Chapel (cat. no. 320). That the Winchester and Eton paintings are nearly monochrome suggests a concern not to compete with polychrome three-dimensional imagery placed further east and on the central axis of the same spaces; and it is worth noting that the Eton paintings, despite their superlative quality, were in the nature of an improvisation, for they occupied bare walling that had originally been intended to be concealed behind choir-stalls.

In the eyes of the great Dutch scholar Erasmus, who visited Canterbury in 1513, there was nothing worth seeing in the nave of the cathedral except a tomb and some chained books (Halkin, Bierlaire and Hoven 1972, p.487). But the vast majority of people entering the naves of great churches in the late Middle Ages were not blinkered by the disdainful attitude of humanists like Erasmus, and they would have taken a keen interest in the numerous images to be found there. Many of these were not associated with altars, and such informality of setting would no doubt have lent them a certain immediacy in the minds of those using them for prayer and empathetic devotion. The traditional focus for lay devotion in the more accessible parts of great churches

was the sculptured and painted wooden crucifixion group, which could be suspended either above a separate rood-screen near the east end of a nave, as at Canterbury, or over a pulpitum (choir-screen) at the west end of a choir. The pulpitum that now terminates the view eastwards in the nave at Canterbury (plate 118) dates from the 1450s and is one of many such structures commissioned by major ecclesiastical corporations in the fifteenth century as replacements for older screens (plate 119). The exquisite refinement of its micro-architecture cannot conceal the fact that Canterbury's choir-screen is a massive optical and physical barrier between the spaces allocated to the laity and to the clergy. Its excluding function is only reinforced by the line-up of kings flanking the narrow central portal (cat. no. 35) – royal founders and benefactors such as had been represented on English choir-screens since the twelfth century.

The sculptors of the Canterbury kings were probably London-based, as the screen's designer Richard Beke had been until his appointment as cathedral architect in 1435; certainly there was a long-standing tradition at Canterbury and other major religious houses of employing metropolitan artificers on particularly important commissions. Away from the south-east, the cachet of London workmanship is likely to have been less consistently acknowledged. At Durham Cathedral Priory, whose high altar screen had been dispatched in crates from London in the late 1370s, the most ambitious undertaking of around 1500 was the installation of sumptuous woodwork in an utterly non-metropolitan style around the Jesus altar at the east end of the nave (Fowler 1902, pp.32–55, 220–22). The screen-coving that survived from this ensemble until very recently probably came either from the loft on the south side of the altar, where the prior could hear the Jesus mass in privacy, or from its northern counterpart, where choristers and an organ were housed. The coving was decorated in a way that has no exact parallels in English late medieval woodwork (plate 120). Its delicate and remarkably varied tracery panels were mostly Flamboyant, a style banished from large-scale masonry architecture more than a hundred years earlier, but preferred to Perpendicular by many carpenters and joiners, particularly in the northernmost counties of England, East Anglia and Wales. One panel (centre row, third from the left) even betrayed the influence of one of the cross-carpet pages of the late seventh-century Lindisfarne Gospels, which were one of Durham's greatest treasures; another panel (bottom row, second from the right) included passable imitations of the acanthus foliage used in late twelfth-century sculpture and wall-painting at Durham. The exoticism of the Durham coving reminds us that before they were ransacked in the name of religious reform, England's great churches would

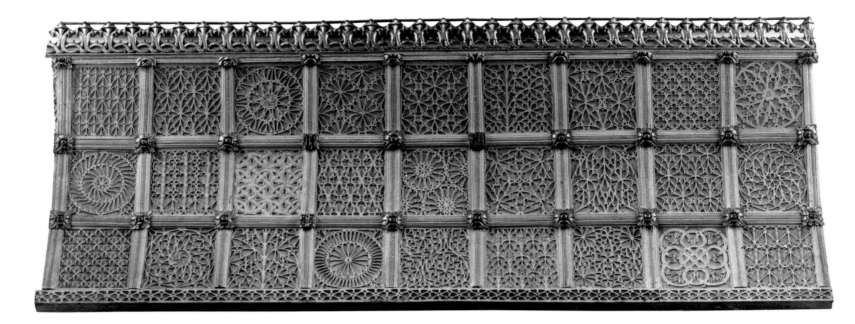

have contained late medieval artworks of types not represented in the pitifully small sample that has survived down to our own time.

Almost all the works mentioned so far were the sorts of projects that could be funded either by the institution itself or by individual benefactors. Funerary monuments were of course normally paid for by the individuals commemorated (or by their executors), and for that reason they are likely to have given considerable scope for the exercise of patronal preference. As supports for sculptural ensembles, and as virtuosic exercises in micro-architecture, chantry chapels (cat. no. 109) could rival high altar screens, and probably for that reason they were normally sited some distance away. A prime example of the avoidance of such a breach of decorum is to be seen at Ely Cathedral, where the extraordinarily rich chantries of Bishops Alcock (d. 1500) and West (d. 1533) – between them originally housing just under 500

polychrome stone sculptures – are tucked into the most easterly bays of the aisles of the east arm. At St Albans Abbey space for chantries was running out by the early sixteenth century, and Abbot Thomas Ramryge (d. 1522) evidently felt there was no option but to take the prime position north of the high altar for his own chapel. How the monastic community as a whole reacted to this development is unknown, but the probability is that it was made palatable by the fact that the Masses celebrated there represented an enhancement of the abbey's devotional resources; that the decoration of the chapel celebrated the abbey's history; and that the high altar screen erected some 40 years earlier was simply too big and too splendid to be jostled, even by this visually assertive newcomer.

FURTHER READING

Marks 1993; Nilson 1998; Tracy 1990; Vallance 1947.

120 Brancepeth parish church (County Durham), wooden coving from Durham Cathedral (destroyed in 1998)

228 Canterbury Cathedral, Lady Chapel

1448–55

From the late eleventh century until 1455 Canterbury Cathedral's main Lady Chapel occupied the eastern-most bays of the north nave aisle. The move into what had hitherto been St Benedict's Chapel on the east side of the north transept was probably due to a desire for a more secluded and self-contained setting comparable to those of other major monastic Lady Chapels. Much of the money for the new chapel, and for the concurrently pursued remodelling of the north transept, will have come from the £500 bequeathed to the fabric of the cathedral by Cardinal Beaufort, Bishop of Winchester (d. 1447).

The designer of the Lady Chapel was Richard Beke, master mason to the cathedral from 1435 until his death in 1458. He had been employed at Canterbury on a consultancy basis since 1432, and it is almost certain that his main task was to have been the rebuilding of the crossing tower, whose first stone was laid in 1433. But work on the tower ceased once the crossing arches had been built, and Beke's ener-gies were channelled into a series of smaller projects, including the choir-screen (plate 119 and cat. no. 35), the Lady Chapel and two other chapels. The hiring of Beke, who had previously been the master mason of London Bridge, was just one episode in a long history of reliance on London-based artificers by Canterbury Cathedral Priory. All his works display a thorough knowledge of the capital's century-old traditions of Perpendicular architecture, but an aware-ness of recent developments in Oxford is evident in the Lady Chapel vault, the oldest large-scale masonry fan-vault to have survived in south-east England. Further evidence of the eclectic spirit informing Beke's design is the derivation of the exquisite foliage carving from the nearby late thirteenth-century tomb of Archbishop Pecham.

It is tempting to think that the aesthetic refinement and technical ambition of this and other late medieval monastic Lady Chapels were consciously conceived as counterparts to the same qualities in the magnificent polyphonic music performed in them during the daily Masses of the Virgin.   CW

LIT. Leedy 1980, pp.147–8; Woodman 1981, pp.181–4.

228

229

Numerous sets with scenes of the Life of Christ or the Life of the Virgin were produced between about 1500 and 1520, but few survive. Three tapestries with scenes from the Life of Christ, woven from the same cartoons as the Canterbury set and of a similar date, are in the Fine Arts Museums in San Francisco (Bennett 1992, cat. no. 17). LW

PROV. Canterbury Cathedral until after 1640; Paris, 1656; Cathedral of St-Sauveur, Aix-en-Provence, from about 1656.

LIT. James 1903–6; Krotoff 1977.

230 Tapestry with St Martin of Tours and St Dunstan

Southern Netherlands, dated 1466

h. 109.5 cm, w. 201 cm

The Worshipful Company of Vintners, London

This small devotional tapestry shows, on the left, St Martin dividing his cloak with the beggar, and on the right, St Dunstan saying Mass. It was made to hang as an altar frontal in Canterbury Cathedral, perhaps intended for use in front of the altar dedicated to St Martin of Tours. The inscription at the bottom refers to the couple who donated the tapestry and their son:

229 Tapestry with scenes of the Life of the Virgin*

Brussels, 1511

Wool warps and wool and silk wefts; Virgin greeting the Apostles, h. 187 cm, w. 133 cm; Death of the Virgin, Max. h. 243 cm, w. 603 cm

Cathedral of St-Sauveur, Aix-en-Provence, France

The tapestry has four scenes separated by pillars, those illustrated showing the Virgin greeting the Apostles and the Death of the Virgin. It comes from an incomplete set of 11 panels with scenes from the Life of Christ and the Virgin, of which 26 scenes survive. These 11 panels have been cut down from an original set of six tapestries, probably containing about 30 scenes.

The set was woven in Brussels in 1511 on the orders of Prior Thomas Goldstone and the cellarer, Richard Dering, to be hung above the choir stalls in Canterbury Cathedral. A Latin inscription referring to Dering with the date 1511 and his coat of arms appear in the borders above the Life of Christ scenes. Goldstone's initials TGP (Thomas Goldstone, Prior) appear in the lower borders of the Life of the Virgin scenes, including that of the Death of the Virgin: they are also carved on the stonework of the central tower ('Bell Harry') of the cathedral. The coats of arms of Archbishops Deane, Morton and Warham are also to be seen in the borders of the tapestries.

230

Although the designer cannot be identified with certainty, it has been suggested that it was the artist Quentin Massys (1464/5–1530), or that the design was influenced by him.

From as early as the twelfth century, long narrow hangings of this kind were made specifically to decorate the choirs of cathedrals, although apparently this was less common in England than on the Continent.

Orate p[ro] animab[us] joh[ann]is bate et joh[ann]e uxoris sue vill[e] d[e] ware et p[ro] do[m]pno waltero hertford filio erud[ito] monacho hui[us] eccl[es]ie ano dni M°cccclxvj (Pray for the souls of John Bate and his wife Joan of the town of Ware and for Walter Hertford their son a monk of this church AD 1466). Walter Hertford was a monk of Christchurch Canterbury from about 1427 to 1475 and became sub-prior there.

Both saints are closely associated with Canterbury. St Martin is also the patron saint of the Vintners' Company, but when the tapestry was acquired by them is unknown and it can be traced back with certainty only to 1783. It has been suggested that it was sold in 1640–50 when the Life of Christ and the Virgin tapestries (cat. no. 229) went to Aix-en-Provence. However, as it is not mentioned in the 1540 inventory of the cathedral, it is equally likely that it was removed around the time that Thomas Becket's shrine was despoiled in 1538.

It was woven in the southern Netherlands. A devotional tapestry of about 1500, similarly divided into two panels, is in Angers Cathedral. LW

PROV. Canterbury Cathedral; the Worshipful Company of Vintners from at least 1783.

LIT. French 1870, pp.487–90; London 1927, cat. no. 232, pl. LXVIII; Ramsay and Sparks 1992, p.321.

231 York Minster, crossing tower

*c.*1410–30

When the thirteenth-century central tower of York Minster fell down in 1407, the chapter appealed for help to King Henry IV, attributing the collapse to their masons' carelessness. The master mason Hugh Hedon was dismissed and replaced, on the king's orders, by William Colchester, master mason of Westminster Abbey. This unique instance of a medieval English king appointing a cathedral architect may have arisen from pure altruism, but there must be a good chance that it was politically motivated, for Henry's confidence in the loyalty of the North would have been badly shaken by the recent rebellions of Harry Percy ('Hotspur') and Archbishop Scrope (cat. no. 141), both of whom were buried in the Minster's Lady Chapel. Indeed the tomb of the latter had already become the focus of an anti-Lancastrian cult. The appointment of a southerner as the Minster's architect was certainly seen as a provocation by some of York's masons, who savagely assaulted Colchester in 1408.

By 1409 the damaged crossing piers were being reconstructed, but the building chronology is otherwise obscure until 1471 when the timber vault was installed. The costumes of some of the internal figure sculptures suggest completion dates of *c.*1415 for the lowest parts of the lantern walls and *c.*1430–40 for the window zone. Despite its protracted execution, the tower probably conforms to Colchester's original scheme, although it is obvious that what exists today is just the main, lower storey of a much taller structure. The crossing tower of 1465–88 at Durham Cathedral reproduces the lantern of the York tower quite closely, and its belfry stage may give an idea of what York's unbuilt upper storey would have looked like. CW

231

LIT. Harvey 1977, pp.167, 170–75, 190–91; Harvey 1978, pp.155, 157, 204, 226; Harvey 1984, pp.66–7, 133.

232 A woman cured at the tomb of St William of York*

c.1414

Stained and painted glass; h. 75 cm, w. 83 cm

York Minster, north-east transept, window n.VII, panel 16e

A woman, poisoned by swallowing a frog contained in a loaf of bread, kneels at the shrine of St William (cat. no. 316). A priest points to the regurgitated frog, depicted in the foreground. This depiction of the shrine offers visual evidence of its form. A small altar is located at its gable end.

This is one of the few clearly identifiable miracles of St William, one of the 43 described on a painted table displayed in the revestry of the Minster, recorded in the seventeenth century by antiquarian Roger Dodsworth (Oxford, Bodleian Library MS 125). The cult of St William would have been adversely affected by the rebuilding of the eastern arm of the cathedral, because for much of the period c.1360–1420 the choir shrine would have been largely inaccessible to pilgrims. In 1405 the burial of the 'martyred' Archbishop Richard Scrope attracted large numbers of pilgrims to the new choir. The glazing of the St William window (see also cat. no. 317), exceeded in size only by the east and west windows, was undoubtedly intended to cash in on the benefits of this pilgrim traffic and to rehabilitate the shrine of St William in the popular consciousness. The window was one of a pair in the lantern-like eastern transepts that illuminated the high altar. The shrine itself stood in screened seclusion behind the high altar. The three rows of miracle scenes, with their emphasis on the efficacy of the shrine as a site of healing, were visual propaganda for the revitalized cult. As part of the same glazing scheme St William was also depicted (together with St John of Beverley and St Thomas of Canterbury) in a window in the north choir aisle (n.IX), the gift of Canon Thomas Parker, prebendary of Ampleforth from 1410 to 1423.

The south-east transept was eventually filled with a great window depicting the life of St Cuthbert, associating St William with the pre-eminent saint of the northern province. SB

LIT. Wilson 1977; French 1999; Brown 2002.

233 Winchester Cathedral, high altar screen

Probably begun in the later 1440s; statues late 19th-century

No documentary evidence for the making of this screen is known to exist, but it appears to have been part of an integrated programme of renewing the settings for the high altar and the relics of St Swithun, the cathedral's patron. So ambitious a programme is very likely to have been conceived by the richest prelate of the age, Henry Beaufort, Cardinal Bishop of Winchester (1404–47). What is certain is that in 1451, four years after Beaufort's death, a design for a gold and silver retable had been made, and much bullion had been received from his executors and other sources for use both in the retable and in the new shrine (see p.348). It is inherently likely that the retable was made in tandem with the masonry screen on to which it was to fit. The argument sometimes advanced that the exotic headgear sported by the St Elizabeth carved on a spandrel of the doorway left of the high altar necessitates dating the screen to the late fifteenth century is invalidated by the fact that such hats appear in Netherlandish painting from c.1410–20 onwards. The architecture of the screen appears to be by the same designer as Beaufort's chantry chapel, which was almost certainly built immediately after the cardinal's death in 1447. For fragmentary stone sculptures formerly in the niches of the screen, see cat. no. 234.

Although comparable 'high wall' altar screens were being built in the fourteenth century, this is the earliest example known to have been introduced into a church whose principal shrine had long occupied a site immediately behind the high altar. The construction of the screen would not only have made it impossible to see St Swithun's shrine from the sanctuary, but would also have cramped and darkened its immediate setting; and doubtless it was to overcome those problems that in 1476 the shrine (begun c.1451) was set up on a new site, the accessible, spacious and relatively well-lit thirteenth-century 'retrochoir' at the east end of the cathedral. CW

LIT. Greatrex 1978, pp.102–4; Crook 1993b, p.64; Lindley 1993a.

233▶

232

234 Three heads from the Great Screen of Winchester Cathedral

*c.*1470–80

a) Head of a man wearing a skull-cap

Limestone, with traces of pigment

Losses from chin and left cheek; nose reassembled from fragments

h. 23 cm, w. 16.4 cm, d. 24 cm

Winchester Cathedral (inv. no. 64)

b) Head of a bishop or mitred abbot

Limestone, with traces of pigment

Losses from mitre and damage to face and amice

h. 38.2 cm, w. 21.4 cm, d. 25 cm

Winchester Cathedral (inv. no. 275)

c) Head of a bearded man

Limestone, with traces of pigment

Damage to nose and hair, with chisel marks in the left eyeball

h. 24.4 cm, w. 19.4 cm, d. 19 cm

Winchester Cathedral (inv. no. 60)

The life-size sculptured heads that survive from the Great Screen of Winchester Cathedral are remarkable for their quality of modelling and extraordinary realism. Three are exhibited from a total of 16. None of the bodies of these images survives except for a single gloved hand.

The heads fall into two groups; the first have in common expressions of great calm and dignity (a, b). They are so startlingly lifelike that they must have been carved either from life or from life-casts. The identity of the sculptor is not known, but from the mastery of his work he must have been one of the foremost artists of his time.

The second group (by a second sculptor) have, in contrast, angry expressions, unkempt hair, parted lips and scowling eyes (c). They are less well modelled, slightly smaller in scale and painted in a different style from the first group. Taking into account their lack of identifying attributes such as a crown or a mitre, they might have represented Old Testament figures or Apostles.

The man (c) has shoulder-length hair, parted centrally, and a beard combed into a distinct fork. Hair and beard were painted dark brown. The chisel marks in the left eye may be an indication of the intensity of feeling unleashed when these images were attacked and removed from the Great Screen in 1538 (cat. no. 233).   JH

LIT. Hardacre 1989, cat. nos 37–8, 53; Lindley 1989 and 1993a; Lindley 1993b, pp.113–14, figs 9.19–9.20; Deacon and Lindley 2001, p.49, ill. on p.50; Boldrick, Park and Williamson 2002, cat. nos 31–2 (entry by S. Cather).

235 Virgin and Child

*c.*1470–80

Limestone, polychromed and gilded; h. 48 cm, w. 34 cm, d. 20 cm

Winchester Cathedral (inv. no. 1134)

This was reassembled from fragments in the nineteenth century. The Virgin's left hand is missing, as is the entire lower part of her body. The Christ Child lacks his head and left hand and there is damage to the Virgin's crown and Child's knees.

This exquisite figure, once seated, retains much of its original pigment. The Virgin wears an undergarment with red cuffs, a round-necked bodice painted brilliant red with cuffs edged in black and gold, and a mantle drawn tightly around her shoulders. The mantle is white, with a wide gold hem bordered with black and a rich blue lining. Her crown is decorated with fictive pearls and cabochon gemstones, and traces of gilding remain on her hair. Her flesh was pale pink with darker tones on her cheeks and in her ears; her eyebrows were black. The Virgin's facial expression is calm and reflective, her downward gaze fixing on the now mutilated image of her Son. The traces of paint on his shift suggest that its original colour was green or gold.

The sculpture is usually considered to have been part of the Great Screen of Winchester Cathedral; it is possible, however, that it functioned as an independent devotional image elsewhere in the cathedral.   JH

LIT. Hardacre 1989, cat. no. 31; Lindley 1989 and 1993a; Deacon and Lindley 2001, pp.48–9, col. pl. on p.64.

234a

234b

234c

236 Norwich Cathedral, 'Erpingham Gate'

Between 1415 and 1428

Sir Thomas Erpingham, steward of Henry V's household, veteran of Agincourt (and by tradition commander of the English archers there), is prominently commemorated on this precinct gate sited directly opposite the west door of the cathedral. The arms in the right-hand spandrels are those of Erpingham and his two wives, and the panelling on the flanking turrets frames angels bearing the same arms and small-scale carvings of Henry V's devices. The Erpingham presence is actually greater now than originally, as the niche in the gable contains a kneeling figure of Sir Thomas which, though medieval, does not belong here. That the original occupant was Christ (the dedicatee of Norwich Cathedral) is clear from the Evangelist symbols that formerly perched on the gable. The inner archivolt of the main arch bears the Apostles, the outer one 12 female saints.

The gate was almost certainly built before Erpingham's death in 1428. So expensive a benefaction – it will have cost several hundred pounds – was probably made possible only by Erpingham's childlessness. He and his wives were buried in the sanctuary of the cathedral, a very privileged location and one presumably intended both as a *quid pro quo* for the building of the gate and as recognition of Sir Thomas's long and distinguished royal service (see also cat. no. 299). The few other East Anglian buildings that exhibit idiosyncratic detailing akin to that of the gate belong to the mid-fifteenth century, but this is not necessarily problematic since the best candidate for the authorship of the design, James Woderofe, is documented working at the cathedral from 1415 to 1451. A precocious feature, which eventually passed into the repertory of Tudor Perpendicular, is the pair of slim polygonal turret-cum-buttresses flanking the archway. The height of the archway and the lack of an upper storey and bulky flanking turrets are exceptional in English late medieval gateways. CW

LIT. Fawcett 1982, pp.47–50, 52–3; Sims 2000.

235

236

238

237 Bath Abbey, Somerset, choir interior

Late 15th century to mid-16th century

In 1500 Oliver King, Bishop of Bath and Wells (1495–1503), signed an injunction referring to the state of the priory church of Bath as 'destroyed from the foundations' (Dugdale 1819, II, p.270). He sought advice and alms from 'many nobles, prelates and abbots' to ensure the swift completion of the recently begun new church. King and his close friend Sir Reginald Bray employed William and Robert Vertue to design a vault for the choir: the masons famously state that there shall be 'noone so goodeley neither in england nor in france'. To meet this goal they chose a fan vault, the design of which shows clear links with other works of the royal circle.

By contrast, the design of the choir elevation depends on a local Somerset parish-church tradition. Probably commenced in the 1480s, at which time the building was described as ruinous, the interior of the choir depends for its impact on huge clearstorey windows rather than complex architectural mouldings. Although the appropriation of the works by noble patrons raised hopes for a swiftly completed building with royal pretensions, progress was slow after the deaths of King and Bray in 1503.

The new choir largely replaced the Romanesque choir which extended west of the eleventh-century crossing. The transepts were rebuilt further west to mark architecturally the termination of the new choir, and the intended plan was surely for the eastern extension of the building – with the creation of an ambulatory and Lady Chapel (viz. Great Malvern Priory) – to replace the Romanesque east end. This plan was never achieved and the building was left unfinished at the Dissolution. Despite its grandeur, therefore, the existing choir represents a truncated version of both the plans for the monastic church and of the aspirations of its patrons. LAM

LIT. Robinson 1914; Monckton 1999, ch. 7.

238 Pair of doors

Second quarter of the 15th century

Oak; h. 350 cm, w. 187 cm, d. 14.5 cm; wicket: h. 188 cm, w. 90 cm

St Albans Cathedral, Hertfordshire

These massive doors are of laminated construction. The layers in order from the front are: first, buttresses in the solid; second, the tracery; third, the backing panels, dowelled together; and fourth, the plain panels on the reverse. Wrought-iron nails are used in great numbers to keep the whole construction together. They also play a strong aesthetic role, emphasizing the verticals and complementing the powerful tracery design. There is a wide margin around the central design, which again is decorated with iron nails. The tracery has suffered much damage over time, and the door of the left-hand wicket is now completely denuded of it. John Carter's early nineteenth-century drawings of the doors, still then *in situ*, give a much better impression of their original appearance than can be gained today (Carter 1813, pl.VII). Each leaf is hung on a substantial iron ring, 9 cm in diameter.

The doors were made for the two portals of the now-demolished Early English west end, constructed between 1195 and 1214. They were probably inserted during the first renovation, which included the construction of an early Perpendicular window above, during the abbacy of John of Wheathampstead (1420–40). Use of the prominent ogee arch at the head of the wicket doors, and the piled-up quatrefoils above, refer back to a fourteenth-century stylistic tradition, exemplified in the abbey by another pair of outstanding doors (1396–9), to the cloisters in the south choir aisle. The flat-faced and undecorated mouldings, and the straight-sided quatrefoils on the old west doors, can be paralleled by the tracery of the screens under the north and south chancel arches at Hitchin parish church, Hertfordshire. CT

LIT. Hewett 1974, appendix, p.147 (ill.); Roberts (E) 1993, pp.139–41 (ills), 168–9.

237

239 Head of a mitred saint

Probably *c*.1510

Limestone (Caen stone?); h. 38 cm,
w. (at shoulders) 31 cm

**Dean and Chapter of Westminster,
Westminster Abbey Museum**

The head and shoulders of either a bishop or abbot, wearing a mitre with lappets, sawn off from a complete figure. The mitre, forehead and nose have been badly damaged, presumably by a blow rather

239

than weathering. The back of the head is roughly blocked out and only the front of the mitre is carved, indicating that it was intended to be set in a niche. The bust was 'found in the core of the north-east buttress of the north transept' in about 1887–8, where it had probably 'been put by one of Wren's workmen in the early eighteenth century' (Tanner 1939, p.26).

Lawrence Tanner identified the head as representing Abbot John Islip (d. 1532). There is in reality no evidence for this: it demonstrably did not form part of an effigy and there are no grounds for accepting that a figure of the living abbot would have been placed in the abbey at this date. Stylistically it clearly belongs among the figures of *c*.1505–15 made for Henry VII's Chapel (plate 1), the facial features and detailed decoration of the mitre being close to a number of the bishop saints represented therein. The interior figures are of two sizes, the larger in the eastern chapels, the smaller in the main body of the chapel at triforium level. The head is clearly too big to be asso-

ciated with the latter series, but may once have belonged in one of the empty niches of the eastern chapels, where other bishop saints are to be found (see Mickelthwaite 1882–3, pl. X, and RCHM 1924, pp.63–5, pls 204, 210). There is a possibility that it emanates from one of the niches on the exterior of the chapel, and this would be consistent with its find-spot. However, none of the other exterior figures seems to have survived the eighteenth-century restorations of the building, and carved inscriptions on scrolls in the niches appear to provide evidence for their identification as prophets and apostles, with no bishop saint among them (Mickelthwaite 1882–3, pp.361–2). It cannot be discounted that the head once belonged to a single freestanding or altar image elsewhere in the church.

Wherever its location was within Westminster Abbey, the head is typical of the superb carving of much of the sculpture executed in the orbit of the workshop responsible for Henry VII's Chapel. The realism of the carving and naturalism of the pose may be seen as a continuation of the developments worked out at Winchester and elsewhere in the late fifteenth century (cat. nos 234b, 356), and although Netherlandish influence is often mentioned in connection with the Westminster figures, direct stylistic evidence for this remains elusive.   PW

LIT. Tanner 1939; Tanner 1948, pp.29–30, pl. 63; Gardner 1951, p.235, fig. 457; London 1963, cat. no. 180; Cocke 1995, fig. 8.

240 Misericord of Samson with the Gates of Gaza

1489–94 (the dates are found on a misericord and a bench-end respectively)

Oak; h. 30.5 cm, w. 62 cm, d. 17 cm

Ripon Cathedral, Yorkshire

Samson, an Israelite, passes in front of the fortified walls of Gaza, bearing the city gates – one on his shoulder, the other under his arm. He had dismantled these in order to escape from the Philistines after having slept with a prostitute (Judges 16). This was seen as a parallel to Christ carrying the cross, and as a symbol of Christ breaking down the gates of hell on his descent into limbo.

Old Testament scenes are rare on misericords, and this one, as well as two others of Jonah cast overboard into the jaws of the whale and rising back out of the whale's belly, is found only in Ripon. The Ripon misericords were the first in England to use prints as patterns, and in this case the scene was copied from a *Biblia Pauperum* produced in the 1460s (cat. no. 241). Several high-quality sets of choir-stalls and misericords were produced in this part of Yorkshire in the early sixteenth century and a number of carvers are recorded, including William Brownfleet, Mayor of Ripon in 1511 (Harvey 1984, p.37).   CG

LIT. Purvis 1935; Grössinger 1989a; Grössinger 1997, p.65.

240

241 *Biblia Pauperum**

The Netherlands, *c*. mid-1460s

Paper, ff.24 + 40; h. 29 cm, w. 22 cm; binding by Johann Richenbach of Geislingen in pigskin, dated 1467

John Rylands University Library, Manchester (16119)

The *Biblia Pauperum* gave an illustrated account of Christ's life, with pictures of events in the Old Testament that prefigured it (Henry 1987). In the opening displayed here, Christ rises from the tomb. On the left, Samson carries the city gates from Gaza to a hill, prefiguring Christ's Resurrection and Ascension; on the right, Jonah's delivery from the whale signifies Christ's emergence from the tomb to redeem mankind.

No examples of the *Biblia Pauperum* survive with a medieval English provenance, but use of its compositions in a variety of media, from woodwork to stained glass, indicate that it was widely known (cat. nos 22, 240). Rather than a 'Bible for the Poor', as the title suggests, it was more a synopsis of biblical scholarship for the educated – this copy was owned by a friar – and a convenient handbook for ornamental and decorative programmes.

Blockbooks, each page of text and image printed from a single woodcut, were developed in the Netherlands and Germany in the 1450s, at the same time as printing. All were of a biblical or devotional nature. In northern Europe they were probably the most widely distributed illustrated book until the 1470s,

when images could economically be printed in the same impression as type. This Netherlandish example is fortunately dated by its binding and by the paper used – the watermark is found in paper used in Lorraine in the 1460s and later, as well as in an *Ars moriendi* blockbook of 1466.   RW

PROV. Horn Collection, Regensburg (?); sold in Paris, 1804; Duke of Cassano Serra Collection, Naples; acquired in 1820 by Earl Spencer of Althorp (1758–1834), whose library was bought in 1892 by Mrs John Rylands and presented to Manchester University.

LIT. Nixon 1956, pp.17–19; Mainz 1991; Baurmeister 1994.

242 Wall tiles from Great Malvern Priory, Worcestershire

c.1458–9

Glazed earthenware; each tile h. 21.6 cm, w. 15 cm, d. 3.6 cm

Inscr. on top tile: *Anno r[egni]. r[egis]. h[enrici]. vi xxxvi*

British Museum, London (MME 1947, 5–5, 1329, 1330, 1332, 1334, 1335)

Five tiles forming a vertical panel. The decorative design, inlaid in white slip, is architectural, forming four niches that contain shields of arms and badges (the arms of Christ, the royal arms crowned, IHC crowned, and the pelican in her piety). The inscription on the top tile includes the date 1458–9.

During the mid-fifteenth century the church of the Benedictine Priory of Great Malvern was rebuilt in the late Perpendicular style, and a series of tiles of high quality was made to decorate the floors and walls. They represent a revival of interest in tiles, which occurred at this time in the Severn Valley and is considered to have begun at Great Malvern; a series was also made at the same time for Gloucester Cathedral. In 1833 a kiln was discovered east of the church, with tiles of the type that decorated the priory church. The tilers who made them were probably itinerant, and influenced tile production over a wide area (Eames 1980, pp.237, 248; Clarke and Jackson 1992; see also cat. no. 159). In Great Malvern Priory church, tiles with these designs decorate the wall of the reredos beside the high altar, although it is not certain that this was their original position.   BN

PROV. Great Malvern Priory church, Worcestershire.

LIT. Way 1844; Eames 1980, pp.236–54, cat. nos 1329–30, 1332, 1334–5, design nos 1321–5; Graves 2002, p.23, fig. 1.23.

241

242

243

243 Lectern

*c.*1500

Cast and engraved brass; h. 187.5 cm, w. 86 cm, d. 56 cm

Inscr. *ORATE PRO ANIMABUS RADULPHI SAVAGE ET PRO ANIMABUS OMNIUM FIDELIUM DEFUNCTORUM* (Pray for the soul of Ralph Savage and for the souls of all the faithful dead)

Southwell Minster, Nottinghamshire

The lectern is of conventional type; the desk formed as an eagle with wings displayed, the talons clutching a globe. This is supported on a turned column with eight mouldings with a faceted section above an expanding base. At the base are three cast-brass lions with open mouths and formalized manes, the heads turned to the right.

The Southwell Minster lectern is one of a series of 33 examples, most of which are in English churches (Oman 1930, pp.128–34). All appear to be the product of one workshop, although different models were used for the figure of the eagle and for the lion feet. The lecterns show a variety of finish, especially in the engraving and burnishing of the castings. In general they are characterized by the very distinctive raised head of the eagle and their wings.

The location of the workshop that produced these lecterns is not known. The export trade from the Low Countries in large base metalwares, including lecterns, was very considerable in the fifteenth and sixteenth centuries. So many from this workshop are to be found in English churches, however, that the possibility must remain that the Southwell lectern is from an English workshop. AN

PROV. Found in the lake at Newstead Abbey (Nottinghamshire) in about 1750; acquired in 1778 by Sir Richard Kaye, prebendary of Southwell, from a Nottingham dealer, and presented to Southwell Minster by his widow in 1805.

LIT. Oman 1930, pp.130–31, no. 18, pl. X.

244

244 The Coronation of the Virgin

*c.*1400–20

**Alabaster relief, painted and gilded,
set in a later painted wood frame; h. 103 cm, w. 58.5 cm**

**Barber Institute of Fine Arts, University
of Birmingham (39.25)**

The seated figure of Christ, resting an orb on his left
knee, blesses the Virgin with his outstretched right
hand as she is crowned by an angel behind her. Two
further angels are shown in the act of censing.

The unusually large size of this fine relief, more
common in earlier English alabasters, suggests that it
occupied the central panel of a grand altarpiece, possibly with slightly smaller reliefs of the apostles to
each side. Altarpieces with the Coronation or Glorification of the Virgin at their centre, with flanking
apostles, were popular on the Continent in the fourteenth century (see Williamson 1988, cat. nos 23–33,
for examples), while later in the fifteenth century the
scene of the Coronation – in a different, 'Trinity',
form, with the Virgin at the centre of the composition, flanked by God the Father and God the Son – is
shown as a subsidiary scene in English alabaster Marian
altarpieces, as on the example at Montréal, Yonne
(London 1913, pl. VII, fig. 15; Pitman 1959). The cult
of the Virgin had grown greatly in popularity from the
thirteenth century onwards, so that by the fifteenth
century all of the great churches – and very many of
the smaller ones – would have altars dedicated to her
(Duffy 1992, pp.256–65). PW

PROV. Bought from Clarence Hungerford MacKay, Roslyn,
Long Island, New York, in 1939.

LIT. Pitman 1959, p.208; Cheetham 1973, p.38; Birmingham
1983, p.68; Cheetham 1984, p.208; Blair and Ramsay 1991,
fig. 10.

245

245 Magdalen College, Oxford

Begun 1474

Magdalen College was founded by William Waynflete (d. 1486), a figure of outstanding importance as a patron of architecture in England (see also cat. no. 250). The college was conceived as a commemorative religious foundation in which education and devotion were jointly harnessed in the service of the wider Christian community. It sprang architecturally and institutionally from the circumstances of Waynflete's early career. Appointed Provost of Eton in 1442, he oversaw the initial work of constructing that royal college and was instrumental in forging an institutional connection between it and King's College,

Cambridge. By this alliance they offered a complete school and university education in the manner of William of Wykeham's colleges at Winchester and New College, Oxford.

This experience probably explains why, within a year of his consecration as Bishop of Winchester in 1447, he founded a new hall at Oxford. In 1458, after securing further funds, he refounded this institution as Magdalen College, with a community of graduate scholars governed by a president. Later he was also to establish two feeder schools for this college, in modest imitation of Henry VI's and William Wykeham's great foundations.

Preparations began to be made for new collegiate buildings from 1467 and the following year William

Orchard, a prominent Oxford mason, was put in charge of operations. He probably drew up the designs for the new college, the foundation stone of which was laid on 5 May 1474. By 1481 the college was largely complete, but work to the buildings continued and the great bell tower was not begun until 1492, six years after Waynflete's death.

Essentially the college comprises a great cloister enclosed on three sides by residential ranges and on the fourth by the chapel and great hall, set end to end. This plan is directly derived from New College, Oxford, built in the 1380s.   JG

LIT. Wilson 1899; VCH 1954, pp.193–207; Davis 1993, pp.57–73.

246 Divinity School, Oxford

*c.*1423–83

The decision to construct a purpose-built theology classroom was taken some time before 1423 when a letter soliciting contributions mentions that the work had already begun. Being the most prestigious branch of study in the medieval university, theology was evidently thought to require a setting whose architecture was on an altogether higher plane than the sober version of Perpendicular normally deemed appropriate to collegiate architecture.

The master mason chosen was Richard Winchcombe, who will have been known already in Oxford for the lavishly finished and idiosyncratically detailed chancel that he had recently built for New College at Adderbury in north Oxfordshire. His even more elaborate design for the Divinity School was doubtless formulated in the early 1420s, although he only received a contract in 1430, when a house in Oxford was rented for him and for the masons working under him. It is likely that Winchcombe had died by January 1440, when he was succeeded by Thomas Elkin. Elkin, about whom little is known, was ordered to eschew the original design's 'frivolous curiosities', which were said to have been deplored by important and knowledgeable persons. There is an element of hypocrisy in this critique, for the real problem was the university's failure to attract sponsorship in a period of economic recession, and Winchcombe's design will undoubtedly have been approved by the university authorities in advance of building. The consequence of Elkin's retrenchment most clearly visible in the fabric is the brutally abrupt switch to much plainer window reveals.

The project was probably rescued from the doldrums by Cardinal Henry Beaufort's executors, whose contribution of more than £300 in 1452 would have helped pay for the walls of the first-floor library (an addition agreed on in 1444), and by Thomas Kemp, Bishop of London, who gave more than £666 in 1478. By 1483 Kemp's money had been spent on the magnificent pendant lierne vault that exists today, and which almost certainly follows in its main lines the vault designed by Winchcombe nearly 60 years earlier.   CW

LIT. St John Hope 1914c; Myres 1967; Harvey 1992, pp.750–51.

246

247 Brass rubbing of Prior Nelond of Lewes

*c.*1432

h. 310 cm, w. 130 cm; l. of figure 178 cm

Marginal inscr. in Leonine verses, in *textura*:

Hic terre cumulus . Thome Nelond tegit ossa
Est et ei tumulus . presens sub marmore fossa
Virtutum donis . hic claruit et racionis
Exemplis q[ue] bonis . decus auxit Religionis
Mundo martha fuit . s[ed] [Christo] mente Maria
In mundo viguit . s[ed] erat sibi celsa sophia
In maii mensis . quarto decimo q[ue] kalendas
Ad celi mensis . sedes migrauit habendas.

(This heap of earth covers the bones of Thomas Nelond, and the grave under the present marble is his tomb. He was renowned for the gifts of virtue and reason, and by good example he augmented the honour of religion. To the world he was a Martha, but to Christ a Mary in his mind. In the world he thrived, but heavenly wisdom was his. On the fourteenth day before the kalends of May [18 April], he departed to take his seat at the heavenly table.)

Derrick Chivers Esq. (original in St Peter's church, Cowfold, West Sussex)

Thomas Nelond, prior of the Cluniac monastery of St Pancras, Lewes (East Sussex), from 1414 to 1432, is shown in the cassock and cowl of a Benedictine monk. From his hands proceed three scrolls, addressed to St Pancras, the Blessed Virgin Mary and St Thomas of Canterbury, whose images are in the canopy: *Martir sancte dei duc ad loca me requiei* (Holy martyr of God lead me to the places of rest); *Mater sancta Jh[es]u me serues mortis ab esu* (Holy Mother of Jesus preserve me from the sting of death); *Sit sancti Thome suscepta precatio pro me* (May the supplication of St Thomas on my behalf be received). At the top left is a shield with the verbal symbol of the Trinity; another shield is missing, as is the end of the marginal inscription. This composition, in its elegant simplicity, represents the London B workshop at its very best.

At the Dissolution in 1537 Lewes Priory was utterly razed, but several monuments were preserved. Three of the Arundel tombs were moved to Chichester Cathedral, and the Nelond brass was apparently transferred to Cowfold by a collateral descendant (Hutchinson forthcoming).   NR

PROV. Lewes Priory.

LIT. Davidson-Houston 1936, pp.149–52; Norris 1977, pp.87, 94–5, 99.

247

248 Cope of Cardinal Morton

*c.*1480–1500

Silk and embroidery; h. 140 cm, w. 289 cm

**Roman Catholic Diocese of Arundel and Brighton,
on loan to Arundel Castle**

The woven silk velvet ground is probably Italian.
Applied motifs, orphreys and hood were embroidered
in England in silk and metal threads with spangles.
The velvet ground is powdered with applied motifs of
angels on wheels (see also cat. no. 274), fleurs-de-lis
and double-headed eagles. The hood and orphreys
show prophets and apostles under arches. The cope
was relined in the late nineteenth to early twentieth
century, when the orphreys were reset and a replacement morse added. The rebus below the hood, with a
mort (falcon) on a tun (barrel), shows that the cope
belonged to Cardinal John Morton (d. 1500). Cardinal
Morton had an illustrious career; he was a minister
under Henry VII, became Archbishop of Canterbury
in 1485, Lord Chancellor in 1486 and Cardinal in
1493 (see also cat. no. 309).

Richly decorated church vestments were produced in
large numbers for powerful individuals of church and
state. Although generally used in grand churches, they
might also be donated to smaller parish churches or
used in the private chapels of great houses. They were
colourful and conspicuous symbols of ecclesiastical
power and sometimes included the arms, device or
name of the owner or patron, as in this case. The
embroidery is of the type that was produced in com-
mercially efficient workshops for a market that
demanded a soundly made ornamental product of
sumptuous appearance at an economic price.

Two related copes with Morton's rebus are in
Oscott College, Sutton Coldfield, and in the State
Historical Museum in Stockholm (Berghman 1957).
A number of copes of similar date and style survive
in various private and public collections, including
that of the Victoria and Albert Museum.   LW

PROV. At Slinden House until *c.*1930 (manor owned by the
Archbishops of Canterbury 1106–1542; granted to the
Kempes (a recusant Catholic family) in 1555, remained in
the family through the female line until 1920s); sold to RC
diocese of Southwark *c.*1930, deposited at St Richard's
church, Slinden; deposited at Arundel Castle, 1983.

LIT. Brighton 1989, cat. no. 185.

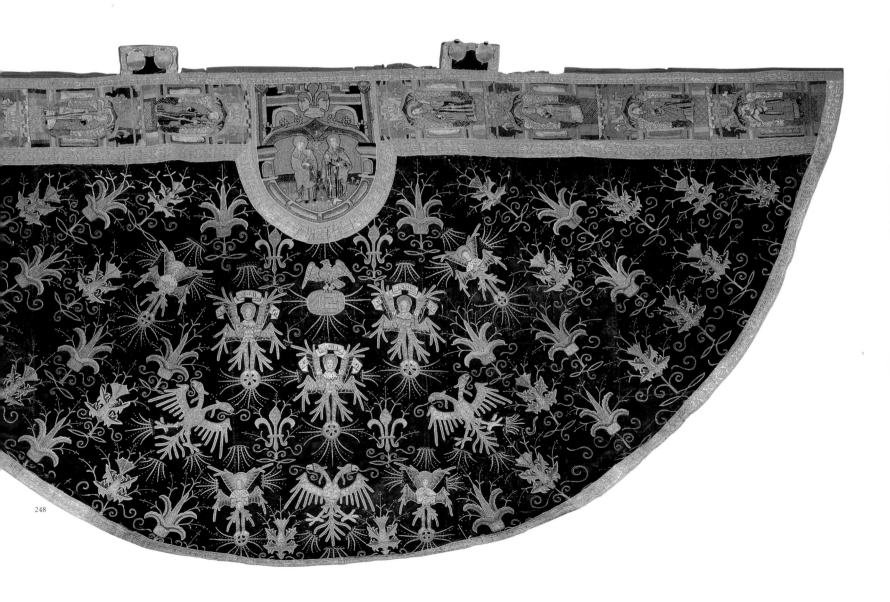

248

249 Pair of ecclesiastical gloves

Probably Spain, c.1500–30

Knitted in silk and silver-gilt thread; each max. l. 18 cm, max. w. 14 cm

New College, Oxford

Hand-knitted in red silk and silver-gilt thread, with details in blue silk, with a central motif of the sacred initials *ihs* and a cross surrounded by floriate rays; at the cuff is a pattern of eight-petalled gold flowers. The gold bands around the thumbs and fingers possibly simulate rings, although the bishop's ring was actually worn outside the glove.

The gloves were traditionally associated with the founder of New College, William of Wykeham (d. 1404). However, as they date from the sixteenth century, they are much more likely to have belonged to William Warham, Archbishop of Canterbury from 1504 to 1532 and Chancellor of the University in 1506–32 (see also cat. nos 180, 188). Ecclesiastical gloves were worn by bishops and other high officers of the church during the celebration of the Mass and were taken off at the consecration of the bread and wine. By the twelfth century most bishops had adopted liturgical gloves and from that time they are increasingly mentioned in service books. There were originally made of white or undyed silk to indicate purity, although red was later introduced for solemn episcopal occasions, and most surviving examples are white or red.

The gloves are typical of the elaborate style favoured in the sixteenth century and belong to a group, examples of which are in various collections, including the Victoria and Albert Museum and the Spence Collection at the Museum of Costume in Bath. They were probably knitted in Spain. LW

LIT. St John Hope 1907, pp.483–4, pl. L; Ashton 1929; Campbell (M) 2002, p.134.

250 Pontifical stockings and ankle boots of William of Waynflete, Bishop of Winchester (b. c.1395–1486)

Magdalen College, Oxford

a) Pontifical stockings

Italian, 1425–50

Lampas silk, pink ground, 2/1 twill; undulating stems, leaves and flowers in polychrome silk; falcons gorged with crowns and collared squirrels brocaded in silver-gilt, 1/2 twill; lining: linen, tabby

h. 52 cm, l. 27 cm

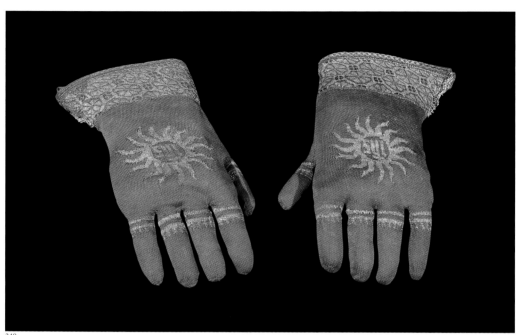

249

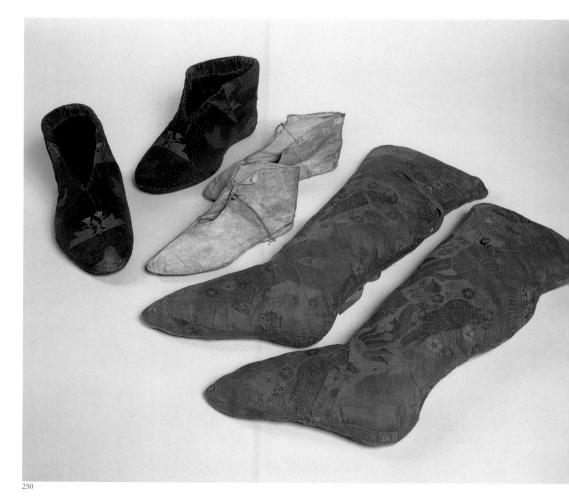

250

b) Ankle boots

Velvet, Italian, 1425–50; boot, English

Uppers: brown felt, later covered with velvet 'tissue'; platform sole rising to wedge heel, black leather; velvet: crimson cut silk pile, with silver-gilt weft loops, extended tabby grounds voided, brocaded with silver-gilt bell-flowers, with parti-coloured leaves and white flowers formed by silk pattern wefts, 1/3 twill

left boot, h. 14.5 cm, l. 29.7 cm; right boot, h. 13.3 cm, l. 31 cm

c) Ankle boots

*c.*1450

Uppers: originally ivory silk; lining (with insocks): white tawed goatskin, grain to the foot; sole: brown tanned goatskin leather

h. (centre back of both boots) 10.2 cm, left boot, l. 26.3 cm, right boot, l. 25.6 cm

Stockings and footwear termed *sandalia* formed part of the pontifical ornaments of a bishop. The bias-cut stockings, fashioned to the leg, were fastened below the knee with a ribbon and button. The silk/goatskin boots were originally front-laced. The silk uppers have all but perished, exposing the lining, yet this pair of ankle boots, complete with insocks, constitutes a rare survival. The other pair was made as felt ankle boots, and later covered with gold-looped velvet 'tissue'.

William of Waynflete, Chancellor of England from 1456, was consecrated Bishop of Winchester at Eton in 1447, and enthroned at Winchester in 1448. He founded Magdalen College in 1458 (cat. no. 245), and subsequently bequeathed his estates to it. His stockings and ankle boots have been connected with an inventory of Magdalen College Chapel in 1495, which described '… two tunicles of white damask lined with blue tartaroun and a pair of sandals of that set … a pair of stockings of silk with divers flowers … a pair of boots of tissue … '

JS & LM

LIT. St John Hope 1907, pp.486–7, pls LI–LII; Campbell (M) 2002, p.135, pl. 22.

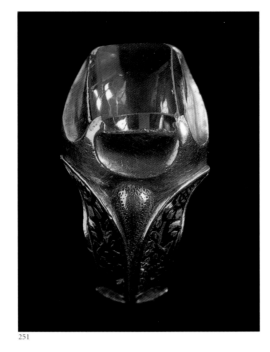

251

251 Bishop Stanbury of Hereford's ring

Mid-15th century

Gold, set with a sapphire; diam. 2.2 cm

Inscr. on the interior in black-letter: *en bon an*

Hereford Cathedral, Herefordshire

The ring is set with a sapphire held by four claws with scooped scallops. The shoulders of the ring are each divided into two panels. Each panel has two flowers on stems set one above the other, reserved against a dark-blue enamelled background.

John Stanbury was a Carmelite friar whose closeness to Henry VI as chaplain and confessor attracted the king's patronage. He was appointed to the See of Hereford in 1453 and remained as bishop until his death in 1474. His alabaster tomb shows a dignified effigy of a bishop, and his chantry chapel is decorated with a series of carved shields combining his own shields with religious heraldry.

If the ring had not been found in the tomb of a bishop, it would have been classified as a secular decorative ring. The inscription '*en bon an*' occurs on a number of late medieval rings of different types, such as signet rings, iconographic rings (those with figures of saints on the bezel), decorative rings set with stones, and plain rings with just the inscription. The form of the inscription suggests that such rings were given as New Year gifts in January.

While the ring is unlikely to have been that used in the consecration of Stanbury as Bishop of Hereford, the panels of decoration and the closeness of its detail to that on the Godstow Ring (cat no. 252) suggest that it was made in the mid-fifteenth century. JC

PROV. Found in the wooden coffin in the tomb of Bishop Stanbury during the restoration of Hereford Cathedral in the 1840s.

LIT. Ward et al. 1981, no. 191; Cherry 1995.

252 The Godstow Ring

Mid-15th century

Gold; diam. 2 cm

Inscr. in the interior in black-letter: *Most in mynd and in myn hert, Lothest from you ferto depart*

British Museum, London (MME AF 1075)

A broad hoop engraved on the outer side with flowers and leaves like those of the Matlask Pendant (cat. no. 208). The floral decoration once stood out against an enamelled background. Within this there are three lozenge-shaped panels engraved with the Trinity, the Virgin and Child, and a bearded male saint. From its discovery at the rich Benedictine nunnery of Godstow near Oxford, and from the inscription, it seems likely that the ring belonged to a nun. It is a surprisingly splendid ring for one who presumably had taken a vow of poverty. JC

PROV. Dug up at the Benedictine nunnery at Godstow, Oxfordshire, before 1868.

LIT. Dalton 1912, no. 962; Ward et al. 1981, no. 196.

252

253 The Abingdon Missal

1461

Parchment, ff.270: h. 35.8 cm, w. 23.7 cm

Bodleian Library, Oxford (MS Digby 227)

The Abingdon Missal is in two volumes: the first, Digby 227, contains the texts necessary for the celebration of feasts and saints' days in the summer part of the liturgical year, and is dated 1461 on f.270v; the second, containing Masses for the winter, is Oxford, Trinity College MS 75. Both volumes are written in an elegant, accomplished script, and numerous historiated initials – all illuminated by the same hand – punctuate the text.

An ambitious production, the missal was apparently made for William Ashenden, abbot of the Benedictine monastery of St Mary's in Abingdon, Berkshire. The abbot kneels in the border of the missal's most impressive miniature, a full-page depiction of the Crucifixion. A scroll rises from Ashenden's hands, inscribed with words of the *Adoramus te*, which praises the Crucifixion as the redemption of the world. The Crucifixion is overlaid with Trinitarian meaning, with God the Father and the Holy Spirit occupying its upper reaches.

Once attributed to William Abell (for whom see cat. no. 20), the Abingdon Missal is now given to an artist dubbed the Abingdon Missal Master. The Master's sophistication is most apparent in the Crucifixion, in which the subtle overlapping of the principal figures and the cross with the border makes the cross appear to be popping out at the viewer. The Master's figure style shows a certain debt to the Fastolf Master (cat. nos 92, 224), a Rouen artist whose career brought him to England sometime in the 1440s, as well as to Abell.

In the borders, muscular acanthus scrolls, flowers and berry stalks are painted in boldly contrasting colours. Scott has noted the striking resemblance of the missal's borders to a group of manuscripts securely tied to Oxford, prompting her to posit an Oxford-based workshop. With Abingdon only a few miles from Oxford, Ashenden would not have had to travel far to commission his missal.   AB

PROV. Probably William Ashenden, abbot (1436–69) of St Mary's, Abingdon, Berkshire; Thomas Allen of Oxford (d. 1632); Sir Kenelm Digby (d. 1635); Bodleian Library, 1634.

LIT. Scott 1996, no. 101a.

254 The Lovel Lectionary

PLATE 4

c.1408

Vellum, ff.17; h. 47 cm, w. 31 cm

British Library, London (Harley MS 7026)

This elaborately decorated gospel lectionary was commissioned by John, Lord Lovel of Titchmarsh (d. 1408) for presentation to Salisbury Cathedral as a memorial to himself and his wife Maud, heiress of the senior branch of the Holland family. The principal illuminator is identifiable as John Siferwas, a Dominican friar who is chiefly celebrated for his work in the Sherborne Missal (Backhouse 1999a), made for the Dorset abbey of that name during the first years of the fifteenth century. Only 17 leaves survive from what must have been 40–50 folios, offering Gospel readings for use at Mass on principal festivals throughout the liturgical year. They are now bound out of order and in some cases reversed. The justly famous double portrait

253

of Lovel and Siferwas with the completed volume (f.4v) is today incorrectly placed to form a frontispiece, facing the opening of the First Mass of Christmas. It originally appeared at the end of the book, providing a pictorial colophon at the end of the readings for the Mass of the Dead. Siferwas's name, now almost illegible, is given below the image. Lovel is named in the inscription to the left of the figures.

Lovel had been a prominent figure at the court of Richard II but, with many of his contemporaries, he successfully transferred his allegiance to the new king when Henry IV seized the throne in 1399. His principal residence was Wardour Castle in Wiltshire, about 20 kilometres west of Salisbury, but he elected to be buried in his wife's family mausoleum at Brackley in Northamptonshire. The bequest of a Gospel lectionary to Salisbury Cathedral is mentioned in his will of 26 July 1408, a copy of which is preserved in Archbishop Arundel's Register at Lambeth. Most of the surviving pages of the manuscript display the Lovel and Holland arms and the family livery badge of a padlock also appears. Lovel and his wife are portrayed in several of the margins.

JMB

PROV. Salisbury Cathedral, after 1408; Joseph Holland, 1600; Thomas Granger (d. 1732); Edward Harley, 2nd Earl of Oxford (d. 1741); British Museum, 1753.

LIT. Scott 1996, no. 10; Backhouse 2003.

255 Cardinal Wolsey's Gospel lectionary

*c.*1529

Vellum, ff.45; h. 40.5 cm, w. 30 cm

Magdalen College, Oxford (MS Lat. 223)

The decoration of Cardinal Wolsey's Gospel lectionary can be dated to the last year of his life, for it includes on many pages representations of his personal arms impaling those of the bishopric of Winchester, surrounded by the Garter. He resigned Durham in exchange for Winchester in 1529. However, the feast of St Swithun of Winchester is not included in the manuscript, though St Cuthbert of Durham is featured, implying that the volume had been written out before the exchange took place. The complementary Epistle lectionary in the library of Christ Church, Oxford (MS 101), is dated 1528. The unusual appearance of St Frideswide suggests that the compilation may have been intended for use at Cardinal College, Oxford (later refounded by Henry VIII as Christ Church), where her shrine is situated.

The manuscript is written in the distinctive script of Peter Meghen, the one-eyed scribe from 's-Hertogenbosch, who produced manuscripts for English clients

255

between 1504 and 1540 and was connected with many of the leading scholars of the period, including Erasmus and Thomas More. The opulent illumination has traditionally been associated with Gerard Horenbout of Ghent, who came to England in the mid-1520s with his son Lucas and daughter Susanna. All three were artists, and Lucas was to become court painter to Henry VIII in 1534. This particular work seems to have acquired a strong Germanic flavour, perhaps through the influence of woodcuts and engravings, and may be due to one of the younger members of Gerard's family. On the Pentecost page (f.28v), Wolsey's arms impale those of the archdiocese of York, which he had held since 1514.

JMB

PROV. Cardinal Wolsey (d. 1530); Royal Library (?); Samuel Chappington, 16th century; Magdalen College, Oxford.

LIT. Trapp 1975, no. 14; Trapp 1981–2, fig. 8; Alexander and Temple 1985, no. 828; Carley 2000, no. H5.4; Kren and McKendrick 2003.

256

256 Binding with image of St George presented to Cardinal Wolsey

*c.*1519

h. 24 cm, w. 16 cm, d. 1.3 cm

Bodleian Library, Oxford (MS Bodley 523)

The binding covers a copy of Robert Whittinton's *Epigrams*, MS *c.*1519. Brown calf, tooled in gold, with two impressions of a large block showing three Tudor emblems above and below a block depicting St George. The blocks were (probably) of metal, engraved in relief to be used with gold leaf, but clearly not made for the binding, on which they only fit sideways. The book was presented to Cardinal Wolsey not later than 1519.

This is the earliest English gold-tooled binding. The technique of decorating bindings with heated tools through gold leaf reached England relatively late. The earliest efforts, dating from about 1519 and the early 1520s, are all of an experimental nature, using blocks, panels, rolls and tools that were clearly neither designed nor cut or cast for the purpose. These first experiments can be linked with the court of Henry VIII. In 1519 Thomas Linacre, the king's physician, presented his royal master and Cardinal Wolsey with copies of his translation of Galen's *Methodus medendi* (Paris, 1519), bound in the atelier of Simon Vostre in brown calf, tooled in blind and gold. Two years earlier Linacre had given Wolsey another Paris binding made in the same atelier, also decorated in blind and gold. It may have been Linacre who pressed for an English experiment. Another of his presents to the king,

Paulus of Middleburg's *De recta Paschae celebratione* (Fossombrone, 1513), was bound *c.*1521–4 by John Reynes, tooled with his signed roll in blind, but with his rose and royal arms panels, cut and cast to be used in blind, impressed through gold leaf. A third experimental binding was also made for Henry VIII in London *c.*1520–25, decorated in gold with individual tools and a roll signed IG and WG. Again, both tools and roll were cut in intaglio for use in blind.   MF

PROV. Cardinal Wolsey.

LIT. Nixon 1964, pp.286–8; Oxford 1968, cat. no. 63; Nixon 1978, nos 5, 6; Fogelmark 1990, p.124; Nixon and Foot 1992, pp.25–6, fig. 19; Foot 2000, p.17; Barber 2000, pp.54, 58–61.

18 THE PARISH CHURCH

PAUL WILLIAMSON

The parish church of Holy Trinity at Long Melford in Suffolk (plate 121) might appear at first sight to be a curious choice as a typical example of the genre. In size and decorative ambition it would be ranked by some as only marginally less important than the famous 'great churches' covered in the previous section of the catalogue; and its liturgical items were, as we shall see, of remarkable quantity. There are advantages, however, in selecting it as a paradigm rather than attempting a general overview of the type, especially as Eamon Duffy has broadly discussed elsewhere (pp.56–67) how the parish church was used by its parishioners in the late Middle Ages.

Long Melford recommends itself because the architectural

121 Holy Trinity church, Long Melford, Suffolk

integrity of the main body of the church, both inside and out, has not been seriously impaired by later additions, and its authenticity as a reflection of the late fifteenth century is guaranteed by the fact that the principal building campaign took place between *c*.1467 and 1497 (Paine 1983, pp.9–18). We also know the names of the major donors to the building of the church, the Clopton and Martin families; and the evocative Clopton chantry chapel to the north of the chancel, the Martin chapel to the south and the various tombs and brasses commemorating the two families serve to illustrate vividly the ever-present links between the sacred and the secular. The visual impact of the interior is heightened considerably by the celebrated remaining panels of stained and painted glass in the north aisle, including members of the Clopton family and other donors, standing saints and angels, but it should be remembered that these are but a fraction of the original number (Woodforde 1950, pp.74–127). The interior of the church is now very much a skeleton – albeit a grand one – but one that may be fleshed out with the help of the extremely full existing documentation.

Like the great churches, not even the most well-preserved parish churches in England can give us an absolutely accurate impression of their appearance in the late Middle Ages. Although the architectural spaces might remain largely unchanged, in most churches key elements of the interior decoration and furnishing have invariably been removed, at the Reformation, during the Civil War in the 1640s or by ecclesiological 'improvements' in the eighteenth and nineteenth centuries. Furthermore, the liturgical vessels so essential for the Mass have all gone from the sacristies (for Suffolk, see Cautley 1982, pp.26–35). Fortunately there are a few contemporary accounts and inventories that help us to reconstruct how the parish church must have looked and how it functioned, and by happy coincidence among the most illuminating of these refer to Long Melford. If one allows for regional differences and the fact that churches varied in size and wealth, Holy Trinity can thus provide a valuable exemplar of the English parish church on the eve of the Reformation.

Two documents are paramount in this connection. The first is *The State of Melford Church and Our Ladie's Chappel at the East End, as I did know it*, written by Roger Martin (*c*.1527–1615) probably in the 1580s or '90s. Martin came from the long-established Long Melford family already mentioned, whose chapel had been built in the early 1480s, and wrote his account in order to record the appearance of the church as it was in his late youth, before the depredations of the mid-century reforms. He was a confirmed recusant who clearly disapproved of the changes forced on the parish, and his short essay – when set against the interior of the church today – paints a poignant picture of the losses suffered. He touches first on the great high altar with the Crucifixion at its centre and with scenes from the Passion of Christ, with 'very fair painted boards, made to shut too, which were opened upon high and solemn feast dayes, which then was a very beautiful shew' (Dymond and Paine 1992, p.1). Although it is not now possible to be sure about this, it is possible – even likely – that this altarpiece was a Netherlandish import: other English patrons, such as the Mercers' Company in London, are known to have ordered such altarpieces from Antwerp and elsewhere (Barron and Erler 2000, p.326; Woods 2002; see also the essay by Kim Woods in this volume). Martin goes on to describe another, smaller altarpiece with the crucified Christ and two thieves in his own family chapel, and mentions that on each side of both this and the high altarpiece were tabernacles containing statues of saints (Dymond and Paine 1992, pp.1–2). To the north of the high altar was the patronal 'fair large gilt image of the Holy Trinity … besides other fair images', and in the chantry chapel the two tabernacles held images of Christ and the Virgin of Pity (see cat. no. 344 for the type), to the north and south respectively. Such sculptures, nearly all now lost, were ubiquitous in parish churches, and Long Melford church had at least 17 images before the Reformation, which included Sts Anne, Leonard, John the Baptist, John the Evangelist, Peter, Anthony, James, Catherine, Margaret (cat. no. 280), Mary Magdalene, Edmund, Sitha (cat. no. 281), George (cat. nos 84, 284), Thomas, Christopher (cat. no. 283), Andrew and Eligius (*ibid.*, pp.24–5, n.79).

The other major feature described by Roger Martin was the rood-loft supporting sculptures of the crucified Christ, the Virgin and St John, which, below 'in 12 partitions in boards, was fair painted [with] the images of the 12 apostles' (*ibid.*, p.3). Rood-lofts, like sculpted altars, were once widespread, but have proved even more vulnerable to destruction. Not a single complete British rood-loft survives, although the reconstructed and repainted example at Eye in Suffolk gives an idea of how such an ensemble must have looked (Cautley 1982, p.139, figs on p.132).

The writer continues by observing that the roof of the church was 'beautified with fair gilt stars' and then concludes his description of its contents by referring to the 'many rich copes' and vestments held in the 'press', or cupboard, of the vestry. Because Martin does not go into any detail over the vestments and does not mention the liturgical objects at all, it is fortunate that we can read his account in tandem with the full inventory of the church compiled in 1529, the second important document to be considered. The 'List of Church Goods' of Long Melford gives an extraordinarily complete picture of the holdings of a parish church – although admittedly a relatively rich one. There is only room here to enumerate briefly the contents (for the full list, see Dymond and Paine 1992, pp.10–26). The inventory starts with plate, including 13 chalices, a grand monstrance for the Blessed Sacrament and a silver reliquary containing a fragment of the Column of the Flagellation of Christ; it continues with numerous other silver vessels, including two basins, three paxes, two crosses, a pyx, two chrismatories, two incense boats, two candlesticks, two censers and four cruets (see cat. nos 303–7 for examples). A fascinating section follows this, specifying all the jewels and rings to be found in the Lady Chapel, many of which were attached to the 'apron of Our Lady' as votive offerings; it goes on to describe the 'Coats belonging to Our Lady' and the Christ Child, in which the figures were dressed on major feast-days (*ibid.*, pp.13–14). The many rich copes and other vestments alluded to by Roger Martin are then referred to in some detail, followed by lists of the altar cloths, the Mass books, antiphoners, graduals, processioners, corporasses, coverlets, brass or 'lattyn' candlesticks of various form and size, two holy water pails and an aspergillum of brass, and various other brass items, including '2 great lectorns in the quire, whereof 2 of the feet be broken' (*ibid.*, p.22; see cat. no. 243). The list closes with descriptions of chests, more crosses, cross cloths and numerous cloths used to hang before images of the saints or to cover them during Lent.

The interiors of parish churches are organic spaces, built up over the centuries with additions and modifications to the fabric, some responding to changes to the liturgy, some the result of the self-aggrandisement of patrons or clergy. Although the stained glass, sculpture, furnishings, books, textiles and liturgical items gathered together in this section of the exhibition are by their nature fragments torn from their original context, they still speak eloquently of the society that produced them. The church at Long Melford may have been exceptionally well appointed, but elements of its fittings and furnishings could be found in every English late medieval parish church.

FURTHER READING

Cox and Ford 1950; Duffy 1992; French 2001; Platt 1981; Swanson 1993, pp.150–63.

257 Church of St Peter and St Paul, Salle, Norfolk, nave

PLATE 37

*c.*1400–10

It is not hard to see why Salle church has long been regarded as the epitome of the late medieval Norfolk parish church, for it conforms to the Perpendicular ideal in being large and unified, and it retains a fair sample of its original high-quality fittings and decoration. The nave also illustrates how an impressive building could be produced by the concerted efforts of a parish elite whose individual members were not spectacularly well-off – a kind of patronage that did not automatically yield satisfactory results. The prime movers in the rebuilding were probably the five men named in a manorial court record of 1408, which refers to the encumbering of a piece of ground by timber belonging to the church. This reference suggests that the nave was well advanced, perhaps ready to be roofed.

The main elevations derive from what was by *c.*1400 the standard formula for a London parish church, but they are saved from dullness by the typically East Anglian elongation of their piers. In a nave of comparable ambition built 10 or 20 years later there would almost inevitably have been more emphasis on articulating the bay design (cat. no. 120). As often happened, the chancel was rebuilt in a separate and later campaign. CW

LIT. Parsons 1937, pp.19–71; Fawcett 1980; Heslop 1988.

258

258 Church of St Peter and St Paul, Lavenham, Suffolk, nave

*c.*1500

In 1400 Lavenham was a small village; in 1524 it was England's thirteenth most prosperous town. Its church is a monument not only to the wealth and piety of the town's rich clothiers, but also to the great deference paid by these men towards the lord of the manor, John de Vere, 13th Earl of Oxford and a close associate of Henry VII. The central vessel of the nave, probably begun shortly after 1500, could scarcely have signalled the earl's involvement more clearly, for the exterior walls of the clearstorey bear his mullet (star) badge, the lost clearstorey glazing was devoted to his and his family's heraldry, and the main internal elevations include many blank shields, which must have been meant to be decorated with his arms as no one else known to have been involved in funding the work was armigerous (entitled to heraldic arms). The absence of inscriptions commemorating donors forms a striking contrast with the earlier nave at nearby Long Melford (see p.376) and almost certainly represents an implicit criticism of the latter.

The main vessel of the nave displays many of the trademarks of the architect to whom it has long been attributed, John Wastell of Bury St Edmunds: capitals with fleuron ornament, bands of cusped diamonds and, most obviously, blind tracery circles and mouchettes on the spandrels of the main arcades. The relative lowness of the arcades is untypical of Wastell, but the low-pitched tie-beam roof is of a kind used in all his parish churches – interesting evidence of the master mason's ability to influence the contribution of the master carpenter.   CW

LIT. Woodman 1978, pp.193–200; Harvey 1984, p.320; Haward 1993, pp.9, 80, 81, 141, 202–4.

259 Church of St Peter and St Paul, Northleach, Gloucestershire, nave

Early and mid-15th century

The south aisle and porch and the west tower were added to a nave of unknown date some time shortly after 1400. The outstanding quality and ambition of all these structures, and the fact that they appear to have been built quickly, suggest patronage by one or more of the wealthy woolmen based in Northleach, rather than a community-wide effort. The south aisle, which is of one build with the porch (plate 74), has pinnacles and window tracery clearly modelled on New College, Oxford, but the façade of the porch possesses a distinctive kind of elegance generated partly by the thinness and elongation of its forms and partly by their juxtaposition next to extensive areas of sheer ashlar masonry.

The north aisle was built a little later, probably by another single donor, but the greatest benefaction came from the highly successful woolman John Fortey (d. 1459), who bequeathed the large sum of £300 'towards the new middle aisle … already begun by me'. Fortey's monumental brass under the second easternmost bay of the north arcade recalls the traditional position for a founder's tomb, and was in this respect an entirely appropriate memorial to the donor of the new central vessel of the nave. Corbels integral with the piers (one of which is visible in the adjacent photograph) show that Fortey's tomb was originally dignified by a wooden tester.

The main elements of the nave elevations illustrate how diverse were the sources drawn on by Cotswold church architects: concave-sided octagonal piers from churches in the vicinity of Oxford, and the recessing of the clearstorey and arcade spandrels from Bristol or Coventry. These borrowings are all fashioned into a unified whole by giving the strips of wall between the clearstorey recesses the same width as the faces of the piers directly below them, and by framing the recesses with a hollow chamfer echoing both the arcade mouldings and the much bolder concavities of the piers and their capitals.   CW

LIT. VCH 2001, pp.137–40.

260 Church of St John the Baptist, Ashton, Devon

PLATE 34

Late 15th century

This small and remote two-aisled church contains an almost complete set of medieval fittings, and fragments of a decorative scheme that would have articulated the relative significance of areas of the building.

Many architectural features in the church are commonly found in Devon churches, for example the wagon vaults over both aisles, the wooden traceried screen stretching across both aisles, and some standard West Country late Perpendicular window tracery. With no architectural distinction between nave and chancel, the screen is the primary liturgical division within the building, providing a significant focus for devotional imagery. Painted on the west face of the screen are figures representing Apostles, church fathers and saints.

The chapel formed by the screen at the east end of the north aisle, dedicated to the Virgin, was in the patronage of the local Chudleigh family, lords of the manor from 1320 to 1745. Heraldic decoration in the surviving medieval glass demonstrates alliances with other local families, identifying their status and their appropriation of the chapel, which would have been served by a priest saying Masses for the souls of the deceased. On the reverse of the rood-screen and on the parclose screen dividing the chapel from the chancel is a remarkable series of painted images holding scrolls bearing Latin inscriptions, identified as relating to the Incarnation and feast of the Transfigu-

ration (instigated after 1457). The image of Christ with the symbols of the Passion on the north wall above the burial vault of the family completes the decorative and iconographical programme.

The significance of the Chudleighs' patronage to the appearance of the church is clearly evident, their status and education implied by the high quality of both glass and paintings, which surpass comparable schemes in the region.   LAM

LIT. Glasscoe 1984 and 1987.

261 St Mary's church, Bury St Edmunds, hammerbeam roof of nave

*c.*1445

Oak carpentry and sculpture

St Mary's church is a major representative of Suffolk's great phase of church rebuilding in the Perpendicular style, demonstrating the wealth of the wool trade and expanding cloth exports. Bury was the regional centre for this industry, and after a successful civic and business career, John Baret II, from one of the most prominent burghal families in the wool trade, left the bulk of his fortune to the town and its two churches on his death in 1467 (see cat. no. 331). The nave roof is not itself documented, but was perhaps completed by 1444, when the parapets were being built, and the presence of Baret's mottoes on the east bay suggests that the roof was provided by him.

The hammerbeam, originating in the late thirteenth

century as a mechanical device for supporting complex roofs, and most famously used in the 1390s rebuilding of Westminster Hall (plate 25), became a medium for spectacular display carpentry in fifteenth-century East Anglia. Westminster's hammerbeams carried angels, and in churches it was the angels rather than mechanical necessity that became the *raison d'être* of this roof type, with the projecting beams allowing the angels to hover between earth and heaven, while the arch-braced rafters provided the main roof structure. The contrast between spacious and relatively simple masonry, and the busy complexity of timberwork, is perfectly exemplified at St Mary's. The sculptural programme of the 10-bay roof includes 42 figures of prophets and saints acting as roof supports, 40 angels on the richly carved coving at the sides, and 18 life-size angels in pairs on the hammerbeams carrying various attributes of a procession to the Mass, with kings and queens at the west end. The timbers are richly moulded, with traceried panels in the apex, the many spandrels providing surfaces for a riot of minor carving, including animals and grotesque figures; this continues in the lean-to roofs of the aisles.   JTM

LIT. Tolhurst 1962; Haward 1999; Paine 2000.

262 Angel corbel

Mid-15th century

Painted oak; h. 26 cm, w. 32 cm, d. 15 cm

York Museums Trust, Yorkshire Museum (YORYM HB 14)

This is in the form of a half figure of a vested angel with flowing hair and arms raised. Behind is the truncated stub of a slip tenon, by which the corbel was attached to the underside of the roof purlin. It was secured to the tenon by means of a long peg driven through its width. The Roman numeral VII, for positioning, is scratched on the back. The original paint is well preserved: pink for the face, hands and lips, the eyes with black pupils, and the hair a reddish-gold colour.

The corbel was salvaged from the central roof of St Martin le Grand, Coney Street, York, in 1870–71, when the latter was replaced. The Yorkshire Museum has five of the series, and that depicting the patron saint also retains its original polychrome mostly intact. The church was extensively rebuilt in 1443–50, and at that time the nave and aisles were provided with new roofs.   CT

PROV. St Martin le Grand, Coney Street, York; acquired before 1921.

LIT. RCHM 1981, pp.25–9; Hills and Oldfield 2001, p.5.

◀261   262

263

263 Angel corbel

Mid-15th century

Oak; h. (excluding tenon) 47 cm, w. 24 cm, d. 21.2 cm

Victoria and Albert Museum, London (W.23–1911)

From the base of a wall post of a roof, this corbel appears in the form of a half-figure of a vested angel with curly hair, holding a lute or gittern, and floating on a cloud. The top consists of a battlemented projection. There is some damage to the right side of the chin, and a split on the left-hand side above the head.

This corbel, and another two in the V&A's collection, is said to have come from St Mary's church in Bury St Edmunds, Suffolk, although it is difficult to imagine where in that church they were located. There is nowhere for them on the timber roof of the nave, with its arch-braced principal rafters and tenoned purlins, the former strengthened with hammerbeams (cat. no. 261). The angels there, in characteristic East Anglian fashion, are cantilevered out from the wall at an angle of 90 degrees. The positioning of a large tenon immediately above all three of the V&A's figures presupposes the placement of these corbel blocks flush against a wall, following the practice in the medium of stone.

The corbels are too small to have been used on the roof of a major space. The use of such figures in lesser contexts is not particularly common, but an instance can be cited in the Lady Chapel at Long Melford, Suffolk. There they are placed beneath the cambered tie-beam of a low pitched roof of modest span (Cautley 1937, pl. on p.109). Stylistically, although different in format, the V&A's corbels seem to be closest to those on the hammerbeam roof at March, Cambridgeshire, of c.1500. Before the fifteenth century the use of wooden corbels on this scale was a rarity.   CT

PROV. Acquired in 1911.

LIT. Tracy 1988, cat. nos 38–40; Haward 1999, p.52.

264 St Mary's church, Attleborough, Norfolk, rood-screen

PLATE 38

c.1470–78

Oak; h. 6 m, w. 15.8 m, d. 1.8 m

The screen covers the full width of the spacious mid-fourteenth- and early fifteenth-century nave, and rests underneath the arch of the crossing tower. The painting on the latter was uncovered in 1844, and revealed a huge cross with attendant adoring figures, comprising angels, archangels and prophets, surmounted by an Annunciation, which must have related to the medieval college's dedication to the Holy Cross. The screen has three exceptionally wide entrances, the central one leading to the now demolished aisled chancel, which was built as a collegiate chantry by the Mortimer family in 1405. The entrance on the north side led to the Chaunticlere chantry. The screen retains most of its original ribbed coving on the west side and its loft veranda. The entrances are surrounded by single light openings without tracery.

Unusually for rood-screens in Norfolk and Suffolk churches, the dado panelling at the base does not accommodate figures of painted saints, just blind tracery heads with flowers below, stencilled in gold on either a red or green background. At Attleborough only six saints are featured, and are placed three each side of the central entrance in the middle zone, where the panels are more than two metres tall. On the north side is the Virgin and Child in the centre, with St John the Baptist and St John the Evangelist on either side. At the feet of the Virgin is a small tonsured figure who, it has been suggested, is John Heyhoo, rector from 1470 to 1478. This period accords with the style of the painting on the north side, which is of exceptional quality. At the centre of the painted panels on the south side of the Attleborough screen, which by contrast are typically East Anglian in style, is the image of the Holy Trinity. This is flanked by a nimbed bishop, possibly St Thomas Becket, and by the figure of St Bartholomew. On neither side does the painting reach the bottom of the panels, and it leaves an unexplained blank portion. What is more, from the more robust style of the joinery below, and the marks of later mutilation, it is clear that nave altars with reredoses originally stood underneath each group of three painted bays.

The loft above is vaulted with tierceron and lierne ribs, which are still whitewashed over. The loft veranda is tall, and the blank spaces in the centre of the bays were painted over in the seventeenth century with the arms of the bishoprics of England and Wales. The screen has suffered many other alterations, including the likely removal of the painted panels to save them from Reformist and even Puritan iconoclasm, and its relocation to the west end of the church from 1845 to 1931. The arches of the coving, instead of being kept in check by a horizontal bressumer beam in the conventional way, are exposed at the front, as exceptionally also at Ranworth in Norfolk, and Southwold and Bramfield in Suffolk.   CT

LIT. Barrett 1848, pp.108–9 (ill.), facing 141 (ill.); Vallance 1936, pp.21, 39, 45–6, 60, 42 (ill.), 250–51 (ills); Duffy 1992, pp.112–13; Duffy 1997.

265 Pair of doors from a rood-screen

15th or early 16th century

Painted oak; h. 223 cm, w. 47 cm (left), w. 50 cm (right)

Exeter City Museums (20/1994)

The doors illustrate the most common form of screen in the West Country: a lower dado of paired panels with painted saints on plain boarding, separated by a heavy central rail from an upper register of four lights with Perpendicular tracery. In this instance the sill and quatrefoil panels at the feet of the doors have been lost, as have the mullions on which they hung, above which ribbed coving would have sprung to support the rood-loft above.

Although these doors are by no means especially grand representatives of the rich tradition of West Country rood-screens, their painting is particularly interesting. The medieval polychromy has survived unrestored. Most unusually, the figures in the dado show two phases of painting, most evident on the right side, where a king with crown and sceptre underlies a bearded saint. The polychromy of the lights is overpainted with limewash, in turn covered with small fragments of further colour; the figures were subsequently defaced. The sequence of painting may reflect the whitewashing of the screen in the reign of Edward VI and subsequent recolouring in Mary's reign.   JA

PROV. St David's church, Ashprington, Devon; removed 1846.

LIT. Bond and Radford 1902; Bond 1908; Bond and Camm 1909.

265

266 Part of a chancel screen with images of prophets and kings

Probably soon after 1463

Oak, painted and gilded; h. 135.5 cm, w. 200 cm;
h. of panels including tracery 87 cm; w. of painted
area of each panel 21 cm

St Mary's church, Kersey, Suffolk

This fragment is all that survives of the chancel
screen of the church, three bays with two adjacent
panels in each, showing three prophets paired with
three kings. None of these is identified by name, but
one of the kings can be recognized as St Edmund,
from the arrow that he holds. Prophet and king in
each bay turn towards each other, gesticulating with
extended hands in active debate. The kings hold scep-
tres and two of the prophets grasp scrolls. All are
dressed in sumptuous ermine-lined garments, in
strong red, green, grey and white, which contrast with
the alternating red and green backgrounds. The
prophets wear extravagant peaked and turban-like
hats and the kings wear crowns trimmed with pearls.

A few screens in East Anglia carry sequences of
prophets (Coddenham, Harpley, Southwold, Thorn-
ham) or kings (Barton Turf, Catfield), but prophets
are rare in this context and kings are usually deployed
in pairs alongside other categories of saint. This combination of prophets and kings is unparalleled in the
region, and was uncommon anywhere in medieval
Europe. It is likely that Edmund's companions are
kings who enjoyed particular veneration in the
region, like Edward the Confessor, Walstan, Olaf and
Henry VI, rather than kings from the Old Testament.
They make strange but dramatic interlocutors with
the prophets.

The panels have suffered serious flaking of their
painted surfaces in places.

The paintings may be associated with a bequest of
John Puske in his will of 1463 (Bury St Edmunds,
Baldwyne, f.337) of 15 marks for painting the candlebeam in the church. In Suffolk wills, the word
'candlebeam' is commonly used to refer to the rood-
screen. This was a large bequest and may well have
been intended to pay for the painting of the whole
screen together with all of its figural panels (pers.
comm., Simon Cotton).   JM

LIT. James 1930, pp.5, 53; Cautley 1975, p. 305, pl. on p.121;
Cotton 1987, p.53.

266

267

267 The Twelve Apostles

Probably mid-15th century

**Alabaster reliefs with substantial traces of paint;
h. 44.5–46.6 cm; w. 14.2–14.8 cm (total w. 174 cm)**

**Victoria and Albert Museum, London (A.148 to
159–1922)**

Each figure is depicted with a scroll painted with the
appropriate section of the Apostles' Creed. Apart
from St Matthias, every apostle holds his traditional
attribute. Each figure has latten wire loops or holes
on the reverse, indicating that they were probably
mounted in a wooden structure.

Cheetham describes them as from an altarpiece,
but this may not have been their original function.
Among 69 alabaster altarpieces recorded by
Cheetham, only Passion, Virgin or saints' altarpieces
are listed, apart from this one, although apostles
occur on altarpieces in other media. Alternatively
they could have decorated the sides of an alabaster
tomb chest, as on the ap Thomas tomb at Abergavenny or the Vernon tomb at Tong, Shropshire, but
another function seems more likely.

Apostles were a popular choice for the painted decoration of rood-screens: in this position they were
located appropriately close to the rood. Apostles with
their creed scrolls, sometimes with prophets, appeared
on both the lower parts and lofts of rood-screens, for
example at Long Melford in Suffolk (Dymond and
Paine 1992, p.3). Carved examples still exist on
rood-lofts in Brittany – at Kerfons and the chapel of
St Nicholas at Priziac – and once did in Wales, at

Llananno (Bond and Camm 1909, pls XIX–XX,
CXXXI; see also Vallance 1936, p.72, for descriptions
of now-lost examples in England). Twelve apostles
were made for the rood-loft at Cranbrook in Kent in
1511 (Duncan and Hussey 1907, p.87). The churchwardens' accounts for the parish of St Helen's,
Leverton (Lincolnshire) for 1526 also describe the
ordering and payment for 'xvii ymage of alybaste' of yᵉ
Rood lofte' (Peacock 1867, p.349); although the
Leverton figures are not identified, it is possible that
the Apostles were among them.   EMT

PROV. A church in the town or province of Zamora, Spain,
until 1919; Grosvenor Thomas, London; gift of the National
Art Collections Fund, 1922.

LIT. Nelson 1920, pp.215–17; Bedford 1923; Cheetham 1984,
p.69 and cat. nos 2, 11, 35, 41, 52, 55, 59, 60, 71, 75, 78, 81;
Franco Mata 1999, pp.79–80, fig. 36.

268 Figure of Christ Crucified

PLATE 39

Early 16th century

Carved oak with traces of polychromy; h. 80.5 cm

**St Anthony's church, Cartmel Fell, Cumbria,
on loan to Kendal Museum**

Christ is shown full length and is now missing his
arms, which were carved from a separate piece of wood
and attached by iron nails, and his feet (which have
been burned). The back of the head is woodworm-

damaged. The remains of the original polychromy
suggest that the figure was painted in flesh colour for
the face and body, with gold leaf on the hair, beard
and robe. The lining of the robe was blue, the crown
of thorns green, with red blood flowing from wounds
on the head and body. Tradition relates that it was
used as a poker for the vestry fire during the early
nineteenth century.

This is a rare survival of an English crucifix figure
from before the Reformation. It probably once
formed part of one of the standard features of any
pre-Reformation church: the rood. This consisted of a
cross bearing the crucified Christ, usually between the
Virgin and St John the Evangelist, set over the screen
between the nave and chancel. Only three other
examples survive in Britain, from Kemeys Inferior
and Mochdre in Wales (Redknap 2000) and South
Cerney in Gloucestershire (Deacon and Lindley 2001,
pp.38–40, cat. no. 19), and all are fragmentary.

The figure is slightly small for a rood figure, but
St Anthony's church is also small. It was founded in
the early years of the sixteenth century as a chapel of
ease under nearby Cartmel Priory, and certainly by
1504, when it is mentioned in the priory records. EMT

PROV. In the vestry of St Anthony's church, Cartmel Fell,
by 1876.

LIT. Lees and Ferguson 1874–5, p.398; Vallance 1909,
pp.233–4; Curwen 1912; Vallance 1936, p.12, figs 3–5;
Behrens 1982.

269

269 Last Judgement

*c.*1500

Oil on oak; h. 198 cm, w. 366 cm

Holy Trinity church, Penn, Buckinghamshire

Christ is seated on a rainbow emerging from stylized clouds, and displays the bleeding wounds in his hands and side. He is flanked by angels holding the Instruments of the Passion, while two others descend blowing the Last Trump. Below, the dead rise from their tombs, while on either side the Apostles kneel in adoration, together with supplicant figures of the Virgin and St John the Baptist.

Typically represented on the wall above the chancel arch, the Last Judgement was less commonly depicted on a tympanum occupying the head of the arch itself; the Penn Doom is one of only a few surviving examples, of which the more elaborate compositions at Dauntsey (Wiltshire) and Wenhaston (Suffolk) include depictions of heaven and hell (Whale 1999). The Penn composition is itself a simplified over-painting of an earlier Doom, which included the inscriptions now visible, as well as a group comprising St Michael weighing souls. Dating evidence for the original painting has recently been provided by dendrochronological analysis, which indicates that

the timber of the support was felled between *c.*1414 and *c.*1448. The star shapes visible on the surface of the tympanum are remnants of a post-medieval decorative scheme. Subsequently, the tympanum was covered with whitewash and lath and plaster, and the Doom was only rediscovered in 1938 after the boards had been thrown into the churchyard during renovation works.   DP

LIT. Rouse 1962; Bubb 2003; Green forthcoming.

270 Bench

*c.*1480–1520

Oak; h. of bench ends 119 cm, h. to top of bench back 74 cm, w. of bench 214 cm, d. 51 cm

St Mary's church, Ufford, Suffolk

The bench is of modest and unergonomic proportions (the seat is 46 cm high and only 27 cm deep). The splayed feet are probably seventeenth-century replacements, as the ends were formerly tenoned directly into an embattled sill, as can still be seen on both sides at the back of the nave. There are elaborate provincial-quality double-buttressed ends. On the right side there are lions sitting on gables and, below,

the panel is traceried with a foliate frieze in the centre. The poppy head above shows two faces, possibly male and female, peeping out at each side. At the left end the seated and crowned figures of St Catherine of Alexandria, holding the sign of her martyrdom, and St Margaret, with a book in her left hand and a sword in her right hand, with which she spears the dragon, surmount another elaborately traceried and foliated bench end. Here the poppy head was probably originally topped by a bird. At the back of the bench is a frieze of leaf and rod type. The style of the Ufford bench ends, although well within the Suffolk genre, is distinctly idiosyncratic.

During the period 1400–1547 congregational seating was introduced into the naves of many English parish churches. This reflected the changing social status of the worshippers and the breaking-down of division by gender, and the decoration of the benches in many cases mirrored the standing of the occupants (French 2001, pp.162–70). The increasing use of preaching must also have contributed to the growth in communal seating (Duffy 1992, pp.57–8; Tracy 1996).   CT

LIT. Cox 1923, p.109, fig. 93; Gardner 1958, pp.9, 69, 126 (ills); Agate 1980, pp.15, 20, 24, 26, 29, 33, frontispiece, pl. 15; Mattingly 1991, p.58.

271 Two bench ends

Early 16th century

Oak; h. 80.3 cm, w. 43.2 cm, d. 8.5 cm (W.18);
W.17 is 38 cm wide

Victoria and Albert Museum, London
(W.17 and W.18–1913)

Two of a set of 14 bench ends from a private museum formed early in the nineteenth century by the Clarkes of Bridwell, near Tiverton, Devon. A slot and mortises at the back are for attachment to a bench. There is old woodworm damage at the base and elsewhere. The shields on cat. no. 271b (W.18) have been detached and reapplied.

These are typical of a very large class of Devon and Cornwall bench ends. The motifs depicted have been identified as the Instruments of the Passion. But if the image on the right side of cat. no. 271b is a book, this hypothesis would be untenable. On the other hand, were it a wrist guard, the implements would be identifiable as the tools of a craftsman's trade. At St Ives church, Cornwall, a range of tools belonging to the master smith Ralph Clies, including a pair of bellows, was carved at the base of a screen (Tracy 1988, fig. 45).

These bench ends are stylistically close to those at Braunton, near Barnstaple in Devon, and at Poughill, just over the county boundary in north Cornwall and about 32 km to the south-west. At Poughill the same kind of decorative circular punching is used, to provide a field for the motifs. CT

PROV. The Clarke family, Bridwell; acquired at Christie's, London, 13 February 1913.

LIT. Tracy 1988, cat. nos 201–2.

270

271a

271b

272 Cantor's desk

Early 15th century

Oak, partly painted; h. 153 cm (h. of desk 56 cm),
w. of desk 44 cm, d. 44 cm, h. of pedestal 94 cm

Inscr. in black-letter, on a vertical board above the lower
book rest: *Gloria tibi, domine, qui natus es de virgine cum
Patre (et) Sancto Spiritu, in sempiterna saecula. Amen;*
and on a scroll below the Evangelist eagle: *In principio
erat verbum* (John I. 1).

St Helen's church, Ranworth, Norfolk

A unique survival, this swivelling desk, or lectern, of
nailed construction is of ingenious design, facilitating
the use of both sides at different levels. Behind the
lower book rest is the painted symbol for St John the
Evangelist, with the opening words of his Gospel. The
desk portion of the lectern has been prepared with
gesso for an overpaint predominantly in red and
green. There are considerable modern restorations,
some of them in mahogany. The black-letter versicle,
with four lines of music, on the vertical board above
the lower book rest was apparently surrounded by a

decorative field in green, small traces of which survive. The pedestal, and plan of the base, is octagonal,
but the outer portion of the latter is modern.

The eagle is too low to be easily visible from a
normal standing position. This suggests that the desk
may have been designed to be used on a pulpitum or
rood-loft. Even from that position the eagle would
have been visible only when the higher book rest was
not in use. The portion of the Gregorian chant above
the lower book rest – a standard versicle suitable for
use throughout the period from Advent to Epiphany
– suggests that this side of the lectern was in more
common use. The desk is likely to have been of local
manufacture. CT

LIT. Cox 1915, pp.187–9 (ills).

272

273 Easter sepulchre*

*c.*1458

Oak; h. 216.5 cm, w. 161 cm, d. 65 cm

St Michael's church, Cowthorpe, North Yorkshire
(The Churches Conservation Trust)

At the base is a chest, 145 cm high, with four stiles
at the corners, meeting the base of the gable above.
The stiles have tracery and sloped offsets in two
zones, and mouldings at the base, now mostly missing or rotted away. The chest is embattled at the
base, and its front has applied traceried panels with
segmental heads, leaf spandrels and flower cusps.
There are two storage compartments, on the left
about 61 cm square and on the right 96.5 × 61 cm,

273

with six original wrought-iron strap hinges with trefoil ends on the chest lid. There are two iron lifting rings, backed by flower escutcheons, and both the original lock plates. The remains of a locking mechanism survives on the back of the right-hand hatch. The hasps and staples are probably more recent in origin.

The superstructure is gabled, and decorated with crockets and cresting at base and top. The finials, which were at each end, are lost. There is a frieze decorated with various motifs under the lower cresting. The spandrels of the openings on the front and left side are decorated with leaves and shields, presumably originally coloured. From the positioning of the decorative carving it is clear that the object's

more common. The Easter ritual took its own course in England, and was centred around the rites of *Depositio* (Deposition of Christ's body), *Elevatio* (Christ Risen from the Grave) and *Visitatio* (the Visit of the Three Maries) during Holy Week. For this liturgical drama the sepulchre would have been decorated with painted cloths (Duffy 2001, p.77). In the *Depositio* ritual the Cross, representing Christ's dead body, might have been placed in the larger compartment of the Cowthorpe chest, and the Host in the other.

The sepulchre was unquestionably made for Cowthorpe church. Bryan Rouclyff – who had been a lawyer in the reign of Henry VI, became a Baron of the Exchequer, and was also Lord of the Manor and

274 Altar frontal

c. 1500–38

h. 90.9 cm, w. 297 cm

Church of St Mary the Virgin, Alveley, Shropshire

The woven silk damask is Italian, early sixteenth century, in two colours: rust (faded from red) and cream; with applied motifs embroidered in silk, silver-gilt and silver thread, English, 1500–38.

The frontal has 12 panes of silk damask, a 13th missing from the right, with a conventional floral pattern with applied motifs of fleurs-de-lis and two kinds of conventional flowers. In the centre the image of All Saints is depicted as God the Father/Abraham, holding up a cloth containing three souls; to either

274

principal viewing point was from the front or left side. At the right end the buttresses were not carved, and the back is completely plain. There are a few repairs and replacements, but the condition is generally authentic. There are traces of a gesso covering on the superstructure, which suggests that it was originally fully coloured.

Apart from this unique North Country portable Easter sepulchre, the examples that have survived are of the permanent and multi-purpose kind, built into the fabric of a church, generally on the north side of the chancel. The number of entries in churchwardens' accounts demonstrates that the temporary and demountable type was by far the

patron of the living at Cowthorpe – was given permission by the Archbishop of York in 1456 to build a church on a new site. The celebrated brass memorial to him and his wife Joan Hammerton displays, among other family armorial motifs, the fleur-de-lis of his maternal uncle's family and the chess rooks of the Rouclyffs. Both appear on the frieze of the sepulchre. CT

LIT. Glynne 1922, p.271; Pevsner 1967, p.172, pl. 31a; Butler 1999.

side and below stands an angel on a wheel with a scroll inscribed '*Da Gloriam Deo*' (see also cat. no. 248). There may originally have been a fringe below the top line of motifs to give the impression of a frontlet, and another at the lower edge. A striped silk braid runs round the frontal, with a part missing at the upper edge.

Altar frontals of this period were often made up of panes of contrasting colours, decorated with embroidered flowers. Related examples are in Baunton (Gloucestershire) and another, belonging to the Butler-Bowdon family, is in the Victoria and Albert Museum (London 1963, cat. no. 145). LW

LIT. Barber 1880, pl. 28; Toulson 2001.

275

275 Altarpiece with the Joys of the Virgin (the Swansea Altarpiece)

Probably *c.*1450–80

Alabaster panels, painted and gilded, set in a wooden framework; h. 83.2 cm (centre), w. 215 cm

Victoria and Albert Museum, London (A.89–1919)

The winged altarpiece is made up of five principal panels, comprising the Annunciation, the Adoration of the Magi, the Ascension, the Assumption/Coronation of the Virgin and, at the centre, a taller relief of the Trinity. At the ends are figures of St John the Baptist

and St John the Evangelist. Both reliefs and figures are surmounted by traceried canopies in alabaster and held in place in the framework with latten wires leaded into their backs and fixed through the wooden boards behind. The alabaster reliefs are painted and gilded, as is the frame, the latter further decorated with raised and gilded gesso panels. The gilded inscriptions on the lower margin of the frame refer in abbreviated form to the figures and scenes above (for a full transcription and detailed physical description of the altarpiece, see Cheetham 1984, pp.70–71).

Alabaster altarpieces of this type were made in large numbers in the fifteenth and early sixteenth centuries. They were not only utilized on the altars of

parish churches and private chapels in England, but were also exported throughout Europe. Of the complete altarpieces, only the foreign exports have survived: in addition to the present altarpiece (which was brought back to England only in the nineteenth century from Germany), Cheetham records nine other altarpieces that include the Joys of the Virgin, and numerous other examples with differing iconographic programmes are to be found on the Continent. The exact date of the English alabasters is in many cases still far from clear, although the present altarpiece was probably made in the third quarter of the fifteenth century: it shares stylistic and physical characteristics with the altarpiece given by the priest

John Goodyear to the cathedral of Santiago de Compostela in 1456, and other comparable altarpieces still surviving in Iceland can be dated convincingly to the period *c*.1460–70 (Cheetham 1984, pp.20–23, 43–4, figs 11 and 26).   PW

PROV. Purchased by John Henry Vivian, Lord Swansea, in Munich in the 1830s; bought by the V&A at the sale of the contents of Singleton Abbey, Swansea (Knight, Frank & Rutley, 13–21 October 1919, lot 125).

LIT. Maclagan 1920; Cheetham 1984, pp.70–71, 114, 122, 170, 185, 206, 292, 306, pl. I; Williamson 1996, p.65.

276 The Ashwellthorpe Triptych

PLATE 49

Master of the Magdalen Legend, *c*.1519

Oil painting on panel; centre: h. 83.9 cm, w. 64.2 cm; wings: h. 83.8 cm, w. 26.7 cm

Norfolk Museums Service (Norwich Castle Museum) (46.983)

The triptych shows the Seven Sorrows of the Virgin in the centre, Christopher Knyvett with St Christopher on the left wing and Catherine van Assche with St Catherine on the right wing. On the exterior of the wings are Sts John the Evangelist and Barbara, painted in grisaille.

The kneeling donors in the wings have been identified from the arms of Knyvett quartered with those of Clifton on his surcoat, and on the shields hanging from the trees above the couple. Christopher Knyvett was a member of the royal household in 1514–20, and owned land in Tournai; he married into the van Assche family from Brabant. The lady's escutcheon is lozenge-shaped, which was the norm for female arms in the Netherlands. The triptych may have been located in either the Knyvett residence at Ashwellthorpe (Norfolk) or the family chapel on the north side of the chancel in Ashwellthorpe parish church.

In the centre the Virgin sits on the ground in an attitude of humility, while in the landscape behind her, in miniature, are episodes of her sorrows: the Presentation in the Temple, the Flight into Egypt, Christ and the Elders, the Carrying of the Cross, the Crucifixion, the Lamentation at the foot of the Cross, and the Entombment. The theme is based on Simeon's words at the Presentation: 'Yea, a sword shall pierce through thine own heart' (Luke 2, 35), expressing the Virgin's co-suffering with Christ and her compassion. This can be depicted literally with one or seven swords piercing her breast or, usually, with roundels and vignettes relating to Christ's Passion surrounding Mary (Schuler 1992).

The Master of the Magdalen Legend was active in Brussels, *c*.1490–1525, and the present triptych has been compared with a triptych of the Annunciation with donors in Brussels. The donors of the Ashwellthorpe Triptych are in Tudor dress and hairstyle, and in about 1700 a date of 1519 was recorded for it, probably found on the original frame.   CG

PROV. In the hands of descendants of the Knyvetts until 1908; sold to Lord Lee of Fareham before 1923; to Norwich Castle Museum from Ashwellthorpe, Norfolk, in 1983.

LIT. Martindale 1989.

277

277 Painted panels

Mid or third quarter of 15th century

Painted oak; Archbishop: h. 115.2 cm, w. 42.4 cm;
Annunciation and Visitation: h. 95.9 cm, w. 42.3 cm;
Resurrection: h. 141.7 cm, w. 51 cm;
Crucifixion: h. 95.9 cm, w. 42.5 cm; St Erasmus: h. 115.1 cm,
w. 42.9 cm; St Margaret: h. 101.7 cm, w. 44.6 cm

Norwich Cathedral, chapel of the Saviour and canons' vestry

Five of these panels were made up into a composite altarpiece in 1958, following their removal from the Norwich church of St Michael at Plea. They show an archbishop, the Annunciation and Visitation, Resurrection, Crucifixion and St Erasmus, identified by the windlass on which his entrails were wound out. The sixth, also from St Michael at Plea, depicts St Margaret (not illustrated). The background of the St Margaret, Annunciation and Crucifixion panels was once gilded and ornamented with elaborate tooled floreate patterns, now hard to distinguish.

The panels derive from more than one context. According to G. W. Minns, who visited the church in 1859, the Crucifixion, an archbishop, St Erasmus and St Margaret formed part of the rood-screen, then *in situ* and forming part of a pew. Other panels, including the Resurrection and the Annunciation, were kept loose in the church. These two may have formed part of an altar retable. As a group, they all give some idea of the richness, sophistication and variety of the painted imagery in urban parish churches of the period.

The individual images from the St Michael at Plea series were chosen in large measure because of the roles that the various saints played in popular devotion of the period. St Erasmus came into vogue in the fifteenth century and was credited with wide thaumaturgical powers (cat. no. 285). St Margaret, the virgin martyr of Antioch, enjoyed widespead popularity and was imaged in all media. She was thought to be one of the most influential helper saints, associated with particular powers of succour and intercession; she was invoked by men in moments of need and peril and by women in childbirth, because of her legendary escape from the belly of a dragon (cat. no. 280).

In the absence of any related documentary evidence, these panels are extremely difficult to situate in the context of painting in England in the fifteenth century. On the one hand, there are elements that recall continental as well as native patterns and practice of the late fourteenth and early fifteenth centuries: the design and elaborate architectural setting of the Annunciation, with its echoes of the work of the Ypres master, Melchior Broederlam; the dramatic diagonal composition of the Resurrection, with exotically attired soldiers about the tomb of Christ, the craggy, sparsely wooded background and star-studded sky, recalling works like the Bohemian Třeboň altarpiece of the 1380s; and the heads and passages of drapery in the Annunciation, which look back to the Wilton Diptych (plate 3). However, there are other details that suggest a considerably later date for all the panels: the fanciful armour and headgear of the soldiers and the sharp silhouette of Christ's robe in the Resurrection, which seems to be by the same hand as the Annunciation; the full, puffy shoulder of St John's tunic in the Crucifixion, the work of another artist; and the half-angels supporting the dossal-cloths behind the two bishops – these are all features current in painting in the region in the later fifteenth and early sixteenth centuries.

All the panels, with the possible exception of the Resurrection and the Annunciation, appear to have been cut down. The panels were restored in the mid-1950s and again treated in 2000.

JM

PROV. Church of St Michael at Plea, Norwich.

LIT. Armstrong 1781, pp.377–8; Blomefield 1806, IV, p.321; Waller 1898; James 1930, p.125; Tudor-Craig 1956a and b; Thurlow 1961; Lasko and Morgan 1973, cat. nos 56–7, pp.39–41; Cotton 1987, pp.44–54; Duffy 1990; Duffy 1992, pp.176–8 (St Erasmus); King 1996b, pp.414–15.

278 Virgin and Child

Late 15th century

Alabaster, painted and gilded; h. 98 cm, w. 35 cm

British Museum, London (MME 1956, 7-1,1)

The Virgin, crowned and enthroned, holds in her left hand the remains of her sceptral lily. With her right arm she supports the figure of Christ, who sits cross-legged in her lap. He is loosely wrapped in a robe and holds an orb in both hands. An element of tenderness, conveyed by the gaze of Christ into the face of his mother, is amplified by the informal detail of his upturned, right foot. The Virgin directs her gaze to the onlooker, with an implication of foreknowledge, and a poignant, psychological dynamic is established. The right foot of the Virgin is supported by an angel who is contorted into a cross-legged pose similar to that of Christ. The Virgin's left foot rests on a grassy mound decorated with the daisy pattern ubiquitous in English alabaster carvings.

The reverse, central section is roughly hollowed out. There are two drill holes; one in the back of the crown and another at the centre between the Virgin's shoulders. Four lead plugs remain; one at each shoulder and one at each side close to the bottom of the figure. The plug to the bottom right still has a latten wire attached, by which means the alabaster was originally secured inside a painted, wooden tabernacle.

Traces of pigments indicate the richness of the figures' original appearance. Gold is combined with red, dark blue and green, while delicate, pink flesh tones survive on the shoulder of Christ and on the exposed sole of his foot.

The large size of this figure suggests that it occupied a prominent space, perhaps in a parish church. Since the thirteenth century it had been obligatory for any parish church in England to have an image of the Virgin on the south side of the high altar, accompanying the patronal image on the north (Marks forthcoming (a)). It is in this context that the alabaster is displayed in the exhibition.

JR

PROV. Purchased from S. W. Wolsey Ltd, London, with the assistance of a contribution from the National Art Collections Fund, 1956.

278

279

279 St Michael

Probably c.1430–50

Alabaster relief, painted; h. 75.6 cm, w. 27.4 cm

Victoria and Albert Museum, London (A.209–1946)

The feathered figure of the archangel Michael is shown trampling on a many-headed dragon, with the Virgin behind him; his upraised right hand holds a falchion, and a shield is suspended by its strap from his left forearm. In his left hand he holds a pair of scales, the arms now broken: on the right, a devil's head sits in the weighing pan, attempting to tip the balance, while on the left the Virgin lays her rosary on the arm of the scales to tilt them in favour of a soul once held in the now-missing weighing pan on the left (for complete examples of this scene in alabaster, see Hildburgh 1930, fig. 3, and Hildburgh 1947, pl. C). The back is flat, cut away at the bottom, with four lead-plugged holes, two with the remains of latten wire, indicating that the relief was fixed into a wooden background.

Judging by its size, the archangel would not have been a terminal figure of an alabaster altarpiece, as seen on the Swansea Altarpiece (cat. no. 275). Instead, like the St Ursula and St Christopher (cat. nos 282–3), it was probably intended as a single devotional image, set within a winged tabernacle. Its size suggests it was an image of some importance. In the exhibition it is displayed in the position of honour reserved in every parish church for the patron saint, on the north side of the high altar (see also cat. no. 278). St Michael, being a symbol of justice, divine power and protection against evil, was one of the most popular saints of the Middle Ages. As the 'guardian spirit of the boundaries between worlds' (Duffy 1992, p.270), the saint was often called upon to aid the passage of the soul after death.   PW

PROV. Given by Viscountess D'Abernon in 1946; believed to have been bought by Lord D'Abernon in about 1926.

LIT. Hildburgh 1947; Cheetham 1984, cat. no. 63, p.134, pl. III.

280 St Margaret

PLATE 43

*c.*1430–1530

Limestone, painted and gilded; h. 78 cm, w. 34 cm, d. 19 cm

An Essex church

St Margaret is carved fully in the round and is clad in a full-length mantle and gown; she has her traditional attributes of a book and cross-staff thrust into the mouth of a dragon at her feet. Most of the upper left side of the head and the upper section of the cross-staff are missing.

One of the comparatively few female saints (apart from the Virgin) popular in parish-church imagery, St Margaret's feast-day is celebrated on 20 July; she was considered particularly efficacious in childbirth. The statue is a rare provenanced survivor of a devotional image in a medium other than alabaster. It was discovered within an elaborate canopied niche in 1968 under the plaster of the east reveal of a nave north-wall window. The figure had been broken and defaced, presumably at some time after Edward VI's accession in 1547, when devotional imagery in parish churches was proscribed. The fact that it was partly repaired, replaced in its niche in a reversed position and then concealed, is suggestive of resistance in the parish to the loss of images during the Reformation. St Margaret is one of a number of late medieval devotional images in this church, including a free-stone image of the Holy Trinity discovered in 1965 walled up in a nave piscina, and nave murals of Christ of the Trades (St Sunday), the Man of Sorrows, St Michael, St Christopher and the Virgin and Child.

Despite its damaged state, the statue reveals that the greater churches did not have a monopoly on high-quality sculpture. Its date is difficult to establish; the static pose and lack of movement in the drapery suggest that it was executed at any time within the century after *c.*1430.   RM

LIT. Boustred and Trace, n.d.; Marks forthcoming (a).

281 St Sitha*

PLATE 28

*c.*1470–1500

Alabaster relief, with remains of paint; h. 46.2 cm,
w. 15.7 cm

The Burrell Collection, Glasgow Museums
(reg. no. 1/44; inv. 12)

The veiled, standing figure of the saint wears a full-length gown over her mantle and holds a book in her left hand; in her right hand she holds a small loaf of bread and a rosary, with a bunch of keys hanging from her girdle. The back is flat, but hollowed out at the base for ease of handling, as was customary with English alabasters; there are also two lead-filled holes for holding the latten wire used to secure the relief in place in a wooden framework, an incised mark at the top and many post-medieval incised names.

The cult of St Zita of Lucca (1218–72) had spread throughout Europe by the late Middle Ages: in England she was known as St Sitha. A maidservant all her life, her pious devotion and the miracles associated with her ensured that a popular following developed shortly after her death. She became the patron saint of servants and housewives, providing a model of moral rectitude, diligence and good works (Sutcliffe 1993). Images of St Sitha appear quite often in English late medieval art, in wall-paintings, stained glass (Woodforde 1946, pp.181–2) and rood-screens (for Barton Turf, Norfolk, see Duffy 1992, pl. 60), and Cheetham has counted four examples in alabaster (Cheetham 1984, p.55). Although St Sitha is represented in the company of other saints, her popularity as a focus of late medieval devotion resulted in the existence of numerous single figures. It is possible that this relief originally belonged at one end of a composite alabaster altarpiece, however, as on the Swansea Altarpiece (cat. no. 275). A similar figure of St Sitha is in the Castle Museum, Nottingham (Cheetham 1973, pp.50–51, ill.).   PW

PROV. Purchased by Sir William Burrell before 1949.

LIT. York 1954, cat. no. 74; Cheetham 1973, p.50;
Tudor-Craig 1973, cat. no. 6; Marks forthcoming (a), ch. 4.

282 St Ursula
and the virgin martyrs

*c.*1475–1500

Alabaster relief, painted and gilded; h. 87 cm,
w. 31 cm, d. 13 cm

Musée national du Moyen Age, Thermes de Cluny,
Paris (Cl. 19336)

St Ursula, crowned and holding three arrows – the instruments of her martyrdom – wears a voluminous mantle under which shelter 10 of the 11,000 virgins who were martyred with her (for her legend, see Ryan 1993, II, pp.256–60). Extensive traces of paint remain, most notably the red of St Ursula's robe and the interior of her mantle and the green of the ground, and her crown retains much of its gilding. The back is flat, hollowed out at the bottom.

Although according to legend St Ursula came from Britain, her celebrity in England never matched that in the area of the Lower Rhine around Cologne, where she was supposedly martyred. Her role as protectress, clearly demonstrated in the standard iconography of the saint, as here, made her attractive to confraternities of young women and also individuals, and her cult spread far and wide in the late Middle Ages (Zehnder 1985). Surviving references and representations suggest that St Ursula featured in England only from the later fifteenth century, perhaps as a result of trade links with Cologne. Single devotional images of the saint were made in large numbers on the Continent, nearly all showing the same arrangement of the diminutive virgin companions sheltering under the mantle; it is likely that the present relief – of excellent quality – was originally contained within a winged tabernacle, perhaps displayed on a pier or wall within a church or on an altar in a side chapel.   PW

PROV. Collection of Alexandre du Sommerard (1779–1842).

LIT. Cheetham 1984, p.156; Prigent 1998, cat. no. 2, p.60.

282

283

283 St Christopher*

First half of the 15th century

Alabaster relief, with traces of painting and gilding; h. 94.7 cm, w. 29.9 cm

Victoria and Albert Museum, London (A.18–1921)

The giant St Christopher is represented in the manner that became commonplace in the late Middle Ages, striding across the river with the Christ Child on his back and supporting himself with a large staff. This episode was popularized through its inclusion in the widely read *Golden Legend* (Ryan 1993, II, p.12; see cat. no. 226) and the image was disseminated throughout Europe with numerous woodcut illustrations (see plate 41; for Germany, see Nuremberg 2000, cat. nos 167, 228–9). The standard image of the saint was repeated in numerous different settings, from the minute to the monumental. Here, an additional, tonsured figure is to be seen kneeling at the bottom right: this is almost certainly the cleric who commissioned the work, and the unfurling scroll above him would originally have contained a painted invocation to the saint. The sculpture is in good condition, although much of the paint and gilding has been abraded and there are some losses and restorations: the Christ Child's right hand is missing, and his left hand and foot have been restored in alabaster. The back is hollowed out in the middle and at the bottom, and six latten wire attachments leaded in. It is likely that the relief was displayed as a single image within a wooden triptych or tabernacle.

Images of St Christopher were often displayed in English parish churches. Usually painted on a colossal scale, they were placed opposite the principal nave entrance (cat. nos 290, 296). The saint was thought to be particularly effective in protecting travellers, and late medieval hymns and inscriptions emphasize his powers: 'If you, whoever you are, look on St Christopher's face, on that day you shall not die a bad death' (Bond 1914, pp.167–9). A bad death meant both an untimely end and death without receiving the sacrament. This alabaster is a particularly fine example: both the quality of the carving and its large size set it apart from the other known alabaster reliefs of the saint, which were probably bought off the shelf rather than commissioned.   PW

PROV. Purchased in Paris and given in memory of Cecil Duncan Jones by his friends, 1921.

LIT. Cheetham 1984, cat. no. 24, p.95 (with earlier lit.); Williamson 1996, pp.66–7; Marks forthcoming (a), ch. 4.

284 St George and the Dragon

Mid–late 15th century

Polychromed oak; h. 72.5 cm, w. 42.5 cm

The Herbert Art Gallery and Museum, Coventry (1993/94)

This is a typical late medieval image of an armoured and mounted St George, sword raised ready to deliver the *coup de grâce* to the dragon lying wounded under the hooves of his horse (see cat. nos 58, 84, 297). Many of the visual motifs are standard at this time, for example the inclusion of a broken lance – which demonstrates the power of the monster that the heroic saint has overcome – and the device of the dragon's tail curling around the horse's leg; the latter is likely to be an evocation of the bestiaries' presentation of the dragon as the mortal enemy of the elephant, who attempts to suffocate its foe with its tail in the manner of a boa constrictor. However, the inclusion of a clearly defined orifice on the dragon's pudendum, which seems to define it as a base, sexualized, female beast, is much less common though by no means unparalleled.

This figure formerly stood in a gate chapel on the city walls of Coventry, where it probably reflected the contemporary identification of St George as a figure of authority and urban government, crushing the threat of chaos and disorder embodied by the dragon. It is a rare survival of an English image of a saint carved in wood.   SR

PROV. Gosford Gate Chapel, Coventry; St Mary's Hall, Coventry.

LIT. London 1930, cat. no. 681; Stone 1972, p.221, pl. 172(B); Riches 2000, pp.169–70.

284

285

285 The Martyrdom
of St Erasmus

1474

Oil on oak panel; h. 51.6 cm (originally taller),
w. 71.6 cm, d. 1.4 cm

Inscr. in Gothic book-hand: *p[er] fr[atr]em Joh[anne]m
holynbourne A[nno] d[omi]ni 1474*

Society of Antiquaries of London (S.12)

The recumbent St Erasmus, semi-naked but for his
mitre, is shown being disembowelled by windlass.
The Emperor Diocletian stands behind, between
two counsellors. In the background is a walled city
and port, and in the bottom right-hand corner is a
half-length figure of the Benedictine monk John
Holynbourne, named in the inscription. It is the
work of a Netherlandish painter, perhaps active in
Canterbury after 1470. A fragment of a larger
painting of the Flagellation at Canterbury could be
by the same artist.

The donor was one of six men from Holynbourne

286

(Kent), who became monks at Christchurch Priory (Greatrex 1997, pp.191–2). He was professed in 1443, student at Canterbury College, Oxford, 1444–9, and priested in 1450. He filled several monastic offices and died between 1489 and 1492.

St Erasmus, a third-century Bishop of Formiae, enjoyed widespread popularity in northern Europe during the later Middle Ages (cat. no. 277). There was no altar to the saint in Canterbury Cathedral, although special offerings before his image in the cathedral were made on his feast-day (2 June) in the fifteenth and sixteenth centuries (Marks forthcoming (a)). The shipping and flocks of sheep in the background of the panel indicate St Erasmus's particular appeal to mariners and those engaged in the wool and cloth industries; his image was found in numerous churches around the Kent coastline and in the Weald. Following the survival of Edward IV and his fleet in a major sea-storm in 1471, Elizabeth Woodeville endowed a chantry chapel dedicated to St Erasmus in Westminster Abbey (Mickelthwaite 1873).   PT-C

PROV. Bought by Thomas Kerrich in Cambridge, 1805; bequeathed by Kerrich to the Society of Antiquaries, 1828.

LIT: Scharf 1865, no. XII, pp.13–14; Tudor-Craig 1974; Collinson, Ramsay and Sparks 1995, p.112, n.209, pl. 27.

286 Reclining figure of Jesse*

Late 15th or early 16th century

Oak; h. 89 cm, w. 293 cm, d. 58 cm

St Mary's church, Abergavenny, Monmouthshire

Thomas Churchyard's 1587 poem 'The Worthines of Wales' mentions, in its marginal notes on St Mary's, Abergavenny: 'In this church was a most famous worke in maner of a genealogie of Kings, called the roote of Iesse, which worke is defaced and pulled down.' In 1645 the cavalier soldier Richard Symonds noted in his diary, 'At the east end of the north yle church lyes a large statue for Jesse, and a branch did spring from him, and on the bough divers statues, but spoyld' (Long 1859, pp.233–8). This is the last mention of the rest of what must have been a stupen-dous sculptural composition of the Tree of Jesse, showing the genealogy of Christ; fortunately the figure of the recumbent Jesse, one of the great masterpieces of British medieval sculpture, survives.

The figure of Jesse lies recumbent, his head supported by a pillow held by an angel. His hat appears to have had a stone fixed into it, and the whole image was lavishly painted, although only traces now remain. The superb swirling draperies are overlapped by his beard and cover the trunk that connected him, in the manner of a family tree, to his descendants, culminating in Christ (see also cat. no. 287). The right hand was separately dowelled on, but the rest of this figure was carved from a single massive oak, which must have been growing at the Norman Conquest. The sculpture, by an unknown British sculptor, is one of the few remaining pieces of wooden religious imagery to have survived Reformation and Common-wealth iconoclasm.   PGL

LIT. Morgan 1872; Graham-Dixon 1996, pl. 7; Deacon and Lindley 2002, pp.50–51, cat. no. 12, ill. on pp.70–71 and cover.

287 Prophet figure

*c.*1470–72

Painted and gilded limestone; h. 115 cm, w. 34 cm, d. 18 cm

St Cuthbert's church, Wells, Somerset (acc. nos 341, 427)

In 1848, a large number of fragments of medieval figure-sculpture were discovered plastered over in two reredoses in St Cuthbert's church, Wells. The sculptures had been smashed at the Reformation and walled up. The original contract for the Jesse reredos in the south transept, from which the figure comes, with a sculptor named John Stowell, still exists. This contract, signed on 25 February, 39 Henry VI (i.e. 1470), between William Vowell, Master of the Town of Wells, and the wardens of the Lady Altar, provided for Stowell to build within 16 months all the workmanship and masonry of a 'frounte' or reredos, from the corner by the northern arch into the angle of the southern corner. It was to rise from the 'growdyng' of the altar to the wall plate in three tiers of tabernacled imagery, 'lynyally' from the figure of Jesse, the precise iconography of the genealogy to be determined by

the master and his associates. Stowell was to have £40 for his work and was to find all materials.

It has been doubted (e.g. Stone and Tudor-Craig) whether the figure and head shown here should be associated with the Tree of Jesse reredos rather than with the north-transept reredos, also discovered in 1848. However, the figure of a prophet self-evidently belongs to the Tree of Jesse iconography, which shows the genealogy of Christ deriving from Jesse (cat. no. 286), and the image fits into the niches of the south-transept reredos. The surviving paintwork of the prophet is of considerable importance, not least because the scroll, bearing a Latin inscription from Deuteronomy 4, 32, can still be read. The stylistic variation of the Wells figures proves that Stowell headed a team of sculptors. PGL

LIT. Ferrey 1851; Serel 1875, pp.19–21; Prior and Gardner 1912, p.402; Stone 1972, p.227; Tudor-Craig 1973, cat. no. 3; Deacon and Lindley 2001, pp.49–50, cat. no. 13, ill. on p.61; Boldrick, Park and Williamson 2002, cat. nos 26–7, pp.92–5 (entry by D. Park and S. Cather).

287

Interior showing the original emplacement of the Jesse figures, St Cuthbert's church, Wells (see cat. no. 287)

288

288 St Mary Magdalene (?)*

c. 1445–55

Stained and painted glass; h. 62.5 cm, w. 27.2 cm

Inscr. in black-letter: *Maria* (monogram)

The Burrell Collection, Glasgow Museums (reg. no. 45.37)

The female saint stands under a canopy with side-shafting, holding what may be an ointment jar in her right hand. On the canopy is a *Maria* monogram. A panel in the Cloisters Collection, Metropolitan Museum of Art, New York, possibly depicting St Barbara, is a companion to this. The adaption from tracery-light to rectangular panel means that it is impossible to know how much of the micro-architecture is original. Part of the background has been renewed, and the upper part of the ointment jar is probably a later

insertion. The identification of this figure is problematic, as the monogram above relates to the Virgin Mary and is an intrusion, and only the bottom part of what may be an ointment jar is definitely original.

This panel is closely comparable with a number of tracery-light panels in Norfolk churches depicting series of female saints. Examples are seen at Cley, Field Dalling, Wighton and Stody, and they can also be paralleled on screens in East Anglia. Duffy sees these saints primarily as intercessory figures for the laity and suggests that Osbern Bokenham's *Legends of Hooly Wummen* of *c*.1447 may have been an inspiration (Duffy 1990, pp.189–90).

Although the rounded folds of the drapery and the delineation of the face suggest a date of *c*.1430–40, comparison with glass of *c*.1450–55 at St Peter Mancroft in Norwich (cat. no. 289), by the same workshop, led by John Wighton, indicates a later dating of *c*.1445–55.   DK

PROV. Ex Hutton Castle, 1956.

LIT. Wells 1965, cat. no. 72; King 1974, pp.8–9; Marks 1984c, pp.18–19; Marks 1993, p.198.

289 The Miraculous Assembly of the Apostles

c. 1450–55

Stained and painted glass; h. 95.5 cm, w. 53.5 cm

The National Trust (Felbrigg Hall, Norfolk; on loan to the church of St Peter Mancroft, Norwich)

The scene is set in a hilly landscape with a castle. In the foreground are three apostles seated on clouds facing right; behind are two similar apostles looking up at an angel who emerges from a cloud and glory, and looks down at them while pointing to the right. The panel is surmounted by a foliage arch. Ruby, purple, blue, light brown and white glass is used for the panel, with yellow stain appearing on both white and blue glass. The panel is extended at the top and bottom with old glass and has been given a modern border of crowned Ws.

The glazing of the major urban church of St Peter Mancroft (cat. no. 120) provides a history of glass-painting in Norwich from the 1450s until the end of the century. This panel was originally in the five-light east window of the north chancel chapel. The window was given by Robert Toppes, a leading Norwich merchant, as recorded (but now missing) heraldic panels from the bottom register attested. The main lights contained two cycles: an Infancy of Christ series, of which seven out of 10 panels are now to be found in the east window, and an extended series depicting the Death, Funeral and Assumption of the

Virgin over 15 panels, of which six panels are wholly or partly extant. The latter series can be almost completely reconstructed because of an eighteenth-century description of the glass. The present panel was the second in the series, after the Annunciation of the Death of the Virgin.

The window is attributed to the workshop of John Wighton, the leading Norwich glazier of the time, and includes in other panels allusions to contemporary local politics.   DK

PROV. Window n.III, St Peter Mancroft, Norwich; *c*.1840, Felbrigg Hall, Norfolk.

LIT. Woodforde 1950, pp.29–30; King 1996a, pp.218–20; King forthcoming.

289

290

290 St Clement, St Christopher and donor figures of Sir Thomas Restwold and his wife Margaret

*c.*1467–77/85

Stained and painted glass; St Clement: h. 120 cm, w. 39.5 cm; St Christopher and donors: h. 260 cm, w. 43 cm

St Peter's church, Stockerston, Leicestershire

Set within side shafts, St Christopher is depicted according to the standard iconography as a giant figure carrying the Christ Child across the stream and with his staff flowering miraculously; a knight wearing a surcoat of the Restwold family and his wife kneel in prayer below within a niche. The fragments at the top include a nimbed head and a shield of the Cokayne family arms. St Clement, also framed by a canopy and side shafts, is clad in pontifical vestments and papal triple tiara, with his double cross-staff and anchor attribute. These panels were all conserved by the York Glaziers Trust in 1983.

The St Christopher and the donor panels are in the nave north-west window and St Clement is in the east window of the nave north aisle. They form part of the embellishment of Stockerston church carried out in the late fifteenth century by John Boyville (d. 1467), lord of the manor, his first wife Elizabeth, their three daughters and their husbands; Margaret, one of these daughters, married Thomas Restwold; another was the wife of John Cokayne.

Because of his protection against sickness and sudden death, representations of St Christopher were ubiquitous in late medieval parish churches (cat. nos 283, 296). As is so often the case with murals of this saint, his window at Stockerston is directly opposite the parishioners' entrance. The manorial donors, therefore, were seeking to benefit the community as a whole, as well as solicit St Christopher's intercession for themselves. As might be expected from his nautical associations, St Clement was more common in counties like Kent, which border the sea, than in the land-locked Midlands.

St Christopher and the donor couple are by a glass-painting workshop based in either Stamford (Lincolnshire) or Peterborough. The former is more likely; if so, the workshop was headed by John Browne, documented in the town between 1474 and 1482/3 and

290

active subsequently. Browne is an example of a late medieval trend of craftsmen attaining high civic office. The figure-style and canopy design of St Clement show that this panel is by another atelier, one that in its accomplished use of imitation 'jewelled' work reveals the influence of the Beauchamp Chapel glazing (cat. no. 89) on glass-painters and their patrons in the Midlands. All three panels are testament to the high quality of late medieval parish-church glazing in this region.   RM

LIT. Nichols 1798, pp.821–2; Marks 1984a, pp.132–5; Marks 1993, p.202, pl. III (b), fig. 171.

291 St Helena presenting the nails and part of the True Cross to the Emperor Constantine

1482

Stained and painted glass; h. 72 cm, w. 62 cm

Holy Trinity church, Tattershall, Lincolnshire (former collegiate church of the Holy Trinity, the Virgin and Sts Peter, John the Baptist and John the Evangelist)

St Helena is presenting Constantine (who wears a triple tiara) with the three nails of the Passion and holds an arm of the cross; attendants flank both figures. The framing and part of the background were restored by Barley Studio in 1988–9.

Now in the chancel east window, this is the only surviving panel from a window originally in the nave of the church which depicted the Story of the Discovery of the True Cross, its capture by the Persians and its recovery and restoration to Jerusalem by the Emperor Heraclius. Pieces of the True Cross were much venerated throughout medieval Europe, and the legend of its recovery by St Helena was particularly popular in England as she was believed to have been the daughter of King Coel of Colchester (cat. nos 125–6). The most famous True Cross relic in England was the Rood of Bromholm in Norfolk (cat. no. 326); nearer to Tattershall, Lincoln Cathedral possessed several True Cross reliquaries. Most relevant of all, in 1416 Maud, grandmother of Ralph, Lord Cromwell – the founder of Tattershall College – bequeathed a relic of the True Cross to Tattershall church; this attracted considerable donations in the 1440s.

The Holy Cross window was executed by one of several teams of glaziers employed by Bishop Waynflete to complete the glazing of Tattershall church. In 1482 Robert Power of Burton-on-Trent (Staffordshire) was paid for glazing this window; the quantity and range of coloured glass and the use of the 'jewelled' technique on St Helena's robes explain the high cost of 1s. 2d. per square foot. Power's work differs markedly from that of Twygge and Wodshawe (cat. nos 37, 292) and of the Stamford/Peterborough workshop (cat. no. 290), and demonstrates the stylistic diversity shown by late medieval Midlands glass-painters.   RM

LIT. Marks 1984a, pp.32, 63–4, 208–15, 264–5; Hebgin-Barnes 1996, p.319.

291

292a

292b

292 Baptism from the Seven Sacraments* and Clothing the Naked from the Corporal Works of Mercy

*c.*1480–82

Stained and painted glass; both panels: h. 72 cm, w. 62 cm

Holy Trinity church, Tattershall, Lincolnshire (former collegiate church of the Holy Trinity, the Virgin and Sts Peter, John the Baptist and John the Evangelist)

a) In the Baptism panel, a priest attended by an acolyte dips a baby into a font, observed by the mother and two male figures. A ruby stream representing Christ's blood flows diagonally to the font. The original parts of the scroll at the top read '/squaloris quicsquid abundant/'.

b) The Clothing the Naked panel depicts a richly dressed man with the speech scroll '/Vestio/' dressing a kneeling, half-naked pauper; the benefactor's servant holds a garment ready for a second pauper, clad in rags.

Both panels conserved by Barley Studio in 1988–9.

The Seven Sacraments and Corporal Works of Mercy formed part of the catechistical programme drawn up in the thirteenth century for the instruction of the laity and were common subjects in late medieval English art. The panels are now in the chancel east window, but come from windows in the nave or transepts (that is, the parochial part of Tattershall church), where they provided exemplary models for a lay audience. Originally the Sacraments window would have had the Crucifixion as its centrepiece, with streams of blood emanating from Christ's

wounds to each sacrament, making explicit that its virtue derived from His sacrifice. Performance of the Works of Mercy was one of the actions considered to earn redemption, and had a societal value in terms of helping the less fortunate. The purse worn by the benefactor was a signifier of wealth and also had a particular resonance at Tattershall, in respect of the repeated representations of the founder Ralph, Lord Cromwell's purse-badge (cat. no. 67).

In 1482 Richard Twygge and Thomas Wodshawe, glaziers of Malvern, were paid at the rate of 1s. 2d. per square foot for the Seven Sacraments window. The Works of Mercy window is undocumented, but can be attributed to the same craftsmen on stylistic grounds. Other panels from both series also survive. Twygge and Wodshawe were one of several workshops employed in the 1480s at Tattershall (cat. nos 290–91). Their commissions ranged from Malvern (cat. no. 37) to

Westminster Abbey and included numerous churches in Worcestershire and Gloucestershire. Both exhibited panels testify to the rich and varied colours, clarity of design and attention to detail that were characteristic of the best indigenous glass-painting of the late fifteenth and early sixteenth centuries. RM

LIT. Marks 1984a, pp.33, 61–2, 202–8, 270–71, 273–4; Hebgin-Barnes 1996, pp.309, 329, pl. 21.

293 Lay donor figures; roundel of the Virgin and Child*

PLATE 35

Late 15th or early 16th century

Stained and painted glass; h. 59 cm, w. 60 cm

Church of St Nicholas, Stanford on Avon, Northamptonshire

The donors are a couple kneeling in prayer in front of a crested seat and prie-dieu bearing an open book. They are clad in red gowns, the man's with fur trimmings and with a purse at his waist, and the woman with a pedimental headdress and girdle. The roundel above is enclosed with large flowers and contains an enthroned Virgin and Child with a black-letter bidding prayer '/S[an]c[t]a Maria Ora pro n(o)bis/'. The glass was conserved by Barley Studio in 1987–97.

Although the donors and roundels are probably contemporary, they did not belong together originally, nor are they *in situ* in their present location in a nave south-aisle window. Both the roundel panel and the donor couple form part of extensive series in this church. The former, along with several other roundels, is on a scale reminiscent of contemporary roundels from domestic contexts (cat. no. 160); possibly they were removed to the church together with a number of shields of arms after the former manor house at Stanford was demolished in 1698. The couple are typical examples of the pictorial commemoration of benefactors that proliferated in parish churches during the fifteenth and early sixteenth centuries and reflected burgeoning lay investment in their fabric and fittings. This pair are unidentified, but the richness of their attire and accoutrements denotes people of substance, perhaps members or associates

of the Cave family, which held the manor by 1432 and whose tombs are ubiquitous in the church. In their original location in a north window, the couple would have faced east, towards a nave altar or the high altar. They are thus partaking in public worship and their representations were designed to preserve their memory and elicit prayers for their souls from their fellow-parishioners; at the same time, the open prayer book and enclosed space in which the couple are placed create an atmosphere of private – even exclusive – devotion and contemplation. RM

LIT. Marks 1998a, p.255, pl. 34.

294 The Appearance of the Risen Christ to the Virgin Mary, the Transfiguration of Christ and the Appearance of the Risen Christ to the Three Marys

PLATE 36

*c.*1500–15

Stained and painted glass; h. 351 cm, w. 271 cm

Inscr: in light b:/S/alue s/ancta/ parens/: in light c, on the tablets held by Moses: /CR(E)D/O IN/DEV/M P/ATR/EM/OMN(I)/PO/TEN/TEM/CRE/ATO/REM/ CEL/(I)ET/

Church of St Mary the Virgin, Fairford, Gloucestershire, east window of the Corpus Christi chapel (window s.III)

This is the best-preserved window in a complete glazing scheme of 28 early sixteenth-century windows, a unique survival in an English parish church. Eight windows in the chancel and eastern chapels recount the Birth and Infancy of the Virgin Mary, the Nativity, Infancy, Passion, Resurrection and Ascension of Christ and the Descent of the Holy Spirit at Pentecost in a continuous narrative sequence, drawing on biblical and apocryphal sources. There is a long tradition in the parish of using these windows in a didactic manner.

This window is positioned directly above the altar of the Corpus Christi chapel. The scenes of the appearance of Christ to his Mother and to the Three Marys in the Garden are spread across two lights and both are set in a convincing spatial environment, one an architectural interior and the other a landscape set-

ting. The Transfiguration is confined to a single central light and its image of elevation fits it for a position above the site of the elevation of the Host, the body of Christ (the Corpus Christi), during the Mass. A golden host appears on Christ's breast. The head of Christ is a recent restoration based on nineteenth-century drawings. The painting on the original head had been scraped away, probably by post-Reformation iconoclasts, and replaced by plain glass in the 1880s. The Transfiguration has been taken out of its correct position in the narrative sequence: its depiction here suggests a careful adjustment of the narrative to fit the liturgical requirements of the church and its topography. The actual Resurrection of Christ is nowhere depicted, although it is implicit in the other scenes in this window.

The first two lights depict the apocryphal first appearance of the Resurrected Christ to his Mother. His salutation to her – 'Hail, Holy Parent' – uses words familiar from the Mass of the Virgin Mary. The inclusion of this scene is evidence of one of a number of ways in which the Fairford windows give especial prominence to the Virgin, to whom the church is dedicated. Derived from the fourth-century writings of St Ambrose, elaborated by Pseudo-Bonaventura's thirteenth-century *Meditationes Vitae Christi*, the story was popularized in England in the fifteenth century by Nicholas Love's English translation, *The Mirrour of the Blessed Lyf of Jesu Christ*, available in printed form from the 1480s. It was a scene often included in extended cycles of the Joys of the Virgin Mary (cat. nos 217, 275).

The reconstruction of the church is associated with the patronage of the wealthy wool merchant John Tame (d. 1500) and his son, Edmund (d. 1534). The Lady Chapel on the north side must have been complete by 1497 when John's will specified it as his place of burial. His tomb, placed between the chancel and Lady Chapel, is in the position often reserved for founders. On his brass, Tame is dressed not as a merchant but as a knight, expressing the social aspirations of his class. His munificent will makes no mention of the glazing of the church, but stylistically it can be attributed to the Anglo-Netherlandish glass-painters established in Westminster and Southwark by the end of the fifteenth century. SB

LIT. Wayment 1984; Marks 1993, pp.209–12, fig. 179; Brown and MacDonald 1997.

295 Vidimus for a stained-glass window for Cardinal Wolsey

*c.*1525–30

Pen and brown ink with watercolour washes on paper; h 42 cm, w. 30.5 cm

National Galleries of Scotland, Edinburgh (D 959A)

Design on two pieces of paper for a 13-light window divided into two registers by a transom. In the centre of the upper row is the Crucifixion, with Christ flanked by the two thieves; on either side are (left) St Peter and the Carrying of the Cross and (right) the Deposition and St Paul. The lower row has the Resurrection in the centre, flanked by St Thomas Becket and the Entombment (left) and the Ascension and St William of York (right). The tracery lights are left blank.

One of Cardinal Wolsey's many ecclesiastical offices was that of Archbishop of York, and the presence of St William of York suggests that this was a commission for a chapel in one of his residences or foundations, either York Place (later Whitehall Palace), Hampton Court or (most likely) Cardinal College, later Christ Church, Oxford (see also cat. no. 255). The sacramental iconography of the central panels and size of the window show that it was intended for an east window. The drawing style has been related to both Nuremberg prints and paintings and to Netherlandish art. The annotations have been attributed to the glazier James Nicholson from the latter region, who worked for Wolsey at Cardinal College and other locations. He was also one of the principal glass-painters employed on the King's College Chapel, Cambridge, windows from 1526 (cat. no. 22). The annotations provide an alternative series of subjects (including several changes of mind) and a reordering of a few of those depicted; they may well represent the changes demanded by Wolsey as patron after viewing the original design. Whatever the final form of the glazing was to be, it has not survived. There is a closely related series of vidimuses in the Musées royaux des Beaux-Arts, Brussels, for the glazing of a Wolsey chapel. RM

PROV. William Esdaile; David Laing Bequest to the Royal Scottish Academy; transferred to the National Galleries of Scotland, Edinburgh, 1910.

LIT. Wayment 1988; Clifford 1999, cat. no. 1, pp.36–7.

296 St Christopher

*c.*1427

Wall-painting

Haddon Hall, Chapel, Derbyshire

The gigantic figure of St Christopher, carrying the Christ Child on his shoulder, strides through a river teeming with fish. To the right, part of the figure of the hermit survives standing before his cell, while other figures are shown on a smaller scale beside the river, all set against a dense foliage background.

Occupying the entire south wall of the nave, this subject forms part of an overall scheme of painting no doubt executed at the same time as the remodelling of the chapel and the glazing of the chancel by Sir Richard Vernon; he and his wife are represented in the stained glass of the east window, with the date 1427 (Marks 1993, p.96). Although in this case in a private chapel, St Christopher is one of the most common subjects in parish church paintings of the later Middle Ages (see also cat. nos 283, 290). Typically, as here, he is prominently represented opposite the entrance, in the belief that sight of the saint would protect the viewer from sudden or 'evil' death (that is, without benefit of the last rites). Executed in a delicate semi-grisaille, this is the finest of all surviving English St Christopher paintings, and like other late medieval examples includes a wealth of anecdotal detail. Here, two of the smaller figures are shown as anglers, one bearded and with a wickerwork basket strapped to his waist, the other with a net in the water. DP

LIT. Hussey 1949, pp.1655 (ill.), 1656.

296

297 St George and the Dragon

*c.*1500

Wall-painting, oil on plaster

Inscr. in black-letter, at base: *Pray ffor the soul off* […]

St Gregory's church, Norwich

Occupying the entire west wall of the north aisle, this enormous painting shows St George about to strike the dragon with his sword, having already impaled it with his lance. In the elaborate landscape behind, the princess kneels and holds a lamb on a lead, while her parents watch from a tower in the city and a soldier stands at the gate. The dragon's cubs peer apprehensively from their lair at the right of the painting.

The most elaborate of all surviving wall-paintings of this popular subject, this example is datable (from details of costume and armour) to not earlier than the late fifteenth century. The remarkable *pteruges* at the saint's shoulders are deliberately exotic, derived from the pendent straps employed in classical Roman armour (Pyhrr and Godoy 1998, pp.9–14), though they are paralleled in a yet more elaborate form in the depiction of the saint on the rood-screen at nearby Ranworth (*c.*1480). The wall-painting is doubtless approximately contemporary with the equally splendid paintings of the Annunciation and the Four Latin Doctors recently uncovered on the south wall of the opposite aisle, which include the arms apparently of John Reede, fishmonger, who bequeathed his funeral pall to the church in 1517; this still survives, and is similarly decorated with dolphins on a black ground (Lasko and Morgan 1973, cat. no. 99). Reede was a councillor of Norwich's famous Guild of St George, which held annual processions in which a man representing the saint rode on horseback through the streets, both 'saint' and horse attired rather similarly to their depiction in the painting (Grace 1937, pp.16–17, 31–2). Possibly Reede was the donor referred to in the inscription, the form of which does not necessarily imply that the painting was executed after the donor's decease. DP

LIT. Kent 1935; Grace 1937, p.7; Carus 1999.

298 Warning to Swearers

*c.*1410

Wall-painting

St Lawrence's church, Broughton, Buckinghamshire

The seated Virgin supports on her lap a horrifically mutilated figure of Christ, while the surrounding figures hold the missing parts of his body, including his heart, hand and bones. Another figure holds the Host, while directly below the Pietà group two men quarrel over a board game, one striking the other with his sword.

Moralizing subjects, including warnings against particular sins such as breaking the Sabbath or gossiping in church, are characteristic of late medieval wall-painting in parish churches (Caiger-Smith 1963, pp.44–63). In this case, the warning is of the injury caused to Christ through the practice of swearing by parts of his body (see also cat. no. 97). It is a theme referred to in many medieval sermons, and in Chaucer's *Pardoner's Tale*, where gaming is cited as one of the causes of such blasphemous oaths. Only one other wall-painting of the same subject survives, at Corby Glen in Lincolnshire (*c.*1400), where the central Pietà is surrounded by men shown being

298

encouraged as well as stabbed by devils, and whose oaths were inscribed in scrolls above their heads (Rouse 1943, pp.157–63, pl. VII). Other examples formerly existed in wall-painting at Walsham-le-Willows (Suffolk) and in stained glass at Heydon (Norfolk) (Woodforde 1950, pp.183–92, pl. XL). The Broughton painting, located on the north wall of the nave, is essentially reliable in its details, despite heavy restoration; the exaggerated headgear and other aspects of the costume are characteristic of the early fifteenth century. DP

LIT. Rouse 1943, p.159, pl. Va; Woodforde 1950, pp.185–8, pl. XLI; Gill 2001, pp.351–5; Marks 2002b, p.112, fig. 10.

◀297

299 The Erpingham Chasuble

Early 15th century (brocaded silk lampas ground Italian, 1400–15; embroidery in silk and silver-gilt thread English, 1400–30)

h. 148.5 cm, max. w. 77 cm

Victoria and Albert Museum, London (T.256–1967)

The silk design, an oriental fantasy of gold camels bearing flower baskets, is in the International Gothic style favoured in the late fourteenth and early fifteenth centuries and may recall Erpingham's travels in Italy and the Near East. The embroidered cross orphrey shows Christ crucified and pairs of saints beneath decorated arches. The chasuble has been drastically cut down to suit a later style in vestments, and some of the fragments of silk have been used to make a matching stole and maniple (T.256A and 256B–1967).

The chasuble bears the shield of arms of Sir Thomas Erpingham (d. 1428) under the cross orphrey on the left and his personal devices on the right: an eagle rising inscribed with the word *yenk* (think), and the red rose of Lancaster. Erpingham championed the Lancastrian cause and achieved high office under both Henry IV and Henry V, acquiring land and property in London and Norfolk (see also cat. no. 236). Although the chasuble cannot be identified among the records of the many vestments that Sir Thomas gave to Erpingham (Norfolk) and other churches, it may have been made for his personal chaplain or for a church with which he was connected.

Richly decorated church vestments with the heraldry of the donor or patron were commonly used as symbols of secular power and spiritual devotion.   LW

PROV. 'Said to have been for many years in the possession of a Catholic family in Monmouthshire' (King 1968, p.59); St Dominic's Priory, London; acquired in 1967.

LIT. King 1968; Williamson 1998, pp.230–31, col. pl. 23.

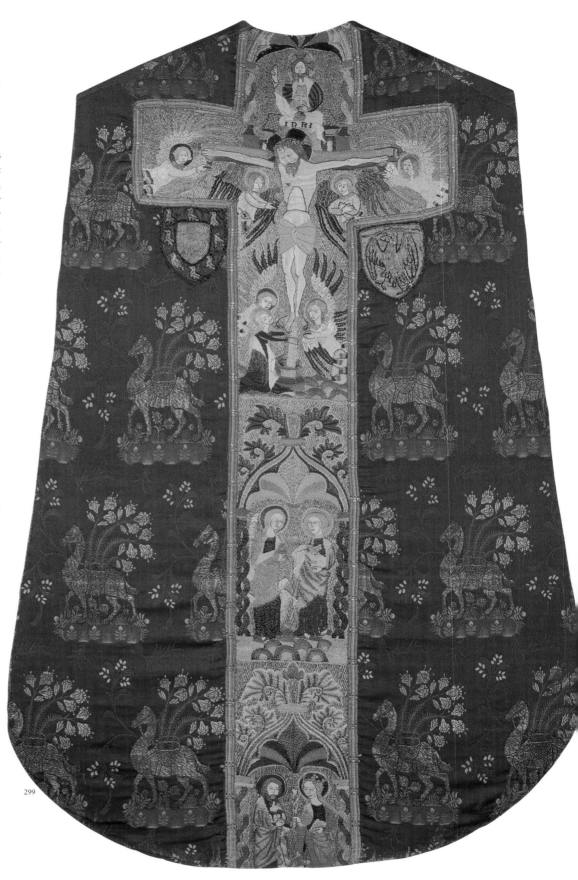

299

300 Vestments from Whalley Abbey

*c.*1415–35

Silk fabrics, Italian; embroidered orphreys, English

Chasuble*: h. 130 cm, w. (shoulders) 86 cm; dalmatic:
h. 119.5 cm, w. (across sleeves) 128 cm; maniple*: l. 101 cm

Towneley Hall Art Gallery, Burnley (T. 141–1974,
T.142–1974, T.147–1974)

These vestments are part of a set recorded in the
second Dissolution inventory of the Cistercian abbey
at Whalley (Lancashire) in 1536/7: '… one vestment
of red clothe of gold with an image on a crosse on the
bak with tynnacles [tunicles] for a deacon and subdeacon belonging to the same … '

Reputedly taken by Sir John Towneley (1473–1541)
from Whalley Abbey at the Dissolution, these vestments descended through the Towneley family to
Lord O'Hagan. A dalmatic or tunicle from this set is
in the Burrell Collection, Glasgow.

The vestments were intended for the celebration of
High Mass, performed by the priest, wearing the chasuble, with the maniple over his left forearm, assisted

300

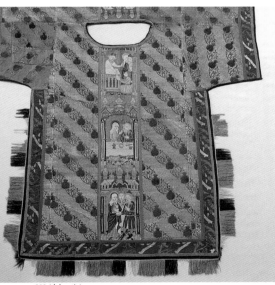

300 (dalmatic)

by his deacon in a dalmatic and his subdeacon in a
tunicle. They were made probably in around 1420–35
from irregular pieces of two expensive fabrics. The
principal fabric is velvet cloth-of-gold, with pomegranates and flowers in polychrome cut silk pile, and
crowns joined by knotted ropes woven into the gold
ground. The border fabric is a voided, brocaded satin
velvet with a vegetal design. The dalmatic is edged
with polychrome silk fringes; the chasuble has been
cut down from a voluminous 'Gothic' shape, and

both are lined with blue linen. The maniple is made
from offcuts of the cloth-of-gold, lined partly with
cream silk twill, and a seventeenth-century silk and
linen damask (not illustrated).

The orphreys are embroidered on linen in silver-
gilt and silver thread and coloured silks, with scenes
from the Life of the Virgin and the Infancy of Christ
set beneath architectural canopies. Although their
style is reminiscent of the 1390s, these orphreys are
datable from *c.*1415 to the early 1430s, on the basis of

the middle king's dress in the *Adoration of the Magi*
on the chasuble. The narrative scenes were drawn
from the Apocrypha as well as the Bible, evoking not
only important feasts of the Church, but also scenes
enacted in mystery plays.   LM

LIT. London 1963, cat. no. 102, p.46; Linnell 1988; Monnas
1994; Palmer 2002, pp.99–102, 129–30.

301

301 Burse

Early 15th century

Linen, painted in colours and gold; h. 20.8 cm
(24.5 cm including tassels), w. 20.5 cm

St Ethelbert's church, Hessett, Suffolk;
on loan to the British Museum, London

The burse is painted on both sides. On the illustrated side is Christ's head and shoulders, within a quatrefoil. In the four corners are the symbols of the four Evangelists with identifying scrolls: an eagle, labelled '*johannes*', at the top left; an angel, '[m]*atheus*', at the top right; a winged lion, '*marcus*', at the bottom left; and a winged ox, '*lucas*', at the bottom right. This side is more faded than the reverse (ill. Cautley 1982, p.15), which shows the *Agnus Dei* holding a flag with a red cross, also set within a quatrefoil. The Lamb stands on a patch of green grass, sprinkled with red flowers, with traces of gold on the background. Outside the quatrefoil is stylized foliage in dark ink. On both sides, around the four edges, a spiralled band is striped in red and white. Around the outer edge, apart from on the top folded edge, runs a light-green band of later fabric (present in 1869) holding the burse together. The bottom edge is open. The tassels are green and red, though much faded.

Burses are used in the Catholic church to carry and store the corporal, a plain linen cloth placed under (and sometimes over) the consecrated Host and chalice during the Mass. The iconography on the Hessett example is traditional, and is also found on an embroidered burse from *c*.1300 in the Victoria and Albert Museum (inv. no. 1416–1874). No other painted burses like this one survive. In fact very few examples at all of medieval painted textiles still exist, although according to records these were common, being cheaper than embroidery (see also cat. no. 155).   EMT

PROV. Found in a chest in the church before 1869.

LIT. Cooke 1869; Knight Watson 1867–70; Cooke 1874; London 1905, p.55; London 1930, cat. no. 438; London 1963, cat. no. 109; Lasko and Morgan 1973, cat. no. 58; Cautley 1982, p.295.

302 Chalice and paten

London hallmark, 1479–80 (maker's mark: a fleur-de-lis)

Silver-gilt, engraved and enamelled; h. 14.2 cm (chalice), diam. 11.3 cm (paten)

St Mary's church, Nettlecombe, Somerset;
on loan to the Victoria and Albert Museum, London

This set is the first known example of English church plate to display full hallmarks, including a date letter. Like many medieval examples, the foot of the chalice features a depiction of the Crucifixion. Unusually, the image is deeply engraved on a separate silver plate attached to the foot by three rivets. The most likely reason for this is that the image was originally enamelled, as it would have been practical to use a separate plate that could be enamelled or fired without damage to the chalice. It is certainly original to the chalice, as the figure of Christ has been engraved in an unusual pose designed specifically to fit the compartment. The face of Christ (or the Vernicle) on the paten is also depicted on a separate engraved panel, which still retains its enamel.

According to parish records, a silver chalice and several other pieces of church plate were handed over to John Trevelyan, owner of the Nettlecombe estate,

302

workmanship, and the Latin inscription is muddled, it is most likely that it was made for a parish church. Chrismatories of very similar design are to be found in the British Museum, the Liverpool Museum and Sir John Soane's Museum, London.

The inscription reveals the function of this casket as a chrismatory. The roughly executed Latin lettering appears to be a misquotation of a line from Psalm 67. During the Middle Ages these words were chanted at the end of the confirmation service. The most important part of this service was the ritual anointing of the recipient with the chrism, a mixture of oil and balsam, in the sign of the cross (Pascal 1844, pp.426–8). Chrism was also used in the administration of Holy Orders, the coronation of kings and the consecration of churches, altars and ecclesiastical objects. This substance was kept in a chrismatory along with other holy oils used for anointing: *oleum infirmorum*, for anointing the sick, and *oleum catechumenorum*, used in baptism.   AW

PROV. Alfred Williams Hearne Bequest, 1923.

LIT. London 1930, cat. no. 462; Oman 1962a.

between 1549 and 1551, presumably for safe-keeping. Although it is not certain that this is the chalice mentioned, it would certainly explain the survival of the set in good condition.   AW

LIT. Morgan 1870; Jackson 1911, pp.133–5; Cripps 1914, p.234; Oman 1957, pp.13, 44, 48, 52.

303 Chrismatory

Late 15th century

Sheet brass, engraved; h. 13 cm, l. 15.5 cm, w. 7.5 cm

Inscr.: *Confer deus via hoc quod.* This is likely to be a misquotation of *Confirma hoc Deus quod operatus es in nobis* (Strengthen, O Lord, that which You have wrought for us: Psalms 67, 29)

Victoria and Albert Museum, London (M.108–1923)

This oblong chrismatory, with a sloping hinged cover, rests on six feet. It is made of sheet brass engraved with an inscription and foliate decoration. Chrismatories were designed to be portable and surviving examples are mostly of base metal or occasionally silver. As this chrismatory is not of high-quality

303

304

304 The Exning Pyx

*c.*1450–1500

Copper alloy, engraved; h. 11.6 cm

Inscr.: MAGNIFICAT AI'A (?) ('My soul doth magnify')

British Museum, London (MME 51.11-27.1)

This is in the form of a covered cup, with a conical spire, standing on a hexagonal foot, all made from sheet copper alloy. The cover is surmounted by a cast crucifix, above which is fixed a large ring. The whole is decorated with engraved stylized foliage and geometric patterns; the lid is prominently inscribed.

It was no doubt to such pieces that Henry VII referred in his will: 'we have often and many times to our inwarde regrete and displeasure … seen in many Churches of oure Reame, the Holie Sacrament of the Aulter kept in full simple and in honest pixes, specially pixes of copre and tymbre'. In the absence of their grander gold and silver counterparts, which vanished at the Reformation, these comparatively humble objects form the principal evidence for the

appearance of English pre-Reformation church plate. They also provide an interesting illustration of the early practice of mass-production. Although we have no evidence as to where this might have been carried out, it was probably in London.

This pyx is of a sort found all over Europe in the late medieval period, though its decoration is distinctively English. The 'Magnificat' inscription is of more general significance; it must be intended for 'Magnificat anima mea Dominum', the opening words of the Magnificat (Luke 1, 46–55), which was from an early date the canticle of Vespers of the western church.

The pyx is almost identical to a slightly smaller one from Ripley, Yorkshire, in the V&A. Both are clearly related stylistically to a series of English fifteenth-century liturgical objects, mostly chrismatories, made of sheet copper or brass (Oman 1962a).   MLC

PROV. Found in Exning churchyard, Suffolk, in 1845; Museum of the Archaeological Institute, 1845; Albert Way Collection; given by Way to the British Museum, 1851.

LIT. London 1850, cat. no. 119; Ipswich 1985, cat. no. 109; Campbell (M) 1985, pp.466–7.

305

305 Pax

*c.*1520

Silver, parcel-gilt, unmarked; h. 13.7 cm

New College, Oxford

Made from one sheet of silver (the upper section has split and been reinforced from the back), to which a rope moulding border and a cast cresting of trefoils are soldered. A handle consisting of a strip of sheet silver is fixed to the back. The figures of Christ, the Virgin and St John, which make up the Crucifixion group, are separately cast and pinned into place on a background engraved with the cross. The border is finely engraved with acanthus leaves, a large bird amid foliage and two double roses, and a daisy with a backward-looking monster with a leafy tail.

Paxes originated in the Early Christian custom in which members of the congregation gave each other a kiss of peace at Mass (Way 1845, p.145). At an uncertain date, but certainly not later than 1250 (*ibid.*, pp.146–7; Oman 1957, p.56), the custom was modified in England, and the pax became an object that was passed around the congregation to be kissed, and known variously as an *osculatorium* and *tabula pacis* (tablet of peace). There are numerous medieval literary allusions to quarrels over the order of precedence for kissing the pax (Duffy 1992, pp.126–7); attacked by English Protestants, the ceremony was abolished at the time of the Reformation (Bossy 1973, pp.141–3). Paxes formed part of the furnishings of all churches and might be made of precious or base metal, enamel or wood, and often depicted the Crucifixion (cat. no. 306). Few English examples have survived, mostly of brass, and only two in silver. While the techniques used vary, their basic designs are close, suggestive of widely diffused pattern books.

By *c.*1500 England was full of alien goldsmiths, many from Germany and the Low Countries, skilled in engraving. One of these may have engraved the pax. The design sources for the border were probably several, and perhaps included a woodcut of *c.*1500 of the Crucifixion for Richard Pynson's *Sarum Missal* (cat. no. 309 and Oman 1978, pp.25–6). A more obvious source is a woodcut border in a Book of Hours produced in Paris in 1500–1, printed by Philippe Pigouchet for Simon Vostre. Here a figure of zodiacal man has a border of pastoral scenes, including the distinctive detail of the leafy-tailed monster and daisy (for an illustration of which, see Harthan 1977, p.170; see also cat. no. 225b). Such close design links between media are rarely demonstrable in silver of this date.   MLC

LIT. Oxford 1928, cat. no. 4a; Oman 1957, pp.76–8 and pl. 40b; Oman 1978, pp.25–7; Oman 1979, p.298.

306

306 Pax*

*c.*1500

Wood (probably beech) frame, gessoed, with traces of gilding and a painting in watercolour on vellum; h. 15.6 cm, w. 12.1 cm

St Andrew's church, Sandon, Essex

This pax consists of a recessed frame in which is displayed a simple miniature (possibly French) of the Crucifixion with the Virgin and St John the Evangelist. Originally the front of the frame, which is much damaged, was gilded, and traces of tooled decoration remain. Holes remain where ornaments were attached. The reverse is also gessoed, though apparently not gilded. It is ornamented with punched circles and dots, and on the right-hand side the letter A is scratched. There are marks where a handle was, and a worn area where the fingertips of those holding it have rubbed away the gesso. This identifies it as a pax, one of only two known surviving wooden examples in England (Nelson 1932).

Many churches had an everyday or 'ferial' pax, and another of greater value for festivals (cat. no. 305). Many of the ferial paxes were probably made of wood, and it is unsurprising that hardly any survive, though they are mentioned in inventories.   EMT

PROV. Found under the floorboards of a cottage near the church in Sandon, Essex, before 1910.

LIT. Layard 1904, pp.126–7; Williams 1940; Bush 1999, pp.26–9.

307 Processional or altar cross

1500–20

Gilded copper; h. 34 cm, w. 30.5 cm

Victoria and Albert Museum, London (824–1901)

This cross shows Christ crucified, with cast, pierced and engraved reliefs of three of the symbols of the Evangelists in roundels on a blue enamelled ground; the backs of the roundels are engraved with stylized roses. The symbol for St Matthew and sockets to hold detachable branches supporting images of John the Evangelist and the Virgin Mary are missing from the bottom of the cross, which has been adapted to fit a later stand.

The cross was found with ecclesiastical vestments in an oak chest in a farmhouse in Abbey Dore, Herefordshire, in 1901. The group is said to have been preserved by the recusant Vaughan family, whose estate at Courtfield had been used for the upbringing of Henry V (born at nearby Monmouth) before the family acquired it in the sixteenth century.

Church processions were an important expression of community identity in the late Middle Ages and were undertaken on numerous occasions, ranging from the parish Mass every Sunday to annual feasts such as Corpus Christi and Candlemas. Parishioners were considered uncharitable and lacking in piety if they did not attend.

Henry VIII's Injunctions of 1547 abolished the celebration of feast-days with processions, with the exception of Rogationtide, which was formally retained by the Elizabethan Injunctions of 1559. Rogationtide was celebrated with processions to the boundaries and natural landmarks of the parish. The purpose of the feast was to petition for the crops to be blessed (hence its name, from the Latin *rogare*, to beseech), to encourage reconciliation between divided neighbours, to raise alms for the poor and to reinforce the boundaries of the parish. Prayers and hymns were offered at important sites, which were given appropriate names such as 'Gospel Oak'.   AS

PROV. Abbey Dore, Herefordshire.

LIT. Oman 1962a, p.207 (wrongly listed as inv. no. 821–1901).

307

308 Missal of St Botolph without Aldersgate*

*c.*1420–30

Vellum, ff.i + 254; h. 35 cm, w. 22.5 cm

Muniment Room, Guildhall Library, London (MS 515)

An entry in its calendar, commemorating the anniversary of the dedication of the London city church of St Botolph without Aldersgate on 4 October, almost certainly indicates that this missal was in use there soon after it was made. The London connection is further stressed by the inclusion of the feast of the Translation of St Erkenwald. The calendar, though contemporary, is an addition to the body of the book, which appears to have been written and illuminated in East Anglia. Three feasts in the *sanctorale* are qualified as being in accordance with the synod of Norwich. One of these is the entry for St Botolph himself, who was widely honoured in East Anglia. The inclusion of the feast of St John of Beverley suggests a date after 1416, when it was formally accepted at Canterbury.

The style of the Crucifixion miniature and its accompanying decoration (ff.108v–109) is consistent with an origin outside London. The choice of pigments, achieving some wonderfully subtle contrasts of colour, is unusual and distinctive. The manuscript may well have been a gift to his local or guild church from one of the many merchants who combined business connections in London with a presence in one of the numerous commercial centres in the eastern counties.   JMB

PROV. St Botolph without Aldersgate; Thomas Dackomb (d. *c.*1572); S. Smith, 17th century; Thomas Bateman (d. 1861); Guildhall Library, 1894.

LIT. Ker 1969, pp.73–75; Scott 1996, no. 46.

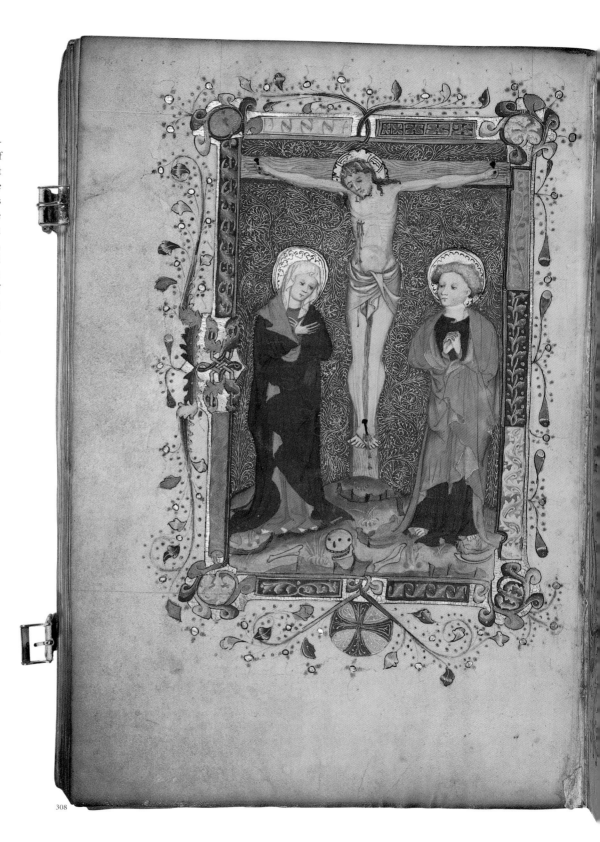

308

309 *Missale ad usum Sarum*

Printed by Richard Pynson, London, 10 January 1500

Vellum, ff.242; h. 27.5 cm, w. 20 cm

John Rylands University Library, Manchester (16904)

Every church had to have a missal. Proper church government needed modern, standardized editions to replace manuscript versions. Until the 1530s, the enormous demand for service books of this kind was mostly supplied by foreign printers (in Paris, Rouen, Venice, Basel); in addition, booksellers such as Caxton and Wynkyn de Worde sometimes commissioned editions from abroad. Pynson's missal of 1500 was a landmark in English printing. It was commissioned and financed by the Archbishop of Canterbury, John Morton (*c*.1420–1500). The archbishop's rebus (a barrel or 'Tun' with the letters MOR) was included in border ornament cut specially for this edition, where it sits among grotesques, birds and foliage, and in the large initials, printed in red, that imitate the design of illuminated letters (see cat. no. 248).

Chancellor from 1487, Morton dominated the government of Henry VII before his death in September 1500. The magnificence of this missal led to further commissions: in 1504 Henry VII ordered another missal from Pynson, which (like that of 1500) stressed its modern, reformed nature. From 1506 Pynson was styled 'Printer to the king'; he is significant as well in being the first printer in England to use Roman founts, in 1508.   RW

PROV. In France in the third quarter of the 18th century (binding by Devers, Paris or Lyons?); acquired before 1822 by Earl Spencer of Althorp (1758–1834), whose library was bought in 1892 by Mrs John Rylands and presented to Manchester University.

LIT. Duff 1917, p.329; Hind 1935, pp.722–3, 733; Chrimes 1972, pp.104–7; Hodnett 1973, no. 1357; STC, no. 16173.

310 *Manuale ad usum insignis ecclesie Sarum**

Printed by Richard Pynson, Fleet Street, London, 1506

Vellum, ff.110; h. 29.8 cm, w. 20.5 cm (slightly cropped)

Stonyhurst College, Lancashire

The manual contains everything needed by a priest. Apart from texts for Mass and offices, there are texts for Extreme Unction and for specialized services. Prominent are the blessings that sanctified everyday objects and activities, from ships and pilgrims with their equipment, to apples on St James's Day and the swords of newly dubbed knights. The only portion in English is the text of marriage vows, spoken by the laity.

Pynson's manual included a full-page image of the royal arms with the Beaufort portcullis (his 1504 missal, printed at the king's command, used the same cut), which suggests royal support for the venture. The work was an outstanding piece of printing. It included two woodcuts, continental rather than English work. That illustrated, a full-page image of

the saints in glory around God the Father (ff.1v–2), had been used by the Paris publisher, Antoine Vérard, for an edition in French of the *Ars moriendi* in 1492; a magnificent woodcut initial O follows a design widely used in manuscripts from the northern Netherlands and Germany. The design circulated in an alphabet engraved by Israhel van Meckenem (*c*.1440/45–1503); Pynson's O was made from the letter Q in this series with the tail removed (Hollstein, XXIV and XXIVA, no. 569).

This copy was used by the parish church of Loddon in Norfolk in the sixteenth century, a church patronized by Sir James Hobart (d. 1507), Privy Councillor of Henry VII. Carefully corrected to allow for Henry VIII's break with Rome after 1533, it shows the predicament faced by those loyal to traditional religion: liturgical practices remained untouched, but where recourse to the Pope's jurisdiction was involved, with excommunicates for example, details of the procedure leading to Rome or to a papal legate were excised.   RW

PROV. Loddon church, Norfolk; owned by Augustin Balles in the 18th (?) century.

LIT. Monceaux 1896, I, pl. between pp.164–5, 255–8; Hodnett 1973, nos 1358, 1482; STC, no. 16140.

309

310

311 The Lambeth Choirbook*

*c.*1521

Parchment, ff.95; h. *c.*66.6 cm, w. 45.7 cm

Lambeth Palace Library, London (MS 1)

On 28 March 1502 Elizabeth of York, queen to Henry VII, paid a considerable sum of 20s. to Robert Fayrfax 'for setting an Anthem of oure lady and Saint Elizabeth'. The anthem that he produced is thought to be *Eterne laudis lilium*, which stands as one of Fayrfax's most accomplished works. The text, which traces the female line of Christ's genealogy, contains a number of tributes to Elizabeth, while the first letter of each line spells out the phrase ELISABETH REGINA ANGLIE.

Robert Fayrfax (1464–1521), a Gentleman of the Chapel Royal, was a favourite musician of Henry VIII and was among the leading composers of his generation. The chief repositories of his works are the so-called Caius and Lambeth Choirbooks, which, with the Eton Choirbook (cat. no. 24), represent the only intact English manuscripts of their type to have survived from the early Tudor period. Caius and Lambeth are considered to be sister productions in that they are of similar size, contain much overlapping repertoire and are copied by the same scribe. Both books were produced with the financial support of Edward Higgins, Master of Arundel College from 1521, who from 1518 also held a canonry at St Stephen's, Westminster, where Nicholas Ludford, the other principal com-

poser in the choirbooks, was based. Caius seems to have been a presentation manuscript from Higgons to St Stephen's, while Lambeth was assembled for use at Arundel College itself. DS

PROV. Library of Henry Fitzalan, 12th Earl of Arundel; John Lord Lumley; Richard Bancroft, Archbishop of Canterbury; Lambeth Palace.

LIT. Lyon 1985; Skinner 1997 and 2003.

312 Wollaton Antiphonal

Probably *c.*1430

Vellum, ff.413; h. 57.5 cm, w. 36.5 cm

St Leonard's church, Wollaton, on loan to the Hallward Library, University of Nottingham (MS 250)

In its complete state, this majestic book contains the materials required for the performance of the daily office during the different seasons of the liturgical year. It must have been intended for use on a lectern (cat. nos 243, 272), from which the musical notation would have been visible to several singers simultaneously. Major festivals such as Easter (f.135) are introduced by large historiated initials and there is lavish and colourful marginal decoration in which heraldry plays a major role. Several different artists contributed to the book, which was probably made in East Anglia or in the north-east Midlands in about 1430.

The heraldry identifies the original patrons as Sir Thomas Chaworth of Wiverton in Nottinghamshire and his wife, Isabella de Ailesbury. Their arms and those of other members of their families appear throughout the book, sometimes separately and sometimes in combination. The right-hand margin of the Easter page displays the arms of Isabella's Bassett mother and of her Ailesbury father, first individually and then quartered. The achievement at the foot of the page represents Sir Thomas's maternal grandmother, Joan Brett, through whom the family acquired Wiverton. Sir Thomas died in 1458–9 and a number of manuscripts, both liturgical and secular, are mentioned in his will. Some of his books can still be identified. This particular item was, however, sold in 1460 to the executors of William Husse, rector of Wollaton, for the perpetual use of his parish church. It was removed to Wollaton Hall by the Willoughby family (possibly at the Reformation, when the office of Becket was formally taken out of the volume) and was returned to the church by Lord Middleton in 1924. It has more recently been transferred to Nottingham University Library for safe-keeping. JMB

PROV. Sir Thomas Chaworth (d. 1458–9); executors of William Husse, rector of Wollaton, 1460; Wollaton parish church.

LIT. Hill 1932; Ker and Piper 1992, pp.667–8; Scott 1996, no. 69.

313 Tenor ('Jesus') bell

*c.*1425–50

Bell-metal; h. 85 cm, w. 80 cm

Inscr. in black-letter: + *Est michi collatum ihc istud nomen amatum* ('To me is given Jesus that beloved name')

Exeter City Museums (37/1995)

This bell comes from the parish church of St James at Halse, Somerset. Its particular interest lies in the founder's mark in the inscription band, which incorporates the initials *r* and *n*, flanking a bell and enclosed within a cabled circle. These allow the maker to be identified as Robert Norton of Exeter, who became a freeman of the city in 1423 and was still working in the 1440s.

Norton was a prolific founder: more than 20 of his bells are known in Devon, with a scattering of others in the adjacent counties of Cornwall, Somerset and Dorset. These have long been admired, both for their beauty of tone and for their clean and precise workmanship. Norton was a progressive figure in English foundry practice, adopting at an early date or even introducing the use of stock legends, in which each word of the inscription was impressed from a single stamp, superseding the earlier and more laborious practice of impressing each letter of the inscription individually into the mould.

Archaeological excavations at Mermaid Yard, Exeter, in 1977–8 recovered evidence of the city's late medieval foundry, including fragmentary clay-loam moulds in which bells and domestic metalwork such as cauldrons and skillets were cast. JA

PROV. Tower of St James, Halse, Somerset; removed 1976.

LIT. Ellacombe 1867; Scott 1968; Blaylock 1996.

313

314 Chandelier

Netherlandish or German, c.1480

Cast, engraved and pierced brass; h. 83 cm, w. 74 cm

Bristol Cathedral, Berkeley Chapel

The chandelier is composed of 12 branches with candle sockets, four above and eight below. The candle sockets are mounted on scrolling branches with formalized twigs and leaves. The leaves are formed as square plates pierced with holes and roughly incised with a floral pattern. The faceted sockets are pierced with keyhole-shaped apertures; the bases are in the form of open rings with screws. These pass through shallow concave drip trays and are screwed to the ends of the branches.

The central section is framed by cast Gothic pinnacles. Above is the figure of the Virgin Mary surmounted by a crown, standing on a turned waisted circular base, with a pierced lower gallery surrounding a half-globe. Below is a cast figure of St George and the Dragon; the figure in Late Gothic armour of full plate with fluted breastplate and formalized mail; the dragon is roughly depicted with upturned jaws grasping a spear. The figure is fixed to a circular platform decorated with mouldings terminating in a formalized lion's head with incised mane, the jaws holding an open ring. The chandelier is suspended from an open trefoil ring set above the Virgin's crown.

The chandelier has been badly damaged. The pedestal on which the figure of St George is set has been crushed and some of the branches appear to be replacements. This was probably caused by a fall when a suspension chain broke.

Although late fifteenth-century Netherlandish chandeliers with figures of the Virgin are reasonably common, those with two figures are rare. This example can be compared with an example in the town hall of Goslar (Germany), dated to about 1480 (Jarmuth 1967, pl. 67), although the workmanship on the latter is of much better quality. The lion-mask terminal is a feature of early brass chandeliers and appears on a number of Netherlandish examples (Ter Kuile 1986, cat. nos 170–73).   AN

PROV. Temple church, Bristol, until the Second World War.

LIT. Tavenor-Perry 1910, pp.145–6, fig. 47.

315 Seal matrix of St Stephen's church, Bristol

Probably c.1450–70

Silver; seal matrix: diam. 2.8 cm; belt attachment: h. 7.8 cm, l. of whole object stretched out 26.5 cm

Inscr. in black-letter: *sigillum+eccl* [les]*ie* +*s*[an]*c*[t]*i*+*steph*[an]*i*+*brist*[o]*ll* (Seal of the church of St Stephen, Bristol)

St Stephen's church, Bristol, on loan to Bristol Museums and Art Gallery

The circular seal matrix shows the patron saint in deacon's vestments, holding three stones (symbols of his martyrdom) within a border of cusped arches. The seal has a conical handle of hexagonal form ending in a trefoil. It is linked to the belt attachment by an elaborate swivel and a heavy chain of 11 links with a further trefoil and swivel under the attachment. The belt would have been inserted through the loop, and the front of the attachment contains a niche with a heavily gilt standing figure of the Virgin and Child on a corbel above two quatrefoils.

The church of St Stephen was entirely rebuilt in the mid-fifteenth century. It is said that the expense of rebuilding was borne jointly by the parishioners and the Abbey of Glastonbury. The fine west tower was erected at the sole cost of John Shipward, twice Mayor of Bristol, in about 1470. The seal could well date from the period of the rebuilding of the church.

This rare survival of a matrix, chain and belt attachment was presumably used by the rector and church wardens for the community of the church. Other church seals, of sixteenth-century date, are known from St Thomas's, Bristol, and St Mary-le-Bow, London.   JC

LIT. *Gentleman's Magazine*, Dec. 1852, pl. opp. p.585; Birch 1887–92, no. 2728.

◀ 314

315

19 PILGRIMAGE

ELEANOR TOWNSEND

'Whoever goeth on pilgrimage … left his father and mother and brethren for the time that he was away from home; therefore Our Lord's promise applied to him; therefore, let him put in the box at the shrine of the saint whatever he would he should receive a hundred times as much in the present world and in the world to come everlasting life'.

Dr Edward Powell, 1553 (Webb 2000, pp.xiii–xiv)

Between 1400 and the Reformation, English people of all backgrounds embarked on pilgrimages for similar reasons to their ancestors. Erasmus's alter ego Ogygius explains that he sought 'those usual petitions, the health of my family, the increase of my estate, a long and healthy life in this world and eternal happiness in the next' (Nichols 1849, p.11). Though Erasmus was writing a satire, the balance between physical and spiritual goals held good for most pilgrims. Margery Kempe's quest for intense religious experiences does not seem to have been the norm among her contemporaries. Most pilgrims sought or gave thanks for cures, or chased indulgences as they were available, to buy time out of Purgatory. John Paston made pilgrimages to Canterbury and Santiago de Compostela at times when indulgences were offered (Webb 2000, p.209). A pilgrimage could be a transaction: Good Works and offerings presented in return for remission from Purgatory or for cures. Such a system was open to abuse particularly as the number of indulgences available increased sharply during the fifteenth century. This was one of the main criticisms made by Lollards and by later reformers.

A pilgrimage did not have to be a long journey – Margery Kempe specifically refers to a two-mile journey as a pilgrimage (Meech and Allen 1940, p.200). People continued to travel to the Holy Land, and to the great shrines of Europe and England during the fifteenth century; we have their accounts and the pilgrim badges to prove it. But increasingly the 'sacred geography' of England became a tighter network of small shrines, with a particular bias towards cults dedicated

122   Henry VI prays at the shrine of St Edmund at Bury St Edmunds, Lydgate's *Lives of Sts Edmund and Fremund* (cat. no. 318)

to the Virgin, such as Our Lady of Woolpit (Suffolk) and Our Lady of Cleeve (Somerset). The emphasis was firmly on the local. Many of the new, non-Marian shrines were devoted to unofficial cult figures, often of local significance, rather than to official saints. Even the shrine of Our Lady at Walsingham was known as 'Our Nazareth', providing a local equivalent to the greatest pilgrimage destination of all: the Holy Land (Coleman and Elsner 1995, p.106).

The journey aspect of a pilgrimage is crucial, even if it is short, as it distinguishes a pilgrimage from other forms of devotion. But the socio-anthropological theory (Turner 1978, pp.34–5) that a pilgrimage is a 'liminoid phenomenon' which necessarily involves a complete removal from the familiar is not easy to maintain when looking at fifteenth-century practice, which mingled the complete unknown of the 'long-haul' pilgrimage with the straightforward journey to a nearby shrine. The journey of a pilgrimage could form a ritual in itself – certain clothes might be worn, or penances observed. But this did not necessarily mean complete abandonment of community ties. The

authorities did show concern about the potential of pilgrimage to allow people to escape normal constraints (Webb 2000, pp.231–2), and there was no doubt a sense of camaraderie on the road, but it was not exactly the otherworldly 'communitas' envisaged by Turner (Coleman and Elsner 1995, p.201ff.).

The pilgrim's progress through the site itself constituted a ritual, a pilgrimage in microcosm. The only written evidence survives for the larger shrines like Canterbury, where the processional for the 1420 Jubilee, descriptions of Margaret of Anjou's 1447 visit, the entertaining Tale of Beryn and Erasmus's account all confirm that visitors were ushered around the site in a very particular order (Nilson 1998, pp.97–8, 118–19; Furnivall and Stone 1909, pp.5–7). The common experience at Canterbury seems to have consisted of a move from public areas (generally the nave) through increasingly protected spaces, via subsidiary relics and shrines, culminating at the main shrine of St Thomas. Pilgrims at Walsingham followed a similarly organized route, though here they were carefully guided first of all to the key focal points of the shrine, the Holy House and image of Our Lady, en route to other relics, in particular the famous Relic of the Holy Milk (Nichols 1849, pp.14–42).

The shrine or image itself was of course the apogee of the pilgrimage experience (cat. no. 316). The great shrines like Canterbury or St Edward's at Westminster were richly ornamented with gilt and jewels (plate 122), and had wooden covers that were removed at certain times, no doubt increasing the suspense. Guardians at some of the smaller chapels must have struggled to maintain sufficient space for pilgrims, among all the clutter. At the shrine to Our Lady of Caversham, Cromwell's commissioner 'pullyd down the place sche stode in, with all other ceremonyes, as lightes, schrowdes, crowchys [crutches], and imagies of wax, hangyng abowt the chapell' (Webb 2000, p.258). Pilgrims presented money, jewels or votive offerings, often made of wax in the form of the afflicted body part, or candles with a wick as long as the sick person (Swanson 1993, pp.175–95; cat. no. 321). The borderline between asking a saint for intercession with God for a cure, and believing that the concentration of holiness at their shrine provided magical healing properties, was a thin one, which reformers found worrying.

All tourists like a souvenir of their trip, and fifteenth-century pilgrims were no different. Badges (plate 123, cat. no. 325) and paper souvenirs (cat. no. 326) were produced at both large and small shrines and avidly collected. They performed a multiple function. Bought as mementoes, souvenirs could also carry something of the saint's power, and act as an advertisement for the shrine, if worn. They were also frequently stuck into prayer books as devotional aids (as in the Pavement Hours, York Minster Library MS XVI.K.6), as pilgrims sought to appropriate the shrine's power on their own locality.

The destruction of the shrines started in 1536 and was more or less complete by 1540. Its suddenness is shocking – Henry VIII was still paying for candles at Walsingham in early 1538, but by October of that year the great shrine of St Thomas at Canterbury was gone (Webb 2000, p.289, n.134). Offerings declined at the great cathedral shrines in the sixteenth century, and it has been argued that, with the increasing emphasis on local devotion, people were turning away from pilgrimage, in a period of decreasing individual wealth and increasing life expectancy (Nilson 1998, p.178). But a closer inspection shows a phenomenon in transition rather than in crisis. Local pilgrimage thrived and new cults, like those of Richard Scrope at York and Henry VI at Windsor, were still flourishing on the eve of the Reformation (Duffy 1992, p.195; Swanson 1993, pp.180–81, 197–200). This context of shifting fashions had always been the pattern for cult devotion in England.

The reformers reserved particular bitterness for certain shrines: the newly fashionable Marian shrines, for example, which were based around images rather than relics. Of course the ingenious frauds which the reformers discovered received the most public of humiliations. The Boxley Rood (cat. no. 324c), which famously wiggled its head and moved its eyes by means of hidden wires, became a *cause célèbre* throughout the country (Finucane 1977, pp.208–10). When it was publicly burned in 1538, the whole phenomenon of pilgrimage in medieval England went onto the fire with it.

FURTHER READING
Coleman and Elsner 1995; Nichols 1849; Webb 2000.

124 Pilgrimage sites mentioned in the text (and some other important 15th- and early 16th-century sites)

123 Pilgrim badges (cat. no. 324)

Durham ▲

York ● ● Bridlington

Doncaster ■

Holywell ●

Bromholm ●
Walsingham ■
Norwich ●
Ely ●
Bury St Edmunds ● ■ Woolpit
Worcester ■
Ipswich ■
Hailes ●
North Marston ●
St Albans ●
Caversham ■ Eton ■ Willesden ■
Windsor ● Westminster ▲ London
Boxley ● Canterbury ▲
Cleeve ■
Winchester ●
Exeter ■

■ Popular cult images of the Virgin
● Other pilgrimage sites
▲ Pilgrimage sites with multiple attractions

Wilsnack ●
Boulogne ■
Aachen ▲ Cologne ●

Compostela ●

Assisi ●
Rome ●

Jerusalem ▲

316 Components from the base of the principal shrine of St William, formerly in York Minster

Begun 1469–70

Teesdale 'marble'; h. 337.5 cm (complete base without step)

York Museums Trust, Yorkshire Museum
(YORYM 1980.52)

This is one of the latest of the long series of shrine bases made for major English churches from the thirteenth century onwards. Typical of that tradition are the material – marble-like, polishable fossiliferous limestone – and the format – a rectangular block with three of its vertical faces hollowed out by prayer niches. Most of the relics of St William (Archbishop of York 1143–7, 1153–4) had been enshrined behind the high altar of the Minster in 1284, and it is likely that the *feretrum* (precious-metal superstructure) of that shrine continued in use until the general destruction of shrines ordered by Henry VIII in 1538. The replacement of the 1284 base was probably due to the desire to make the shrine match the style of its renewed setting, the enormous Perpendicular east arm constructed from 1361. The start of work on the new base is signalled by a payment in the 1469–70 Minster fabric accounts for expenses incurred by the master mason of the church, Robert Spillesby, in riding for four weeks to seek out marblers.

Consideration of the proportions and parallels with other English shrine bases suggests that there were four prayer niches on each long side and two on the short east side. On the west side an altar

316

dedicated to St William was flanked by diagonally projecting screens. The Green Man in one of the quatrefoils formerly below the prayer niches exemplifies the high quality of the decorative sculpture on the base as a whole. The most remarkable architectural details are the miniaturized vaults over the prayer niches. Three of the four extant patterns are fan vaults that differ strikingly from full-size Perpen-

dicular fan vaults in incorporating flowing tracery – a throwback, it would seem, to the distinguished early fourteenth-century Decorated architecture of York and its region. CW

PROV. Several central York sites; acquired at various dates, mostly in the late 19th and early 20th centuries.

LIT. Wilson 1977, pp.18–21; Wilson 1982.

Reconstruction of St William's principal shrine and its setting in York Minster, looking north (*feretrum* and movable cover hypothetical) (see cat. no. 316)

317 Pilgrims collect healing oil at the shrine of St William of York

*c.*1414

Stained and painted glass; h. 75 cm, w. 83 cm

York Minster, north-east transept, window n.VII, panel 16a

A rectangular panel in which five pilgrims, one of them a cripple, collect the healing oil that flows from the spigots in the recessed niches of the shrine structure. Two of the pilgrims press their bodies into the niches in order to bathe their faces directly in the flow of oil.

Until the thirteenth century York Minster lacked a 'resident' saint, as other cathedrals had benefited from the relics of York's saintly bishops and archbishops. In 1223 sweet-smelling oil flowed from the tomb of Archbishop William FitzHerbert (d. 1154). FitzHerbert, a former treasurer of the Minster, had secured the archiepiscopal throne after a long period of dispute and died in suspicious circumstances only a few hours after celebrating the Mass following his enthronement. He was buried beneath a Roman coffin lid at the east end of the nave. In 1226 Archbishop Walter de Gray (1216–55) secured his canonization, although no immediate efforts were made to enshrine the new saint in an appropriately splendid new tomb. In 1284 Anthony Bek, bishop-elect of Durham, paid for St William's translation to a new shrine behind the high altar in the choir, an event attended by Edward I. The original site of William's burial in the nave was enhanced by a new tomb-shrine, the gift of Archbishop William de Melton (1316–40). The cult of St William never enjoyed more than local popularity and until the fifteenth century there was no major pictorial cycle of his life and miracles in the Minster.

The baronial Ros family of Hamlake (Helmsley) emerged as donors of this enormous window in about 1414 (see also cat. no. 232). Nine members of the family kneel at the foot of the window and the greatest prominence was given to Beatrice (née Stafford), dowager Lady Ros, whose arms are also depicted in the choir clearstorey above. The window has been attributed on stylistic grounds to the workshop of John Thornton, who came to York from Coventry to glaze the great east window (1404–8). The glazing of the choir aisles, the choir clearstorey and the St William window followed this in the years immediately afterwards. SB

LIT. Wilson 1977; French 1999.

317

318 John Lydgate, *Lives of Sts Edmund and Fremund*

PLATE 122

*c.*1434–9

Vellum, ff.iii+119+I; h. 25 cm, w. 17 cm

British Library, London (Harley MS 2278)

Visits to shrines formed part of the ceremonial of medieval kingship. Henry VI's visit to the Benedictine abbey of St Edmund at Bury, Suffolk, was unusual only in its length. From Christmas Eve 1433 to St George's Day (23 April) 1434 the royal household was quartered with the abbot and convent. In addition to formal veneration of the relics of St Edmund, and participating in the Holy Week liturgy, the 12-year-old king was able to spend time in hunting, fishing and falconry. At the end of the visit Henry was admitted to the confraternity of the abbey. As a souvenir, Abbot Curteys commanded Lydgate (see also cat. no. 172) to compile a verse life of the martyr king of the East Angles and his shadowy cousin Fremund. It was probably completed in 1439, when Lydgate began to receive a royal pension and Abbot Wheathampstead of St Albans commissioned a similar work.

Harley MS 2278, the presentation copy of the 3,774-line poem, in a fine *anglicana* hand, is illustrated by no fewer than 120 miniatures, by three, or possibly four, artists based in Bury St Edmunds. One, Hand III, can be identified as the painter Robert Pygot, the artist associated with the St Etheldreda panels (cat. no. 319). Their style displays a variety of influences, from London, Flemish and Dutch miniaturists. There is evidence of an awareness of Eyckian realism. Several of the miniatures attempt to portray a specific topographical setting. The exhibited miniature on f.4v, by Hand II, depicts the moment at the start of the king's visit when he prayed at the shrine. He is shown kneeling on a carpet, attended by four courtiers and two monks. This accompanies an indulgenced prayer to St Edmund, the original copy of which was kept at the shrine. NR

PROV. Henry VI; Henry VIII; Thomas, Baron Audley of Walden (d. 1538); Mrs L. D., early 18th century; Mr Colston; bought by Robert Harley, 1st Earl of Oxford, 1720; Edward Harley, 2nd Earl of Oxford; bought with the Harley Collection, 1753.

LIT. Horstmann 1881, pp.376–440; Scott 1996, no. 78, ills 310–13; Rogers 1998.

Hic rex dat votum: quod sancta petit sine totum
Mans corde rata: permansit virgo beate

Hic aqua triumpla deo

319

319 Scenes from the Life of St Etheldreda

Probably by Robert Pygot, 1455

Oil on oak; two panels, each h. 120 cm, w. 56 cm with bevelled edges, showing the panels were originally framed

Society of Antiquaries of London (S.11)

Inscr. in black-letter in rhyming couplets:

a) *... Ecgfrid reg ... non carnis su ...*
   . . . .

b) *Hic rex dat votum: quod sancta petit fore totum*
   Extans corde rata: permansit virgo beata

c) *Hic nova templa deo fund ...*
   ... in ipsa virgineis . . . .

d) *Quarter quaternas est ut tumulata per annos*
   Integra spectatur ... cutis medicatur

The inscriptions come from a thirteenth-century metrical hymn, of which the last couplet can be exactly matched in British Library MS Cotton Domitian xv (Maddison 2000, text to pl. 11; Blake 1962, p.235, footnote).

The panels show:
a) The second marriage of St Etheldreda (*c*.630–79) to King Egfrith of Northumberland

b) The saint leaving her husband in 672 for the Abbey of Coldingham

c) The saint supervising the building of her own double monastery at Ely.

d) The translation of St Etheldreda's body to a marble coffin found at Grantchester, 16 years after her death. The picture illustrates the incident, recorded, like all the scenes, by Bede. The incision in Etheldreda's neck made by the surgeon a few days before she died was found incorrupt.

Thomas Kerrich insisted that there had been a third panel, cut up to eke out the other two (Kerrich notes in Society of Antiquaries). In 1896 the Misses Hartshorne, granddaughters of Thomas Kerrich, exhibited a 'Head of St Etheldreda' at the Society of Antiquaries, which has not been traced since. The third panel could have preceded the others and shown the birth of the saint, and below it Etheldreda hiding in her flight to Ely, but more probably it carried a full-length frontal standing figure of the saint, originally flanked by these, the most important scenes from her life. The painting is thoroughly English, indeed East Anglian (see cat. no. 318), and was probably executed by Robert Pygot of Bury St Edmunds.

The shrine of St Etheldreda, of which considerable portions of the thirteenth-century base survive, had suffered thefts and vandalism in the fourteenth century. However, the saint's popularity had not flagged. In 1439 income from offerings at her shrine was £64

(Wharton 1691, pp.592–98). The panels were surely part of the refurbishing of the shrine done to welcome the new bishop, William de Gray (d. 1478), who returned from Italy to take up his see in 1454 (*ibid.*, pp.672–3). The Ely inventory made at the Reformation includes 'A folding table for an altar', which could have stood at the west end of the shrine (Atkinson 1933, p.177).
PT-C

PROV. Bequeathed to the Society of Antiquaries in 1828 by Thomas Kerrich, to whom James Bentham, author of *The History of the Conventual and Cathedral Church of Ely* (1771), had given them. Bentham discovered the panels serving as cupboard doors in a cottage in Ely (Kerrich notes in Society of Antiquaries).

LIT. Scharf 1865, no. XI, pp.11–13; Rickert 1954, p.202, pl. 180; Fletcher 1974a and 1974b.

320 The Empress Takes the Veil

c.1479–87

Oil on stone

Eton College Chapel, Berkshire

This is the last of eight scenes on the south wall of the chapel, which illustrate the story – familiar from Chaucer's *Man of Lawe's Tale* – of the falsely accused empress aided by the Virgin. The empress, having cured the emperor's brother of leprosy (despite his malicious accusation of infidelity during her husband's absence on pilgrimage), is later vindicated and enters a nunnery. She kneels before the abbess, her conspicuously discarded crown separating her from the emperor and symbolizing her rejection of secular life. Fictive statues on pedestals flank the scene: St Juliana with a devil

320

on a chain and St Winifred holding the sword of her decapitation.

Part of the college founded by Henry VI in 1440–41 (cat. no. 23), the Chapel of Our Lady of Eton possessed a cult image of the Virgin, and was a significant centre of pilgrimage (cat. no. 324h, plate 93). This pilgrimage role is reflected in its wall-paintings, by far the finest late medieval scheme to survive in England, and dated by documentary evidence to *c.*1479–87. Originally comprising two tiers of subjects featuring the Virgin on the north and south walls, now only a single tier of individual Virgin miracles survives on the north wall, facing the empress cycle on the south. Astonishingly, the two upper tiers were almost entirely destroyed in the nineteenth century, the lost scenes being known only from drawings (James and Tristram 1928–9, pls I–III). Only one of the upper scenes survives: the Miracle of the Jew of Bourges, with its accompanying inscription, directly above the empress taking the veil. Executed throughout in grisaille, though with many touches of colour, the paintings are stylistically comparable with contemporary paintings by Dirk Bouts and Hugo van der Goes, as well as with Flemish manuscripts illuminated in the 1480s for Edward IV (see cat. no. 43); they may well be, at least partly, the work of artists from the Low Countries.   DP

LIT. James and Tristram 1928–9; Martindale 1995; Williamson 2000b; Gill forthcoming.

321 Votive offerings

PLATE 45

Late 15th century

Mould-cast wax; h. (of female figure) 19 cm, w. 6 cm

Exeter Cathedral Library

These wax fragments are part of a large group, the only surviving English example of a genre of image production that was widespread throughout Europe in the later Middle Ages and subsequently. Pilgrims coming to shrines could buy an image in wax representing the particular focus of their supplication to the saint or cult figure (Swanson 1993, pp.179–95). This group includes a figure of a woman, as well as animal and human body parts. Several have strings, for suspension at the shrine. The figure of the woman has two holes for string in her head. Similar *ex votos* appear in the Bodleian woodcut of Henry VI (plate 46) and are mentioned in accounts.

These were found over the tomb of Edmund Lacy, Bishop of Exeter from 1420 to 1455 and chaplain to Henry V at Agincourt (see Orme 1986). After Lacy's death, a cult began: John Vowell wrote in 1583 that 'many Miracles were said, and devised, to be done at his Tomb; whereupon great Pilgrimages were made by the Common People to the same' (Radford 1949, p.165). Offerings are recorded in cathedral records and a local will. Like most cults at Exeter, the attraction seems predominantly to have been a local one,

reflecting the long-standing relationship Lacy had had with the area. The *ex votos* show a particular interest in the shrine's healing properties. The bishop suffered from a disease of the shinbones, which may explain the prevalence of limbs found in this group. The shrine lost its status at the Reformation, and the radical Dean Heynes had defaced the tomb by the time the antiquary John Leland visited Exeter in 1543.   EMT

PROV. Found after an air raid in 1943, on top of the north side of the enclosure surrounding the choir, over Bishop Lacy's tomb, Exeter Cathedral.

LIT. Radford 1949; Webb 2000, pp.71–2; Moreno 2001.

322 Mortuary chest*

*c.*1425

Oak, painted on gesso, with original iron nails; l. 124 cm, h. 40 cm, w. 33.5 cm

Winchester Cathedral (inv. no. 1099)

The box is of simple four-sided rectangular construction, with no surviving lid. Each long side is painted with latticework on a green ground, containing roses and crowns with four heads, two bearded. On the reverse the bearded heads are crowned, possibly representing the kings whose remains were within. On both sides a scroll is inscribed: '*hic Rex Egbert pausat*

322

cum Rege Kynulpho' (Here rests King Egbert with King Kynulph). The short sides are painted in a less sophisticated style with red latticework, with red and green rosettes. The box was conserved by Professor Tristram in 1933 and by Harrison Hill Ltd in 1988.

The royal bones originally in this box were moved to the present Norman building from the Saxon Old Minster and placed, according to a chronicler, in lead sarcophagi in the mid-twelfth century. From here they were moved to a succession of wooden chests like this one, of which one other survives at Winchester. In 1525 Bishop Fox completed new sides to the choir enclosure, replacing previous screens on which the chests had stood. He also ordered eight new chests, in which the two boxes were placed.

The Old Minster was a major burial place for Saxon kings and bishops, including most famously St Swithun. Kenulph (d. 714) built the church that preceded the present cathedral, while Egbert (d. 836) was grandfather of Alfred the Great and was crowned 'King of all England' in the Old Minster. They were buried there with at least 11 others, according to inscriptions on Fox's chests. There is no evidence for any major cults involving Anglo-Saxon kings or bishops at Winchester Cathedral, apart from St Swithun (Ridyard 1988, p.115 ff.). Perhaps therefore the remaining chests show an increasing interest in pre-Conquest history in the fifteenth and early sixteenth centuries, as shown also in genealogical rolls of the period (e.g. cat. no. 96).   EMT

PROV. Found inside one of Bishop Fox's chests on the north side of the Winchester Cathedral presbytery screen in 1874.

LIT. Vaughan 1919, p.27; Atkinson and Goodman 1933; Jervis 1976, pp.31–2; Hardacre 1989, pp.46–7; Biddle 1993, pp.275–8.

323 Henry VI

PLATE 21

Late 15th century

Alabaster with traces of polychromy; h. 49 cm

Rijksmuseum, Amsterdam (BK-18310)

The crowned figure is shown as a young man, standing full-length, dressed in a red cloak with a gold edge and blue lining, over a belted gown. There are extensive remains of original colouring, particularly on the cloak, belt and ground. He has a collar with a scalloped edge, probably originally painted to resemble ermine, and holds a sceptre in his left hand and an orb in his right. At his feet are a lion and an antelope with serrated horns, gorged with a coronet. These creatures were used by Henry VI as supporters for the royal arms.

This image is unusual among surviving English alabaster figures in showing Henry VI, who became a cult figure after his death in 1471 (see also cat. no. 36).

Other carved devotional representations do exist, including a sandstone figure in Alnwick, Northumberland, and a fragmentary alabaster figure at Toft, Cambridgeshire. Further examples – which have been lost – are mentioned in church accounts and wills. The orb and sceptre, as well as the crown, signify Henry's true kingship, asserted strongly under his anti-Yorkist successors, the Tudors. The inclusion of the heraldic beasts also constitutes a particular political statement and they were found on many images of Henry VI created after his death.

The evidence of wills, images and pilgrim badges (cat. no. 324i) show that the cult of Henry VI was national in scope in the later fifteenth century, and that it thrived until the Reformation.   EMT

LIT. Leeuwenberg and Halsema-Kubes 1973, cat. no. 854; Cheetham 1984, fig. 4; Marks 2003.

324 Group of pilgrim badges

PLATE 123

a) St Thomas of Canterbury

Second half of 15th century

Tin-lead alloy; h. 2.7 cm, w. 1.6 cm

Museum of London (86.202/4)

Until the 1490s Canterbury was England's pre-eminent pilgrim centre. Its most popular souvenirs purported to be miniature replicas of Becket's head reliquary, which housed the top of his skull, hacked off by his assassins in 1170. The 'Head of Thomas' became one of the most important stations in the pilgrim's conducted tour of Canterbury Cathedral. Several hundred badges of this class have been found at London alone. During the fifteenth century these badges diminished markedly in size, but nevertheless remained – apart from Compostela's scallop-shells – the best-known pilgrim souvenirs of the medieval world.

PROV. Found in 1977 on a Thames-side site in Bankside, Southwark, along with 279 other badges and numerous contemporary artefacts, deposited during the period *c.*1450–*c.*1500.

LIT. Spencer 1998, pp.102–19; Spencer 2000, pp.322–4.

b) The Sword, Canterbury Cathedral

Second half of 15th century

Tin-lead alloy; h. 9 cm, w. 2.2 cm

Museum of London (86.202/14)

At an altar set up on the spot where Becket had been slain, the chief murder weapon was preserved and exhibited to pilgrims, becoming a major attraction in

Chaucer's time. In the early sixteenth century even Erasmus took the opportunity to kiss the sword's 'sacred rust'. Souvenirs incorporated a buckler and a scabbard, into which the miniature sword was slotted.

PROV. Recovered from the Bankside site specified above (a).

LIT. Spencer 1998, pp.93–9.

c) The Rood of Grace, Boxley Abbey, Kent

Early 15th century

Tin-lead alloy; h. 9.4 cm, w. 7 cm

Inscr.: *INRI* (*Iesus Nazarenus Rex Iudeorum*)

Museum of London (8676)

Throughout the fifteenth century this miracle-working rood was a favourite stopping-off place for Canterbury pilgrims. Other closely related versions of the badge add a tiny altar, inscribed '*gras*', and a shrine-keeper taking note of coins and other offerings. At the Dissolution, the rood's life-size figure of Christ was dismantled and publicly exposed as an automaton, capable of registering facial expressions of approval or disapproval.

PROV. Recovered from the Thames at London.

LIT. Spencer 1998, pp.165–7.

d) The Instruments of the Passion

Second half of 15th century

Tin-lead alloy; h. 5.9 cm, w. 4 cm

Museum of London (85.79/1)

Bridging the narrow gap between pilgrim badges and secular, heraldic badges, this shield is blazoned with the arms of Christ, the spear and sponge on a reed in saltire across the Crucifixion, together with the pillar, cords and scourges. The subject appears more often on die-struck flans of brass foil, as well as on devotional woodcuts. Substantial indulgences could be earned by devotions performed in the presence of the Instruments.

PROV. Retrieved in 1981 from the Thames foreshore.

e) The Holy House, Walsingham

First half of 15th century

Tin-lead alloy; h. 6 cm, w. 6.2 cm

Museum of London (SWA81 [2102], <989>)

Walsingham Priory, Norfolk, was incomparably the most important Marian shrine in England. Among the many attractions was the Holy House, deemed to be a replica of the house at Nazareth where Gabriel greeted Mary with the words of the Annunciation. The Annunciation scene was therefore adopted as the principal Walsingham pilgrim souvenir. In this example it was cast in openwork at the centre of a rose. Later these badges were also stamped out of brass and silver foil.

PROV. Excavated at the site of a car park in Swan Lane, Upper Thames Street, London, 1981.

LIT. Spencer 1998, pp.141–5.

f) Our Lady's Milk, Walsingham

Second half of 15th century

Tin-lead alloy; h. 7.2 cm, w. 3.1 cm

Museum of London (86.202/26)

The Virgin's milk was one of Walsingham Priory's minor attractions. First mentioned in 1300 and noted by Erasmus some 200 years later, the milk was commemorated for pilgrims by badges in the form of a monstrance enclosing a small phial. The hexagonal foot and fringe of knobbly crockets are consistent with the date established by associated archaeological evidence at the badge's find-spot.

PROV. Found at the Bankside site specified above (a).

LIT. Spencer 1998, p.147.

g) Richard Caister, Norwich

Mid-15th century

Tin-lead alloy; h. 3.8 cm, w. 3.3 cm

Inscr. at the foot in black-letter: *r kast* **(R. Caister);
an ornate letter R forms the badge's frame**

Museum of London (86.202/18)

Noted for his piety and learning, Caister was vicar of St Stephen's, Norwich, from 1402 until his death in 1420. On the evidence of wills and the testimony of Margery Kempe, the mystic of King's Lynn, he was proclaimed to be a saint by the local populace (Meech and Allen 1940, pp.38–40). The scattered distribution of his badges indicates that Caister's appeal reached well beyond East Anglia. St Stephen's became a satellite shrine of Walsingham and may, for a time, have shared the same badge-maker.

PROV. Found at the Bankside site specified above (a).

LIT. Spencer 1990, pp.46–7; Spencer 1998, pp.196–8.

h) The Blessed Mary
of the Assumption, Eton

Mid-15th century

Tin-lead alloy; h. 5 cm, w. 3.4 cm

**Inscr. at the Virgin's feet: a letter E,
followed by a cask or tun**

Museum of London (84.134)

Henry VI founded Eton College in 1440–41 and dedicated its chapel to the Blessed Mary of the Assumption (plate 93, cat. no. 320). On this badge and others like it, the Virgin, crowned and with hands joined in prayer, is borne up by angels and surrounded by an almond-shaped glory. At her feet is the rebus for Eton and below that a fragment of the royal arms.

By securing many benefits for Eton's devotees, Henry helped to add to the wide range of options open to pilgrims in the Windsor area at the end of the fifteenth century.

PROV. Retrieved from spoil recovered from the site of Billingsgate Market lorry park, Lower Thames Street, London, 1983.

LIT. Spencer 1990, pp.29–30; Spencer 1998, pp.148–9.

i) Henry VI, Windsor

*c.*1485

Tin-lead alloy; h. 6 cm, w. 2.9 cm

Museum of London (97.22)

A badge celebrating King Henry VI, who is shown in regal splendour. At his feet is an antelope, his heraldic badge. After defeat by Edward IV in 1471, Henry, last of the Lancastrian dynasty, was put to death in the Tower of London and buried at Chertsey Abbey. To the chagrin of the Yorkist kings, Henry soon began to emerge as a saint of the people (cat. no. 323). In 1484 Richard III took steps to place the cult under closer supervision by having Henry's body transferred to the new St George's Chapel, Windsor. When the Yorkist dynasty ceased to exist in 1485, all restraints on the cult were removed and the pious followers of Henry VI flocked to his miracle-working tomb at Windsor. On the evidence of pilgrim badges alone, it is possible to suggest that from c.1480 to c.1510 Windsor was the primary English pilgrimage.

PROV. Retrieved from the Thames foreshore at Queenhithe, London.

LIT. Knox and Leslie 1923, p.5; Spencer 1978; Spencer 1998, pp.189–92.

j) The Three Kings, Cologne

Second half of 15th century

Tin-lead alloy; h. 10.7 cm, w. 5.9 cm

Museum of London (94.102)

From 1162 Cologne Cathedral possessed the supposed relics of the Magi. The Magi are depicted here, riding to Bethlehem. Pilgrims everywhere were led to expect that their badges could be pressed against the relics or images concerned and would thereby absorb some of their virtue. With the emergence of mass pilgrimages, it was often no longer practicable for pilgrims to touch relics with their badges. At Cologne

and other major pilgrimage centres, mirrors (in supplementary circular frames) were therefore built into the badges' design, in the belief that by catching a reflection of inaccessible relics, the mirrors would encapsulate some of the radiated grace.   BS

PROV. Retrieved from the Thames foreshore at Angel Passage, Upper Thames Street, London.

LIT. Spencer 1998, pp.261–6; van Beuningen, Koldeweij and Kicken 2001, p.260.

325 Pilgrim badge and mould of John Schorn

a) Mould

Second half of 15th century

Stone; h. 13.8 cm, w. 5.4 cm, d. 1.8 cm

**Ashmolean Museum, Oxford (Brian North Lee gift),
1997.20**

This is part of a three-piece mould yielding (when complete) at least three badges at every casting. Such implements of multiple production were required to

325a

meet the demand among pilgrims for inexpensive, eye-catching souvenirs of the places they had visited.

The badges produced by this mould commemorated an obscure Buckinghamshire priest, John Schorn, rector of North Marston from 1282 until his death in 1314. Though never canonized, he became a saint by popular consent (Marks 2002a). His tomb at North Marston was the focus of a cult that flourished until the very eve of the Reformation.

PROV. Found in 1986 in a well-head at Edlesborough and made from stone quarried at Totternhoe, both places near North Marston, Buckinghamshire.

LIT. Spencer 1978, pp.239–40, 248–9, 257–8; Spencer 1998, pp.192–5.

b) Badge

Second half of 15th century

Tin-lead alloy; h. 5 cm, w. 3.8 cm

Inscr. at the foot: *MA IO SCO* (Magister Johannes Schorn)

Museum of London (8774)

A badge similar to those produced by the mould above (a), with the same distinctive canopy. The presence of a flower (or, in the mould, a flowering staff) probably alludes to Schorn's discovery, in a drought, of a health-giving well that was especially effective in the treatment of the ague and gout. The presence of a thigh-boot in which the devil has been trapped may again refer to gout, but also to Schorn's reputation as an exorcist. In 1478 Schorn's relics were removed to St George's Chapel, then under construction at Windsor Castle, thereby providing a much grander setting for Schorn's clientele (cat. no. 25). Badges designed without a canopied frame may have been made for the Windsor pilgrimage.   BS

PROV. Retrieved from the Thames foreshore at Queenhithe, London, 1866.

LIT. Cuming 1867.

325b

326 The Lewkenor Hours

1390s and 1490s

Vellum, ff.iv+195; h. 15 cm, w. 10 cm

Lambeth Palace Library (MS 545)

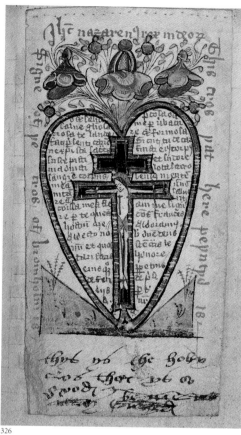
326

Sometime between 1206 and 1223 a relic of the True Cross was given to the Cluniac priory of Bromholm, Norfolk, by an English priest who had been a chaplain to Baldwin I, the Latin Emperor of Constantinople. The Rood of Bromholm soon became famous nationally; it was referred to by Chaucer and Langland. The appearance of the reliquary, a patriarchal cross, is known from the thirteenth-century seal of the priory and two late fifteenth-century miniatures. That in the Lewkenor Hours is a rare surviving example of a prayer card, glued to f.136v. Usually the only traces of such devotional images in Books of Hours are stitch-marks or glue-stains. On this vellum leaf, presumably sold at Bromholm, the reliquary is shown within a heart-shaped frame, representing the Sacred Heart. Around it is the text of a hymn used at Bromholm. This book also contains a prayer card depicting the wound in Christ's side.

The Lewkenor Hours, originally London work of the 1390s, was expanded in the 1490s by a London-based atelier, presumably for Sir Thomas Lewkenor of Trotton, Sussex, who was in the service of Lady Margaret Beaufort. The added devotions include prayers to Henry VI and Sts Dorothy, Sitha, Roch and Bridget, all popular in early Tudor court circles. On the leaf preceding the prayer card is a fair copy of the Bromholm hymn to the holy cross, suggesting that the image may already have been in Sir Thomas's possession when the Book of Hours was enlarged for him.   NR

PROV. Sir Thomas Lewkenor; Roger Lewkenor the Elder of Tangmere (d. 1509); Roger Lewkenor the Younger; ?Edmund Lewkenor; Mary Everard.

LIT. James and Jenkins 1930–32, pp.747–50; Wormald 1937, pp.32–4, 42, pl. 7b.

20 THE ART OF DEATH

PAUL BINSKI

Johan Huizinga's remark in *The Waning of the Middle Ages* that 'no other epoch has laid so much stress as the expiring Middle Ages on the thought of death. An everlasting call of memento mori resounds through life' has provided a bold and enduring historical metaphor (Huizinga 1919 and 1924; McConica 1996; Binski 1996, p.130). In his view the art and life of the late Middle Ages in France, Burgundy and Flanders crystallized the epoch's pessimism, empty concern for form, nostalgia and morbidity. Even a cursory reading of our textbooks on English art reveals the influence of this way of seeing the period, as death-obsessed and also itself dying (Rickert 1954, p.226; Stone 1972, p.213). Huizinga's history, like T. S. Eliot's post-First World War poetry, offered a commentary on the end of an old European order which made decadence not merely interesting, but compelling (Page 1993, pp.143–88).

Huizinga was not especially concerned with England, but the present exhibition has made clear that English medieval visual culture remained part of the European mainstream. And so too with death; for England's Purgatory, its suffrages, intercessions, indulgences, liturgies of death and burial, offices, Masses, tombs, pastoral literature and morbid images like the Dance of Death are all those of European Catholicism (Duffy 1992, pp.299–376; Llewellyn 1991). By our period most major doctrinal issues had been resolved: belief and practice had settled into a widespread and durable institutional life within which individuals lived and died. As Jacques Le Goff put it of Purgatory, scholastic systematization had been followed by social victory (Le Goff 1984, chapter 9). This victory was broadly based, for the visual conceits of death and dying were now common to most of the social orders, whether in commissioning the most modest memorial brasses or grander tombs, screens or altarpieces, rebuilding parish churches, founding chantries and colleges, erecting guildhalls (cat. no. 123) or furnishing mausolea, as at Warwick (cat. nos 86–9) and Cobham (Saul 2001). The wills of citizens and gentry become a vital source of knowledge about methods of commissioning and paying

125   Abbot John Islip's hearse before the high altar of Westminster Abbey, Islip Roll, 1532 (Westminster Abbey, London)

through a widespread and perfectly orthodox literature of *contemptus mundi* of older monastic origin, in which the idea of the morbid epitomized fallen and imperfect human nature; and through the new literature of practical wisdom, such as the *Ars moriendi* or craft of dying (plate 126; O'Connor 1942; Beaty 1970). Printing and sermonizing were becoming powerful vehicles for such ways of thinking. And its attendant ideas of Christian compunction – the *Prick of Conscience* – evolved harmoniously within the broader economy of affective late medieval devotional art, which placed increasing stress on the sharp immediacy of the images of Christ's suffering, defeat and triumph, as in Our Lady of Pity (cat. no. 344), the Man of Sorrows (cat. no. 345) and the cult of Corpus Christi. The refashioning of the late medieval parish church in accordance with contemporary taste and ideals of piety, the spread of indulgenced images (cat. nos 344–5), and religious lyrics of death and the Passion of Christ make the interconnectedness of this public and private discourse of religious and devotional life very clear (Woolf 1968).

Huizinga's evocative and poetic turn of mind was not concerned with origins and causes. The notion that the art of death and commemoration had been affected permanently by the Black Death, for example, has been not so much discredited as made subject to questioning. Certainly no authority on English art or architecture has proposed the kind of analysis of the post-plague period proffered by Millard Meiss for Florence and Siena, which identified in that period a profound spiritual and aesthetic crisis (Meiss 1951; van Os 1981). Interest has shifted instead towards the practical effects of the plague of the 1340s and to the impact of its frequent recurrence in the later fourteenth and fifteenth centuries (Ormrod and Lindley 1996). The plague's economic consequences boosted income to major saints' shrines, and in the later fourteenth century the cult of memory, especially in the form of the establishment of chantry foundations, accelerated; the plague too may have heralded the demise of the labour-intensive and hence costly Decorated style (Cook 1963; Wood-Legh 1965; Rosenthal 1972; Nilson 1998). But art and theology were taking a more austere turn well before 1350 or 1400, and at a deeper imaginative level it is likely that the plague simply served to accelerate existing trends. The earliest manifestations of the art of the macabre on tombs, such as the modest shroud brass to the wealthy peasant John the Smith of *c*.1370 at Brightwell Baldwin (Oxon), indicate the importance of rapid post-plague social mobility and wealth redistribution (Norris 1965, fig. 96). By the time of the great cadaver or 'transi' tombs of the fifteenth century, commissioned by Wykehamist bishops like Chichele and Bekynton

for, as well as understanding, works of art (Duffy 1997). The rationale as well as the fact of death was universal, for death and commemoration were part of the dense local networks of social obligation of medieval society (Goodall 2001). Death, and especially the doctrine of Purgatory, mobilized art because art was not only beautiful, but effective in strengthening that universal human bond of charity between the quick and the dead, of which Thomas Aquinas had written in the thirteenth century and which patrons did so much to put into physical effect in the fifteenth.

But death – and here Huizinga's instincts were sound – was also 'good to think with' in our period, since its concepts informed and allegorized human experience in ways less true earlier on. It informed ideas of human conduct

at Canterbury and Wells (plate 105; see also cat. no. 331), the social victory of such imagery was complete (Panofsky 1964; Cohen 1973; King 1990; Binski 1996, pp.123–63).

Which art-forms are peculiarly indicative of the history of death in England? Two should perhaps be singled out. Monumental brasses survive in vastly greater numbers – about 8,000 – in England than on the Continent, and their social basis was broad and representative (Norris 1977, 1978). Our imagination of the period is probably most influenced by this remarkable and attractive archive. Though quasi-serial production of brasses in large numbers had begun by the early fourteenth century, by the 1400s and until the end of the Reformation brass production was even more widespread, with London as well as other regional manufacturers catering for a large market. The religious, personal and 'gentilitial' imagery of brasses provides a valuable index of attitudes, though their epitaphs remain neglected. Many brasses of the period, such as those at Felbrigg or Trotton (cat. no. 53), are of superb quality. But our second form, the stone-cage chantry chapel, deserves special emphasis. A chantry is essentially an endowed institution (and not necessarily a building) for the chanting or saying of Masses for the souls of the dead in Purgatory. Such institutions were widespread in Europe, not least after the final formulation of the doctrine of Purgatory itself in 1274. But 'closet' chantries – intimate vaulted enclosures within churches designed to house these Masses, of the type first founded and built by Bishops Edington (1366) and Wykeham (1404) at Winchester – are a peculiarly English phenomenon of the period after 1350 in the province of Canterbury (Cook 1963; Wood-Legh 1965). In such chantries, the versatility and beauty of the Perpendicular style, which was to be deployed to such effect by the great bishops, magnates and gentry of the fifteenth century, is especially apparent (cat. no. 109); and it is to such edifices in our greater and lesser churches that we should turn for a really distinctive sense of the English devotional mind in the period before the chantries – and with them the entire edifice of Purgatory – were swept away by the state in 1547 (Duffy 1992).

Pre-Reformation England produced no imaginative response to the afterlife to match Dante's poetry. But its thoroughly orthodox outlook on death served instead to create a landscape of art and institutions which, despite the Reformation, has proved extraordinarily durable. Many works of art and architecture miraculously survive. English educational culture owes much to the pre-Reformation landscape: the bishops' colleges – academic chantries – at Winchester and Oxford, model foundations, as well as the king's colleges at Cambridge and Eton, still adhere to their original purposes even if many other collegiate foundations

126 Death scene, *Ars moriendi* (cat. no. 341)

(like that at Cobham) had no such future. Episcopal injunctions required that great mass of unbeneficed clergy, the chantry priests, to run schools that were later reformed and re-endowed as grammar schools (Krieder 1979, p.60). Prayers for the dead mutated inconspicuously into Founder's Day, and though the 'phantasing vain opinions of purgatory and masses satisfactory to be done for them which be departed' vanished at the Reformation, their legacy is still with us (Elton 1972, pp.382–5; Duffy 1992, p.454).

FURTHER READING

Beaty 1970; Binski 1996; O'Connor 1942.

327 Former collegiate church of St Mary and All Saints, Fotheringhay, Northamptonshire, nave

Begun 1434

Just enough fragments of the story of the rebuilding of Fotheringhay church survive to make it feasible to propose the following partly hypothetical reconstruction. In 1412 Edward, 1st Duke of York, founded a college in the existing parish church, and three years later Stephen Lote, king's chief master mason, began work on a new choir (destroyed in the sixteenth century). At an unknown date before 1434 the choir was finished to Lote's design by Thomas Mapilton, the former's friend and successor in his royal office. In 1434, when Mapilton is known to have been cutting back on his commitments, his former subordinate at Fotheringhay, the Londoner William Horwode, then resident in Fotheringhay, was hired by the 2nd Duke to build the nave. Horwode's contract, which survives, requires that the design follow the choir in all but small details.

The Fotheringhay nave closely resembles Archbishop Courtenay's collegiate church at Maidstone, Kent (begun 1395), almost certainly a work of Henry Yevele, Lote's predecessor as king's chief master mason. Both buildings derive from the standard late fourteenth-century pattern for London parish churches, from which they are differentiated by the East Anglian device of substituting downward extensions of the arcade arch mouldings for the shafts usually found on the north and south sides of the piers. Fotheringhay betters Maidstone in having wall-shafts towards the central vessel and in elaborating slightly the arch mouldings and clearstorey treatment. Historically, Fotheringhay is of interest as an example of the tendency of exalted patrons to employ metropolitan artificers in the provinces, apparently on the assumption that this would guarantee superior quality. It also illustrates the enormous gulf separating a royal duke's patronage and a monarch's, for it does not begin to compare with St George's Chapel, Windsor, built by the 3rd Duke of York after he became King Edward IV (cat. no. 25).

The destruction of the choir of Fotheringhay church after the Reformation encompassed the tombs of the 1st and 2nd Dukes.   CW

LIT. Salzman 1967, pp.505–9; Marks 1978, pp.79–81; Harvey 1984, p.149.

327

328 Five choir-stalls*

*c.*1460–80

Oak; h. of ends 153 cm, of seating capping 93 cm,
l. 310 cm, d. (max.) 32.5 cm

Church of St Peter and St Paul, Hemington,
Northamptonshire

From the north side of the chancel at Hemington, this
bank of stalls consists of four seat standards, or
dividers, and five misericords. There is another run of
five stalls on the south side of the church. The stall
ends are unique in their design. Instead of finishing in
a conventional way with a flat top, or poppy head, the
finial continues upwards, curving tightly forward to
form a swan's-neck profile. The lower section of these
ends is filled with blind tracery, carved in the solid.
Their spandrels contain both non-specific royal and
Yorkist heraldic badges, such as a feather rising out of
a ducal coronet, a falcon within a fetterlock, a rosette
and boar, the last probably for Richard III. The misericords show a mermaid with fish supporters, a
falcon within a fetterlock with two empty ones on
each side, a coronet with two small ones as supporters
with feathers hanging down, and a dragon with
dragon-head supporters.

The Yorkist emblems and the proximity of Hemington to Fotheringhay indicate that the stalls came
from the church of the college founded at Fotheringhay by Edmund of Langley, fifth son of Edward III
and 1st Duke of York. Edmund and his son Edward,
Earl of Rutland, and their wives featured prominently
among those whose souls were to be prayed for in the
college. Building work on the choir, which became
the principal mausoleum of the house of York, was
under way in 1414 and was finished by the time of
the 1434 contract for the nave (cat. no. 327). The
choir-stalls were made to accommodate the establishment of the college, consisting of a master, eight
clerks and 13 choristers.

After the dissolution of the college in 1548, the
choir-stalls were removed to a number of local parish
churches, including Tansor, Hemington, Benefield
and Great Gidding. These refugees, however, are not
all stylistically homogeneous. The woodwork from
Hemington and Great Gidding was made by the same
craftsman, but some 40 years later than that at Tansor
and Benefield, which is of more refined manufacture,
comparable with the furniture of the late 1420s at
Ludlow (Tracy 1990, pp.12–13, pls 40a, 40b). The style
of the heraldic boar on the back of the pulpit at

Fotheringhay, which must have been made during the
reign of Edward IV, since it bears his arms, is close to
the treatment of the boars on the misericords.   CT

LIT. Bonney 1821, p.67; RCHM 1984, p.90; Grössinger 1997,
pp.53–4.

329 St Mary's church, North Leigh, Oxfordshire, Wilcote Chapel

*c.*1438

Construction of this chapel probably began immediately after Elizabeth Wilcote obtained a licence to
found a chantry here in 1438. The highly accomplished architecture was attributed by F. E. Howard to
Richard Winchcombe, first master mason of the
Divinity School at Oxford (cat. no. 246). If, as seems
likely, Winchcombe was dead by 1440, the Wilcote
Chapel would be one of his last works. Recently the
validity of the attribution has been challenged, on the
grounds that the chapel does not exhibit Winchcombe's characteristic trait of extremely shallow and
almost straight-sided four-centred arches and because
it contains moulded rear-arches of a profile not
found elsewhere in his documented oeuvre. But
Winchcombe's designs amount to much more than
shufflings of a fixed set of motifs; they are eclectic
and very varied blends of ideas drawn from Oxford,
Warwick, Coventry and Gloucester sources. The fact
that the Wilcote Chapel is in some respects untypical
of Winchcombe's work is therefore inadequate
grounds for discarding Howard's attribution.

It has also been suggested that the use of window
tracery copied from that of the late fourteenth-century
chancel of St Mary's, Warwick, represents a quotation
designed to express Elizabeth Wilcote and her husband's familial links to the Earls of Warwick. But to
argue thus is to attribute to tracery patterns an allusive
capacity for which there is no known parallel at this
period. It also necessitates discounting the fact that at
least one other of Winchcombe's works incorporates a
wholesale 'lift' from the Warwick chancel, a building he
would have known on account of working elsewhere
in the town for the Earl of Warwick in 1408–9. The use
of fan vaulting over the Wilcote Chapel exemplifies the
sudden upsurge of interest in this vault type in the
Oxford region during the late 1430s.   CW

LIT. Howard 1926, pp.38–9; Leedy 1980, pp.188–9;
Harvey 1984, pp.336–7; Heard 2001.

328

330 Tomb of Ralph Greene and Katherine Mallory*

PLATE 8

Carved by Thomas Prentys and Robert Sutton, 1419–20

Alabaster

St Peter's church, Lowick, Northamptonshire

Ralph and Katherine Greene are shown hand-in-hand, a pose popular among contemporary funeral monuments in both brass and alabaster, but achieved more awkwardly here than on most. Unusually, the monument originally had an alabaster canopy. Only the lower portions of the shafts survive. The 'gablettes' behind the effigies' heads are found on few other monuments. Many details are common to other tombs of the time and make an interesting comparison with the Wilcote monument (cat. no. 329). The distinctive standing angels around the chest are the basis on which other monuments by the same carvers, Thomas Prentys and Robert Sutton, have been identified. They were based at Chellaston, Derbyshire, site of the alabaster quarry that provided material for altarpieces and devotional figures made in Nottingham. The 1419 contract for the Greene tomb specified that his effigy represent an esquire, but the monument was otherwise more appropriate to a knight or nobleman. Prentys and Sutton undertook to complete the tomb by Easter 1420 for the sum of £40. Sutton was still active in 1443.

Ralph was the eldest son of Sir Henry Greene, Richard II's unpopular minister, who was summarily executed in 1399 during Henry IV's invasion. Ralph did not recover full control of his father's holdings from the king until 1411. Despite serving as Sheriff of Northamptonshire three times and of Wiltshire once, he was never knighted. He died in 1417. JCB

LIT. Ryde 1977; Bayliss 2001, pp.23–8.

331 Cadaver tomb effigy of John Baret

PLATE 58

1450s

Limestone, with traces of paint, Purbeck marble; effigy: l. 161 cm; tomb chest: l. 170 cm, w. 73 cm

Inscr. at the end:

Ion   Ho that wil sadly beholde me with his Ie.   Baret
       May se hys owyn merowr & lerne for to die.

On the side:

Wrappid in a schete . as a ful rewli wrecche.
No mor of all myn good . to me ward wil strecche.
From erthe I kam . & on to erthe I am browht.
This js my natur . for of erthe I was wrowht.
Thus erthe on to erthe . to gedir now is knet.
So endith ech creature . Q'd John Baret.
Qwerfor [y]e pepil . in weye of charite.
W[i]t[h] [y]o[u]r good p[re]yeris . I prey [y]u help me.
For sych as I am . right so schal [y]e be.
Now God on my sowle haue m[er]cy & pite. Amen.

St Mary's church, Bury St Edmunds, Suffolk

John Baret (d. 1467) was a wealthy clothier of Bury St Edmunds who also served as an official in the household of the Abbot of Bury. He is represented as an emaciated corpse in a shroud, on which, over his head, is the inscription 'Ecce nu[n]c in puluere dormio' (Behold now I sleep in the dust). Around the effigy runs a scroll inscribed with a text from the Office of the Dead: 'D[omi]ne secundu[m] actu[m] meu[m] noli me iudicare. nichil dignu[m] i[n] [con]spectu tuo egi. Ideo dep[re]cor magestate[m] tua[m] ut tu deus deleas i[n]iquitate[m] mea[m]. John Baret.' (O Lord judge me not according to my deeds. I have done nothing worthy in thy sight. Therefore I beseech thy majesty that thou, O God, shalt blot out my iniquity.) On the front of the tomb chest Baret is shown as he was in life, in a fur-trimmed gown, wearing the collar of SS (cat. no. 71), probably given at the time of Henry VI's visit in 1433–4 (see cat. no. 318), and holding part of his motto 'Grace me gou[er]ne'. The other panels have his monogram and shields, formerly with his arms in brass. At the head is the Lamb of God, surrounded by a scroll inscribed 'Deus propicius esto michi Peccatori' (God be merciful to me a sinner).

The cadaver tomb is a form of monument, derived from continental models (the so-called *transi* tombs), which was adopted in England in the 1420s. As the inscriptions on Baret's tomb make clear, it is meant to prompt the viewer both to consider his own fate and to pray for the deceased. The decaying body represents the soul suffering in Purgatory (King 1990). Such images of mortality were often executed during the lifetime of the person commemorated. Baret's tomb was in place by the time he made his will in

1463. It is probably the work of a sculptor in the employ of Simon Clerk (*fl.* 1434–d. ?1489), master mason of Bury St Edmunds Abbey, whom Baret mentions in his will. The tomb was the focus of a chantry chapel of which the painted roof, set with mirrors, by Henry Peyntour (?Henry Albreed), still survives. NR

LIT. Tymms 1850, pp.233–8; Duffy 1992, pp.307–8, 329, pl. 113; Paine 2000, pp.6–7.

332 Brass rubbing of Sir Thomas Stathum and wives

*c.*1470

l. of figures 46 cm, 47 cm, 45 cm;
inscription h. 12 cm, w. 59 cm

Inscr. in *textura*: *Orate p[ro] a[n]i[m]ab[us] Thome Stathum Milit[is] nup[er] d[omi]ni huius ville q[ui] obiit xxvij die Julij A[nn]o d[omi]ni M° CCCC° lxx° Et d[omi]ne Elisabeth vx[or]is ei[us] filie Rob[er]ti langley Armigeri ac Thomasine alterius vxoris ei[us] Filie Joh[ann]is Curson Armigeri quor[um] a[n]i[m]ab[us] p[ro]piciet[ur] deus Amen.* (Pray for the souls of Thomas Stathum, knight, sometime lord of this town, who died on 27 July in the year of our Lord 1470, and Lady Elizabeth his wife, the daughter of Robert Langley, gentleman, and Thomasine, his second wife, the daughter of John Curson, gentleman, on whose souls may God have mercy. Amen.)

Derrick Chivers Esq. (original in St Matthew's church, Morley, Derbyshire)

Sir Thomas Stathum, in plate armour of German type, with large pauldrons, his head on a helm with a stork crest, is shown between his two wives, in fur-trimmed gowns. From them proceed prayer scrolls to their patron saints, St Anne, St Christopher and the Virgin and Child. This is one of a remarkable series of brasses in Morley church commemorating the Stathum family, including one to Thomas's parents, John (d. 1454) and Cecily, which enumerates their benefactions to the church, and a rare obit reminder brass (Dufty 1952). Sir Thomas carefully specified the appearance of this brass in his will: 'a stone of marble with iij ymages of laton oon ymage maade after me and the othir ij aftir both my wifis we all knelyng on our kneys with eche on of us a rolle in our handis unto our Lady saint Marye and to saint Christophore over our heedis with iiij scochons of myn armes and both my wifis armes quarterly to gedir and to ware on the said stone vj marcs'. The London D workshop did not follow these instructions completely; the posture of the figures was changed and another patron saint was introduced, making the composition more balanced. NR

LIT. Field 1904, pp.33, 35; Norris 1978, pp.52, 77, 90, fig. 72; Lack, Stuchfield and Whittemore 1999, pp.146, 149 (illus.).

332

333 Brass rubbing of Joan, Lady Cromwell

PLATE 59

*c.*1490

h. 198 cm, w. 76 cm; l. of figure 152 cm

Inscr. in *textura: Orate p*[ro] *a*[n]*i*[m]*a Johanne d*[omi]*ne Cromwell que obiit decimo die marcii Anno d*[omi]*ni mill*[esi]*mo CCCCº lxxxx cui*[us] *a*[n]*i*[m]*e p*[ro]*piciet*[ur] *deus amen.* (Pray for the soul of Joan, Lady Cromwell, who died on the 10th day of March in the year of our Lord 1490. On whose soul may God have mercy, Amen.)

Derrick Chivers Esq. (original in Holy Trinity church, Tattershall, Lincolnshire)

Lady Cromwell is depicted in the ceremonial robes of a peeress: an ermine-trimmed sideless cote and a mantle held together by a jewelled clasp. She wears her hair loose, with a jewelled circlet. In the canopy are figures of the Virgin, St Christopher and St Dorothy on the left, and St Anne, St George and St Edmund on the right. Joan Stanhope, the niece of Ralph, Baron Cromwell, married Sir Humphrey Bourchier, who was created Lord Bourchier de Cromwell in 1461 and died fighting for Edward IV at Barnet. Her second husband was Sir Robert Radclyffe of Hunstanton, Norfolk. This Norfolk link explains the commissioning of the brass from the Norwich 3 workshop, which was run by the glazier William Heyward (*fl.* 1485–d. 1506) (on the Norwich 3 series, see Greenwood and Norris 1976, pp.28–32). There are stylistic links with the glass at East Harling, Norfolk, and also with certain panel paintings, such as the rood-screen at Filby, Norfolk.   NR

LIT. Stephenson 1908, pp.333–7; Norris 1977, pp.182–3, fig. 207.

334

334 Brass of Thomas and Emme Pownder

Southern Netherlands, *c.*1525

Latten; h. 116 cm, w. 76 cm

Inscr. in calligraphic *textura: Here lieth beried Thomas Pownder Marchauns* [sic] *and som*[e] *time Balie of Ipswiche whiche departid in the yere M^l v^c xxv yeris and vii day of Noue*[m]*byr And Emme Pownder his wiffe whiche departid in the yere M^l v^c* [blank]

Ipswich Borough Council Museums and Galleries (R.1948–270)

Thomas and Emme Pownder are shown in an intimate family group that is reminiscent of donor groups in contemporary Flemish paintings. He wears a doublet and a gown with false sleeves, she a kirtle, gown and English hood with hanging lappets. From her girdle hangs a rosary. At their feet kneel their two sons Richard and Thomas, the younger shown as a schoolboy with book satchel, and six daughters, of whom only Joan, Elizabeth and Agnes were alive in 1525. Behind them are disposed three shields, with the merchant's mark of Thomas Pownder flanked by the arms of Ipswich and the Merchant Adventurers' Company. In the background a damask hanging is suspended between two ornate classical columns, and the canopy work is composed of classical motifs.

Thomas Pownder was one of the bailiffs, or joint mayors, of Ipswich. He was a ship-owner and, according to his will, owned houses in two Ipswich parishes. After her husband's death, Emme traded as a merchant in her own right, and survived to 1564 (Webb 1962, p.22).

Pownder's trading connections prompted the ordering of his monument in Flanders. The design is by a talented artist, perhaps in the circle of Adriaen Isenbrant. A comparison can be made with the involvement of the painter Jan Mandijn of Antwerp in the making of the brass of Bishop George Crichton in 1537. The classical motifs can be paralleled in Antwerp glass of the 1520s.   NR

PROV. Parish church of St Mary Quay, Ipswich; transferred to Christchurch Mansion Museum, 1948.

LIT. Norris 1977, p.105; Norris 1978, pp 79, 105, fig. 65.

335 Three memorial effigies

1529

Oak; l. of figures 188.5 cm, 193 cm, 193 cm

Inscr. on the tomb-chest in black-letter (*textura quadrata*): *Bonys emonge stonys lys ful steyl qwylste the sawles wanderis were that god wyle[.] ihc. Anno d[omi]ni mill[es]imo quingentissimo v[i]gesimo + vono [recte nono].* (Bones among stones lie full still while the souls wander where that God wills. Jesus. The year of the Lord 1529.)

Church of St Michael and All Angels, Thornhill, Yorkshire (WR)

The tomb is located in the Savile family chapel. The wooden effigies, of a man in armour and two ladies with uncovered hair, lie on a wooden tomb-chest (not exhibited), round the top of which, on three sides, is the above inscription. The knight's sword and dagger are missing; there are some other minor losses and repairs. The remains of painted arms (including Savile) on two of the shields on the south side are not original.

In 1669 Henry Johnston noted that the effigies were painted and his drawing (see ill.) shows a lost canopy, similar to that on the monument by the same hand or workshop at Worsborough (Yorkshire, WR), commemorating Sir Roger Rockley (d. 1533–4). The military effigy (there is a cadaver effigy below) is very similar to that at Thornhill.

Incomplete heraldry, recorded on the Thornhill tomb-chest by various antiquaries, is inconclusive, but the monument most probably commemorates Sir John Savile (d. 1504–5) and his wives Alice Vernon (d. 1503–4?) and Elizabeth Paston (d. 1541–2) (Clay 1920, pp.8–11). The last was a member of the East Anglian family made famous by its correspondence. As none of these died in 1529, it appears that the date on the monument is that of its erection, though this is early for a tomb to be dated in this way. Unusually, the remainder of the inscription is in a local (northern English) dialect. The locally produced wooden tombs at Thornhill and Worsborough are only of moderate quality and no doubt provided a cheaper alternative to equivalent monuments in stone (e.g. cat. nos 330–31)

RK & PJL

LIT. Fryer 1924, pp.58, 106–7, pl. XXV, fig. 56.

335

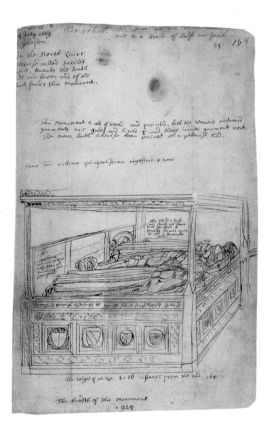

Drawing of the Savile monument in Thornhill church, West Yorkshire, Henry Johnston, 1669 (Bodleian Library, University of Oxford, MS Top. Yorks. C. 13, f.23) (see cat. no. 335)

336

336 Tomb relief from Thetford Priory*

*c.*1536–9

Limestone; h. 22.8 cm, l. 41.5 cm, d. 9.6 cm

British Museum, London (MME 1886, 9-8, 2)

A rectangular panel with relief carving of the bust of a prophet holding a scroll and set in a scallop-shell niche. Masons' mark on top: IIII+. Traces of red distemper on the underside.

This and a companion panel with a king and several fragments were intended for a pair of tombs in the church of the Cluniac priory of Thetford (Norfolk) and were unfinished at the time of its dissolution in 1540. Thetford Priory was the Howard family mausoleum and the tombs were intended for Thomas, 3rd Duke of Norfolk (d. 1554) and his son-in-law Henry Fitzroy (d. 1536), bastard son of Henry VIII. Elaborate

Tomb of the 3rd Duke of Norfolk, Framlingham church, Suffolk, c.1536–9 and 1555–9 (see cat. no. 336)

tombs incorporating some elements of the original monuments were eventually erected for both men between 1555 and 1559 in the new family burial site of Framlingham parish church in Suffolk (see ill.). The two tombs as originally conceived were modelled on contemporary French sepulchral monuments, which the duke may have seen on one of his ambassadorial missions. A conservative in matters religious, Thomas Howard was at the centre of political affairs under Henry VIII and only escaped execution through the king's death. RM

PROV. Thetford Priory; acquired in 1886.

LIT. Stone and Colvin 1965; Marks 1984b; Lindley 1997a, pp.83–6.

337 Tomb of Thomas Manners, 1st Earl of Rutland, and Eleanor Paston*

Carved by Richard Parker, 1543–4

Polychromed alabaster

St Mary's church, Bottesford, Leicestershire

The design of the Rutland tomb breaks with earlier alabaster monuments in dispensing with Gothic details in favour of setting the weepers along plain sides with simple mouldings at top and bottom. The Renaissance pilasters at the corners probably derived more from continental prints than from direct contact with the work of continental craftsmen. The effigies of the earl and countess convey an air of calm dignity. Carefully cut and detailed, they are still very much in the late medieval tradition. Traces of paint remain on the earl's tabard and the mantle worn by the countess, showing their respective arms. The male figures around the sides also wear heraldic tabards. At the west end, the eldest son Henry kneels at prayer under festoons of bay leaves. Richard Parker of Burton-upon-Trent was paid £20 for the earl's tomb. Parker was active from 1534 until his death in 1570, but his later tombs did not evolve much beyond his work on the Rutland monument.

Thomas Manners, who succeeded his father as Lord Ros in 1513, was a contemporary and companion of Henry VIII, who made him Earl of Rutland in 1525. At the Reformation, the earl removed the Ros monuments from Belvoir Priory to Bottesford, two of them with the same type of standing angels that appear on the Greene tomb at Lowick (cat. no. 330). He died on 20 September 1543 and his own tomb was erected at Bottesford in 1544. JCB

LIT. Manners 1903, pp.272–4, ill.; Bayliss 1990, pp.40–52.

338 Armet and funerary crest from the tomb of Sir George Brooke

Italian (armet) and English (crest), late 15th century

Steel, wood; h. 53 cm

St Mary Magdalene's church, Cobham, Kent, on loan to the Royal Armouries, Leeds (AL30.4/6)

This type of helmet, with large hinged cheek-pieces, is known as an armet. With its missing visor, rondel and mail collar, it would have had an active life as part of a field (battle) armour. It was subsequently converted for funerary use by the addition of the Saracen's head and a wrapper and bevor across the face-opening. It was then hung above the tomb of Sir George Brooke, 8th Lord Cobham (d. 1558). There was a strong English tradition from the late fourteenth century (for example, the achievements of the Black Prince, Canterbury Cathedral) of hanging weapons and armour, mostly helmets, above tombs. This tradition of chivalric symbolism became widespread in parish churches during the fifteenth and sixteenth centuries, even for those who had not borne arms in their lifetime. This differs from the Continent, where arms and armour in churches were invariably placed as *ex votos*. KW

LIT. Cobham 1844, pp.9–10; de Cosson and Burges 1881, pp.55–6; Cripps-Day 1922, p.196.

337

338

339 Grave goods of Abbot John Dygon (d. 1510)*

a) Mitre with three pendants ('infulae')

*c.*1510

Sheet lead, painted; h. of mitre *c.*37.3 cm, w. 25.2 cm, d. 18.8 cm

English Heritage, St Augustine's Abbey Museum, Canterbury (AML 749380, 782310-12)

The thick sheet lead is bent and soldered into the shape of a full-size mitre, and painted entirely in red-purple, with details in white.

John Dygon was elected abbot of St Augustine's, Canterbury, in 1496–7, and died on 10 May 1510. His

coffin was discovered in 1901 in the centre of the rectangular chapel there, which he possibly built (Potts 1920, p.146). The grave was identified by an inscribed coffin plate, and also contained two finger rings.

This funerary mitre is a unique survival in an English context. The painting on it imitates the gems and pearls that would have adorned a 'pretiosa' mitre, used on important religious occasions. The painting on the mitre pendants imitates the patterned bands of textile pendants, as on the de Gray pieces (Ramm et al. 1971, p.128). The shape of the mitre closely resembles that shown in the painting of 1527 by Holbein of William Warham, Archbishop of Canterbury between 1504 and 1532 (Potts 1920, p.147).

According to one account, Dygon's head was enclosed by this mitre when the coffin was found (Routledge 1902, p.242). The decorative pendants – which would have hung from the back lower edge of the mitre – had been deliberately folded in two, no doubt to symbolize Dygon's death (Thorn 1981, p.76). It was normal for the clergy to be buried with the symbols of their office, commonly chalices.

b) Chalice (not illustrated) and paten

*c.*1510

Sheet lead, painted; h. 15 cm, diam. of paten 11.8 cm

Inscr. on the paten: *Iohs Dygon* and *1510*

English Heritage, St Augustine's Abbey Museum, Canterbury (AML 78203076 & 78)

A shallow cup on a long square stem, with a circular foot, painted a deep purple-red with black lines (Thorn 1981, pp.79–80). Funerary chalices are the most common form of grave goods from the medieval period, and were generally of pewter or lead, though sometimes of silver (Ramm et al. 1971, pp.126–7; Oman 1957, p.40). Their shape is stylized and the decoration non-existent. It is rare to find any inscription, as here, where the owner's name and date of death are incised on the paten, which is also painted with the sacred monogram 'ihs'.   MLC

PROV. St Augustine's Abbey, Canterbury, excavated 1901; St Augustine's College Museum; English Heritage.

LIT. Routledge 1902, pp. 238–42; Potts 1920, pp.146–7; Thorn 1981, pp. 74–84.

340 *The Desert of Religion (Vado mori)*

*c.*1420–30

Vellum, ff.24; h. 25.5 cm, w. 20 cm

British Library, London (Cotton MS Faustina B. VI, pt II)

The double frontispiece to this manuscript (ff.1v–2) is devoted to the theme of death, based on lines from the English version of a thirteenth-century Latin poem, *Vado mori*. The figures on the left – a knight, a king and a bishop – represent different ranks of society, their status and achievements futile in the face of the last enemy. On the right, Christ and His Mother petition God the Father on behalf of a dying man, whose prayer rises from the soul just leaving his body. Death himself stands over the man, and an angel and a devil struggle for possession of the soul.

The bulk of the book contains a copy of the *Desert of Religion*, a popular devotional poem in English, written and illuminated during the 1420s. Its text is accompanied by diagrammatic paintings of trees of the Virtues and Vices, which it describes, and by delicately coloured images of various saints and other religious figures. Two of these, Richard Rolle of Hampole (d. 1349) and the seventh-century abbess Hilda of Whitby, are particularly connected with Yorkshire, and the poem itself is in a northern dialect. The style of the painting suggests that the artist was trained in the Low Countries. The technique lies somewhere between tinted drawing and full painting. No gold is

339a

339a

339b

340

used, except for two monograms of the Holy Name of Jesus, one carried on a shield by an angel and the other applied to the breast of the figure of Richard Rolle, who was specially associated with the establishment of the cult.
JMB

341 *The art or craft to die well (Ars moriendi)*

PLATE 126

Printed by Wynkyn de Worde, London, 1505

Paper, ff.142; h. 26.4 cm, w. 18 cm

John Rylands University Library, Manchester (14869)

The *Ars moriendi* is a treatise instructing all mortals on how to fulfil a religious life and prepare for approaching death by observing the sacraments and resisting temptation. All through the later Middle Ages it was read as a text of universal importance. From the beginning of printing, it appeared in many different versions and languages: Latin, German, French, Dutch, Italian, Spanish, Catalan and English. Towards the end of his life, William Caxton translated from the French and printed two short versions, both reprinted in Westminster and London before Wynkyn de Worde decided in 1505 to publish a version on a grander scale. He chose as his model another French version, printed twice in Paris in the 1490s, and had its numerous woodcuts copied in mirror-image. His printing type was obtained from France and the decorated woodcut initial F is also French in style.

On the exhibited page (f.CCIV, 2r) we see the end of the *Ars moriendi* itself. The patient in bed, holding the burning candle of faith and supported by angels, saints and a religious friend, dies in sight of the crucifix. His soul leaves his body and rises to heaven. By his faith he has defeated the devils of temptation clustering below the bed and yelling with rage, their ranks thrown into confusion. The cries of frustration, printed on banderols, are an almost audible dissonant in the harmonious death-bed scene.

Wynkyn de Worde included the additional tracts present in his French model. The prologue to the next text, 'The Needle of the Fear Divine', follows immediately. In the woodcut its anonymous author is represented as writing the book. The translation is thought to be the work of Andrew Chertsey (*fl.* 1502–32), who translated several works printed at this time by de Worde.
LH

342a

342b

342c

342 Four panels of the 'Last Things' from an altarpiece

*c.*1430–75

Alabaster, painted and gilded; (a) h. 38.5 cm, w. 23.2 cm;
(b) h. 37 cm, w. 23 cm; (c) h. 60.5 cm, w. 22 cm;
(d) h. 35 cm, w. 22 cm

a) Victoria and Albert Museum, London (A.118–1946)

b–d) British Museum, London (MME 1872, 5-20, 30;
1910, 12-8, 2-3)

The 'Last Things' were 15 signs that were believed to precede the Last Judgement. They were thought to derive from the teachings of St Jerome and are detailed in the *Golden Legend* (Ryan 1993, I, p.8).

The Fifth Sign (a) describes how the trees and grass will give forth dew of blood while all species of birds will gather together in fear. This heavily congested scene arranges a variety of birds in the branches of trees in three distinct registers. In the centre, three male figures witness the chaos, while above the topmost branches of the trees, two angels (their heads now missing) indicate to a fragmentary

scroll that would have identified the scene by its inscription (now lost). The Sixth Sign (b) illustrates how buildings will collapse and be consumed by fiery thunderbolts. Long flames lick around five male figures arranged in various states of collapse, while above them two buildings topple at divergent angles. An angel issues from the roof of one building and gestures to the remains of a scroll. The Tenth Sign (c) depicts how men will emerge from caves, out of their senses and unable to speak. Standing figures of five men and two women, with hands raised helplessly, turn their heads in all directions in total distraction.

teynynge in length ij yardes di'; and a further 'altar of Doomsday' was until 1550 in the church of St Mary the Great in Cambridge (Nelson 1918, p.6). JR

PROV. (a) Collection of G. McNeil Rushforth; Philip Nelson; Dr W. L. Hildburgh; given to the V&A in 1946.
(b) Purnell Collection; acquired 1872.
(c and d) Collection of Max Rosenheim; acquired through the National Art Collections Fund, 1910.

LIT. London 1913, cat. nos 35–7, pls XVII–XVIII; Nelson 1918; Cheetham 1984, cat. no. 240; Cheetham 2001, cat. no. 16; Boldrick, Park and Williamson 2002, cat. no. 10 (entry by D. Park).

343 Head of God the Father

Probably c.1525–30

Limestone, with traces of paint; h. 24.2 cm, w. (at shoulders) 27.2 cm

The National Trust (The Vyne, Hampshire)

The head and shoulders of a bearded and crowned figure, broken from a larger composition; the surface condition is good, with slight traces of red paint and gesso on the shoulders. There are small abrasions to the nose and left eyebrow, and the hair on the left side and the fleurons of the crown have been damaged. The back is flat up to the neck, indicating that it was set against a background, but the head is fully carved in the round.

It is clear that the head represents God the Father,

and that it formed part of a Trinity group: this would either have shown God the Father holding the crucified Christ in front of him, as on English alabasters, with the Dove of the Holy Ghost in between (see Cheetham 1984, cat. nos 223–35, for examples), or might have followed the form of the Netherlandish 'Throne of Grace', with the Dead Christ held in God the Father's arms (Steyaert 1994, cat. no. 5; see also cat. nos 347, 356). It is thus highly likely that the sculpture emanates originally from the chapel of the Holy Trinity, to the south of the Holy Ghost Chapel in Basingstoke, probably built by Lord Sandys of The Vyne in the years immediately following 1524 to house the tombs of his family (Wayment 1982, pp.141–2), and that it was brought to The Vyne together with the celebrated contemporary painted glass at some time after the dereliction of the chapel in the seventeenth century. It is not now possible to be sure whether this Trinity group formed part of a small altar or was a single patronal image. Images of the Trinity were extremely appropriate for family mausolea: the Trinity is frequently mentioned in preambles to medieval wills and is quite often represented on English sepulchral monuments (see, for example, Gardner 1940, figs 16, 18).

The head shares the high quality of the products of the nearby Winchester workshops associated with Bishop Fox's chantry chapel, of a decade earlier (Lindley 1995, pp.211–12). PW

LIT. Howard 1998, p.23.

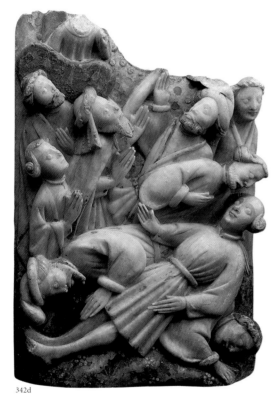

342d

They stand beneath golden rays, above which an angel holds the customary scroll under an elaborate, architectural canopy. The Thirteenth Sign (d) shows how all the living shall die in order to rise again. Nine figures are arranged in prayer or in the throes of death. Above them, an angel occupies a tree, its head and scroll now missing along with the top right-hand corner of the panel.

The panels derive from an altarpiece or altarpieces similar to that described in 1534 as belonging to the Guild of St Mary in Boston, Lincolnshire: 'a table of Alabaster with the storry of the dome [doom] con-

343

344 Pietà

Early 15th century

Alabaster with traces of polychromy; h. 107 cm, w. 62 cm, d. 12 cm

Musée national du Moyen Age, Thermes de Cluny, Paris (Cl.11906)

The Virgin is enthroned, with the diminutive body of the crucified Christ across her knees and displaying His wounds to the spectator. The Virgin gazes into the distance with a contemplative expression and holds her veil in her left hand. The throne is set on a hillock, representing Golgotha, and strewn with skulls and bones. The traces of polychromy include some of the Virgin's blue mantle. The carving is in low relief and the absence of any working on the reverse shows that the image was designed to be viewed from the front.

The Pietà, or Our Lady of Pity, was one of the most popular late medieval images in western Christendom. Originating in south Germany around 1300, it had been introduced into England by the late fourteenth century. At the Reformation it could be found in numerous parish churches and greater churches throughout the country. The image's popularity lay in its potent emotive appeal. Simultaneously it fused the roles of Our Lady as grieving mother, who nevertheless remained steadfast in her conviction of the coming Resurrection, and as *mediatrix* for mankind. Prayers before the image carried an indulgence, and burial in proximity to it was coveted. The iconography exhibits considerable variations in detail. The veil-touching gesture, emphasizing the Virgin's participation in both the Incarnation and the Redemption, is a feature of most of the score or so surviving English carved and mural images of the Pietà. The sweeping drapery folds suggest a date in the early fifteenth century. This is one of the largest existing English carved representations of the Pietà.   RM

PROV. Acquired 1889.

LIT. Prigent 1998, cat. no. 1, p.59; Marks 2002b and forthcoming (a).

344

345

345 Man of Sorrows and St Michael

c.1500 (frame is modern)

Painted panel; h. 72.4 cm, w. 17.5 cm

Inscr. in black-letter: *Vis indulta patru*[m] *tibi prosint … portor … / Hanc . ur gregorius faverat assumtem / N… … or aut maior est illa recita … na / Rome q*[uod] *presens iam patet effigies*

St Oswald's church, Ashbourne (Derbyshire)

Christ is shown as Man of Sorrows above a lengthy indulgence inscription; his half-length figure is set against a brocade background, the horizontal arm of the cross appearing at the top. St Michael below, wearing a red cope like a cloak, impales the dragon with his cross-staff. On the reverse is a full-length female figure in grisaille, her left hand raised, and a blank speech scroll above.

This panel must have formed the left wing of a folding altarpiece, the Man of Sorrows and accompanying inscription reflecting the late medieval belief in the power of indulgences to reduce the duration of Purgatorial suffering. The half-length figure is of

346

346 Triptych

Picardy (?), *c*.1480 (frame is modern)

Painted oak panels; centre: h. 99 cm, w. 127 cm;
wings: h. 99 cm, w. 58.4 cm

Chapel of the almshouse of Sts John, Sherborne, Dorset

The Raising of Lazarus is shown in the central panel,
Christ casting out the Devil on the left wing, the Raising of the Son of the Widow of Nain on the right
wing; on the exterior of the wings are standing saints
in grisaille: Sts Paul and James (left wing) and Sts
Thomas and Peter (right wing).

In the Raising of Lazarus scene, Lazarus does not
have his hands untied by St Peter, as is usual, but by a
man who unwinds the shroud from his head. St Mary
Magdalene kneels by his side, and Christ blesses him,
surrounded by the disciples, including Sts Peter and
Martha. In the left wing a father brings his son before
Christ, who drives out his evil spirit in the shape of a
little demon. In the background is shown the healing
of the blind Bartimaeus. The glass roundels in the
windows depict the Queen of Sheba visiting King
Solomon (left) and the Sacrifice of Isaac (right). The
background to the main scene on the right wing
depicts the Raising of Jairus's Daughter.

The almshouse at Sherborne received its royal

Byzantine derivation, conflating the Crucifixion and
Resurrection by the inclusion of both the cross and
Christ's folded hands. The most celebrated such
image, a mosaic icon in Santa Croce in Gerusalemme
in Rome, was believed to derive from a vision of St
Gregory – the 'Mass of St Gregory' – and images of
both the Mass and the Man of Sorrows alone are frequently associated with indulgence inscriptions (van
Os 1994, pp.106–13). In its use of a textile background, the Ashbourne painting is comparable with
the widely disseminated engraving after the Santa
Croce icon by Israhel van Meckenem of *c*.1490 (*ibid.*,
pl. 33). The figure of St Michael below, in clerical
attire, is of Netherlandish type (de Vos 1994, p.205),
as is the grisaille figure on the reverse. Although this
female figure has no attribute, she is clearly the Virgin
from an Annunciation, a subject typically represented
in grisaille on the reverse of altarpieces and to be displayed at Lent (Smith 1957–9).   DP

PROV. First recorded at Ashbourne in 1844, as the gift of the
Rev. T. J. Jones, rector of Atlow (Derbyshire). Previously he
had been curate at Tideswell (Derbyshire), which still
possessed several sections of wooden screens in the 19th
century (pers. comm. George E. Shaw).

LIT. Eeles 1944–5; Hulbert 1986; Gill forthcoming.

charter from Henry VI in 1437, and a licence was
granted for 20 brethren, 12 poor or sick and impo-
tent men and four women, with a chaplain. Although
it is not known when the altarpiece was acquired for
the chapel of the almshouse, the iconography of the
panels would always have been extremely appropriate
in such a context, concentrating as it does on curing
and revival.

A panel with fewer figures in the collection of the
Marquesa de Camporreal in Madrid, by a follower of
Rogier van der Weyden, is identical to the central
composition in Sherborne. However, the angularity
and stiffness of the figures' style and the use of haloes
would point to the latter's creation in the north of
France, possibly Picardy, by an artist who had an intimate knowledge of the work of van der Weyden's successors, such as the Master of the Legend of St
Catherine and Vrancke van der Stockt.   CG

PROV. According to local tradition, in the almshouse since
before the Reformation.

LIT. Grössinger 1979; Grössinger 1992, cat. no. 54, pp.194–9,
figs 190–93, 195–7, col. pl. XV.

347 Register of the Fraternity of the Holy and Undivided Trinity and Blessed Virgin Mary, Luton, Bedfordshire

PLATE 30

1475–1546

Vellum, ff.130; h. 28.6 cm, w. 20.5 cm

Luton Museum Service (1984/127)

In common with its Dunstable counterpart and the London Skinners' book (cat. nos 133, 348), the Luton Register is one of the most lavishly decorated guild books to have survived. The names of the annual admissions to the fraternity are entered from its foundation in 1474 until its dissolution in 1546, together with the office-bearers for each year. The exhibited frontispiece (f.13v) is by a highly accomplished south Netherlandish illuminator and bears witness to the high status of those who were instrumental in its inception. The founder-members kneel before the Holy Trinity within an ecclesiastical setting: in the foreground is Thomas Rotherham, Bishop of Lincoln, between groups separated by gender and led respectively by Edward IV and Queen Elizabeth; next to the latter is the king's mother, Cecily, Duchess of York. The royal theme is continued in the opening initial on the opposite page, which has the king's arms and supporters enclosed by a collar of the Order of the Golden Fleece. The subsequent decoration, mostly borderwork with occasional representations of prominent fraternity members, is by 20 or so English miniaturists, of varying abilities. The manuscript was updated each year, apparently at the Master's expense and probably in London.

The illumination and the Gothic *textualis* book-hand indicate that the manuscript was a fair copy for use on important occasions in the fraternity calendar, such as banquets, processions on major feast-days and at the guild altar in Luton church on the patronal festival. Religious fraternities were very popular late medieval institutions. In addition to functioning as collective chantries, offering Masses for the souls of deceased brothers and sisters, they also acted as social clubs for the membership, which in Luton was drawn mainly from the town's artisans and tradesmen and their wives.   RM

PROV. James I (?); James Mathews; Andrew Ducarel, FSA (d. 1785); Thomas Astle (d. 1803); the Earl of Bute (d. 1792) and subsequent members of the Bute family; acquired in 1984.

LIT. Gough 1906; Marks 1998b; Scott 2000a.

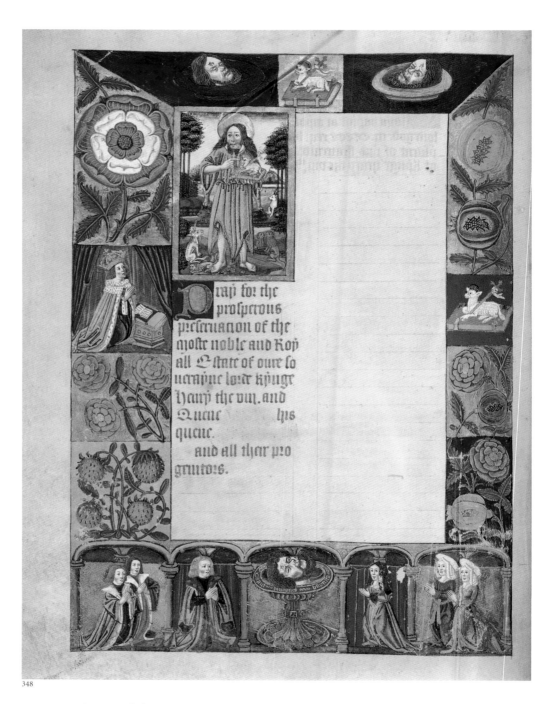

348

348 Register of the Fraternity of St John the Baptist, Dunstable, Bedfordshire

1506–8, 1522, 1525–41

Vellum, ff.83; h. 38.6 cm, w. 28 cm

Luton Museum Service (191/46)

The register is a composite. The folios for 1506–8 are only lightly decorated and were probably extracted from an earlier register and incorporated in a new one begun in 1522. Between this year and 1541 a basic design formula was followed, comprising a miniature of St John the Baptist with full border decoration containing the figures of the fraternity president and two wardens for each year, together with their wives, the

Baptist's head on a charger and a repertoire of fruit and foliage motifs derived from Ghent–Bruges illumination. The exhibited folios for 1522 (5v and 6r) are the most lavishly decorated in the manuscript and depict Henry VIII and Queen Catherine of Aragon, the royal arms and members of the fraternity.

Like the Luton Register (cat. no. 347), the Dunstable book was probably decorated annually in London. It was not executed by the same artists, but the differences stem chiefly from the later date of most of its figurative imagery, which is much more extensive than in the Luton Register, and the different social status of its leadership. The Dunstable guild was established in 1442 by three of the town's leading burgesses and, like its Luton counterpart, for its entire existence the membership was dominated by artisan and mercantile families (cat. nos 349–50). However, the gulf between the landowning upper echelons of the Luton fraternity and the rank-and-file membership was not a feature of the Dunstable St John the Baptist guild. In the latter, the pinnacle of social advancement was election to the offices of president or warden. Whereas it is the rich and powerful who feature in the Luton frontispiece and other pages, irrespective of whether they were office-holders, in the Dunstable Register the presidents and wardens and their spouses are represented.   RM

PROV. Sir Thomas Phillipps; acquired in 1946.

LIT. Buck 1947; Marks 1998b.

349 Funeral pall of the Fayrey family

PLATE 31

Top: velvet cloth-of-gold, crimson silk cut and uncut pile and silver-gilt weft loops; Florence, *c.*1516

Side panels: violet velvet, applied embroideries of silver-gilt, silver and coloured silks on linen, in brick, satin and split stitches, with laid and corded work; embroidery, English, *c.*1516

l. 264 cm, h. 132 cm

St Peter's church, Dunstable, Bedfordshire, on loan to the Victoria and Albert Museum, London

In the centre of each side panel is St John the Baptist, preaching. On the short side panels, two kneeling figures are identified by inscribed scrolls as John (*iohn*) and Mary Fayrey; two bales bear a merchant's mark and initials I. F. On the long sides are two groups of standing figures (14 men and 13 women). The foremost figure of each group is identified by a scroll as Henry and Agnes Fayrey. Four shields bear the arms of the Merchants of the Staple (a lion), Fayrey

(eagles), the Mercers' Company (bust), and Butler (Lord Mayor of London, 1515: crosses).

The pall is thought to have been given to the Fraternity of St John the Baptist, Dunstable (cat. no. 348) by Henry Fayrey (d. 1516). Draped over the coffin at the Fraternity members' funerals, the pall provided a splendid reminder of the Fayreys' patronage. Henry and Agnes Fayrey are buried in Dunstable Priory (cat. no. 350).   LM

PROV. The Priory church of St Peter, Dunstable.

LIT. Kendrick 1923; London 1963, cat. no. 150, pp.57–8, pl. 24; Chambers 1963–5.

350 Brass of Henry and Agnes Fayrey with their sons

*c.*1516

Latten; h. of figures 54 cm, 52 cm, 12 cm

Inscr. in *textura*: *Of yo[u]r charite p[ra]y for the soule of henry Fayrey & Agnes his wife the which lyeth buried under this stone & the said henri decessid the xxviii dai of december A[nno] d[omi]ni M° ccccc xvi*

Victoria and Albert Museum, London (M.126, 127–1922, M.2267–1931, M.33–1932)

Henry and Agnes Fayrey are shown naked, wrapped in their shrouds and with their hands raised in prayer or supplication, perhaps representing the moment of their resurrection at the Last Judgement. Their five sons, depicted as alive, kneel in prayer below. The plates showing the four daughters and the four evangelistic symbols are missing and the top knots of the shrouds have been restored. The brass is a late example of the London F series (Emmerson 1978a, pp.61–5, 77–8).

One of the sons is John, a mercer and merchant of the Staple. Henry and Agnes were residents of Dunstable and, like John, were members of the Fraternity of St John the Baptist (cat. no. 348). Both Henry and John are depicted on the Fayrey Pall with their wives and children (cat. no. 349). Like the Baret tomb (cat. no. 331), this brass presents the viewer with an image of mortality in order to elicit prayers.   NR

PROV. The nave of Dunstable Priory church, Bedfordshire.

LIT. Lack, Stuchfield and Whittemore 1992, pp.32, 35 (ill.); Norris 1992, pp.198, 249.

350

21 POSTSCRIPT

RICHARD MARKS

Henry VIII, as portrayed in the Walker Art Gallery painting (cat. no. 351), is the epitome of omnipotent regality: powerfully built, magnificently attired, swaggeringly self-confident – even priapic – in pose and exuding authority. Like its prototype, Hans Holbein's dynastic mural in Whitehall Palace (cat. no. 2), the image was designed to leave an abiding impression on its viewers of a monarch in his full glory, cast in the heroic Renaissance mode and in the prime of life, lord of all he surveyed. To the end, Henry continued to be a model of princely magnificence. During the last decade of his life he added to the stock of royal residences by the acquisition of Oatlands and the building of the new palace of Nonsuch, both in the newly created honour of Hampton Court. Sumptuously decorated in the most up-to-date Renaissance fashion under the direction of Nicholas Bellin of Modena, who had worked for Henry's arch-rival, Francis I, at Fontainebleau, Nonsuch's imagery proclaimed the authority of the House of Tudor and extolled the king's personal virtues (cat. no. 352). At his death, his mountain of possessions included more than 2,000 tapestries and 2,000 items of gold and silver plate (Starkey 1998; plate 94).

At the same time as Nonsuch was rising, Henry's realm was thrown into strife and turmoil by his actions in matters religious, in which opposition to the royal will was ruthlessly crushed. What began as an issue over his marriage led to the break with Rome and the attack on the religious houses. The impact on the visual arts was profound. In the short space of five years, every monastery, nunnery and friary was dissolved, their buildings rendered inhabitable or ruined and their contents and treasures, accumulated over centuries, dispersed, defaced or for the most part destroyed (cat. nos 95, 234–5, 356–7). Many, like Bisham Abbey, served as aristocratic mausolea, but even these were not spared. Tombs might survive in those monastic churches that were retained in part or as a whole; only occasionally were they transferred to a parish

127   *Henry VIII* (cat. no. 351)

church (cat. no. 336). Some houses had recently been, or still were, engaged in the endless cycle of rebuilding and refurbishment. The unfinished west tower of Bolton Abbey (plate 128) is testament to the suddenness and speed of the attack. Every one of the numerous shrines and miraculous images, whether associated with monasteries or not, was proscribed and destroyed, with the offerings and embellishments going to swell the royal coffers. So great was the quantity of jewels and other adornments stripped from Becket's shrine at Canterbury that they were said to have filled twenty-six wagons. Although not the focus of attack at this stage, parish churches did not remain unaffected. Those that housed cult images or relics saw them removed. Apart from the reviled Thomas Becket (cat. no. 89), their non-miraculous images were permitted to remain; but deprived of their devotional purpose, they became mere furnishings and embellishments, on a par with stained-glass windows and screen paintings. The English landscape was no longer a landscape of the sacred. People continued to use their primers, but they now bore the imprints of the new dispensation, with the erasure of Becket's name and symbols of papal authority like the tiara (cat. no. 140). With the instruction to every parish to acquire a copy of the Bible in the vernacular by Easter 1539, another kind of spiritual reading was introduced (cat. no. 355). Its title-page spelled out to every parish with unprecedented frankness that the king, not the Pope, was now God's agent in England.

More than the French wars and the Wars of the Roses, the religious crisis affected every man, woman and child in the kingdom. Until the 1530s, people continued to contribute, as their ancestors had done, to the enhancement of their parish churches. With the exception of a few critics within the church and small groups of heretical Lollards, the traditional faith went largely unquestioned. Not only did the abolition of the shrines and monasteries destroy the treasures of past centuries, but the first signs of doctrinal attack on traditional religious practices led to the drying-up of the stream of benefactions. New commissions for church fabric and furnishings came to a halt. For many of the craftsmen whose livelihood had depended largely on the now-overturned religious order, the first stages of the Reformation already spelt ruin. The Church ceased to be a major focus of artistic patronage, a position not reversed until the nineteenth century. However, it is important to remember that not every aspect of production was affected by the religious changes and the destruction of shrines, monastic buildings and their contents. High-quality and costly textiles, goldsmiths' work, jewellery and miniature and large-scale portraiture (the

last increasingly fashionable) continued to be in demand from the king, and from those who served him as courtiers and officials. The elite continued to embellish their houses with heraldic glass and costly furnishings (cat. no. 152). Before long, some of the new owners of former monastic lands began to invest in splendid residences, some quite literally rising from the ruins of the dissolved religious houses.

Henry himself, *Fidei Defensor* and Supreme Head of the Church (cat. nos 353–5), remained conservative in doctrinal matters until the end, but religious policy was fiercely contested between evangelicals and traditionalists; the king contributed to the uncertainty by oscillating between the two parties. The outcome would determine the future direction of the Church in England: would it remain in the Catholic fold, albeit without the Pope – or would it join one of the Reformed camps? In this struggle, images were a principal *casus belli*. The attack on the monasteries and on pilgrimage was a harbinger of what was to come under Edward VI; but to contemporaries, this outcome was neither predictable nor inevitable. At his death, Henry ruled over a realm confused and divided about religion, and uneasy and uncertain about the future. The fate of much of England's artistic heritage was hanging in the balance.

FURTHER READING

Aston 1988; Duffy 1992.

128   Bolton Abbey, West Yorkshire, west tower, begun in 1540 and left unfinished at the Dissolution

351 Henry VIII

PLATE 127

1540–60

Oil on oak panel; h. 237.9 cm, w. 134 cm

National Museums and Galleries on Merseyside, Walker Art Gallery, Liverpool (WAG 1350)

This full-length image of Henry VIII is one of the most accomplished of the paintings produced after Holbein's portrait of the king, which formed part of the dynastic mural painting at Whitehall Palace, completed in 1537 and destroyed by fire in 1698. This showed Henry VIII and his third wife Jane Seymour with his parents, Henry VII and Elizabeth of York, with a Latin inscription in praise of the Tudors (cat. nos 2, 39). Other versions are at Belvoir, Chatsworth, Parham, Petworth and Trinity College, Cambridge, the last signed by Hans Eworth and dated 1567. Recent dendrochronological investigation has dated the present panel to after 1530; infrared investigation has refuted a suggestion that it too might be the work of Eworth (Strong 1969, I, p.159).

Comparison between versions of portraits of Henry VIII by Holbein and others suggests that such versions of the king were created using patterns derived from Holbein's original painting, since they accord closely with the dimensions of Holbein's cartoon. However, the 1667 copy of the lost Whitehall portrait shows that Holbein changed the head of the king from the three-quarter-face view of the cartoon to the full-face view that the Walker portrait of Henry VIII follows, and therefore copyists must have had access to the different, final version of the pattern for the head.

Portraits of Henry VIII are recorded in inventories from the second half of the sixteenth century (Foister 1981). Individual images such as this may have served to reinforce the message conveyed by the Whitehall wall-painting of the strength of the Tudor dynasty.

SF

PROV. Probably by descent from Edward Seymour, Duke of Somerset, to the Seymours of East Knoyle, Wiltshire. Bought 1945, from the sale of Miss Jane M. Seymour of Knoyle House.

LIT. Strong 1969, I, p.159; Brooke and Crombie 2003.

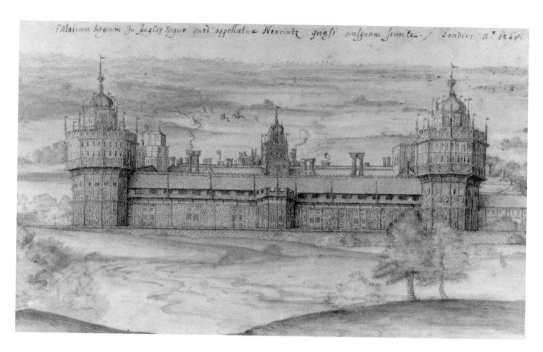

352 Nonsuch Palace, Surrey

Begun 1538

Previously occupied by the village of Cuddington, the site of Nonsuch was selected because of the excellent hawking and hunting. Work began in April 1538, and though the structure was complete by 1541, decoration continued until 1545. The palace was demolished in 1682–3. No doubt its boastful name arose from the truly unparalleled nature of the ornamentation applied to the interior and exterior fronts of the inner court: large figural panels executed in *stucco duro*, all enclosed in a grid formed of sheets of black slate. The slate, which was richly carved and gilded, served as cladding to the timber-framed structure. From afar the inner court must have appeared like an unusually large timber-framed house, a not inappropriate image given its hunting-lodge function.

The starting-point for the concept of exterior elevations covered with stucco figure-sculpture was undoubtedly such Italian garden buildings as the *giardino segreto* of the Palazzo del Te at Mantua. The possibility of realizing that concept in England did not exist until 1537 when Nicholas Bellin of Modena entered Henry VIII's service. In 1533 Bellin had been employed by Francis I on decorations at Fontainebleau

Nonsuch Palace, garden front of inner court, pen and watercolour drawing by Joris Hoefnagel (1568), private collection (cat. no. 352)

that featured large-scale stucco figures. A few architectural elements of the inner court would have recalled earlier English royal palaces, for example the 'onion' domelets surmounted by heraldic, vane-bearing beasts, the two-storey bay windows and the jettied-out upper storeys. Others, notably the bulkiness of the corner towers and the classical columns applied to their angles, would have struck an unfamiliar note. Influence from the medievalizing drum towers on early sixteenth-century French châteaux such as Bury or Le Lude is highly likely, although the Nonsuch towers differ in being polygonal in plan – presumably a consequence of their timber construction. Bellin could well have suggested both the towers and the use of slate to clad structural timbers, for though new to England, the latter technique was already current in France. No sources have yet been identified for the iconographic scheme governing the selection of the classical subjects shown in the stuccoes.

CW

LIT. Biddle 1966, pp.106–21; Colvin 1982, pp.179–205; Biddle 1984; Turner 1996, XXIII, pp.197–8.

353

353 Medal of Henry VIII as Defender of the Faith

1545

Gold; diam. 5.2 cm, wt 62.31 g

Obv.: bust of Henry VIII facing right, wearing a jewelled cap, ermine robe and jewelled collar

HENRICUS OCTA ANGLIAE FRANCI ET HIB REX FIDEI DEFENSOR ET IN TERR ECCL ANGLI ET HIBE SUB CHRIST CAPUT SUPREMUM (Henry VIII king of England, France and Ireland, defender of the faith, and on earth supreme head under Christ of the church of England and Ireland)

Legend in two concentric circles, divided into four by the Tudor royal badges: rose, portcullis, lis and harp

Rev.: the same legend as above, across the field, in Hebrew and Greek, with HR above and *Londini 1545* below

British Museum, London (CM MI.47, 44)

The role of the medal as an instrument of royal propaganda and policy was very restricted in England, in contrast to France and the Italian and Habsburg courts, and such medals as were made in England, or for the king, in the first half of the sixteenth century were mostly the work of foreign artists. However, the end of Henry VIII's reign saw the appearance of the first undoubted English medal, attributed to Henry Basse, chief engraver at the London mint. This medal celebrates Henry's position as head of the church in England, but does not appear to commemorate any specific development, his titles and position having been confirmed by parliament in 1534 and formally proclaimed in 1535. It is thus unclear whether its creator made it by commission, or perhaps as a demonstration of personal skill in this relatively novel medium. It was successful enough to inspire a similar follow-up, the coronation medal of Edward VI. BC

LIT. Hawkins 1885, pp.47–8; Hill 1916; Jones 1990, p.18; Starkey 1991, cat. no. V.54, p.93.

354 Henry VIII, *Assertio septem sacramentorum*

Printed by Richard Pynson, London, 1521

Paper, ff.95; h. 23.5 cm, w. 16.5 cm

British Library, London (9.a.9)

On the European stage, Henry sought leadership in religious as well as political and cultural matters. His *Assertio*, composed with the discreet help of more qualified scholars, defended traditional teachings on the sacraments against Luther's attack in *De captivitate Babylonie* (Wittenberg, 1520). Twenty-eight copies were dispatched in August 1521 to Rome for the cardinals and the Pope, that for the latter beautifully illuminated and inscribed by Henry. The king sought a title that matched those of Francis I (*Rex Christianissimus*) and Ferdinand of Spain (*Rex Catholicus*); by a papal bull of 11 October 1521, Henry was awarded the title *Fidei Defensor* (Defender of the Faith), confirmed as a hereditary title by the English parliament in 1543.

This edition of Henry's text includes the address to the Pope of John Clerk, royal representative in Rome, and related documents. It was intended for an international readership. Pynson's use of a Roman fount and Renaissance ornament aimed to match other works of humanist learning published in continental Europe. The frontispiece, a copy of an image by Holbein the Younger, first used in 1516 by the great humanist publisher Froben in Basel, depicted the story of Mucius Scaevola, a Roman who infiltrated the camp of the Etruscan king Porsenna, then besieging the Republican government in Rome. Mucius killed the king's secretary by mistake, rather than the king, and when threatened with torture, burned his own right hand to show his defiance of pain. The story evidenced classical learning, but contained ambiguous political messages not totally in accord with Henry's defence of orthodoxy. RW

PROV. Royal Collection.

LIT. McKerrow and Ferguson 1932, nos 8, 11; Vian 1962; Scarisbrick 1968, pp.110–17; STC, no. 13083; Gwyn 1990, pp.481–5; Müller 1997, pp.33, 241.

355 *The Byble in Englyshe*

Printed by Richard Grafton and Edward Whitchurch, London, 1540

Vellum, vol. I of III, ff.124; h. 43 cm, w. 30 cm

British Library, London (C.18.d.10)

The title-page of the 'Great Bible', first published in 1539, contained a major statement of royal authority, one that was clearly Protestant: the king in imperial majesty, as the agent of God, distributes the Holy Scriptures to the clergy and laity, the Archbishop of Canterbury and the Chancellor representing

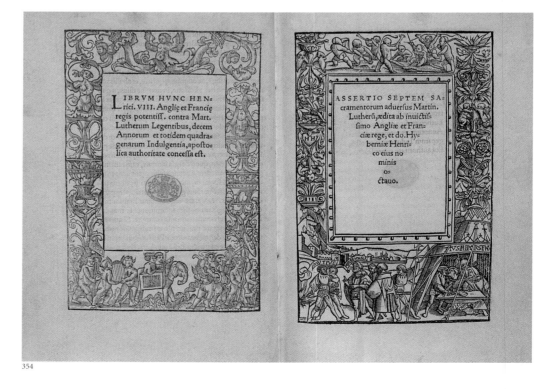

354

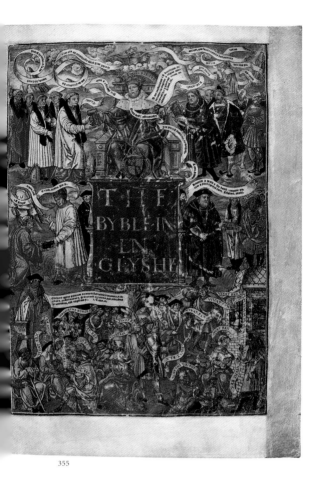

355

ecclesiastical and civil government; between a preacher and a prison, the populace cry '*Vivat Rex*' and '*God save the kinge*'. The title-page of this copy was illuminated for Henry VIII himself, probably in 1542.

In the mid-1530s Thomas Cromwell encouraged the king to support a Protestant translation of the Bible into English. In 1538 he prevailed on Henry VIII to order that every church have a Bible in English, and hastened what became the first official Bible of the Anglican Church. Printing began in Paris (by François Regnault) in 1539, but was completed in London. The title-page was probably designed for Archbishop Cranmer and Chancellor Cromwell by Lucas Horenbout (the illumination attributed to him in the *Valor Ecclesiasticus*, PRO E.344/22, has similar design elements) and engraved in Paris. The title-page had the arms of both Cranmer and Cromwell, those of the latter being excised from the woodcut for editions printed after his execution on 28 July 1540.

In April 1541 the London businessman Anthony Marler obtained the patent for printing bibles and the renewal of the directive that every church should have one. This coloured copy was probably offered to Henry by way of thanks.   RW

PROV. Presented by Anthony Marler of London, Haberdasher, to Henry VIII, 1542.

LIT. McKerrow and Ferguson 1932, no. 45; Herbert 1968, pp.25–30; STC, no. 2070; Strong and Murrell 1983, p.43; King 1989, pp.70–74; String 1996; Hellinga and Trapp 1999, pp.592–4.

356 Head of God the Father

Late 15th century

Polychromed limestone; h. 37.4 cm, w. 28.7 cm, d. 16.2 cm

Winchester Cathedral (276)

This head was discovered in rubble infill during work in the north transept of Winchester Cathedral in 1885. Wearing a papal triple tiara decorated with ornamental ribbons, the head is that of an elderly bearded man, with lined cheeks and brow and with pronounced eyebrows and heavily lidded eyes. Almost certainly it formed part of an image of the Holy Trinity, with God the Father holding the body of the dead Christ: this version of the Trinity occurs on the Continent from the early fifteenth century (cat. nos 343, 347). On much the same scale as the Virgin and Child (cat. no. 235), it too may have been an independent image and may not have belonged to the Cathedral Great Screen (cat. no. 233).

The quality of this and the other exhibited Winchester sculptures gives an indication of the catastrophic effect of the Dissolution of the monasteries and later of the Reformation on English medieval religious art. The destruction of the Winchester Cathedral images took place after 21 September 1538, when Thomas Cromwell's commissioners came to demolish the shrine of St Swithun. The screen and high altar were then stripped of all precious ornament and the imagery removed at the same time or shortly afterwards. The figures suffered a variety of fates: most were sawn up and reused as building blocks, some were used as hard core, and others – especially the heads of the large figures – are thought to have been buried under the floor in the area behind the screen. Only in the nineteenth century were they gradually rediscovered, as a result of repairs or reconstruction work in the cathedral or close, and, with all the other sculptural fragments found in and around the cathedral, brought together as objects of curiosity.   JH

LIT. Hardacre 1989, cat. no. 32; Lindley 1989 and 1993a; Lindley 1993b, p.113, fig. 9.18.

356

357 The Risen Christ

*c.*1500, overpainted *c.*1540–53

Oak, painted; h. 81 cm, w. 24.5 cm

The Priory church of St Mary and the Holy Cross, Binham, Norfolk

This fragmentary panel carries two phases of painting; on the lower, earlier level an image of the glorious risen Christ; and over this nine lines of text in large black Gothic characters.

357

Christ is shown standing full-length, more or less frontally, his head gently inclined to one side, against a red ground. He holds a tall-shafted cross and wears a golden cape, which falls down to reveal his body. He displays his wounds, which shed profuse patterned streams of blood.

The panel comes from the chancel- or rood-screen, which divided the part of the church reserved for the laity from the sanctuary in the old nave of the Benedictine priory church at Binham. Four bays of the parapet that formed the base of the southern section of the wooden screen survive, painted with figures of saints, four to each bay, now visible only in part

through the flaking paint of the superimposed texts. The panel with Christ may be the only surviving fragment from the northern half. The overlying inscription, of which only the ends of lines are preserved, shows that this figure was at the extreme right of a bay of four. As he gestures to the left, he may originally have formed a pair with another figure, possibly Mary Magdalene meeting her risen lord in the Garden, who greets her with the words *'Noli me tangere'*. The five wounds of Christ, more commonly displayed in the image of the dead Christ upright in his tomb (the Man of Sorrows), were a popular focus of veneration, of compunctive meditation and prayer, in the late Middle Ages.

Traces of an original dedicatory inscription can be made out on the upper rail of the parapet, in black characters overwritten in red. The initial words seem to read *'Orate pro bono fratu […] et […]'*, which suggests that the screen may have been a bequest of two of the monks – brothers – of the community at Binham. The presence of Henry VI among the saints on the screen means that it cannot have been painted before 1471, the date of Henry's death.

Binham Priory was suppressed in 1539. Subsequently, the images on this screen were obliterated, painted over with texts in the English of Cranmer's Great Bible of 1539 (cat. no. 355), written in black characters on a white ground. The text painted over the panel with Christ is from I Timothy 6, 10–12: '[For coveteousnes of money is the] roote of all [evyll …]'   JM

LIT. James 1930, p.171; Duffy 1992, pp.238–48; Duffy 1997, p.160, pl. 8.9; Duffy n.d.

358 Archbishop Parker's ewer and basin

London, 1545–6 (maker's mark: a queen's head)

Silver-gilt and enamel; h. of ewer 22 cm; diam. of basin 45.8 cm

Corpus Christi College, Cambridge

The ewer is of octagonal form, with faceted spout and angular handle; it is stamped around the foot with foliage and chased on alternate panels of the body with Moresque ornament. The circular basin is similarly chased around the rim and central boss. The basin and the cover of the ewer are both applied with an enamelled coat of arms within an inscription dated 1570.

The Latin inscription on the reverse of the basin records its gift by Archbishop Matthew Parker (1504–75) to the college in 1570. Parker was admitted to Corpus as an undergraduate in 1521, became a fellow in 1527 and was elected Master of the college

358a

in 1544. In 1559 he was appointed Archbishop of Canterbury by Elizabeth I and under his doctrinally moderate and efficient leadership the foundations of the reformed Anglican Church were laid. As archbishop, he was to become the greatest benefactor of the college, leaving not only his library but a substantial group of plate, of which this ewer and basin are the most imposing. The set could have been commissioned by Parker to mark his election as Master, but could equally have been acquired at a later date. Certainly the enamelled coats of arms replace whatever

was there originally and were clearly added at the time of the gift to reinforce the identity of its donor.

The form and ornament of the ewer and basin represent a transitional phase in English silver and reflect continental influence. The swirling lobes at the centre of the basin still have a Gothic feel, but the naturalistic leaves around them, the Moresque foliage on the rim and the stamped dentils at the edge are all features of current Renaissance style. These were reaching England through engraved books of ornament, such as Hans Brosamer's *Neu Kunstbüchlein*, pub-

lished in Frankfurt in around 1545 (see also cat. no. 13). The design of the ewer has a strong affinity with contemporary Antwerp silver and it is quite possible that the maker, whose name is not known, was one of the many Flemish goldsmiths working in London at the time.　　　　　　　　　　　　　　　TS

LIT. Foster and Atkinson 1896, p.14, pl. XIII; Jones 1910, p.42, pl. XLIX; Jackson 1911, pp.574–5; Crighton 1975, p.32; Oman 1978, p.33; Schroder 1988, pp.29–30; Glanville 1990, p.62; Ellory, Clifford and Rogers 1997, pp.4–11 (H. Clifford).

358b

359 *Angliae figura*

*c.*1534–46

Ink and colours on vellum; h. 63.5 cm, w. 42 cm

British Library, London (Cotton MS Augustus I.i.9)

The ultimate source for the depiction of England and Wales on this map – particularly the unindented west coast of Wales – was a map of about 1290 that also provided the basis for the Gough Map of about 1360, now in the Bodleian Library. There are, however, significant additions. The inclusion of Ireland (albeit like the egg it was then supposed to resemble) and the improved outline of Scotland on a map of 'England' reflect the expansionist policies of Henry VIII, though Scotland and Ireland are differentiated from England and Wales by yellow outlines. The content also reflects the new Renaissance spirit. It is the earli-est surviving map of Britain to be graduated for lati-tude and longitude (apparently from the Azores), to improve on the incorrect Ptolemaic outline for Scot-land and to be drawn on a projection, that devised for Ptolemaic maps in the late fifteenth century by Nicolaus Donus Germanus. It has many new English place-names, which are generally well fixed. A link with the south German mathematician and instru-ment-maker, Nicolaus Kratzer, Henry VIII's court astronomer, who had written to Albrecht Dürer of creating an improved Ptolemaic map of England in 1524, cannot be excluded.

The map may date from the late 1530s since it shows no sign of the improved Welsh and Scottish outlines known at court after 1540 and it still names shrines like Walsingham.

Many of the maps collected by Sir Robert Cotton can be traced back to Henry VIII. The Holbein-influ-enced decorative cartouche with its arched, imperial crown, the elegance of execution and the scientific vocabulary that would have appealed to the king strengthen the chances that this map was probably one of the 'Mappe[s] of England' that are recorded as hanging in the galleries of several of Henry's palaces. The naming of 'ha*mp*ton corte', its first-known men-tion on any map, might even suggest the specific palace.   PB

PROV. [Hampton Court; William Cecil, Lord Burghley; Robert Cecil, Earl of Salisbury, d. 1616?]; Sir Robert Cotton (1571–1631); British Museum.

LIT. Crone 1961, pp.8, 20–22, pl. 12; Starkey 1991, p.151, no. XI.15; Barber 1998, pp.45, 46, 49, 50.

SELECT GLOSSARY

ACANTHUS: a Classical, Byzantine and Romanesque carved ornament based directly or indirectly on the leaves of the acanthus plant.

ALL'ANTICA: in the manner of Classical prototypes.

ALMAIN: one of a series of rivets or short pieces of metal sliding in slot-holes formed in the overlapping plates of armour, so that the plates yielded to the movement of the body.

AMICE: the neckerchief of a priest's vestments, embroidered with a cross.

ANTIPHONAL/ANTIPHONER/ANTIPHONARY: a service book containing all the antiphons, collects, etc. – that is, all that is said or sung in the choir, except the lessons.

ANTIQUE: pertaining to Classical Antiquity or based on prototypes of that period.

ARABESQUE: Antique-style surface decoration incorporating scrolling foliage and animal, human or architectural motifs.

ARMET: a helmet used in the fourteenth, fifteenth and sixteenth centuries.

ASPERGILLUM: a rod having a long handle with a brush or perforated globe at the end for sprinkling holy water at the asperges and blessings.

BACINET/BASINET: a form of helmet introduced in the thirteenth century, but most widely used in the fourteenth and fifteenth centuries; at first small and hemispherical, it was subsequently given a high conical form.

BANDEROL: a little banner.

BARD: the trappings of a horse.

BEVOR: a chin defence, usually of plate.

BLACK-LETTER (TEXTURA): a form of Gothic lettering commonly used from the fourteenth century; its name derives from its having been used by the earliest Gothic painters. Its main characteristic is angularity and verticality of form.

BORDURE: a narrow band around the edge of a shield of arms.

BREVIARY: a book containing all the offices for the daily hours of the public liturgy of the Church.

BURSE: a flat wallet used to hold the corporass.

CANTLE: the protuberant part behind the saddle.

CAPARISON: a cloth or covering, more or less ornamented, laid over the saddle of a horse.

CARTOON: a preparatory full-scale design, often for stained glass or tapestry.

CASCABEL: a little bell, a button or knob at the end of a cannon; the rear part of a cannon; the part that is behind the base ring and includes the base and knob.

CAVETTO: a cornice or horizontal moulding of concave profile.

CHANTRY CHAPEL: a chapel where Masses were celebrated for the soul of the founder. (The term 'chantry' denotes the endowment supporting the celebrant priests, but is commonly applied to the chapel.)

CHASUBLE: a sleeveless vestment worn by a priest during the Mass.

CHRISMATORY: a utensil for holding chrism, a mixture of olive oil and balsam used in the sacraments.

CLASSICISM: a style based on Classical precedents.

CLEARSTOREY/CLERESTORY: ranges of windows forming the uppermost storey of the central vessel of a church.

CONOID: in Gothic vaults, a configuration of ribs and cells approximating in form to an inverted cone or part-cone.

COPE: a cloak-like vestment worn by a priest in various church ceremonies.

CORBEL: a projecting bracket supporting a statue or architectural member.

CORPORASS/CORPORAL: cloth used in the celebration of the Mass.

COWTER: a plate elbow-defence.

CRINET: a very fine, hair-like feather.

CRUPPER: a covering for the rear of a horse.

DALMATIC: a shin-length tunic worn by deacons assisting the priest at Mass.

DAMASCENE: a watered pattern on steel, mainly on sword blades, originating in Damascus, but adopted elsewhere.

DECORATED: the phase of English Gothic architecture lasting from c.1290 to c.1360.

DENTIL: a small rectangular block, of which a series is arranged like teeth under a cornice.

DIAPER: all-over surface decoration composed of small repeated patterns, either carved in relief or painted, or both.

DIPTYCH: two hinged tablets of equal size; often an altarpiece.

DONJON: the principal tower or keep of a castle, usually containing residential quarters for the lord.

DOSSAL: a hanging behind a seat or altar.

EARLY ENGLISH: the phase of English Gothic architecture lasting from c.1190 to c.1250.

ÉMAIL EN RONDE-BOSSE: a technique of enamelling the irregular surface of figures, or of objects, in the round or in very high relief. These small-scale sculptural compositions were invariably of gold or silver, whose surface was roughened to hold the enamel coating in place.

FALCHION: a sword with a broad, curved, convex-edged blade.

FAN VAULT: a vault incorporating (usually) regular conoids whose surfaces are decorated with blind tracery arranged in radiating panels as in Rayonnant rose windows. Between the horizontal bounding ribs at the top of the conoids is a spandrel panel, also decorated with blind tracery.

FIRE-BLUING: the process of heating iron and other metals in the fire until they assume a blue colour.

FLAMBOYANT: the final phase of French Gothic architecture, lasting from c.1390 to 1540, named after the flame-like forms of the curvilinear window tracery characteristic of this period.

FLEURON: a carved floral motif, square or diamond-shaped in format; often used to decorate hollow mouldings.

FLORIATED: decorated with floral ornament.

FORTE: the strong portion of a sword-blade or rapier.

FULLER: one whose occupation is to full (make denser) cloth in a mill.

GABION: a large wickerwork basket of cylindrical form, but without a bottom, filled with earth and serving to shelter men from an enemy's fire; especially used in sieges.

GADROON: a convex curve or inverted fluting, usually applied as an edging.

GAUFFERED: crimped or fluted, especially in cloth.

GRADUAL: a book of hymns and prayers.

GRISAILLE: panels or windows of predominantly white glass leaded or painted to form geometric or foliage designs; monochromatic painting in grey or beige.

GROTESQUE: a monstrous or deformed creature, sometimes in human form.

GUIGE: a strap for suspending a shield round the neck.

HAMMERBEAM ROOF: a roof incorporating hammerbeams, short horizontal beams which project inwards from the wall-head and function as brackets, carrying on their inner extremities vertical posts ('hammer posts'), connected to collars by means of curved, arch-like braces.

HISTORIATED: a form, often an initial letter, enclosing a figural representation.

INTAGLIO: an engraved stone or gem, the opposite of cameo.

INTERNATIONAL GOTHIC: the style or series of styles employed in painting and sculpture throughout Europe in the years c.1370–1430.

JESSE, TREE OF: an image, taken from Isaiah XI, showing the ancestors of Christ in the form of a family tree ascending from Jesse.

KNOP: a decorative knob, often spherical, usually a feature of the stem of (for example) candlesticks, chalices, croziers and cups.

LADY CHAPEL: a chapel dedicated to the Virgin Mary, usually sited at the east end of a church.

LAPPET: a flap on a headdress, especially on a bishop's mitre.

LATE GOTHIC: a general term (pan-European in scope) for the last phase of Gothic, in English architecture extending from c.1400 to c.1540.

LATTEN: copper alloy resembling modern brass, but usually containing tin as well as zinc.

LECTIONARY: a book for use in public worship, containing portions of Scripture to be read on particular days.

LENTICULAR: resembling a lentil in size or form.

LIERNE VAULT: a vault incorporating liernes, short ribs unconnected to any of the springings and usually arranged so as to form decorative patterning on the upper parts of the vault surfaces.

'LIGHTS' (E.G. PLOUGH-LIGHTS/MAIDEN-LIGHTS): candles or tapers in churches, set before images.

LINENFOLD: a carved motif resembling a piece of cloth arranged in shallow parallel folds; used to decorate wooden panelling.

LOGGIA: a longitudinal space with an open arcade on one side.

LOLLARDY: the principles or doctrines of the Lollards, the followers of John Wyclif.

MACHICOLATION(S): a projecting parapet on a castle wall or tower, with openings in the floor between the supporting corbels, through which missiles could be dropped.

MANIPLE: a Mass vestment comprising a strip of cloth suspended from a priest's left arm.

MANUAL: a book containing the forms prescribed for a priest to administer the sacrament.

MAZER: a drinking vessel made of wood, often burr maple, the name deriving from the word *maserle* (the maple tree).

MINUSCULE: a minute sort of letter or character used in manuscripts.

MISERICORD: from the Latin *misericordia* (pity); a hinged seat, often carved on the underside, that gives support to standing clergy when tipped up.

MISSAL: a service book, containing Masses for feast-days and saints' days.

MORSE: a clasp used to fasten a cope, the ceremonial cape worn by a priest or bishop.

MULLION: a slender upright of masonry or wood dividing windows into lights.

MURREY: a dark-red colour, derived from mulberry.

NIMBED: with a halo or nimbus.

NOCK: a notch, specifically the notch of an arrow or that of the bow where the string is fastened.

OGEE ARCH: an arch composed of two double-curved lines (ogees) meeting at the apex.

ORIEL: a bay window projecting from an upper storey.

ORPHREY: a band of gold embroidery decorating chasubles, copes, etc.; according to its shape it may be called a cross-orphrey or a pillar-orphrey.

PATEN: a shallow dish on which the bread and, later, the consecrated host is placed during the Mass; usually made of gold or silver, it was invariably made to match a chalice.

PATTÉE: in heraldry, spreading out at the extremity.

PAULDRON: an armoured shoulder defence.

PAX: a tablet, often of ivory or precious metal, decorated with a sacred image, for transferring the Kiss of Peace from the celebrant at Mass to the clergy and laity.

PERPENDICULAR: the phase of English Gothic architecture lasting from *c*.1330 to *c*.1550.

PEYTRAL: the breastplate of a horse.

PIETÀ: an image of the Virgin lamenting over the body of the dead Christ lying across her knees.

POLEYN: armour for the knee, usually of plate.

POLYCHROME/POLYCHROMY: coloured surface decoration, especially of sculpture.

POMMEL: the knob at the top of the hilt of a sword, designed to counterbalance the blade.

POPPY HEAD: a generic term applied to the groups of foliage or other ornaments placed on the summits of bench ends, desks and other woodwork in ecclesiastical buildings of the Middle Ages.

POUNCING: hammering, usually on silver, to give a powdered effect.

PSALTER: a service book containing the psalms, a selection of prayers and other items, like a calendar; a popular book for private devotion, often lavishly decorated.

PULPITUM: a screen of solid construction, normally stone, at the west end of a choir.

PURLIN: a longitudinal timber giving support to the common rafters of a roof, and placed parallel to the wall plate and ridge beam some way up the slope of a roof.

PUTTO: a small child, cherub.

PYX: a small vessel in which the sacrament is reserved for later use; usually a round ivory or metal box.

QUARRY: a diamond- or square-shaped piece of window glass.

QUATREFOIL: a four-lobed shape formed by part circles, sometimes enclosed within a full circle.

QUILLON: a sixteenth-century French term, commonly used by modern writers on swords, for the arms of the cross.

RAGULY: in heraldry, a term used of any charge or ordinary that is jagged or notched in an irregular manner.

RAYONNANT: the phase of French Gothic architecture lasting from *c*.1230 to *c*.1350, named after the radiating arrangement of lights in rose windows; its main characteristics are the extreme thinness of

all members and the maximum extension of tracery and glazing.

REBUS: a representation of words, especially a name, by the use of figures or pictures instead of words.

REFORMATION: the religious revolution of the sixteenth century, begun by Luther and others *c*.1517, and which divided the western church into the two sections known as Roman Catholic and Protestant.

RELIQUARY: a container for a relic, usually made of precious materials.

REREDOS: a high screen, often with carved decoration, behind and above an altar.

RESPOND: a group of shafts forming part of a system of supports and receiving some major arched feature such as the ribs of a vault.

RETABLE: a carved or painted panel placed above the back of an altar.

ROOD: a cross or crucifix, especially one placed over the screen at the entrance to the choir.

SABATON: armour for the foot, usually of plate.

SALLET: a light helmet, with a projection behind; sallets were made of various forms, with and without a visor.

SALTIRE: a heraldic term for a diagonal cross.

SARUM USE: the calendar, liturgical texts and practices codified by Bishop Richard Poore (1217–28) of Salisbury (New Sarum); used increasingly outside the Province of York (see also YORK USE). Indicative of an English provenance.

SHAFFRON: armour for a horse's head.

SKIPPET: a small cylindrical turned box with a lid or cover for keeping records or seals.

SLIPWARE: lead-glazed earthenware decorated with slip (a mixture of fine clay and water) in relief, before firing.

SPANDREL: the approximately triangular area between two arches, or between an arch and an adjacent wall or vertical moulding.

STRAPWORK: ornament consisting of strap-like interlaced bands.

STRING-COURSE: a projecting moulding running horizontally along the face of a wall and usually dividing one register from another.

STUCCO DURO: hard plaster.

TANG: a projecting part of an object, which is inserted into and so secured to another.

TASSET: armour for the thighs.

TEXTURA: see BLACK-LETTER.

TIE-BEAM ROOF: a roof incorporating transverse horizontal timbers (tie-beams) whose outer ends are joined to the lower ends of rafters.

TIERCERON VAULT: a vault incorporating tiercerons, ribs linking one of the springings to the longitudinal or lateral ridge.

TONDO: a painted or sculpted roundel.

TORSE: in heraldry, a wreath or twisted scroll.

TRACERY: openwork geometrically based patterns of cut stone, principally used in the arched heads of Gothic windows. Blind tracery is unglazed tracery incorporated into a solid masonry surface.

TRACERY LIGHT: a stained-glass panel inserted in tracery.

TRANSLATION: the solemn moving of a saint's remains from one place to another, usually followed by the insertion of the relics into a shrine.

TREFOIL: a three-lobed shape.

TRESSURE: in heraldry, a twisted or plaited border around the shield of arms, usually borne double, following the form of the escutcheon.

TRIFORIUM: in Rayonnant and some other phases of Gothic church architecture, a wall passage whose side next to the central vessel is formed by an open arcade. Normally placed between the clearstorey and the main arcade.

TRIPTYCH: like a diptych, but with three panels instead of two.

TRUNNION: a knob projecting on each side of a gun, mortar, etc., and serving to support it on the cheeks of the carriage.

TYMPANUM: the vertical field defined by the head of an arch.

VAMBRACE: plate armour for the arm.

VIDIMUS: a preliminary design drawing.

VOLUTE: a spiral scroll.

YELLOW STAIN: a technique developed in the early fourteenth century which colours white glass yellow, or blue glass green, by applying a solution of a silver compound to the exterior surface and firing it.

YORK USE: the calendar, liturgical texts and practices of the Province of York (see also SARUM USE).

BIBLIOGRAPHY

Agate, J., *Benches and Stalls in Suffolk Churches*, Ipswich, 1980.

Ainsworth, M. and Martens, M. P. J., *Petrus Christus: Renaissance Master of Bruges*, exh. cat., Metropolitan Museum of Art, New York, 1994.

Alexander, J. J. G., 'William Abell "lymnour" and 15th-century English illumination', in A. Rosenauer and G. Weber (eds), *Kunsthistorische Forschungen Otto Pächt zu seinem 70. Geburtstag*, Vienna, 1972, pp.166–72.

Alexander, J. J. G., 'Painting and manuscript illumination for royal patrons in the Later Middle Ages', in V. J. Scattergood and J. W. Sherborne (eds), *English Court Culture in the Later Middle Ages*, London, 1983, pp.141–62.

Alexander, J. J. G., 'The Pulpit with the Four Doctors at St James's, Castle Acre, Norfolk', in Rogers 1994, pp.198–206.

Alexander, J. and Binski, P. (eds), *Age of Chivalry: Art in Plantagenet England 1200–1400*, exh. cat., Royal Academy of Arts, London, 1987.

Alexander, J. and Crossley, P., *Medieval and Early Renaissance Treasures in the North West*, exh. cat., Whitworth Art Gallery, University of Manchester, 1976.

Alexander, J. J. G. and Temple, E., *Illuminated Manuscripts in Oxford College Libraries, the University Archives and the Taylor Institution*, Oxford, 1985.

Allan, J. and Timms, S., *Treasures of Ancient Devon*, Exeter, 1996.

Allison, K. J. (ed.), *The City of Kingston upon Hull* (Victoria County History, Yorkshire, East Riding, I), Oxford, 1969.

Allmand, C. T., *The Hundred Years War*, Cambridge, 1989.

Andersson, A., *Medieval Drinking Bowls of Silver found in Sweden*, Stockholm, 1983.

Anglo, S., *The Great Tournament Roll of Westminster*, 2 vols, Oxford, 1968.

Anglo, S., *Chivalry in the Renaissance*, Woodbridge, 1990.

Anglo, S., *Images of Tudor Kingship*, London, 1992.

Anglo, S., *The Martial Arts of Renaissance Europe*, New Haven and London, 2000.

Anstis, F., *The Register of the Most Noble Order of the Garter . . .* , 2 vols, London, 1723.

Archbold, W. A. J., 'Sir Thomas Lovell', *Dictionary of National Biography*, XII, Oxford, 1917 (reprinted 1973), pp.175–6.

Archibald, E. and Edwards, A. S. G. (eds), *A Companion to Malory*, Cambridge, 1996.

Archibald, M., 'Fishpool, Blidworth (Notts.)

1966 Hoard: Interim Report', *Numismatic Chronicle*, VII, 1967, pp.133–46.

Armstrong, C. A. J., 'The piety of Cicely, Duchess of York: a study in late medieval culture', in D. Woodruff (ed.), *For Hilaire Belloc: Essays in honour of his 72nd birthday*, London, 1942, pp.73–94.

Armstrong, E., 'English Purchases of Printed Books from the Continent 1465–1526', *English Historical Review*, XCIV, 1979, pp.268–90.

Armstrong, M. J., *History and Antiquities of the County of Norfolk*, vol. X, Norwich, 1781.

Arnould, A. and Massing, J.-M. (eds), *Splendours of Flanders, Late Medieval Art in Cambridge Collections*, exh. cat., Fitzwilliam Museum, Cambridge, 1993.

Asaert, G., *Documenten voor de Geschiedenis van de Antwerpse scheepvart voornamelijk de Engelandvaart (1404–1485)*, Collectanea Maritima III, Wetenschappelijk comité voor maritieme geschiedenis, Koninklijke Academie voor Wetenschappen, Letteren en Schone Kunsten van België, Brussels, 1985.

Ashbee, A., 'Groomed for service: musicians in the Privy Chamber at the English court, c.1495–1558', *Early Music*, XXV, 1997, pp.185–97.

Ashley, K. and Sheingorn, P. (eds), *Interpreting Cultural Symbols: Saint Anne in Late Medieval Society*, Athens (Georgia) and London, 1990.

Ashton, L., 'The so-called Gloves of William of Wykeham', *The Burlington Magazine*, LIV, 1929, pp.34–9.

Astle, T. (ed.), *The Will of King Henry VII*, London, 1775.

Aston, M., 'Huizinga's Harvest: England and the Waning of the Middle Ages', *Medievalia et Humanistica*, new ser., IX, 1979, pp.1–24 (reprinted in Aston 1993, pp.133–54).

Aston, M., *England's Iconoclasts*, Oxford, 1988.

Aston, M., *Faith and Fire: Popular and Unpopular Religion 1350–1600*, London, 1993.

Atkinson, C., *Mystic and Pilgrim. The Book and World of Margery Kempe*, Ithaca, 1983.

Atkinson, D. W., *The English Ars Moriendi*, New York, 1992.

Atkinson, T. D., *An Architectural History of the Benedictine Monastery of St Etheldreda at Ely*, Cambridge, 1933.

Atkinson, T. D. and Goodman, A. W., 'The Mortuary Chests', *Winchester Cathedral Record*, II, 1933, pp.11–14.

Attreed, L. (ed.), *York House Books, 1461–1490*, II, Stroud, 1991.

Auerbach, E., *Tudor Artists*, London, 1954.

Avril, F. and Reynaud, N., *Les manuscrits à peintures en France 1440–1520*, exh. cat., Bibliothèque nationale, Paris, 1993.

Avril, F. and Stirnemann, P., *Manuscrits enluminés d'origine insulaire, VIII–XX siècle*, Bibliothèque nationale, Paris, 1987.

Axton, M., 'Lord Morley's *Tryumphes of Petrarch*', in M. Axton and J. Carley (eds), *Triumphs of English, Henry Parker, Lord Morley, Translator to the Tudor Court*, London, 2000, pp.171–200.

Ayre, K., *Medieval English Figurative Roundels*, Corpus Vitrearum Medii Aevi Great Britain, Summary Catalogue 6, Oxford, 2002.

Babington, C. (ed.), *R. Pecock. The Repressor of Over Much Blaming of the Clergy*, 2 vols, Rolls Series, London, 1860.

Backhouse, J., 'A re-appraisal of the Bedford Hours', *British Library Journal*, VII, 1981, pp.47–69.

Backhouse, J., 'Founders of the Royal Library: Edward IV and Henry VII as collectors of illuminated manuscripts', in Williams 1987, pp.23–41.

Backhouse, J., *The Bedford Hours*, London, 1990.

Backhouse, J., 'Sir John Donne's Flemish Manuscripts', in Monks and Owen 1994, pp.48–57

Backhouse, J., 'Illuminated manuscripts associated with Henry VII and members of his immediate family', in Thompson 1995, pp.175–87.

Backhouse, J., *The Illuminated Page*, London, 1997.

Backhouse, J., *The Sherborne Missal*, London, 1999.

Backhouse, J., 'The Royal Library from Edward IV to Henry VIII', in Hellinga and Trapp 1999, pp.267–73.

Backhouse, J., 'The Lady Margaret Beaufort Hours at Alnwick Castle', in Mitchell and Moran 2000, pp.336–48.

Backhouse, J., 'Memorials and Manuscripts of a Yorkist Elite', in Richmond and Scarff 2001, pp.151–60.

Backhouse, J., 'A further illuminated devotional book for the use of Lady Margaret Beaufort', in B. J. Muir (ed.), *Reading Texts and Images: Essays on Medieval and Renaissance Art and Patronage in honour of Margaret M. Manion*, Exeter, 2002, pp.221–35.

Backhouse, J., 'The Lovel Lectionary: a Memorial Offering to Salisbury Cathedral', in J. Backhouse (ed.), *The English Medieval Cathedral: Papers in Honour of Pamela Tudor–Craig* (Proceedings of the 1998

Harlaxton Symposium), Harlaxton Medieval Studies, X, Donington, 2003, pp.112–25.

Backhouse, J. and Carley, J. P., 'Remembrances of Lady Margaret Beaufort: her Foundation Document and her Signatures', *Christ's College Magazine*, CCXXII, 1997, pp.14–17.

Badham, S., 'The Suffolk School of Brasses', *Transactions of the Monumental Brass Society*, XIII/1, 1980, pp.41–67.

Badham, S., 'Monumental Brasses: the development of the York workshops in the fourteenth and fifteenth centuries', in Wilson 1989, pp.165–85.

Badham, S. F., 'The Fens 1 Series: an early fifteenth-century group of monumental brasses and incised slabs', *Journal of the British Archaeological Association*, CXLII, 1989, pp.46–62.

Badham, S. F., 'London standardisation and provincial idiosyncrasy: the organisation and working practices of brass-engraving workshops in pre-Reformation England', *Church Monuments*, V, 1990, pp.3–25.

Badham, S. and Blatchley, J., 'The Bellfounder's Indent at Bury St Edmunds', *Proceedings of the Suffolk Institute of Archaeology and History*, XXXVI, 1988, pp.288–97.

Bain, J. (ed.), *Hamilton Papers*, 2 vols, Edinburgh, 1890–92.

Barber, G., 'The advent of gold tooling in English bookbinding and the intermediary role of Thomas Linacre', in D. Pearson (ed.), *For the Love of the Binding*, London, 2000, pp.53–65.

Barber, M., *Some Drawings of Ancient Embroidery*, London, 1880.

Barber, P., 'The Evesham World Map: A Late Medieval English view of God and the World', *Imago Mundi*, XLVII, 1995, pp.13–33.

Barber, P., 'The British Isles', in M. Watelet (ed.), *The Mercator Atlas of Europe*, Oregon, 1998, pp.43–77.

Barker, N. J., 'A Register of Writs and the Scales binder', *The Book Collector*, XXI, 1972, pp.227–44, 356–79.

Barnard, F. P., *Edward IV's French Expedition of 1475, the Leaders and their Badges*, Oxford, 1925.

Barnes, H. D., *A Fifteenth Century Armourer's Letter*, privately printed, n.d. [but 1932], and subsequently published in *Zeitschrift für historische Waffen- und Kostümkunde*, XIV, 1935–6, pp.65–6.

Barnum, P. H. (ed.), *Dives and Pauper*, Early English Text Society, original series, 275, 280, 1975–.

Barr, H. (ed.), *The Piers Plowman Tradition*, London, 1993.

Barrett, J. T., *Memorials of the Parochial Church, the Collegiate Chantry, and the Chapel of St Mary, commonly called Mortimer's Chapel in the Parish of Attleborough*, London, 1848.

Barron, C. M., 'Richard Whittington: the Man behind the Myth', in A. E. J. Hollaender and W. Kellaway (eds), *Studies in London History presented to Philip Edmund Jones*, London, 1969, pp.197–248.

Barron, C. M., *The Medieval Guildhall of London*, London, 1974.

Barron, C. M., 'Johanna Hill (d. 1441) and Johanna Sturdy (d. *c*.1460), bell founders', in C. M. Barron and A. F. Sutton (eds), *Medieval London Widows*, London and Rio Grande, 1994, pp.99–112.

Barron, C. and Erler, M., 'The making of Syon Abbey's altar table of Our Lady *c*.1490–96', in Mitchell and Moran 2000, pp.318–35.

Barron, C. and Saul, N. (eds), *England and the Low Countries in the Late Middle Ages*, Stroud, 1995.

Baumstark, R. (ed.), *Das Goldene Roessl. Ein Meisterwerk der Pariser Hofkunst um 1400*, exh. cat., Bayerisches Nationalmuseum, Munich, 1995.

Baurmeister, U., 'Das Blockbuch – Vorläufer oder Konkurrent des mit bewegliched Lettern gedruckten Buchs?', in P. Rück, *Rationalisierung des Buchherstellung im Mittelalter und in der frühen Neuzeit*, Marburg an der Lahn, 1994, pp.147–64.

Bayliss, J., 'Richard Parker "The Alablasterman"', *Church Monuments*, V, 1990, pp.39–56.

Bayliss, J., 'An indenture for two alabaster effigies', *Church Monuments*, XVI, 2001, pp.22–9.

Bayne-Powell, R., *Catalogue of Portrait Miniatures in the Fitzwilliam Museum*, Cambridge, 1985.

Beadle, R., 'Prolegomena to a literary geography of late medieval Norfolk', in F. Riddy (ed.), *Regionalism in Late Medieval Manuscripts and Texts*, Cambridge, 1991, pp.89–108.

Beard, C. R., 'The Emperor Maximilian's Garter', *The Connoisseur*, CXXXI, 1953, pp.108–9.

Bearman, F., 'The origins and significance of two late-medieval textile chemise bookbindings in the Walters Art Gallery', *Journal of the Walters Art Gallery (Essays in honor of Lilian M. C. Randall)*, LIV, 1996, pp.163–87.

Beaty, N. L., *The Craft of Dying: a study in the literary tradition of the Ars Moriendi in England*, New Haven, 1970.

Beaven, A. B., *The Aldermen of the City of London*, 2 vols, London, 1908–13.

Bedford, R. P., 'An English set of the twelve Apostles in alabaster', *The Burlington Magazine*, XLII, 1923, pp.130–34.

Begent, P. J. and Chesshyre, H., *The Most Noble Order of the Garter, 650 Years*, London, 1999.

Behrens, G. A., 'Conservation work on the Cartmel Fell figure of Christ', *Transactions of the Cumberland and Westmorland Antiquarian and Archaeological Society*, LXXXII, 1982, pp.125–34.

Bell, P. (ed.), *Bedfordshire Wills 1484–1533*, Bedfordshire Historical Record Society, LXXVI, 1997.

Bell, R., 'The Royal Visit to Acton Court in 1535', in Starkey 1991, pp.120–23.

Benham, H., *Latin Church Music in England 1460–1575*, London, 1977.

Benham, W. G., 'Ancient legends connected with the Arms of Colchester', *The Essex Review*, IX, 1900, pp.202–20.

Benham, W. G., 'The town charters and other borough records of Colchester', *Archaeological Journal*, LXIV, 1907, pp.203–9.

Bennett, A. G., *Five Centuries of Tapestries from the Fine Arts Museums of San Francisco*, rev. edn, San Francisco, 1992.

Benson, L. D. (gen. ed.), *The Riverside Chaucer, based on the works of Geoffrey Chaucer, edited by F. N. Robinson*, 3rd edn, Oxford, 1987.

Bent, M., 'Sources of the Old Hall Music', *Proceedings of the Royal Musical Association*, XCIV, 1967–8, pp.19–35.

Bent, M., *Dunstaple*, London, 1981.

Bent, M., 'The Progeny of Old Hall: More Leaves from a Royal English Choirbook', in L. A. Dittmer (ed.), *Gordon Athol Anderson (1929–1981) in memoriam*, Henryville, PA, 1984, pp.1–54.

Bent, M. and I., 'Dufay, Dunstable, Plummer – A New Source', *Journal of the American Musicological Society*, XXII, 1969, pp.394–424.

Beresford, M. and Hurst, J. G., *Wharram Percy. Deserted Medieval Village*, London and New York, 1990.

Bergen, H. (ed.), *Lydgate's Troy Book. A.D. 1412–20*, 4 vols, Early English Text Society, XCVII, CIII, CVI, CXXVI, London, 1906–35.

Berghman, A., 'An Armorial Bishop's Cope from the Fifteenth Century', *The Coat of Arms*, IV/30, 1957, pp.235–7.

Biddle, M., 'Nicholas Bellin of Modena', *Journal of the British Archaeological Association*, 3rd series, XXIX, 1966, pp.106–21.

Biddle, M., 'The Stuccoes of Nonsuch', *The Burlington Magazine*, CXXVI, 1984, pp.411–16.

Biddle, M. (ed.), *Object and economy in medieval Winchester*, 2 vols, Oxford, 1990.

Biddle, M., 'Early Renaissance at Winchester', in Crook 1993a, pp.257–304.

Biddle, M., 'Nonsuch Palace', in J. Turner (ed.), *The Dictionary of Art*, London, 1996, XXIII, pp.197–8.

Bindoff, S., *The History of Parliament. The Commons 1509–1558*, 3 vols, London, 1982.

Binski, P., *Medieval Death: Ritual and Representation*, London, 1996.

Birch, W. de Gray, *Catalogue of Seals in the British Museum*, 6 vols, London, 1887–92.

Birmingham 1936: *Catalogue of an Heraldic Exhibition . . .*, exh. cat., City Museum & Art Gallery, Birmingham, 1936.

Birmingham 1983: *Handbook of the Barber Institute of Fine Arts, with a list of the collection*, 2nd edn, Birmingham, 1983.

Black, W. H., *History and Antiquities of the Worshipful Company of Leathersellers of the City of London*, London, 1871.

Blackmore, H. L., *The Armouries of the Tower of London, I, Ordnance*, London, 1976.

Blair, C., *European Armour, circa 1066 to circa 1700*, London, 1958.

Blair, C., *European and American Arms, c.1100–1850*, London, 1962.

Blair, C., 'The Emperor Maximilian's gift of armour to King Henry VIII and the silvered and engraved armour at the Tower of London', *Archaeologia*, XCIX, 1965, pp.1–52.

Blair, C., 'A drawing of an English medieval royal gold cup', *The Burlington Magazine*, CXXI, 1979, pp.370–73.

Blair, C., 'Ci-git Richard Beauchamp', *Connaissance des Arts*, 333, 1979, pp.72–9.

Blair, C., *The Goldsmith and the Grape: Silver in the Service of Wine*, exh. cat., Goldsmiths' Hall, London, 1983.

Blair, C., 'The word "Baselard"', *Journal of the Arms and Armour Society*, XI, 1983–5, pp.193–206.

Blair, C., 'Sir Giles Capel's Funerary Instructions, 1556', *The Church Monuments Society Newsletter*, II/2, Winter 1987, pp.14–15.

Blair, C., 'King Henry VIII's tonlet armour', *Journal of the Arms and Armour Society*, XV/2, September 1995, pp.85–108.

Blair, C., 'The Lullingstone Helm', *The Antiquaries Journal*, LXXVIII, 1998, pp.289–305.

Blair, C. and Blair, J., 'Copper Alloys', in Blair and Ramsay 1991, pp.81–106.

Blair, C. and Delamer, I., 'The Dublin Civic Swords', *Proceedings of the Royal Irish Academy*, LXXXVIIIc, 1988, pp.5–142.

Blair, J., 'English monumental brasses before 1350: types, patterns and workshops', in Coales 1987, pp.133–74.

Blair, J. and Ramsay, N. (eds), *English Medieval Industries, Craftsmen, Techniques, Products*, London, 1991.

Blake, E. O. (ed.), *Liber Eliensis*, Camden Society, 3rd series, XCII, 1962.

Blake, H., 'De Nomine Jhesu: an Italian export ware and the origin of Renaissance maiolica pottery-making in the Low Countries', in Gaimster 1999, pp.23–56.

Blake, H., Egan, G., Hurst, J. and New, E., 'The cult of the holy name of Jesus and the Reformation: from popular devotion to resistance and revival', in D. R. M. Gaimster and R. Gilchrist (eds), *Archaeology of the Reformation*, forthcoming.

Blake, N., *Caxton's own prose*, London, 1973.

Blanchett, C., 'The floor tiles at The Vyne, Hampshire, England', *Glazed Expressions*, 41, 2000, pp.1–32.

Blaylock, S. R., 'Bell and cauldron founding in Exeter', *Historical Metallurgy*, XXX, 1996, pp.72–82.

Blockmans, W. and Prevenier, W., *The Promised Lands: the Low Countries under Burgundian Rule, 1369–1530*, trans. and ed. by E. Fackelman and E. Peters, Philadelphia, 1999.

Blomefield, F., *An Essay towards a Topographical History of the County of Norfolk . . .*, Lynn, 11 vols, 1739–75 (2nd edn, 1805–6).

Blore, T., *A History of the Manor and Manor-house of South Wingfield in Derbyshire*, London, 1793.

Blunt, C. E. and Whitton, C. A., 'The coinage of Edward IV and Henry VI restored', *British Numismatic Journal*, XXV, 1945–9, pp.4–59, 130–82, 291–339.

BM 1924: *A Guide to the Mediaeval Antiquities and Objects of Later Date in the Department of Mediaeval Antiquities*, British Museum, London, 1924.

BMC: *Catalogue of Books printed in the XVth Century now in the British Museum*, vols I–, London, 1908–.

Boldrick, S., Park, D., Williamson, P. et al., *Wonder: Painted Sculpture from Medieval England*, exh. cat., Henry Moore Institute, Leeds, 2002.

Bologna, G., *Tutte le dame del re. Ritratti di dame milanesi per Francesco I re di Francia*, Milan, 1989.

Bolton, J. L., *The Medieval English Economy, 1150–1500*, London, 1980.

Bond, F., *Screens and Galleries in English Churches*, Oxford, 1908.

Bond, F., *Dedications & Patron Saints of English Churches: Ecclesiastical symbolism, Saints and their emblems*, Oxford, 1914.

Bond, F. Bligh and Camm, F., *Rood Screens and Rood Lofts*, 2 vols, London, 1909.

Bond, F. Bligh and Radford, A. L. F., 'Devonshire screens and rood lofts', *Report and Transactions of the Devonshire Association*, XXXIV, 1902, pp.531–50.

Bonney, H. K., *Historical Notes on Fotheringhay*, Oundle, 1821.

Bonney, R. (ed.), *Economic Systems and State Finance*, Oxford, 1995.

Bonney, R. (ed.), *The Rise of the Fiscal State in Europe, c.1200–1815*, Oxford, 1999.

Boon, K. G., 'Two designs for windows by Dierick Vellert', *Master Drawings*, II, 1964, pp.153–6.

Borchgrave d'Altena, Comte J. de, 'Statuettes malinoises', *Bulletin des Musées royaux d'Art et d'Histoire*, XXXI, 1959, pp.2–98.

Borg, A., 'A Royal Axe', *Connoisseur*, CLXXXVIII, 1975, pp.296–301.

Bosanquet, E. F., *English Printed Almanacs and Prognostications. A Bibliographical History to the Year 1600*, Bibliographical Society, London, 1917.

Bossy, J., 'Blood and Baptism: kinship, community and Christianity', *Studies in Church History*, X, 1973, pp.129–43.

Boulton, D'A. J. D., *The Knights of the Crown*, Woodbridge, 1987.

Boustred, R. and Trace, K., *The Parish Church of St Ouen commonly known as St Andrew's Fingringhoe. A Guide for Visitors*, n.d.

Bowers, R., 'Some observations on the life and career of Lionel Power', *Proceedings of the Royal Musical Association*, CII, 1975–6, pp.103–27.

Bowers, R., 'To chorus from quartet: the performing resource for English church polyphony, c.1390–1559', in J. Morehen (ed.), *English Choral Practice*, Cambridge, 1995, pp.1–47.

Bowers, R., *English Church Polyphony: Singers and Sources from the 14th to the 17th Century*, Aldershot, 1999.

Bowman, S. G. E. and Stapleton, C. P., 'The All Souls Jewel: the enameller's art, deliberate or accidental tinting?', *Jewellery Studies*, VIII, 1998, pp.1–10.

Bradley, H., 'Lucia Visconti, Countess of Kent, d. 1424', in C. M. Barron and A. F. Sutton (eds), *Medieval London Widows*, London and Rio Grande, 1994, pp.77–84.

Bradner, L., 'Some unpublished poems by John Leland', *Publications of the Modern Language Association*, LXXI, 1956, pp.827–36.

Branca, V. (ed.), *Boccaccio visualizzato*, 3 vols, Turin, 1999.

Brandeis, A. (ed.), *Jacob's Well*, part 1, Early English Text Society, 115, 1900.

Brewer, J. S., Gairdner, J. and Brodie, R. H. (eds), *Letters and Papers, Foreign and Domestic, of the Reign of Henry VIII, 1509–47*, 21 vols and addenda, London, 1862–1932.

Brighton 1989: *Treasures from Sussex Churches*, exh. cat., Brighton Museum and Art Gallery, 1989.

Brighton, T., 'Art in the Cathedral from the Foundation to the Civil War', in M. Hobbs (ed.), *Chichester Cathedral: An Historical Survey*, Chichester, 1994, pp.69–84.

Brindley, D., *Richard Beauchamp: medieval England's greatest knight*, Stroud, 2001.

Brinkmann, B., *Die Flämische Buchmalerei am Ende des Burgunderreiches. Der Meister des Dresdener Gebetbuchs und die Miniaturisten seiner Zeit*, Turnhout, 1997.

Britnell, R. H., *The Commercialisation of English Society, 1000–1500*, Cambridge, 1993 (2nd edn, Manchester, 1996).

Britton, J., *The Architectural Antiquities of Great Britain*, 5 vols, London, 1807–20.

Britton, J., *Cathedral Antiquities: historical and descriptive accounts . . .* , 5 vols, London, 1836.

Brodrick, A. and Darrah, J., 'The fifteenth century polychromed limestone effigies of William Fitzalan, 9th Earl of Arundel, and his wife, Joan Nevill, in the Fitzalan Chapel, Arundel', *Church Monuments*, I/2, 1986, pp.65–94.

Brooke, G. C., *English Coins*, 3rd edn, London, 1950.

Brooke, X. and Crombie, D., *Henry VIII Revealed: The Legacy of Holbein's Portraits*, London, 2003.

Brooks, C., *The Gothic Revival*, London, 1999.

Brown, M., and McKendrick, S. (eds), *Illuminating the Book, Makers and Interpreters, Essays in Honour of Janet Backhouse*, London and Toronto, 1998.

Brown, R. (ed.), *Calendar of State Papers and Manuscripts relating to English affairs in the Archives and State Papers of Venice and other libraries of Northern Italy*, III, London, 1867.

Brown, R. Allen, *English Castles*, London, 1976.

Brown, S., *'Our Magnificent Fabrick'. An Architectural History of York Minster*, London, 2002.

Brown, S. and MacDonald, L. (eds), *Life, Death and Art: The Medieval Stained Glass of Fairford Parish Church*, Stroud, 1997.

Bruce, J. (ed.), *Historie of the arrivall of Edward IV in England*, Camden Society, I, 1838.

Bubb, R. E., 'The Penn Doom: a technical examination and treatment', *The Conservator*, XXVII, 2003.

Buchanan, A., *Robert Willis and the Rise of Architectural History*, unpublished doctoral dissertation, University of London, 1995.

Buck, A., 'The Register of the Fraternity of St John the Baptist, Dunstable, 1506–8, 1522–41', *Bedfordshire Historical Record Society*, XXV, 1947, pp.10–14.

Buhler, C. F. (ed.), *The Dicts and Sayings of the Philosophers*, Early English Text Society, original series, CCXI, 1941 for 1939.

Bull, G. (trans.), *Benvenuto Cellini, Autobiography*, Harmondsworth, 1956.

Burgess, C., 'For the Increase of Divine Service: Chantries in late medieval Bristol', *Journal of Ecclesiastical History*, XXXVI, 1985, pp.48–65.

Burgess, C. (ed.), *The Pre-Reformation Records of All Saints Bristol: Part I*, Bristol Record Society, 1995.

Bush, R., *Sandon, A Village History*, Peterborough, 1999.

Butler, L., 'Symbols on medieval memorials', *Archaeological Journal*, XLIV, 1987, pp.246–55.

Butler, L., *St Michael's Church, Cowthorpe, North Yorkshire*, The Churches Conservation Trust, 1999.

Caiger-Smith, A., *English Medieval Mural Paintings*, Oxford, 1963.

Camille, M., 'Seeing and Reading: some visual implications of medieval literacy and illiteracy', *Art History*, VIII, 1985, pp.26–49.

Camille, M., 'The Language of Images in Medieval England, 1200–1400', in Alexander and Binski 1987, pp.33–40.

Camille, M., *The Gothic Idol: Ideology and Image-making in Medieval Art*, Cambridge, 1989.

Camille, M., 'The Iconoclast's Desire: Deguileville's Idolatry in France and England', in Dimmick, Simpson and Zeeman 2002, pp.151–71.

Campbell, B. M. S., *English Seigneurial Agriculture*, Cambridge, 2000.

Campbell, B. M. S., Galloway, J. A., Keene, D. and Murphy, M., *Medieval Capital and its Grain Supply: Agrarian Production and Distribution in the London Region c.1300* (Historical Geography Research Paper Series), 1993.

Campbell, L., 'The Art Market in the Southern Netherlands', *The Burlington Magazine*, CXVIII, 1976, pp.188–98.

Campbell, L., *The Early Flemish Pictures in the Collection of Her Majesty The Queen*, Cambridge, 1985.

Campbell, L., 'Holbein's miniature of "Mrs Pemberton": the identity of the sitter', *The Burlington Magazine*, CXXIX, 1987, pp.366–71.

Campbell, L., *Renaissance Portraits*, London and New Haven, 1990.

Campbell, L., 'Holbein's miniature of Jane Pemberton: a further note', *The Burlington Magazine*, CXXXII, 1990, pp.213–14.

Campbell, L., 'Approaches to Petrus Christus', in M. Ainsworth (ed.), *Petrus Christus in Renaissance Bruges, an Interdisciplinary Approach*, New York and Turnhout, 1995, pp.1–10.

Campbell, L., 'The Donne Triptych', in H. Verougstraete et al. (eds), *Memling Studies, Proceedings of the International Colloquium (Bruges, 10–12 November 1994)*, Leuven, 1997, pp.71–80.

Campbell, L., *The National Gallery Catalogues, The Fifteenth Century Netherlandish Schools*, London, 1998.

Campbell, L. et al., 'Quentin Matsys, Desiderimus Erasmus, Pieter Gillis and Thomas More', *The Burlington Magazine*, CXX, 1978, pp.716–24.

Campbell, L. and Foister, S., 'Gerard, Lucas and Susanna Horenbout', *The Burlington Magazine*, CXXVIII, 1986, pp.719–27.

Campbell, M., 'A fifteenth-century copper pyx from the Victoria and Albert Museum', *The Antiquaries Journal*, LXV, 1985, pp.465–7.

Campbell, M., 'English Goldsmiths in the Fifteenth Century', in Williams 1987, pp.43–52.

Campbell, M., 'The Shrewsbury bowl', *The Antiquaries Journal*, LXVIII, 1988, pp.312–13.

Campbell, M., 'Gold, silver and precious stones', in Blair and Ramsay 1991, pp.107–66.

Campbell, M., '"White harts and coronets": the jewellery and plate of Richard II', in Gordon, Monnas and Elam 1997, pp.95–114.

Campbell, M., 'Medieval founders' relics: royal and episcopal patronage at Oxford and Cambridge colleges', in Coss and Keen 2002, pp.126–42.

Campbell, T., 'School of Raphael tapestries in the Collection of Henry VIII', *The Burlington Magazine*, CXXXVIII, 1996, pp.69–78.

Campbell, T., 'Cardinal Wolsey's tapestry collection', *The Antiquaries Journal*, LXXVI, 1996, pp.73–137.

Campbell, T., *The English Royal Tapestry Collection: 1485–1547*, unpublished doctoral dissertation, Courtauld Institute of Art, University of London, 1998.

Campbell, T. P., *Tapestry in the Renaissance: Art and Magnificence*, exh. cat., Metropolitan Museum of Art, New York, 2002.

Capp, B., *Astrology and the popular press. English almanacs 1500–1800*, London, 1979.

Carley, J., '*Her moost lovyng and fryndely brother sendeth gretyng*: Anne Boleyn's manuscripts and their sources', in Brown and McKendrick 1998, pp.261–80.

Carley, J., 'The Royal Library under Henry VIII', in Hellinga and Trapp 1999, pp.274–81.

Carley, J., *The Libraries of King Henry VIII* (Corpus of British medieval library catalogues, 7), London, 2000.

Carlin, M., 'Fast food and urban living standards in medieval England', in Carlin and Rosenthal 1998, pp.27–52.

Carlin, M. and Rosenthal, J. (eds), *Food and eating in medieval Europe*, London, 1998.

Carpenter, C., *Locality and Polity: Study of Warwickshire Landed Society, 1401–1499*, Cambridge, 1992.

Carpenter, C., *The Wars of the Roses: politics and the constitution in England, c.1437–1509*, Cambridge, 1997.

Carrington, J. B. and Hughes, G. R., *The Plate of the Worshipful Company of Goldsmiths*, Oxford, 1926.

Carter, J., *Specimens of the Ancient Sculpture and Painting now remaining in this Kingdom . . .* , 2 vols, London, 1780, 1787.

Carter, J., *Some Account of the Abbey Church of St Alban*, London, 1813.

Carus, C., 'Wall painting discovery in Norwich', *Church Archaeology*, III, 1999, pp.34–5.

Carus-Wilson, E. M., *Medieval Merchant Venturers*, London, 1954.

Carus-Wilson, E. M., *The Overseas Trade of Bristol in the Later Middle Ages*, London, 1967 (reprint of 1937 edition by Bristol Record Society).

Castor, H., *The King, the Crown and the Duchy of Lancaster: public authority and private power 1399–1461*, Oxford, 2000.

Catto, J., 'Religious change under Henry V', in Harriss 1985, pp.97–115.

Catto, J. I., 'The Origins of Court English, 1350–1400', unpublished paper, given at Oriel College, Oxford, May 2001.

Cautley, H. M., *Suffolk Churches and their Treasures*, London, 1937; 4th edn, Ipswich, 1975; 5th edn, Woodbridge, 1982.

Cavallo, A. S., *Medieval Tapestries in the Metropolitan Museum of Art*, New York, 1993.

Caviness, M. H., 'Fifteenth-century stained glass from the Chapel of Hampton Court Herefordshire: the Apostles' Creed and other subjects', *The Walpole Society*, XLII, 1970, pp.35–60.

Caviness, M. H., *The Windows of Christ Church Cathedral, Canterbury*, Corpus Vitrearum Medii Aevi Great Britain, II, Oxford, 1981.

Caviness, M. H., 'Biblical stories in windows: were they Bibles for the Poor?', in B. S. Levy (ed.), *The Bible in the Middle Ages: its influence on literature and art*, Binghamton, NY, 1992, pp.103–47.

Caviness, M. H., *Paintings on Glass: Studies in Romanesque and Gothic Monumental Art*, Aldershot, 1997.

Challis, C. E., 'The ecclesiastical mints of the early Tudor period: their organisation and possible date of closure', *Northern History*, X, 1975, pp.88–101.

Challis, C. E., *The Tudor Coinage*, Manchester, 1978.

Challis, C. E., 'The first gold sovereigns', *Spink's Numismatic Circular*, 1990, pp.347–8.

Chamberlain, A., *Hans Holbein the Younger*, 2 vols, New York, 1913.

Chambers, B., 'The Fayrey Pall', *Bedfordshire Magazine*, IX, 1963–5, pp.311–15.

Chaney, E., 'Henry VIII's tombs, "Plus catholique que le pape"?', *Apollo*, October 1991, pp.234–8.

Chappell, E., *New Light on the 'Little Men' of Naworth Castle in the Victoria and Albert Museum*, unpublished MA thesis, Courtauld Institute of Art, University of London, 2002.

Charles, F. and Down, K., 'A 16th-century drawing of a timber–framed town house', *Transactions of the Worcestershire Archaeological Society*, III, 1970–72, pp.67–78.

Charleston, R. J., *English glass and the glass used in England c.400–1940*, London, 1984.

Chatwin, P. B., 'Monumental effigies in the County of Warwick', *Birmingham and Midland Archaeological Society Transactions and Proceedings*, XLVI, 1921, pp.35–88.

Chatwin, P. B., 'The effigy of Richard Beauchamp at Warwick', *The Antiquaries Journal*, VI, 1926, pp.448–9.

Chatwin, P. B., 'Recent discoveries in the Beauchamp Chapel, Warwick', *Birmingham and Midland Archaeological Society Transactions and Proceedings*, LIII, 1928, pp.145–57.

Chatwin, P. B., 'The decoration of the Beauchamp Chapel, Warwick, with special reference to the sculptures', *Archaeologia*, LXXVI, 1928, pp.313–34.

Cheetham, F. W., *Medieval English Alabaster Carvings in the Castle Museum Nottingham*, rev. edn, Nottingham, 1973.

Cheetham, F., *English Medieval Alabasters. With a catalogue of the collection in the Victoria and Albert Museum*, Oxford, 1984.

Cheetham, F., *The Alabaster Men: Sacred Images from Medieval England*, exh. cat., Daniel Katz Ltd, London, 2001.

Cherry, J., 'The Dunstable Swan Jewel', *Journal of the British Archaeological Association*, XXXII, 1969, pp.38–53.

Cherry, J., 'The Medieval Jewellery from the Fishpool, Nottinghamshire, Hoard', *Archaeologia*, CIV, 1973, pp.307–21.

Cherry, J., 'The three rings preserved in the College associated with Bishop Fox', *The Pelican*, 1981–2, pp.45–51.

Cherry, J., 'Cauldrons and skillets: metal and pottery in cooking', in B. Vyner and S. Wrathmell (eds), *Studies in medieval and later pottery in Wales*, Cardiff, 1987, pp.145–60.

Cherry, J., 'Rochester Silver Plate in the British Museum', *Friends of Rochester Cathedral Report*, 1988, pp.7–8.

Cherry, J., 'Symbolism and survival: medieval horns of tenure', *The Antiquaries Journal*, LXIX, 1989, pp.111–18.

Cherry, J., 'The seal matrix of Henry, Prince of Wales, later Henry V, for the Lordship of Carmarthen', *The Antiquaries Journal*, LXX, 1990, pp.461–2.

Cherry, J., *The Middleham Jewel and Ring*, York, 1992.

Cherry, J., 'The rings of John Stanbury and Richard Mayo, Bishops of Hereford', in Whitehead 1995, pp.150–56.

Cherry, J., 'Purse Frame', *National Art Collections Fund 1998 Review*, p.72.

Cherry, J., 'A purse frame saved from the Thames and from export', *Minerva*, Jan./Feb. 1999, pp.6–7.

Cherry, J., 'Healing through Faith: the continuation of medieval attitudes to jewellery into the Renaissance', *Renaissance Studies*, XV/2, 2001, pp.154–71.

Chinnery, V., *Oak Furniture, the British tradition: a history of early furniture in the British Isles and New England*, Woodbridge, 1979.

Chrimes, S. B., *Henry VII*, London, 1972.

Christ, W. and Minkenberg, G., *Gemälde und Skulpturen des Aachener Domes in Blickfeld von Konservierung und Restaurierung. 30 Jahre Restaurierungswerkstatt für Gemälde und Skulpturen am Dom zu Aachen* (Karlsverein Schriftenreihe, 1), Aachen, 1995, pp.24–9.

Christensen, C., *Princes and Propaganda: Electoral Saxon Art of the Reformation*, Sixteenth Century Essays and Studies XX, Kirksville, MO, 1992.

Christianson, C. P., *A Directory of London Stationers and Book Artisans 1300–1500*, New York, 1990.

Clark, G. T., 'The chronology of the Louthe Master and his identification with Simon Marmion', in Kren 1992, pp.195–208.

Clarke, H., *The Archaeology of Medieval England*, London, 1984.

Clarke, S. and Jackson, R. and P., 'The discovery of the site of a medieval encaustic floor tile kiln in Monmouth, Gwent', *Medieval Ceramics*, XVI, 1992, pp.72–6.

Clarke, T. H., 'Lattimo – a group of Venetian glass enamelled on an opaque-white ground', *Journal of Glass Studies*, XVI, 1974, pp.22–56.

Clay, J. W., 'The Savile Family', *Yorkshire Archaeological Journal*, XXV, 1920, pp.1–47.

Clayton, M., *The Collectors' Dictionary of the Silver and Gold of Great Britain and North America*, London, 1971.

Clifford, T., *Designs of Desire. Architectural and Ornamental Prints and Drawings 1500–1850*, exh. cat., National Galleries of Scotland, Edinburgh, 1999.

Clifton-Taylor, A., *The Pattern of English Building*, 2nd edn, London, 1965.

Coad, J., *Deal Castle, Kent*, English Heritage Guidebook, London, 1998.

Coales, J., *The Earliest English Brasses: Patronage, Style and workshops, 1270–1350*, London, 1987.

Cobb, H. S., *The overseas trade of the London exchequer customs accounts 1480–81*, London Records Society, XXVII, 1990.

Cobham 1844: *The Pictorial Guide to Cobham*, London, 1844.

Cocke, T., *900 Years: The Restorations of Westminster Abbey*, London, 1995.

Cohen, K., *Metamorphosis of a Death Symbol: the Transi Tomb in the Late Middle Ages and the Renaissance*, Berkeley and Los Angeles, 1973.

Cokayne, G. E., *The Complete Peerage*, 14 vols, London and Stroud, 1910–98.

Coleman, S. and Elsner, J., *Pilgrimage: Past and Present in the World Religions*, London, 1995.

Collins, A. J., *Jewels and Plate of Queen Elizabeth I. The Inventory of 1574*, London, 1955.

Collinson, P., Ramsay, N. and Sparks, M. (eds), *A History of Canterbury Cathedral*, Oxford, 1995.

Colvin, H., 'Gothic Survival and Gothic Revival', *Architectural Review*, CIII, 1948, pp.91–8; revised and reprinted in ibid., *Essays in English Architectural History*, New Haven and London, 1999, pp.217–44.

Colvin, H. M. (ed.), *The History of the King's Works, I–II*, London, 1963, *III*, London, 1975, *IV*, London, 1982.

Colvin, H. and Simmons, J. S. G., *All Souls: An Oxford College and its Buildings*, Oxford, 1989.

Connolly, M., *John Shirley: book production and the noble household in fifteenth-century England*, Aldershot, 1998.

Cook, B. J., 'Showpieces: medallic coins in early modern Europe', *The Medal*, XXVI, 1995, pp.3–25.

Cook, B. J., 'The afterlife of a coinage: the Lancastrian salut in England and elsewhere', *Numismatic Chronicle*, CLXI, 2001, pp.302–7.

Cook, G. H., *Medieval Chantries and Chantry Chapels*, London, 1963.

Cook, T., 'The bronze medallion in Henry VII's Chapel in Westminster Abbey', *Monthly Review*, XII, August 1903, pp.89–97.

Cooke, W., 'Ancient burse and veil preserved at Hessett Church, Suffolk', *The Ecclesiologist*, XXIX, pp.86–9.

Cooke, W., 'Materials for a History of Hessett', *Proceedings of the Suffolk Archaeological Institute*, IV, 1874, pp.301–32.

Cooper, C. H., *Memoir of Margaret, Countess of Richmond and Derby*, Cambridge, 1874.

Cooper, J. K. D., 'A reassessment of some English late Gothic and early Renaissance plate. Part I', *The Burlington Magazine*, CXIX, 1977, pp.408–22.

Cooper, N., *Houses of the Gentry 1480–1680*, London, 1999.

Coote, L. A., *Prophecy and Public Affairs in later medieval England*, York, 2000.

Corder, J. S., 'The Guildhall of Corpus Christi, Lavenham', *Suffolk Institute of Archaeology*, VII, 1891, pp.113–19.

Coss, P. and Keen, M. (eds), *Heraldry, Pageantry and Social Display in Medieval England*, Woodbridge, 2002.

Cosson, C. A., Baron de, 'The Capells of Rayne Hall, Essex', *The Archaeological Journal*, XL, 1883, pp.64–79.

Cotehele 1998: *Cotehele, Cornwall*, National Trust Guidebook, rev. edn, London, 1998.

Cotton, C., 'The Screen of the Six Kings in Canterbury Cathedral', *Canterbury Cathedral Chronicle*, XX, 1935, pp.12–20.

Cotton, S., 'Mediaeval roodscreens in Norfolk – their construction and painting dates', *Norfolk Archaeology*, XL/1, 1987, pp.44–54.

Coulson, C., 'Structural symbolism in medieval castle architecture', *Journal of the British Archaeological Association*, CXXXII, 1979, pp.73–90.

Courcelle, P., *La Consolation de philosophie dans la tradition littéraire*, Études Augustiniennes, Paris, 1967.

Cox, J. C., 'The Parish Churches of Northamptonshire, illustrated by wills', *Archaeological Journal*, LVIII, 1901, pp.113–32

Cox, J. C., *Pulpits, Lecterns and Organs in English Churches*, Oxford, 1915.

Cox, J. C., *English Church Fittings, Furniture and Accessories*, London, 1923.

Cox, J. C. and Ford, C. B., *The Parish Churches of England*, 6th edn, London, 1950.

Cranage, D. H. S., 'The Monastery of St Kilburga at Much Wenlock, Shropshire', *Archaeologia*, LXXII, 1922, pp.105–32.

Crighton, R. A., *Cambridge Plate*, exh. cat., Fitzwilliam Museum, Cambridge, 1975.

Cripps, W. J., *Old English Plate*, London, 1914.

Cripps-Day, F. H., 'On Armour preserved in English Churches', vol.V/2 of Laking 1920–22.

Croft-Murray, E., 'Lambert Barnard: an English Early Renaissance Painter', *Archaeological Journal*, CXIII, 1957, pp.108–25.

Crofts, H. H. S. (ed.), *The Boke named the Gouernour, deuised by Sir Thomas Elyot, knight*, 2 vols, London, 1883.

Crone, G. R., *Early Maps of the British Isles AD 1000–AD 1579* (Royal Geographical Society Reproductions of Early Maps, 17), London, 1961.

Crook, J. (ed.), *Winchester Cathedral: Nine Hundred Years 1093–1993*, Chichester, 1993.

Crook, J., 'St Swithun of Winchester', in Crook 1993, pp.57–68.

Crossley, F. H., *English Church Monuments A.D. 1150–1550*, London, 1921.

Crossley, F. H., 'The Renaissance of Cheshire Church Building in the late Fifteenth and early Sixteenth Centuries', *Journal of the Chester and North Wales Architectural, Archaeological and Historic Society*, new ser., XXXIV, 1939, pp.53–160.

Crowfoot, E., Pritchard, F. and Staniland, K., *Textiles and Clothing c.1150–1450*, Museum of London, 1996.

Cullum, P. and Goldberg, J., 'How Margret Blackburn taught her daughters: reading devotional instruction in a book of hours', in J. Wogan-Browne et al., *Medieval Women: Texts and Contexts in Late Medieval Britain. Essays for Felicity Riddy*, Turnhout, 2000, pp.217–36.

Cuming, H. S., 'On signacula found at London', *Journal of the British Archaeological Association*, XXI, 1867, pp.331–2.

Currin, J. M., 'Henry VII and the Treaty of Redon (1489): Plantagenet ambitions and early Tudor foreign policy', *History*, LXXXI, 1996, pp.343–58.

Curtis, G. and Wathey, A., 'Fifteenth-century English liturgical music: a list of the surviving repertory', *Royal Musical Association Research Chronicle*, XXVII, 1994, pp.1–69.

Curwen, J. F., 'St Anthony's Chapel, Cartmel Fell', *Transactions of the Cumberland and Westmorland Antiquarian and Archaeological Society*, XXII, 1912, pp.285–96.

Curzon, N. and Tipping, H. A., *Tattershall Castle, Lincolnshire*, London, 1929.

Cust, L., untitled note in *Proceedings of the Society of Antiquaries*, XVIII, 1901, pp.280–84.

Dalton, O. M., *Catalogue of the Finger Rings . . . in the Museum*, British Museum, London, 1912.

Dalton, O. M., 'A late medieval Bracer in the British Museum', *The Antiquaries Journal*, XI, 1922, pp.208–10.

Darr, A. P., 'The sculptures of Torrigiano: the Westminster Abbey tombs', *Connoisseur*, CC, 1979, pp.177–84.

Darr, A. P., *Pietro Torrigiano and his Sculpture for the Henry VII Chapel, Westminster Abbey*, unpublished doctoral dissertation, New York University, 1980.

Darr, A. P., 'New documents for Pietro Torrigiani and other early cinquecento Florentine sculptors active in Italy and England', in M. Cämmerer (ed.), *Kunst des Cinquecento in der Toskana*, Munich, 1992, pp.108–38.

Darr, A. P., 'Verrocchio's Legacy: observations regarding his influence on Pietro Torrigiani and other Florentine sculptors', in S. Bule, A. P. Darr and F. S. Gioffredi (eds), *Verrocchio and Late Quattrocento Italian Sculpture*, Florence, 1992, pp.125–39.

Darr, A. P., 'Pietro Torrigiano', in J. Turner (ed.), *The Dictionary of Art*, vol. 31, London, 1996, pp.188–92.

Davenport, C., *Royal English Bookbindings*, London, 1896.

Davenport, C., *English Embroidered Bookbindings*, London, 1899.

Davidson-Houston, C. E. D., 'Sussex Monumental Brasses. Part II', *Sussex Archaeological Collections*, LXXVII, 1936, pp.130–94.

Davidson-Houston, C. E. D., 'Sussex Monumental Brasses. Part V', *Sussex Archaeological Brasses*, LXXX, 1939, pp.93–147.

Davies, C. S. L., 'The Wars of the Roses in European context', in A. J. Pollard (ed.), *The Wars of the Roses*, Basingstoke, 1995, pp.162–85.

Davies, C. S. L., 'Henry VIII and Henry V: the wars in France', in Watts 1998, pp.235–62.

Davies, M., *The Earlier Italian Schools*, National Gallery, London, 1957.

Davies, R., *A Memoir of the York Press*, London, 1868.

Davis, N. (ed), *Paston Letters and Papers of the Fifteenth Century*, 2 vols, Oxford, 1971–6.

Davis, N. (ed.), *The Paston Letters: A Selection in Modern Spelling*, Oxford, 1983.

Davis, R. H. C., 'The Chronology of Perpendicular Architecture in Oxford', *Oxoniensia*, XI–XII, 1946–7, pp.75–89.

Davis, V., *William Waynflete*, Woodbridge, 1993.

DCMS 1999–2000: *Export of Works of Art 1999–2000*, Forty-sixth Report of the Reviewing Committee, Department for Culture, Media and Sport, London, 2000.

Deacon, R. and Lindley, P., *Image and Idol: Medieval Sculpture*, exh. cat., Tate Britain, London, 2001.

de Backer, A., *Essai bibliographique sur le livre De imitatione Christi*, Liège, 1864; reprinted 1966.

de Beer, E. S., 'Gothic: Origin and Diffusion of the Term; the Idea of Style in Architecture', *Journal of the Warburg and Courtauld Institutes*, XI, 1948, pp.143–62.

de Cosson, Baron F. and Burges, W., *Ancient Helmets and Examples of Mail*, Royal Archaeological Institute, London, 1881.

de Hamel, C., *A History of Illuminated Manuscripts*, 2nd edn, Oxford, 1994.

de Laborde, L., *Les ducs de Bourgogne*, 3 vols, Paris, 1849–52.

de la Mare, A. C. and Hunt, R., *Duke Humfrey and English Humanism in the Fifteenth Century*, exh. cat., Bodleian Library, Oxford, 1970.

de la Mare, A. C. and Gillam, S., *Duke Humfrey's Library and the Divinity School 1488–1988*, exh. cat., Bodleian Library, Oxford, 1988.

Delmarcel, G., 'Text and image: some notes on the tituli of Flemish Triumphs of Petrarch tapestries', *Textile History*, XX, 1989, pp.321–9.

Delmarcel, G., *Flemish Tapestry*, London, 1999.

Derveaux-van Ussel, G., *Retables en bois*, Musées royaux d'Art et d'Histoire, Brussels, 1977.

de Schryver, A., 'The Louthe Master and the Marmion Case', in Kren 1992, pp.171–80.

de Smedt, O., *De Engelse Natie te Antwerpen 1496–1582*, II, Antwerp, 1950.

Detsicas, A. (ed.), *Collecteana Historica: essays in memory of Stuart Rigold*, Maidstone, 1981.

de Vos, D., *Hans Memling*, exh. cat., Groeninge Museum, Bruges, 1994.

Dibdin, T. F., *Bibliotheca Spenceriana or a descriptive catalogue of the books printed in the fifteenth century and of many valuable first editions in the library of George John Earl Spencer*, 4 vols, London, 1814–15.

Dillon, H. A., untitled note, *Proceedings of the Society of Antiquaries*, 2nd series, VII, 1877, pp.299–306.

Dillon, Viscount, 'On a manuscript collection of ordinances of chivalry of the 15th century belonging to Lord Hastings', *Archaeologia*, LVII, 1901, pp.29–70.

Dimmick, J., Simpson, J. and Zeeman, Z. (eds), *Images, Idolatry and Iconoclasm in Late Medieval England: Textuality and the Visual Image*, Oxford, 2002.

Dixon, P. and Lott, B., 'The Courtyard and the Tower: Contexts and Symbols in the Development of the Late Medieval Great House', *Journal of the British Archaeological Association*, CXLVI, 1993, pp.93–101.

Dobson, R. B., *The Peasants' Revolt of 1381*, 2nd edn, London, 1983.

Driver, M., 'Pictures in Print: late fifteenth-century and early sixteenth-century English religious books for lay readers', in M. G. Sargent (ed.), *De Cella in Seculum: Religious and Secular Life and Devotion in Late Medieval England*, Woodbridge, 1986, pp.229–44.

Driver, M. W., 'Nuns as patrons, artists, readers: Bridgettine woodcuts in printed books produced for the English market', in C. G. Fisher and K. L. Scott (eds), *Art into Life: Collected Papers from the Kresge Art Museum Medieval Symposia*, East Lansing, 1995, pp.237–67.

Driver, M., 'The illustrated Wykyn de Worde: an overview', *Studies in Iconography*, XVII, 1996, pp.349–403.

Druitt, H., *A Manual of Costume illustrated by Monumental Brasses*, London, 1906.

Dubuc, B. D., 'Le Chemin de Vaillance: mis à point sur la date de composition et la vie de l'auteur', in Monks and Owen 1994, pp.276–83.

Duff, E. G., *A Century of the English Book Trade . . . 1457 to . . . 1557*, London, 1905.

Duff, E. G., *The English Provincial Printers, Stationers and Bookbinders to 1557*, Cambridge, 1912.

Duff, E. G., *Fifteenth century English books. A bibliography of books and documents printed in England and of books for the English market printed abroad*, The Bibliographical Society Illustrated Monographs, XVIII, London, 1917.

Duffy, E., 'Holy Maydens, Holy Wyfes: the cult of women saints in fifteenth- and sixteenth-century England', in W. J. Sheils and D. Wood (eds), *Women in the Church* (Studies in Church History, vol. 27), Oxford, 1990, pp.175–96.

Duffy, E., *The Stripping of the Altars: Traditional Religion in England c.1400–c.1580*, New Haven and London, 1992.

Duffy, E., 'The parish, piety and patronage in late medieval East Anglia: the evidence of rood screens', in French, Gibbs and Kümin 1997, pp.133–62.

Duffy, E., *The Voices of Morebath: Reformation and Rebellion in an English Village*, New Haven and London, 2001.

Duffy, E., Notes on the painted screen in Binham Abbey (typescript), n.d.

Dufty, A. R., 'The Stathum Book of Hours; an existing MS. mentioned on a 15th-century brass', *Archaeological Journal*, CVI, supplement, 1952, pp.83–90.

Dugdale, W., *Antiquities of Warwickshire*, London, 1656; 2nd edn by W. Thomas, London, 1730.

Dugdale, W., *Monasticon Anglicanum*, 6 vols, London, 1730 (later edition, London, 1819).

Dugdale, W. (ed.), *The Restoration of the Beauchamp Chapel, at St Mary's Collegiate Church, Warwick 1674–1742*, Oxford, 1956.

Duggan, L. G., 'Was art really the "book of the illiterate"?', *Word and Image*, V, 1989, pp.227–51.

Dumortier, C., 'Maiolica production in Antwerp: the documentary evidence', in Gaimster 1999, pp.107–11.

Duncan, L. L. and Hussey, A., *Testamenta Cantiana*, Kent Archaeological Society (Kent Records), 1907.

Duru, L. M., *Bibliothèque historique de l'Yonne*, 2 vols, Auxerre, 1850–64.

Dyer, A. D., *Decline and growth in English towns*, Cambridge, 1995.

Dyer, C., 'English diet in the later Middle Ages', in T. H. Aston, P. R. Coss et al. (eds), *Social relations and ideas: essays in honour of R. H. Hilton*, Oxford, 1983, pp.191–216.

Dyer, C., *Standards of Living in the Later Middle Ages: Social Change in England, c.1200–1520*, Cambridge, 1989.

Dyer, C., *Everyday Life in Medieval England*, London, 1994.

Dyer, C., 'Peasants and coins: the uses of money in the middle ages', *British Numismatic Journal*, LXVII, 1997, pp.31–47.

Dymond, D. and Paine, C., *The Spoil of Melford Church: the Reformation in a Suffolk Parish*, 2nd edn, Ipswich, 1992.

Eames, E., *Catalogue of Medieval Lead-Glazed Earthenware Tiles in the Department of Medieval and Later Antiquities, British Museum*, London, 1980.

Eames, P., *Medieval Furniture*, London, 1977.

Eaves, I., 'The Tournament Armours of King Henry VIII of England', *Livrustkammeren*, exh. cat., Stockholm, 1993, pp.15–18.

Eden, F. S., 'The Arms of Battle Abbey', *The Connoisseur*, LXXXVI, 1930, pp.174–5.

Edinburgh 1982: *Angels, Nobles & Unicorns: Art and Patronage in Medieval Scotland*, exh. cat., National Museum of Antiquities, 1982.

Eeles, F. C., 'Mediaeval triptych: remains discovered at Ashbourne Church', *Journal of the Derbyshire Archaeological and Natural History Society*, new ser., XVIII, 1944–5, pp.83–8.

Egan, G., *Playthings from the Past*, London, 1996.

Egan, G. (ed.), *The Medieval Household: daily living c.1150–1450 (Medieval Finds from Excavations in London, 6)*, London, 1998.

Egan, G., *Urban Material Culture in an Age of Transition: Finds from Bermondsey, South London, c.1450–1700*, forthcoming.

Egan, G. and Forsyth, H., 'Wound wire and silver gilt: changing fashion in dress accessories c.1400–c.1600', in Gaimster and Stamper 1997, pp.215–38.

Egan, G. and Pritchard, F., *Dress Accessories c.1150–c.1450*, London, 1991.

Eikelmann, R., 'Goldemail um 1400', in Baumstark 1995, pp.106–30.

Elias, E. R. D., *The Anglo-Gallic Coins*, Paris–London, 1984.

Eliot, G., *Scenes of Clerical Life*, ed. D. Lodge, London, 1980.

Ellacombe, H. T., 'The church bells in the towers of all the parish churches of Devonshire', *Transactions of the Exeter Diocesan Architectural Society*, 2nd series, I, 1867, pp.221–427.

Ellis, H., 'Badges of the House of York', *Archaeologia*, XVII, 1814, pp.226–7.

Ellis, H. D., *Ancient Silver Plate belonging to the Worshipful Company of Armourers and Brasiers*, London, 1892.

Ellory, C., Clifford, H. and Rogers, F. (eds), *Corpus Silver: patronage and plate at Corpus Christi College, Oxford*, Barton-under-Needwood, 1999.

Elton, G. R., *The Tudor Constitution. Documents and Commentary*, Cambridge, 1972 (2nd edn, Cambridge, 1982)

Emden, A. B., *A Biographical Register of the University of Oxford to A.D. 1500*, 3 vols, Oxford, 1957–9.

Emery, A., 'Ralph, Lord Cromwell's Manor at Wingfield (1439–c.1450): its construction, design and influence', *Archaeological Journal*, CXLII, 1985, pp.276–339.

Emery, A., *Greater Medieval Houses of England and Wales, 1300–1500*, Cambridge, vol. I, 1996, vol. II, 2000.

Emery, A. and Binney, M., 'Wingfield Manor, Derbyshire', *Country Life*, CLXXI, 8 and 15 April 1982, pp.946–9, 1042–5.

Emmerson, R., 'Monumental Brasses: London Design c.1420–85', *Journal of the British Archaeological Association*, CXXXI, 1978, pp.50–78.

Emmerson, R., 'William Browne's taste in brasses', *Transactions of the Monumental Brass Society*, XII, 1978, pp.322–5.

Erbe, T. (ed.), *Mirk's Festial: a Collection of Homilies*, Early English Text Society, extra series, XCVI, 1905.

Erler, M. C., 'The maner to live well and the coming of English in François Regnault's Primers of the 1520s and 1530s', *The Library*, 1984, pp.229–43.

Erler, M. C., 'Devotional Literature', in Hellinga and Trapp 1999, pp.495–525.

Evans, J., *English Art 1307–1461* (Oxford History of English Art, V), Oxford, 1949.

Evans, J., *Dress in Medieval France*, Oxford, 1952.

Evans, J. and Cook, N., 'A statue of Christ from the ruins of Mercers' Hall', *Archaeological Journal*, CXI, 1955, pp.168–80.

Evelyn, J., *An Account of Architects and Architecture, together, with an Historical, Etymological Explanation of certain terms, particular Affected by Architects*, London, 1706.

Fairbrass, S. and Holmes, K., 'The Restoration of Hans Holbein's Cartoon of Henry VIII and Henry VII', *The Conservator*, X, 1986, pp.12–16.

Fairfield, L. P., *John Bale: Mythmaker for the English Reformation*, West Lafayette, 1976.

Falcke, S., 'A triptych by Antonio da Solario', *The Burlington Magazine*, LXIX, 1936, pp.229–30.

Fallows, D., 'Henry VIII as a Composer', in C. Banks, A. Searle and M. Turner (eds), *Sundry Sorts of Music Books: Essays on the British Library Collections Presented to O. W. Neighbour on his 70th Birthday*, London, 1993, pp.27–39.

Farmer, D. H., *The Oxford Dictionary of Saints*, 2nd edn, Oxford, 1987.

Fawcett, R., 'Salle Church', *Archaeological Journal*, CXXVII, 1980, pp.332–3.

Fawcett, R., 'St Mary at Wiveton in Norfolk, and a group of churches attributed to its mason', *Antiquaries Journal*, LXII, 1982, pp.35–56.

Fehrmann, A., 'The Chantry Chapel of King Edward IV', in Keen and Scarff 2002, pp.177–91.

Ferrey, B., 'St Cuthbert's, Wells', *Proceedings of the Somersetshire Archaeological and Natural History Society*, II, 1851, pp.93–6.

Ffoulkes, C., *Inventory and Survey of the Armouries of the Tower of London*, II, London, 1916.

Field, H. E., 'The Monumental Brasses of Derbyshire', *Transactions of the Monumental Brass Society*, III, 1898–9, pp.194–6, 209–15; V, 1904–9, pp.1–7, 29–39, 101–11, 129–38, 171–80, 380–89.

Fines, J., 'Cathedral and Reformation', in M. Hobbs (ed.), *Chichester Cathedral: An Historical Survey*, Chichester, 1994, pp.47–68.

Finucane, R. C., *Miracles and Pilgrims: Popular Beliefs in Medieval England*, London, 1977.

Fiorato, V., Boyston, A. and Knusel, C.

(eds), *Blood Red Roses: the Archaeology of a Mass Grave from the Battle of Towton*, Abingdon, 2001.

Fisher, J. H., 'The Portraits in the Bedford Psalter Hours (B.M. MS Add. 42131) and the Lancastrian Literary Affinity', in N. M. Reale and R. E. Sternglantz (eds), *Satura: Studies in Medieval Literature in Honour of Robert R. Raymo*, Donington, 2001.

Fitch, R., 'Engraving of a gold niello', *Norfolk Archaeology*, III, 1852, pp.97–104.

Fletcher, D., 'The Lancastrian Collar of Esses: its origins and transformation down the centuries', in J. Gillespie (ed.), *The Age of Richard II*, Stroud, 1997, pp.191–204.

Fletcher, J., 'Four scenes from the life of St Etheldreda', *The Antiquaries Journal*, LIV, 1974, pp.287–9.

Fletcher, J., 'Slices from a deep cake: dating panel paintings of St Etheldreda from Ely', *Country Life*, 28 March 1974, pp.728–30.

Fogelmark, S., *Flemish and related panel-stamped bindings*, New York, 1990.

Foister, S., 'Paintings and other works of art in sixteenth-century English inventories', *The Burlington Magazine*, CXXIII, 1981, pp.273–82.

Foister, S., 'A Lady with a squirrel and a starling by Holbein: Illusion and invention for an unknown sitter', *National Art Collections Fund Review*, 1992, pp.30–34.

Foister, S., 'Humanism and art in the early Tudor period: John Leland's poetic praise of painting', in J. Woolfson (ed.), *Reassessing Tudor Humanism*, Basingstoke, 2002, pp.129–50.

Foister, S., Wyld, M. and Roy, A., 'Hans Holbein's "A Lady with a Squirrel and a Starling"', *National Gallery Technical Bulletin*, XV, 1994, pp.6–19.

Foot, M. M., 'English decorated bookbindings', in Griffiths and Pearsall 1989, pp.65–86.

Foot, M. M., *Studies in the History of Bookbinding*, Aldershot, 1993.

Foot, M. M., 'A binding by the Scales binder, 1456–65', in Foot 1993, pp.121–4.

Foot, M. M., *The History of Bookbinding as a Mirror of Society*, London, 1998.

Foot, M. M., 'The earliest-known European gold-tooled bookbindings', *The New Bookbinder*, XX, 2000, pp.15–17.

Forsyth, H. and Egan, G., *Toys, Trifles, Trinkets: Base metal Playthings c.1150–1800*, forthcoming.

Foster, J. E. and Atkinson, T. D., *An Illustrated Catalogue of the Loan Collection of Plate exhibited in the Fitzwilliam Museum, May 1895*, Cambridge, 1896.

Foucart, E., *Les peintures de Hans Holbein le Jeune au Louvre*, exh. cat., Musée du Louvre, Paris, 1985.

Fowler, J. T. (ed.), *Rites of Durham*, Surtees Society, CVII, 1902.

Franco Mata, A., *El retablo Gótico de Cartagena y los alabastros ingleses en España*, Murcia, 1999.

Frankl, P., *The Gothic. Literary sources and interpretations through eight centuries*, Princeton, 1960.

French, G. R., 'Description of the Plate and Tapestry of the Vintners' Company', *Transactions of the London and Middlesex Archaeological Society*, III, 1870, pp.472–91.

French, K. L., 'Maidens Lights and Wives stores: women's parish guilds in late medieval England', *Sixteenth Century Journal*, XXIX, 1998, pp.399–425.

French, K. L., *The People of the Parish. Community Life in a Late Medieval English Diocese*, Philadelphia, 2001.

French, K. L., Gibbs, G. G. and Kümin, B. A. (eds), *The Parish in English Life 1400–1600*, Manchester, 1997.

French, T., *York Minster: The Great East Window*, Corpus Vitrearum Medii Aevi Great Britain, Summary Catalogue 2, Oxford, 1995.

French, T., *York Minster: The St William Window*, Corpus Vitrearum Medii Aevi Great Britain, Summary Catalogue 5, Oxford, 1999.

Fretton, W. G., *The Fuller's Guild of Coventry*, Warwick, 1879.

Friedberg, E. (ed.), *Corpus Iuris Canonici*, 2 vols, Leipzig, 1879–81.

Friedländer, M. J. and Rosenberg, J., *Lucas Cranach*, New York, 1978.

Friedman, J. B., *Northern English Books, Owners, and Makers in the Late Middle Ages*, Syracuse, NY, 1995.

Friedman, J. B., 'Harry the Hay警de and Talbot his dog: an illustrated girdlebook from Worcestershire', in C. G. Fisher and K. L. Scott (eds), *Art into Life: Collected Papers from the Kresge Art Museum Medieval Symposia*, Michigan, 1995.

Fritz, J. M., *Goldschmiedekunst der Gotik in Mitteleuropa*, Munich, 1982.

Fritz, R., *Die Gefässe aus Kokosnuss in Mitteleuropa 1250–1800*, Mainz, 1983.

Fryer, A. C., *Wooden Monumental Effigies of England and Wales*, rev. edn, London, 1924.

Fulman, W. (ed.), *Historia Croylandensis Continuatio*, in *Rerum Anglicarum Scriptorum Veterum*, Oxford, 1684, pp.451–546.

Furnivall, F. J. (ed.), *Hoccleve's Works, III: The Regement of Princes*, Early English Text Society, extra series 72, 1897.

Furnivall, F. J. and Stone, W. G. (eds), *The Tale of Beryn*, Early English Text Society, extra series, CV, 1909.

Gage, J., *The History and Antiquities of Hengrave in Suffolk*, London, 1822.

Gaimster, D. R. M., 'Post-medieval ceramic stove-tiles bearing the royal arms: evidence for their manufacture and use in southern Britain', *Archaeological Journal*, CXLV, 1988, pp.314–43.

Gaimster, D. (ed.), *Maiolica in the North: the archaeology of tin-glazed earthenware in north-west Europe c.1500–1600*, British Museum Occasional Paper 122, London, 1999.

Gaimster, D., 'Imported maiolica vases bearing the Royal arms of England: a reconsideration', in Gaimster 1999, pp.141–46.

Gaimster, D., 'Pots, Prints and Protestantism: changing mentalities in the urban domestic sphere c.1480–1580', in Gaimster and Gilchrist, forthcoming.

Gaimster, D. et al., *German Stoneware 1200–1900: archaeology and cultural history*, London, 1997.

Gaimster, D. and Gilchrist, R. (eds), *The Archaeology of the Reformation*, London, forthcoming.

Gaimster, D. and Nenk, B., 'English households in transition 1450–1550: the ceramic evidence', in Gaimster and Stamper 1997, pp.171–95.

Gaimster, D. R. M. and Redknap, M. (eds), *Everyday and Exotic pottery from Europe c.650–1900: Studies in Honour of John G. Hurst*, Oxford, 1992.

Gaimster, D. and Stamper, P. (eds), *The Age of Transition: The Archaeology of English Culture c.1400–1600*, Oxford, 1997.

Gaimster, D. and Weinstein, R., 'A pipeclay lion figurine from Utrecht, the Netherlands', *Post Medieval Archaeology*, XXIII, 1989, pp.11–14.

Gairdner, J. D., (ed.), *Letters and Papers Illustrative of the Reigns of Richard III and Henry VII*, 2 vols, London, 1861–3.

Gairdner, J. D., (ed.), *The Paston Letters, A.D. 1422–1509*, 6 vols, London, 1904 (reprinted Gloucester, 1986).

Galloway, J. A., 'Driven by drink? Ale consumption and the agrarian economy of the London region, c.1300–1400', in M. Carlin and J. T. Rosenthal (eds), *Food and Eating in Medieval Europe*, London and Rio Grande, 1998, pp.87–100.

Galloway, J. A. (ed.), *Trade, Urban Hinterlands and Market Integration c.1300–1600*, London, 2000.

Galloway, J. A., Keene, D. and Murphy, M., 'Fuelling the city: production and distribution of firewood and fuel in London's region, 1290–1400', *Economic History Review*, XLIX, 1996, pp.447–72.

Galvin, C. and Lindley, P., 'Pietro Torrigiano's portrait bust of King Henry VII', *The Burlington Magazine*, CXXX, 1988, pp.892–902.

Ganz, P., 'An unknown portrait by Holbein the Younger', *The Burlington Magazine*, XLVII, 1925, pp.113–15.

Gardner, A., *Alabaster Tombs of the Pre-Reformation Period in England*, Cambridge, 1940.

Gardner, A., *English Medieval Sculpture*, Cambridge, 1951.

Gardner, A., *Minor English Wood Sculpture 1400–1550*, London, 1958.

Garvey, P. A., *Silver Heritage: a History of Hedon's Civic Plate*, Withernsea and Hornsea, 1979.

Garvey, P. A., *The Hedon Silver*, revised by M. Craven and J. Markham, Beverley, 2000.

Gay, V., *Glossaire archéologique du Moyen Age et de la Renaissance*, 2 vols, Paris, 1887 and 1928.

Geddes, J., *Medieval Decorative Ironwork in England*, Society of Antiquaries, London, 1999.

Geddes, J., 'John Tresilian and the Gates of Edward IV's Chantry', in Keen and Scarff 2002, pp.166–76.

Gee, S., 'The printers, stationers and bookbinders of York before 1557', *Transactions of the Cambridge Bibliographical Society*, XII/1, 2000, pp.27–54.

Giles, K. F., *An Archaeology of Social Identity: Guildhalls in York, c.1350–1630*, British Archaeological Report 315, Oxford, 2000.

Gill, M. C., *Late Medieval Wall Painting in England: Content and Context (c.1350–c.1530)*, unpublished doctoral dissertation, Courtauld Institute of Art, University of London, 2001.

Gill, M., 'The wall paintings in Eton College Chapel: the making of a late medieval Marian cycle', in P. Lindley (ed.), *Making Medieval Art*, forthcoming.

Girouard, M., 'Three Gothic drawings in the Smithson Collection', *RIBA Journal*, 3rd series, LXIV, 1956, pp.35–6.

Girouard, M., *Life in the English Country House*, New Haven and London, 1978.

Glanville, P., *Silver in England*, London, 1987.

Glanville, P., *Silver in Tudor and Early Stuart England*, Victoria and Albert Museum, London, 1990.

Glasscoe, M., *Ashton Church, Devon*, Exeter, 1984.

Glasscoe, M., 'Late Medieval paintings in Ashton Church, Devon', *Journal of the British Archaeological Association*, CXL, 1987, pp.182–90.

Glynne, S., 'Notes on Yorkshire Churches', *Yorkshire Archaeological Journal*, XXVI, 1922, pp.259–99.

Goldberg, P. J. P., *Women, work and life cycle in a medieval economy: women in York and Yorkshire, c.1300–1520*, Oxford, 1992.

Goodall, J. A., 'The use of armorial bearings by London aldermen in the middle ages', *Transactions of the London and Middlesex Archaeological Society*, XX, 1959–61, pp.17–21.

Goodall, J. A. A., *God's House at Ewelme: Life Devotion and Architecture in a Fifteenth-century Almshouse*, Aldershot, 2001.

Goodall, J. A. A., 'Henry VI's Court and the construction of Eton College', in Keen and Scarff 2002, pp.247–63.

Goodison, J. W., *Catalogue of the Portraits in Christ's, Clare and Sidney Sussex Colleges*, Cambridge, 1985.

Goodman, A., *The New Monarchy*, Oxford, 1988.

Gordon, D., Monnas, L. and Elam, C. (eds), *The Regal image of Richard II and the Wilton Diptych*. London, 1997.

Görlach, M., 'Regional and social variation' in R. Lass (ed.), *The Cambridge History of the English Language*, III, *1476–1776*, Cambridge, 1999, pp.459–538.

Goronwy-Roberts, A., *Mask: Torrigiano's Bust of Bishop Fisher Reconsidered*, privately published, 1992.

Gough, H. (ed.), *The Register of the Fraternity or Guild of the Holy and Undivided Trinity and Blessed Virgin Mary in the Parish Church of Luton*, Luton, 1906.

Gough, R., *Sepulchral Monuments in Great Britain*, I, London, 1786.

Gough, S., *Treasures for the Nation: Conserving our Heritage*, London, 1988.

Grace, M., *Records of the Gild of St George in Norwich, 1389–1547: a Transcript with an Introduction*, Norfolk Record Society, IX, 1937.

Graham-Dixon, A., *A History of British Art*, London, 1996.

Gransden, A. (ed.), *Bury St Edmunds:*

Medieval Art, Architecture, Archaeology and Economy (British Archaeological Association Conference Transactions, XX), Leeds, 1998.

Gras, N., *The Early English Customs System*, Cambridge, MA, 1918.

Graves, A., *Tiles and Tilework of Europe*, Victoria and Albert Museum, London, 2002.

Graves, P., 'Social Space in the English Parish Church', *Economy and Society*, XVIII/3, 1990, pp.297–322.

Gray, D., 'The Five Wounds of Our Lord', *Notes and Queries*, CCVIII, 1963, pp.50–51, 82–9, 127–34, 163–8.

Greatrex, J. (ed.), *The Register of the Common Seal of the Priory of St Swithun, Winchester, 1345–1497*, Hampshire Record Series, II, 1978.

Greatrex, J., *Biographical Register of the English Cathedral Priories of the Province of Canterbury, c.1066 to 1540*, Oxford, 1997.

Green, M., 'The Penn Doom', *Records of Bucks*, XLIV, 2003, forthcoming.

Greenhill, F. A., *Incised Effigial Slabs*, 2 vols, London, 1976.

Greenwood, J. R., 'Haines's Cambridge School of Brasses', *Transactions of the Monumental Brass Society*, XI/1, 1969, pp.2–12.

Greenwood, R. and Norris, M., *The Brasses of Norfolk Churches*, Holt, 1976.

Grenville, J., *Medieval Housing*, Leicester, 1997.

Grierson, P., 'The origin of the English sovereign and the symbolism of the closed crown', *British Numismatic Journal*, XXXIII, 1964, pp.118–34.

Grierson, P., 'Notes on early Tudor coinage. 4. The origin of the portrait groats', *British Numismatic Journal*, XLI, 1972, pp.80–94.

Griffiths, J. and Pearsall, D. (eds), *Book Production and Publishing in Britain 1375–1475*, Cambridge, 1989.

Griffiths, R., *The Reign of Henry VI*, Berkeley, 1981.

Grimme, E. G., *Der Aachener Domschatz*, (*Aachener Kunstblätter*, XLII), Aachen, 1972.

Grössinger, C., 'The Raising of Lazarus; a French Primitive in Sherborne (Dorset)', *Journal of the British Archaeological Association*, CXXXII, 1979, pp.91–101.

Grössinger, C., *Ripon Cathedral Misericords*, Ripon, 1989.

Grössinger, C., 'The Misericords in Beverley Minster: their relationship to other misericords and fifteenth-century prints', in Wilson 1989, pp.186–94.

Grössinger, C., *North-European Panel Paintings: A Catalogue of Netherlandish & German Paintings before 1600 in English Churches & Colleges*, London, 1992.

Grössinger, C., *The World Upside-Down: English Misericords*, London, 1997.

Grove 2001: *The New Grove Dictionary of Music and Musicians*, 2nd edn, London, 2001.

Guiffrey, J., *Inventoires de Jean, Duc de Berry*, 2 vols, Paris, 1894.

Guildhall Museum 1908: *Catalogue of the Collection of London Antiquities*, London, 1908.

Gunn, S. J., *Early Tudor Government, 1485–1558*, Basingstoke, 1995.

Gunn, S. J. and Lindley, P. G. (eds), *Cardinal Wolsey: Church, State and Art*, Cambridge, 1991.

Gunn, S. J. and Lindley, P. G., 'Introduction', in Gunn and Lindley 1991, pp.1–53.

Gutch, J., *Collectanea Curiosa*, Oxford, 1781.

GW: *Gesamtkatalog der Wiegendrucke*, vols I–, Leipzig and Stuttgart, 1925–.

Gwyn, P., *The King's Cardinal: The Rise and Fall of Thomas Cromwell*, London, 1990.

Gwynne, P., 'The frontispiece to an illuminated panegyric of Henry VII: a note on the sources', *Journal of the Warburg and Courtauld Institutes*, LV, 1984, pp.266–70.

Hadley, G., *Citizens and Founders: A History of the Worshipful Company of Founders, 1365–1975*, London, 1976.

Halkin, L.-E., Bierlaire, F. and Hoven, R. (eds), *Opera Omnia Desiderii Erasmi Roterodami, Ordinis Primi, Tomus Tertius, Colloquia*, Amsterdam, 1972.

Hall, E., *The Union of the two Noble and illustrious families of Lancastre and Yorke . . .*, 1548/50, London, 1809.

Halliwell, J. O., *The Early History of Freemasonry*, 2nd edn, London, 1844.

Hamer, R., 'Introduction' in C. Stace (ed.), *Jacobus de Voragine, The Golden Legend: Selections*, London, 1998, pp.ix–xxxi.

Hamilton Thompson, A., *The English Clergy and their Organisation in the Later Middle Ages*, Oxford, 1947.

Hammond, P. W., 'The Coronet of Margaret of York', *The Ricardian*, VI, September 1984, pp.362–5.

Hand, J. O., *The Collections of the National Gallery of Art, Systematic Catalogue, German Paintings of the Fifteenth through Seventeenth Centuries*, Washington and Cambridge, 1993.

Hanham, A. (ed.), *The Cely Letters 1472–1488*, Early English Text Society, 273, 1975.

Hanham, A., *The Celys and their World: An English merchant family of the fifteenth century*, Cambridge, 1985.

Hardacre, J., *Winchester Cathedral Triforium Gallery: Sculpture, Woodwork and Metalwork from Eleven Centuries*, Winchester, 1989.

Harding, V., 'Cross-Channel trade and cultural contacts – London and the Low Countries in the later 14th century', in Carlin and Rosenthal 1998, pp.153–68.

Hardman, P., 'Interpreting the incomplete scheme of illustration in Cambridge, Corpus Christi College MS 61', *English Manuscript Studies 1100–1700*, VI, 1997, pp.52–69.

Hardy, C. F., 'On the music in the painted glass of the windows in the Beauchamp Chapel at Warwick', *Archaeologia*, LXI, 1909, pp.583–614.

Hardy, R., *Longbow*, Sparkford, 2000.

Harper, J., *The forms and orders of western liturgy from the tenth to the eighteenth century: a historical introduction and guide for students and musicians*, Oxford, 1991.

Harris, K. 'The Patron of British Library Arundel MS 38', *Notes and Queries*, XXXI, 1984, pp.462–3.

Harris, K., 'The patronage and dating of Longleat House MS 24, a prestige copy of the Pupilla Oculi illuminated by the Master of the *Troilus* Frontispiece', in Riddy 2000, pp.35–54.

Harrison, D. F., 'Bridges and economic development, 1300–1800', *Economic History Review*, XLV, 1992, pp.240–61.

Harrison, F., 'Sutton Place, Guildford', *Surrey Archaeological Collections*, IX, 1888, pp.1–18.

Harrison, F. L. (ed.), *The Eton Choirbook*, 3 vols, London, 1956–61.

Harrison, F. L., *Music in Medieval Britain*, London, 1958.

Harriss, G. L., 'Medieval government and statecraft', *Past and Present*, XXV, July 1963, pp.8–39.

Harriss, G. L., 'Henry V's Books', in McFarlane 1972, pp.233–8.

Harriss, G. L. (ed.), *Henry V. The Practice of Kingship*, Oxford, 1985.

Harriss, G. L. 'The King and his Subjects', in Horrox 1994, pp.13–28.

Harthan, J., *Books of Hours and their Owners*, London, 1977.

Hartshorne, A., 'Blythborough Church, Suffolk', *Archaeological Journal*, XLIV, 1887, pp.1–14.

Harvey, A. S., *The Trinity House, Kingston upon Hull*, Hull, 1950.

Harvey, J. H., *The Heritage of Britain. Our historic past through 53 centuries*, London, 1940.

Harvey, J. H., 'The Medieval Office of Works', *Journal of the British Archaeological Association*, 3rd series, VI, 1941, pp.20–86.

Harvey, J. H., *Gothic England. A Survey of National Culture 1300–1550*, London, 1947.

Harvey, J. H., *An Introduction to Tudor Architecture*, London, 1949.

Harvey, J. H., 'Early Tudor Draughtsmen', in L. G. G. Ramsey (ed.), *Connoisseur Coronation Book*, London, 1953, pp.97–102.

Harvey, J. H. (ed.), *William Worcestre: Itineraries*, Oxford, 1969.

Harvey, J. H., *The Mediaeval Architect*, London, 1972.

Harvey, J. H., *Mediaeval Craftsmen*, London and Sydney, 1975.

Harvey, J. H., 'Architectural History from 1291 to 1558', in G. E. Aylmer and R. Cant (eds), *A History of York Minster*, Oxford, 1977, pp.149–92.

Harvey, J., *The Perpendicular Style, 1330–1485*, London, 1978.

Harvey, J. H., 'The Church Towers of Somerset', *Transactions of the Ancient Monuments Society*, XXVI, 1982, pp.157–83.

Harvey, J. H., *English Mediaeval Architects. A Biographical Dictionary down to 1550*, rev. edn, Gloucester, 1984.

Harvey, J. H., 'Architecture in Oxford 1350–1500', in J. I. Catto and R. Evans (eds), *The History of the University of Oxford, Vol. II, Late Medieval Oxford*, Oxford, 1992, pp.747–68.

Haskell, F., *History and its Images. Art and the Interpretation of the Past*, New Haven and London, 1993.

Haskell, F. and Penny, N., *Taste and the Antique*, New Haven and London, 1981.

Hatcher, J., 'England in the aftermath of the Black Death', *Past & Present*, CXLIV, 1994, pp.3–35.

Hatcher, J., 'The great slump of the mid-fifteenth century', in R. Britnell and J. Hatcher (eds), *Progress and Problems in Medieval England: Essays in Honour of Edward Miller*, Cambridge, 1996, pp.237–72.

Haward, B., *Suffolk Medieval Church Arcades, 1150–1550*, Ipswich, 1993.

Haward, B., *Suffolk Medieval Church Roof Carvings: a Photographic Survey of Carvings on Hammerbeam Roofs*, Ipswich, 1999.

Hawkins, E., *Medallic Illustrations of the History of Great Britain and Ireland to the death of George II*, I, London, 1885.

Hawkyard, A. D. K., 'Thornbury Castle', *Transactions of the Bristol and Gloucestershire Archaeological Society*, XCV, 1978, pp.51–8.

Hay, D., 'The Church of England in the later middle ages', in D. Hay, *Renaissance Essays*, London, 1988, pp.233–48.

Hayward, J. F., 'The Pearl Sword of the City of Bristol', *The Connoisseur*, May 1956, pp.85–7.

Hayward, J. F., *Virtuoso Goldsmiths and the Triumph of Mannerism 1540–1620*, London, 1976.

Heard, K., 'Death and representation in the fifteenth century: the Wilcote chantry chapel at North Leigh', *Journal of the British Archaeological Association*, CLIV, 2001, pp.134–49.

Hearn, K. (ed.), *Dynasties: Painting in Tudor and Jacobean England 1530–1630*, exh. cat., Tate Gallery, London, 1995.

Heenan, M. G., 'The French quartering in the arms of King Henry IV', *Coat of Arms*, X, 1968–9, pp.215–21.

Hegbin-Barnes, P., *The Medieval Stained Glass of the County of Lincolnshire*, Corpus Vitrearum Medii Aevi Great Britain, Summary Catalogue 3, Oxford, 1996.

Hellinga, L., 'Wykyn de Worde's native land', in R. Beadle and A. J. Piper (eds), *New science out of old books: Studies in manuscripts and early printed books in honour of A. I. Doyle*, Aldershot, 1995, pp.342–59.

Hellinga, L. and Trapp, J. B. (eds), *The Cambridge History of the Book in Britain, III, 1400–1557*, Cambridge, 1999.

Henisch, B. A., *Fast and Feast: Food in Medieval Society*, Pennsylvania and London, 1976.

Henry, A. (ed.), *Biblia Pauperum. A facsimile and edition*, Aldershot, 1987.

Hepburn, F., 'The Portraiture of Lady Margaret Beaufort', *The Antiquaries Journal*, LXXII, 1992, pp.118–40.

Hepburn, F., 'Three Portrait Busts by Torrigiani: A Reconsideration', *Journal of the British Archaeological Association*, CLIV, 2001, pp.150–69.

Herbert, A. S., *Historical catalogue of printed editions of the English Bible* (rev. and expanded from the edn of T. H. Darlow and H. F. Moule, 1903), London and New York, 1968.

Heslop, T. A., 'The construction and furnishing of the parish church of Salle, Norfolk', in B. Ford (ed.), *The Cambridge Guide to the Arts in Britain, Vol. 2, The Middle Ages*, Cambridge, 1988, pp.194–9.

Hewett, C. A., *English Cathedral Carpentry*, London, 1974.

Hicks, M. A., 'The Piety of Margaret, Lady Hungerford', *Journal of Ecclesiastical History*, XXXVIII, 1987, pp.19–38.

Hicks, M.A., *Warwick the Kingmaker*, Oxford, 1998.

Hieatt, C., 'Making sense of medieval culinary records – much done but more to do', in Carlin and Rosenthal 1998, pp.101–10.

Higgins, A., 'On the work of Florentine Sculptors in England in the early part of the sixteenth century; with special reference to the tombs of Cardinal Wolsey and King Henry VIII', *Archaeological Journal*, LI, 1894, pp.129–220.

Hildburgh, W. L., 'Further notes on English alabaster carvings', *The Antiquaries Journal*, X, 1930, pp.34–45.

Hildburgh, W. L., 'An English alabaster carving of St Michael weighing a Soul', *The Burlington Magazine*, LXXXIX, 1947, pp.129–31.

Hill, A. du B., 'The Wollaton Antiphonal', *Transactions of the Thoroton Society*, XXXVI, 1932, pp.42–50.

Hill, G. F., 'A medal of Henry VIII as Supreme Head of the Church', *Numismatic Chronicle*, 1916, pp.194–5.

Hill, G. F., *A Corpus of Italian Medals of the Renaissance before Cellini*, 2 vols, London, 1930.

Hill, G., *Medals of the Renaissance*, rev. and enlarged by G. Pollard, London, 1978.

Hills, A., 'The Capel Helm and a recently discovered Sacring Bell', *Transactions of the Essex Archaeological Society*, N.S. XXI, 1937, pp.209–18.

Hills, P. J. and Oldfield, A. L., *St Martin le Grand, Coney Street, York. A Brief Guide*, York, 2001.

Hind, A. M., *An Introduction to the History of Woodcut*, 2 vols, London, 1935.

Hind, A. M., *Engraving in England in the Sixteenth and Seventeenth Centuries*, I, Cambridge, 1952.

Hindman, S., Camille, M., Rowe, N. and Watson, R., *Manuscript Illumination in the Modern Age*, Evanstown, 2001.

Hobhouse, E., 'An indenture of agreement between the Warden of Merton College, and John Fisher, citizen of London, for making a roodloft within the Quire of the Church AD 1486', *Archaeological Journal*, II, 1846, pp.181–2.

Hobson, G. D., *English Binding before 1500*, Cambridge, 1929.

Hodgson, P. and Liegey, G. M., *The Orchard of Syon, edited from early manuscripts*, Early English Text Society, original series, 258, London, 1966.

Hodnett, E., *English Woodcuts 1480–1535*, 2nd edn, Oxford, 1973.

Hollstein 1986: *Hollstein's German engravings, etchings and woodcuts, c.1400–1700*, vol. XXIV, Amsterdam, 1986.

Homer, R. F., 'Crowned feather plates and Henry VIII's Coronation', *Journal of the Pewter Society*, VII/2, 1989, pp.47–8.

Homer, R. F., 'Pewter in a Somerset church', *Journal of the Pewter Society*, X/1, 1995, pp.19–22.

Honey, W. B., *A Catalogue of the Collection of Italian and other Maiolica . . . and other Ceramic Wares, formed by William Ridout of London and Toronto*, London, 1934.

Honey, W. B., 'Augustin Hirschvogel and the Tyrolese Owl-Jugs', *The Burlington Magazine*, LXIX, 1936, pp.111–20.

Horrox, R. *Richard III: a study of service*, Cambridge, 1989.

Horrox, R. (ed.), *Fifteenth-century Attitudes: perceptions of society in late medieval England*, Cambridge, 1994.

Horrox, R., 'Caterpillars of the Commonwealth? Courtiers in late medieval England', in R. E. Archer and S. Walker (eds) *Rulers and Ruled in late medieval England*, London, 1995, pp.1–15.

Horstmann, C., *Altenglische Legenden. Neue Folge*, Heilbronn, 1881.

How, G. E. P. and J. P., *English and Scottish Silver Spoons*, 3 vols, London, 1952–7.

Howard, F. E., 'Richard Winchcombe's work at the Divinity School and elsewhere', in T. F. Hobson (ed.), *Addersbury 'Rectoria'*, Oxfordshire Record Society, VIII, 1926, pp.34–41.

Howard, M., *The Early Tudor Country House: Architecture and Politics 1490–1550*, London, 1987.

Howard, M., *The Vyne, Hampshire*, The National Trust, London, 1998 (revised 2000).

Howard, M. and Wilson, C., *The Vyne: The Archaeology of a Great Tudor House*, forthcoming 2003.

Howarth, D., *Images of Rule: art and politics in the English Renaissance, 1485–1649*, Basingstoke, 1997.

Hübner, W., Paradis-Vroon, M. and Minkenberg, G., *Der Schatz des Gnadenbildes im Dom zu Aachen*, Domschatzkammer Aachen Aachen, 1996.

Hudson, A., *The Premature Reformation*, Oxford, 1988.

Hudson, A. (ed.), *Two Wycliffite Texts: The Sermon of William Taylor of 1405, The Testimony of William Thorpe 1407*, Early English Text Society, original series, 301, 1993.

Hughes, A. and Bent, M. (eds), *The Old Hall Manuscript* (Corpus Mensurabilis Musicae, 46), 1969–73.

Hughes, J., *The Religious Life of Richard III*, Gloucester, 1997.

Huizinga, J., *Herfsttij der middeleeuwen*, Amsterdam, 1919.

Huizinga, J., *The Waning of the Middle Ages. A survey of the forms of life, thought and art in France and the Netherlands in the XIVth and XVth centuries*, trans. by F. Hopton, London, 1924.

Huizinga, J., *The Autumn of the Middle Ages*, trans. by R. J. Payton and U. Mammitzsch, Chicago, 1996.

Hulbert, A., 'St Oswald's Church, Ashbourne, Derbyshire: Panel Painting', unpublished conservation report, 1986.

Hunt, A., *Governance of the Consuming Passions: a History of Sumptuary Law*, London, 1996.

Hurst, J., 'Medieval pottery: England to 1550', in R. J. Charleston (ed.), *World Ceramics*, London, 1968, pp.111–14.

Hurst, J. G., 'Sixteenth-century South Netherlands Maiolica imported into Britain and Ireland', in Gaimster 1999, pp.91–106.

Hurst, J. G., Neal, D. S. and Van Beuningen, H. J. E., *Pottery produced and traded in North-West Europe 1350–1650*, Rotterdam Papers IV, Rotterdam, 1986.

Husband, T., *The Wild Man: Medieval Myth and Symbolism*, exh. cat., Metropolitan Museum of Art, New York, 1980.

Husband, T., 'The Winteringham Tau Cross and *Ignis Sacer*', *Metropolitan Museum Journal*, XXVII, 1992, pp.19–35.

Hussey, C., 'Ockwells Manor, Bray', *Country Life*, LV, 1924, pp.52–60, 92–9, 130–37.

Hussey, C., 'Haddon Hall, Derbyshire', *Country Life*, CVI, 1949, pp.1651–6.

Hutchinson, F. E., *Medieval Glass at All Souls College*, London, 1949.

Hutchinson, R., 'Tombs of Brass are Spent', in Gaimster and Gilchrist, forthcoming.

Illingworth, W., 'Transcript of a Draft of an Indenture of Covenants for the erecting of a Tomb to the memory of King Henry the Eighth, and Queen Katherine his wife; found among the papers of Cardinal Wolsey, in the Chapter House at Westminster', *Archaeologia*, XVI, 1812, pp.84–8.

Imray, J., *The Charity of Richard Whittington*, London, 1968.

Ipswich 1985: *Selig Suffolk*, exh. cat., Christchurch Mansion Museum, 1985.

Jackson, C. J., 'The spoon and its history', *Archaeologia*, LIII, 1893, pp.107–46.

Jackson, C. J., *An Illustrated History of English Plate, Ecclesiastical and Secular*, London, 1911.

Jacob, E. F., 'The Building of All Souls College 1438–1443', in J. G. Edwards, V. C. Galbraith and E. F. Jacob (eds) *Essays in Honour of James Tait*, Manchester, 1933, pp.121–35.

Jacob, E. F., *Archbishop Henry Chichele*, London, 1967.

Jacob, E. F. and Johnson, H. C. (eds), *The Register of Henry Chichele, Archbishop of Canterbury 1414–1443*, 4 vols, Canterbury and York Society, XLII, XLV–XLVII, 1937–47.

James, M. R., *A descriptive catalogue of the second series of fifty manuscripts in the collection of Henry Yates Thompson*, London, 1902.

James, M. R., 'The Tapestries at Aix-en-Provence and at La Chaise Dieu', *Proceedings of the Cambridge Antiquarian Society*, XI, 1903–6, pp.506–11.

James, M. R., *Suffolk and Norfolk: a Perambulation of the Two Counties with Notices of their Ancient Buildings*, London, 1930, reprinted Bury St Edmunds, 1987.

James, M. R. and Jenkins, C., *A Descriptive Catalogue of the Manuscripts in the Library of Lambeth Palace*, Cambridge, 1930–32.

James, M. R. and Tristram, E. W., 'The wall-paintings in Eton College Chapel and in the Lady Chapel of Winchester Cathedral', *Walpole Society*, XVII, 1928–9, pp.1–43.

Janson, H. W., *Apes and ape lore in the Middle Ages and the Renaissance*, London, 1952.

Jarmuth, K., *Lichter leuchten im Abendland*, Brunswick, 1967.

Jefferson, L., 'Gifts given and fees paid to Garter King of Arms at Installation ceremonies of the Order of the Garter during the 16th century', *Costume*, XXXVI, 2002, pp.18–35.

Jenkinson, H., 'The Great Seal of England: deputed or departmental seals', *Archaeologia*, LXXXV, 1936, pp.293–338.

Jervis, S., *Woodwork of Winchester Cathedral*, Winchester, 1976.

Jewitt, L. and St John Hope, W. H., *The Corporation Plate and the Insignia of Office of the Cities and Corporate Towns of England and Wales*, 2 vols, London, 1895.

Jones, A. H. M., 'All Souls College, Buildings', *Victoria County History, Oxfordshire, III*, London, 1954, pp.183–93.

Jones, E. A., *The Old Plate of the Cambridge Colleges*, Cambridge, 1910.

Jones, E. A., *Catalogue of the Plate of Eton College*, London, 1938.

Jones, M., 'The medal in Britain', *Médailles*, 1990, pp.17–28.

Jones, M. K., 'Collyweston – an early Tudor Palace', in Williams 1987, pp.129–41.

Jones, M. K. and Underwood, M. G., *The King's Mother: Lady Margaret Beaufort, Countess of Richmond and Derby*, Cambridge, 1992.

Jones, P. M., 'Medicine and Science', in Hellinga and Trapp 1999, pp.438–42.

Jones, P. M. and Olsan, L. T., 'Middleham Jewel: Ritual, Power, and Devotion', *Viator*, XXXI, 2000, pp.249–90.

Jones, W., *Finger Ring Lore*, London, 1877.

Kaeuper, R. W., *Chivalry and Violence in Medieval Europe*, Oxford, 1999.

Kamerick, K., *Popular Piety and Art in the late Middle Ages: Image Worship and Idolatry in England 1350–1500*, New York and Basingstoke, 2002.

Keen, L. and Scarff, E., *Windsor: Medieval Archaeology, Art and Architecture of the Thames Valley* (British Archaeological Association Conference Transactions, XXV), Leeds, 2002.

Keen, M., *Chivalry*, New Haven and London, 1984.

Keen, M. H., 'The end of the Hundred Years War: Lancastrian France and Lancastrian England', in M. Jones and M. G. A. Vale (eds) *England and her Neighbours, 1066–1453. Essays in Honour of Pierre Chaplais*, London, 1989, pp.297–311.

Keen, M. H., *English Society in the Later Middle Ages, 1348–1500*, London, 1990.

Keene, D., 'Medieval London and its region', *The London Journal*, XIV, l989, pp.99–111.

Keene, D., 'Wood', in Biddle 1990, pp.959–62.

Keene, D., 'Small towns and the metropolis: the experience of medieval England', in J.-M. Duvosquel and E. Thoen (eds), *Peasants and Townsmen in Medieval Europe: Studia in Honorem Adriaan Verhulst*, Ghent, 1995, pp.223–38.

Keene, D., 'Metalworking in medieval London: an historical survey', *The Journal of the Historical Metallurgy Society*, XXX/2, 1997 for 1996, pp.95–102.

Keene, D., 'Changes in London's economic hinterland as indicated by debt cases in the Court of Common Pleas', in Galloway 2000, pp.59–82.

Keene, D., 'Metropolitan values: migration, mobility and cultural norms, London 1100–1700', in Wright 2000, pp.93–114.

Keiser, G. R., *Works of Science and Information: A Manual of the Writings in Middle English 1450–1500*, New Haven, 1998.

Kemp, W., *The Narratives of Gothic Stained Glass*, Cambridge, 1997.

Kendrick, A. F., 'The Fayrey Pall at Dunstable', *The Embroideress*, I, 1923, pp.123–4.

Kent, E. A., 'The mural painting of St George in St Gregory's Church, Norwich', *Norfolk Archaeology*, XXV, 1935, pp.167–9.

Kent, J. P. C., 'Monumental brasses: a new classification of military effigies c.1360–c.1485', *Journal of the British Archaeological Association*, 3rd series, XII, 1949, pp.70–97.

Kent, J. P. C., 'A new type of George noble of Henry VIII', in Detsicas 1981, pp.231–4.

Ker, N. R., *Medieval Manuscripts in British Libraries, I, London*, Oxford, 1969.

Ker, N. R., *Medieval Manuscripts in British Libraries, II, Abbotsford-Keele*, Oxford, 1977.

Ker, N. R. and Piper, A. J., *Medieval Manuscripts in British Libraries, IV, Paisley-York*, Oxford, 1992.

Kermode, J., *Medieval Merchants. York, Beverley and Hull in the Later Middle Ages*, Cambridge, 1998.

Kerry, C., *The History and Antiquities of the Hundred of Bray in the County of Berks*, London, 1861.

Kidson, P., 'The architecture of St George's Chapel', in M. Bond (ed.), *The Saint George's Chapel Quincentenary Handbook*, Windsor, 1975, pp.29–38.

King, D., 'A relic of "Noble Erpingham"', *Victoria and Albert Museum Bulletin*, IV, 1968, pp.59–64.

King, D. J., *Stained Glass Tours around Norfolk Churches*, Woodbridge, 1974.

King, D. J., 'A glazier from the Bishopric of Utrecht in fifteenth-century Norwich', E. de Bièvre (ed.), *Utrecht: Britain and the Continent, Archaeology, Art and Architecture*, British Archaeological Association Conference Transactions XVIII, 1996, pp.216–25.

King, D. J., 'The panel paintings and stained glass', in I. Atherton et al. (eds) *Norwich Cathedral: Church, City and Diocese, 1096–1996*, London and Rio Grande, 1996, pp.410–30.

King, D. J., *The Medieval Stained Glass of St Peter Mancroft, Norwich*, Corpus Vitrearum Medii Aevi Great Britain, IV, forthcoming.

King, J. N., *Tudor Royal Iconography. Literature and Arts in an Age of Religious Crisis*, Princeton, 1989.

King, P. M., 'The Cadaver Tomb in England: novel manifestations of an old idea', *Church Monuments*, V, 1990, pp.26–38.

Kingsley, N., *The Country House of Gloucestershire, Vol. I, 1500–1660*, Cheltenham, 1989.

Kipling, G., *Enter the King: theatre, liturgy and ritual in the medieval civic triumph*, Oxford, 1998.

Kirk, R. E. G. and Kirk, E. F., *Returns of Aliens 1523–71*, Huguenot Society, X/1, 1900.

Kisby, F., 'Music and musicians of early Tudor Westminster', *Early Music*, XXIII, 1995, pp.223–40.

Kisby, F., 'Royal minstrels in the city and suburbs of early Tudor London: professional activities and private interests', *Early Music*, XXV, 1997, pp.199–219.

Kisby, F., 'A mirror of monarchy: Music and musicians in the household chapel of the Lady Margaret Beaufort, mother of Henry VII', *Early Music History*, XVI, 1997, pp.203–34.

Knight Watson, C., untitled note in *Proceedings of the Society of Antiquaries*, IV, 1867–70, pp.86–7.

Knighton, C., 'Copes transform the most inelegant cleric', *The Westminster Abbey Chorister*, XXIX, Winter 1999–2000, pp.50–53.

Knowles, D., *The Religious Orders in England, III, The Tudor Age*, Cambridge, 1959.

Knowles, D. and Hadcock, R. N., *Medieval Religious Houses: England and Wales*, 2nd edn, London, 1971.

Knowles, J. A., *Essays in the History of the York School of Glass-Painting*, London, 1936.

Knox, R. and Leslie, S. (eds) *The Miracles of King Henry VI*, Cambridge, 1923.

Korteweg, A. S. et al. (eds), *Praal, ernst & emotie*, exh. cat., The Hague, 2002.

Kovacs, E., 'Le reliquaire de l'Ordre du Saint-Esprit: la "dot" d'Anne de Bretagne', *Revue du Louvre*, IV, 1981, pp.246–51.

Kowaleski, M., *Local Markets and Regional Trade in Medieval Exeter*, Cambridge, 1995.

Kowaleski, M., 'The expansion of the south-western fisheries in late medieval England', *Economic History Review*, LIII, 2000, pp.428–54.

Kren, T. (ed.), *Margaret of York, Simon Marmion and the Visions of Tondal*, Malibu, 1992.

Kren, T. and McKendrick, S. (eds), *Illuminating the Renaissance: the Triumph of Flemish Manuscript Painting in Europe 1467–1561*, exh. cat., Getty Museum, Los Angeles, 2003.

Krieder, A., *English Chantries: The Road to Dissolution*, Cambridge, MA, 1979.

Krotoff, M.-H., *Les tapisseries de la vie du Christ et de la Vierge d'Aix-en-Provence*, exh. cat., Musée des Tapisseries, Aix-en-Provence, 1977.

Kurath, H. (ed.), *Middle English Dictionary*, Ann Arbor, 1956–99.

Laborde, L., *Les ducs de Bourgogne: études sur les lettres, les arts et l'industrie pendant le XVe siècle et plus particulièrement dans les Pays-Bas et le duché de Bourgogne*, I, Paris, 1849.

Lack, W., Stuchfield, H. M. and Whittemore, P., *The Monumental Brasses of Bedfordshire*, London, 1992.

Lahoz, L., *Escultura funeraria gótica en Alava*, Vitoria, 1996.

Laking, G. F., *A Record of European Armour and Arms through Seven Centuries*, 5 vols, London, 1920–22.

Lander, J. R., *Government and Community: England 1450–1509*, London, 1980.

Lasko, P. and Morgan, N. J. (eds), *Medieval Art in East Anglia 1300–1520*, exh. cat., Norwich, 1973.

Law, A. S., 'Another Feather dish', *Journal of the Pewter Society*, V/2, 1985, pp.61–5.

Lawler, T. M. C. et al., *Complete Works of St Thomas More*, vol. 6, New Haven and London, 1981.

Lawton, L., 'The illustration of Late Medieval secular texts, with special reference to Lydgate's "Troy Book"', in D. Pearsall (ed.), *Manuscripts and Readers in fifteenth-century England: the literary implications of manuscript study*, Cambridge, 1983, pp.41–69.

Layard, N. F., 'Notes on some English paxes, including an example recently found in Ipswich', *The Archaeological Journal*, LXI, 1904, pp.120–30.

Leach, M. (ed.), *Dictionary of Folklore, Mythology and Legend*, 2 vols, New York, 1949, 1959–62.

Leedy, W. C., *Fan Vaulting: A Study of Form, Technology and Meaning*, London, 1980.

Lees, T. and Ferguson, R. S., 'On the remains of ancient glass and woodwork at St Anthony's Chapel, Cartmel Fell', *Transactions of the Cumberland and Westmorland Antiquarian and Archaeological Society*, II, 1874–5, pp.389–99.

Leeuwenberg, J. and Halsema-Kubes, W., *Beeldhouwkunst in het Rijksmuseum, Catalogus*, Amsterdam, 1973.

Le Goff, J., *The Birth of Purgatory*, translated by A. Goldhammer, Chicago, 1984.

Lepie, H., *Die Domschatzkammer zu Aachen. Katalog*, 6th edn, Aachen, 1990.

Leroquais, V., *Les bréviaires manuscrits des bibliothèques publiques de France*, 6 vols, Paris, 1934.

Lester, G. A., 'Sir John Paston's *Grete Boke*: a bespoke book or mass-produced?', *English Studies*, LXI, 1985, pp.93–104.

Letts, M. (trans. and ed.), *The Travels of Leo of Rozmital through Germany, Flanders, England, France, Spain, Portugal and Italy 1465–1467*, Hakluyt Society, 2nd series, CVIII, Cambridge, 1957.

Levey, M., 'Dürer and England', *Anzeiger des Germanischen Nationalmuseums*, 1971–2, pp.157–64.

Lewis, J., 'Lathom House: the Northern Court', *Journal of the British Archaeological Association*, CLII, 1999, pp.150–71.

Lieftinck, G., *Boekverluchters uit de omgeving van Maria van Bourgondië* (Verhandelingen van de Koninklijke Vlaamse Academie voor Wetenschappen, Letteren en Schone kunsten van België, Klasse der Letteren 31, no. 66), Brussels, 1969.

Lightbown, R. W., *Secular Goldsmiths' Work in Medieval France: A History*, London, 1978.

Lightbown, R. W., *Mediaeval European Jewellery, with a catalogue of the collection in the Victoria and Albert Museum*, London, 1992.

Lilley, K. D., *Urban Life in the Middle Ages, 1000–1450*, Basingstoke, 2002.

Lindley, P., 'The sculptural programme of Bishop Fox's chantry chapel', *Winchester Cathedral Record*, LVII, 1988, pp.33–7 (reprinted in Lindley 1995, pp.207–12).

Lindley, P., 'The Great Screen of Winchester Cathedral, I', *The Burlington Magazine*, CXXXI, 1989, pp.604–15.

Lindley, P. G., 'Playing check-mate with royal majesty? Wolsey's patronage of Italian Renaissance sculpture', in Gunn and Lindley 1991, pp.261–85.

Lindley, P., 'The Great Screen of Winchester Cathedral, II', *The Burlington Magazine*, CXXXV, 1993, pp.796–807.

Lindley, P., 'The medieval sculpture of Winchester Cathedral', in Crook 1993, pp.97–122.

Lindley, P., *Gothic to Renaissance: Essays on Sculpture in England*, Stamford, 1995.

Lindley, P., 'Innovations, tradition and disruption in tomb-sculpture', in Gaimster and Stamper 1997, pp.77–92.

Lindley, P., 'Absolutism and Regal image in Ricardian Sculpture', in Gordon, Monnas and Elam 1997, pp.61–83, 288–96.

Lindley, P., 'The Great Screen and its Context', in M. Henig and P. Lindley (eds), *Alban and*

St Albans. Roman and Medieval Architecture, Art and Archaeology (British Archaeological Association Conference Transactions, XXIV), Leeds, 2001, pp.256–70.

Linnell, C., 'The Burrell Dalmatic and the Whalley Vestments', in *Rarer Gifts than Gold: Fourteenth-century Art in Scottish Collections*, exh. cat., The Burrell Collection, Glasgow, 1988, pp.47–8.

Llewellyn, N., *The Art of Death: visual culture in the English death ritual c.1500–1800*, London, 1991.

Lloyd, A. H., *The Early History of Christ's College, Cambridge*, Cambridge, 1934.

Lloyd Parry, H., *The History of Exeter Guildhall and the Life Within*, Exeter, 1936.

Loach, J., *Parliament under the Tudors*, Oxford, 1991.

London 1850: *Catalogue of Antient and Medieval Art*, exh. cat., Royal Society of Arts, 1850.

London 1890: *Exhibition of the Royal House of Tudor*, exh. cat., New Gallery, Regent Street, 1890.

London 1894: *Illustrated Catalogue of the Heraldic Exhibition*, exh. cat., Burlington House, 1894.

London 1896: *Catalogue of Exhibition of English Mediaeval Paintings and Illuminated Manuscripts*, exh. cat., Society of Antiquaries, 1896.

London 1905: *Catalogue of English Embroidery*, exh. cat., Burlington Fine Arts Club, 1905.

London 1908: *Exhibition of Illuminated Manuscripts*, exh. cat., Burlington Fine Arts Club, 1908.

London 1909: *Exhibition Illustrative of Early English Portraiture*, exh. cat., Burlington Fine Arts Club, 1909.

London 1913: *Illustrated Catalogue of the Exhibition of English Medieval Alabaster Work held in . . . 1910*, exh. cat., Society of Antiquaries, 1913.

London 1924: *Exhibition of British Primitive Paintings from the twelfth to the early sixteenth century. With some related illuminated manuscripts, figure embroidery, and alabaster carvings*, exh. cat., Royal Academy of Arts (Oxford, 1924).

London 1927: *An Exhibition of Works of Art belonging to the Livery Companies of the City of London*, exh. cat., Victoria and Albert Museum, rev. and ill. edn, 1927.

London 1929: *Catalogue of Loan Exhibition of English Decorative Art . . .* , exh. cat., Lansdowne House, 1929.

London 1930: *Exhibition of English Mediaeval Art, c.700–1500*, exh. cat., 2 vols, Victoria and Albert Museum, 1930.

London 1934a: *Guide to an Exhibition of English Art gathered from various departments and held in the Prints and Drawings Gallery*, British Museum, 1934.

London 1934b: *Exhibition of British Art c.1000–1860*, exh. cat., Royal Academy of Arts, 1934.

London 1936: *Heralds' Commemorative Exhibition 1484–1934 Held at the College of Arms. Enlarged and Illustrated Catalogue*, exh. cat., College of Heralds, 1936.

London 1939: *Catalogue of an Exhibition of British Mediaeval Art*, exh. cat., Burlington Fine Arts Club, 1939.

London 1951: *Catalogue of the Historic Plate of the City of London*, exh. cat., Goldsmiths' Hall, 1951.

London 1952: *Corporation Plate of England and Wales*, exh. cat., Goldsmiths' Hall, 1952.

London 1953: *Treasures of Oxford*, exh. cat., Goldsmiths' Hall, 1953.

London 1955: *Catalogue of Silver Treasures for English Churches: an Exhibition of Ecclesiastical Plate of Domestic Origin*, Christie's, 1955.

London 1959: *Treasures of Cambridge*, exh. cat., Goldsmiths' Hall, 1959.

London 1963: *Opus Anglicanum*, exh. cat., Victoria and Albert Museum, 1963.

London 1967: *Hungarian Art Treasures*, exh. cat., Victoria and Albert Museum, 1967.

London 1977: *The Burrell Collection*, exh. cat., Hayward Gallery, 1977.

London 1978: *Touching Gold and Silver: 500 Years of Hallmarks*, exh. cat., Goldsmiths' Hall, 1978.

London 2000: *The Image of Christ*, exh. cat., National Gallery, 2000.

London, H. S., *The Life of William Bruges, the first Garter King of Arms*, Harleian Society, CXI–CXII, 1970.

London Museum 1940: *Medieval Catalogue, London Museum Catalogues No. 7*, London, 1940.

Long, C. E. (ed.), *Diary of the Marches of the Royal Army, During the Great Civil War*, London, 1859.

Lowry, M., 'John Rous and the survival of the Neville circle', *Viator*, 1988, pp.327–38.

Luton 1936: *Loan Exhibition of Furniture of the Gothic and Early Tudor Periods*, exh. cat., Luton Museum, 1936.

Lyell, L. and Watney, F. D., *Acts of the Court of the Mercers' Company 1453–1527*, Cambridge, 1936.

Lyon, M. (ed.), *Sacred Music from the Lambeth Choirbook* (Recent Researches in Music of the Renaissance, 69), Madison, WI, 1985.

Lyons, L.-C., untitled note in *Proceedings of the Society of Antiquaries*, XXII, 1907–9, p.540.

Macauley, G. C. (ed.), *John Gower, The English Works*, 2 vols, Early English Text Society, extra series, LXXXI–LXXXII, 1900–1.

McCarthy, M., *The Origins of the Gothic Revival*, New Haven and London, 1987.

McCleod, E., *Charles of Orleans, Prince and Poet*, London, 1969.

McConica, J. K., *English Humanists and Reformation Politics under Henry VIII and Edward VI*, Oxford, 1965.

McConica, J. K., *The Waning of the Middle Ages: an essay in historiography*, Toronto, 1996.

MacCulloch, D., *Suffolk and the Tudors*, Oxford, 1986.

Macfarlane, J., *Antoine Vérard*, Bibliographic Society, London, 1900 (for 1899).

McFarlane, K. B., *Lancastrian Kings and Lollard Knights*, Oxford, 1972.

McFarlane, K. B., *The Nobility of Later Medieval England*, Oxford, 1973.

McFarlane, K. B., 'Henry V, Bishop Beaufort and the red hat', in K. B. McFarlane, *England in the Fifteenth Century*, London, 1981, pp.79–113.

MacGregor, A., 'Antler, bone and horn', in Blair and Ramsay 1991, pp.355–78.

MacGregor, A., with M. Mendonça and J. White, *Manuscript Catalogues of the Early Museum Collections 1683–1886 (Part I)*, BAR International Series 907, Oxford, 2000.

McHardy, A. K., 'Some reflections on Edward III's use of propaganda', in J. S. Bothwell (ed.), *The Age of Edward III*, Woodbridge, 2001, pp.171–92.

McKendrick, S., 'Edward IV: An English royal collector of Netherlandish tapestry', *The Burlington Magazine*, CXXIX, 1987, pp.521–4.

McKendrick, S., '*La Grande Histoire Cesar* and the Manuscripts of Edward IV', in P. Beal and J. Griffiths (eds), *English Manuscript Studies 1100–1700*, 2, Oxford, 1990, pp.109–38.

McKendrick, S., 'The *Great History of Troy*: a Reassessment of the Development of a Secular Theme in Late Medieval Art', *Journal of the Warburg and Courtauld Institutes*, LIV, 1991, pp.43–82.

McKendrick, S., 'The *Romuléon* and the Manuscripts of Edward IV', in Rogers 1994, pp.149–69.

McKendrick, S., 'Tapestries from the Low Countries in England during the Fifteenth Century', in Barron and Saul 1995, pp.43–60.

McKenna, J. W., 'Popular canonization as political propaganda: the cult of Archbishop Scrope', *Speculum*, XLV, 1970, pp.608–23.

McKerrow, R. B. and Ferguson, F. S., *Title-page borders used in England and Scotland 1485–1640*, London, 1932.

Maclagan, E., 'An English alabaster altarpiece in the Victoria and Albert Museum', *The Burlington Magazine*, XXXVI, 1920, pp.53–65.

Maclagan, E. and Oman, C. C., 'An English Gold Rosary of about 1500', *Archaeologia*, LXXXV, 1935, pp.1–22.

Maddison, J., *Ely Cathedral: Design and Meaning*, Ely, 2000.

Mainz 1991: *Blockbücher des Mittelalters: Bilderfolgen als Lektüre*, exh. cat., Gutenberg Museum, Mainz, 1991.

Mallet, C. E., *A History of the University of Oxford*, 3 vols, London, 1924–7.

Mallon, A. H., 'Cotehele, a feudal manor house of the West', *Pall Mall Magazine*, 1894, pp.180–97.

Manchester 1958: *Ecclesiastical Art*, exh. cat., Whitworth Art Gallery, Manchester, 1958.

Mane, P., 'Emergence du vêtement de travail à travers l'iconographie médiévale', *Le Vêtement (Cahiers du Léopard d'or*, I, 1989), pp.93–122.

Mann, J. G., 'A Sword and a Helm in Westminster Abbey', *The Antiquaries Journal*, XI, 1931, pp.405–9.

Manners, V., 'The Rutland Monuments in Bottesford Church', *The Art Journal*, 1903, pp.269–74.

Margeson, S. and Goodall, I. H., various reports on metalwork in S. Margeson (ed.), *Norwich Households: Medieval and post-medieval finds from Norwich Survey excavations 1971–78 (East Anglian Archaeology, 58)*, Norwich, 1993.

Marius, R., *Thomas More*, New York, 1985.

Marks, R., 'The Glazing of Fotheringhay Church and College', *Journal of the British Archaeological Association*, CXXXI, 1978, pp.70–109.

Marks, R., *The Stained Glass of the Collegiate Church of the Holy Trinity, Tattershall (Lincs.)*, New York and London, 1984.

Marks, R., 'The Howard Tombs at Thetford and Framlingham: new discoveries', *The Archaeological Journal*, CXLI, 1984, pp.252–68.

Marks, R., 'Recent discoveries in Medieval Art', *Scottish Art Review*, XVI/1, 1984, pp.13–20.

Marks, R., *Stained Glass in England during the Middle Ages*, London, 1993.

Marks, R., 'The glazing of Henry VII's Chapel, Westminster Abbey', in Thompson 1995, pp.157–74.

Marks, R., *The Medieval Stained Glass of Northamptonshire*, Corpus Vitrearum Medii Aevi Great Britain, Summary Catalogue 4, Oxford, 1998.

Marks, R., 'Two illuminated guild registers from Bedfordshire', in Brown and McKendrick 1998, pp.121–42.

Marks, R., 'A Holbeinesque "royal" window in England', *Österreichische Zeitschrift für Kunst und Denkmalpflege*, LIV/2–3, 2000, pp.385–91.

Marks, R., 'A late medieval pilgrimage cult: Master John Schorn of North Marston and Windsor', in Keen and Scarff 2002, pp.192–207.

Marks, R., 'Viewing Our Lady of Pity', in *Magistro et Amico amici discipulique. Lechowi Kalinowskiemu w osiemdziesięciolecie urodzin*, Cracow, 2002, pp.101–21.

Marks, R., 'Images of Henry VI', in J. Stratford and J. Boffey (eds), *The Lancastrian Court* (Harlaxton Symposium, 2001), Stamford, 2003.

Marks, R., *Image and Devotion in Late Medieval England*, forthcoming.

Marks, R., 'Entumbid Right Princely': *The Beauchamp Chapel at Warwick and the Politics of Interment* (inaugural lecture, University of York, 1996), forthcoming.

Marks, R. et al., *The Burrell Collection*, London and Glasgow, 1983.

Marks, R. and Morgan, N., *The Golden Age of English Manuscript Painting 1200–1500*, London, 1981.

Marks, R. and Payne, A., *British Heraldry from its origins to c.1800*, exh. cat., British Museum, London, 1978.

Martin, C. T., *Catalogue of the Muniments in the Muniment Room of All Souls College, Oxford*, London, 1877.

Martindale, A., 'The Ashwellthorpe triptych', in D. Williams (ed.), *Early Tudor England (Proceedings of the 1987 Harlaxton Symposium)*, Woodbridge, 1989, pp.107–23.

Martindale, A., 'The wall-paintings in the Chapel of Eton College', in Barron and Saul 1995, pp.133–52.

Mattingley, J., 'The dating of bench-ends in Cornish churches', *Journal of the Royal Institute of Cornwall*, n.s. ii, I/1, 1991, pp.58–72.

Mattingley, J., 'Stories in the glass – reconstructing the St Neot pre-Reformation glazing scheme', *Journal of the Royal Institute of Cornwall*, n.s. ii, III/3–4, 2000, pp.9–55.

Maxwell-Lyte, H., *A History of Eton College 1440–1874*, London, 1875.

Mayer-Thurmann, C., *Raiment for the Lord's Service*, exh. cat., Art Institute of Chicago, 1975.

Mead, W. E., *The English Medieval Feast*, London, 1931.

Meale, C. M., 'Patrons, Buyers and Owners: Book Production and Social Status', in J. Griffiths and D. Pearsall (eds), *Book Production and Publishing in Britain 1375–1475*, Cambridge, 1989, pp.201–38.

Meech, S. B. and Allen, H. E. (eds), *The Book of Margery Kempe*, Early English Text Society, CCXII, 1940.

Meiss, M., *Painting in Florence and Siena after the Black Death*, Princeton, 1951.

Melville, N., 'Towards the identification of a group of fifteenth century English two-handed swords', *Handbook to the Eighteenth Park Lane Arms Fair*, London, 2001, pp.19–25.

Mennell, S., *All manners of food, eating and taste in England and France from the Middle Ages to the present*, Oxford, 1985.

Metcalf, D. M., *Sylloge of Coins of the British Isles, 23. Ashmolean Museum, Oxford, III. Coins of Henry VII*, London, 1976.

Meyrick, S. R., Letter of 26 November 1826 to Henry Ellis, Secretary of the Society of Antiquaries, on the sword of Battle Abbey, *Archaeologia*, XXII, 1829, pp.414–16.

Mickelthwaite, J. T., 'A description of the Chapel of St Erasmus in Westminster Abbey', *Archaeologia*, XLIV, 1873, pp.93–9.

Mickelthwaite, J. T., *Modern Parish Churches: their Plan, Design and Furniture*, London, 1874.

Mickelthwaite, J. T., 'Notes on the imagery of Henry the Seventh's Chapel, Westminster', *Archaeologia*, XLVII, 1882–3, pp.361–80.

Middeldorf, U., *Sculptures from the Samuel H. Kress Collection, European Schools XIV–XIX Century*, London, 1976.

Middleton, A., 'The idea of public poetry in the reign of Richard II', *Speculum*, LIII, 1978, pp.94–114.

Miglio, M., *Storiografia pontificia del quattrocento*, Bologna, 1975.

Miller, E. (ed.), *The Agrarian History of England and Wales, III, 1348–1500*, Cambridge, 1991.

Milner, J., *A Treatise on the Ecclesiastical Architecture of England, during the Middle Ages*, London, 1811.

Milroy, J., 'Middle English dialectology', in N. Blake (ed.), *The Cambridge History of the English Language*, II, *1066–1476* (Cambridge, 1992), pp.156–206.

Milsom, J., 'Songs and society in early Tudor London', *Early Music History*, XVI, 1997, pp.235–9.

Mireille, M., 'Cornes et cornettes', in M. Smeyers and B. Cardon (eds), *Flanders in a European Perspective: Manuscript Illumination around 1400 in Flanders and Abroad (Proceedings of the International Colloquium, Leuven, 7–10 September 1993)*, Leuven, 1995, pp.417–26.

Mitchell, J., assisted by M. Moran, *England and the Continent in the Middle Ages: Studies in Memory of Andrew Martindale, (Harlaxton Medieval Studies, VIII)*, Stamford, 2000.

Mitchell, J., 'Painting in East Anglia around 1500: The Continental Connection', in Mitchell and Moran 2000, pp.365–80.

MME: *A Manual of the Writings in Middle English 1050–1500*, 10 vols, New Haven, 1967– (I–II ed. by J. B. Severs, III–X by A. E. Hartung).

Moffat, H. C., *Old Oxford Plate*, London, 1906.

Monceaux, H., *Les Le Rouge de Chablis, calligraphes et miniaturistes, graveurs et imprimeurs. Étude sur les débuts de l'illustration du livre au XVe siècle*, 2 vols, Paris, 1896.

Monckton, L., *Late Gothic Architecture in South West England*, unpublished doctoral dissertation, University of Warwick, 1999.

Monks, P. R. and Owen, D. D. R. (eds), *Medieval Codicology, Iconography, Literature, and Translation: Studies for Keith Val Sinclair*, Leiden, 1994.

Monnas, L., 'New documents for the vestments of Henry VII at Stonyhurst College', *The Burlington Magazine*, CXXXI, 1989, pp.345–9.

Monnas, L., 'Silk cloths purchased for the Great Wardrobe', *Ancient and Medieval Textiles: Studies in Honour of Donald King (Textile History*, XX/2, 1989), pp.283–307.

Monnas, L., 'Opus Anglicanum and Renaissance Velvet: the Whalley Abbey Vestments', *Textile History*, XXV/1, 1994, pp.3–27.

Monnas, L., '"Tissues" in England during the fifteenth and sixteenth centuries', *CIETA Bulletin*, LXXV, 1998, pp.62–80.

Monnas, L., 'Textiles from the Funerary Achievement of Henry V', *Proceedings of the 2001 Harlaxton Symposium*, forthcoming.

Mooney, L. R., 'English almanacs from script to print', in J. Scattergood and J. Boffey (eds), *Texts and their Contexts: Papers of the Early Book Society*, Dublin, 1997.

Moore, A., with Crawley, C., *Family and Friends: A Regional Survey of Portraiture*, exh. cat., Norwich Castle Museum (London, 1992).

Moore Smith, G., *The Family of Withypoll*, Walthamstow Antiquarian Society Official Publications 34, 1936.

Morehen, J. (ed.), *English Choral Practice, 1450–1625*, London, 1995.

Moreno, T. K., *A Collection of 15th-century Wax Votive Images: Identification, Analysis and Conservation*, unpublished MA dissertation, University of Durham, 2001.

Morgan, O., 'On a Chalice and Paten belonging to the Parish Church of Nettlecombe in the County of Somerset, with remarks on Early English Chalices', *Archaeologia*, XLII/2, 1870, pp.405–16.

Morgan, O., *Some Account of the Ancient Monuments in the Priory Church, Abergavenny*, Newport, 1872.

Morganstern, A., *Gothic Tombs of Kinship in France, the Low Countries, and England*, University Park, PA, 2000.

Morris, C. (ed.), *The Journeys of Celia Fiennes*, London, 1949.

Müller, C., *Hans Holbein d. J. Die Druckgraphik im Kupferstichkabinett Basel*, Basel, 1997.

Muller, J., *Laiton, Dinanderie*, Musées royaux d'Art et d'Histoire, Brussels, 1983.

Muller, L. A. (ed.), *The Letters of Stephen Gardiner*, Cambridge, 1933 (reprinted Westport, CT, 1970).

Munby, A. N. L., *Connoisseurs and Medieval Miniatures, 1750–1850*, Oxford, 1972.

Munby, J., 'Richard Beauchamp's Funeral Car', *Journal of the British Archaeological Association*, CLV, 2002, pp.278–87.

Murdoch, J., Murrell, J., Noon, P.J. and Strong, R., *The English Miniature*, New Haven and London, 1981.

Murdoch, T. (ed.), *Treasures and Trinkets: Jewellery in London from pre-Roman Times to the 1930s*, exh. cat., Museum of London, 1991.

Murdoch, T., 'The Dacre Beasts', *V&A Magazine*, May–August 2000 (2000), pp.14–16.

Murdoch, T., 'The Dacre Beasts', *National Art Collections Fund 2000 Review*, 2000, pp.128–9.

Myers, A. R., *The Household of Edward IV: the Black Book and the Ordinance of 1478*, Manchester, 1959.

Myers, A. R., 'Parliament, 1422–1509', in R. G. Davies and J. H. Denton (eds),

The English Parliament in the Middle Ages, Manchester, 1981, pp.141–84.

Myers, H. W., 'The Mary Rose "Shawm"', *Early Music*, XI, 1983, pp.358–60.

Myres, J. N. L., 'Recent discoveries in the Bodleian Library', *Archaeologia*, CI, 1967, pp.151–68.

Nelson, P., 'A Doom Reredos', *Transactions of the Historic Society of Lancashire and Cheshire*, LXX, 1918, pp.67–71.

Nelson, P., 'Some unpublished English medieval alabaster carvings', *Archaeological Journal*, LXXVII, 1920, pp.213–25.

Nelson, P., 'An English medieval wooden Pax', *The Antiquaries Journal*, XII, 1932, pp.445–6.

Nelson, P., 'The Warwick Signet-Ring', *Transactions of the Historic Society of Lancashire and Cheshire*, CI, 1949, pp.65–7.

Nelson, W., 'Thomas More, grammarian and orator', *PMLA [Publications of the Modern Language Association of America]*, LVIII, 1943, pp.337–52.

Newton, P. A., 'William Browne's Hospital at Stamford', *Antiquaries Journal*, XLVI, 1966, pp.283–6.

New York 1975: *The Secular Spirit: Life and Art at the End of the Middle Ages*, exh. cat., Metropolitan Museum of Art, 1975.

New York 1986: *Gothic and Renaissance Art in Nuremberg 1300–1550*, exh. cat., Metropolitan Museum of Art, 1986.

Nichols, A. E., *Seeable Signs. The Iconography of the Seven Sacraments, 1350–1544*, Woodbridge, 1994.

Nichols, J., *The History and Antiquities of the County of Leicester*, vol. II, part II, London, 1798.

Nichols, J. G., *Description of the Church of St Mary, Warwick, and of the Beauchamp Chapel*, London, 1838.

Nichols, J. G. (trans. and ed.), *Erasmus, Pilgrimages to St Mary of Walsingham and St. Thomas of Canterbury*, London, 1849.

Nichols, J. G. and Bruce, J., *Wills from Doctors Commons. A Selection of the Wills of Eminent Persons*, Camden Society, 1st series, LXXXIII, 1862–3.

Nicols, N. H., *Testamenta Vetusta*, London, 1826.

Nightingale, P., *A Medieval Mercantile Community: the Grocers' Company & the Politics & Trade of London, 1000–1485*, New Haven and London, 1995.

Nilson, B., *Cathedral Shrines of Medieval England*, Woodbridge, 1998.

Nixon, H. M., *Broxbourne Library. Styles and designs of bookbindings from the 12th to the 20th century*, London, 1956.

Nixon, H. M., 'Early English gold-tooled bookbindings', in *Studi di bibliografia e di storia in onore di Tammaro de Marinis*, Verona, 1964, III, pp.283–308.

Nixon, H. M., *Five Centuries of English Bookbindings*, London, 1978.

Nixon, H. M. and Foot, M. M., *The History of Decorated Bookbinding in England*, Oxford, 1992.

Nocq, H., *Le Poinçon de Paris . . . depuis le Moyen Age*, 5 vols, Paris, 1926–31.

Norman, A. V. B., *Arms and Armour in the Royal Scottish Museum*, Edinburgh, 1972.

Norman, A. V. B. and Wilson, G., *Treasures from the Tower of London*, exh. cat., London, 1982.

Norris, M., *Brass Rubbing*, London, 1965.

Norris, M., *Monumental Brasses: The Memorials*, 2 vols, London, 1977.

Norris, M., *Monumental Brasses: The Craft*, London, 1978.

Norris, M., 'Later medieval monumental brasses: an urban funerary industry and its representation of death', in S. Bassett (ed.), *Death in Towns: Urban Responses to the Dying and the Dead, 100–1600*, Leicester, 1992, pp.184–209, 248–51.

Norris, T. G., 'On the statue of St Peter, High Street, Exeter', *Transactions of the Exeter Diocesan Architectural Society*, 2nd series, I, 1867, pp.159–62.

North, J. J., *English Hammered Coinage*, II, London, 1991.

Nuremberg 2000: *Spiegel der Seligkeit. Privates Bild und Frömmigkeit im Spätmittelalter*, exh. cat., Germanisches Nationalmuseum, 2000.

Oakeshott, R. E., 'A fifteenth-century "Royal" sword preserved in Westminster Abbey Library', *The Connoisseur*, May 1952, pp.104–8, 128.

O'Connor, D., 'Iconography', in French 1995, pp.6–11.

O'Connor, M. C., *The Art of Dying Well: the development of the Ars Moriendi*, New York, 1942.

Oman, C. C., 'Medieval Brass Lecterns in England', *Archaeological Journal*, LXXXVII, 1930, pp.117–49.

Oman, C., 'English medieval drinking horns', *Connoisseur*, CXIII, 1944, pp.20–23.

Oman, C., *English Domestic Silver*, 2nd edn, London, 1947.

Oman, C., 'Belted Will Howard', *Country Life*, CIII, 1948, pp.1076–8.

Oman, C., *English Church Plate 597–1830*, London, 1957.

Oman, C., 'English Medieval Base Metal Church Plate', *The Archaeological Journal*, CXIX, 1962, pp.195–207.

Oman, C., 'The Winchester College Plate', *Connoisseur*, CXLIX, 1962, pp.24–33.

Oman, C., *Medieval Silver Nefs*, Victoria and Albert Museum, London, 1963.

Oman, C., 'The Eton College Plate: Part 1 (1430–1760)', *Connoisseur*, CLXXVII, 1971, pp.100–7.

Oman, C., *British Rings 800–1914*, London, 1974.

Oman, C., *English Engraved Silver 1150–1900*, London, 1978.

Oman, C., 'The College Plate', in J. Buxton and P. Williams (eds), *New College Oxford 1379–1979*, Oxford, 1979, pp.293–306.

Orme, N., 'Two Saint-Bishops of Exeter: James Berkeley and Edmund Lacy', *Analecteca Bollandiana*, CIV, 1986, pp.403–18.

Orme, N., 'John Holt (d. 1504), Tudor schoolmaster and grammarian', *The Library*, 6th series, XVIII/4, December 1996, pp.283–305.

Orme, N., *The Saints of Cornwall*, Oxford, 2000.

Orme, N., *Medieval Childhood*, New Haven and London, 2001.

Ormerod, G., 'Observations on several ancient Swords of State belonging to the Earldom of Chester', *Vetusta Monumenta*, V, Society of Antiquaries of London, 1835.

Ormrod, W. M. and Lindley, P. G. (eds), *The Black Death in England*, Stamford, 1996.

Osborne, J., 'Politics and popular piety in fifteenth-century Yorkshire: Images of "St" Richard Scrope in the Bolton Hours', *Florilegium*, XVII, 2000, pp.1–19.

Ouy, G., 'Charles d'Orléans and his brother Jean d'Angoulême in England: what their manuscripts have to tell', in M. -J. Arn (ed.), *Charles d'Orléans in England 1415–1440*, Cambridge, 2000.

Oxford 1904: *Illustrated Catalogue of a Loan Collection of Portraits of English Historical Personages who died prior to the year 1625*, exh. cat., Examination Halls, University of Oxford, 1904.

Oxford 1928: *Catalogue of a loan exhibition of silver plate belonging to the Colleges of the University of Oxford*, Oxford, 1928.

Oxford 1968: *Fine Bindings 1500–1700 from Oxford Libraries*, exh. cat., Bodleian Library, 1968.

Oxford 1988: *Duke Humfrey's Library and the Divinity School*, exh. cat., Bodleian Library, 1988.

Page, C., *Discarding Images: Reflections on Music and Culture in Medieval France*, Oxford, 1993.

Paine, C., 'The Building of Long Melford Church', in *A Sermon in Stone: The 500th anniversary book of Long Melford Church*, Lavenham, 1983.

Paine, C. R., *St Mary's Bury St Edmunds*, rev. edn, Bury St Edmunds, 2000.

Palliser, D. M. (ed.), *The Cambridge Urban History of Britain, I, 600–1540*, Cambridge, 2000.

Palmer, B. D., 'Recycling "The Wakefield Cycle": the records', *Research Opportunities in Renaissance Drama*, XLI, 2002, pp.88–130.

Palmer, F., 'Musical instruments from the Mary Rose: a report on work in progress', *Early Music*, XI, 1983, pp.53–9.

Panofsky, E., *Tomb Sculpture: its changing aspects from Ancient Egypt to Bernini*, New York, 1964.

Pantin, W. A., *The English Church in the fourteenth century*, Toronto, 1980.

Paris 1981: *Les Fastes du Gothique: le siècle de Charles V*, exh. cat., Galeries nationales du Grand Palais, 1981.

Parker, J. H. and Turner, T. N., *Some Account of Domestic Architecture in England from Richard II to Henry VIII*, Oxford, 1859.

Parker, K. T., *Catalogue of the Collection of Drawings in the Ashmolean Museum, I, Netherlandish, German, French and Spanish Schools*, Oxford, 1938.

Parker, K. T., *The Drawings by Holbein in the Collection of His Majesty the King*, Oxford, 1945 (reprinted with appendix by S. Foister, 1983).

Parkes, M. B. and Salter, E., *Troilus and Criseyde, Geoffrey Chaucer. A Facsimile of Corpus Christi College Cambridge MS 61*, Cambridge, 1978.

Parsons, W. L. E., *Salle. The Story of a Norfolk Parish, its Church, Manors and People*, Norwich, 1937.

Pascal, J. B. E., *Origines et raison de la liturgie catholique en forme de dictionnaire*, Paris, 1844.

Paul, J. Balfour, *Memorial catalogue of the heraldic exhibition, Edinburgh, MDCCCXCI*, Edinburgh, 1892.

Payne, A., 'The Salisbury Roll of Arms, c.1463', in Williams 1987, pp.187–98.

Payne, A., 'Sir Thomas Wriothesley and his heraldic artists', in Brown and McKendrick 1998, pp.142–61.

Peacock, E., 'Extracts from the churchwardens' accounts of the parish of Leverton', *Archaeologia*, XLI, 1867, pp.333–70.

Pearce, J. and Vince, A. G., *Surrey Whitewares*, London and Middlesex Archaeological Society Special Paper 10, 1988.

Pedrick, G., *Borough Seals of the Gothic Period*, London, 1904.

Pegge, S., 'Of the horn, as a charter or instrument of conveyance', *Archaeologia*, III, 1775, pp.13–14.

Perceval, C. S., 'Seal of the borough of Colchester', *Proceedings of the Society of Antiquaries*, X, 1883–5, pp.343–6.

Peters, E. and Simons, W. P., 'The New Huizinga and the Old Middle Ages', *Speculum*, LXXIV, 1999, pp.587–620.

Petre, J. (ed.), *Richard III: crown and people*, London, 1985.

Pevsner, N., *An Outline of European Architecture*, 7th edn, London, 1963.

Pevsner, N., *The Buildings of England: Yorkshire, The West Riding*, 2nd edn, rev. E. Radcliffe, Harmondsworth, 1967.

Pfaff, R. W., *Montague Rhodes James*, London, 1980.

Philadelphia 2001: *Leaves of Gold, Manuscript Illumination from Philadelphia Collections*, exh. cat., Philadelphia Museum of Art, 2001.

Pinto, E., *Treen and other wooden bygones: an encyclopedia and social history*, London, 1969.

Piponnier, F. and Mane, P., *Dress in the Middle Ages*, London, 1997.

Pirovano, C. (ed.), *Segni e Sogni della Terra: il disegno del mondo dal mito di Atlante alla geographia delle reti*, exh. cat., Milan, Novara, 2001.

Pitman, C. F., 'Nottingham Alabasters', *Museums Journal*, LIX, 1959, pp.208–12.

Platt, C., *The English Medieval Town*, London, 1976.

Platt, C., *The Parish Churches of Medieval England*, London, 1981.

Plenderleith, H. J. and Maryon, H., 'The Royal Bronze Effigies in Westminster Abbey', *The Antiquaries Journal*, XXXIX, 1959, pp.87–90.

Plummer, C. (ed.), *The Governance of England . . . by Sir John Fortescue, Knight*, Oxford, 1885.

Plunkett, S., 'Finger-ring depicting the Annunciation', *National Art Collections Fund 1997 Review*, pp.73–4.

Pollard, A. J., *North-Eastern England during the Wars of the Roses: Lay Society, War and Politics, 1450–1500*, Oxford, 1990.

Pollard, A. J. (ed.), *The Wars of the Roses*, Basingstoke, 1995 (2nd edn, 2001).

Pollard, A. J., *Late Medieval England, 1399–1509*, Harlow, 2000.

Pope-Hennessy, J., *Catalogue of Italian Sculpture in the Victoria and Albert Museum*, 3 vols, London, 1964.

Postan, M. M., *The medieval economy and society: an economic history of Britain in the Middle Ages*, London, 1975.

Potter, D., *War and Government in the French Provinces: Picardy, 1470–1560*, Cambridge, 1993.

Potter, W. J. W. and Winstanley, E. J., 'The coinage of Henry VII. Chapter VI. The profile coins', *British Numismatic Journal*, XXXI, 1962, pp.109–17.

Potts, R. U., 'St Austin's Abbey Canterbury', *Archaeologia Cantiana*, XXXIV, 1920, pp.139–48.

Powell, E., *Kingship, Law and Society: criminal justice in the reign of Henry V*, Oxford, 1989.

Powell, S., 'Lady Margaret Beaufort and her Books', *The Library*, 6th series, XX, 1998, pp.197–240.

Power, E., *Medieval People*, London, 1963.

Prevenier, W. and Blockmans, W., *The Burgundian Netherlands*, Cambridge, 1986.

Prigent, C., *Les sculptures anglaises d'albâtre*, Musée national du Moyen Age, Thermes de Cluny, Paris, 1998.

Prior, E. S., *Gothic Art in England*, London, 1900.

Prior, E. S. and Gardner, A., *An Account of Figure-Sculpture in England*, Cambridge, 1912.

Proctor, R., 'The Accipies woodcut', *Bibliographica*, I, 1895, pp.52–63.

Pugh, T. B., 'Richard Plantagenet (1411–60), Duke of York, as the King's Lieutenant in France and Ireland', in J. G. Rowe (ed.), *Aspects of late medieval government and society*, Toronto, 1986, pp.107–42.

Pugin, A. W. N., *Contrasts: or, a parallel between the noble edifices of the fourteenth and fifteenth centuries, and similar buildings of the present day; shewing the present decay of taste*, London, 1836.

Purvis, J. S., 'The use of continental woodcuts and prints by the Ripon school of woodcarvers', *Archaeologia*, LXXXV, 1935, pp.107–28.

Pyhrr, S. W. and Godoy, J.-A., *Heroic Armor of the Italian Renaissance: Filippo Negroli and his Contemporaries*, exh. cat., Metropolitan Museum of Art, New York, 1998.

Quirk, R. N., 'Sir William de Lillebon, the Lady Anastasia and their Painted Panel', *Winchester Cathedral Record*, XXIV, 1955, pp.17–23.

Rackham, B., *Early Netherlands Maiolica, with special reference to the tiles at The Vyne*, London, 1926.

Rackham, B., *Medieval English Pottery*, 2nd edn, rev. J. G. Hurst, London, 1972.

Radford, U. M., 'The wax images found in Exeter Cathedral', *The Antiquaries Journal*, XXIX, 1949, pp.164–8.

Radice, B. (trans.), *Erasmus, Praise of Folly*, Harmondsworth, 1993.

Ramm, H. G. et al, 'The tombs of Archbishop Walter de Gray (1216–55) and Godfrey de Ludham (1258–65) in York Minster, and their contents', *Archaeologia*, CIII, 1971, pp.101–48.

Ramsay, N., 'Alabaster', in Blair and Ramsay, 1991, pp.29–40.

Ramsay, N. and Sparks, M., 'The Cult of St Dunstan at Christ Church, Canterbury', in N. Ramsey, M. Sparks and T. Tatton-Brown (eds), *St Dunstan: His Life, Times and Cult*, Woodbridge, 1992, pp. 311–23.

Ransome, D. R., 'The struggle of the Glaziers' Company with foreign glaziers, 1500–1550', *Guildhall Miscellany*, II/1, September 1960, pp.12–20.

Rapp-Buri, A. and Stucky-Schürer, M., *Burgundische Tapissereien*, Munich, 2001.

Rashdall, H., *The Universities of Europe in the Middle Ages*, 3 vols, 2nd edn by F. M. Powicke and A. B. Emden, Oxford, 1936.

Raven, J. J., *The Church Bells of Suffolk*, London, 1890.

RCHM 1924: Royal Commission on Historical Monuments (England), *An Inventory of the Historical Monuments in London, Vol. I, Westminster Abbey*, London, 1924.

RCHM 1939: Royal Commission on Historical Monuments, England, *An Inventory of the Historical Monuments in the City of Oxford*, London, 1939.

RCHM 1959: Royal Commission on the Historical Monuments of England, *An Inventory of the Historical Monuments in the City of Cambridge*, London, 1959.

RCHM 1981: Royal Commission on the Historical Monuments of England, *An Inventory of the Historical Monuments in the City of York, Volume 5, The Central Area*, London, 1981.

RCHM 1984: Royal Commission on the Historical Monuments of England, *An Inventory of the Historical Monuments of North Northamptonshire*, London, 1984.

Read, C. H., untitled note in *Proceedings of the Society of Antiquaries*, XVIII, 1899–1901, pp.114–15.

Reddaway, T. F. and Walker, L., *The Early History of the Goldsmiths Company 1327–1509*, London, 1975.

Redknap, M., 'The medieval wooden crucifix figure from Kemeys Inferior, and its church', *The Monmouthshire Antiquary*, XVI, 2000, pp.11–43.

Rees-Jones, S. and Riddy, F., 'The Bolton Hours of York: female domestic piety and the public sphere', in A. Mulder-Bakker and J. Wogan-Browne (eds), *Women and the Christian Tradition*, Turnhout, 2002.

Reineking-von Bock, G., *Steinzeug (Kataloge des Kunstgewerbemuseums Köln, IV)*, 2nd edn, Cologne, 1976.

Remington, P., 'A Portrait of an English Ecclesiastic of the sixteenth century', *Bulletin of the Metropolitan Museum of Art*, XXXI, 1936, pp.223–9.

Reynolds, C., 'Les Angloys de leur droicte nature veullent touzjours guerreer': Evidence for Painting in Paris and Normandy, c.1420–1450', in C. Allmand (ed.), *Power, Culture and Religion in France c.1350–1550*, Woodbridge, 1989, pp.37–55.

Reynolds, C., 'The Shrewsbury Book, British Library, Royal MS 15 E VI', in J. Stratford (ed.), *Medieval Art, Architecture and Archaeology at Rouen*, British Archaeological Association Conference Transactions XII, 1993, pp.109–16.

Reynolds, C., 'English Patrons and French Artists in Fifteenth-century Normandy', in D. Bates and A. Curry (eds), *England and Normandy in the Middle Ages*, London and Rio Grande, 1994, pp.299–313.

Reynolds, C., 'The Bedford Master', in J. Turner (ed.), *The Dictionary of Art*, London, 1996, vol. 20, pp.624–66.

Reynolds, C., 'The Function and Display of Netherlandish Cloth Paintings', in C. Villers (ed.), *The Fabric of Images, European Paintings on Textile Supports in the Fourteenth and Fifteenth Centuries*, London, 2000, pp.89–98.

Reynolds, C., 'The Workshop of the Master of the Duke of Bedford: Definitions and Identities', in G. Croenen (ed.), *Patrons, Authors and Workshops: Books and Book Production in Paris c.1400* (Papers from the Conference at the University of Liverpool, July 2000), Leuven, forthcoming.

Reynolds, S., *An Introduction to the History of English Medieval Towns*, Oxford, 1977.

Reynolds, S., *Fiefs and Vassals. The Medieval Evidence Reinterpreted*, Oxford, 1994.

Richardson, T., 'Recently acquired armour from the Gwynn collection', *Royal Armouries Yearbook*, VI, 2001, pp.13–21.

Richardson, T., *The Armour & Arms of Henry VIII*, Royal Armouries Museum, Leeds, 2002.

Riches, S., *St George: hero, martyr and myth*, Stroud, 2000.

Richmond, C., *John Hopton: A Fifteenth-century Suffolk Gentleman*, Cambridge, 1981.

Richmond, C., 'Religion and the fifteenth-century Gentleman', in R. B. Dobson (ed.), *The Church, Politics and Patronage in the Fifteenth Century*, Gloucester, 1984.

Richmond, C., 'The visual culture of fifteenth-century England', in Pollard 1995, pp.186–250.

Richmond, C. and Scarff, E., *St George's Chapel, Windsor, in the Late Middle Ages*, Windsor, 2001.

Richmond, V. B., *The legend of Guy of Warwick*, New York and London, 1996.

Rickert, M., *Painting in Britain: The Middle Ages*, Pelican History of Art, Harmondsworth, 1954.

Rickert, M., 'The so-called Beaufort Hours and York Psalter', *The Burlington Magazine*, CIV, 1962, pp.238–46.

Rickman, T., *An Attempt to discriminate the Styles of English Architecture from the Conquest to the Reformation; preceded by a sketch of the Grecian and Roman Orders . . .* , London, n.d., but 1817.

Riddy, F. (ed.), *Prestige, Authority and Power in Late Medieval Manuscripts and Texts*, York, 2000, pp.35–54.

Ridyard, S., *The Royal Saints of Anglo-Saxon England: A Study of West Saxon and East Anglian Cults*, Cambridge, 1988.

Rimer, G., *Wheel lock Firearms of the Royal Armouries*, Leeds, 2001.

Roberts, E., *The Hill of the Martyr: an Architectural History of St Albans Abbey*, Dunstable, 1993.

Roberts, J., *Holbein and the Court of Henry VIII*, exh. cat., National Gallery of Scotland, Edinburgh, 1993.

Robinson, J. Armitage, 'Correspondence of Bishop Oliver King and Sir Reginald Bray', *Proceedings of the Somerset Archaeological and Natural History Society*, LX/2, 1914, pp.1–10.

Robinson, M. (ed.), *The Concise Scots Dictionary*, Aberdeen, 1985.

Robson-Scott, W. D., *The Literary Background to the Gothic Revival in Germany*, Oxford, 1965.

Rogers, N. J., 'Fitzwilliam Museum MS 3-1979: A Bury St Edmunds Book of Hours and the Origins of the Bury Style', in Williams 1987, pp.229–43.

Rogers, N. (ed.), *England in the Fifteenth Century, Proceedings of the 1992 Harlaxton Symposium (Harlaxton Medieval Studies, IV)*, Stamford, 1994.

Rogers, N., 'The Bury artists of Harley 2278 and the origins of topographical awareness in English art', in Gransden 1998, pp.219–27.

Rogers, N., 'Some *Curiosa Hagiographica* in Cambridge Manuscripts Reconsidered', in L. Dennison (ed.), *The Legacy of M. R. James*, Donington, 2001, pp.194–210.

Rogers, N., 'Patrons and purchasers: evidence for the original owners of books of hours produced in the Low Countries for the English market', in B. Cardon, J. Van der Stock and D. Vanwijnsberghe (eds), *'Als Ich Can': Liber Amicorum in Memory of Professor Dr Maurits Smeyers*, Leuven, 2002, vol.II, pp.1165–81.

Rohlmann, M., *Auftragskunst und Sammlerbild. Altniederländische Tafelmalerei im Florenz des Quattrocento*, Alfter, 1994.

Rosenthal, J., *The Purchase of Paradise: Gift Giving and the Aristocracy, 1307–1485*, Toronto, 1972.

Ross, C. D., *The Rous Roll, with an historical introduction*, Gloucester, 1980.

Ross, W. O. (ed.), *Middle English Sermons*, Early English Text Society, original series, 209, 1940.

Rotuli Parliamentorum, 6 vols, London, 1767–77.

Rouen-Evreux 1998: *D'Angleterre en Normandie: Sculptures d'albâtre du Moyen Age*, exh. cat., musée départemental des Antiquités, Rouen, and musée de l'Ancien Evêché, Evreux, 1998.

Round, J. H., 'The Arms of Colchester', *Transactions of the Essex Archaeological Society*, n.s., V, 1895, pp.247–9.

Rouse, E. C., 'Wall paintings in the Church of St John the Evangelist, Corby, Lincolnshire', *Archaeological Journal*, C, 1943, pp.150–76.

Rouse, E. C., 'The Penn Doom', *Records of Bucks*, XVII, 1962, pp.95–104.

Routledge, C. F., 'Excavations at St Austin's Abbey, church of Saints Peter and Paul Canterbury', *Archaeologia Cantiana*, XXV, 1902, pp.238–42.

Rowlands, J., *The Paintings of Hans Holbein the Younger*, Oxford, 1985.

Rowlands, J., with Bartrum, G., *Drawings by German Artists . . . in the British Museum. The Fifteenth Century and the Sixteenth Century by Artists born before 1530*, 2 vols, London, 1993.

Rude, D. (ed.), *A Critical Edition of Sir Thomas Elyot's 'The Boke named the Governour'*, New York and London, 1992.

Rudge, T., *The History and Antiquities of Gloucester, from the earliest period to the present time*, Gloucester, n.d., but *c*.1815.

Rule, M., *The Mary Rose: The Excavation and Raising of Henry VIII's Flagship*, London, 1990.

Rundle, D., 'Two unnoticed manuscripts from the collection of Humfrey, Duke of Gloucester', *Bodleian Library Record*, XVI, 1998, pp.211–24, 299–313.

Rushforth, G. McN., *Medieval Christian Imagery as Illustrated by the Painted Windows of Great Malvern Priory Church, Worcestershire*, Oxford, 1936.

Rushforth, G. McN., *The Windows of St Neot, Cornwall*, Exeter, 1937.

Russell, J. G., *Diplomats at Work: Three Renaissance Studies*, Stroud, 1992.

Ryan, W. G. (trans.), *Jacobus de Voragine, The Golden Legend: Readings on the Saints*, 2 vols, Princeton, 1993.

Ryde, C., 'An alabaster angel with shield at Lowick – a Chellaston shop pattern', *Derbyshire Archaeological Journal*, XCVII, 1977, pp.36–49.

Saint, A., *The Image of the Architect*, New Haven and London, 1983.

St John Hope, W. H., 'Seals of the Colleges and of the University of Cambridge', *Proceedings of the Society of Antiquaries*, 2nd series, X, 1883–5, pp.225–52.

St John Hope, W. H., 'On the English medieval drinking bowls called Mazers', *Archaeologia*, L, 1887, pp.129–93.

St John Hope, W. H., 'On the sculptured alabaster tablets called St John's Heads', *Archaeologia*, LII, 1890, pp.669–708.

St John Hope, W. H., 'Municipal Seals of England and Wales', *Proceedings of the Society of Antiquaries*, XV, 1893–5, pp.434–54.

St John Hope, W. H., 'The Episcopal Ornaments of William of Wykeham and William of Waynflete, sometime Bishops of Winchester, and of certain Bishops of St Davids', *Archaeologia*, LX, 1907, pp.465–92.

St John Hope, W. H., *Windsor Castle: An Architectural History*, 3 vols, London, 1913.

St John Hope, W. H., untitled note in *Proceedings of the Society of Antiquaries*, 30 January 1913, pp.39–44.

St John Hope, W. H., 'The Funeral Monument and Chantry Chapel of King Henry the Fifth', *Archaeologia*, LXV, 1914, pp.129–86.

St John Hope, W. H., 'The inventory of John de Vere, Earl of Oxford', *Archaeologia*, LXVI, 1914, pp.328–38.

St John Hope, W. H., 'The heraldry and sculptures of the vault of the Divinity School at Oxford', *Archaeological Journal*, LXXI, 1914, pp.217–60.

St John Hope, W. H. and Fallow, T. M., 'English medieval chalices and patens', *Archaeological Journal*, XLIII, 1886, pp.137–61, 364–402.

Saltmarsh, J., 'The Muniments of King's College', *Proceedings of the Cambridge Antiquarian Society*, XXXIII, 1933, pp.83–97.

Salzman, L. F., 'Medieval Glazing Accounts', *Journal of the British Society of Master Glass-Painters*, III, 1929–30, pp.25–30.

Salzman, L. F., *Building in England down to 1540: a documentary history*, Oxford, 1967 (enlarged reprint of 1952 edn).

Sammut, A., *Unfredo duca di Gloucester e gli umanisti italiani*, Padua, 1980.

Sandon, N., 'The Henrician Partbooks at Peterhouse, Cambridge', *Proceedings of the Royal Musical Association*, CIII, 1976–7, pp.106–40.

Sanna, L., *Tra immagini e parole: I 'Pageants of Richard Beauchamp'*, Pisa, 1991.

Saul, N., *Death, Art and Memory in Medieval England. The Cobham Family and their Monuments 1300–1500*, Oxford, 2001.

Saunders, A., *Fortress Britain. Artillery Fortification in the British Isles and Ireland*, Liphook, 1989.

Saygin, S., *Humphrey, Duke of Gloucester (1390–1447) and the Italian Humanists*, Leiden, Boston and Cologne, 2002.

Scarisbrick, J. J., *Henry VIII*, London, 1968; 2nd edn, New Haven and London, 1997.

Scase, W., 'Writing and the "Poetics of Spectacle": Political Epiphanies in *The Arrivall of Edward IV* and some contemporary Lancastrian and Yorkist texts', in Dimmick, Simpson and Zeeman 2002, pp.172–84.

Scattergood, J., 'Fashion and Morality in the Late Middle Ages', in Williams 1987, pp.255–72.

Scattergood, J., '*Pierce the Ploughman's Crede*: Lollardy and Texts', in M. Aston and C. Richmond (eds), *Lollardy and Gentry in the Later Middle Ages*, Stroud and New York, 1997, pp.77–94.

Scharf, G., *A Catalogue of the Pictures belonging to the Society of Antiquaries*, London, 1865.

Schmeller, J. A. (ed.), *Des böhmischen Herrn Leo's von Rozmital Ritter-, Hof- und Pilge- –Reise durch die Abendlande 1465–1467. Beschreiben von zweien seiner Begleiter*, Bibliothek des literarischen Vereins in Stuttgart, VII, Stuttgart, 1844.

Schofield, J., *Medieval London Houses*, London, 1994.

Schofield, J., 'Social perceptions of space in medieval and Tudor London houses', in M. Locock (ed.), *Meaningful Architecture: Social Interpretations of Buildings*, Aldershot, 1994, pp.188–206.

Schofield, J. and Vince, A., *Medieval Towns*, Leicester, 1994.

Schroder, T., *The National Trust Book of English Domestic Silver*, London, 1988.

Schuler, C., 'The Seven Sorrows of the Virgin: popular culture and cultic imagery in pre-Reformation Europe', *Simiolus*, XXI, 1992, pp.5–28.

Scofield, C. L., *The Life and Reign of Edward the Fourth*, 2 vols, London, 1923.

Scott, J. G. M., 'Casting a bell for Exeter Cathedral, 1372', *Report and Transactions of the Devonshire Association*, C, 1968, pp.191–203.

Scott, K. L., *The Caxton Master and his patrons*, Cambridge Bibliographical Society Monograph 8, Cambridge, 1976.

Scott, K. L., *Later Gothic Manuscripts 1390–1490 (A Survey of Manuscripts Illuminated in the British Isles, 6)*, 2 vols, London, 1996.

Scott, K.L., 'The illustration and decoration of the Register of the Fraternity of the Holy Trinity at Luton Church, 1475–1546', in A. S. G. Edwards, V. Gillespie and R. Hanna (eds), *The English Medieval Book: Studies in Memory of Jeremy Griffiths*, London, 2000, pp.155–84.

Scott, K. L., 'Limner-Power: a Book Artist in England c.1420', in Riddy 2000, pp.55–75.

Scott, M., *Late Gothic Europe, 1400–1500 (The History of Dress Series)*, London, 1980.

Scott, R. F., 'On the Contracts for the Tomb of the Lady Margaret Beaufort, Countess of Richmond and Derby, mother of King Henry VII, and Foundress of the Colleges of Christ and St John in Cambridge', *Archaeologia*, LXVI, 1915, pp.365–76.

Scribner, R., 'Popular Piety and Modes of Visual Perception in Germany', *Journal of Religious History*, XV, 1989, pp.448–69.

Sedding, J. D., 'The Architecture of the Perpendicular Period', *Transactions of the St Paul's Ecclesiological Society*, I, 1881–5, pp.31–44.

Serel, T., *Historical Notes on the Church of Saint Cuthbert in Wells*, Wells, 1875.

Shaw, W. A., *Letters of Denization and Acts of Naturalisation for Aliens in England 1509–1603*, Huguenot Society, VIII, 1893.

Sheppard, J. B. (ed.), *Literae Cantuarienses*, III, London, 1889.

Sherborne, J. W., *William Canynges (1402–1474), Mayor of Bristol and Dean of Westbury College*, Bristol, 1985.

Sim, A., *Food and Feast in Tudor England*, Stroud, 1997.

Simpson, W. D., 'The Building Accounts of Tattershall Castle 1434–1472', *The Lincoln Record Society*, LV, 1960.

Sims, T., 'The Erpingham Gate', in A. Curry (ed.), *Agincourt 1415. Henry V, Sir Thomas Erpingham and the Triumph of the English Archers*, Stroud, 2000, pp.91–103.

Sinclair, A., *The Beaufort Pageant*, Richard III and Yorkist History Trust, Donington, 2003.

Skeat, W. W. (ed.), *Piers Plowman. The Vision of William concerning Piers the Plowman*, 2 vols, Oxford, 1886.

Skinner, D., 'Discovering the provenance and history of the Caius and Lambeth choirbooks', *Early Music*, XXV, 1997, pp.245–66.

Skinner, D. (ed.), *Nicholas Ludford I*, London, 2002.

Skinner, D., *The 'Arundel' Choirbook*, Roxburghe Club, 2003.

Slater, T. R. and Rosser. G. (eds), *The Church in the Medieval Town*, Aldershot, 1998.

Smeyers, M. (ed.), *Vlaamse miniaturen voor van Eyck (ca.1380 – ca.1420)*, Corpus van Verluchte Handschriften uit de Nederlanden 6, exh. cat., Cultureel Centrum Romaanse Poort, Leuven, 1993.

Smeyers, M., *L'Art de la Miniature flamande du VIIIe au XVIe siècle*, Tournai, 1998.

Smit, H. J., *Bronnen tot de Geschiedenis van der Handel met Engeland, Schotland en Ierland, 1150–1585*, 2 vols in 4, Rijks Geschiedkundige Publicatiën 65, 66, 86 and 91, The Hague, 1928–50.

Smith, A., 'The Chantry Chapel of Bishop Fox', *Winchester Cathedral Record*, LVII, 1988, pp.27–32.

Smith, C. J., 'The Bear and Ragged Staff', *Amateur Historian*, III/5, 1957, pp.217–19.

Smith, J., *The Panorama of Science and Art*, 2 vols, Liverpool, 1815.

Smith, L. T., *The Maire of Bristowe is Kalendar by Robert Ricart, Town Clerk of Bristol, 18 Edward IV*, Camden Society, New Series, V, 1872.

Smith, M. T., 'The use of grisaille as a Lenten observance', *Marsyas*, VIII, 1957–9, pp.43–54.

Sneyd, C. A. (trans. and ed.), *A Relation [. . .] of the Island of England [. . .] about the Year 1500*, Camden Society, XXXVII, 1847.

Spencer, B., 'King Henry of Windsor and the London Pilgrim', in J. Bird, H. Chapman and J. Clark (eds), *Collectanea Londinensia: Studies presented to Ralph Merrifield*, London and Middlesex Archaeological Society Special Papers 2, 1978, pp.235–64.

Spencer, B., 'Fifteenth century collar of SS, and a hoard of false dice and their container, from the Museum of London', *The Antiquaries Journal*, LXV/2, 1985, pp.449–53.

Spencer, B., *Pilgrim Souvenirs and Secular Badges*, Salisbury Museum Medieval Catalogue, 1990.

Spencer, B., *Pilgrim Souvenirs and Secular Badges: Medieval Finds from Excavations in London vol. 7*, Museum of London Catalogue, 1998.

Spencer, B., 'Medieval pilgrim badges found at Canterbury, England', in D. Kicken, A. M. Koldeweij and J. R. ter Molen (eds), *Gevonden Voorwerpen: Lost and Found. Essays on Medieval Archaeology for H. J. E. Van Beuningen*, Rotterdam, 2000, pp.316–26.

Spindler, R. (ed.), *The Court of Sapience*, Leipzig, 1927.

Sprague Allen, B., *Tides in English Taste (1619–1800)*, 2 vols, Cambridge, MA, 1937.

Spufford, P., *Handbook of Medieval Exchange*, London, 1986.

Stamp, G., *An Architect of Promise: George Gilbert Scott Jr. (1839–97) and the Late Gothic Revival*, Stamford, 2002.

Starkey, D. (ed.), *Henry VIII: a European court in England*, National Maritime Museum, Greenwich, 1991.

Starkey, D. (ed.), *The Inventory of King Henry VIII. Society of Antiquaries MS 129 and British Library MS Harley 1419. Vol. I: The Transcript*, Reports of the Research Committee of the Society of Antiquaries of London, 56, London, 1998.

STC: *Short title catalogue of books printed in England, Scotland and Ireland, and of English books printed abroad, 1475–1640*, first compiled by A. W. Pollard and G. R. Redgrave, 2nd edn, rev. and enlarged, begun by W. A. Jackson and F. S. Ferguson, completed by K. F. Pantzer, 3 vols, London, 1976–91.

Steane, J., *Archaeology of the Medieval English Monarchy*, London, 1993.

Stenning, D. F. and Andrews, D. (eds), *Regional Variation in Timber-Framed Building in England down to 1550*, Chelmsford, 1998.

Stephenson, M., 'Brasses in Tattershall Church, Lincolnshire', *Transactions of the Monumental Brass Society*, V, 1908–9, pp.326–37, 371–80.

Steppe, J. K., 'Lambert van Eyck en het portret van Jacoba van Beieren', *Mededelingen van de Koninklijke Academie voor wetenschappen, letteren en schone kunsten van België, Klasse der Schone Kunsten*, XLIV/2, 1983, pp.53–86.

Stevens, J. (ed.), *Music at the Court of Henry VIII* (Musica Brittanica, 18), 2nd edn, London, 1973.

Stevens, J., *Music and Poetry at the Early Tudor Court*, London, 1961, reprinted with corrections, Cambridge, 1979.

Steyaert, J. W., *Late Gothic Sculpture: The Burgundian Netherlands*, exh. cat., Ghent, 1994.

Stone, L., *Sculpture in Britain: the Middle Ages*, The Pelican History of Art, 2nd edn, Harmondsworth, 1972.

Stone, L. and Colvin, H. M., 'The Howard Tombs at Framlingham, Suffolk', *The Archaeological Journal*, CXXII, 1965, pp.159–71.

Stothard, C. A., *The Monumental Effigies of Great Britain*, rev. edn, London, 1876.

Stratford, J., 'The Manuscripts of John, Duke of Bedford: Library and Chapel', in Williams 1987, pp.329–50.

Stratford, J., *The Bedford Inventories: the Worldly Goods of John, Duke of Bedford, Regent of France (1389–1435)*, Reports of the Research Committee of the Society of Antiquaries of London, XLIX, London, 1993.

Stratford, J., 'The Early Royal Collections and the Royal Library to 1461', in Hellinga and Trapp 1999, pp.255–66.

Stratford, J. and Reynolds, C., 'The Foyle Breviary and Hours of John, Duke of Bedford, in the British Library', *Festschrift for Lucy Freeman Sandler*, forthcoming.

Stratford, N., 'All Souls lends Flower Jewel', *British Museum Magazine*, 28, 1997, p.32.

String, T., 'Henry VIII's Illuminated "Great Bible"', *Journal of the Warburg and Courtauld Institutes*, LIX, 1996, pp.315–24.

Strohm, P., *England's Empty Throne: usurpation and the language of legitimation 1399–1422*, Yale, 1998.

Strohm, R., *The Rise of European Music 1380–1500*, Cambridge, 1993.

Strong, P. and Strong, F., 'The Last Will and Codicils of Henry V', *English Historical Review*, XCVI, 1981, pp.79–102.

Strong, R., *Tudor and Jacobean Portraits*, National Portrait Gallery, London, 1969.

Strong, R., *Holbein, The Complete Paintings*, London, 1980.

Strong, R. and Murrell, V. J., *Artists of the Tudor Court: the Portrait Miniature*

Rediscovered, 1520–1620, exh. cat., Victoria and Albert Museum, London, 1983.

Stubbs, W., The Constitutional History of England, 5th edn, III, Oxford, 1903.

Sutcliffe, S., 'The cult of St Sitha in England: an introduction', Nottingham Medieval Studies, XXXVII, 1993, pp.83–9.

Sutton, A. F., 'Christian Colborne, Painter of Germany and London, died 1486', Journal of the British Archaeological Association, CXXXV, 1982, pp.55–61.

Sutton, A. F., 'Caxton was a Mercer: his social milieu and friends', in Rogers 1994, pp.118–48.

Sutton, A. F., 'Malory in Newgate: a new document', The Library, 7th series, I, 2000, pp.243–62.

Sutton, A. F. and Hammond, P. W. (eds), The Coronation of Richard III: the extant documents, Gloucester, 1983.

Sutton, A. F. and Visser-Fuchs, L., The Hours of Richard III, Stroud, 1990.

Swanson, H., Medieval Artisans: An Urban Class in Late Medieval England, Oxford, 1989.

Swanson, H. C., Medieval British Towns, Basingstoke, 1999.

Swanson, R. N., 'Standards of livings: parochial revenues in pre-Reformation England', in C. Harper-Bill (ed.), Religious Belief and Ecclesiastical Careers in Late Medieval England, Woodbridge, 1991, pp.151–96.

Swanson, R. N. (trans. and annotated), Catholic England: Faith, Religion and Observance before the Reformation, Manchester and New York, 1993.

Swenarton, M., Artisans and Architects. The Ruskinian tradition in architectural thought, Basingstoke and London, 1989.

Symondson, A., Sir Ninian Comper: the last Gothic revivalist, exh. cat., RIBA Heinz Gallery, London, 1988.

Tait, H. (ed.), Jewellery through 7,000 Years, British Museum, London, 1976.

Tait, H., Catalogue of the Waddesdon Bequest in the British Museum, I, The Jewels, London, 1986.

Tanner, L. E., 'A fifteenth-century sword and a medieval bronze figure from Westminster Abbey', The Antiquaries Journal, X, 1930, pp.146–8.

Tanner, L. E., 'A Mediaeval Abbot', The Westminster Abbey Quarterly, I/1, 1939, pp.26–8.

Tanner, L. E., Unknown Westminster Abbey, Harmondsworth, 1948.

Tatton-Brown, T., 'The constructional sequence and topography of the Chapel and College buildings at St George's', in Richmond and Scarff 2001, pp.3–38.

Tavenor-Perry, J., Dinanderie: A History and Description of Mediaeval Art Work in Copper, Brass and Bronze, London, 1910.

Taylor, G. and Scarisbrick, D., Finger Rings from Ancient Egypt to the Present Day, London, 1978.

Ter Kuile, O., Koper & Brons (Catalogi van de verzameling kunstnijverheid van het Rijksmuseum te Amsterdam, Deel 1), The Hague, 1986.

Thielemans, M.-R., Bourgogne et Angleterre, Relations politiques et économiques entre les Pays-Bas Bourguignons et l'Angleterre 1435–1467, Université libre de Bruxelles, Travaux de la Faculté de Philologie et Lettres, XXX, Brussels, 1966.

Thomas, A. H. and Thornley, I. D. (eds), The Great Chronicle of London, London, 1938.

Thomas, B. and Gamber, O., Kunsthistorisches Museum, Wien, Waffensammlung: Katalog der Leibrüstkammer, I, Vienna, 1976.

Thompson, B., 'The laity, the alien priories and the redistribution of ecclesiastical property', in Rogers 1994, pp.19–41.

Thompson, B. (ed.), The Reign of Henry VII (Harlaxton Medieval Studies, V), Stamford, 1995.

Thompson, M., The Decline of the Castle, Cambridge, 1987.

Thoms, W. J., Franks, A. W. and Scharf, G., 'Instructions given by Henry VI to Edward Grimston . . . with additional observations . . . ', Archaeologia, XL, 1866, pp.451–82.

Thorn, J. C., 'The burial of John Dygon, Abbot of St Augustine's', in Detsicas 1981, pp.74–84.

Thrupp, S., The Merchant Class of Medieval London, Ann Arbor, 1962.

Thurley, S., The Royal Palaces of Tudor England: Architecture and Court Life 1460–1547, New Haven and London, 1993.

Thurley, S., Whitehall Palace: An Architectural History of the Royal Apartments 1240–1690, London, 1999.

Thurlow, G., The Medieval Painted Retables in Norwich Cathedral, Norwich, 1961.

Thysius, A. (ed.), Polydore Vergil, Historia Anglica, Leiden, 1651.

Ticehurst, N. F., The Mute Swan in England, London, 1957.

Tillott, P. M., The Victoria History of the County of York. City of York, Oxford, 1961.

Tipping, H. A., 'Hengrave Hall, Suffolk', English Homes Period II, Vol. 1, Early Tudor 1485–1558, London, 1926, pp.231–43.

Tipping, H. A., 'Herstmonceux Castle, Sussex', English Homes Periods I and II, Vol. 2, 1066–1558, London, 1937, pp.281–306.

Tolhurst, J. B. L., 'The Hammer-beam figures of the nave roof of St Mary's Church, Bury St Edmunds', Journal of the British Archaeological Association, 3rd series, XXV, 1962, pp.66–70.

Toulmin Smith, L. (ed.), The Itinerary of John Leland in or about the Years 1535–1543, 5 vols, London, 1906–10 (reprinted Carbondale, 1964).

Toulson, W., 'The Conservation of the Late Medieval Altar Frontal from the Church of St Mary, Alveley', unpublished report, 2001.

Townsend, C. D., 'Pots from the Mary Rose', Ceramic Review, no. 85, Jan.–Feb. 1984, pp.32–4.

Tracy, C., English Medieval Furniture and Woodwork, Victoria and Albert Museum, London, 1988.

Tracy, C., English Gothic Choir-Stalls 1440–1540, Woodbridge, 1990.

Tracy, C., 'Pew', in J. Turner (ed.), The Dictionary of Art, London, 1996, vol. 24, pp.575–8.

Tracy, C., Continental Church Furniture in England: A Traffic in Piety, Woodbridge, 2001.

Trapp, J. B., 'Notes on manuscripts written by Peter Meghen', The Book Collector, XXIV, 1975, pp.80–96.

Trapp, J. B., 'Peter Meghen, 1466/7–1540: scribe and courier', Erasmus in English, XI, 1981–2, pp.28–33.

Trapp, J. B. and Schulte-Herbrüggen, H., 'The King's Good Servant': Sir Thomas More 1477/8–1535, exh. cat., National Portrait Gallery, London, 1977.

Trio, P., 'L'enlumineur à Bruges, Gand et Ypres (1300–1435). Son milieu socio-économique et corporatif', in M. Smeyers and B. Cardon (eds), Flanders in a European Perspective. Manuscript Illumination c.1400 in Flanders and Abroad (Proceedings of the International Colloquium, Leuven, September 1993), Leuven, 1995, pp.721–9.

Tudor-Craig, P., Exhibition of Medieval Paintings from St Michael at Plea, Victoria and Albert Museum, London, 1956.

Tudor-Craig, P., 'Medieval panel paintings from St Michael at Plea', Burlington Magazine, XCVIII, 1956, pp.333–4.

Tudor-Craig, P., Richard III, exh. cat., National Portrait Gallery, London, 1973.

Tudor-Craig, P., 'Fragment of panel painting of the Flagellation in the possession of Canterbury Cathedral and the Martyrdom of St Erasmus belonging to the Society of Antiquaries', The Antiquaries Journal, LIV, 1974, pp.289–90.

Turner, D. H., 'The Bedford Hours and Psalter', Apollo, LXXVI, 1962, pp.265–70.

Turner, D., The Hastings Hours, London, 1983.

Turner, V. and E., Image and Pilgrimage in Christian Culture, Oxford, 1978.

Turner, W., A new booke of spirituall physic for dyverse diseases [Emden], 1555.

Turville-Petre, T., England and the Nation: Language, Literature and National Identity: 1290–1350, Oxford, 1996.

Tyack, G., Oxford: an Architectural Guide, Oxford, 1998.

Tymms, S., Wills and Inventories from the Registers of the Commissary of Bury St Edmund's and the Archdeacon of Sudbury, Camden Society, XLIX, 1850.

Uden 1992: Heilige Anna, Grote Moeder. De cultus van de Heilige Moeder Anna en haar familie in de Nederlanden en aangrenzende streken, exh. cat., Museum voor Religieuze Kunst, Uden, 1992.

Unwin, G., The Gilds and Companies of London, 4th edn, London, 1963.

Utrecht 1989: The Golden Age of Dutch Manuscript Painting, exh. cat., Rijksmuseum het Catharijneconvent, Utrecht, 1989.

Vallance, A., 'Roods, screens and lofts in Lancashire', in Lt-Col Fishwick and P. H. Ditchfield (eds), Memorials of Old Lancashire, II, London, 1909, pp.228–58.

Vallance, A., Old Crosses and Lychgates, London, 1920.

Vallance, A., English Church Screens, London, 1936.

Vallance, A., Greater English Church Screens, London, 1947.

van Beuningen, H. J. E., Koldeweij, A. M. and Kicken, D. (eds), Heilig en Profaan 2: 1200 laatmiddeleeuwse insignes uit openbare en particuliere collenties, Rotterdam Papers 12, Cithen, 2001.

van der Velden, H., The Donor's Image. Gerald Loyet and the Votive Portraits of Charles the Bold, Turnhout, 2000.

van der Velden, H., 'A prayer roll of Henry Beauchamp, earl of Warwick', forthcoming.

van Mander, K., The Lives of the Illustrious Netherlandish and German Painters, ed. H. Miedema, Doornspijk, 1994.

van Os, H., 'The Black Death and Sienese Painting: a problem of interpretation', Art History, IV/3, 1981, pp.237–47.

van Os, H. (ed.), *The Art of Devotion in the Late Middle Ages in Europe 1300–1500*, exh. cat., Rijksmuseum, Amsterdam, 1994.

van Uytven, R., 'Splendour or Wealth: art and economy in the Burgundian Netherlands', in *Fifteenth-century Flemish Manuscripts in Cambridge Collections*, Transactions of the Cambridge Bibliographical Society, X, 2, 1992, pp.101–24.

Vaughan, J., *Winchester Cathedral: Its Monuments and Memorials*, London, 1919.

VCH 1937: *Victoria County History, Sussex, Vol. IX*, London, 1937.

VCH 1954: *Victoria County History, Oxford, Vol. III*, London, 1954.

VCH 1969: *Victoria County History, Warwickshire, Vol. VIII*, London, 1969.

VCH 2001: *Victoria County History, Gloucestershire, Vol. IX*, Oxford, 2001.

Veale, E. M., *The English Fur Trade in the Later Middle Ages*, Oxford, 1966.

Venables, E., 'The Castle of Herstmonceux and its Lords', *Sussex Archaeological Collections*, IV, 1851, pp.125–202.

Versailles 1994: *Versailles et les Tables Royales en Europe, XVIIème–XIXème siècles*, exh. cat., Musée national des châteaux de Versailles et de Trianon (Paris, 1994).

Vertue, G., *Notebooks, IV*, Walpole Society, XXIV, 1936.

Vian, N., 'La presentazione e gli esemplari Vaticani della "Assertion septem sacramentorum" di Enrico VIII', in *Collectanea Vaticana in honorem Anselmi M. Card. Albareda a Bibliotheca Apostolica edita*, Vatican City, 1962, I, pp.355–75.

Vienna 1962: *Europäische Kunst um 1400*, exh. cat., Kunsthistorisches Museum, 1962.

von Euw, A. and Plotzek, J., *Die Handschriften der Sammlung Ludwig, II*, Cologne, 1982.

Wagner, A. R., *Aspilogia I: A Catalogue of English Mediaeval Rolls of Arms*, Society of Antiquaries and Harleian Society, C, 1950.

Wagner, A. R., *Aspilogia II: Rolls of Arms. Henry III (with Additions and Corrections to Aspilogia I)*, Society of Antiquaries and Harleian Society, CXIII–CXIV, 1967.

Wagner, A., Barker, N. and Payne, A., *Medieval Pageant: Writhe's Garter Book. The Ceremony of the Bath and the Earldom of Salisbury Roll*, Roxburghe Club, London, 1993.

Waller, J. G., 'On the retable in Norwich Cathedral and paintings in St Michael-at-Plea', *Norfolk Archaeology*, XIII, 1898, pp.315–42.

Wallis, R. Ransome, Note in *Goldsmiths' Review*, 1975–6, pp.33–5.

Walpole, H., *Anecdotes of Painting in England; with some Account of the principal Artists; and incidental notes on other arts; collected by the late Mr Geroge Vertue*, 4 vols, Strawberry Hill, 1762–71.

Walsingham, T., *Historia Anglicana*, 2 vols, London, 1863.

Walters, H. B., *Church Bells of England*, London, 1912.

Ward, A., Cherry, J., Gere, C. and Cartlidge, B., *The Ring from Antiquity to the Twentieth Century*, London, 1981.

Warner, G. F., *Descriptive Catalogue of Illuminated Manuscripts in the Library of C. W. Dyson Perrins, D.C.L., F.S.A.*, Oxford, 1920.

Warner, G. (ed.), *The Libelle of Englyshe Polycye*, Oxford, 1926.

Warner, G. F. and Gilson, J. P., *Catalogue of Western Manuscripts in the Old Royal and King's Collections*, British Museum, 4 vols, London, 1921.

Warner, R., *An History of the Abbey of Glaston*, Bath, 1826.

Warton, T., *Observations on the Fairy Queen of Spencer*, 2nd edn, London, 1762.

Washington 1979: *Treasures from Chatsworth: The Devonshire Inheritance*, exh. cat., National Gallery of Art and other venues, 1979.

Washington 1991: *Circa 1492: Art in the Age of Exploration*, exh. cat., National Gallery of Art, 1991.

Wathey, A., 'Dunstable in France', *Music and Letters*, LXVII, 1986, pp.1–36.

Wathey, A., 'Lost books of polyphony in England: a list to 1500', *Royal Musical Association Research Chronicle*, XXI, 1988, pp.1–19.

Wathey, A., *Music in the Royal and Noble Households in Late Medieval England: Studies of Sources and Patronage*, New York, 1989.

Watkin, D., *The Rise of Architectural History*, London, 1980.

Watson, N., 'Censorship and cultural change in late medieval England: vernacular theology, the Oxford Translation Debate, and Arundel's Constitutions of 1409', *Speculum*, LXX, 1995, pp.822–64.

Watson, N., 'Middle English Mystics', in D. Wallace (ed.), *The Cambridge History of Medieval English Literature*, Cambridge, 1999, pp.539–65.

Watts, J. L., *Henry VI and the Politics of Kingship*, Cambridge, 1996.

Watts, J. L. (ed.), *The End of the Middle Ages?*, Stroud, 1998.

Watts, J. L., 'Introduction: history, the fifteenth century and the Renaissance', in Watts 1998, pp.1–22.

Watts, J. L., 'Looking for the State in Later Medieval England', in Coss and Keen 2002, pp.243–67.

Way, A., 'Ornamental tiles in Great Malvern Church', *Gentleman's Magazine*, CXIV/2, 1844, pp.25–31.

Way, A., 'Notices of ancient ornaments, vestments and appliances of sacred use. The pax, tabula pacis, osculatorium, or porte-paix', *Archaeological Journal*, II, 1845, pp.145–51.

Way, A., 'The will of Sir John de Foxle of Apuldrefield, Kent, dated November 5th 1378', *Archaeological Journal*, XV, 1858, pp.267–77.

Way, A., 'Gold pectoral cross from Clare', *Archaeological Journal*, XXV, 1868, pp.60–71.

Wayment, H., 'The great windows of King's College Chapel and the meaning of the word "vidimus"', *Proceedings of the Cambridge Antiquarian Society*, LXIX, 1979, pp.53–69.

Wayment, H., 'The Stained Glass of the Chapel of the Vyne and the Chapel of the Holy Ghost, Basingstoke', *Archaeologia*, CVII, 1982, pp.141–52.

Wayment, H., *The Stained Glass of the Church of St Mary, Fairford, Gloucestershire*, London, 1984.

Wayment, H., 'Twenty-four vidimuses for Cardinal Wolsey', *Master Drawings*, XXIII–XXIV/4, March 1988, pp.503–17.

Wayment, H., 'Wolsey and stained glass', in Gunn and Lindley 1991, pp.116–30.

Wayment, H., 'The late glass in King's College Chapel: Dierick Vellert and Peter Nicholson', *Proceedings of the Cambridge Antiquarian Society*, LXXXIV, 1995, pp.121–42.

Webb, D., *Pilgrimage in Medieval England*, London, 2000.

Webb, J., *Great Tooley of Ipswich: Portrait of an Early Tudor Merchant*, Ipswich, 1962.

Webb Ware, T. G., 'Dies and designs: the English gold coinage 1465–1485. Part I', *British Numismatic Journal*, LV, 1985, pp.95–116.

Webster, C. and Elliott, J. (eds) *'A church as it should be': the Cambridge Camden Society and its influence*, Stamford, 2000.

Weever, J., *Ancient Funerall Monuments . . . ,* London, 1631.

Weinstein, R., 'Kitchen chattels: the evolution of familiar objects 1200–1700', in *The Cooking Pot: Oxford Symposium on Food and Cookery 1988*, Oxford, 1988.

Weinstein, R. et al., *Pewter, a celebration of the craft 1200–1700*, exh. cat., Museum of London, 1989.

Weiss, R., 'Portrait of a Bibliophile XI: Humfrey, Duke of Gloucester d. 1447', *The Book Collector*, XIII, 1964, pp.161–70.

Weiss, R., *Humanism in England during the Fifteenth Century*, Oxford, 1967.

Wells, W., *Stained and Painted Heraldic Glass: Burrell Collection*, Glasgow, 1962.

Wells, W., *Stained and Painted Glass, The Burrell Collection: Figure and Ornamental Subjects*, Glasgow, 1965.

Wells-Cole, A., *Art and Decoration in Elizabethan and Jacobean England*, London and New Haven, 1997.

Whale, K., 'The Wenhaston Doom: a biography of a sixteenth-century panel painting', *Proceedings of the Suffolk Institute of Archaeology and History*, XXXIX, 1999, pp.299–316.

Wharton, H., *Anglia Sacra*, London, 1691.

Whitaker, E. C. (ed.), *Martin Bucer and the Book of Common Prayer*, Alcuin Club Collections, 55, 1974.

White, G., *The Church of St Mary, Warwick, and the memorials of the last Beauchamp Earls: an interpretative study*, unpublished MA thesis, University of York, 1988.

White, J. F., *The Cambridge Movement: the Ecclesiologists and the Gothic Revival*, Cambridge, 1962.

Whitehead, D. (ed.), *Medieval Art, Architecture and Archaeology at Hereford* (British Archaeological Association Conference Transactions, XV), Leeds, 1995.

Whitehouse, D., 'Chinese porcelain in medieval Europe', *Medieval Archaeology*, XVI, 1972, pp.63–78.

Whitton, C. A., 'The heavy coinage of Henry VI', *British Numismatic Journal*, XXIII, 1938–41, pp.59–90, 206–67, 399–439.

Whitton, C. A., 'The coinages of Henry VIII and Edward VI in Henry's name', *British Numismatic Journal*, XXVI, 1949–51, pp.56–89, 171–212, 290–332.

Wiedemer, J. E., Jr, *Arms and Armour in England, their cost and distribution*, University Park, PA, and London, 1967.

Willemsen, A., *Kinder Delijt: Middeleeuws Spielgoed in de Nederlanden*, Nijmeegse Kunsthistorische Studie 6, Nijmegen, 1998.

Williams, B., 'Late medieval floor tiles from Acton Court, Iron Acton, Avon, 1974', in

Rescue Archaeology in the Bristol Area, 1, City of Bristol Museum and Art Gallery Monograph no. 2, Bristol, 1979, pp.61–76.

Williams, B., 'Medieval floor tiles', in K. Rodwell and R. Bell (eds), *Acton Court: the evolution of an early Tudor courtier's house*, English Heritage, forthcoming.

Williams, D. (ed.), *England in the Fifteenth Century (Proceedings of the 1986 Harlaxton Symposium)*, Woodbridge, 1987.

Williams, G. (ed.), *Official Correspondence of Thomas Bekynton*, 2 vols, Rolls Series, LVI, 1872.

Williams, J. F., 'A wooden Pax at Sandon', *Transactions of the Essex Archaeological Society*, XXII, 1940, pp.37–44.

Williamson, M., 'The Eton Choirbook: collegiate music-making in the reign of Henry VII', in Thompson 1995, pp.213–28.

Williamson, M., 'The early Tudor court, the provinces and the Eton Choirbook', *Early Music*, XXV, 1997, pp.229–43.

Williamson, M., 'Royal image-making and textual interplay in Gilbert Banaster's *O Maria et Elizabeth*', *Early Music History*, XIX, 2000, pp.237–78.

Williamson, M., '*Pictura et scriptura*: the Eton Choirbook in its iconographical context', *Early Music*, XXVIII, 2000, pp.359–80.

Williamson, P., 'The collecting of medieval works of art', in Williamson, P., *The Thyssen-Bornemisza Collection: Medieval sculpture and works of art*, London, 1987, pp.9–19.

Williamson, P., assisted by P. Evelyn, *Northern Gothic Sculpture 1200–1450*, Victoria and Albert Museum, London, 1988.

Williamson, P. (ed.), *European Sculpture at the Victoria and Albert Museum*, London, 1996.

Williamson, P. (ed.), *The Medieval Treasury: the Art of the Middle Ages in the Victoria and Albert Museum*, 3rd edn, London, 1998.

Williamson, P., *Netherlandish Sculpture 1450–1550*, Victoria and Albert Museum, London, 2002.

Williamson, P., *Medieval and Renaissance Stained Glass in the Victoria and Albert Museum*, London, 2003.

Willis, R. and Clark, J. W., *The Architectural History of the University of Cambridge*, 3 vols, Cambridge, 1886.

Willmot, G. F., 'A Discovery at York', *The Museums Journal*, LVII/2, 1957, pp.35–6.

Wilson, A., '*Banquetting Stuffe*': the fare and social background to the Tudor and Stuart Banquet, Edinburgh, 1991.

Wilson, C., 'The original design of the City of London Guildhall', *Journal of the British Archaeological Association*, CXXIX, 1976, pp.1–14.

Wilson, C., *The Shrines of St William of York*, York, 1977.

Wilson, C., *The Origins of the Perpendicular Style and its Development down to c.1360*, unpublished doctoral dissertation, Courtauld Institute of Art, University of London, 1980.

Wilson, C., 'The Neville Screen', in N. Coldstream and P. Draper (eds), *Medieval Art and Architecture at Durham Cathedral* (British Archaeological Association Conference Transactions, III), Leeds, 1980, pp.90–104.

Wilson, C., unpublished typescript catalogue of fragments from the late 15th-century shrine base of St William formerly in York Minster, now in the Yorkshire Museum, York, 1982.

Wilson, C. et al., *Westminster Abbey*, New Bell's Cathedral Guides, London, 1986.

Wilson, C. (ed.), *Medieval Art and Architecture in the East Riding of Yorkshire* (British Archaeological Association Conference Transactions, IX), Leeds, 1989.

Wilson, C., *The Gothic Cathedral. The Architecture of the Great Church 1130–1530*, rev. edn, London, 1992.

Wilson, C., 'The Designer of Henry VII's Chapel, Westminster Abbey', in Thompson 1995, pp.133–56.

Wilson, C., 'Rulers, artificers and shoppers: Richard II's remodelling of Westminster Hall, 1393–99', in Gordon, Monnas and Elam 1997, pp.33–59, 274–88.

Wilson, C., 'The Royal Lodgings of Edward III at Windsor Castle: Form, Function, Representation', in Keen and Scarff 2002, pp.15–94.

Wilson, C., 'The functional design of Henry VII's Chapel: a reconstruction', in R. Mortimer (ed.), *Westminster Abbey. The Lady Chapel of Henry VII*, Woodbridge, 2003.

Wilson, H. A., *Magdalen College*, The University of Oxford College Histories, London, 1899.

Wilson, T., 'Spoons with a taste of history', *British Museum Society Bulletin*, 46, July 1984.

Windeatt, B. A. (trans.), *The Book of Margery Kempe*, Harmondsworth, 1985.

Wingfield Digby, G., assisted by W. Hefford, *The Devonshire Hunting Tapestries*, Victoria and Albert Museum, London, 1971.

Wingfield Digby, G., assisted by W. Hefford, *The Tapestry Collection: Medieval and Renaissance*, Victoria and Albert Museum, London, 1980.

Winn, M. B., *Anthoine Verard, Parisian publisher 1485–1512: prologues, poems and presentations*, Travaux d'humanisme et Renaissance, Geneva, 1997.

Winston, C., *An Inquiry into the difference of Style Observable in ancient Glass Paintings, especially in England*, Oxford, 1847.

Winston, C., *Memoirs Illustrative of the Art of Glass-Painting*, London, 1865.

Wolffe, B. P., *Henry VI*, London, 1981.

Wood, M., *The English Medieval House*, London, 1965.

Woodforde, C., *Stained Glass in Somerset, 1250–1830*, London, 1946.

Woodforde, C., *The Norwich School of Glass-Painting in the Fifteenth Century*, Oxford, 1950.

Woodhead, P., *Sylloge of Coins of the British Isles, 47. Herbert Schneider Collection, Part I: English Gold Coins and their Imitations 1257–1603*, London, 1996.

Wood-Legh, K. L., *Perpetual Chantries in Britain*, Cambridge, 1965.

Woodman, F., *John Wastell of Bury, Master Mason*, unpublished doctoral dissertation, Courtauld Institute of Art, University of London, 1978.

Woodman, F., *The Architectural History of Canterbury Cathedral*, London, 1981.

Woodman, F., *The Architectural History of King's College Chapel*, London, 1986.

Woodman, F., 'The rebuilding of St Peter Mancroft', in A. Longcroft and R. Toby (eds), *East Anglia Studies. Essays presented to J. C. Barringer on his retirement, August 30, 1995*, Norwich, 1995, pp.290–95.

Woods, K. W., *Netherlandish carved wooden altarpieces of the fifteenth and early sixteenth centuries in Britain*, unpublished doctoral dissertation, Courtauld Institute of Art, University of London, 1988.

Woods. K., 'The pre-Reformation altarpiece of Long Melford Church: an investigation', *The Antiquaries Journal*, LXXXII, 2002, pp.93–104.

Woolf, R., *The English Religious Lyric in the Middle Ages*, Oxford, 1968.

Woolley, L., *Medieval Life and Leisure in the Devonshire Hunting Tapestries*, Victoria and Albert Museum, London, 2002.

Wordsworth, C. and Littlehales, H., *The Old Service-books of the English Church*, London, 1904.

Wormald, F., 'The Rood of Bromholm', *Journal of the Warburg Institute*, I/1, 1937, pp.31–45.

Wormald, F., 'An Italian Poet at the Court of Henry VII', *Journal of the Warburg and Courtauld Institutes*, XIV, 1951, pp.118–19.

Wormald, F. and Giles, P., *A descriptive catalogue of the Additional illuminated manuscripts in the Fitzwilliam Museum acquired between 1895 and 1979*, 2 vols, Cambridge, 1982.

Wright, C. E., *English Heraldic Manuscripts in the British Museum*, London, 1973.

Wright, L., 'About the evolution of standard English', in E. M. Tyler and M. J. Toswell (eds), *Studies in English Language and Literature: 'Doubt Wisely', Papers in Honour of E. G. Stanley*, London, 1996, pp.99–115.

Wright, L. (ed.), *The Development of Standard English, 1300–1800: Theories, Descriptions, Conflicts*, Cambridge, 2000.

Wright, P. P., *The Parish Church Towers of Somerset. Their Construction, Craftsmanship and Chronology 1350–1550*, Avebury, 1981.

Wright, S., 'The Author Portraits in the Bedford Psalter Hours: Gower, Chaucer, and Hoccleve', *British Library Journal*, XVIII, 1992, pp.190–201.

Wright, T. (ed.), *Political Poems and Songs*, 2 vols, Rolls Series, 1859–61.

Wüstefeld, W. C. M., 'Een bijzonder gebedsrolletje, toegeschreven aan de Meester van Sir John Fastolf', *Quaerendo*, forthcoming.

Wyon, A. B., 'The great seals of Henry IV, Henry V and Henry VI', *Journal of the British Archaeological Association*, XXXIX, 1883, pp.139–67.

Wyon, A.B ., *The Great Seals of England*, London, 1887.

York 1954: *English Medieval Alabaster Carvings*, exh. cat., York City Art Gallery, York, 1954.

Young, B., 'John Dynham and his tapestry', *Metropolitan Museum of Art Bulletin*, n.s. XX, 1961–2, pp.309–16.

Zehnder, F. G., *Sankt Ursula: Legende, Verehrung, Bilderwelt*, Cologne, 1985.

Zeuner, D., *The Bayleaf Medieval Farmstead. The Research – A Road to Discovery*, Weald and Downland Open Air Museum, Singleton, 1990.

LIST OF LENDERS

Gothic: Art for England 1400–1547, Victoria and Albert Museum, London, 9 October 2003–18 January 2004

The following individuals and institutions have lent objects to the exhibition. The catalogue number of each object is given after the lender's name. Note: the List of Lenders was correct at time of going to press.

BELGIUM

Louvain, Université Catholique de Louvain 215

FRANCE

Paris, Bibliothèque nationale de France 72, 74

Paris, musée du Louvre, département des Objets d'art 10

Paris, musée national du Moyen Age 282, 344

GERMANY

Aachen, Domkapitel, Domschatzkammer 11

THE NETHERLANDS

Amsterdam, Rijksmuseum 323

Utrecht, Museum Catherijneconvent 92

UNITED KINGDOM

Her Majesty The Queen 55, 56, 65, 209

Alveley, Shropshire, church of St Mary the Virgin 274

Arundel & Brighton, Roman Catholic Diocese of 248

Ashbourne, Derbyshire, St Oswald's church 345

Binham, Norfolk, The Priory Church of St Mary and the Holy Cross 357

Birmingham, The University of Birmingham, The Trustees of The Barber Institute of Fine Arts 244

Bristol Cathedral, Chapter 314

Bristol City Council 127

Bristol, Bristol Museums and Art Gallery 135, 198

Bristol, St Stephen's church 191, 315

Buccleuch and Queensberry, Duke of 95

Burnley, Lancashire, Towneley Hall Art Gallery 300

Bury St Edmunds, Suffolk, St Mary's church 331

Cambridge, Master and Fellows of Christ's College 110, 111, 112, 113

Cambridge, Master and Fellows of Corpus Christi College 171, 358

Cambridge, Syndics of the Fitzwilliam Museum 17, 94

Cambridge, The Provost and Scholars of King's College 20, 21

Cambridge, Magdalene College 169

Cambridge, University Museum of Archaeology and Anthropology 57

Cartmel Fell, Cumbria, St Anthony's church 268

Chatsworth, Derbyshire, the Duke of Devonshire and the Chatsworth Settlement Trustees 45

Chivers, Derrick A. 53, 139, 247, 332, 333

Cirencester, Gloucestershire, church of St John Baptist 13

Cobham, Kent, St Mary Magdalene's church 338

Colchester Castle Museum 125

Colchester Council 126

Coventry, Herbert Art Gallery and Museum 59, 284

Dunstable, Bedfordshire, St Peter's church 349

Edinburgh, National Galleries of Scotland 295

Edinburgh, Trustees of the National Museums of Scotland 61

English Heritage 69

Essex church, an 280

Eton, The Provost and Fellows of Eton College 24, 190

Exeter Cathedral, Dean and Chapter 321

Exeter City Council 129

Exeter, Exeter City Museums 121, 265, 313

Fairford, Gloucestershire, church of St Mary the Virgin 294

Glasgow Museums, the Burrell Collection 38, 152, 160, 178, 217, 219

Hedon Town Council, East Riding of Yorkshire 128

Hereford Cathedral, Dean and Chapter 251

Hessett, Suffolk, St Ethelbert's church 301

Ipswich Borough Council Museums and Galleries 210, 334

Kersey, Suffolk, St Mary's church 266

Lacock, Wiltshire, St Cyriac's church 184

Little Malvern Priory church, Worcestershire 37

Liverpool, National Museums and Galleries on Merseyside 97, 351

London, All-Hallows-by-the-Tower church 136

London, British Library Board 14, 15, 27, 33b, 41, 42, 43,46, 47,49, 73, 77, 80, 85, 90, 93, 96, 116, 173, 223, 225, 254, 318, 340, 354, 355, 359

London, Trustees of the British Museum 32, 34, 40, 68, 70, 132, 165, 166, 189, 195, 204, 205, 206, 211, 221, 242, 252, 278, 304, 342, 353

London, College of Arms 76

London, Guildhall Library, Corporation of London 130, 142

London, His Grace the Archbishop of Canterbury and the Trustees of Lambeth Palace Library 44, 103, 227, 326

London, Museum of London 62, 71, 122, 176, 177, 200, 202, 203, 212, 221, 222, 324, 325

London, National Gallery 135, 162, 213

London, Public Record Office 30

London, Society of Antiquaries of London 285, 319

London, Board of Trustees of the Victoria and Albert Museum 6, 8,18, 151,153, 156, 157, 160, 164, 167, 182, 183, 187, 199,2 01, 218, 220, 222, 263, 267, 271, 275, 279, 299, 303, 307, 342, 350

London, Westminster Abbey, Dean and Chapter 9, 54, 114, 239

London, Worshipful Company of Armourers and Brasiers 58, 134, 193

London, Worshipful Company of Founders 75

London, Worshipful Company of Goldsmiths 186, 192

London, Worshipful Company of Leathersellers 131

London, Worshipful Company of Mercers 137, 138

London, Worshipful Company of Pewterers 197

London, Worshipful Company of Skinners 133

London, Worshipful Company of Vintners 230

Luton Museum and Art Gallery 347, 348

Manchester, John Rylands University Library 172, 174, 309, 341

Mendlesham, Suffolk, church of St Mary the Virgin 60

National Trust 81, 216, 289, 343

Nettlecombe, Somerset, St Mary's Church 302

Northumberland, Duke of 115

Norwich Cathedral, Dean and Chapter 277

Norwich, Norfolk Record Office 168

Norwich, Norfolk Museums Service 155, 208, 276

Nottingham University Library 312

Oxford, Warden and Fellows of All Souls College 36, 99, 100, 101, 102, 179, 207

Oxford, Visitors of the Ashmolean Museum 12, 325

Oxford, Bodleian Library, University of Oxford 253, 256

Oxford, Corpus Christi College 104, 105, 106, 107, 108

Oxford, Magdalen College 250, 255

Oxford, New College 180, 181, 188, 249, 305

Penn, Buckinghamshire, Holy Trinity church 269

Portsmouth, Mary Rose Trust 63

Portsmouth, Royal Armouries at Fort Nelson 66

Ranworth, Norfolk, St Helen's church 272

Ripon Minster 240

St Albans, The Cathedral and Abbey Church of St Alban 238

Sherborne, Dorset, Master and Brethren of the Almshouse of St John the Baptist and St John the Evangelist 346

The Society of Jesus (Stonyhurst College, Lancashire) 31

Southwell Minster, Dean and Chapter 243

Stanford-on-Avon, Northamptonshire, church of St Nicholas 39

Stockerston, Leicestershire, St Peter's church 290

Strategic Rail Authority 194

Tattershall, Lincolnshire, Holy Trinity church 291, 292

Thornhill, West Yorkshire, church of St Michael and All Angels 335

Ufford, Suffolk, St Mary's church of the Assumption 270

Verulam, Earl of 161

Warwick, St Mary's church 87, 88, 89

Wells, Somerset, St Cuthbert's church 287

Winchester Cathedral, Dean and Chapter 234, 235, 356

Winchester, Warden and Scholars of Winchester College 185

York, The Mansion House, City of York Council 82

York Minster, Dean and Chapter 48, 141, 317

York Museums Trust (Yorkshire Museum) 98, 262, 316

U.S.A.

Brunswick, Maine, Bowdoin College Museum of Art 22

New York, Metropolitan Museum of Art 8, 79, 154, 163

Philadelphia Free Library 140

Pierpont Morgan Library 91

Washington, National Gallery of Art 84